MANNINGHAM, John. The diary of John Manningham of the Middle Temple, 1602–1603: newly edited in complete and unexpurgated form from the original manuscript in the British Museum, with introd., notes, and life of the author by Robert Parker Sorlien. University Press of New England, 1976. 467p index 74-22553. 25.00 ISBN 0-87451-113-5

CHOICE   MAR. '77
History, Geography &
Travel

Europe

John Manningham's diary or copy book has long been considered an important source of Tudor-Stuart literary and social history. However, the only previous edition of the work, which was published in the mid-19th century, was both incomplete and inaccurate (John Bruce, ed., *The diary of John Manningham,* Camden Society, 1868). Consequently, historians and literary scholars will welcome this new edition. Manningham was a law student in London during the critical years that witnessed the transition between Tudor and Stuart England. He was present at the court during Elizabeth's final hours and recorded both a description of the queen's death as well as the reaction to the proclamation of the new king. His copy book also includes popular anecdotes, reports of contemporary events, notes of sermons he heard and impressions of the personalities he encountered, including some of the leading literary and political figures of the age. The edition is an im-

Travel

Europe

pressive work of careful scholarship. It includes a useful introduction, extensive notes (which unfortunately are placed at the end of the text), and a short biography of Manningham. Recommended for graduate libraries.

THE DIARY OF
JOHN MANNINGHAM
OF THE MIDDLE TEMPLE
1602–1603

Warren D. Smith is Professor of English at the University of Rhode Island, author of many articles on Shakespeare and Marlowe, and former theater director and actor.

27.

of the femme had the orange, of the substance
and the deitie, of the good and the body: the
person and the land hath bin divided: by his death.
a division without violence: this applye[n]g to
them to the roote, made them hto bleed at the
verey heart.

This gospell makes mention of an excellent woman
that sang not to his selfe and his nurse: but
went amongst the multitude: and blessed as an
other woman more excellent then she selfe: yea
the blessed her it is mother for his babes sake.
Tho here are two excellent women, one that
bare Christ, and an other that blessed Christ.
So that may we come to Christ, she that bare
and blessed him both: she bare him in her
heart as in the wombe: she nourished him in
faith, she brought him fforth in aboundaunce
of good workes: and nursed him with faith and
discretion: she blessed him in the middest
of a froward and wicked generation, when
the bulle of Basan roared: and the counsaile
raged and bound themselves with oathes and
swore against the Lorde and his annoynted.
And him g[od] extoled into his maiestie: and so. and
now is the tyme of praise: for praise now
before his death: And thou gratissima hu[...]
allio cum nullus frigendi, aut assentandi
locus restinguitur: yet will praise her but
like the moste of meate that uppon a dead wo[...]
graue why she cannot last: or like the light
behind a ward back will cannot direct forth:
the would say little: non quod ingratus, sed qu[...]
oppressus multitudine et magnitudine rerum
dicendarum: onely she would say that his

governe[...]

27. Sir govermt ought bin too clement, temporal
and godly: that so may say sic
mibuti sumus, non possumus nisi optimū
ferre. / Those usd in Theodosius hys Empower
tyme went to Rome called their travel
Felix peregrinatio; becaurse they had Rome
home. they had Rome Theodosius: they had Rome
Rome and Theodosius togither: so have had
only strangers that have bin to visit our kingdom
thinke them selves happie that had Rome England,
and Q: Elizabeth: had England and Q: Elizabeth
beth togither. / But hir her Panegyricks
provided for sir, faythfully registred, had also too
recited. / she was pretritis melior: better
then those usd went before sir, and may be to
precedent to those that shall follow sir; Hir
takeing sir from us us unto a great division
but god safe shewed it as agayne: it was a
grievous sore but god safe sealed it. he sth
given us a worthy successor, a somer of y
nobles. our that is flose of our floser: god
shewed to say unto us, opend thy mouth wide and
I will fill it with aboundant blessing: so mens
thy — to so did to so our's what shod
I sawe done that I save not don unto too
O England. noo vacuum, noo interregnū
noo interruption of govermt, as in somme
tim other places, whan in suche tymes the peristed
fly opon egos. / but a quiet, a peosable, and
reofull succession of thing a long: quem populus
et proceres voce petebant, hir best wished, and
hir onely agreed upon: The Lord from his
holy sanctuary blesse him in his throne;

**The University Press of
New England**

Sponsoring Institutions

Brandeis University
Clark University
Dartmouth College
The University of New Hampshire
The University of Rhode Island
The University of Vermont

THE DIARY OF

John Manningham

OF THE MIDDLE TEMPLE

1602 – 1603

newly edited in complete and
unexpurgated form from the
original manuscript in the
British Museum, with introduction,
notes, and life of the author, by

ROBERT PARKER SORLIEN

Published for the University of Rhode Island

by The University Press of New England

Hanover, New Hampshire 1976

FOR BARBARA MEREDITH

Contents

Preface   ix

Introduction   1

Text of the Diary   27

The Life of Manningham   249

Appendixes   281

A. Final Agreement on Ownership of Land   283

B. Will of Richard Manningham   284

C. Inscription on Richard Manningham Monument   288

D. Will of John Manningham   289

Notes to the Text of the Diary and to the Life   293

Index   421

Preface

Preparation of this edition of Manningham's uncommon commonplace book has had two main motives: first, to provide a complete and accurate text for the use of scholars and other readers; second, by annotation, particularly in the form of identification of Manningham's *dramatis personae*, his informants, and other associates, to assist the reader in comprehending what the Diarist wrote.

Fortunately for the modern editor, Manningham—though he seldom indented—divided his entries by drawing a short line beneath each passage, at the left margin. The present text scrupulously observes these divisions (in contrast to the only earlier published version, of 1868, which often ignores them).

Manningham's capitalization and spelling have been preserved, except for abbreviations, which have been extended to the forms most commonly encountered in the manuscript when the Diarist chose to write them out in full: e.g., m^{ty} for *majesty*. Manningham's pointing has generally been followed, except that his various virgules (/, ·/., //., etc.) have been rendered by commas or full stops according to the sense of the passage. Tudor *i–j* and *u–v* reversals have been normalized according to modern practice. Latin passages have been transcribed as written, except that single words and short phrases have been italicized.

The following excerpts illustrate the method employed:
On fo. 25 of the manuscript the third passage reads as follows:

> Yf any should aske why it was comaunded in Levitic: that the people should offer primitias, and in Exod^{s}./ that they should alsoe giue decimas./ I should make noe other aunswer, but that wee should not onely remember our creator in the dayes of our youth, but alsoe serue him in holines and righteousnes all the dayes of our lyfe/./

This becomes in the present edition:

> Yf any should aske why it was commaunded in Levitic[us]
> that the people should offer *primitias,* and in Exodus that
> they should alsoe give *decimas,* I should make noe other
> aunswer but that wee should not onely remember our
> Creator in the dayes of our youth, but alsoe serve him in
> holines and righteousnes all the dayes of our lyfe.

My initial interest in Manningham's book I owe to Dr. Powel M.
Dawley, who during our conversations at the Conference in
Theology for College and University Faculty, at Trinity College,
Hartford, Connecticut, in 1955, regarding Donne's sermons and
the Elizabethan preaching tradition, called it to my attention.
Since then, while engaging in this "playing labor" (to use Robert
Burton's phrase), I have had encouragement, advice, and assistance
from many other people.

The project has been aided by a Faculty Summer Fellowship
from the University of Rhode Island, for which grant I am grateful
particularly to Professors Walter L. Simmons and Warren D. Smith,
and to Dean Ernest W. Hartung (now president of the University
of Idaho). I wish also to thank, for aid of various sorts, Professors
Allan H. MacLaine, William Young, and Clare Murphy, the late
Harold W. Harrison, and Mr. Peter Hicks.

At Brown University Professor Leicester Bradner has been not
only a kind friend but a wise and helpful guide, offering valuable
suggestions on many occasions. The same may truly be said of
Professor Philip J. Finkelpearl of Vassar, who read the introduction.

In England I have had generous and courteous assistance from
numerous scholars, archivists, and library personnel: Mr. Derek
V. A. Sankey, Librarian and Keeper of the Records of the Middle
Temple, his assistant Roderick Walker, and Lawrence Stanley
Sheppard, F.R.I.C.S., Surveyor; the staff in the Manuscript Room
of the British Museum, at the Public Record Office, and at Somer-
set House; Mr. C. W. Ringrose, Librarian of Lincoln's Inn; and Miss
Mildred Wretts-Smith.

For permission to have the Manningham MS in the Middle
Temple photographed, I am indebted to the Master Treasurer,
William Latey, Esq., C.B.E., Q.C.

At Clare College, Cambridge, Dr. Geoffrey Elton has been especially helpful, along with Mr. James Claydon, Mr. Donald Missen, and Mr. and Mrs. A. E. Bowen at the Cambridge University Library. Also the late Alan L. Maycock and Mr. Derek Pepys-Whitely at the libraries of Magdalene College; Miss H. E. Peek, Cambridge University Archivist; Mr. J. Michael Farrar, Cambridgeshire County Archivist; the Rev. Raymond Pearson, Vicar of Fen Drayton, and Mrs. Pearson; the Rev. Harold J. Scott, Vicar of Swavesey, and Mrs. Scott; Professor William Rushton, F.R.S., Fellow of Trinity College, and Mrs. Rushton, and their guest from the Folger Library, Mrs. Laetitia Yandel (a fortunate acquaintance for me); and Dr. F. Brittain of Jesus College.

In Kent I have benefited from the knowledge and courtesy of the Rev. Derek Chapman, Vicar of East Malling, and Mrs. Chapman; Dr. S. C. Pearce at the East Malling Research Station; Dr. Felix Hull, Kent County Archivist; the Rev. Canon N. K. Nye, Rural Dean, All Saints' Church, Maidstone, and his secretary, Mrs. K. L. Kidman; Dr. William Urry, Archivist at Canterbury Cathedral; and the Rev. M. G. Hewett, Rector of Chevening, Sevenoaks.

Others to whom I am indebted are Mr. Godfrey Thompson, Librarian of the Guildhall Library in London; Drs. Frederick H. Shriver and Robert Kreuger; Miss Patricia Bell, Assistant Archivist, Bedford County Record Office; Mr. Peter Walne, Herts. County Archivist; Miss Clare Talbot, Librarian of Hatfield House.

Also staff members of the libraries at Harvard, Brown, Yale, and the University of Rhode Island, particularly Mr. Francis P. Allen, librarian at URI, and a succession of interlibrary loan personnel: Mr. Robert Rhodes, Miss Marianne Gelbert, Mr. David Taylor, and Mrs. Kathleen Schlenker. Also a succession of efficient and cooperative typists: Mrs. Louis Kutcher, Mrs. Everett C. Greene, Miss Elizabeth Lee Pratt, and Mrs. Jean Parrish.

Finally, I wish to thank the staff of the University Press of New England, and for her help in innumerable ways, my wife, Barbara Meredith Sorlien.

Cambridge, England   R.P.S.
June 1975

THE DIARY OF
JOHN MANNINGHAM
OF THE MIDDLE TEMPLE
1602–1603

Introduction

"My tables,—Meet it is I set it down," declares
Hamlet, probably referring to the sort of copy book that young
Elizabethan gentlemen were in the habit of carrying. Such a book
from the Elizabethan age, fortunately surviving among the Harleian
manuscripts in the British Museum, has come down to us in the
"Diary" of a young law student, John Manningham of the Middle
Temple. This work, long known to Shakespearean scholars since
the mid-nineteenth century but never published in full, is here
presented in its gusty entirety, with nothing excluded, nothing
expurgated.

The little book in which the young law student entered his jottings in 1602 and 1603, though listed in the British Museum catalogue of the Harleian manuscripts (III, 1808, pp. 261-262) as "A
small paper Book of various Collections," numbered 5353, and of
unknown authorship—"Who was the writer does not appear," reads
the annotation—first came to the notice of modern scholars in 1831,
when John Payne Collier published his *Annals of the Stage,* in
which he devoted sixteen pages to what he had learned from his
study of the manuscript. Then Joseph Hunter, who had first seen
it in 1828, by following up leads in the Diary mentioning journeys
into Kent and the names of several cousins—Cranmer at Canterbury,
Watts at Sandwich, Chapman at Godmersham, as well as "my
cousin in Kent," at Bradbourne (identified as Richard Manningham)—determined the name of the author. Sometime before 1850
the manuscript was rebound by the British Museum.[1] To the find-
ings of Hunter, who printed them in his *Illustrations of Shakespeare*
(1845), John Bruce added details when in 1868 he brought out his
useful but incomplete and bowdlerized Camden Society edition of
Manningham's text.

1. According to Mr. B. Schofield, deputy keeper of the Department of
MSS. See Sidney Race, "Manningham's Diary, the Case for Re-examination,"
NQ, 199 (1954), 380.

The original manuscript is a duodecimo volume measuring not quite 4″ × 6″. Its 133 leaves are, with some exceptions, close-packed in a small but fairly legible secretary hand. It begins in January 1601/02, and runs through April 1603, though the order of entries is not entirely chronological, because the writer seems at times to have entered his notes and impressions wherever he had vacant space.

Manningham's book has been called a social diary;[2] a notebook, "a curious patchwork ... a miscellany of odds and ends";[3] "an entertaining medley";[4] and a commonplace book.[5] It is all of these.

To keep commonplace books was a fashion in the sixteenth and seventeenth centuries, and students turned them to good account. Thomas Fuller recommended them as instructional aids when he advised, "Adventure not all thy learning in one bottom, but divide it betwixt thy memory and thy Notebooks."[6] As R. E. Bennett correctly observes, Manningham did not use his for original literary effort.[7] Rather the young law student used it to record conversations, anecdotes, witticisms, rumors and reports of contemporary events, sermons he heard preached, books and poems he read, and impressions of personalities he encountered, as well as some of his own activities.

Because of its copious examples of witty anecdote and verbal horseplay, it is related to the jestbook tradition, on the one hand— as represented by Sir Nicholas L'Estrange's *Merry Passages and Jests*[8]—and because of its realistic observations and depiction of personality, it is related to both character writing and serious biography, on the other.

The result is a valuable record of men and events that helped to shape the age, the last years of Queen Elizabeth and the Jacobean

2. William Matthews, *British Diaries* (Berkeley, 1950), p. 7.

3. John Bruce, ed., *The Diary of John Manningham*, Camden Society (1868), preface, p. xi.

4. Sidney Lee, *DNB*, 12:959.

5. This term has been used by Bruce, Matthews, and almost every other commentator on Manningham.

6. *The Holy State* (1642), III, x, 175–176.

7. "John Manningham and Donne's Paradoxes," *Modern Language Notes*, 46 (1931), 312.

8. MS Harl. 6395, portions of which have been published in W. J. Thoms's *Anecdotes and Traditions*, Camden Society, 1839.

and Caroline periods that followed, as well as of the social customs, attitudes, and ways of life in that turbulent and colorful era.

As a reporter and raconteur Manningham was observant as well as witty. His keen, wide-ranging curiosity—the desire to *know* so characteristic of the Renaissance—led him into many paths, including, besides law and politics, theology, medicine, sports, and sex. Consequently the Diary contains something of interest to everyone. For the historian it is a primary source, particularly Manningham's account of the Queen's final hours. For the student of literature and literary history, including the stage, it offers memorabilia of many of the writers of the age, some major, some now all-but-forgotten, together with extracts from some of the works then popular.

Through the pages of Manningham's tiny book we catch glimpses of the great Elizabethan figures—Ralegh before his eclipse; Bacon rising to great place; Cecil, already a power. We sense the contemporary concern over the succession, reflected in the Diarist's reading of Dolman's *Conference* and Hayward's *Answer,* and the interest in the rival claimants to the throne—the beauteous and scholarly Arabella Stuart, victim of intrigues, of circumstances, and of her own limitations; the ambitious Seymours; and of course James—a concern and an interest that mounted to anxiety and fear of civil war at the time of the great Queen's death. We feel, too, the release of tension and the mood of celebration when the problem was peaceably settled.

We see and hear, or hear about, lawyers, judges, and future statesmen, both good and bad: Whitelock, Bramston, and Pym; Justices Anderson, Fenner, Yelverton, and Hele and Dr. Caesar; John Davies in disgrace; and the fine old barristers and benchers of the Inns of Court: Henry Haule of the Middle Temple, William Towse of the Inner Temple, Foster of Lincoln's Inn—the latter pair telling memorable anecdotes about Spenser, Shakespeare, Burbage, and Thomas More.

Poets, playwrights, and satirists appear too, in scraps of their verse or prose, in conversations overheard, or in rumor or tale: paradoxical Donne and rare Ben Jonson themselves; Thomas Overbury, handsome but tartly outspoken; John Marston in merry acerbity.

The Diary shows that Manningham was on intimate terms with

several witty verse-writing friends of both Jonson and Donne—
effervescent, fun-loving Richard Martin; jolly Benjamin Rudyerd;
John Hoskyns, author of a treatise on rhetoric; and one of his own
kinsmen, John Chapman of Godmersham, Kent. All of these
poetical lawyers were members of the Jonson-Donne circle of wits.
Hoskyns and Chapman were Manningham's sureties upon his
admission to the Middle Temple in 1598.

They were a hearty, ebullient, earthy lot, these sociable and
affable young intellectuals, these "learned, civil, merry men," as
Jonson termed them in his "Sociable Rules for the Apollo,"[9] and
they placed a premium on talking wittily. Samples of their repartee,
including Rabelaisian bawdry, enliven the leaves of the original
manuscript.

Manningham was fortunate to be at the Middle Temple with some
of the vivid personalities, the boon companions, of the age. Among
them the art of banter and a talent for clever expression were assid-
uously, if informally, cultivated.

The Inns of Court, Maitland has aptly said, were "associations of
lawyers which had about them a good deal of the Club, something
of the College, something of the trade union."[10] Although most of
the students were training for legal practice in Westminster Hall or
elsewhere, or for public business, they had ample opportunity to
be convivial. Middle Templars met together for dinner and supper
in Plowden's Great Hall and in less formal gatherings at the buttery
bar or around the hall fire, or in summertime in the garden. On
such occasions they talked frankly, pungently, and sometimes
sarcastically, and the Diarist, keeping his ear cocked, remembered
these quips and jotted them down. For example, he heard the
lawyer-poet John Hoskyns, author of *Dirreccōns for Speech and
Style* and future Serjeant-at-Law, make the following racy pun—
one of several dozen passages the Victorian editor declined to print:

> One told Sergeant Harrys howe many there were newe prickt
> sergeantes. "Would I were newe-prict to," q[uoth] he; "it
> would be the better for my wife then." (Hoskins)

The jest reflects the temper of the scholarly but spirited Hoskyns,

9. Transl. Alexander Brome, *Songs and Other Poems,* 1661.
10. As quoted, George Godwin, *The Middle Temple, The Society and
Fellowship* (London, 1954), p. 47.

from whom Manningham received his first supervision at the Middle
Temple. Hoskyns had recently married a charming and wealthy
widow, Benedicta ("Bennet") Bourne, with whom he was passionately in love.

Though not all the wit in the Diary is as lively and pointed as this
entry on fo. 98, much of it is. Jocularity was part of the age, a sport
indulged in by all, from greybeard clergy and justices down to the
most recent graduate of Oxford and Cambridge. To be a good companion, friendly, affable, and pleasant, was considered an asset in
those times. Shakespeare was so regarded, and praise of other men
often stressed this attribute. Evidence of congeniality was a man's
facility for clever and merry expression.

Such love of wit was so pervasive that even the prelates were given
to it, as Manningham shows by recording an anecdote about a Bishop
of Bath and Wells, Dr. John Still, who when he was summoned to
the court and offered the see of Ely turned it down with these
words: "that Bishopricke was the onely mayden Bishopricke in
England, and he would not be the first should deflour it" (fo. 102).

Among Manningham's chief informants were his chambermate,
Edward Curle of Hatfield (John would later marry Curle's sister
Anne), and Charles Danvers of Edington, Wilts. From Curle he
heard a beast fable (fo. 33b) and learned how Thomas Bodley
wooed and won a "riche widdowe" by letting a rival suitor hold her
cards (fo. 46). Danvers (often spelled "Davers" in the Diary), was
admitted to the Middle Temple about five months before Manningham but called to the bar with him in 1605; he seems to have been
a close friend, if we may judge from the number of times he is
mentioned or quoted in the Diary. In later years he would father
many daughters, one of whom, Jane, would marry the poet George
Herbert. That Danvers also kept a notebook is indicated by an entry
on fo. 44, where Manningham cites "Ch. Danvers booke" as his
source. In another place (fo. 6b) he copied sermon notes taken by
Danvers. Those two—Curle and Danvers—supplied many of the
anecdotes and jests recorded in the Diary.

A third was Benjamin Rudyerd (sometimes abbreviated to "B.
Rud." in the MS and mistranscribed "B. Reid" in the 1868 published edition). This elegant man-about-town, this future knight,
who would become the "silver-trumpet" of the Long Parliament
and enjoy poetical fellowship with the Mermaid Tavern wits and

William Herbert, Earl of Pembroke, had been educated at Winchester and St. John's, Oxford, then admitted to the *Societate Medii Templi* in the spring of 1590, when he was 18. After ten years' study he was called to the bar, in October 1600. Presumably his *Noctes Templariae,* a sprightly account of the "Prince d'Amour" Christmas revels of the Templars in 1597/8 (when Richard Martin was chosen to reign as the Prince of Love) was written in 1599, when he was only 27.[11] His pleasantries, as recorded by Manningham, are then of a man of 30.

Another quipster oft-quoted in the Diary was the brilliant but ill-starred Thomas Overbury—talented, handsome, outspoken, an Oxford B.A. at 17, in 1598, and in residence at the Middle Temple since 1599. His father, Nicholas Overbury, was a prominent bencher of the society. At that time no one could have predicted young Tom's meteoric rise to power and prestige as guide and tutor to King James's favorite, Sir Robert Carr, Viscount Rochester, and his miserable end—his murder in the Tower by poisons administered by agents of the Countess of Essex.

Many of the Overburian utterances recorded by Manningham are sarcastic, such as his description of George Snigg, a bencher and future Chancellor of the Exchequer:

> Sniges nose loked downe to see howe many of his teethe were lost, and could never get up againe. (fo. 39b)

Ridiculous and trivial though they are, such caricatures show, besides enthusiasm for clever expression, a keen interest in people, their appearance and behavior, especially the idiosyncracies of human nature. To a considerable extent the age was given to caricature, in which "humors" were being portrayed in satire and exhibited on the stage. The Diary shows that colorful eccentrics at the Middle Temple gave Overbury good practice for composing his Theophrastan prose "characters," which would become a popular seventeenth century genre—ingenious, often satirical, epigrammatic in style.

In a sense, the Diarist himself was working this vein by describing from observation or hearsay actual individual representatives of

---

11. See J. A. Manning, *Memoirs of Sir Benjamin Rudyerd,* Knt. (London, 1841), p. 8, and P. J. Finkelpearl, "Sir John Davies and the 'Prince d'Amour,' " *NQ,* 208 (1963), 300–302.

Elizabethan character types. One was Steven Beckingham of Hert-fordshire, who possessed a "hott collerick disposicion, a creaking loud voyce, a greasy whitish head, a ruddish beard, of long staring *mouchetons*" and who wore a satin doublet and "an outworne muff with two old gold laces ... his cuffs wrought with coloured silk and gold" (fo. 45b).

One contemporary Middle Temple sport was Davies-baiting, for in the Diary are several jibes at John Davies, the author of the celebrated poem on dancing entitled *Orchestra* and the future Sir John. Davies' quarrel with his friend Richard Martin, one of the merriest and best-liked men in the kingdom, and his infamous and brutal cudgeling of Martin while the latter was "sitting quietly at dinner" at the barristers' table in the Hall on the night of February 9, 1597/8, together with Davies' abrupt departure and subsequent expulsion, were undoubtedly still resounding when Manningham was admitted to the society only a month later. John Hoskyns had been closely associated with the poet, having been "bound" with him when Hoskyns entered the society (13 March 1592/3).[12] More than likely he, with "Cousin" Chapman, Curle, Rudyerd, and many another Middle Templar with whom Manningham became acquainted, had been present in the Hall when Davies applied his bastinado. Though Davies, after sojourning at Oxford for several years, had been permitted to make his submission (on All Saints' Day, 1601) and been reinstated, it is clear from the Diary that his reputation had not been restored.

That the Diarist's sympathies were with Martin is shown in the following portrait of Davies (omitted by Bruce when he transcribed fo. 127b):

> Jo[hn] Davys goes wadling with his arse out behinde as though he were about to make every one that he meetes a wall to pisse against (B. Rudyerd, or Th. Overb[ur]y). He never walkes but he carries a clokebag behinde him, his arse stickes out soe farr.

This passage is one of several that indicates the dislike and contempt in which the lawyer-poet was then held—and there may have been truth in the description.

12. Louise B. Osborne, *Life, Letters and Writings of John Hoskyns* (New Haven, 1937), p. 20.

That baiting Davies was not confined to the Middle Temple is shown by John Donne's satire of the author of *Orchestra* in his Latin jeu d'esprit of around 1600, the mock *Catalogus Librorum Aulicorum,* or "Courtier's Library," in which Donne—termed by Bacon "a master of scoffing"—ridiculed a number of his contemporaries by attributing to their authorship imaginary books, in the manner of Rabelais. The ironical title of Davies' alleged work reads as follows:

> 16. *The Justice of England.* Vacation exercises of John Davies on the Art of forming Anagrams approximately true, and Posies to engrave on Rings. [13]

The Middle Templars and "Lincolnians" like Donne—i.e., members of Lincoln's Inn—enjoyed a close sociability, "an ancient and general league," as Rudyerd called it: [14] and Donne and Martin were warm friends.

In this connection it should be mentioned that Manningham refers to Donne's nearly disastrous marriage and the now familiar pun that the poet himself is reported to have started when after his arrest he and his bride wryly signed a letter "John Donne, Anne Donne. Undone" (fo. 75b).

More important from a literary point of view is the direct evidence the Diary offers of the kind of audience for the early work of Donne, whose prose paradoxes, a verse epigram, and a verse letter are quoted or paraphrased—perhaps copied from manuscript versions then circulating among Inns of Court friends of the poet. From Manningham we have concrete indications of who comprised this audience: men like himself, young, intelligent, sophisticated, satirical, appreciative of ironic reversals, startling images, and "strong lines."

Among the paradoxes of Donne that Manningham copied into his book—"That Women Ought to Paint" and "That a Wise Man is Known By Much Laughing" (fo. 101)—is another, "Hee That Weepeth is Most Wise," which corresponds to no known paradox

---

13. *The Courtier's Library, or Catalogus Librorum, Aulicorum incomparabilium et non vendibilium,* ed. and tr. Evelyn Mary Simpson (London: Nonesuch Press, 1930).

14. *Le Prince d'Amour* (1660), p. 78.

by Donne but which R. E. Bennett has proved beyond reasonable
doubt is of Donne's composing.[15]

These entries are important for several reasons: they are the
earliest dated references to Donne's paradoxes; they show the
appeal that this genre had for the young Templars, interested as
they were in legal disputation; and they indicate that Manningham
was one of the appreciative readers of the poet's early work. Martin,
Hoskyns, Rudyerd, or Cousin Chapman could have supplied him
with copies; or, since he had acquaintances in the other Inns of
Court, he could have had them from William Hackwell (Hakewell),
the Lincoln's Inn friend of Donne and the other wits and a nephew
of Sir John Peryam and kinsman of Thomas Bodley. (Hackwell himself is quoted in fo. 45b.)

Manningham also knew another Lincoln's Inn lawyer, Thomas
Foster, who, as they walked or went by boat together to the courts
at Westminster, told jests about Sir Thomas More. One of these
anecdotes, based on a bilingual pun, recounts Sir Thomas' showing
an old acquaintance a picture of a death's head with the words
Memento morieris, which More made use of to remind the friend
that he owed him some money: "It is not much [said More], and
though I be Chauncellor I have use for as little. And now me thinkes
this picture speakes unto you *Memento Mori aeris:* Remember to
pay Moore his money" (fo. 29).

The Diarist's version of this story does not appear in the usual
sixteenth-century printed works that allude to More; in fact it
anticipates by more than a dozen years the briefer and less circumstantial version of it by Cresacre More, the first of More's biographers to tell it, in his *Life of Thomas More,* composed about
1615–20 but not published till about 1626 (see below, note to
fo. 29).

Manningham's chief connection at the Inner Temple was William
Towse, a prominent and active bencher, who told him about living
personages, such as Sergeant John Heale—noted for his drinking;
Dr. Julius Caesar, the Treasurer of the Inner house, who held such
important posts in government as Master of Requests, Chancellor
of the Exchequer, and Master of the Rolles (Dr. Caesar was another
friend of Donne's); Sir Henry Yelverton; the unscrupulous judge

15. *Modern Language Notes,* 46 (1931), 309–313.

Sir Roger Manwood, Lord Chief Baron of the Exchequer; Chief
Justice Edmund Anderson; and others.

It was Towse who gave Manningham the lines Spenser was said
to have written when he could not get payment from the Queen
for his verses:

> It pleased your Grace upon a tyme
> To graunt me reason for my ryme,
> But from that tyme untill this season
> I heard of neither ryme nor reason.
>
> (Touse) (fo. 31b)

From Towse, too, came what is probably the best-known entry
in the Diary, the merry tale of Shakespeare's clever vanquishing of
Burbage in their rival pursuit of a woman of easy virtue, a tale that
James Joyce would borrow from Manningham and incorporate into
Ulysses.[16]

> Upon a tyme when Burbidge played Rich[ard] 3. there was a
> Citizen grewe soe farr in liking with him, that before shee
> went from the play shee appointed him to come that night
> unto hir by the name of Ri[chard] the 3. Shakespeare, over-
> hearing their conclusion, went before, was intertained, and at
> his game ere Burbidge came. Then message being brought that
> Richard the 3d. was at the dore, Shakespeare caused returne
> to be made that William the Conquerour was before Rich[ard]
> the 3. Shakespeare's name William.
>
> (Mr. Touse) (fo. 29b)

This contemporary reference to the playwright from Stratford,
though naturally not relished by the idolators, corroborates
Aubrey's description of him as "very good company, and of a very
readie and pleasant smoothe Witt."[17]

Although Manningham made no reference to having attended a
playhouse, he at least mentioned a few theatre personalities: besides
Shakespeare and Burbage, the satirist Marston—a Middle Templar
from 1595 till 1602, though his heart was not in legal studies—and
the fencers Turner and Dun at the Bankside.

16. New Random House Edition (1961), p. 201.
17. John Aubrey, *Brief Lives*, ed. Oliver L. Dick (London, 1950), p. 275.

He also heard about and mentioned the celebrated "hoax" allegedly "perpetrated" by Richard Vennar of Lincoln's Inn at the Swan in November 1602, when Vennar advertised an entertainment called *England's Joy,* lured in an audience, took their money, and attempted—or was forced by bailiffs chasing him for debt—to abscond, thereby provoking the enraged customers to riot (fo. 59b). For details of this incident we have to turn to Vennar's own *Apology,* printed in 1614 and reprinted by J. P. Collier in 1866, and to the letters of John Chamberlain. Manningham, unlike Chamberlain, not only knew of the existence of Shakespeare, but knew of him as a formidable and jolly theater personality.

A more important entry relating to Shakespeare is the Diarist's brief eye-witness report of a performance of *Twelfth Night* in the Great Hall of the Middle Temple (fo. 12b). Although we wish he had given details about this entertainment provided for the Candlemas Feast of 1601/02, at least he was there, and he enjoyed the Malvolio plot device enough to record it in his book.

Both the Shakespeare passages are justly famous, one for evidence of the playwright's amorous proclivities, the other for its record of a production of his most festive high comedy.

If Manningham tended to slight the public theaters, his curiosity did lead him to read about and explore all manner of other subjects, from popular writers of the day like Samuel Rowlands to controversialists like Thomas Stapleton, and from medical remedies to the latest popular craze, shuttlecock. One of the Diarist's principal recreations was hearing sermons, on which he took notes, varying in length according to preacher and message (and sometimes depending upon audibility)[18] from a few lines to as many as thirteen pages.

It was the beginning of the golden age of Anglican preaching, and he savored the vigorous, eloquent, reasoned, and witty presentation of the Christian faith by a host of illustrious pulpit orators, including the learned Lancelot Andrewes, then Dean of Westminster; John Spenser of Corpus Christi College, Oxford, newly granted a D.D. and preaching in his flowing, figurative style; Andrew Downes, the celebrated Regius Professor of Greek at Cambridge, John King, future bishop of London, then at St. Andrew, Holborn; Thomas

18. After straining in vain to hear Francis Marbury at the Temple Church, in October 1602, he wrote: "I love not to heare the sound of the sermon, except the preacher will tell me what he says" (fo. 55).

Holland, Regius Professor of Divinity at Oxford; and adventurous John Layfield, who had been to the New World and had survived to tell about it. These were scholars all, soon to distinguish themselves as bishops or Bible revisers, or both, using wit to make the Gospel meaningful and, without knowing it, providing patterns and models for the future Dean of St. Paul's, the great John Donne. Manningham also heard Roger Fenton, admired by Francis Bacon and the elite and favored by wealthy patrons, and the colorful popular preachers Clapham and Egerton.

Besides such prominent figures, less notable preachers received his attention too. Some of these are sharply depicted, such as one, unnamed, "at Paules," who had "a long browne beard, a hanging looke, a gloting eye, and a tossing learing jeasture" (fo. 79).

Many of the preaching clergy seem to have heeded the advice given by Bishop Gardiner in 1547 that the congregation had better be delighted or entertained or they would go home and drink. Manningham heard some vigorous and homely homilies on a variety of points theological and ethical. For example, he heard Edward Philips declare, "The drunkard makes his belly noe better than a bucking tubb, a vessell to poure into, and put out at" (fo. 8).

The Diarist was by no means uncritical and could, when occasion warranted, react acidly, as he did to the "sounding laboured artificiall pronunciacion" of the Dean of Windsor, Dr. Giles Thompson, whom he heard at Whitehall in April 1603: "he regards that soe muche that his speache hath no more matter then needes in it" (fo. 125b). He was also quick to perceive ironic incongruities. For instance, after hearing the rector of St. Clement Danes, Dr. John Layfield, preach on laboring not for personal gain or advancement but for the service of God and the state, he commented ironically: "Mr. Hill told me that Mr. Layfeild married a rich wife, worth above 1000£. He speakes against covetousnes, but will exact the most of his dutyes in his parishe" (fo. 126).

Often the young lawyer attended two sermons on a Sunday. On December 12, 1602, after going to St. Clement's, he went to the little second-story church of St. Anne's, Blackfriars, to hear Stephen Egerton, who was attracting large crowds—"specially of women," says Manningham—with his winsome piety. Egerton would soon be one of those chosen by the Puritan leaders to present the Millenary petition for additional reform of the Church.

Among the most colorful of these pulpit orators was another of
Puritan persuasion, Henoch Clapham, who is mentioned eight times
in the Diary. His regular church was St. Peter's at Paul's Wharf, but
Manningham heard him in various places. On the afternoon of December 19, 1602, when Clapham preached at a church in Foster
Lane end, Manningham described him as "a black fellowe, with a
sower looke, but a good spirit, bold, and sometymes bluntly witty"
(fo. 80). Discoursing on Canticles 4:3, "Thy lips are like a thred of
skarlett," Clapham was heard to say, "An harlot is like a pantofle
or slipper at an Inne, which is ready to serve for every foote that
comes" (fo. 81). The following February at the Temple Church,
the Diarist heard Dr. George Abbot (the future Archbishop of
Canterbury) preach in the forenoon and Clapham in the afternoon.
Evidently the preaching of the latter appealed to the Inns of Court
students, for Manningham also quotes several witticisms attributed
to Clapham.

Manningham's note-taking methods seem to have varied. His full
and detailed notes of Dr. John King's sermon at Paul's Cross in
October 1602, for instance, suggest that he may have had his little
book with him while listening; that is, he wrote in longhand on the
spot; or if not, he took notes in some form of shorthand and later
transcribed them.[19] Although ordinarily he was content merely to
list the main heads of a sermon, on occasions when a star attraction
like Dr. King or Dr. Spenser preached, he paraphrased and quoted
extensively, writing down nearly everything he heard.[20] The result
is an oral quality: the distinctive tones and idiom of the preacher,
together with something of the flavor of his personality. Thus
Manningham caught one of Dr. King's favorite expressions, "the
apple of his eye."

Several of the churchmen heard by Manningham would within a
few years become Bible revisers: Overall, Holland, Abbot, Thompson, as well as Andrewes, Spencer, Downes, and Layfield. These
men, along with Fenton, Lively, Chaderton, Harding, Reynolds,
Ravis, and other scholarly divines—and Sir Henry Savile—were

19. These inferences run counter to the opinion of W. Fraser Mitchell that
the Diarist's sermon notes were "clearly written up from memory day by day
and probably owe nothing to note-taking at the moment." *English Pulpit
Oratory from Andrewes to Tillotson* (New York, 1962), p. 36.

20. See notes to fo. 40, below.

rising to the literary heights of the King James version. As Manningham's extracts of their sermons show, they were already steeped in
the diction and rhythms of the earlier versions—the Vulgate,
Tyndale, Coverdale, the Geneva.[21]

A passage from a sermon delivered at St. Paul's by Jeffrey King,
a Fellow of King's College, Cambridge, who became Regius Professor of Hebrew at Cambridge and served in Andrewes' Hebrew group
of translators at Westminster, affords a brief example of this Scriptural flavor:

> Fayth is the evidence of things not seene; as we hold our
> temporal inheritaunce by our writinges, which we call our
> evidence, soe wee clayme our eternall inheritaunce in the
> heavens by fayth, which is our evidence.   (fo. 103)

For students of late Elizabethan and Jacobean preaching, the
Diary is a rich source; it affords abundant evidence that the basic
themes, methods, structure, and stylistic qualities, such as the serious
use of wit, striking imagery, and homely analogies—and sometimes,
too, the eloquence, fervor, and poetry—that we have come to admire in the sermons of John Donne were being employed some
dozen years or more before Donne began his ministry.

Among the many attractive personalities that emerge from the
pages of Manningham is Dr. Henry Parry, one of the Queen's chaplains and a future prelate, who on April 20, 1602, entertained the
young lawyer as an overnight guest, probably at Sundridge, in Kent,
where Parry held benefices.

On that occasion the older man reminisced about his upbringing:

> Dr. Parry told how his father was deane of Salisbury, kept a
> sumptuous house, spent above his revenewe, was carefull to
> preferr such as were men of hope, used to have showes at his
> house, wherein he would have his sonne an actor to embolden
> him.   (fo. 38b)

Clearly such training in acting had been beneficial. According to
Sir John Harrington, who often heard him preach before the Queen

21. This is perhaps the answer to the question raised by Gustavus Paine in
The Learned Men (1959), p. 44: "How could such men as Barlow, Spenser,
and Fenton have risen to the literary heights reached by the King James
version?"

(as Dr. Parry had recently done on Good Friday—see fo. 38), Parry was "greatly respected and reverenced at the court" because "it was not possible to deliver sounder matter, nor with better method."[22] Manningham reinforces this tribute, for when Parry showed him the sermon he had preached on "My God, My God, why hast thou forsaken me?" the Diarist liked it for its eloquence, "sound doctrine, grave exhortacions, and heavenly meditacions," and he remembered its main heads (fo. 38b). Later (fo. 133) he mentioned the honor accorded Parry by Archbishop Whitgift in "soliciting" him to prepare a funeral oration for the Queen. This worthy parson would become Dean of Chester, then of Rochester (where Donne's friend John Pory, the indefatigable newsletter writer and future secretary of state in Virginia, heard him preach in Latin before the royal brothers-in-law, James I and Christian IV of Denmark),[23] then Bishop of Gloucester and finally of Worcester, where he erected a pulpit in the nave of the cathedral.

From Dr. Parry the Diarist obtained a recipe for making "ale for the spring":

> Of the juyce of Scourvy-grasse, one pint; of the juyce of water-cresses, as much; of the juyce of succory, halfe a pint; of the juyce of fumitory, halfe a pint: proportion to one gallon of ale: they must be all tunned up togither.   (fo. 34)

This worthy chaplain also told him of an Elizabethan experiment with a new psychedelic drug, laudanum, which could be obtained at Dr. Turner's, apothecary, in Bishopgate Street, and which "will for a tyme lay a man in a sweete trans, as Dr. Parry told me he tryed in a fever" (fo. 34). The physician referred to was a prominent member of the medical fraternity and Parry's brother-in-law, Peter Turner.

Through the accounts of Dr. Parry, we catch glimpses of the Queen—in a bitter mood after the execution of Essex and also in a merry mood. In these brief sketches Gloriana seems very human, even pathetic.

In her final hours, Dr. Parry, in his capacity as chaplain, attended

22. *Nugae Antiquae,* ed. Henry Harington and Thomas Park, 2 (1804), 205.

23. Pory to Sir Robert Cotton, August 12, 1606, in Brit. Mus. MS Jul. C. III, 298. A portion of this letter was printed in *Court and Times of James I,* ed. Thomas Birch, 1 (1948), 65–67.

at her bedside. At this time when she was dying and rumors were rampant, Manningham went to the court at Richmond, to find out at first hand whether she was still living. At the chapel he found himself in illustrious company, with Archbishop Bancroft, Lord Keeper Egerton, and many other high officials. After hearing Dr. Parry preach "a verry learned, eloquent, relligious, and moving sermon" and offer a fervent prayer "for hir Majestie" that "left few eyes drye" (fo. 110), he dined with him in the Privy Chamber. There he heard from Parry and other clergy, including the Bishop of Chichester and the Deans of Canterbury and Windsor, of the Queen's melancholy during the previous three or four months and learned details of her pensiveness and silence followed by her renewal of faith during the final days of her life.

> Shee tooke great delight in hearing prayers, would often at the name of Jesus lift up hir handes and eyes to Heaven. Shee would not heare the Arch[bishop] speake of hope of hir longer lyfe, but when he prayed or spake of Heaven and those joyes, shee would hug his hand, &c. It seemes shee might have lived yf she would have used meanes; but she would not be persuaded, and princes must not be forced. Hir physicians said shee had a body of a firme and perfect constitucion, likely to have lived many yeares.
>
> A royall majesty is noe priviledge against death.   (fo. 111)

So ends the entry of March 23rd. The next, written the following day, reads as follows:

> This morning about 3 at clocke hir Majesty departed this lyfe, mildly like a lambe, easily like a ripe apple from the tree, *cum leve quadam febre, absque gemitu.* Dr. Parry told me that he was present and sent his prayers before hir soule; and I doubt not but shee is amongst the royall saintes in heaven in eternall joyes.   (fo. 111b)

Later that same morning James VI of Scotland was proclaimed King. Manningham describes the reading of the proclamation by Cecil at Whitehall Gates and again in Cheapside, amid the panoply, the pageantry, of "Many noblemen, lords spirituell and temporell, knightes, 5 trumpets, many herauldes."

The fears of civil strife, the solemn relief when no uprisings

occurred—attitudes shared by the bulk of the population—are
reflected in statements like the following:

> There was a diligent watch and ward kept at every gate and
> street, day and night, by housholders, to prevent garboiles:
> which God be thanked were more feared then perceived.
>
> (fo. 111b)

These accounts, together with the next describing the reactions
of the citizenry to the proclamation, provide an eloquent and
dignified climax for the book. Here the Diarist is at his best: sorrow-
ful, anxious, hopeful, and sincerely thankful for a peaceful outcome
to a dangerous crisis. He has put aside his customary cool objectivity
and spoken out with personal feeling.

> The proclamacion was heard with greate expectacion, and
> silent joye, noe great shouting. I thinke the sorrowe for hir
> Majesties departure was soe deep in many heartes they could
> not soe suddenly shew anie great joy, though it could not be
> lesse then exceeding greate for the succession of soe worthy a
> King. And at night they shewed it by bonefires, and ringing.
>
> (fo. 112)

There was, he continued,

> Noe tumult, noe contradicion, noe disorder in the city; every
> man went about his busines, as readylie, as peaceably, as
> securely, as though there had bin noe change, nor any newes
> ever heard of competitors. God be thanked, our king hath his
> right: *magna veritas et prevalet.*   (fo. 112)

Some ten days later Manningham recorded a footnote to the
Queen's passing, one that strongly suggests an historical basis for
(the germ of truth within) the romantic legend of Elizabeth and the
Earl of Essex. The source was one of the Queen's ladies, Frances, the
Countess Kildare (daughter of the first Earl of Nottingham, now
married to Henry Brooke, Lord Cobham), who had told Dr. Parry
that "the Queene caused the ring wherewith shee was wedded to
the Crowne, to be cutt from hir finger some 6 weekes before hir
death, but wore a ring which the Earl of Essex gave hir unto the
day of hir death" (fo. 119b). Besides reports of this sort, recorded
at first or second hand, the Diary abounds in anecdotes of historical

interest, some of the Queen, some of illustrious courtiers like Sir Walter Ralegh, some of lesser known figures. One on fo. 38, for instance, records Elizabeth's irony toward Dr. William Barlowe when he ventured to come into her presence against her express command, given because he had preached at Paul's against Essex.

The current dislike of Ralegh is reflected in several passages. One story Manningham heard from Charles Danvers:

> A lewde fellowe comming before Sir W. Rawley to be examined concerninge some wrecke which he had gotten into his handes, and being demaunded whether he would sweare to such articles as they would propound, answerd that he would sweare to anie thinge they would aske him, and then being admonished he should not be soe rashe in soe serious a matter, as concerned his soule soe nearely, "Fayth," said he, "I had rather trust God with my soule, then you with my goodes."
>
> (fo. 24b)

"Bold-faced" Ralegh, brilliant but proud to the point of brazenness, is also commemorated in a verse exchange that puns insultingly on his name, reflects his disgrace following his clandestine marriage to Elizabeth Throckmorton, alludes to his poem "The Lie," and expresses the contumely with which he was generally regarded: Raw Ly (fo. 83).

Other colorful personalities appear: Serjeant Daniel, judge of the assizes at Rochester (fo. 16); Richard Ousley, or Oseley, of the Middle Temple, evidently a madcap (fo. 39b); the old Recorder William Fleetwood, and his son Thomas, on whom John Bramston, the future Lord Chief Justice, exercised his wit and judgment (fos. 29b, 31b); Barbara Ruthven, sister of the ill-fated principals in the Gowry Conspiracy, which had nearly cost King James his life (fos. 117, 127b); and old Stow, the antiquary (fo. 78).

Because of his wide acquaintance, which included Peter Saltonstall, son of a prominent goldsmith of London and ancestor of a family that has since been prominent in the political life of Massachusetts, Manningham met a number of celebrities to whom he might not otherwise have had entrée.

The more one reads or studies Manningham, the more one becomes engrossed in the personalities whose lives are glimpsed for a few moments and who seem alive as one encounters them. Such immediacy is an attribute of the best personal writing, but it is particularly characteristic of letters and diaries. Part of Manningham's success is due to his style, which is nearly always lucid and vigorous. Like most Elizabethan prose it has an oral, colloquial ring; despite its formal echoes of classical rhetoric, it has the tang of speech.

Although the Diarist tells us little of his private life and seldom states directly what he is thinking and feeling—his is not the intimate candor of Pepys, but rather an elusive charm of another sort, perhaps to be found in ironic detachment—he has recorded a few personal or domestic episodes. In these is reflected his friendly interest in people, in human nature and psychology.

From his "father-in-love," Richard Manningham, the old squire of the manor of Bradbourne, in East Malling, Kent, he garnered odd bits of information about the cloth business, trade, politics and legal customs in the Low Countries, local property transactions, the custom in Goa of burning widows with the bodies of their husbands, the new surgical method of cutting for the stone with a catheter and "an other toole which they call a duckes bill" (fo. 15), and the way wolves generate.

Because of his periodic visits to Bradbourne, several entries refer to his foster-father's second wife, who seems to have given her husband a hard time. For instance, he observed the following family squabble:

> Cos. shee would have sent a part of a gammon of bacon to their servantes; my cousin said he loved it well, &c. And, because he would not send that shee would, shee would not that he would, and grewe to strange hott contradiction with him. After, when shee sawe him moved (and not without cause), shee fell a kissing his hand at table with an extreeme kinde of flattery, but never confest shee was to violently opposite.   (fo. 38b)

Another day, when she had received some fish from one Joane Bachellor but, for some reason not stated, had sent them back and had been chided by her husband for her unforgiving nature, the Diarist tells us that "this shee tooke in such snuffe that she could not afford him a good looke all that day, but blubberd, &c." (fo. 14b).

Nevertheless John seems to have enjoyed her company. Once he rode with her to Maidstone, where they dined at the home of a physician and family friend, Dr. Gellibrand. Together they inspected a skull in the doctor's study and heard about how the doctor had given a feverish clergyman, Mr. Alane, both a "glyster" (clyster, or enema) and a blood-letting on the same day (fo. 10b). (We never learn whether the patient survived such ungentle treatment.)

The doctor had a brother, Thomas Gellibrand, and we have this delightful bit of dialogue concerning two congenial wives:

> My Cosen shee said that the Gellibrands 2 wives lived like a couple of whelpes togither, meaninge sportingl[y]—but I sayd like a payre of turtles, or a couple of connies: sweetely and loveingly. (fo. 10b)

Sometime that same day, Mrs. Manningham confided in her young companion, telling him of a traumatic experience in her first marriage when, riding behind her husband, Marche, she fell off the horse and was left to walk while her husband rode off without her (fo. 10b). This comical-pathetic adventure of a real-life Kate and Petruchio may have endeared the lady to him.

Besides the many shrewd and pungent appraisals of men and manners (on fo. 39 "one Parkins" of the Inner Temple is described as "a very complementall gent[leman]. A Barrester, but noe lawyer"), and besides the salty humor and the youthful tendency to scoff and ridicule (he and his cousin Thomas Cranmer enjoyed jibing at the eminent Oxford divine Dr. John Reynolds for his tendency to display his prodigious learning and memory by excessive quoting—fo. 66), humanitarian sympathies appear. On the violence with which Turner ended his fencing match with his opponent Dun by mortally running him "soe far in the brayne at the eye," Manningham commented, "A goodly sport in a Christian state, to see one man kill an other" (fo. 98).

In numerous such passages of ironic comment the Diarist reveals himself as an observer with a cutting edge. Concerning gossip that George Snigge, the Middle Temple Bencher and Treasurer, was offering £800 to be named Serjeant-at-Law, Manningham adds with characteristic wit: "Argent makes Sargent" (fo. 91).

If he took conscious pride in his own talent for clever phrase-making and skill in repartee (see fo. 11, for example), his vanity is pardonable when we recall the sparkling company he had to compete with at the Middle Temple. It seems obvious that he used the Diary partly as a training ground to exercise his wit, as well as his memory, and we can be glad that he did.

Like his counterparts at the other Inns of Court in this period, the Middle Templar was naturally and uninhibitedly male. Elizabethan in upbringing and temperament, he was accustomed to juxtapositions of splendor and filth, of the glories of mind and spirit and the delights and absurdities of the body. While seriously concerned with Christian theology and polemics, as well as the law, he seems to have been almost as curious about the lower divinity of Eros. Manningham, for instance, could, on the same page, jot down an apt analogy in a sermon by Dr. Rowland Searchfield of St. John's College, Oxford, and also some doggerel advice on marital relations:

> Offer noe love rights, but lett your wife
>   still seeke them,
> For when they come unsought, they seldome
>   like them.   (fo. 9)

When John Bruce, the Victorian editor, omitted entries like this, on grounds of sensibility, he distorted the portrait that the Diary gives us. Comparison of the original MS with the 1868 edition printed by the Camden Society shows that Bruce omitted 54 passages. Of these, 37 were left out because of their alleged coarseness or indecency. Of the other 17, 14 are brief, including several that are virtually illegible (such as the one at the top of the fly leaf, fo. 1) and a few that are unclear.

Of the three longer omissions, one, on fos. 95 and 95b, lists fifteen lottery mottos, which formed part of an entertainment that Sir Thomas Egerton and his wife, the Countess of Derby, put on for the Queen and her ladies at Harefield, near Uxbridge, in July 1602. A full account of this device, misdated 1601, was printed by Francis Davison in *A Poetical Rhapsody* (1602). Another version, a manuscript in the Conway collection, gives a slightly different text of the mottos. Comparison shows that Manningham's version matches the latter, suggesting that he had a manuscript copy, either the Conway or one like it, and that where they differ from

Davison's, the Manningham and Conway MS texts are usually superior.

Bruce also omitted nine pages of extracts from Sir John Hayward on the Succession, in reply to Dolman, and six pages of extensive notes on a Latin polemical work by Thomas Stapleton, the academic oration *An Politici sint in numero Christianorum habendi.* These passages together with quotations and paraphrases from other contemporary works, such as William Warner's *Albion's England* and Samuel Rowlands' lively genre piece *'Tis Merrie When Gossips Meet,* show us explicitly what Inns of Court students were reading in 1602 and 1603.

Decidedly more entertaining, however, are the clever anecdotes and other bits of bawdry that Manningham seems to have picked up wherever he went—even in the tiltboat between London and Gravesend (fo. 102b). In thus savoring the Rabelaisian or risqué, the complete Middle Templar was reflecting an interest shared by most men of his age and probably by most normal men and women in all periods. Certainly, in this respect he was like other, more important writers, including Jonson and Henry Wotton, who, as we learn from William Drummond of Hawthornden, dabbled in erotica.[24]

However dubious the literary value of such jocularities (some of them are silly or trivial), the several sexual and the few scatalogical jokes that Manningham recorded suggest that his interest in these matters was secondary to other considerations: to satire, story-telling, and wit; and they help to round out the portrait of the complete Middle Templar.

Because of its broad range of interests—it touches on many different aspects of Elizabethan and Jacobean life, including the new science, medicine, politics, sports, and even fashions—it exhibits concretely the curiosity and versatility that distinguish its era and is a characteristically Renaissance book. Aside from its importance as a repository of entertaining anecdotes and witty sayings in the jest-book tradition, it is a valuable historical record of the persons, trends, events, and public attitudes of the times.

24. Conversations, 5, ll. 78–81, in *Ben Jonson*, ed. C. H. Herford and Percy Simpson, I (1925), 134.

Its principal value as history is in the way it reflects the temper of the *fin de siècle,* the general apprehension, with the old regime breaking up amid nervous concern for the succession to Elizabeth's throne. The Diary illustrates the contemporary interest both in the theoretical questions stimulated by the 1594 publication of Dolman's *A Conference about the next Succession to the Crown of England* and by Hayward's Reply, and in such actual claimants as Arabella Stuart, who at the end of 1602 had been indulging in dangerous intrigue and on whom the Queen had set a close watch.[25]

We glimpse Elizabeth, aging, declining into melancholy and debility, pathetically human, but imperious to the end. As history the Diary is, as its Victorian editor declared, virtually a primary source of information about her death and the attitudes of fear and hope prevailing in that crisis. As Hunter declared, Manningham's account "rises to the dignity of an historical document."[26]

One passage reports a rumor, later proved false, of armed opposition by the Lord Beauchamp (Edward Seymour), who as the son of the Earl of Hertford was a possible claimant to the throne.

At this time all "schemers for advancement"[27] were looking toward the Scottish court, and in the entries of March and April 1603 the Diarist provides clear and immediate evidence of the jockeying for position of courtiers and would-be courtiers to gain the favor of their new sovereign. These included Robert Carey; John Davies; Sir Henry Bromley; Edward Neville, Lord Latimer; and Ralegh's Kentish henchman, Henry Brooke, Lord Cobham.

Among the many notices of historical interest is the release from the Tower, on April 10, 1603, of the Earl of Southampton, Shakespeare's patron, and Sir Henry Nevil. Also mentioned is Lord Henry Howard, son of the Earl of Surrey and a cousin of the Queen but an old supporter of the Queen of Scots—he had been working to effect an alliance between King James and Cecil and had been poisoning the King's mind against Ralegh.[28]

25. J. E. Neale, *Queen Elizabeth* (New York, 1934), p. 387.

26. *Illustrations of Shakespeare* (1848), p. 369.

27. Agnes M. C. Latham, *The Poems of Sir Walter Ralegh* (London, 1951), introd., p. xviii.

28. Fo. 121. See A. L. Rowse, *Sir Walter Ralegh, His Family and Private Life* (New York, 1962), pp. 228, 230; also Willard M. Wallace, *Sir Walter Ralegh* (Princeton, 1959), pp. 183–184.

Such scraps and fragments on the fringes of history and biography have their place, however modest, by contributing to our understanding of the personalities that have made history. Manningham is, of course, not a conscious historian, and he is seldom tendentious or eulogistic. Herein lies part of his charm. But like some of the best of the early historians and biographers, from Foxe on Bishop Latimer in the *Actes and Monuments* (1563), to Cotton Mather in the *Magnalia Christi Americana* (1702), he had an ear for anecdote and often makes use of directly quoted conversation.

The Diary, too, is not without antiquarian value. It records on fo. 16b, for instance, inscriptions on tombs that have since disappeared from Rochester Cathedral. As one might expect, some of Manningham's notes are primarily of legal interest, such as that on fo. 30b regarding the controversy over rank and precedence in the seating of officers at the York assizes. Several portray customs and procedures (and even furniture) at the Middle Temple, such as the following entry, with its pun on "Dunce's table":

> There is nowe a table placed for the barristeres crosse over the Hall by the cuppord, which one called St. Albanes because he said it was in the ways to Dunstable.　　　　　(fo. 26b)

And after eleven new Serjeants had been called (February 1, 1602/03–fo. 91), Manningham described the ceremony in the Hall:

> This day at dynner Mr. Snig tooke Mr. Nichols by the hand and led him up from the lower end of the table, where his place was, and seated him, on the benche highest at the upper end.

This custom is similarly described by Dugdale in *Origines Juridiciales* (1666).

Sufficient examples to indicate the importance of the work as social history have been cited. As a source book on contemporary preachers, their theological stance and their artistry in the pulpit, it is invaluable. The notes on sermons suggest the serious concerns of the Elizabethans—a deeper note that is never long absent from the thoughts of the finer men of the period.

Perceptive readers will find other elements of literary significance besides those already emphasized: the glances at writers like Donne and Jonson, the examples of wit in action among members of their circle, the evidence of their appeal to the intellectual elite at the Inns of Court, the concrete indication of who comprised their coterie, at once both audience and stimulus for prose paradoxes and avant garde verse, and the proof of what was being read by at least one member of that audience. In the Shield Gallery at Whitehall (fo. 3) the Diarist observed the empresas; by recording the various "scucheons," mottos, and verses there, he has provided thirty-five examples of the emblem tradition that influenced the verse of Quarles, Herbert, and Crashaw.

Since Manningham's Diary was obviously not intended to be a work of literature, it cannot be ranked high in the scale of literary art. It is too unsystematic, unorganized, fragmentary, the inevitable faults of a medley. Yet it warrants a respectable place in literary history, in that heterogeneous group of journals, letters, notebooks, and diaries that we call memoir literature. Thus it belongs with the records and jottings of Henry Machyn, the merchant-tailor and undertaker; of Samuel Ward, the Puritan divine; of Roger Wilbraham, the lawyer, and James Whitelock, Manningham's fellow barrister at the Middle Temple; of Simonds D'Ewes' autobiography with its valuable Inns of Court material; of Lady Anne Clifford; and of the letter-writers Chamberlain, Dudley Carleton, Joseph Mead, and John Pory. Of such works surviving from the Elizabethan and Jacobean periods there can never be enough.

TEXT OF THE DIARY

FOLIO 1

A puritan is a curious corrector of thinges indifferent.

[*line illegible in MS*]
[Rec?] [1]St. Dunstanes [2]Paules [3]Christ church [4]Salsbury [5]Windsor

SONG TO THE QUEENE AT THE MASKE AT COURT

Nov. 2.

Mighty Princes of a fruitfull land,
   In whose riche bosome stored bee
   Wisdome and care, treasures that free
Us from all feare; thus with a bounteous hand
You serve the world which yett you doe commaund.
     Most gracious Queene, wee tender back
      Our lyves as tributes due,
     Since all whereof wee all partake
      Wee freely take from you.

Blessed Goddess of our hopes increase,
   Att whose fayre right hand
Attend Justice and Grace,
   Both which commend
True beauties face;
Thus doe you never cease
To make the death of warr the life of peace.
Victorious Queene, soe shall you live
   Till tyme it selfe must dye,
Since noe tyme ever can deprive
   You of such memory.

[*fo. 1b blank in MS*]

FOLIO 2

In Motleyum
O cruell death to murder in thy rage
Our ages flower in flower of his age.—Holland

In Spenserum
Famous alive and dead, here is the od's
Then god of Poets, nowe poet of the Gods.

March 29, 1602.
I sawe Dr. Parryes picture with a bible in his hand, the word upon
it *huic credo,* and over his heade an heaven, with a motto, *Hoc
Spero.*

Epigr[am] (Mr. Kedgwyn)
lustre
The radiant *splendor* of Tom Hortons nose
Amates the ruby and puts downe the rose.
Had I a jewell of soe rich an hewe
I would present it to some monarchs viewe.
Subjects ought not to weare such gemms as those
Therefore our Prince shall have Tom Hortons nose.

Eiusdem in Luce Morgan
I say that Luce's bodie's chast
Downe from hir head unto hir wast,
But to hir wast up from hir thyes
Whoe sayth she's chast I say he lyes.

FOLIO 2b

Epitaph in the Chauncery at Sandey in Bedford[shire]

Cur caro laetatur dum vermibus esca paratur?
Terrae terra datur, caro nascitur ut moriatur;
Terram terra tegat, demon peccata resumat,
Mundus res habeat, spiritus alta petat.

Why growes our fleshe so proud,
Whiles 'tis but made wormes foode?
This earth must turne to earth,
To dye flesh tooke it birth,
The earth our earth must hyde,
Our synnes the devill betyde,
The world our goodes must have,
And God our soules will save.

FOLIO 3

**Certayne Devises and Empresaes
taken by the Scucheons in the
Gallery at Whitehall. 19 Martij, 1601.**

The scucheon, twoe windemilles crosse sailed, and all the verge
of the scucheon poudred with crosses crosselets; the word, *Vndique
cruciatus.* Under written these verses:
When most I rest behold howe I stand crost,
When most I move I toyle for others gayne,
The one declares my labour to be lost,
The other shewes my quiet is but payne.
Unhappy then whose destiny are crosses,
When standinge still and moveing breedes but losses.

The devise manie small tapers neere about a great burning; the
word, *Nec tibi minus erit.*

The devise a taper newe blowen out, with a fayre blast from a
cloude; the word, *Te flante relucet.*

The scucheon argent with a hand and a pen in it; the word, *Solus
amor depinget.*

Two garlandes in a sheild, one of lawrell, the other of cypresse; the
word, *Manet vna cupressi.*

A ship in the sea; the word, *Meus error ab alto.*

A man falling from the top of a ladder; the word, *Non quo, sed unde cado.*

A scrole of paper full of cypheres; the word, *Adde vnum.*

A sunne with a sweete face in it averted from an armed knight, shaddowed in a cloud all but his handes and knees, which were bended; the word, *Quousque auertes?*

FOLIO 3b

The scucheon, a grayhound coursing, with a word, *In libertate labor;* and an other grayhound tyed to a tree and chafinge that he can not be loosed to followe the game he sawe; the word, *In servitute dolor.*

A fayre sunne; the word, *Occidens occidens.*

A glorious lady in a cloud in the one syde, and a sunne in the other. Beneath a sacrifice of hands, harts, armes, pennes, &c.; the word, *Soli, non soli.*

A kingfisher bird, sitting against the winde; the word, *Constans contrariae spernit.*

A palme tree laden with armor upon the bowes; the word, *Fero, at patior.*
An empty bagpipe; the word, *Si impleueris.*

An angle with the line and hooke; *Semper tibi pendent.*

A viall well strunge; the word, *Adhibe dextram.*

A sable field; the word, *Par nulla figura dolori.*

A partridge with a spaniell before hir, and a hauke over hir; the word, *Quo me vertam.*

The man in the moone with thornes on his backe looking down-warde; the word, *At infra se videt omnia.*

A large diamond well squared; the word, *Dum formas minuis.*

A pyramis standinge, with the mott *Ubi* upon it, and the same fallen, with the word *Ibi* upon it.

A burning glas betwixt the sunne, and a lawne which it had sett on fire; the word, *Nec tamen cales.*

A flame; the word, *Tremet et ardet.*

A torch light in the sunne, the word, *Quis furor.*

FOLIO 4

A stag having cast his head and standing amazedly, weeping over them; the word over, *Inermis et deformis;* under, *Cur dolent habentes.*

A torche ready to be lighted; the word, *Spero lucem.*

A man attyred in greene, shoting at a byrd in the clowdes, the one arrowe over, the other under, the 3rd in his bowe drawne to the heade, with this word upon it, *Spero vltimam.*

A foote treading on a worme; *Leviter ne peream.*

A dyall in the sunne; *In occasu desinit esse.*

A ballance in a hand; *Ponderare est errare.*

A fly in an hors eye; *Sic ultus peream.*

A scucheon argent; *Sic cum forma nulla placet.*

A ship sayling in the sea; *Portus in ignoto est.*

An eagle looking on the sunne; *Reliqua sordent.*

A branche sprung forth of an oake couped; the word, *Planta fuit quercus.*

[*fo. 4b blank in MS*]

FOLIO 5

Marche 28: 1602.
At the Temple:
sermon, the text, Mark, 10:20.

---

notes: All the commandementes must be observed with like respect; it is not sufficient to affect one and leave the rest unrespect, for that were to make an Idoll of that precept.

Obedience must be seasoned with love; yf any other respect be predominat in our actions, as feare of punishment, desyre of estimacion, &c., they are out of temper.

  Christ propoundes these commaundementes of the 2nd table, because, yf a man cannot observe these, he shall never be able to keepe them of the first, for yf a man love not his neighbor whom he hath seene, howe shall he love God whom he hath not seene? And he that is bound to observe the lesse must keepe the greater commaundement.

The doctrine of justificacion consistes upon these pillars, 1. *ex merito, si non ex condigno, at ex congruo.* 2. and this upon free-will, for noe merrit with[out] a free agent. 3. and this upon a possibilitie of keeping the commaundementes, for *liberum arbitrium* is a power of performing what wee would and should, and *libertas voluntatis* and *liberum arbitrium* are severall.

Noe man can performe anie any action soe well but he shall fayle either in the goodnes of the motion efficient, the meanes, or end.

Justificacion by workes is but old Pharisaisme and newe papisme;

FOLIO 5b

the papistes distinguishe and make *Justiciam legalem* and *evangelicam;* the 1st in performaunce of outward required accions; the 2nd in the intent supplied.

All the sacrifices that God was most delighted with are for the most part sayd to be yonge: a lambe, &c., and the exhortacion of him which was more the agent and more learned then anie, for he was a King and the wisest that ever was, is. Remember thy Creator in the dayes of thy youth, &c.

There is a generall and a speciall love of Christ wherewith he embraceth men; the 1st is here ment and mentioned, and with that he loves all which doe but endevour to be morrally good; soe doubteles he loved Aristides for his justice, which was a worke of God in him, and so being a good, God could not but love it, and him for it.

But the speciall is that whereby he makes us heires of eternall lyfe, and adoptes us for his children.

Beholding him, God regardes the least perfections or rather imperfect affections in us; he will not breake a crazed reede.

FOLIO 6

At St. Clementes the preacher.

note. The breade in the sacrament becoming a nourishment is a *medicina* to our whole bodye.

The manner of receyving Christes body in the sacrament, as to make a question of it by way of doubting, is dangerous; soe to enquire of it to knowe it, is relligious.

Wee receive it *non per consubstantialitatem, sed per germanissimam societatem.* (Chrisostom.)

It must be received with 5 fingeres: the first the hand, the 2nd the understanding, 3rd fayth, 4th application, 5th affection and joy; and this makes it a Communion.

Take and eate, the wordes of the serpent to Eva, the wordes of the brasen serpent to us; those were beleved and brought in perdicion, these yf beleived are the meanes to salvation.

FOLIO 6b

Out of a booke called
the Picture of a Perfect
Commonwealth.

A wicked king is like a crazed ship, which drownes both selfe and
all that are in it.

Pleasures are like sweete singing birds, which yf a man offer to
take they fly awaye.

Dr. Mounfordes Sermon. (Ch. Davers.)
Of pleasure. *Momentaneum est quod delectat, Aeternum quod
cruciat.*
It is better to eate broken fishes with Christ, then a messe of pottage with Esau.

Nil turpius quam plus ingerrere quam possis digerere.

The glutton eates like a dogge, and lives like a hogg, having his
soule as salt onely to keep his body from stinkinge. He that filleth
his body emptieth his soule.

Id pro Deo colitur quod prae omnibus diligitur.

Vtinam, sayth Augustine, *tam finiatur quam definitur ebrietas.*

Bacchus painted yonge because he makes men like children, unable
to goe or speake, naked because discovers all.

It is noe better excuse for a drunkard to say that it was his owne
that he spent, then yf one should say he would cut his owne throate
for the knife that should doe it is his owne.

Drunkennes is the divells birding synne; the drunkard like the stale
that allures other to be taken like it selfe.

Matt. 12.
Envie and mallice will barke though it be so musselled that it cannot bite.

FOLIO 7

It is almost divine perfection to resist carnal affection. When wee censure other men wee should imitate that good imitator of nature Apelles, whoe being to drawe a face of an great person which wanted an eye, drewe that side only which was perfect.

The malicious man is like the vultur, which passeth over manie sweete gardens and never rests but upon some carrion or garbage; soe he never takes notice of anie thing but vices. Libellers are the Divels herauldes.

Invidus alienum bonum suum facit peccando malum.

Envy, though in all other respectes it be a thing most execrable, yet in this it is in some sort commendable, that it is a vexacion to it selfe. It is like gunpowder, which consumes itselfe before it burnes the house. Or the fly *pyrausta,* which would put out the candle, but burnes it selfe.

Honor is like a buble, which is raysed with one winde and broken with an other.

MR. DOWNES.

The love of the world is the Divels eldest sonne.
Honour, riches, and pleasure are the wordly mans trynitie, wherewith he committs spirituall idolatry.

Thankefullnes is like the reflex of the sunne beame from a bright bodie.

After a full tyde of prosperitie cometh a lowe ebbe of adversitie. After a day of pleasure a night of sorrowe.

FOLIO 7b

Honour is like a spiders webbe, long in doinge, but soone undone, blowne down with every blast. It is like a craggy steepe rocke, which a man is longe getting upon, and being up, yf his foote but slip, he breakes his necke. Soe the Jewes dealt with Christ; one day they would have him a king, an other day none; one day cryed Hosanna to him, an other nothing but Crucifie him.

The world is like an host; when a man hath spent all, body, goodes, and soule with it, it will not vouchsafe to knowe him.

Laban chose rather to loose his daughters than his Idols, and the riche man had rather forsake his soule then his riches.

If a citisen of Rome made him selfe a citizen of anie other place, he lost his priviledge at Rome; yf a man wilbe a citizen of this world, he cannot be a citizen of heaven.

Ambitious men are like little children, which take great paynes in runninge up and downe to catch butterflyes, which are nothing but painted winges, and either perishe in takinge or fly away from them.

Covetous man like a child, which cryes more for the losse of a trifle then his inheritance; he laments more for losse of wealth then soule.

A covetous man proud of his riches is like a theife that is proud of his halter.

MR. PHILLIPS.

The proverbe is that building is a theife, because it makes us lay out more money then wee thought on. But pride is a theife and a whore too, for it robbes the maister of his wealth, and the mistress of hir honesty.

FOLIO 8

The drunkard makes his belly noe better then a bucking tubb, a vessell to poure into, and put out at.

Bona opera habent mercedem, non ratione facti, sed ratione pacti.

Non est refugium a Deo irato, nisi ad Deum placatum.

Synn is Adams legacy bequeathed to all his posteritie: nothing more common then to committ synn, and being committed, to conceale it.

A concealed synn is *tanquam serpens in sinu, gladius in corde, venenum in stommacho;* it is like a soare of the body: the closer it is kept, the more it festers.

Scelera quandoque possunt esse secreta, nunquam secura.

Confession must be *festina, vera, et amara.*

Confession of synne onely at the houre of death is like a theifes confession at the gallowes, or a traytors at the racke, when they cannot choose.

Sine confessione justus est ingratus, et peccator mortuus.

The mercy of God is never to be despayred of but still to be expected, even *inter pontem et fontem, jugulum et gladium.*

Dissembled righteousness is like smoake, which seemes to mount up to heaven, but never comes neare it.

Prayse is a kinde of paynt which makes every thing seeme better then it is. (Cha. Davers.)

To prayse an unworthy man is as bad as to paint the face of an old woman. (*Idem.*)

Sorrowe is the punishment and remedy for synn: *Sic deus quod poenam dedit, medicinam fecit.* (Augustine.)

FOLIO 8b

Mr. Munnes of Peterhouse in Cambridge.

Primum querite regnum Dei, et omnia adjicientur vobis.

Tullies brother, in a sort reprehendinge or discouraging his suit for the Consulship, tells him that he must remember that he is *novus, consulatum petit,* and *Romae est;* the Divell, perhaps least any should attempt to put this precept in practise, will terrifie us by shewinge us our weakenes, and that greatnes. *Terrae filius es; Regnum quaeris? Coelum est, &c.*

Sit modus amoris sine modo.
Beatus est domine qui te amat propter te, amicum in te, et inimicum propter te.

Quere, 3:[1.] *Quere Deum et non aliud tanquam illum;* 2. *non aliud praeter illum;* 3. *non aliud post illum.*

Diuitiae non sunt bonae, quae te faciant bonum, sed unde tu facias bonum.

Baeda interpreted those letters, S. P. Q. R. written upon a gate in Rome, *Stultus Populus Quaerit Romam,* intimating they were but fooles that went thither for true relligion.

Yf Christ had thought well of wealth he would not have bin soe poore himselfe. He was *pauper in ingressu,* borne in a manger; *in progressu,* not a hole to hide his head in; *in egressu,* not a sheet of his owne to shroude him in.

The covetous persons like the 7 leane kine that eate up the 7 fatt, and yet remaine as illfavoured as before.

Yf thou carest not to live in such a house as hell is, yett feare to dwell with such a companion as the Divel is.

FOLIO 9

Serchfeild of St. Johns in Oxford.

Cursus celerimus, saepe pessimus.

Sit opus in publico, intentio in occulto.

A dissembled Christian, like an intemperate patient, which can gladly heare his physicion discourse of his dyet and remedy, but will not endure to observe them.

Minus prospere, qui nimis propere.

MR. SCOTT, TRINIT. CANT'BR.

Dum sumus in corpore peregrinamur a domino.

Non contemnenda sunt parva, sine quibus non consistunt magna.

The soules of the just men are like Noahs dove sent out of the arke; could finde noe resting place upon the earth.

He that hath put on rich apparrail will be carefull he stayne it not; he that hath put on Christ, as a garment, must take heede he soile not himself with vices.

Offer noe love rights, but lett your wife still seeke them, For when they come unsought, they seldome like them.

An high calling is noe priviledge for an impious action.

All our new corne comes out of old fields, and all our newe learning is gathered out of old bookes. (Chaucer.)

Words spoken without consideracion are like a messinger without an errand.

Our owne righteousnes at the best is but like a beggares cloke, the substance old and rotten, and the best but patches.

FOLIO 9b

At Bradborne with my Cosen this Christmas.

1601

My Cosen told me that Mr. Richers would give his cosen Cartwright 8,000£. for his leas of the Abbey of towne mallinges, the Reversion whereof the L. Cobham hath purchased of hir Majestie.

An old child suckes hard; *i.* [*e.*], children when they growe to age prove chargeable.

Peter Courthope said it would be more beneficiall yf our woll and cloth were not to be transported but in Colours; but my cosen said, we may as well make it into clokes and garmentes, as dye it in colours before we carry it over; for both variable, and as much change in colour as fashion.

January.
To furnishe a shipp requireth much trouble,
But to furnishe a woman the charges are double.
(My Cosens wife said.)

The priviledge of enfranchising anie for London is graunted, to every Alderman at his first creation, for one: to every Sherif for 2: to every maior for 4. (Cosen.) And almost any man for some 40£. may buy his freedome, and these are called free by redemption.

If a man prentice in London marry, he shall be forced to serve of his time, and yet loose his freedome. But yf a woman prentice marry, shee shall onely forfayte hir libertie, but shall not be forced to serve. (Cosen.)

To be warden of the companie of mercers is some 80£. charge; to be one of the livery, a charge but a credit. A Bachelor is charged at the maiors feast some 100 markes.

FOLIO 10

January: 1601

The Flushingeres wanting money since hir Majesties tyme, and while they were our frends, seised certayne merchantes ships, forced them to give 40,000£; the merchantes complayned, but could not be relieved. Oftymes the Princes dutys are defrayed with the subjectes goodes.

Sir Moyle Finche of Kent married Sir Frauncis Hastinges daughter

and heir, worth to him 3,000£. per annum. All his livinge in Lincoln-
shire and Kent, &c., worth 4,000£. per annum. (Drue Chapman.)

8: Dyned at Mr. Gellibrandes, a physicion at Maidstone.

Mr. Fr[ancis] Vane, a yong gent. of great hope and forwardnes,
11: verry well affected in the Country already, in soe much that
the last parliament the Country gave him the place of knight before
Sir H. [?] Nevell; his possibilitie of living by his wife verry much,
shee beinge daughter and heire to Sir Antony Mildmay; and thought
hir mother will give hir all hir inheritance alsoe; the father worth
3,000£. per annum, the motheres 1,200£. (Mr. Tutsham.)

The Duke of Albues [Alva's] negligence in not fortifying Flushinge
before other places in the Netherlands was the cause he lost the
Country, for when he thought to have come and fortified, the
towne suddenly resisted his Spanish souldieres and forced them to
returne. (Cos[en].)

18: I rode with my cosens wife to Maidstone, dyned at Gellibrands.
As wee were viewinge a skull in his studye, he shewed the seame
in the middle over the heade

FOLIO 10b

Jan. 1601

and said that was the place which the midwife useth shutt in
women children before the wit can enter, and that is a reason that
women be such fooles ever after.

My Cosen shee said that the Gellibrands 2 wives lived like a couple
of whelpes togither, meaning sportingl[y]—but I sayd like a payre
of turtles, or a couple of connies: sweetely and loveingly.

Th. Gellib[rand] said that such a tall man lookt over the hedge as
other mens beastes doe, i.[e.] like a cuckold.

Husband, said a wife, I lay a wager you cannot put downe my

middle finger (yf he sh'uld shee might shewe him what shee gave him).

Mr. Alane, a minister, was verry sicke. Gellibrand gave him a glyster and lett him bloud the same day, for a fever; his reason was that not to have lett him bloud had bin verry dangerous but to lett bloud is doubtfull—it may doe good as well as harme.

My Cos., as I was walking with him, upon a suddein ranne into Hastons house, and out, and in againe straungelly.

My Cosen shee told me that when shee was first married to hir husband Marche, as shee rode behinde him, shee slipt downe, and he left hir behinde—never lookt back to take hir up; soe shee went soe long afoote that shee tooke it soe unkindely that she thought never to have come againe to him, but to have sought a service in some unknowne place, but he tooke hir at last.

Wee were at Mrs. Cavils, where she practised some wit upon my cosen shee.

Cosen she called double Anemonies "double enimies."

Mrs. Cavill desired some rootes, and shee referd hir to hir man Thomas Smith.

FOLIO 11

Jan: 1601

My cose sh[e] speaking lavishly in commendacions of one Lovell of Cranebrooke (a good honest poore silly puritane), "O," said shee, "he goes to the ground when he talks in Divinitie with a preacher." "True," said I, "tis verry likely a man shall goe to the ground when he will either venture to take upon him a matter that is to waightie for him, or meddle with such as are more then his matche."

"I put him downe yfayth," said one, when he had outtalked a wiser

then himselfe. "Just," said I, "as a drumme putes down sweete
still musicke, *not* as *better,* but *mor soundinge.*"

22: At London.

in a booke of newes from Ostend.

Touchinge the parly which Sir Fr. Vere held with the Archduke
there till he had reenforced himself, Sir Franc[is] said that the
banes must be thrice askt, and yf at the last tyme anie lawefull
cause can be showen, the marriage may be hindred. The Duke
answered, he knewe that was true, yet, he said, it was but a whore
that offered hir selfe.

Divers merchantes arrested by Leake for shipping over cloth above
the rate of their licence. (Theroles [?] *nar.*)

The companie of pewterers much greived at a licence graunted to
one Atmore to cast tynne, and therefore called him perjured knave;
whereupon he complayned to the Counsel, and some of them were
clapt up for it.

"I will be even with him for it, yfayth," said one that thought he
had bin disgraced by his credit. "Then you will pay him surely,"
quoth I.

FOLIO 11b

Jan: 1601.

Nature doth check the first offence with loathing,
But use of synn doth mak[e] it seeme as nothing.

The spending of the afternoones on Sundayes, either idly or about
temporall affayres, is like clipping the Q[ueenes] coyne; this treason
to the Prince, that prophanacion and robbing God of his owne.—
(Leydall.)

Rashnes ridiculous: One had fouled his finger with some reverence
and would have taken it of[f] in great haste but in his hast he stroke

his finger against a bord; and then as many use in such cases, forgetting where his finger had bin, clapt it presently in his mouth to have easd the payne. Mer[c]y [?] foh. (Mr. Davers).

Hide to Tanfeild: "It is but a matter of forme you stand so much upon." "But it is such a forme," said Tanfeild, "as you may chaunce to breake your shins at, unless you be the nimbler."

Certaine in the Country this last Christmas chose a jury to finde the Churle of their parishe, and when they came to give their verdict, they named one whose frende, being present, began to be verry collerick with the boys for abusing him. "Hold you content, gaffer," said one of them. "Yf your boy had not bin one of the jury, you had bin found to have bin the Churle."

The gaine of untimely reprehension, and the verry course of common Inquests, all led by some frend!

The L[ord] Paget upon a tyme thinkinge to have goded Sir Tho. White (an Alderman of London) in a great assembly, askt him what he thought of that cloth, shewing him a garment in present.

FOLIO 12

Jan. 26.

"Truly, my L[ord]," said he, "it seemes to be a verry good cloth, but I remember when I was a yong beginner I sold your father a far better to make him a gowne, when he was Sergeant to the L[ord] Maior; truly he was a very honest sergeant!" None so ready to carpe at other mens meane beginnings as such as were themselves noe better. (Reeves.)

Tarlton called Burley house gate in the Strand towardes the Savoy, the Lo[rd] Treasurers Almes gate, because it was seldome or never opened. (Ch. Davers.)

Repentaunce is like a drawebridge, which is layd downe for all to passe over in the day tyme, but drawne up at night: soe all our life wee have tyme to repent, but at death it is to late. (Ch. Davers *recit.*)

26. It was ordered by our bencheres that wee should eate noe breade but of 2 dayes old. Mr. Curle said it was a binding lawe, for stale breade is a great binder; but the order held not 3 dayes, and soe it bound not.

EPITAPHE OF JOHN FOOTE.

Reader look to'it: Here lyes John Foote,
He was a minister, Borne at Westminster.

ALIUD OF MR. CHILD.

If I bee not beguild,   (Overbury *recit.*)
Here Lyes Mr. Child.

I will be soe bolde as to give the Assise the Lye:
(Ch. Davers in arg[umen]t.)

"I came rawe into the world, but I would not goe out rosted," said one that ment to be noe martyre. (Curle *nar.*)

"They say London stones are proud, but I made them kisse myne arse," q[uoth] the country man when he had a fall.

FOLIO 12b

Jan. 1601

This last Christmas the Conny-catcheres would call them selves Country-gentl[emen] at dyce.

When a gent[le]woman told Mr. Lancastre he had not bin soe good as his word, because he promised shee should be gossip to his first child (glaunceing at his bastard on his landres), "Tut," said he, "you shall be mother to my next, if you will."

ANAGRAM.

Margaret Westfalinge
My greatest welfaring.   (Streynsham *nar.*)

Dauis.   Aduis.   Iudas.   (Martin.)

FEBR. 1601.

2. At our feast wee had a play called "Twelve night, or what you will"; much like the commedy of errores, or Menechmi in Plautus, but most like and neere to that in Italian called Inganni.

A good practise in it to make the steward beleeve his Lady widdowe was in Love with him, by counterfayting a letter, as from his Lady, in generall termes, telling him what shee liked best in him, and prescribing his gesture in smiling, his apparraile, &c., and then when he came to practise, making him beleeve they tooke him to be mad.

Quae mala cum multis patimur laeviora putantur.

12. Cosen Norton was arrested in London.
11. He put up a supplicacion to Sir R[o]b[er]t Cecile presented by his wife, whome he tooke notice of the next day, which remembering, with out being remembred, what he had done in it.

FOLIO 13

Febr. 1601.

The effect of this petition was that, whereas Copping had their goodes forth of Mr. Cranmers hand (whoe had dealt but to honestly for such unthankefull persons), and they should have a certaine summe yearely, they could neither gett payment nor have him account; he said twenty pounds were enough to keepe the Lunaticke their mother, when Cranmer had the goodes; now he deductes 50£. for hir and yett keepes hir far more basely, &c. And therefor humbly desyre Copping might be brought to some order. Norton tels me this Copping is a notable riche practiser, &c.

Cosen Norton told me that one Mr. Cokayne of Hertfordsh[ire] gott his brother H. Norton by a wile to his house, and their married him upon a pushe to a kinswoman of his, and made a serveing-man serve the purpose in sted of a preist.

14. Bounty is wrong'd interpreted as duty.

My Cosen Garnons told me that the old E[arle] of Sussex, being in service in the north, was intangled by his marshall, but extricated by the E[arle] of Leycest[er], whose overthrowe afterward he covertly practised. *Quaedam beneficia odimus; vitam nulli debemus libenter.*

The office of the L[ord] Keep[er] better worth then 3000£. per annum; of the Admirall more, of the Secretary little lesse. (*Idem.*)

FOLIO 13b

Febr. 1601

My Cosen Garnons told me that the Court of Wardes will send 14. a prohibicion to anie other Court to cease from proceeding in anie suite, whereof them selves may have colour to hold plea in that Court. Soe praedominat a Court is that nowe become.

18. Went to my Cosen in Kent.
19. I was at malling with Mr. Richeres.
The Bishop of London is Dr. Parrys crosse frend. (Mr. Richers.)
In discourse of Mr. Sedley, he told me that his Lady said he is gone over sea for debt, which Mr. Richers thinkes was caused by his lavishe almes; for Mr. Sedley would not sticke him selfe to say, yf any gent[leman] spent not above 500£. a yeare, he gave as muche to the poure; and as he was prodigall in givinge, soe was he indiscreet in bestowinge, appointinge vile fellowes to be the distributors of it; he is now at Padua, without anie man attendant.

He went into Italy to learne discourse; he was nothing but talke before. "I marvaile what he will be when he returnes," said he. Reade muche but not judicious. (*Idem.*) Mrs. Frauncis Richers said he was a gentle gentleman. F. is open in talke. Plotters for him.

Miller, a rich yeoman about Rotham, when he came to entreate he might be abated in the assessment for subsidies, threwe in a note that he was worth but 550£. land fee simple: one of Mr. Sedleys almesmen.

This day Mr. Cartwright had bin with my Cosen to knowe whether he denied to hold anie land of him. My Cosen acknowledged

FOLIO 14

Febr. 1601.

that he held diverse parcells of him but doth not certainely
19. knowe howe it is all bounded. My cosen told me it was con-
cealed land, and recovered by Mr. Cartwrightes father against Mr. Catlin, of whom my Cosen bought Bradborne.

Sir Robert Sydney hath bought Otford house, and sells it againe by parcells.

Mr. Cartwrightes father and Mr. Richers mother were brother and sister, soe they [are] first cosens. (Cos.)

Mr. Jo[hn] Sedley hath built a house in Aylesford, which cost him above 4000£.; hath not belonging to it above 14 acres of ground. Perhaps he purposed to have bought the Lor[d]ship, which indeede was afterward offered unto him; but he soe delayed the matter that particuler men have it nowe. It is thought the L[ord] Buckhurst would buy the house, &c. (Cos.)

20. Yf a man in the Lowe countryes come to challenge a man out of his house, and because he comes not forth, throwes stones at his

windowes, this [is] a crime capitall, because an assault in his house, which is his castle, Cosen told me.

> Out of a book intituled Quodlibets written
> by a secular preist called Watson, against
> the Jesuites, fol. 151 & 152.

His sp[ecia]ll argumentes for a tolleracion in relligion:
1. that yf a tolleracion were induced, then there should be noe collor to publishe bookes howe tyrannicall the persecution of Catholiks is.

FOLIO 14b

Febr. 1601.

2. Then England should not be called the nursery of faction.
3. Then the Spaniard should have noe Prince to band on his side.
6. The subjects would not be so fitt to be allured to rebellion.
7. The safety of hir Majesties person mutche procured. All slight.

One Kent, my cosen's brother by his mothers side, living in Lincoln-shire, bought a jewell, part of a price [prize?] that was brought in to that Country. The Earle of Lyncolne hearing of it, sent for Kent, and desyred him to bestowe it on him, but when Kent would not part from it for thankes, the Earle gave him a bill of his hand for the payment of 80£. at a certaine day. At the day, came and de-maunded it, the E[arl] would not see his bill; and when he had it he put it in his pocket, and fell in talke with some gent. then present; but when Kent continued still in the roome, expectinge either his bill or his monie, the E[arl] gave him hard wordes and sent him away without either. (Durum.)

19. Mr. Cartwright demaundes some three acres of land of my Cosen, which he saith one John Sutor of Bradborne gave unto the Abby of Towne Mallinge, by the name of Sutors Croft, lying betwixt his house and the churche. My cosen denies it.

21. My Cosen shee told him that Joane Bachellor upon Thursday last had sent hir some fishe, which she sent back againe. Whereupon he said shee was of an ill nature that could not forgive. And this shee tooke in such snuffe that she could not afford him a good looke all that day, but blubberd, &c.

FOLIO 15

Febr: 1601

21. This day there came certaine bags of pepper to Newhide to be conveyed to one Mr. Clarke of Ford, but they were seised by the Searcher of Rochester as goodes not Customed, &c.

A gent. of Nottinghamshire called an other whore maister. "Why," said the other, "I had rather be a whore maister then maistered by a whore as thou art." (My Cosen *narr.*)

S[i]r Jarvis Clifton being at a Bare Baytinge in Nottinghamshire, when the beare brake loose and followed his sonne up a stayres towards a gallery where him selfe was, he apposed himselfe with his rapier against the fury of the beast, to save his sonne. This same his beloved sonne not long after dyed and his death was opened unto him very discreetely by a gent. that fayned sorrowe as the case had been his owne, till S[i]r Jarvis gave him words of comfort, which after he applied to S[i]r Jarvis himselfe. (My Cosen).

One Burneham of London, whoe was the watergate officer at Flushinge, being troubled with the stone soe mutche that it was a hindraunce unto him in the execution of his office, ventured a dangerous cure and was cutt for it, but dyed of it. This cure by cutting is a newe invention, a kinde of practise not knowne to former ages. There is a seame in the passage of the yard neere the fundament, which the surgeons searche with a crooked instrument concaved at the one end (called a catheter) whereinto they make incision and then grope for the stone with an other toole which they call a duckes bill. Yf the stone be greater

FOLIO 15b

Febr. 1601.

then may be drawne forth at the hole made by the seame, the partie dyes for it. (My Cosen.)

A certaine goldsmith in Cheape was indebted to my Cosen above 100£. and after executed for clipping gold. Sir Rich[ard] Martin seised the goodes for the Q[ueen]. After hir Majestie gave commaund by word of mouth that all debtes should be p[ai]d; but, because there was noe warraunt under hir Majesties hand, Sir Rich[ard] refused to pay; yet he delivered certaine of the goodes to my Cosen, to be sold by him, which he made 30£. of and retained it. All the satisfaccion he could have.

Vita coelibis, bis coelestis, considering the crosses of marriage, and the advise of the apostle.

24. At Rochester at the Assises.
Mr. Thomas Scott of Scottes Hall in Kent is Sherife of Kent.

One Tristram Lyde a surgeon, admitted to practise by the Archbishops letteres, was arraigned for killing divers women by annoyntinge them with quicksylver, &c. Evidence given that he would have caused the women to have stript themselves naked in his presence, and himselfe would have anoynted them; that he tooke upon him the cure, and departed because they would not give him more then their first agreement. He pleaded theire diseases were such as required that kinde of medicine; that it was there owne negligence, by takinge cold in going abroade sooner then he prescribed;

FOLIO 16

Febr. 1601.

soe he was acquited.

Sergeant Daniel sitting there as Judge sayd he knewe that there might be a purgacion by a fume. And that to cure by cutting a gutt was a dangerous venture, and a rare skill, for he could never heare of anie had that cunning but onely one man, and that was learned in Turkie.

If a man kill an other (as they say) in hott bloud, excepte there appear some cause to heate his bloud, the jury must finde it murder. (*Per* Sergeant Danyell.)

There was one gave an other rude wordes; whereupon a third standing by said to him to whome they were spoken, "Will you endure such an Injury, fayth? Putt up them, and put up any thinge." Hereupon the party present fetcht his weapon, mett with the other that gave him those wordes, and [in] the presence of the setter-on, fought with him and slewe him, the other standing by and doinge noe more. Yet they were both condemned at this assises, and after executed.

There was one had his booke given him at the prisoners barr, where the ordinary useth to heare and certifie there readinge. And one Mr. Gylburne start up, sayinge, "He will reade as well as my horse;" which wordes Serg[eant] Daniel, havinge before allowed the cleargy, took verry ill, telling him playnely that he

FOLIO 16b

24 Febr. 1601.

was too hasty and yet caused the prisoner to be brought nearer that Gylburne might heare him reade, and he reade perfectly.

IN THE CATHEDRALL CHURCHE AT ROCHESTER.
Monuments. Of Jo. Somer of Newland, clerke of the Privy Signet, and Martin [*sic*] his wife, daughter to Ed. Ridge, late widdowe of Th. Colepepper. They had 6 sonnes, but all deade, and 2 daughters: whereof the one called Frances was married to James Cromer, by

whome one daughter called Frances. *Versus.*
   Sunt nisi praemissi, quos periisse putas.

IN NAVI ECCLESIAE

Thomas Willowbee, Decanus 3^d, *obiit Anno 25 Reg.*
Elizab., 76 aetatis suae, et 10° *decanatus.*
   Gualterus Phillips, nouissimus prior et primus decanus, obijt
23° *Nouemb.* 1576, *aetatis* 70, *decanatus* 30°.

[*fo. 17 blank in MS*]

FOLIO 17b

May. 1602.

2. At Glastonbury there are certaine bushes which beare mayflowers
at Christmas and in January; and there is a walnut tree which hath
noe leaves before Barnabies day in June, and then it beginnes to bud,
and after becomes as forward as any other. (Mr. Towse *narravit.*)

I heard that the old Earle of Hartford maried Alderman Parnels
[Pranell's] sonnes widdowe; shee was the daughter of Viscount
Bindon.

FOLIO 18

May 9, 1602.

Att the Temple churche. Dr. Montague, his text Joh. 3:14: "As
Moses lift up the serpent in the wildernes so must the sonne of man
be lift up."

Speaches are either historicall, of a thing past; propheticall, of a thing to come; legall, of a thing to be done; or figurative, when one thing is said and an other ment. [Of] figures there are in scripture two almost peculiar—Typicall and Sacramentall: the one shewing one thing by an other, the other declaring what is conferred by an other.

Moses had speciall commaundment to erect this serpent, and yet God did not dispense with the 2[n]d commaundment, for this Serpent was not made to be worshipped, but to be looked upon.

God cannot dispense with anie commaundment of the first table but he should cease to be God; as the first, "Thou shalt have none other Gods but me"; admit a pluralitie, and himselfe should be none, &c., but with the 2nd table he often dispenseth, for those concerne man immediately.

The text is hystoricall (Numb. 21:9) and typicall. Christ resembled by the brasen serpent, syn by the stinging.

Moses while he was in the Wilderness had onely the place of a mediator, not a judge, and therefore we read that whensoever the people murmured, God punished them.

FOLIO 18b

May 9, 1602.

But when Moses left his station, and would at any tyme become a judge over them, God never punished the people that murmured, but Moses, that forgot his place. Christ, untill the latter day, hath the place of an advocate, but then he shalbe a judge of the quicke and dead.

Wee reade of three exaltacions of our Savior, one upon the crosse to purchase our pardon; 2, from the grave for the publicacion thereof; 3, to heaven for the application of his resurrection; and all these were necessarilie to be performed by him, for the consummacion of our salvacion.

The serpent was not lifted up in the wildernes before the people were stung by the serpentes, and Christ is not to be propounded on the Crosse as a comfort untill the sting of synn be felt throughly.

The scripture telleth us that of all beasts the serpent is the most subtill, and his subtilty is observed in three points: first when those nations in Syria and other hott countries found themselves often endangered by the stinging of venomous beastes, amongst other remedies they invented charming, which the serpent percevinge, to avoyd there cunning and effect his malice, he would stop both his eares, the one by laying it close to the earth, the other by stopping it with his tayle. Soe fareth the synner; lett the preacher speake never soe heavenly, yet will he close one eare with worldly thoughts, and the other with fleshly imaginacions.

FOLIO 19

May 9, 1602.

The 2[n]d property of his subtilty is in defending his heade, where his lyfe lyes; it will soe winde it selfe about that part, that [it] is a matter of greate difficulty to cutt of a serpentes heade. In every man there is some radicall and capitall synn, which is predominant, and this the devil endeavours by all slightes to preserve. The 3[r]d point of the serpentes subtilty is accounted the attractive power which remayneth in the heade devided from the body, for it is proved by experience that yf a serpent be cutt in many peeces, yf his heade remaine alive, yet that part will gather the rest togither againe; soe leave the head synn alive, and it will gather a whole body againe.

As Christ is the heade of the churche he never suffered nor dyed.

The brasen serpent was made like the live and true serpentes in all thinges, the sting onely excepted; Christ was made like man in all things saving synn.

All which beheld the brasen serpent were cured: all that beleeve in Christ are saved.

Remedies are either naturall, by virtue of some inherent qualitie in the medicine applied; or by divine influence and institution, when some thing is effected either beyònd or contrary to the force and nature of that which is used. And this is miraculous. Soe was the curing of the blind by laying spittle and clay upon the eyes of the blinde. Soe the cure of the lame by washing in the poole of Bethesdas, and soe the healing of the Israelites by beholdinge the brasen serpent.

Fayth properly in things beyond, or contrary to, reason.

FOLIO 19b

May 9, 1602.

As by the institucion of marriage the heate of the flesh is abated, soe by our mysticall connection with Christ the heate of syn is allayed.

May 13
At the Temple churche. One moore of Baliol colledge in Oxford; his text: Amos 3:6: "Shall there be evil in the City and the Lord hath not done it?"

Malum culpae, et Malum poene; of the latter onely God is the author. God may be said to be the author of synn permissive. And an actor in synn, though not the author of the synne, for ther is noe action but he is the first cause of it: and yet he is noe partner or cause of the il in the action, noe more than he which rideth upon a lame jade can be said to be the cause of his limpinge, though he be the cause of his paceinge, nor a cunning musician the cause of discordes when he playeth on a lute that is out of tune.

FOLIO 20

May 13, 1602.

There is a twofold power in every thing, and both derived from God; the one of creacion, whereby every thing worketh according to nature, as the fyre to burne, &c., and the other of preservacion, whereby that force is continued. And yf the 2nd be withdrawne, the first perisheth, for God is not a mere efficient externall, as the taylour of the garmente, or a carpenter of the house, whose effects may continue though their labour continue not; but he is an inherent continuall assistant cause, soe that yf he with drawe his power of preserving, the power of creacion is idle. Soe the fire in furnace could not burne the children, &c.

DE ASCENSIONE DOMINI

Non omnis questio est doctrinae inquisitio,
Sed quaedam etiam est ignorantiae professio.

Cicatrices Dominus seruauit post resurrectionem et in iudicio seruaturus est: Vt fidem resurrectionis astruat; 2. Vt pro omnibus supplicando ea patri representet; 3. Vt boni quam misericorditer sint redempti videant; 4. Vt reprobi quam iuste sint damnati recognoscant; 5. Vt perpetuae victoriae seu [suae?] triumphum deferat.   (*Beda.*)

FOLIO 20b

May 16, 1602.

At Paules crosse, one Sanders made a Sermon, his text 1 Timoth. 6:17. "Charge them that are riche in this world that they be not high mynded, and that they trust not in uncertayne riches, but in the living God (which giveth us abundantly all thinges to enjoye)."

Charge them that they lift up their soules to God in heavenly meditacion, not against God by worldly presumption.

Charge the Riche, therefore there were diversitie of condicion and
estates of men in the primitive churche, not all thinges common in
possession as the Anabaptists would have it. When there came one
to Pope Benedict to entreat him to make more Cardinals, he
demaunded first yf he could devise how he might make more
worldes, for this was to litle for the Cardinals which were already.
Such an ambitious covetousness the pope noted in these holie ones.

Good meate is often tymes corrupted by a bad stommacke, and
good doctrine of small effect with bad heareres. Yett the minister
must not be discouraged, but proceed in his calling, that yf synn
cannot be avoyded, yet it may become unexcusable. Ephesus,
whereof Tymothie was Bishop, was the confluence of honour and
wealth, like our London.

The surgeon is not to be blamed that findes and shewes the corrupt and rotten parts of the body, but the body which is soe corrupt as to breed them. Soe the preacher not to be disliked for
reprehending our synnes, but our selves for committing things
worthy reprehension.

FOLIO 21

May. 1602.

Good thinges, though common, are not to be contemned for their
commonness, noe more then the sunne, the light, the ayre, &c.
The usurour sometymes looseth both his principall and interest,
the husbandman his labour and his seede, the merchant adventu[rer]
lyfe and goods; but the profession of the preacher is subject to
greater then all these, for he may loose both his owne and the
peoples soules.

It is one of the most heavie judgments that God useth to threatnen to anie nation with whom he is displeased, that he will remove their candlesticke and send a famine of the world amongst them.

God made some riche, and some poore, that twoe excellent virtues might flourish in the world, charitie in the riche, and patience in the poore.
Pride is the sting of riches. *Tolle superbiam, et diuitiae non nocebunt.*
A man may speake of his owne riches, soe it be without arrogancy. For it is a good thinge to speake of the loving kindenes of the Lord.

Magistrates and richmen must not be like the filling stones in a building, but arche and corner stones, which support otheres.
(When persons of meane worth thrust them selves into places beyond their condicion and hability, it is all one as yf the rough mortar and pebles should appeare in the roomes of the squared stones in a fayre building. M[?])

Themistocles said there was no musicke soe sweete unto him as to heare his owne prayses.

In the primitive churche the richmen were soe proud that they refused to receive the sacrament with the poore. The examples of the Incertaintie of riches, by often and suddain casualtyes, should be like Lottes wife to the beholders, to remember and avoid the like.

The multitude followe the richmen, as a swarme of bees followe a man that carries the hive of honie combes rather for love of the honie then his person, more for the love of his mony then his manhood.

FOLIO 21b

23 May, 1602.

At Westminster Dr. Androes, Deane of that Churche, made a sermon, his text John: 16:7: "Yet I tell you the truth. It is expedient for you that I goe away, for if I goe not away the

Comforter will not come unto you, but if I depart I will send him unto you."

These words have reference to the feast which is celebrated this day: whereupon St. Augustine said, *In verbo fuit promissio missionis, et in festo missio promissionis:* for soe is it in the 2nd of the Acts. "When the day of Pentecost was come, they were all filled with the Holy Ghost."

These words were spoken to the disciples when their heartes were full of sorrowe that Christ must part from them; and therefore had neede of comfort, for they had cause of sorrowe; for yf a man would not willingly be forsaken of any, as Paule complayneth, 2 Tim. 4:10, that Demas had forsaken him, would it not greive the disciples to [be] for saken by such a frend as Christ had bin unto them, whoe in one place speaking unto them asketh this question, "Which of you hath wanted any thing since you followed me?" And in an other place he compareth them while he continues with them to the Children of the bridechamber.

Besides the tyme of his departure might aggravate their sorrowes, for it was then when he foretold soe many persecutions should come upon them. And therefore he ministeres words of comfort, telling them that [it] is expedient, and expedient for them, that he should leave

FOLIO 22

23 May, 1602.

them, for thereby they should receive a benefit, and that of soe high a nature as they were better to want him then it. And further for their comfort he added that though he would forsake them, yet he would not leave them like orphanes destitute of all frendes, but would send them a Comforter.

And here he made his prayer, which being ended with the Lordes prayer, he proceeded with his text: and first noted that Christ rendred a reason of his departure (though it be not requisit always

that governors should render a reason to their subjectes of all their
commaundments, for in the 1 Sam. the Kinge gives noe other reason but it was his pleasure). 2. It is a mylde reason, not harshe like
that in Marke 9. cap. 19 v: "O, ye faythles generacion, howe long
shall I bee with you, how long nowe shall I suffer you?"; but here
he deliveres it meekely, and moves them with expediency, and that
not for himselfe, *non nobis, sed vobis expedit.* And therefore
because it is expedient it ought not to greive them, in soe much as
the profit they shall gayne will countervayle the pleasure which
they must forgoe by his departure.
And yet it might seeme strange that they should gayne by loosing
him; it is reade, *dissolve coelum et veni ad nos, Domine,* and againe,
Veni ad nos, et mane nobiscum. But to goe from them what desyre
could they have?
Here may arise three difficulties: 1. The disciples might have
rejoyned, and sayde, What neede, what care wee for any other comforter? soe long as you are with us, wee desyre noe other.

FOLIO 22b

23 May, 1602

2. Why might not the Holy Ghost have come, and yet Christ tarried
with them; could they not be togither? 3. Howe can it be expedient
for anie to lose Christ? What comfort can there be in those wordes
which tell them Christ will forsake them?
1. Our happines is to be reunited to God, from whom wee were fallen
by our first fathers synn; for as it is the perfection of a branche that
is broken of to be ingrafted againe that it may growe with the body,
soe is it the felicitie of man to be united to his Creator. And in this
Union, as well as God must be partaker of man, soe must man be
made partaker of God, otherwise there can arise noe Union; the
former was effected by Christes incarnacion, and the 2[n]d is perfected by the inspiration of the Holy Ghost, whoe is as it were the
connexion and love knot of the Deitie. Christ hath as it were made

his testament, and the Holie Ghost is the executor (1 Cor. 12). Christ is the Word, and the Holy Ghost is the seale of it (2 Corin. 1:22). "Christ hath purchased redemption for us," and the Holy Ghost must give us seisin (Eph. 1:14). And in conclusion Paule sayth, 8th Rom. 9, "He that hath not the Spirit of Christ is not his." And therefore was it expedient and necessary that the Holy Ghost should come; for as Christ was *complementum legis,* soe is the Holy Ghost *complementum Evangelii.*

2. They may stand togither, they may beare one an otheres presence, for the manhood of

FOLIO 23

23 May, 1602.

Christ was conceived by the Holy Ghost, and the Evangelist sayth, *Vidi Spiritum descendentem et manentem super eum.* But yet it was expedient they should not be togither upon the earth; expedient, as Augustine noteth, *Non necessitatis pondere, sed divini consilii ordine.*

And two reasons are given for [it] in the part of the Holy Ghost: 1. Yf the Holy Ghost should have come downe while Christ was upon the earth, whatsoever the Holy Ghost should have done in his person would have bin ascribed to Christ. 2. He would have appeared to have bin sent from the Father alone. And soe it would not have bin so apparant that he proceeded from the Father and the Sonne bothe. 3. Expedient it was that Christ should depart from them, howe good soever his presence was unto them. Wee knowe that bread is the strength of mans hart, yet sometymes it may be expedient to fast: our bloud is the treasury of our lyfe, yet sometymes it is expedient to loose it; our eyesight is deare and precious unto us, yet sometymes it is expedient to sitt in a darke roome. And here it is expedient that Christ should withdraw his presence, not corporal onely, but his invisible presence of grace

alsoe. It is expedient that children which growe fond of their
parentes should be weaned. The Apostles were to full of carnall
and terrene cogitacions even after his resurrection; they asked him,
"Wilt thou restore the Kingdome to Israell?" Therefore nowe it was
highe tyme they should put of Childishnes and be taught, as Paule
sayth that henceforth they knowe him noe more in

FOLIO 23b

23 May, 1602.

the fleshe; and this must be effect by withdrawing his corporall
presence, which they began to dote upon; and for the taking away
the presence of his grace, that was expedient alsoe: 1. least being
to full they should begin to loath it, as the Children of Israel did
manna in the Wildernes; and upon this reason did the prophet
threaten a famine of the word when the people, being full, contemned it. 2. that they should not growe proud with abundaunce,
the Psalmist sayth, "Yf I say I cannot be removed," and "It is
good that I was in trouble, for before I went wronge." Peter was
soe sure and confident upon him selfe, that yf all the world should
have for saken Christ, he would not; and therefore because he stoode
soe much upon himselfe, it was expedient that suche a swollen
bladder should be prickt, as he was till he denied and forswore his
master; And even this withdrawing of grace was a kind of grace,
that seeing his owne weaknes he might possesse his soule in humility, with[out] which there is noe grace to be expected. And therefore, *expedit superbo vt in peccatum incidat.* And to this purpose
are these wordes of Paules that the messengers of Sathan, i.[e.],
temptacions, were sent to punish him, least he should growe proud.
Christ is our advocate in defending us when the divel accuseth us
falsely; he is our intercessor and mediator by pleading a pardon for
us when Sathen layes his greatest and truest accusacions against us;
he is our high Priest to offer sacrifice for us.

Christ left them not as orphanes, but sent an other unto them whoe was equall with himselfe, otherwise they should have lost by the change.

FOLIO 24

23 May, 1602.

The Holy Ghost hath divers offices and soe divers effects: he in-lightens the understandinge, and soe is called the Spirit of truth: he rectifies the will, and soe is named the Spirit of Holines: he deliveres from the bondage of Sathan and soe is the Spirit of Comfort, which is the cheife and very consummacion of all.

The Holy Ghost is not given to all in the same measure, nor the same manner. When Christ breathed upon his disciples they received the Holy Ghost; and, when the Holy Ghost came like fyrey tongues, they were filled with him: breath was warme, but fyre is hotter: there was heate in both but not equally. Elias prayed that the Spirit of [Elijah] might be doubled upon him.

The gifts of the Holy Ghost are obteyned and perfected divers wayes: understanding and fayth by the word, which is the truthe; holynes of lyfe, by prayer, meditacion, and good workes; consola-cion by receiving the sacramentes.

FOLIO 24b

7 Junij, 1602.

A lewde fellowe comming before Sir W. Rawley to be examined concerninge some wrecke which he had gotten into his handes, and being demaunded whether he would sweare to such articles as they would propound, answerd that he would sweare to anie thinge they would aske him, and then being admonished he should not be soe rashe in soe serious a matter, as concerned his soule soe nearely, "Fayth," said he, "I had rather trust God with my soule, then you with my goodes." (Ch. Da.)

Mr. Stevens of our house said Mrs. Fouler was a verry p[ro]p[er] woman, yf shee were prop[er?] (as she is common). (Th.)

"Were is your husband?" said Mr. Reeves to a girl. "He is a build-ing," said shee. "The worse lucke for you," q[uo]t[h] hee; a bild-ing in Wiltsh. signifies a male with one stone. (Ch. Da.)

FOLIO 25

At Paules Crosse, Junii 6th, 1602.

Mr. Barker: his text Luke 9, and the last verse, "Noe man that putteth his hand to the plough and looketh back is apt to the King-dome of God."

The fyre from Heaven which consumed the sacrifices in the old lawe was preserved by continuall addicion of fuell. Soe the heavenly virtue of Chrystian charitie being kindled in the hart of man must be preserved by continuall meditacions on the word of God.

Yf any should aske why it was commaunded in Levitic[us] that the people should offer *primitias,* and in Exodus that they should alsoe give *decimas,* I should make no other aunswer but that wee should not onely remember our Creator in the days of our youth, but alsoe serve him in holines and righteousnes all the dayes of our lyfe.

Aliud est incepisse, aliud perficisse.

Some in their lives, like the image in Nebuchadnezers dreame, Dan. 2, goodly beginninges, but earthie endinges.

The Divel laboureth most against our perseveraunce because that virtue onely hath a promise of coronacion.

There be but 7 steps in the ladder that leades downe to hell, and the lowest, saving desperacion, is a custom of synning.

These combined discommodities ensue the custome of synning; *fit diabolus ad oppugnandum audacior, anima ad peccandum promptior, deus ad condonandum difficilior.*

FOLIO 25b

6th Junii, 1602

This virtue of Christian magnanimity or perseveraunce consisteth in *Patiendo et Faciendo:* in *patiendo,* 1., in *ferendo* 2. *et perferendo; faciendo,* by continuance in preaching fayth, and in good lyfe.

Christ compared Christian profession to a plough. And why, 1. to soe base a thing, 2. to soe laborious a thing, 3. to that onely? 1. That none howe base soever by condicion or profession should despayre of attayning Heaven; and meane thinges may be compared with the greatest. Christ sayth the Kingdom of Heaven is like a litle leaven, and to a smaller thing then that, it is like a grayne of mustard seede; and here to a plough, that none might despayre. Simon a tanner, Peter a fisher, Paul a tent-maker, Joseph a carpenter. Some great ones, Theophilus. Some ladyes, in the Acts. Some customers, and some from the beggars, as Lazarus.

And yet, that rich men might not contemne it for the basenes, he compares it to a riche jewell, a precious stone, &c.

2. The place of the preacher is a calling of great paynes and travaile. He selected and spake of the Archbish[op] of Canterbury as the sunne amongst ministeres, and the old Deane of Paules compared to the moone. And Dr. Overall, the new Deane, to the newe moone, gravity & learning and life. The ministeres to starrs.

FOLIO 26

Junii 9, 1602.
Marti Lib. 10, Epig. 47.

I take noe care to gett, my wealth was left me,
I reape the harvest of what 'ere I sowe,
I stur not muche a broade, home best befits me,
I ne're received wronge, nor none I owe.
I travaile not in publique busines,
Nor ought's within my charge but myne owne soule,
My body's healthfull, fitt for exercise,
Myselfe enjoyes myselfe without controule.
I have a harmeles thought, an aequal frend,
My clothes are easy, and my face wants art,
I greive not when I rest, nor doe I spend
More tyme in sleepe then nature can impart.
I cast the world behinde, heaven is my guide,
I would be what I am, and nought beside;
But above all, which is all and summe,
I neither wishe nor feare the day to come.
Th. Sm.

  Georgius Savile
Egregious Vile as.

FOLIO 26b

June. 1602.

  Vrsula
Du feare and love won all.

Arbella Stuarta: tu rara es et bella.

Henricus Burbonius: rex bonus orbi.

12. Common preachers worse then common swearers, for these doe abuse but Gods name, but they abuse Gods worde. (Curle.)

15. Upon a tyme when the làte Lord Treasurer, Sir William Cecile, came before Justice Dyer in the Common Place with his rapier by his side. The Justice told him that he must lay a side his long pen-knife yf he would come into that court. This speache was free, and the sharper, because Sir William was then Secretary. (Bradnux.)

There is nowe a table placed for the barresteres crosse over the Hall by the cuppord, which one called St. Albanes because he said it was in the waye to Duns-table.

Laetus doth keepe his sister and his whore.
Laetus doth keepe his sister and noe more.
                              (G. M.)

16. "Roome! roome!" said one, "here comes a woman with a cup-bord on hir head" (of one that had sold hir cupboard to buy a taffaty hat). (Franklin.)

FOLIO 27

June. 1602.

16. Kentish tayles are nowe turned to such spectacles, soe that yf a man put them on his nose he shall have all the land he can see. (*Idem.*)

ANAGR[AM]

    Martyne: myne art. (W [?])

22. Sergeant Heale, since he became the Queens Sergeant, came to the L[ord] Keeper, desyring that he would hereafter give him more gratious hearinge; otherwise, his clients already beginning to fall from him, he would nowe betake him selfe to his ease in the country,

and leave this troublesome kinde of lyfe. The L[ord] Keeper made him noe other answere but said yf that were his resolucion he doubt it not but the blessing of Issakar would light upon him. (Mr. Bennet *nar.*) *Vide* Gen. 49. 14: "Issachar shall be a stronge asse couching downe betweene two burdens; and he shall see that rest is good; and that the land is pleasaunt, and he shall bowe his shoulders to beare, and he shalbe subject unto tribute."

FOLIO 27b

June 20, 1602.

At Paules one of Baliol colledge in Oxeford.
His text 3. Jonah 4 et 5.

"Yet fourty dayes and Ninivy shall be destroyed. 5. So the people of Nineveh beleeved God," &c.

He divided his text into Jonahs sermon to the people of Nineveh, and the peoples repentaunce at the sermon; the former consists of mercy, "yett fourty dayes," and justice, "and Nineveh shall be destroyed;" Gods patience and his judgment. He might have sayd, as the prophet David sayd, "My song shall be of mercy and judgment."

4 things in the effect of the Sermon; fayth in beleving God, and that was not fruitles. 2. fasting, and that was not frivolous. 3. their attyre, and that was not costly, but sack cloth. 4. their number, that was not small, from the greatest to the lowest.

As Noahs dove came from the floud with an olive braunch in the mouth, soe this heavenly Dove (for soe Jonah signifieth) came from the waters of the sea with a sermon of mercy in his cry, "Yett fourty dayes."

God is pitifull; it was Christ's commaundment to His Apostles that they should say "Peace be unto you" when they entred into anie house.

Noted by Jonahs crying in the middest of such a city, that the
preachers must not be timerous to tell anie of their faults, nor feare
the person of anie man. Yet he reprehended those which are to
sharpe reprehenders without circumstaunce. Such as Bernard
calleth *non correptores, sed corrosores.* Such may be termed *bilis
et salsugo,* like the people of India which are said to barke in
stead of speakinge. (*Canis et tuba vitiorum*).

FOLIO 28

June, 1602

But, as he misliked those sharpe biters, soe must he needes speake
against such preachers as flatter greate men, and sowe cushions
under their elbowes.

They are like Heliotropium, which turnes the flower with the sunne,
though a cloud be interposed, soe they follow greatnes though
clouded with synn.

Like the river Jordan, turnes and windes every way; speake nothing
but silken wordes. At last the[y] become *serui multitudinis,* say
anie thing to please the people.

Nineveh, as St. Augustine, in his booke *De Civitate Dei,* signifieth
not the citie but the synns of the people; and soe the prophecy
verryfied, for that synn was destroyed by their repentaunce within
40 dayes. But he rather inclined to expound it by way of an implyed
condicion, that they should be oerthrowen unles they repented; soe
was that prophecie of Isah understoode to Hezekiah, Isaiah 38.
"Thou shalt dy and not live."

God is slowe in punishing, yet *tarditas poenae gravitate pensetur.*
Gratious and righteous is the Lord in sparinge and punishing.

The synne of Nineveh was Idolatry.

FOLIO 28b

June. 1601.

20. Dr. Buckridge, at the Temple churche.
Compared the lawe of nature to the night, reason to the starres,
the written lawe to the morning or dawning of the day, and the
lawe of grace to the sunnshine of the day; the first to the blade,
the second to the eare, the third to the seede of corne.

Synn must be like an hedge of thornes sett about, not within, our
garden, to keepe us in goodnes.

In tymes past men were a shamed feard to committ synn, but ready to
make confession; nowe the world is changed, for nowe every one
dares comitt anie synne, but is ashamed to make confession.

FOLIO 29

June. 1602.

25. Mr. Foster of Lyncolnes Inn told these jeastes of Sir Th. Moore
as we went to Westminster.

One which had bin a familiar acquaintaunce of Sir Th. Moores in
his meaner fortunes, came to visit him when he was in the height
of his prosperitie. Sir Th. amongst other parts of entertaynement
shewed him a gallery which he had furnished with good variety of
excellent pictures, and desyred his frendes judgment which he liked
best; but he making difficulty to prefer anie, Sir Tho. shewed him
the picture of a deathes head with the word *Memento morieris,*
which he commended as most excellent for the devise and conceit.
The gent. being desyrous to knowe what he conceived extraordinary in soe common a sentence, he told him, "Sir, you remember

sometymes you borrowed some monie of me, but I cannot remember you have remembred to repaye it; it is not much, and though I be Chauncellor I have use for as little, and nowe me thinkes this picture speakes unto you *Memento Mori aeris:* Remember to pay Moore his money."

After he was deprived of his place and dignity, whereas his gentlemen were wont after he was gone forth of Church to signifie to their lady that his Lordship was gone before, himselfe upon a Sunday came from his seate when prayer was ended, opened his ladyes pue dore, saying, "Madame, his Lordship is gone before" (alluding to the losse of his place); and then, "Come, wife, nowe wee may goe togither and talke."

FOLIO 29b

Marche. 1601.

11. Sergeant Yelverton and Serg. Heale being upon a tyme in the Companie of gentlewo[men] which were merryly disposed, Yelverton began to take exception against Heale that he went noe oftner then once by the yeare to pay his wife hir duty. Heale said that the gent[le]women were fittest judges in this controversie and therefore he would but put the case and referr it to them. Yf a man be to pay you a good round summe, whether had you rather receive it by driblets or the whole togither? After the gent[lewomen] had strayned courtesie whoe should breake silence, at last one of them made him this answere: Lett me be paid as I neede it. (M^r· Ed Curle, *n.*)

13. Mr. Watts and Mr. Danvers had fiery wordes.

Commonly those which speake most against Tullie are like a dog, which comming into a roome where he espies a shoulder of mutton lying upon some high place, falls to barking at it, because he cannot reach it. (Watts.)

Upon a tyme when Burbidge played Rich[ard] 3. there was a Citizen grewe soe farr in liking with him, that before shee went from the play shee appointed him to come that night unto hir by the name of Ri[chard] the 3. Shakespeare, overhearing their conclusion, went before, was intertained, and at his game ere Burbidge came. Then message being brought that Richard the 3^d. was at the dore, Shakespeare caused returne to be made that William the Conquerour was before Rich[ard] the 3. Shakespeare's name William. (Mr. Touse.)

14. Mr. Fleetewood the Recorder sitting in judgment when a prisoner was to have his clergy and could not read, he saved him with this jeast: "What, will not that obstinat knave reade indeede? Goe take him away and whip him." (Mr. Bramstone.)

He imprisoned one for saying he had supt as well as the Lord Maior, when he had nothing but bread and cheese.

FOLIO 30

Marche. 1601.

2^d This day there was a great Court of Merchant Adventurers; two were sent from the Counsell to sitt and see their proceedinges at their Courtes, and to make relacion. At this Court 2 questions were moved: 1. Whether their companie were able to vent all the clothes made in England, yf they might choose their place in the Lowe Countries, and be ayded by hir Majestie for the execution of their orderes. Resolved that they are able. 2. Whether they can continue a Companie to trade yf the Earle of Cumberlandes licence take effect, wherby he hath liberty to ship over what cloth he pleaseth, contrary to his Majesties patentes and grauntes to the merchauntes. Resolved by handes that they cannot. (Mr. Hull *narr.*)

Their Courts consist of one Governour, one Deputy, a Secretary, and these sitt at a table raysed a little, and 24 Assistantes sitt about;

the autority of these continues but 6 moneths; these speake, heare, and judge of other mens speaches in Court. The greater part of the present at any Court carries the judgment. (*Idem.*)

FOLIO 30b

May. 1602.

3. Mr. Touse told that in the last cirquit into Yorkeshire the Vice President of Yorke would have had the upper hand of Justice Yelverton, but he would not yeeld. (Mr. Touse.)

Long since, when Justice Manwood roode Somersetshire Circuit with Lorde Anderson, there happened a great quarrell betweene the Lord Sturton and Sir Jo. Clifton, in which affray the Lord Anderson himselfe, onely with his cap in his hand, tooke a sword from a verry lustie tall fellowe. Of such a courage is Anderson. (*Idem.*)

My Chamberfellowe told me of Mr. Longs opposicion against him, and howe he had overmatcht him; told me of his owne preferment to Sir Robert Cecile by the Lord Ch[ief] Baron Periams and Lord Ch[ief] Justice Pophams meanes, almost without his owne suite. By Sir Roberts favour he obtayned the cancelling of an obligacion, wherin his father stoode bound to Auditour Tucke not to use that office or receive the profites for a certaine tyme.

4. Those which presume upon repentaunce at the last gaspe by [the] theeves example on the crosse, doe as yf a man should spurr his horse till he speake because wee reade that Balams asse did soe when his maister beate him.

This day Serjeant Harris was retayned for the plaintife, and he argued for the defendant; soe negligent that he knowes not for whom he speakes.

Soe many accions of *Quare impedit* in the Common Place, that it were well a *Quare impedit* were brought against the *Quare impedit* for hindering other accions.

FOLIO 31

June. 1602.

28. One that would needes be married in all the [*sic*] hast, though he were soe verry a beggar that the preist told him he would not marry him because he had not money sufficient to pay him his duty for that service: "Why then," said he, "I pray you, Sir, marry me as farr as that will goe. Nowe I am here I must needes have something ere I goe."

One when he was in marrying and the preist said those wordes "to have and to hold," he follows with "To have and to hole." (Mr. Douglas *n.*)

A Puritan scholemaister that taught litle children in their horne bookes would not have them say "Christ crosse A," &c., but "Black spott A," &c. An other being to invit his frend, desyred him come and take part of a "Nativity pie" at "Christ tyde" with him.

When a Puritan that had lost his purse made great moane as desyrous to have it againe, an other minister (meaning to try his spirit) gave forth that he was able to helpe him to it by figur-casting; whereupon the Puritan resorted unto him; and the day appointed for the purpose, the other told him that when he caste a paper into the chaffing dishe of coales which he placed before them, he should looke in the glasse to see the visage of him that had it; but the flame being too short for him to advise well what face it was, he earnestly entreated to see it againe. "Oh," said the other, "I perceve well the cause why you could not discerne it was that you trust to much in God." "Whoe, I?" said the Puritan. "I trust noe more in God then the post doth. Lett me see it once againe." Such hyppocrytes are those professours. (Ch. Da[nvers].)

FOLIO 31b

May 4.

Mr. Fleetwood, after he was gone from supper, remembered a case to the purpose he was talking of before he went, and came againe to tell us of it, which Mr. Bramston said was as yf a reveller, when he had made a legg at the end of his galliard, should come againe to shew a tricke which he had forgotten.

This day there was a strange confused pressing of souldieres carrying soe to the ships that they were thrust togither under hatches like calves in a stall.

6. When hir Majestie had given order that Spenser should have a reward for his poems, but Spenser could have nothing, he presented hir with these verses:
It pleased your Grace upon a tyme
To graunt me reason for my ryme,
But from that tyme untill this season
I heard of neither ryme nor reason.
(Touse.)

A gent[leman] whose father rose by the lawe, sitting at the benche while a lawyer was arguying in a case against the gent[leman], touching land which his father purchased, the gent[leman], more collerick then wise, sayd the lawyer would prate, and lye, and speake anie thing for his fee. "Well," said the lawyer, "yf your father had not spoken for a fee, I should have noe cause to speake in this cause to day."

The posterity of Lawyers hath more flourished then that either of the Clergy or Citisens.

FOLIO 32

August. 1602.

Notes out of a copie of a letter written by way of dedicacion of
Charles the 5th his instructions to his sonne Phillip: Translated out of Spanish, and sent to hir Majestie by L[ord] H. Howard.

Hir Majesties affections are not carved out of flint, but wrought out of virgin wax, and hir royall hart hath ever suted him in mercy whom hir state doth represent in majesty.

If anie sentence were mistaken by equivocacion of wordes, or ambiguity in sence, I onely blame the stintles rage of destinie, which ever carryeth the best shaftes of my unluky quiver to such endes as are most distant from the white I aymed at.

Since I began, each fruit hath answered his blossom, each grayne his seede, all eventes there hopes; my selfe onely, more unfortunate then all the rest, have sowne with teares, but can reape with noe revolucion.

I have presumed once againe (least the ground of my devocion, by lying to long fallowe, might seeme either waxen wyld or overgrowne with weedes,) to breake the barren soyle of myne unfruitfull brayne, that prosperous successe may rather want at all tymes to myne endevours, then endevour to my loyall determinacion.

You are that sunne to me, whose going downe leaves nothing but a night of care.

The divel, like those painteres which are skilfull in the art of perspective, taketh pleasure, by false colours and deceitful shadowes, to make those things seeme farthest of which are nerest hand (as death), and to abuse our nature with vayne hopes.

FOLIO 32b

August. 1602.

As the glasse of tyme is turned every hour upside downe, soe is the course of our uncertaine lyfe; as that part which before was full is emptied, and that other which was emptied is replenished, soe fareth this world interchangeably.

As the highest region of the ayre is cleare and without stormes, soe hir minde free from all distemperes of affection.

These that live not in the safe arke of your gracious conceit, &c.

The sea can brooke noe carcasses, nor hir Majesties thoughtes admit of castaways.

The fig tree never bare fruit after it was blasted by the breath of Christ; noe plant can prosper that never feeles the comfort of the same; soe, &c.
In this the difference, Adam dyed because he eat of it (i.e., the tree of lyfe), but I shall dye before I looke on it.

Manie find frendes to cover faultes; my cloke is innocency. An eye may be cleare enough yet not discerne without your light; a course may be direct, yet endles without your clewe. My dealinges may be free from base alloy, but yet not currant amongst honourable persons without the lively print of your cherefull countenaunce. What dangerous diseases breed in bodyes naturall by putrefaction springing out of the sunnes eclipse, the same, or rather greater by proportion, must growe in well affected myndes by the darke vayle of your discouragement.

FOLIO 33

August, 1602.

Patience like a pill by continuall use looseth his virtue. I wonder at your matchles worth as they that are borne under the North Pole doe at the sunne, whose comfort they feele not at all, or without anie great effect.

Praye that since there is but one period and bounder, one high water marke, both of your happie life and our countryes good, the same may be inlarged above ordinary termines, defended by all extraordinary meanes, and augmented with all speciall favour which either death possesseth or heaven promiseth.

That ever in the Zodiack, our Princely Virgin may assend with assistance of all happie planetes.

Such is my beliefe in your administracion of right, as with the faythfull daughter of Darius, while I live I will deeme *Me captum esse
quamdiu Regina vixerit.*
(The world is governed by planets, not fixed starrs.)

FOLIO 33b

August. 1602.

8. One Mr. Palmes told at supper that one Mr. Sappcottes, a Northamptonshire gent[leman], married his owne bastard, had never anie
issue by hir; after his death shee was with child, would not discover
the father. Sappcottes left hir worth some 400£. yearely, yet none
will marry hir.

October. 1602. Mr. Kempe in the King's bench reported that in
tymes past the counsellours wore gownes faced with satten, and
some with yellowe cotten, and the benchers with jennet furre; nowe
they are come to that pride and fa[n]tasticknes that every one
must have a velvet face, and some soe tricked with lace that Justice
Wray in his tyme spake to such an odd counsellour in this manner:
"*Quomodo intrasti, domine, non habens vestem nuptialem?* Get
you from the barr, or I will put you from the barr for your folish
pride." (Ch. Da[nvers]: *narr.*)

9. Every man serves to serve himselfe.

October 25. As the fox and the Asse were travayling by the way,
they overtooke a mule, a strange beast as they thought, and began
to be verry inquisitive, like a couple of constables, to know whence
he came and what his name might be. The mule told them his name
was written in his foote, and there they might reade it yf they would;
the foxe, dissembling, sayd he was not bookish, and askt the asse
what he could doe. He, like an asse, without feare or witt, went
about to shewe his schollership; but while he was taking up the
foote to reade what was told him, the mule tooke him such [a]
blowe with his foote that the asse payd for his cuning[?]. Such are
meere scholleres. (Ed. Curle.)

FOLIO 34

*Maiores in sacris litteris progressus praemia maiora postulant, et
plures in vita necessitates plura vitae necessaria subsidia requirunt:*
these causes of a plurality in a dispensacion.

DR. PARRYES ALE FOR THE SPRING.

R$_x$. Of the juyce of Scourvy-grasse one pint; of the juyce of water-
cresses, as much; of the juyce of succory, halfe a pint; of the juyce
of fumitory, halfe a pint: proportion to one gallon of ale: they must
be all tunned up togither.

There is a certaine kinde of compound called Laudanum, which
may be had at Dr. Turners, appothecary, in Bishopgate Streate; the
virtue of it is verry soveraigne to mitigate anie payne; it will for a
tyme lay a man in a sweete trans, as Dr. Parry told me he tryed in a
fever, and his sister Mrs. Turner in hir childbirth.

The L[ord] Zouche, a verry learned and wise nobleman, was made
Lord President of the Marches of Wales after the death of the old
Earle of Pembroke.

FOLIO 34b

My cosen told me that the Custome of burning women with their
husbandes in Goa began upon this occasion: the women of that
Country being skilfull in poysoninge, and exceedingly given to the
synn of Lechery, could noe sooner like an other but presently their
husband would dye, that they might marry him whom they best
liked; whereupon it came to passe that one woman burried manie
husbands, and soe the king lost many subjectes. And therefore to
prevent this mischeife the king ordeined, that, whensoever the husband died, the wife should be burned with him, in great sollemnitie
of musike and assembly of frendes; esteeming by this meanes to

move the wives to make much of their husbandes, yf not for the love of their companie, yet for love of their owne lives, since their safety consisted in their preservacion.

EPITAPHES IN THE TEMPLE CHURCHE.

Hic jacet corpus H. Bellingham Westmerlandiensis, generosi, et nuper Socij Medij Templi, cuius relligionis Synceritas, Vitae probitas, morumque integritas, eum maxime commendabant. Obijt 10 Decembr. 1586, aetatis suae 22°.

FOLIO 35

D:O:M: on the South Syde
on a pillar.

Rogerio Bisshopio, illustris interioris Templi Societatis quondam studioso, in florentis aetatis limine morte immatura praerepto, qui ob faelicissimam indolem, moresque suauissimos, magnum sui apud omnes desiderium relinquens, corpus humo, amorem amicis, coelo animum dicavit.
    Monumentum hoc amoris et maeroris perpetuum testem charissimi posuere parentes.
    Obijt 7° Sept, 1597: aetatis suae 23.

EPITAPHE IN THE CHURCH AT HYTHE IN KENT

    Whiles he did live which here doth lye
        Three suites gott of the Crowne,
    The Mortmaine, fayre, and Mayralty,
        For Heith this auncient Towne;
    And was himselfe the Baylif last,
        And Mayor first by name;
    Though he be gon, tyme is not past
        To prayse God for the same.
    (Of John Bridgman; obijt 1591.)

FOLIO 35b

May.

W. Wats, antagonista. Summum jus non est summa injuria jure positivo, sed equitate.

9. [Name heavily cancelled] showed me certaine love letteres from [name heavily cancelled], whom he should have married, but himselfe crost it, though both the [name cancelled] sollicited and the gent[lemen] word him.

14. Mr. Curle, my chamberfellowe, was called alone by parliament to the barr.

29. There have bin 5 Bishops of London in hir Majesties tyme: Grindall, Sandes, Elmar, Fletcher, and Bancroft nowe.

Those which goe to church onely to heare musicke goe thither more for *fa* then *soule*. (B. Rud[yerd].)

One said yong Mr. Leake was verry rich, and fatt. "True," said B. Ru[yerd], "Pursy men are fatt for the most part."

"He takes the stronger part still," of one that would be sure to drinke stronge beare yf he could come to it.

[*fo. 36 blank in MS*]

FOLIO 36b

Aprill. 1602.

À MEDICINE FOR THE WINDINES IN THE STOMACH.

R_x. A quarter of a pint of lavanda spike water, halfe as much balme water, a fewe cloves, and a little long pepper, beaten togither; drinke this at twise. (Mrs. Cordell exper[t].)

FOR THE HAYMEROYDS.

R_x. Two ounces of shoemacke brayed, and put it to halfe a pint of red rose water, warme them over the fyre, and bath the place with it. (My Cosen exper[t].)

The covetous man rides in a coache which runnes upon 4 wheeles: the 1. Pusillanimity. 2. Inhumanity. 3. Contempt of God. 4. Forgetfulnes of death (*Dr. Chamberlayne*); it is drawne with two horses: 1. *Rapacitas*. 2. *Tenacitas*. The divel the coachman, and he hath two whippes: 1. *Libido acquirendi*. 2. *Metus amittendi*.

6. This day there was a race at Sapley neere Huntingdon, invented by the gent[lemen] of that Country: at this Mr. Oliver Cromwell's horse won the sylver bell, and Mr. Cromwell had the glory of the day. Mr. Hynd came behinde.

FOLIO 37

April. 1602.

While I was at Hemmingford Dr. Chamberlayne told me that Dr. Bilson was made Bishop of Winchester by the meanes of the Earl of Essex. Nowe the Bishop, being visitour of Trinity Colledge in Oxeford by his place, promised to the Lady Walsingham, that he would make him, that nowe is, President after Dr. Yeilderes decease. And for this purpose expelled such fellowes as he thought would be opposite, and placed such in their roomes as he knew would be sure unto him. By this meanes Dr. Chamberlaine was defeated of his right, being an Oxefordshire man, whom by their statutes they are bound to preferr before anie other.

The fellowes of that Colledge are to nominat 2, and the Visitour within 6 weekes must elect the one of them to be President.

Upon marriage with the Lady Polivizena, Sir Henry Cromwell convayed his landes unto his sonne Mr. Oliver in marriage. Soe Mr. Oliver with his owne and his ladyes living is the greatest esquire in those partes, thought to be worth neere 5000£. per annum. There lives a housefull at Hinching brooke, like a kennell.

Mrs. Mary Androes, daughter and heir to Mr. Androes of Sandey, was married to one Mr. Mayne of Grayes In; had 1000£. present; and yf Androes have issue, to have an other. Mayne had but 150£. per annum.

FOLIO 37b

Aprill. 1602.

I hear that the yong Lord North was married to Mrs. Brocket, Sir Jo. Cutts his Ladies sister; being constrayned in a manner through want of money while he lived in Cambridge, he had some 800£. with hir. Shee is not yong nor well favoured, noe marvaile yf he love hir not.

On Easter day Dr. Chamberlaine was at Sir Henry Cromwells, and ministred the Communion, but without booke.

15. I was with my cosen in Kent, and he told me that there is one [blank], a rich broker in London, whose first wife had such a running strong conceit in hir head that the sherifes sought still to apprehend hir, that, noe perswasion to the contrary prevayling with hir, first shee cutt hir owne throate, and that being cured, she brake hir necke by leaping out at hir garret windowe.

Jo. Vermeren, a Dutchman, of kin to my cosens first wifes sisters husband, had issue a daughter, married to one Niepson. Their daughter was married to one Hoofman, a notable rich man, whoe in his beginning was but a pedler of pottes, yet after by his good fortune and industry he proved soe wealthie that he gave 10,000£. with his daughter in marriage to Sir Horatio Polivizena, now deceased, and the widdowe married to Mr. Oliver Cromwell, the sonne and heir of Sir H[enry] Cromwell. This marriage and certaine land he had from his Uncle Warrein cleared him out of debt.

FOLIO 38

Aprill. 1602.

18. My cosen concluded with William Tunbridge of Ditton to give
him 115£. for a leas of Ditton ruffe for 25 yeares.

16. Dr. Parry told howe Dr. Barlowe, nowe one of hir Majesties
chapleins, received a checke at hir Majesties, because he presumed
to come in hir presence when shee had given speciall charge to the
contrary, because shee would not have the memory of the late Earl
of Essex renewed by him, who had preached against him at Paules.
"O, Sir," said shee, "wee heare you are an honest man! you are an
honest man, &c."

Hir Majestie merrily told Dr. Parry that shee would not heare him
on Good Friday; "Thou wilt speake against me, I am sure," quoth
shee. Yet shee heard him.

18. Duke de Neveurs, a Frenchman, departed for France this day.

19. My cosen told me that Vicares, King Henry the 8. his Sergeant
Surgeon, was at first but a meane practiser in Maidstone, such a one
as Bennett there, that had gayned his knowledge by experience,
untill the King advanced him for curing his sore legge.
A light hand makes a heavy wound.

20. I rode to Dr. Parryes. He said there was noe greater evidence to
prove a man a foole then yf he leave the University to marry a wife.

FOLIO 38b

Aprill.

21. Dr. Parry told howe his father was deane of Salisbury, kept a
sumptuous house, spent above his revenewe, was carefull to preferr
such as were men of hope, used to have showes at his house, wherein he would have his sonne an actor to embolden him.

He shewed me the sermon he made at Court last Good Fryday; his text was, "My God, my God, why hast thou forsaken me?" It was right eloquent and full of sound doctrine, grave exhortacions, and heavenly meditacions.

Vox horrentis, forsaken; *Vox sperantis,* My God; *Vox admirantis,* Why hast thou, &c.

Meẽ. There was in Christ *Esse naturae, Esse gratiae, Esse gloriae.*

God's presence 2^x $\begin{cases} \text{by essence,} \\ \text{by assistance;} \end{cases}$
dereliction, withdrawing, and retyring.

I returned to Bradborne.

Cos. shee would have sent a part of a gammon of bacon to their servantes; my cosen said he loved it well, &c. And, because he would not send that shee would, shee would not that he would, and grewe to strange hott contradiction with him. After, when shee sawe him moved (and not without cause) shee fell a kissing his hand at table, with an extreeme kinde of flattery, but never confest shee was to violently opposite.

FOLIO 39

Aprill.

22. The *fleur de luce,* as wee call it, takes his name, I thinke, as *Fleur de Lis,* which *Lis* is a river in Flanders neere Artoys.

26. I came from my cosens to London.

27. Perpetuityes are so much impugned because they would be prejudiciall to the Queenes proffites, which is raysed dayly by fines and recoveryes.

One Parkins of the Inner house a very complementall gent[leman]. A Barrester, but noe lawyer.

28. In the Starchamber the benche on that part of the roome where the Queenes armes are placed is alwayes vacant; noe man may sitt on it, as I take it, because it is reserved as a seate for the Prince, and therefore before the same are layd the purse and the mace as notes of autority.

29. "It is a great thing must stopp a feme covert," said Justice Fennar.

30. Those which name such as they ought not, and such as they knowe to be unfitt, to be Sherives of London, doe but goe a woll-gathering, purposing to fleece such men. (Cosen Onsloe.) And they goe a fishinge for some 100£. or 2, as they nominated my cosen this yeare.

FOLIO 39b

October. 1602.

One Mr. Ousley of the Middle Temple, a yong gallant, but of a short cutt, overtaking a tall stately stalking cavalier in the streetes, made noe more a doe but slipt into an iron mongeres shop, threwe of his cloke and rapier, fitted himselfe with bells, and presently cam skipping, whistling, and dauncing the morris about that long swaggerer, whoe staringly demaunding what he ment, "I cry you mercy," said the gent[leman], "I tooke you for a May pole." (Ch. Da[nvers] *nar.*)

Mr. Buttler beinge askt by a gent[leman] why he did not marry, "Why," said he, "the Hole needes not the Physicion." (Overbury.)

9. Sniges nose loked downe to see howe many of his teethe were lost, and could never get up againe. (Th. Overbury of Snigs crooked nose.)

Sir Frauncis Englefields house overthrowne by the practice of Mr. Blundell of the Middle Temple, whoe, being put in speciall trust, tooke a spleen upon a small occasion against the heir, and presently in his heate informed the Earl of Essex, that such a conveyaunce was made of soe goodly an inheritaunce in defraud of the Queen, and soe animated him to begg it, to the utter ruine of that house. (Mr. Curle *nar.*)

One told a jest and added that all good wittes applauded it; a way to bring one to a dilemma, either of arrogance in arriding, as though he had a good witt too, or of ignoraunce, as thoughe he could not conceive of it as well as others.

FOLIO 40

October. 1602

10. At Paules Crosse, Dr. Spenser preached. He remembred in his prayer the Companie of the Fishmongers, as his speciall benefactours while he lived in Oxford; his text the 5th of Isay, v. 4.

We are soe blind and perverse by nature that wee are soe farre from the sence of our owne imperfections and the terror of our synn, that either not seeing or not acknowledging our owne weaknesses, wee runne headlong into all wickednes, and hate soe much to be reformed, that God is fayne to deale pollitikely with us, propounding our state unto us in parables as it were an others case, that thereby drawing man from conceit of himselfe which would make him partiall, he might draw an uncorrupt judgment of him self from him selfe. Soe dealt the Lord with David by the parable of the poor mans sheepe, and soe here he taketh up a comparison of the vine, to shewe Israel their ingratitude.

Parables are proportionable resemblances of thinges not well understoode; they be vayles indeed, which cover things, but being removed give a kind of light to the[m] which before was insensible, and makes them seeme as though they were sensible.

The things considerable in the text are, first, the churche, resembled by the vine; 2. Godes benefites towards the churche expressed in the manner of his dressing the vine; 3. the fruit expected: grapes:

judgment and righteousnes; 4. the fayling and ingratitude, by bringing forth sower

FOLIO 40b

and wild grapes: oppression and crying; 5. Godes judgment, vers. 6.

In the Church, he considered what it is and where it is.

The churche is compared most aptly to the vyne, for neither of
them spring naturally: *Non sumus de carne, nec voluntate hominis,
sed beneplacito Dei.* 2. Both spring and growe first in weaknes, yet
then they claspe their little hands and take hold on[e] of an other;
and soe going on *crescunt sine modo,* the increase without measure,
as Plini sayth. 3. Noe plant more flourishing in the summer, none
more poore and bare naked in winter. All followe the church in
prosperitie, and the rich, the mighty, the wise, in persequution fall
away like leaves. 4. Bring forth fruit in clusteres, which cheres the
hart. God and men and angels rejoyce when the church aboundes
in workes of righteousnes and true holines. 5. Both have but one
roote, though manie branches: Christ is the true foundacion, other
then this can no man lay. 6. The branches are ingrafted; and as in
planting all are tyed alike with the outward bond, yet all prove not
alike, soe all have the same profession and outward meanes, yet all
growe not nor fructifie alike: but it is the inward grace that maketh
the true branche, as he is a Jewe that is one within. (Rom. 2: 28 et
29.)

FOLIO 41

2. The Lordes Vineyard is not to be knowne by the fruit (for we
reade here that it bringeth forth wyld grapes), but where the roote
is planted, where Christ is professed, there the Church is; it is nowe
Universall, not tyed to anie place; we reade of 7 Churches in the

Revelacions, though all not alike pure, yet all churches; Israell is his eldest sonne, though a prodigall; as betwixt man and woman after a publique contract celebrated, though the woman play the harlot and bring forth children of fornicacion unto hir husband, yet continues shee his wife whose name shee beares untill a publique divorce be sued. Some churches are soare, some sicke, some soe leprous that noe communion ought to [be] continued with them, yet churches still.

Yf anie aske, as manie Papistes use to doe, where our church was before Martin Luther was borne, we aunswer that it is the same churche that was from the beginninge, and noe newe on[e] as they terme it, for the weeding of a vyneyard is noe destroyinge, nor the pruning any newe planting; for we have removed but Idolatrie and a privat masse of ceremonies, which with the burying the author [?] of life in a hidden and unknowne language had almost put the heavenly light out of our Candlesticke; and when the trashe of humaine inventions had raysed themselves to soe high esteeme, it was tyme to say, "Yf Ephraim play the harlot, yet lett not Israell synn."

FOLIO 41b

Jerusalem litterally is the mother churche of all.

The churche, like the vine that hath many branches but one roote, may have severall members, but all knit together with the unity of 3 bondes: one Lord, one fayth, one baptisme. But nowe Rome, usurping over hir fellowes, speakes like Babilon in the 18. Revel. "I cannot erre," and have encroched an article upon the Creede that must be beeleeved upon payne of damnation, that there is one Visible heade of the Churche (which must be the Pope). And yet in an oecumenical counsell of 330 catholike bishops it was decreed that Constantinople should have equall authority with Rome, which plainely confuted their usurped universall supremacy. Yet the popes, by the assistaunce of the emperours, have, like ivy,

risen higher then the oke by which it climbed: soe much that our
countriman Stapleton doubts not to call his holines *Supremum in
terris numen.*

3. The benefites and manner of dressing the vine: Genesis is but the
nurse of it; Exodus, the removing; Leviticus, the ordering and manner of keeping it; Josua, the weeding, &c. God soe loved it that he
gave his onely sonne to redeeme it, and when he gave him, what
gave he not with him?

Might not the church use the wordes of the leaper in the Ghospell:
"Lord, if thou wilt, thou canst make me cleane"? (and why then
complaynest thou?)

FOLIO 42

True it is, yf we consider his power: for he that is able to rayse up
children to Abraham of stones, to make the iron sweate, &c., can
purifie our corruptions yf wee regard his power, and that without
our meanes; but God hath tyed himself to ordinary meanes, by his
eternall decree: and he that will not heare Moses and the prophetes
neither will he beleeve though on[e] should rise from the dead.
Many were foule with the leprosie in Nathans tyme, yet none cured
but Naman.

4. The fruit.
All things, even the meanest, imitate the Creatour in doing something
in their kind for the common good, not themselves alone; the olive
doth not anoint it self with it[s] owne oyle; the trees and plants
which spend themselves in bringing forth some fruit or berry holdes
it noe longer then till it be ripe, and then lettes it fall at his masters
feete; the grape is not made drunke with it[s] owne juyce.

"He that receiveth a benefit hath lost his liberty," saith Seneca; and
since we have received such benefites of God as we can not, we
would not, renounce, lett us glorifie him in our bodies whose we
are, (not our owne).

Aeternitie cometh before we worke: therefore our workes merit
not eternall life. And infantes incorporat into the mysticall vyne
are saved though they dy before they are able to bring forth anie
good worke.

Our good workes growe as it were in a cold region: the best of
them, even our prayers, scarce come to perfection throughe the
imperfection of our nature.

Good workes to be performed for mutuall helpe, and though we
holde our selves sufficient, yet they are to be done even as every
thing

FOLIO 42b

bringeth forth something yf for noe other purpose yet to continue
in its owne state; like the spring, which, because it yeildeth water,
is therefore continually fed with water. *Bona opera sunt via regni,
non causa regnandi.* (Bernard.)

   The fruites brought forth: wyld grapes, an heavy sight to a carefull husbandman, to have noe better reward of his paynes.

I pray God the church of England may not justifie the synns of
Sodome and Judas. Covetousnes, the roote of all wickednes, maketh
men desyre to be greate rather then good, and this desyre causes
them to sucke even the lyfe from one an other. There is a synn
amongst us which hath not bin heard of amongst the gentiles, that
wee should robb God, and that is in tithing. Howe manie desyrous
that the labouring man, the minister, might be put out, that themselves might have the inheritaunce. It is the corruption of the
ministery that all the dores of entraunce are shut up but the dore
of symony, soe that the most and best places are for the most possessed by the worst; and, yf anie of the better be forced to come in,
they are constrayned to make shipwracke of a good conscience.

If it be true which is published in the names of the popish faction,
the Pope hath sent a dispensation that the popish patrons may sell

their presentations, soe be it the money come to the maintenance of the Jesuites. And will Peters successour thinke it lawefull to sell the guiftes of the Holie Ghost? Will Simon Peter become Simon Magus? But he will nowe

FOLIO 43

become a fisher for men, because he findes in their mouths greater peices then twenty pence. The ministeres are like the hart and liver, from whence are derived lyfe and nourishment by sound doctrine and good example unto the members of the church, and yf these be corrupt it is much to be feared the whole body is like to languishe in a dangerous consumption.

In defrauding the ministery, we pull downe the pillers of the house wee dwell in.

FOLIO 43b

October. 1602.

11. The L[ord] Zouche, L[ord] President of the Marches of Wales, begins to knowe and use his authoritie soe muche that his jurisdiction is allready brought in question in the common place, and the Cheif Justice of that bench thinkes that Glostershire, Herefordshire, &c., are not within his circuit.

When he came to sitt on the benche at Ludlowe, there were, as it was wont, two cushions layd, one for the Chief Justice Leukenour, another for the President, but he tooke the on[e], and casting it downe said, one was enough for that place. (Th. Overbury.)

Sir Walter Rhaleighs sollicitor on Sheborough was verry malapert and saucy in speache to Justice Walmesley at the bench in the Common place; soe far that, after wordes past hotly betwixt them, he said he thought it fitt to commit him for his contemptuous behaviour, but the other judges were mum. *Quantus ille!* His wordes: "Before God, you do not well to lay their practises upon us. You knowe me well enough, yf you list, &c."

At Guildhall, Mr. Long saies [?], Serg[ean]t Heale came to move a cause which he said was betwixt the cuckhold and the cuchold maker, but his client was the honester man, for he came to prove him selfe the cuckhold. His mayd, in hir aunsweres to my lord upon his examinacion, said still, "And it like you, my Lordship."

FOLIO 44

October. 1602.

10. I heard that Sir Robert Cecile is fallen in dislike with one of his secretaries of greatest confidence, Mr. [blank], and hath discarded him, which moves manie conjectures and much discourse in the Court. This secretary was a sutour to be on[e] of the clerkes of the signet, as a place of more ease and lesse attendaunce then a clarke of the Counsell, which it is though[t] he might have.

The Irish Earle of Clanrichard is well esteemed of by hir Majestie, and in speciall grace at this tyme; hath spent lavishly since he came over, yet payes honestly. (Mr. Hadsor.)

The E[arl] of Ormond is purposed and hath licence to marry his daughter to one of his cosens, not to the Lord Mountjoy as was thought. (*idem.*)

Evil companie cuttes to the bone before the fleshe smart. It is like a fray in the night, when a man knowes not howe to ward. (Ch. Davers *booke.*)

The libertines from the rose of *Sola fides,* sucke the poyson of security—*idem.*

A souldier being challenged for flying from the camp said, *Homo fugiens denuo pugnabit.*
Booth, being indited of felony for forgery the 2[n]d time, desyred a day to aunswere till Easter terme; "Oh!" said the Attorny, "you would have a spring; you shall, but in a halter." (*Ch. Da*[vers].)

Mr. Tanfeild, speaking of a knave and his queane, said he was a little to inward with hir.

25. I heard that Sir Rich[ard] Basset is much seduced, indeed gulled, by one Nic. Hill, a great profest philosopher, and nowe abuseth this yong knight by imagined Alchymie. (Jo. Chap[man].)

FOLIO 44b

October. 1602.

12. The E[arl] of Sussex keepes Mrs. Sylvester Morgan (sometyme his ladies gent[lewoman]) at Dr. Daylies house as his mistress, calls hir his Countesse, hyres Capt[ain] Whitlocke, with monie and cast suites, to brave his countes, with telling of hir howe he buyes his wench a wascote of 10£., and puts hir in hir velvet gowne, &c. Thus, not content to abuse hir by keeping a common wench, he strives to invent meanes of more greife to his lady, whoe is of a verry goodly and comely personage, of an excellent presence, and a rare witt. Shee hath brought the E[arl] to allowe hir 1700£. a yeare for the maintenaunce of hir selfe and hir children while she lives apart. It is conjectured that Capt[ain] Whitlocke, like a base pander, hath incited the E[arl] to followe this sensuall humour, of preferring strang fleshe before his owne, as he did the E[arl] of Rutland. (J. Bramstone *nar.*) The Countesse is the daughter to the Lady Morrison in Hartfordshire, with whom it is like she purposeth to live.

("I would be loath to come after him to a wench for feare of the pox," said Mr. Curl of E[arl] of Su[ssex].)

(A practise to bring the nobilitie into contempt and beggery, by nourishing such as may provoke them to spend all upon lechery and such base pleasures.)

When there came one which presented a supplicacion for his master to the Counsell, that upon sufficient bond he might be released out of Wisbishe Castle, where he lay for recusancy, that he might looke to his busines in harvest, the L[ord] Admirall thought the petition reasonable, but the old L[ord] Treasurour, Sir W. Cecil, said he would not assent, "For," said he, "I knowe howe such men would use us yf they had us at the like advantage, and therefore while we have the staffe in our handes lett us hold it, and when they gett it lett them use it." (Mr. Hadsor *narr.*)

FOLIO 45

October. 1602.

Out of a poeme called "It is merry when Gossips meete."
S. R. Such a one is clarret proofe, *i.*[*e.*], a good wine bibber.

There's many deale upon the score for Wyne,
When they should pay, forgett the Vintners Syne.

of Dido and Aeneas:
She ply'd him with the Wyne in golden cup,
Turning the liquor in the bottom up.

I pray goe up the stayres;
Good Cosin no, let's take it standing here.

A drapers man and shee were mighty In. (lovers)

Maydes take fewe thinges to which they say not nay.

Tis maydens modesty to use denyall;
A willing offer commeth twise or thrice.

Wine and Virginity kept stale drink flatt.

Taurus soe rules and guides your husbands head,
That every night they sleepe in hornework cap.

The devils picture on your husbands browes.

I knowe tis better to take[?] wrong then doe it,
But yet in such a case flesh leades us to it.

A man whose beard seemes scard with sprites to have bin
And hath noe difference twixt his nose and chin;
But all his hayres have gott the falling sicknes,
Whose forefront lookes like jack an Apes behind.

A Gossips round, thats every on[e] a cup.

FOLIO 45b

October. 1602.

12. Mr. Steven Beckingham of Hartfordshire was brought into the
Kings benche at the suit of two poore joyners whom he hath undone; they seeled his house, which came to a matter of some 80£.,
and they could hardly obtain anie thing by suit. A man of a hott
collerick disposicion, a creaking loud voyce, a greasy whitish head,
a ruddish beard, of long staring *mouchetons;* wore an outworne
muff with two old gold laces, a playne falling band, his cuffs
wrought with coloured silk and gold, a satten doublet, a wrought
wastcoate, &c. *Ut facile quis cognoscat haud facile si cum alijs
convenire posset, qui voce, facie, vestitu ita secum dissidet.*

One of his witnesses would not aunswere any thing for him untill
he were payd his charges in the face of the Court. Soe little confidence had he in his credit, whoe had dealt soe hardly with his
joyners.

On[e] Fossar, an old joyner dwelling Paules Churchyard, a common and a good measurer of joyners worke.

Mr. Prideaux, a great practiser in the Eschequer, and one that usurpes upon a place certaine at the bar, left his man one day to keepe his place for him; but Lancaster of Grayes In comming in the meane tyme, would needes have the place, though the man would have kept it. "For," said L., "knowes[t] thou not that I beeleve nothing but the reall presence?" meaning that he was a Papist; and besydes could not thinke it to be *corpus meum* except Mr. Prideaux himselfe were there. (Mr. Hackwell *nar.*)

FOLIO 46

October. 1602.

16. When Mr. Dodridge in his argument of Mr. Darsies patentes, and soe of the prerogative in generall, he began his speache from Godes government. "It is done like a good archer," quoth Fr[ancis] Bacon, "he shootes a fayre compasse."

There was an action brought to trie the title of one Rooke an infant for a house and certaine land. "All this controversye," said the attorny, "is but for a little rookes nest."

AN EPITAPHE UPON A BELLOWE MAKER.

Here lyes Jo. Potterell, a maker of bellowes,
Maister of his trade, and king of good fellowes;
Yet for all this, att the houre of his death,
He that made bellowes could not make breath. (*B. J.*)

24. Mr. Bodly, the author, promoter, and the perfecter, of a goodly library in Oxford, wan a riche widdowe by this meanes: comming to the place where the widdowe was with one whoe is reported to have bin sure of hir, as occasion happened, the widdowe was absent; while he was in game, he, finding his opportunity, entreated the surmised assured gent[leman] to hold his cardes till he returned.

In which tyme he found the widdowe in a gardein, courted, and obteined his desyre; soe he played his game, while an other held his cardes. He was at first but the sonne of a merchant, untill he gave some intelligence of moment to the Counsell, whereupon he was thought worthie employment, whereby he rose. (Mr. Curle.)

FOLIO 46b

October. 1602.

24. Mr. Dr. King, preacher at St. Andrews in Holborn, at Paules Crosse this daye. His text:
2 Peter 2. v. 4, 5, 6, 7, 8, 9. The length of his text might make some tedious semblance of a long discourse, but the matter shortly cutt it self into two parts: example and rule; one particular, the other generall; the one experiment, the other science; the one of more force to prove, the other to instruct. The argument is not *a posse ad esse,* but *ab esse ad posse;* it hath bin, and therefore may be; nay, by this place it shalbe, for *lege mortali quod vnquam fuit, et hodie fieri potest;* but *lege aeterna,* that which hath bin shalbe agayne.

Here is an acted performaunce, a demonstracion, το ὅτι, which are most forceable to persuade, being of all thinges, saving the thinges themselves, neerest our apprehension, leading from the sense to the understanding, which is our certaynest meane of acquiring knowledge, since philosophie teacheth *quod nihil est intellectu, quod non prius fuit in sensu; sicut audivimus, et fecerunt patres nostri.* Hystory and example the strongest motives to imitation. Rules are but sleeping and seeming admonitions. Thomas would not beleeve unles he thrust his fingeres into Christes sydes and felt the print of his nayles; and we are so obstinat wee will hardly beeleve, except Godes judgmentes thrust fingeres and nayles into our sydes.

FOLIO 47

October. 1602.

The examples are bipartite: each containing contrary doctrines, like the language of them in the last ch[apter] of Nehemias, halfe Jewishe, halfe Ashdoch; like the bandes of the Levites, that parted themselves one companie to one mount to blesse, the other to an other to curse the people; soe the one part denounceth judgment, the other declareth mercy: they may be compared to the cleane beastes, Deut. 14, which had parted hoofes and chewed the cudd; soe here on the one syde is the old world drowned, on the other Noach saved; on the one Sodom burned, on the other Lott preserved. They are three of the strangest and fearefullest examples in nature: the fall of the Angells, the drowning of the world, the burning of Sodome; they stretch from one end to an other, alpha and omega, heaven and earth, men and angels, the most excellent payre of Godes creatures, and the deluge oecumencall and universall. But God in his punishment like a wise prince will begin at his owne sanctuary, at his owne house, *non habitabit mecum iniquus,* "I will not suffer a wicked person to dwell in my house," and therefore first turned the Angels from his habitacion. Angells in their creacion, *vere δεύτερον,* the second light, the eyes and eares of the great king, continuall attendantes in his court and assistauntes of his throne; they are farr above the greatest saint, for wee shalbe but like them,

FOLIO 47b

October. 1602.

and they are next to the Sonne of God, otherwise he had said nothing when he said, to which of the angels sayd he at anie tyme, &c. *Hebr.:* they were *in summo, non in tuto,* or rather *non in summo sed in tuto,* untill they synned; but what their synne was, I may safely say I knowe not. One sayth *non seruarunt principatum,* and St. Jo[hn] sayth *non steterunt in veritate,* their synn was treason, they continued not in their allegeaunce and fidelity; an other, *et in Angelis vacuitatem, prauitatem, infamiam reperiit.* An other, though an absurd opinion, that it was fleshly lust, and concupiscence, by carnall copulacion with women upon earth, and this they would lay upon these wordes, "and the Sonnes of God tooke the daughters of men"; but of this it was well sayd, *perquam noxium audire et credere.* And yet it became as common as it was absurd, because men thereby thought they might sooth themselves in that synn, and thinke it tollerable when Angells had done the like before them. An other opinion more probable, that it was noe carnall, but spirituall luxury that overthrewe them, a kinde of selfe love, when they overvalued their owne excellency, and forgat their Creator; and this opinion that their synn was pride is the most received, and most like because after his fall the first temptation that he made was of pride to Adam in paradise, *enim similis altissimo.*

FOLIO 48

October. 1602.

The divel never desyred to be like God in his essence, for that being impossible, he could never conceive it, and that is never in appeticion which was nott first in apprehension. Yet he may be sayd to affect it *desyderio complacentiae, non efficaciae,* because he might please himself with such conceites, not conceave howe he might attaine to those pleasures, and to this purpose some there be that write as though they had bin taken up into the third heaven, and heard and seene the conflict betwixt Michael and the Divel: and will not stick to affirme that Michael had his name, because when the divel like a great giant bellowed out blasphemie against the most highest, denying that he had any creator or superior, Michael should resist and tell him, *Quis ut Deus;* which is the interpretacion of Michael. Soe though it be incertaine what was the synn of Angells, yet is it most certayne that they fell from the highest happines to the lowest wretchednes; the fall was like ligh[t]ning, suddein, and the place of it not possible to be found; it passeth the capacitie of man to expresse it by comparison soe perfectly that he may say *hoc impetu.* And for their payne it is *transcendens, et transcendentia transcendit:* it is invaluable, incomprehensible, passeth all hyperbole; there was a present amission of place, grace, glory, the fruition of Godes presence, &c., which is the greatest of miseries;

FOLIO 48b

October, 1602.

felicem fuisse: but their remaines a fearefull expectacion of future miseryes, *et nihil magis adversarium quam expectatio; et quo me vindicta reservas?*

It was the opinion of Origen, long since condemned for erronius, that the Divels might be saved, and his reason was because they had *liberum voluntatis arbitrium,* which might perhaps change and encline to the desyre of good, and soe through repentaunce obteyne mercy; but the Divels are soe obdurate in their malice that though they may have *stimulum conscienciae,* yet they can never come *ad correptionem gratiae,* and in that opinion Origen is said Πλατονιϛεῖν non Χριϛιανιϛεῖν. An other prop to his opinion was Jacobs ladder, where he imagined the descending and ascending of Angels could meane nothing but the fall and restitution of Angels.

The 2^d example is the drowning of the world, a descent from heaven to earth in judgmentes. The world is termed Χοσμος of the Grecians, from the excellent beauty thereof, and of the Lattynes *Mundus, quia nihil mundius;* but here it is used to expresse the universalitie of the destruction, as the hystorye declares it, Gen. 6:7, *et.* 7:21, 22, 23, 24: God destroyed everything that was upon the earth from

man to beast, to the creeping thing, and to the foule of the heaven,
onely the fishes escaped, and the reason one rendreth was because
the sea onely was undefiled at that tyme; there was then noe sayling upon that element, noe pyracie and murder committed upon it,
noe forrein invasions intended over it, noe trafficque with the
nations for strang comodities, nor for one an others synnes and
vices; all the other creatures were polluted by man, and were [to]
be purged with that floud. The ayre as farr as our eyes could looke
and fascinate, even the foules as far as our breath could move, were
infected

FOLIO 49

October. 1602.

with the contagion thereof; all were uncleane, all were to be clensed
or punished. The greatnes of their number cannot excuse, but aggra-
vates the offence. A mulitude may synn and their synn is more
grievous, *qui cum multitudine peccat, cum multitudine periet;* and
for the most part, the most are the worst. It is noe sound argument,
it is well done because many doe so. The fox brings forth many
cubbes, and the lyon hath but one whelpe at once, yet that is a
lyion, and more then manie foxes. The harlot boasts that shee had
many moe resorted to hir house then Socrates to his schole, but hir
followers went the way of darknes.

"And brought in the floud:" and therefor a miracle supernaturall
wrought by the finger of God, not as some imagine by the conjunction of waterishe planetes, soe attributinge all to and confirming
all by naturall meanes, they say the world shalbe destroyed by fire,
as it was by water, when there shall happen the like conjunction of
firy as there was of watery planetes; but beleeve God, whoe sayth
Ego pluam. And this was against nature to destroy hir owne workes.
The length of the rayne, 40 dayes, the continuaunce of the waters,
for twelve moneths, the dissolucion of soe muche ayre with water
as should make a generall deluge—these are directly against the rules

of naturall philosophie, besydes the influence of a planet never stretcheth beyond his hemisphere, all which shewe plainely, that it was the miraculous worke of God, not effected by the course of nature. This was not *imber in furore missus,* to destroy or famishe some particular city or country, of which kinde of baptismes our land hath within fewe yeares felt many. But this made the sea, which before made but one spheare with the earth, as man and wife make but one flesh, breake the boundes of modesty and over-flowe the whole; that which before was the girdle of the earth, nowe girt it, but in such a fashion, that it stiffled all. It was such a dropsie in the world, that our simples having lost their former virtue, we were permitted to eat flesh for the preservacion of our lives, which before

FOLIO 49b

October. 1602.

were prolonged with the naturall herbes and fruites of the earth, more hundreds then nowe they can bee scores with our best helpes of art or nature.

But it may be said, What, will God punishe the goode with the wicked? Will he drownd, all togither, the righteous and the bad? Will he say *Pereant amici, modo pereant inimici?* Will he command *stragem tam amicorum quam hostium?* Shall his judgmentes be like the nett in the Gospell, that catcheth good and bad togither? Noe, for he punished the old world. This floud was his sope and nitar to scoure of the filth, to sever the good from the evill, the wheat from the chaffe. He brought the floud upon the Ungodly, but he saved Noah, the 8th person a small number, a child may tell them, a poore number, *pauperi est numerare*—but eight persons saved. Those tymes were evil, but there are worse dayes not instant but extant, wherein iniquitie prescribes hypocrisie, settes hir hand to many false bills, settes downe 100 for 10; the whole is overflowne with all wickednes, &c.

The 2^d part is Godes mercy, "but he saved Noah," like a ring on his finger; he kept him as writing in the palme of his hand, as the apple of his eye, and as a seale on his heart. He built him a castle stronger then brasse, and lockt him up in the arke like a jewell in casket. He preserved him safe in a wodden vessell amongst the topps of mountains, in a world of waters, without card, tacleing, or pilot. He was saved between judgment and judgment, like Susanna betwixt the twoe elderes, like the Children of Israell betweene two walles of water in the Red Sea, like Christ betweene the two theives; soe that it may be truly sayd, it was noe meaner a miracle in saving Noah then in drowning the whole world.

FOLIO 50

October. 1602.

But "Saved Noah, the eight[h] person, a Preacher of righteousnes." Here is a banner of hope to all that feare God. When Justice was running hir course like a strong giant to have destroyed the whole world, Mercy mett, encountered, and told hir that she must not touch Godes anoynted, nor doe his prophetes anie harme. There was Noah, "a preacher of righteousnes," and he must be spared, he was a preacher, not a whisperer in corners, singing to himselfe and his muses. This Noah was the hemme of the world, the remnant of the old, and the element of the newe; he was *communis terminus,* the first shipwright, and yet "a preacher of righteousnes." Nowe concerninge the estimacion of preachers in auncient tymes, and the contempt of that calling in these dayes, their high account with God, their neglect with men, from hence he said he could paradox manie conclusions which tyme forced him to over slip. But in this age lett a preacher be as aunciently discended and of as good a parentage, bee as well qualified, as soundly learned, of as comely personage, as sweete a conversation, have a mother witt, and perhaps a fathers blessing to, lett him be equall in all the giftes and ornamentes of nature, art, and fortune to a man of an other profession, yet he shall be scorned, derided, and pointed at like a bird of divers strange coloures, and all because he beares the name of a preacher.

FOLIO 50b

October. 1602.

Tymes past were so liberall to the clergy that for feare all would have runne into their handes there were statutes of mortmaine enacted to restrayne that current: but devotion at this day is growne soe cold that the hartes and handes of all are a verry mortmaine it self; the[y] hold soe fast they will part from nothing; noe, not from that which hath bin of auncient given to holie uses. There are in England above 3000 impropriacions, where the minister hath a poore stipend; their bread is broken amongst strangers, the foxes and cubbes live in their ruines, the swallowe builds hir nest and the Satyres daunce and revill where the Levites were wont to sing, the Church livinges are seised upon and possessed by the secular; it was the old lawe that none should eate the bread of the aultar but those that wayted at the altar. Those things, which were provided for the pastors of our soules, with what conscience can they receive, which are not able to feede them?
O miseram sponsam talibus creditam paranymphis.

It is strang that that abhominable synn of symony should be so common, that it is no strang thing for a learned man to purchase his promotion, but the honest must say to their patron, as Paule to the lame, *aurum et argentum non habeo, quod habeo dabo.* I will live honestly, I will preach diligently, I will pray for you devoutly, but that *quid dabitis* liveth still with those of Judas his humour. They thinke all to much for the preacher, nothing to much for themselves; it must be enacted that they may not have to much for fear of surfetting; they would have them according to

the new Dyet brought downe to the skin and bone, to cure them.
All their speaches and actions tend to our impoverishment, saith
he, as though wee were the onely droanes and they the bees of the
state. The Lord commaunded

FOLIO 51

October. 1602.

to bring into his tabernacle, but these strive whoe may carry out
fastest, and blesse themselves in the spoile, saying with that church
robber, *Videtis quam prospera navigatio ab ipsis diis immortalibus
sacriliges detur,* but the hier of these laboureres, this field Of Naboth,
&c., will cry out against them. Christ, when he was upon the earth,
wipped those out the church which bought and sold in the church;
what will he doe with those which buy and sell his church it selfe?
I speake not this, because I would perswade you to give your goodes
unto us; *Non vestra, sed vos,* nay, *non nostra, sed vos quero.* I doe
but advertise you to consider whether the withholding the tenth
may not deprive you of the whole, the spoiling the churche of hir
clothes may not strip you of your living, the impropriating his benefices may not dispropriat the Kingdome of Heaven to you.

"A preacher of righteousnes" or a righteous preacher, such a one
as Jo[hn the] Baptist was; he preached, as all ought to doe, by his
lyfe, by his handes. By his lyfe: *Vel non omnino, vel moribus
doceto.* He preached amendement from synn, he preached the
lawes of nature and the judgmentes imminent, and as some thinke,
he preached Christ alsoe. And wee preache the lawe of nature:
doth not nature teache you, &c? Wee preache fayth: then being
justified by fayth. Wee preache the lawe of Moses: Christ came not
to break but to fulfill the Lawe.

FOLIO 51b

October. 1602.

We preach righteousnes, *semen et germen,* embued, endued; active and contemplative; justificacion and sanctificacion; primitive and imputed, the one in Christ absolute, the other in us. Righteousnes acted by Christ and accepted by us, which is the true justifying righteousnes, and above all the other.

The 3^d Example, of Sodome and Gomorrhe: they were not condemned onely, but condemned to be overthrowne, and soe overthrowne that they should be turned, not into stones which might come togither againe, but into ashes; neither soe onely, for there had bin some mitigacion, yf they might soe have perished that they should not have bin remembred, but they must be an example to all posteritie. Their remembraunce must not dye.
The country is said to have bin a verry pleasaunt and fruitfull soyle, but *terra bona, gens mala fuit,* and therefore it was destroyed with fyre from a 7 tymes hotter myne then that 7 times heated oven. It was hell-fyre out of heaven, fire from coales that were never blowne, it rayned fyre.

As Kayne was sett as a marke to take heede of bloudshed, soe are those places an example to the ungodly; there remaines untill this day such a noysom water that some call it the Divels Sea; others the Sea of Brimstone, for the ill savour; the Dead Sea, for noe fishe can live in it, soe foule that noe uncleane thing can be clensed in it, soe thick a water that nothing can sinke into it.

There are certaine apples fayre to the eye which being touched, *in fumum abeunt, tanquam ardent adhuc, et olet adhuc incendio terra.*

FOLIO 52

October. 1602.

There is seen a cloud of pitche and heapes of ashes at this daye, their woundes are not skinned over, they appeare for ever.

"And delivered just Lott." The word signified a kinde of force, as though he had pulled him out; here is Lottes commendacion, that he lived amongst the wicked, and was not infected with them; *bonum esse cum bonis non admodum laudabile; nihil est in Asia non fuisse, sed in Asia continenter vixisse, eximium.* Soe was Abraham in Chaldea, Moses in the Court of Pharao, and yet noe partakers of the synnes of those places. "Vexed with the uncleane conversacion." *Non veniat anima mea in consilium eorum!* The Justice of Lott was professed enmity with the wicked. When Martiall asked Nazianzeene but a question, Nazianzeene told him he would not answere *nisi purgatus fuerit.* Wee must not say soe much as God save them! to the wicked. But our stomackes are to strong; wee can digest to be drunke for companie, to rend the ayre with prodigious oathes in a bravery, but not rend our garmentes in contrition of heart; wee can telle howe to take 10 in the 100, nay 100 for 10, with a secure conscience; this synne of usury is a synn against nature, like the synn of Sodome. Wee will dissemble with the hyppocrite, temporize with the politician, deride with the Atheist. Men thinke nowe adayes that Arrianisme, Atheisme, Papisme, Libertinisme, may stand togither, and like salt, oyle, and meale be put togither in a sacrifice. Their conscience is sett in binde, like Thamar when shee went to play the harlott; they had rather have

FOLIO 52b

October. 1602.

the shrift of a popishe priest then heare the holsome admonicion of a preacher; they have Metian, Suffetian myndes; *Vertumni, Protei;* any relligion, every relligion will serve their turne.

Rome, that second Sodome, which still battlith[?] our church and relligion, lett it charge hir wherin the gospell hath offended this 44 yeares, and at last it will appeare all hir fault wilbe noe more but innocency and true godlines. *Est mihi supplicii causa fuisse piam,* &c.

Godes mercy in particuler to our nation, in prosperity, in trade, avoydaunce of forrein attemptes, appeasing of inbred treasons and dissensions, &c., soe that wee may say these 44 yeares of hir Majesties happie goverment is the Kalender of earthly felicity, wherein the gospell hath growne old, yf not to old to some which begin to fall out of love with it, but were it as newe as it was the first day of hir Majesties entraunce, wee should hear them cry "Oh howe beautifull are the feete of those that bring glad tydings of salvacion!" *Eamus in domum Domini,* &c. And lett us pray to Christ that, as the Evangelist writes he did, soe the gospell may *crescere aetate et gratia.*

"The rule followeth," s[ai]d he, "which I promised, but tyme and order must rule me. It is but the summe of the examples: it is the same liquor that ranne from those spoutes and is nowe in this cysterne; it runnes like that violl in the gospell with wyne and oyle, wherewith Christ cured the wounded travailer; it runnes like Christes syde, with water and bloud, judgment and mercy; punishment and comfort," &c.

Consciencia est coluber in domo, immo in sinu.

FOLIO 53

October. 1602.

28. In the Chequer, Mr. Crooke, the Recorder of London, standing at the barr betweene the twoe maiors, the succeeding on his right hand, and the resigning on his left, made a speache after his fashion, wherin first he exhorted the magistrate to good desartes in regard of the prayse or shame that attendes such men for their tyme well or ill imployed. Then he remembred manie hir Majesties favours to the citie, their greate and beneficial priviledges, their ornamentes and ensignes of autoritie, their choise out of their owne companies, &c. "Great, and exceeding great," s[ai]d hee, "is hir Majesties good-

nes to this city," for which he remembred their humble due thankefullnes; next he breifly commended the resigning Sir Jo. Jarrett,
saying that his owne performaun[c]es were speaking wittnesses for
him; and the succeeding, for the good hope, &c. and then showing
howe this maior, Mr. Lee, had bin chosen by the free and generall
assent of the Citye, he presented him to that honourable court,
praying their accustomable allowaunce.

The L[ord] Chief Baron Periam comended the recorders speache,
and recommended hir Majesties singular benefites to their thankefull
consideracions, admonished that their might be some monethly
strict searche be made in the Cytie for idle persons and maisterles
men, whereof there were, as he said, at this tyme 30,000 in London;
theise ought to be found out and well punished, for they are the
very scumme of England, and the sinke of iniquitie, &c.

FOLIO 53b

October. 1602.

28. The L[ord] Treasuror, L[ord] Buckhurst, spake sharply and
earnestly, that of his certaine knowledge there were two things hir
Majesty is desyrous should be amended. There hath bin warning
given often tymes, yet the commaundement still neglected. They
are both matteres of importaunce, and yf they be not better looked
unto, the blame wilbe insupportable, and their answere inexcusable.
The former is, nowe in this time of plenty to make provision of
corne to fill the magazines of the citie, as well for suddein occasions
as for provision for the poore in tyme of dearth. This he advised the
maior to have speciall care of, and to amend their neglect by dili-
gence, while their fault sleepes in the bosome of hir Majesties
Clemency. The other matter was the erecting and furnishing hospi-
tals. Theise were thinges must be better regarded then they have bin;
otherwise, howesoever he honour the cytie in his privat person, yet
it is his dutie in regard of his place to call them to accompt for it.

FOLIO 54

October. 1602.

27. Thou carest not for me, thou scornest and spurnst me, but yet like those which play at footeball, spurne that which they runne after. (Hoste to his wife.)

Wee call an hippocrite a puritan, in briefe, as by an Ironized terme a good fellowe meanes a thiefe. (*Albions Engl[and].*)

He lives by throwing a payre of dice, and breathing a horse some-tyme, *i.e.* by cheatinge and robbing. (Towes phrase [?]).

28. *IN PATRES JESUITAS.*

> *Tute mares vitias, non uxor, non tibi scortum,*
> *Dic Jesuita mihi, qui potes esse pater?*

When there was a speach concerning a peace to made with Spayne, a lusty cavallier at an ordinary swore he would be hangd yf there were a peace with Spaine, for which wordes he was sent for to the court and chargd as a busie medler and a seditious fellowe; he aunswered, he ment noe such matter as they imagined, but he ment plainely that because himselfe was a man of armes, yf wee should have a peace he should want employment, and then must take a purse, and soe he was sure he should be hanged yf there were a peace with Spaine. (Mr. Gorson).

One said the Recorder was the mouth of the cytie; then the city hath a black mouth, said Harwell, **for** he is a verry blacke man.

FOLIO 54b

October. 1602.

31. At Paules Dr. Dove made a sermon against the excessive pride and vanitie of women in apparraile, &c., which vice he said was in

their husbandes power to correct. This man the last tyme he was in this place taught that a man could not be divorced from his wife, though she should commit adultery.

He reprehended Mr. Egerton, and such an other popular preacher, that their auditory, being most of women, abounded in that superfluous vanity of appa[raile].

At the Temple church one Mr. Irland, whoe about some three yeares since was a student of the Middle Temple, preached upon this text: "Thy fayth hath saved the, goe thy waye in peace."

The Persians had a lawe, that when any nobleman offended, himselfe was never punished, but they tooke his clothes, and when they had beaten them, they gave them unto him againe; soe when mans soule had synned, Christ took our flesh upon him, which is as it were the apparaile of the soule, and when it had been beaten he gave it us againe.

In the after noone Mr. Marbury at the Temple: text, 21. Isay. 5 v. &c. But I may not write what he said, for I could not heare him; he pronunces in manner of a common discourse. Wee may streache our eares to catch a word nowe and then, but he will not be at the paynes to strayne his voyce, that wee might gaine one sentence.

FOLIO 55

October. 1602.

I love not to heare the sound of the sermon, except the preacher will tell me what he says.

I thinke many of those which are fayne to stand without dores at the sermon of a preacher whom the multitude throng after may come with as greate a devotion as some that are nearer, yet I beleeve the most come away as I did from this, scarse one word the wiser.

FOLIO 55b

November. 1602.

1. A preacher in Cambridge said that manie in their Universitie had long beardes and short wittes, were of greate standing and small understanding; the world sayth *Bonum est nobis esse hic,* and *Solvite asinum,* for the Lord hath neede of him; the good schollers are kept downe in the universitie, while the dunces are preferred. (Cosen Willis *narrav.*)

One Clapham, a preacher in London, said the divell was like a fidler, that comes betymes in the morning to a mans windowe to call him up before he hath minde to rise, and there standes scraping a long tyme, till the window opens and he gettes a peece of sylver, and then he turnes his backe, puts up his pipe and away; soe the divel waites in Godes presence till he hath gotten some imployment which he lookt for, and then he goes from the face of God.

2. Suspicion is noe proofe, nor Jealousy an equall judge.

1. Dr. Witheres, a black man, preached in Paules this day; his text, Mark 9:2, &c.
Of the transfiguracion of Christ: whereby, first, we learne to contemne earth and the pleasure thereof, in regard of the heavenly glory wee shall receive. 2[nd]ly: by the hope of this glorie the paynes of this lyfe are eased. 3[rd]ly: by this transfiguracion of Christ wee are taught that he suffered the indignitie of the crosse not by imposed necessitie, but of his owne good will and pleasure.

In that he tooke but 3 disciples, it may be collected that all thinges are not at the first to be published to all men, but first to some fewe, and after to others.

FOLIO 56

November. 1602.

1. He tooke them up into a mountaine, to shewe their thoughtes
and hopes must be higher then the earth, lifted up to the heavens
like a cloud. The mountaine was high, and alone—two principall
pointes of regard in a fortificacion, that it be difficult of accesse,
and far from an other that may annoy it. The glory of Christes
kingdome is hard to be attayned, the way is steepe and high;
*facilis descensus averni, sed revocare gradum superasque evadere
ad oras; hic labor, hoc opus est;* and it can not be equalled by anie.
The lyfe of a Christian is like Moses serpent, which was terrible to
looke upon in the forepart, but take it by the tayle and it became
a rodd, to slay him. So yf we consider onely the present miseries
of this lyfe, which usually accompanied a true Chrystian, it would
terrifie a man from the profession; but take it by the tayle, looke
to the ende and glory that wee hope fore, and it is lyfe incompar-
ably most to be desyred.

Paule sayth our body shall rise a spirituall body, not a body that
shalbe a spirit, for spirits are noe bodyes: but a body glorious,
nimble, incorruptible, as a spirit.

"At that day," sayth the prophet, "the moone shall shine as the
sunne, and the sunne shall be 7 tymes as bright"; the unconstant
condicion of man is compared to the moone, and Christ is the sunn
of righteousnes, &c.

FOLIO 56b

November. 1602.

1. Christ carried them into a mountayne apart, for commonly the
multitude is like a banquet whether every one brings his part of
wickednes and vice, and soe by contagion infect one an other.

It was a wonder howe the glorious divinity could dwell in flesh, and not showe his brightnes; but it was the pleasure of the Almightie to eclipse the splendor with the vayle of our body; but here like the sunne out a cloud he breaketh forth, and his glory appeareth.

FOLIO 57

November. 1602.

4. Barker told certaine gent[lemen] in the buttry that one of the benchers had sometime come downe for a lesse noyse: "Soe he may nowe too, I think," said Whitlocke, "for I thinke he may finde a lesse noyse anie where in the house then here is."

5. Mrs. Gibbes seing a strangeres horse in their yard, asked a thrasher whose horse? He told hir. "Wherefore comes he?" "Wherefor should he come," said he, "but to buy witt?" (*viz.* a clyent to the Counsellor.) (Mr. Gibbes.)

One said Nel Frengtham[?] kisseth like a neates foote: she turnes hir inside out. (Fraklin.)

Ch[arles] Davers told me he would tell me a jeast, howe that a yong gent[leman] after long suit having obtained a gent[le]woman, the first night they were married, after he had performed his duty and taken that he soe long had longed for: "And is that all," said he, "I soe much desyred? Fayth, I would I were unmarried againe." "And is this all your jeast?" said I; "fayth, you might have kept [it] to your selfe."

6. Mr. Curle told me he heard of certaine that Mr. Cartwright, comming to a certaine good fellowe that was chosen to be maior of a towne, told him soe plainely and with such a spirit of his dissolute and drunken life, howe unfit for the office to governe others when he could not rule himselfe, &c., that the man fell presently into a swound, and within thre dayes dyed. Whether Cartwrightes vehe-

mency, the mans conceit, or both, wrought in him, it was verry straunge. Happened in Warwickshire.

FOLIO 57b

November. 1602.

4. Mr. Hadsor told Mr. Curle and me that he heard lately forth of Irland, that whereas on[e] Burke, whoe followes the L[ord] Deputy, had obteyned the graunt of a Country in Irland, in consideracion of his good service, and this by meanes of Sir Robert Cecile, upon Sir Robert Gardneres certificat under his hand, and all this after passed and perfected according to the course in the Courtes in Irland. Nowe of late an other Burke, one of great commaund and a dangerous person yf he should breake out, hearing of this graunt, envyed, grudged, and upbrayded his owne desertes, intimating as much as yf others of meaner worth were soe well regarded and himselfe neglected, he ment perhaps to give the slip and try his fortune on the other party. The L[ord] deputy having intelligence hereof, and foreseing the perilous consequence yf he should breake out, sent for the otheres patent, as desyrous to peruse the forme of the graunt, but when he had it he kept it; and, upon advise with the Counsaile, cancelled both the patent and the whole record, to prevent the rebellion like to ensue upon the graunt. A strange president.

Sir Robert commendes none but will be sure to have the same under the hand of some other, on whome, yf it fall out otherwise then was suggested or expected, the blame may be translated. (*Idem.*)

He told further that Mr. Plowden had such a checke as he never heard [?] of, for saying to a circumventing justice of peace, upon demaund made what were to be done in such a case, that by the lawe neither a justice nor the counsell could committ anie to prison without a cause, upon their pleasure.

FOLIO 58

3. Mr. Gardner of Furnivals Inne told howe that Mr. Dr. King, preacher at St. Androes in Holborne, beinge earnestly intreated to make a sermon at the funerals of gent[lemen] of their house, because the gent[lemen] desyred he should be requested, made noe better nor other aunswer but told them plainely he was not beholding to that house nor anie of the Innes of Chauncery, and therefore would not. He is greived, it seemes, because the gent[lemen] of the Inns come and take up rooms in his churche, and pay not as other his parishioners doe. He is soe highly esteemed of his auditors, that when he went to Oxeford they made a purse for his charges, and at his return rode forth to meete him, and brought him into towne with ringing, etc.

6. I heard that the E[arl] of Northumberland lives apart againe from his lady nowe shee hath brought him an heire, which he sayd was the soder of their reconcilement. He lives at Sion house with the child, and plays with it, being otherwise of a verry melancholy spirit.

A gentlewoman which had bin to see a child that was sayd to be possessed with the Divel, told howe she lost hir purse while they were at prayer. "Oh," said a gent[lemen], "not unlikely, for you forgott halfe your lesson: Christ bad you watch and pray, and you prayed onely; but had you watched as you prayed, you might have kept your purse still." (W. Scott *na*[*r*].)

5. "I was muzeled in my pleading," said Mr. Martin, when he was out, and could not well open.

"He will clogg a man with a jeast, he will never leave you till he hath told it." (Of Mr. L.)

FOLIO 58b

November.

6. Mr. Overbury, telling howe a knave had stolne his cloke out of his chamber, said the villeine had gotten a cloke for his knavery.

One said of a foule face, "it needes noe maske, it is a maske it selfe." "Nay," said an other, "it hath neede of a maske to hide the deformitie."

I heard that Dr. Redman, Bishop of Norwiche, Dr. Juel, professor at [MS blank] in the low cuntryes, and Mr. Perkins of Cambridge, all men of note, are dead of late.

The preacher at the Temple said that he which offreth himselfe to God, that is, which mortifieth and leaveth his pleasures and affection to serve God, doth more then Abraham did when he offered to sacrifice his sonne, for there is none but loves himselfe more dearly then his owne children.

10. The embasing of the coyne for Irland hath brought them almost to a famine; for the Q[ueen] hath received backe as muche as shee coyned; they have none other left, and for that none will bring anie victuall unto them. (Mr. Curle *nar.*)

I heard that the French king hath reteined the Sytzers [Switzers?] for 8000£. present and 3000£. annuall. [He] hath sold diveres townes to the D[uke] of Bulloine, whoe meanes to be on the part of the Archduke for them.

"I was brough[t] up as my frends were able; when manners were in the hall, I was in the stable," quoth my laundres, when I told hir of hir saucy boldnes.

FOLIO 59

November. 1602.

10. Mr. Curle demaunded of Wake a marke which he layd out for him when they rede with the reader; his aunswere was he lived upon exhibicion, he could not tell whether his friendes would allowe him soe much for that purpose. Sordide.
Soe soone as they began to rate the charges at St. Albans, awaye startes he. "He did justly, a dog would not tarry when you rate him," s[ai]d L.

Mr. Blunt, a great gamester, marvellous franke, and a blunt Cavelier.

Mrs. T., because hir brother would have crost hir lascivious love towardes hir man H., shee would have practised to hang him for a theife, had not Mr. S. p[er]swaded the contrairy. Soe violent and unnaturall a womans malice. Hir owne daughter knowes hir luxurie (*quam incaute, quam inepte, quam indigne.*)

8. Mr. Bacon, in giving evidence in the Lord Morleys case for the forrest of Hatfeild, said it had alwayes flowne an high pitche; i.e., hath bin allwayes in the handes of greate men.

The first Lord Riche was Lord Chauncellor of England in Ed. 6. tyme. (Bacon.)

To stinge a wenche. (Brod [na]x?)
They have lockt us up with delayes. (Darston.)

12. In the Starr chamber, when Mr. Moore urged in defense of Atturnies that followed suites out of thier proper Courtes that it was usuall and common, the L[ord] Keeper said, "*Multitudo peccantium pudorem tollit, non peccatum.*"

"Ha! the Divel goe with the," said the B[ishop] of L. to his boule when himselfe ran after it. (Mr. Cu.)

FOLIO 59b

November. 1602.

"Size ace will not, deux ace cannot, quater tree must," q[uoth]
Blackborne, when he sent for wine.

a common phrase of Subsidies and such taxes: the greate ones will
not, the little ones cannot, the meane men must pay for all.

The old L[ord] Treasurors witt was as it seemes of Borrowe
Englishe tenure, for it descended to his younger sonne, Sir
R[o]b[er]t. (W[?])

A nobleman on horsebacke with a rable of footmen about him is
but like a huntsman with a kennell of houndes after him. (W[?])

A drunken Cunt hath noe porter.

The Dutch which lately stormed the galleys which our ships had
first battered, deserve noe more credit then a lackey for pillaging
of that dead body which his maister had slayne. (Sir Robert
Mansell.)

Sequitur sua poena nocentem.

Bacon said that the generall rules of the lawe were like cometes,
and wandring starrs. Mr. Attorny [Coke] said rather they were like
the sunne, they have light in themselves, and give light to other;
whereas the starrs are but *corpora opaca.*

The Attorny said he could make a lamentable argument for him
in the remainder that is prejudiced by the act of the particular
tenant; but it would be sayd of him as of Cassandra, when he had
spoken much he should not be believed.

A difference without a diversitie, a curiosity.

Vennar, a gent[leman] of Lincolnes, who had lately playd a notable cunnicatching tricke, and gulled many under couller of a play
to be of gent. and reverens, comming to the Court since in a blacke
suit, bootes and golden spurres without a rapier, one told him he
was not well suited; the golden spurres and his brazen face
unsuited[?]

FOLIO 60

November. 1602.

A vehement suspicion may not be a judiciall condemnacion: L[ord] Keeper said he would dismiss one as a partie vehemently suspected, then judicially condemned.

The callender of women saynts was full long agoe. That [there?] are soe fewe nowe that will not yeild to opportunity, yf they be importuned.

A Womans love is river-like, which stopt doth
    overflowe,
But when the river finds noe lett, it often runnes
    too lowe.

---

14. An hypocrite or puritan is like a globe, that hath all in *convexo, nihil in concavo:* all without painted, nothing within included. (Mr. Curle.)

About some three yeares since there were certayne rogues in Barkeshire which usually frequented certaine shipcoates every night. A Justice having intelligence of their rablement, purposing to apprehend them, went strong, and about midnight found them in the shipcoate, some six couple men and women dauncing naked, the rest lying by them; diveres of them taken and committed to prison. (Mr. Pigott *na.*)

Posies for a jet ring lined with sylver.
    "One two": soe written as you may begin with either word.
"This one ring is two": or both sylver and jet make but one ring; the body and soule one man; twoe frends one mynde.
"Candida mens est": the sylver resembling the soule, being the inner part.
"Bell' ame bell' amy": a fayre soule is a fayre frend, &c. "Yet fayre within."
"The firmer the better": the sylver the stronger and the better.

    Mille modis laeti miseros mors una fatigat.

[fo. 60b blank in MS]

FOLIO 61

November. 1602.

Ex oratione Academica Stapletonii. An Politici horum temporum
in numero Christianorum sunt habendi?

Isti politici contendunt, Multa esse tempori concedenda, multa esse
pro tempore dissimulanda; 2. Publicae pacis causam ante occulos
semper habendam, non esse irritandos crabrones; 3. haereses istas
vel debellari non posse quia potentes; 4. vel ex animis hominum
evelli non posse, quia pertinaces haeretici sunt; 5. vel tantis conati-
bus impugnari non esse necesse, quia de rebus leviculis contenditur;
6. vel postremo tanti illas non esse, vel tantum universum religionis
curam nobis incumbere, ut pacem publicam, communesque fortunas,
vel ad illas reprimendas, vel ad hanc conservandam, periclitari sina-
mus; 7. Quin imo prudentis ac politici viri esse, patriae et civium
suorum commodis, ante omnia prospicere, suis rebus consulere;
8. Principum placitis sese accommodare; 9. Invidias aut simultates
superfluas religionis causa non subire; 10. illam curam vel solis
clericis ac monachis; 11. vel etiam ipsi Deo relinquere, qui suas
injurias, si quas per haec nova dogmata acceperit, ipsemet ulcisci ac
vindicare valeat. 12. In summa id agendum, ne quid res vel publica,
vel privata detrimenti capiat; 13. suam sibi cuiusque conscientiam
absque istis certaminibus sanam ac salvam esse posse. Habetis politicorum hominum voces, principia, axiomata, quibus illi confisi
Religionis causam negligent & tractant, laborantis Ecclesiae patro-
cinium turpiter deserunt, fidem catholicam hostibus nefarie produnt,
et penitus profligandam relinquant.

FOLIO 61b

Contra Politicos . . . .

Propositio authoris. Dicimus huiusmodi Politicum qui Religionis
causam atque defensionem, suis fortunis aut commodis, vel etiam

reip. paci et incolumitati postponit, imo qui eam rebus omnibus non anteponit, Christiani hominis loco habendum non esse.

Neopolitic non solum religionis usum et praxim male vivendo, sed et ipsam in se Religionem male sentiendo abiecerunt. Nullam enim religionem tenet, qui nihil ad se attinere religionem putat. (He holdes noe religion that thinkes religion hath noe hold of him.)

Religio magis ad morem, quam ad rem pertinere judicanda est; et illam sapiens servat tanquam legibus jussam, non tanquam Deo gratam (Seneca).

Valeat Religio quantum valere potest. Politicorum hodie voces veterum Paganorum vocibus conformes. Colantur Dii ut voluerint. Ita habeatur vera Religio, in qua faeliciter, et affluenter vivamus. Non curent Reges quam bonis, sed quam subditis imperent. Quid alienae vitae potius, quam quid suae quisque noceat, legibus advertatur? Quid pacem publicam laedat, non quo conscientia, aut religione laesa, quisque sibi noceat, leges dispiciant? Sic istos Politicos vite licentiosae libido ad religionis neglectum, neglectus ad contemptum, contemptus ad Atheismum, perduxit.

Nec maritus dicendus est, qui quolibet conjugii incommodo motus, a conjuge divortium quaerit. Nec Christianus qui periclitantem religionem deserit.

FOLIO 62

Contra Politicos.

Soli simulato et larvato Christiano horrenda paena infligitur. (Matt. 22.)

Tu ne es ille qui conturbas Israel? Achab Eliae. (3 Reg. 27.) Si dimittimus cum sic, omnes credent in eum, et venient Romani et tollent locum nostrum et gentem. Pharisaei. (Jo[hn] 12.)

Sacerdotes ex seminariis Ro[mano] missi, supplicio afficiantur. Ne tota gens pereat, ne veniat Papa, aut veniant Hispani, et tollent locum nostrum et gentem.

Ut quid perditio haec? Judas. (Matt. 26.) de sumptibus in bello sacro factis.

Si hunc dimittis, non es amicus Caesaris. Pilatus. (Jo[hn] 19.)

Isti sunt neopolitiorum praeclari parentes, splendidi majores, antecessores amplissimi. Jeroboam, (3. Reg. 12) Achab, et Achaz (2 Paral. 28). reges impii. Pharasei Christum persequentes. Judas proditor, reprobus Esau, Pilatus perditissimus Judex, Julianus apostata. Arundines vento agitatae.

Volunt uti Deo, et frui mundo; uti ad suum Commodum religione, Frui et conquiescere in bonis terrenis.

Magnus nugator Bodinus (de rep. lib 3, ca. 7). Liberos conventus haereticis concedendos vellet. Politicum agens hostem se Chrystianitatis prodit.

Cui ille peccato, cui sceleri, fraudi, flagitio consensum et operam praebere suam reformidabit qui totius pietatis fontem, atque virtutis uniculum Religionem despexit?

Constantius dixit eos Regi suo nunquam fideles fore, qui Deo infideles exti[ti]ssent (cum promiserat gratiam Diis sacrificantibus famulis [word illegible] et sacrificantes aula dimiserat).

At tu dictis Albane maneres.

Quae illis fides habenda, qui in ipsa fide, fidem non servaverunt?

FOLIO 62b

... Contra Politicos.

Timon, rogatus cur homines oderit, respondit: Improbos odi, quia improbi sunt. Bonos odi, quia improbos non oderunt.

Idololatra est, qui idololatriam concedendam suadet; haereticus tribuendum sentit, in sacro sanctae fidei praejudicium.
Ignavia et cessione Catholicorum vis et potentia crevit haereticorum.

Pompeius inter strepitus armorum clamat "Parcite sanguini."
Caesar autem[?]: Miles faciem feri: sic fugato Pompeio vicit Caesar.
Meliorem causam vicit deterior, quia illa politicè et molliter, haec
zelosè et ferventer tractata fuit.

Magna est vis religionis, multum valet societas fidei, arctissimum est
Christianae charitatis vinculum; portentum atque monstrum certis-
simum est, esse aliquem Christiani nominis, fide ac professione
Christianum, qui p[er] cuius religionis sacramenta renatus est; et
factus lucis filius illam Religionem indignissimè luce privare, nefarie
prodere, deserere, contemnere, non p[er]timescit.

Maior est haereticorum potentia quam ut in ordinem cogi queant,
quare lenienda magis quam exagitanda videtur; consulendumque
magis securitati, quam vindictae, et accuratè considerandum potius
quid ab illis cavere, quam quid in illos quibus impares sumus,
statuere debeamus. Prudentes potius naucleros imitari oportet, qui
tempestati cedendo, naufragium evadunt.

Non opus est rem armis transigi, quae vel in ceremoniarum dis-
crepantia, vel in subtilitatum disquisitione minus necessaria tota
consistat.

FOLIO 63

... Contra Politicos

Controversiae modernae de Religione gravissimae.

An Romana Ecclesia sit vera. An Papa sit caput Ecclesiae. De sacra-
mentorum numero, et usu.

De externo sacrificiae missae.

An sola fide salus comparetur, aut ad salutem bona op[er]a neces-
sario requirantur.

Religio ad humanae societatis vinculum, inventa et tradita est; ergo propter illam ad arma non est veniendum, ne dum pro illa pugnamus, eius primario usu ac fine eam ac nos ipsos praepostere spoliemus. Replique a la Remonstrance du Catholique Anglois (pag. 191). Sed hoc argumento ubi primum ad maenia accedit hostis, ne pax cinium p[er]turbetur, aperiendae confestim hostibus sunt portae. Eleboro purgandum cerebrum.

Ad pacem conservandam bellum est necessarium.

Si Deus justus et potens est, quae eius sacrosanctam religionem violant ab ipso vindicanda relinquii debent? Volet enim quia justus est, et poterit, quia potens. Judaeorum vox Christo: 27 Matt.

Sectas alere est pernicies Religionis (Eph. 4). Nec Deus divisionis Deus est, sed pacis.

Cato ridens eos qui in triumpho Deos hostium Capitolio intulerunt. Ut quid (inquit) eos Deos colitis, qui suos cultores tueri non poterant.

Una vera religio ab omnibus falsis impugnatur, omnia vitia contra unum virtutem, omnia falsa contra unum veritatem; Saducaei, Pharisei, Herodiani, Romani contra unum Christum conspirarunt. Una sanitas quae a quovis morbo corrumpitur; una sacrosancta religio qua uni vero Deo servitur.

FOLIO 63b

Contra Politicos

Volunt isti Politici ut p[er]mixtis nobis cum haereticis ecclesia quoque Christi finem accipiat, sicut ex p[er]mixtione Pharisaeorum et Saducaeorum accepit synagoga Judeorum. Saducaei enim in idem jus admissi cum Pharisaeis, Hircano Pontifice pulso, cuius tamen op[er]a in Sanhedrim cooptati sunt, soli dominari voluerunt. Quod cum efficere non possent, Hircano a Pompeio restituto, ad Herodem extremum imperium detulerunt.

In hac sua execranda Neopolitia si p[er]sistunt et ecclesiam Christi Catholicam simulatione sua perdere, ac prodere, partumque parturientem praepedire p[er]petuo pergunt, hoc hominum genus ab omni reip. et societate Christiana, tanquam hostes eius insensos & studiose cavendos, et si opus fuerit abarcendos, omnique loco et auctoritate dejiciendos censet.

[*fo. 64 blank in MS*]

FOLIO 64b

November. 1602.

Yf foure or five assist one which kills an other, the lawe sayth they shall all be hanged, because they have deprivd the Queene of a subject. But is this a way to preserve the Queens subjectes, when there is one slayne already, to hang up four or five more out of the way? Is this to punishe the fact or the State? (Benet[?])

16. Goe little booke, I envy not thy lott,
Though thou shalt goe where I my selfe cannot.

18. One would needes knowe of a philosopher what reason there was that a man should be in love with beauty; the other made noe other answer but told him it was a blind mans question. Soe one wondred what sweetnes men found in musicke they were soe much delighted in; an other said it was but the doubt of a deaf man, &c.

Flumen orationis, micam vero habuit rationis: hee had a streame of wordes, but scarce a drop of witt.

Beauty more excellent then many virtues, for it makes it selfe more knowne: noe sooner seene but admired, whereas one may looke long enough upon a man before he can tell what virtue is in him, untill some occasion be offered to shewe them.

23. Captaine Whitlocke, a shuttlecock: flyes up and downe from one nobleman to an other; good for nothing but to make sport, and help them to loose tyme.

FOLIO 65

November. 1602.

14. Dr. Dawson of Trinity in Cambridge, at Paules Crosse; his text, 7 Isay. 10.

All the while he prayed he kept on his velvet night cap untill he came to name the Queen, and then of went that to, when he had spoken before both of and to God with it on his head.

Yf Godes words will not move us, neither will his workes. If Dixit will not perswade, neither can Fecit induce us.

A regall not a righteous motive.
Putes on the visard of hypocrisie.

Omne bonum a Deo bono, as all springs from their offspring the sea.

Judge the whole by part, as merchants sell their wares: the whole butt by a tast of a pint, &c.

Jobs patience compared to Godes not soe muche as a drop to the sea, or a mote to the whole earth.

Sinfull man approching Godes presence is not consumed as the stuble with the fyre, because man is Godes worke, and Godes mercy is over all his workes.

What will you make me like unto, or what will you make like unto me, saith God.

Scriptura discentem non docentem respicit, and therefore penned in a plaine and easie manner.

Essentia operis est potentia creatoris.

Here he stumbled into an invective against contempt of ministeres and impoverishing the Clergy. Pharoes dreame is revived, the leane kine eate up the fatt, and were never the fatter; laymens best livings were the Church livinges; yet the gentry come to beggery.

FOLIO 65b

November. 1602.

14. *Magnum solatium est magnum supplicium a magno impositum;*
but intollerable when the basest make it their cheife grace to disgrace the ministeres.

Christ cals them the light of the world, and they are the children of
darknes that would blowe it out.

Pride is a greate cause of unthankefulnes, when he shall thinke
omne datum esse tuum officium et suum meritum.

Bishop Bonner made bonefires of the bones of saintes and martyres
in Queen Maries days.

Praysd our happy government for peace and relligion and soe ended.

FOLIO 66

November. 1602.

21. Though a fashion of witt in writing may last longer then a
fashion in a sute of clothes, yet yf a writer live long, and change
not his fashion, he may perhaps outlive his best credit. It were good
for such a man to dy quickly. (of Dr. Reynold; Th. Cranmer.)

Reynoldes esteemes it his best glorie to quote an author for every
sentence, nay almost every syllable; soe he may indeed shewe a
great memory but small judgment. Alas, poore man! he does as yf
a begger should come and pouer all his scraps out of his wallet
at a riche mans table. He had done what he could, tell where he
had begd this peece and that peece, but all were but a beggerly
showe. He takes a speciall grace to use an old worne sentence, as
though anie would like to be served with cockcrowen pottage, or

a man should take delight to have a garment of shreedes. (Cran. and I.)

The olde Deane of Paules, Nowell, told Dr. Holland that he did *onerare,* not *honorare, eum laudibus.*

That which men doe naturally they doe more justly; subjectes naturally desire liberty, for all thinges tend to their naturall first state. And all were naturally free without subjection. Therefore the subject may more justly seeke liberty then the prince incroach upon his liberty. (Th. Cran.)

Lucian, after a great contention amongst the gods which should have the first place, the Grecian challenging the prioritie for their curious workmanship, though their stuff were not soe rich, the other for the richnes of their substaunce, though they were less curious; at last he determined, the richer must be first placed, and the virtuous next. (Th. Cran.)

FOLIO 66b

November. 1602.

21. Jo. Marstone the last Christmas when he daunct with Alderman Mores wives daughter, a Spaniard borne, fell into a strang commendacion of her witt and beauty. When he had done, shee thought to pay him home, and told him she though[t] he was a poet. "Tis true," said he, "for poetes fayne, and lye, and soe dyd I when I commended your beauty, for you are exceeding foule."

Mr. Tho. Egerton, the L[ord] Keepers sonne, brake a staff gallantly this tilting; there came a page skipping, "Ha, well done yfayth!" said he, "your grandfather never ranne such a course." (*In novitatem.*)

"His mouth were good to make a mouse trap;" of one that smels of chese-eating.

A good plaine fellowe preacht at night in the Temple churche; his text, 86 Psal. v. 11: "Teache me thy wayes, O Lord, and I will walk in thy truth."

1. Note Davides wisdome in desyring knowledge, before all thinges. 2. Our ignoraunce: that we must be taught. 3. Our imperfection. David was an old scholler in Godes schole, and yet desyred to be taught. 4. Thy wayes, not false decretals, &c., nor lying legendes, &c.

Soe soone as the Arke came into the temple, the idol Dagon fell downe and brake its necke; when God enters into our hartes, our idol synnes must be cast out.

FOLIO 67

November. 1602.

21. At Paules Crosse: Mr. Fenton, reader of Grays Inn. His text, Luke 19. 9: "This day is salvacion come unto this house: insoemuch as this man alsoe, is become the sonne of Abraham." This is an absolution, and a rule of it; 1. He that pronounceth the Absolucion is Christ. 2. The person absolved is Zachee. An example that may most move this auditorie to followe Christ: since this man was rich, and a ruler of the people, whereas the most of them that followed Christ had nothing to loose.

3. The ground of his absolucion, that he was the sonne of Abraham, which he proved to Christ by his fayth, to the world by his workes.

He observed 5 parts: 1. The nature of the absolution, that it is a declaracion of salvacion. 2. By whom it is declared, viz., by Christ. 3. Howe far it extended, to Zachee and his family. 4. Upon what ground, that is, his fayth and repentaunce. 5. Howe soone, "This day."

Salvacion is come, wee are not able to seeke it; therefore Christ
sayd, "Enter into thy fathers joy," for wee are not capable that it
should enter into us; but enter into that joye as the bucket into
the fountayne.

Yf he should endeavour to prefix a preface for attention, he could
not finde a better then to tell them, he must tell them of Salvation.
None under the degree of an Angell was thought worthie to publishe the first tydings of it to a fewe shepheardes. Noe preacher
able to give his auditorie a tast of Salvacion.

FOLIO 67b

November. 1602.

21. It is one thing to forgive, an other thing to declare forgivenes
of synnes; the former is personall, and that Christ carried to heaven
with him, the other ministeriall, and that he left behind to his
disciples and apostles: "Whose synnes you binde shall be bound,
whose synnes you remitt shalbe loosed."

The raysing of Lazarus, a resemblaunce of absolucion. Lazarus
had [bin] laying 3 days when Christ came to rayse him; he bad
him come out; here is his voyce, which being seconded by divine
power restored him to lyfe. Soe the word of God preached to a synner, being seconded with divine grace, rayseth the synner.

Popishe priests and Jesuites play fast and loose with mens
consciences.

Jesuites come into riche mens houses, not to bring them salvacion,
but because there is something to be fisht for. Jesus and the Church
wee knowe, but whoe are these? Soe they are sent away naked and
torne, like those presumptuous fellowes that would have cast out
divels in Christs name without his leave; and the God of heaven
will laugh them to scorne.

Not all poore blessed, but the poore in spirit onely; nor all rich cursed, but the riche in the world onely; for here is Zache blessed. Howesoever Christs wordes import a greate difficulty for rich men to enter into heaven, when, after he had compared heaven gate to a needles eye, and the rich man to a cammel, hee aunswered his disciples wonder, that all things are possible with God, and as though it were a miracle with men. Hardly can he runne after Christ when his hart is lockt up in his coffer.

FOLIO 68

November. 1602.

21. But the scripture tells us there is a rich Abraham in heaven, as well as a Dives in hell.

Yf anie have inriched themselves by forged cavillacion lett them not despayre, for soe did Zache. Yf anie have a place that he must have under him as many officers as Briareus had handes, through whose handes many thinges may be ill carried, lett him not be discouraged, for soe had Zache. Yf anie be branded with infamie lett him yet be comforted by the example of Zache, for soe was hee, and yet became a true Christian.

Salvacion came unto Zache by a threefold convayaunce: 1. By his riches, which to the good are sacramentes of his favor. 2. That himself being convert, his whole family was soe; the servantes and attendantes are the shaddowes of their master; they move at his motion. 3. That all his houshould was blessed for his sake; such are the braunches as the roote; the whole lumpe was made holie by the first fruites.

Thrice happie land, whose prince is the daughter of Abraham crowning it with the sacramentes of temporall blessinges; add, O Lord, this blessing, that hir dayes may be multiplied as the starrs of heaven.

To become the sonne of Abraham is to receive the image of Abraham. He hath two images, his fayth and his workes.

Imitate him: 1. In rejoycinge in God, As Simeon did when he had Christ in his armes; and this joy made the burden seeme light to the lame man when he carried his bed after Christ had cured him.

FOLIO 68b

November. 1602.

21. 2. In hospitallitie; he received Angels, and amongst them God, for one was called Jehova. 3. In despising to growe rich by ill meanes; Sodome could not make him rich, because he would not have it said that the divel had made him riche.

There is none but would spend the best bloud in his body, and stretch his verry hart stringes, to be made sure of his salvacion; but the matter is easier: you must stretch your purse-stringes, and restore what you have gotten wrongefully, otherwise noe security of salvacion.

To peremptory to conclude before his premisses.

What motives to restitution? Should I propound the rigor of the lawe, you will say that is taken away by the gospell. Should I sett before you the commendable examples of such as professed restitution, you will alledge your owne imperfection—they were perfect and rare men, wee must not look for such perfection. Shall I tell you there are but 4 crying synnes, and this is one of them (Jame), "The syn of them that have taken from others by fraud or violence cryeth before the Lord of Hosts," as though nothing could appease but vengeance,

yet, you will say, though the syn be heynous, yet the mercy of God is over all his workes, and there is more virtue in the seede of the woman to heale then there can be poison in the serpent to hurt us. And God forgiveth all upon repentaunce. 'Tis true, God absolveth the penitent, but upon condicion that he restore the pledge that he withheld, and that which he hath robbed. But may not this be dispensed withall by the gospell? The shaddowe pointes at the truthe;

FOLIO 69

November. 1602.

21. in the 5th of Numbers, 7 [v.] besides the ransom for the attonement, the goodes that were deteyned must be restored. Christ resembleth the ramm, &c. *Ob.* Hath not Christ paid all our debts for us? Yes, but such as thou couldst not pay thy selfe; he hath satisfied God for thy syn, and thou must satisfie thy brother for the wrong thou hast done him, yf thou beest able, otherwise thou must looke for noe absolucion, for without repentaunce and amendment noe absolucion; and without restitucion, noe true repentaunce.

It may be you will say you are sorry for that you have gayned wrongfully, and meane to doe soe noe more. This is noe true sorrowe, noe sufficient repentaunce; for soe long as you reteine the thing, there is a continuaunce of the syn, for thou holdest that willingly which was gotten wrongfully. Surely yf a theife had taken your purse, and should tell you he were sorry, but could not finde in his heart to give you it againe, you would thinke he did but mocke you; but be not deceived, God will not be mocked. Glaunces make noe impression.

There is a worldly sorrowe, and there is a godly sorrowe. Soe long as the goodes are reteined *poenitentia non agitur, sed fingitur.* But *poenitentia vera, non est poenitenda.* But you will say, yf I should make restitution, I should empty manie of my bags and make a greate hole in my lands, and this would make me sorry againe; but this is worldly. Soe there would followe a certaine kinde of shame upon restitucion. But the point is to resolve first to restore, and then doubt not but the wisdome of God will cause you to restore without shame, as the cunning of the Divel made you gett without shame.

FOLIO 69b

November. 1602.

21. This day. When God came to reprehend and denounce judgment against Adam in Paradise, it is sayd he walked; but when he comes with salvacion he comes with hindes feet, swiftly. This day. Against procrastinacion and deferring repentaunce. It is a fearefull saying, they shall strive to enter in and cannot, because they came not soone enough; too many think they have the Spirit of God in a string, and are able to dispatch all while the bell is tolling.

But God sayth, they shall cry, but I will not hear them; then they shall seeke me earely, but they shall not finde me; because they cry and seeke too late. The example of the theife on the crosse is noe example. It was a miracle, that Christ might shewe the power of his divinity in his greatest humiliacion; besides, the theife had moe and greater graces then manie of the disciples at that time, for some had forsaken and none durst confesse him. And besydes, he were but a desperat theife that would presume because the prince had graunted one pardon.

Outward actions of Christ point at inward and spirituall matters: the raysing of Lazarus that had bin dead three dayes was with great difficulty—Christ was fayne to cry out and grone ere he could get him up. And the Disciples could not cast out the divel that had possessed the man from his infancy. And when Christ cast him out it was with wonderfull tormentinges to the possessed; soe dangerous delay, for the difficulty to repent, syn growing as deare as old, &c.

FOLIO 70

November. 1602.

22. I heard that one Daniel, an Italian, having appeached one
Mowbray, a Scott, of treason against his Kinge, Mowbray challenged the combat, and it was appointed to be foughten—foughten
verry lately, wherein they were slayne.

25. L[ord] Cheife Baron Manwood, understanding that his sonne
had sold his chayne to a goldsmith, sent for the goldsmith, willed
him to bring the chaine, enquired where he bought it; he told, in
his house; the Baron desyred to see it, and put it in his pocket,
telling him it was not lawefully bought. The goldsmith sued the
L[ord], and fearing the issue would prove against him, obteined
the Counsels letters to the L[ord], whoe answered, *"Malas causas
habentes, semper fugiunt ad potentes. Ubi non valet veritas, prevalet authoritas. Currat lex, Vivat Rex*, and soe fare you well, my
Lordes"; but he was committ. (Curle.)

Take heede of your frend,
    You are in the right;
Your foe strikes by day,
    Your freind in the night.

Mr. Nichols, of Eastwell in Kent, wrote a booke which he called
the Plea of Innocents; wherein it seemes he hath taken upon him
the defense of Puritans more then he ought, for I heard that he is
deprived, and must be degraded for it, besides imprisonment and
perpetuall silence, before the high commissioners at Lambeth.

Women, because they cannot have their Wills when they dye, they
will have their will while they live.

27. *Dum spero pereo.* (J. Coupers motto.)

ANAGRAMMATA

Henricus Borbonius: Rex bonus orbi.
Rex orbus boni.

Lady Elisabeth Bridget: Bright Lady Bes.

John Sweete: wee shine to. A companie of stars about the moone (his devise).

FOLIO 70b

November. 1602.

27. There were called to the bar by parliament, Shurland, Branstone, Bradnux, Bennet, Gibbes, Jeanor, Rivers, Paget, Horton, and Crue.

The Divine, the lawyer, the physicion must all have these three things: reason, experience, and authority, but eache in a severall degree; the Divine must begin with the autoritie of scripture, the lawyer rely upon reason, and the physicion trust to experience.

The happiest lyfe that I can fynd,
Is sweete content in a setled mynd.

A wenching gent[leman], desyrous to put an opinion on some that he spent his tyme well, told them he laid close and did nothing but looke on his booke. One told him that his booke was a fayre volume, but it had but twoe leaves (legs) to open, and he was a bad scholler—could doe nothing without his festcue (i.[e.], his p').

Serjeant Harris, standing on day at the common place barr with the other sergeants, and having scarce clients enough to hold motion; "They talke of a call of sergeants," said he, "but for ought I can see wee had more neede of a call of clientes."

When one said that Vennar the graund connicatcher had golden spurres and a brazen face, "It seemes," said R. R., "he hath some mettall in him."

A proud man is like a rotten egge, which swymmes above his betteres.

FOLIO 71

November. 1602.

28 At Paules Mr. Tolson of Queenes Colledge in Cambridge; his text in Ephes. 5 25: "As Christ alsoe hath loved the Church, and hath given himself for hir, that he might sanctifie it."

The blessinges of God to man are infinit and exceeding gracious; many being given which we knowe not of, many before wee aske them, manie which wee are unthankefull for; but of all this gift is most admirable, most inestimable, Christ gave himselfe.

He considered the person giving, the party receiving.

There is noe creature soe base and little but if it be considered with reason it may shewe, as were written in greate Caractars, that there is a God.

God is infinit and eternall, therefore can be but one in essence. One person doth not differ from another really in the essence of Diety. Yet each person differeth really from other, and have their proper personall operacions not common to all. Soe here Christ is said to have given himselfe, that is, the person of the sonne of God, perfect God and perfect man; he gave not his body, nor his soule, nor his whole humanitie onely—for if all the creatures in the world were heaped up togither to be given, they were noe sufficient sacrifice to satisfie the justice of God—but he gave himselfe, his whole person.

But two deaths of the soule, synn and eternall damnacion; to affirme that the soule of Christ suffered either were horrible blasphemie.

Wee must soe worship God as a trinity in unity, and an unity in trynity; otherwyse wee worship but our owne fantasie.

Christ was *et sacerdos et sacrificium;* he gave himselfe.

FOLIO 71b

November. 1602.

28. *Christus totus mortuus est, non totum Christi;* the whole person of Christ and both his natures suffered; his diety and soule being mortall could not, but his whole person, wherein both natures are indessolubly united. *Christus homo in terra, deus in coelo, Christus in utroque.*

Christ not made in, nor by the Virgin, but of the Virgin; therefore perfect man. Not an essence of a nature above the Angels but inferior to the Godhead, but the splendor or brightnes of Godes glory, the ingraven forme of his person (Hebr. 1. cap.); therefore perfect God.

2 par. He gave himselfe, not for all men, but for his Church; he died for all *sufficienter non efficienter;* he would have all men saved, *revelata non occulta voluntate;* or rather, as a Father sayth, *Deus vult omnes salvos fieri, non quod nullus hominum sit, quem non velit salvum fieri, sed quia nemo salvus fit, nisi quem velit;* he saveth whom he pleaseth, and they are saved because he will.

Christ gave himselfe for the Church, and hence growes the greate quarrell betwixt Papistes and us Protestantes; for, this gift being soe precious that none can be saved without it, every one is ready to intitle himselfe thereunto, and challeng his part therin; noe heretike so damnable, but would hold he was of the Churche, but the point is whether they bee what they pretend, or have what they arrogate. (And here, because, as he said, the text gave him occasion, and he had direction from the supervisor of this sea, he spake some things against the common enimye.)

Ecclesia dicitur ἀπο τοῦ ἐκκαλεῖν, *ab evocando,* because it is a people called from the rest to be sanctified by Christ.

FOLIO 72

November. 1602.

28. The church is compared to the moone for fayrenes and to the
sonne for brightnes; therefore the church is not a companie of
reprobates, and Idolatrous heretickes, as Rome is. Christ is not the
head of such a body. Those which give him such a body doe, as the
poet sayth, *humano capiti cervicem adjungere equinam.* But if they
define the church such a congregacion, the[y] may easily mainteane
theirs to be one.

The papistes have a trick of appropriatinge the name of the church
to themselves onely; as they reade the Church, it is theirs dead sure;
but this is but the fashion of Cresilaus of Athens, a franticke fellowe,
that would board all ships that arrived, searche and take account of
all thinges as they were his owne, when, poore fellowe, he was
scarse worth the clothes on his backe.

The Papists call their masse a bloudles sacrifice, but yf wee looke
backe but the late tymes before hir Majesties happie entraunce,
wee may see tokens and wittnes enough, that it is the most bloudy
kind that ever was invented.

Christ Gave himselfe: noe virtue that is not voluntary: he gave himselfe willingly; soe saith he, "I lay downe my life, and noe man
taketh it from me," though the Jewes layd violent handes upon
him, which made them inexcusable; yet because yf he would have
resisted, they could not have effected their malice, therefore his
subjection to their violence was voluntary.

FOLIO 72b

November. 1602.

28. Nowe from informing your understandinges, give me leave,
said he, to proceede to the reforming your wills and affections.

Uses. Since Christ hath given himselfe for us such worthles creatures, such nothings indeed, let us dedicate our soules, our selves,
our thoughts, and actions to his service, for a reasonable sacrifice.

Christ gave his whole person for us, wee must give our whole selves
to him; not as some which are content to be present at his service
but have their myndes about other matters; or as other which will
say they have given their mynds to God and serve him in their soule,
though their bodies be present where he is most dishonored, as the
yong degenerat travayler that can be content [to] be present, and
perhaps partaker at a masse, and yet thinke he can be sound at the
hart, for all that. But wee must apply both body and soule to
Christes service.

Most travaylers returne, either worse men or worse subjectes;
caveat in permitting to many travailers.

Some can be content to be fervent and zealous in the halcion dayes
of the gospell, as Peter; but lett the sword of persecution be once
drawne out, the[y] strait withdrawe them selves and leave their
maister. Yf the[y] thinke they spie a tempest but comming afarr
of, strait they runn under hatches. Yf Judas come with a kisse, and
a companie with swordes and staves, they are gone. All were hott
and zealous against the papist in the beginning of hir Majesties
raigne; all cold, as it were a sleepe, nay dead, in these tymes.

Some slaunder the court, as though they were neuters, some the
universities, as yf inclining to Popery, many looking for a tolleracion.

But whither shu'd wee goe? here is the word of lyfe.

FOLIO 73

December. 1602.

5. Mr. Layfeild at St. Clementes. His text, 2 Cor. 3. 7: "Whoe hath
alsoe made us fitt ministers of the Newe Testament, not of the letter,
but of the spirit: for the letter killeth, but the spirit quickeneth."

He had preached heretofore of this text, and had in that sermon observed out of this place that the duty of a Christian and a fitt minister are severall and distinct.

Nowe he considered the object whereabout the office of a minister is imployed, which is the Newe Testament, and to this purpose he shewed the difference betwixt the Old and Newe Testament, the old law and the newe, which consisted not onely in this (which the papistes make to all), that the newe is more plaine then the old, and that Moses was the writer of the first and Christ of the latter; but this the true essentiall difference: the old was a covenant; a mutual sponsion and stipulacion; a promise upon condicion; something to be performed on either part. *Fac hoc,* sayth God to man, this is the lawe to be observed by man, *et vives,* and I will give the[e] lyfe; trust me with that. But the gospell, the Newe Testament, is a covenant absolute, like that "I have made a covenant with myne eyes," and that "I have made a covenant with David that I will not fayle"; a promise on Godes part onely, like a testament in this, that it is a free donacion, without condicion precedent, all meerely of grace and favour from God, noe merit from us. When he assended he gave gifts unto men. When Man had entered into covenant with God, and by breaking of it became soe farre his debtor that he had forfayted body and soule for his synn, God dealt mercifully with him and tooke a sacrifice of some living beast as a bond which deferred, not satisfied, the debt; and this to continue till Christes comming, whose death should be a discharge of that obligacion, and the whole debt alsoe for soe manie as could obteine Christes favour.

FOLIO 73b

December. 1602.

5. In the afternoon, the same man at the same place. After a breife recapitulacion of what he had delivered in the forenoone, he proceeded to shewe the office of a minister of the Newe Testament,

with the difference betweene the preistes of the Old and the ministers of the Newe Testament. The office of those was to teache the
covenant, to denounce the curse, and to take sacrifices of synneres
as obligacions and testimonies against the synner that he had soe
often forfayted his soule and body. The office of the minister of the
New Testament is to preache both the lawe to deject and humble
the synnes by the operacion of the spirit; and the gospell to rayse
and comfort him, that he may not despayre and dye, but beeleeve
and be saved; their office is alsoe as executors of Christes testament to dispose of his legacyes, his promises; that is, to remitt synnes to every penitent beleeving synner; and lastly, to impart and
confirme the graces by ministring his blessed sacramentes.

The letter killeth, for that sayth in the lawe thou must doe this,
thou must not doe that; otherwise God must be satisfied: thou
must be punished, or els thou must have pardon. Man could not
observe them; man was not able to abide the punishment; was like
a man in prison, could not gett forth to sue for pardon; was like a
poore man deepely indebted, had noe meanes to make satisfaction.
The gospell likewise in the letter sayth thou must repent, thou
must beleeve, or els thou canst not be saved; and yet none of them
is in our power. But the spirit quickeneth; that shewes us Christ
hath satisfied, and gives us grace to beleeve it, &c.

FOLIO 74

December. 1602.

5. The lawe of the Old Testament is not abolished by the Newe,
but the old covenant, the condicion of the lawe, is taken awaye;
for the lawe continues and hath a singular use in the ministry of
the Newe Testament, to make a synner knowe and confesse himselfe such a one, for before he finde his synnes greivous he hath noe
neede of a saviour. As Christ sayd, "I came not to call the righteous
but synners to repentaunce," and "Come unto me, all ye that are
weary, and I will easye you," and "The whole neede not the
physitian."

Yf the minister dispense Christes legacyes to a counterfayt and dis-
semblinge penitent, yet they have done their duty. And as Christ
sayd to his disciples, "When you enter into anie place, say 'peace
be with you,' and yf the sonne of peace be not there, your peace
shall returne againe unto you."

Christ made his testament, bequeathed legacyes, made his executors
the disposers of them; therefore there must be certaine markes and
notes, as certaine as the names of persons, to knowe the persons to
whome the legacyes are bequeathed, otherwise the executors cannot knowe how [to] dispose of them. And these markes are fayth
and repentaunce, for to every one that repenteth and beleeveth
remission of syn is given: and therefore it followeth, against the doctrine of the Church of Rome, that a man must beleeve, and knowe
that he beleeveth, hath fayth and repentaunce, for that generall
fayth of that Church in generall is noe more but to beleeve, noe
[more?] but this, that all that is in the Scripture is true, that all
that beleeve shall be saved, and that noe man knoweth whether he
beleeve or repent. But on the contrarie we hold that beleeve and
fayth must be in particuler, and then such a person is become a
legatory certaine in Christ testament, and capable of the disposicion of the promise.

FOLIO 74b

December. 1602.

7. In Justice Catlines tyme one Burchely brought a Replegiar
"quare averia cepit et injuste detinuit," et declare *"quod cepit et
detinuit vnam vaccam,"* and soe it was recorded. After, when Meade
came to argue, he pleaded this in abatement; and Burchely, per-
ceiving the record was faulty, entred the wordes *et vitulum,* and
then said there was a calfe in the case in the roll (an Essex case).
Justice Cataline demaunded to see the record, and the wordes
being written soe newely that they were not dry, "It is true," sayd
he, "your cowe hath newly calved, for shee hath not lickt the calfe
dry yet." (Colebrand.)

The abuse of the statute for reforming errors in the Kings bench, &c., hath frayed the clientes from their suites, when they see they can have noe judgment certaine or speedy.

Mr. Deering held while he was reader at Paules that yf a man and his wife lye togither after either of them knowe the other hath committed adultery, this is adultery in them. (Mr. Colebrand.)

Three mens opinions preferred before five, yf not all togither, as in a writt of error in the Kinges benche to reverse a judgment in the Common place. Yf there be three of one opinion to reverse, and the fourth would have it affirmed; nowe regarding the judgment in the Common place, with this mans opinion there are five on the on syde, and but three one [on?] the other, yet those three shall pre-vaile.

FOLIO 75

December. 1602.

7. Out of a little booke intituled *Buccina Capelli in Laudem juris:*
   Lawe hath God for the author, and was from the beginning. Juris prudentia est Naturae effigies, ut Demosthenes; humanitatis initium, ut Isocrates; libertatis fundamentum, ut Anaxagoras; recte vivendi norma, ut Diodorus; aequi bonique ars, ut Ulpianus. Confert divitias, quibus egenos fulciant, amicos sublevent, patriam vel labentem sustineant, vel precipitantem erigant, vel florentem augeant; honores, quibus illustrati familiam suam obscuram illustrent, novam exornent, insignem decorent, facultatem qua inquinatam improborum vitam retundant et comprimant, et optimorum optimè traductam muneri-bus et mercede digna et laudabili ornent et illustrent, ut majores dicantur.

Quid aliud vult sibi legis nomen quam hoc, ut velit quicquid sit insolutum ligare, quicquid dissolutum legis severitate devincire, quicquid corruptum, quicquid inquinatum, illud resecare vel resar-cire.

Cuidam percontanti quomodo respublica florere, et statu faelicissimo quam diutissimè permanere possit, Respondit Solon, "Si illi quos fortuna ad infimam plebis sortem depresserat, penderent a praescripto magistratuum, et quos fortuna ad altiorem dignitatis gradum erexerat penderent a praescripto legum."

Literis incumbunt juvenes ut fiant judices.

Scio qualis fuerim, immo qualis fuisse non deberem; cognosco qualis sum, timeo qualis futurus sim, et magis timeo quo minus doleo; utinam magis dolerem, ut minus timerem. Doleo, quia semper dolens dolere nescio.
Quo modo nisi per dolores sanabitur, qui per delectationes infirmatur? Doce me salutarem dolorem.

FOLIO 75b

December. 1602.

> Dunne is Undonne; he was lately secretary to the L[ord] Keeper, and cast of because he would match him selfe to a gentlewoman against his Lordes pleasure.

On Munday last the Queene dyned at Sir Robert Secils [sic] newe house in the Stran. Shee was verry royally entertained, richely presented, and marvelous well contented, but at hir departure shee strayned hir foote. His hall was well furnished with choise weapons, which hir Majestie tooke speciall notice of. Sundry devises; at hir entraunce, three women, a maid, a widdowe, and a wife, eache commending their owne states, but the virgin preferred.

An other, on[e] attired in habit of a Turke desyrous to see hir Majestie, but as a straunger without hope of such grace, in regard of the retired manner of hir Lord, complained; answere made, howe gracious hir Majestie in admitting to presence, and howe able to discourse in anie language; which the Turke admired, and admitted, presentes hir with a riche mantle, &c.

FOLIO 76

December. 1602.

12. At St. Clements, a plaine plodding fellowe, sometimes of
Queenes Colledge in Cambridge, his text Heb. cap. 11. v. 8. He
noted the fayth of Abraham, and the fruit thereof, his obedience;
he shewed the kindes of fayth, and sayd this fayth of Abraham was
not hystoricall, not miraculous, not a momentary fayth; such lasts
noe longer then prosperitie, &c., but it was the true justifying fayth,
which was a firme beleife of Christes comminge, with the application of his merites. He named fayth to be the gift of God, because
Abraham is said to be called. God performeth his promises in his
due tyme, or in a better kinde. He promiseth long lyfe to the godly:
yet oftentymes he takes them away in the floure of their age, but
he gives them a better lyfe for it.

Abraham went into a straunge Country; therefore travailing lawefull,
soe it be either specially warranted by Godes call, or to profitt the
Country, not to see and bring home ill fashions, and worse con-
scienses.
He was called, therefore every one must take upon him some calling
and profession, and this calling must be allowed of God; therefore
the trade of stageplayers unlawefull.

The land of promise given to Abraham for the syn of the people;
lett us leave synning least our land be given into the hand of a
strang people againe, as it was sometyme to the Romains, and lastly
to the Normand, for a conquest.

FOLIO 76b

December. 1602.

12 At the Black Friars, Mr. Egerton, a little church or chappell up
stayres, but a great congregacion, specially of women. After "God

be mercifull," reade after the 2^d lesson, having sat a good tyme
before in the pulpit, willed them to sing to the glorie of God and
theire owne edifying, the 66 Psal. 2 part; after he made a good
prayer, then turnd the glas, and to his text, Acts 7. 23, &c. Here he
made a recapitulacion of that he had delivered the last Sabboth and
soe he came to deliver doctrines out of this text. When he had said
what he thought good of it, he went to Catachise; it seemes an
order which he hath but newely begun, for he was but in his
exordium questions; then he prayed, sung a plasme [psalm], gave
the blessing, and soe an end.

He remembred out of his former text these notes, v. 17: That God
performes his promises, not in our tyme, but in his tyme, which is
best, because he is wisest. 2. The pollicy of man folishnes with God.
They may maliciously oppose them selves therein, but cannot alter
his decree. 3. (v. 21) God makes our enimies become our frendes,
and causeth them to doe good unwittingly. 4. Parentes ought to
give their children educacion as well as foode and rayment, and
rather bring them up in learning and trades then proud inheritances
with wronge. 5. Moses a good orator and a good warrior, mighty in
wordes and in deedes, yet modest in all.

Then in his text: Not dispaire of calling, for Moses was 40 yeares
old before he thought of this busines. 2. God put the motion in his
heart. 3. Lawefull to protect the wronged and reprove them that
doe ill, though a man be hated for his labour. 4. The good rejoyce
and are glad to see the magistrate, and every good Cristian and true
subject glad to see the principall magistrat with a gard about, as
well to reward and protect the good, as to revenge the wronged,
glad like

FOLIO 77

December. 1602.

12. one that in a hott sunshine sees a fayre leavy tree, which promiseth a shaddowe yf he be sunburnt; such is the prince to the good
subject.

Those which come to sermons and goe away unreformed are like those which looke in a glas, spie the spott in their face, but will not take the pains to wipe it off.

He defined Catechising to be a breife and familiar kinde of teaching the principles of relligion, in a plaine manner by way of question and aunswere, either publiquely by the minister or privatly by the maister or mistres of the family.

Herein noted the difference betwixt preaching and catechising, that that is.a large continued course of speache, and may be performed onely by the minister.

It is the Custome (not the lawe) in Fraunce and Italy that yf anie notorious professed strumpet will begg for hir husband a man which is going to execution, he shal be reprieved, and shee may obteine a pardon and marry him, that both their ill lives may be bettered by soe holie an action. Hence grewe a jeast, when a scoffing gentlewoman told a gent[leman] shee heard that he was in some danger to have bin hanged for some villanie, his answere: "Truely, madame, I was a feard of nothing soe much as you would have begd me."—intimating shee was a whore, as well as he a theife.

In England it hath bin used that yf a woman will beg a condemned person for hir husband, shee must come in hir smocke onely, with

FOLIO 77b

December. 1602.

12. a white rod in hir hand, as Sterrill said he had seen.

Montagne tells of a Piccard that was going to execution, and when he sawe a limping wenche coming to begg him, "Oh, shee limps! she limps!" sayd hee, "dispatch me quickly," preferring death before a limping wife.

J. Cooper demaunded of Nic. Girlington, whoe is lately returned from Fraunce, what thing he tooke most delight in, in all his travail.

He told him to see a masse in their churches; it was performed with such magnificent pomp and ceremonie, in soe goodly a place, as would make a man admire it. The Hugenotes are coupt up in barnes, as it were, in regard of the Papists churches.

I heard that Geneva is beseiged by the Duke of Savoy.

16. Mr. Hadsor told me that the Earle of Ormondes daughter is come to our Court, and that shee shall be married to yong Ormond, cosen german to the old Earle, which yong man was in prison here in England but is nowe to be released.

17. Mr. Girlington told me there was on[e] Blackewell brought over as apprehended and sent over by Sir Th[omas] Parry, Embassador in Fraunce, because he had confessed under his hand that he came from the Spanyard to murder hir Majestie or burne the navy.

18. Heard that certaine in ragged appairell, offring their service in the navy, were apprehended as suspected, and found worthy suspicion.

FOLIO 78

December. 1602.

16. I brought in a moote with Jo. Bramstone.
18. I was with Stowe the Antiquary. He told me that a modell of his picture was found in the Recorder Fleetwoods study, with this inscription or circumscription: *Johannes Stowe, Antiquarius Angliae*, which nowe is cutt in brasse and prefixed in print to his Survey of London. He sayth of it as Pilat sayd, "What I have written I have written," and thinkes himselfe worthie of that title for his paynes, for he hath no gaines by his travaile.

He gave me this good reason why in his Survey he omittes manie newe monumentes: because those men have bin the defacers of the monumentes of others, and soe thinkes them worthy to be deprived of that memory whereof they have injuriously robbed others.

He told me that the cheife citizens of London in auncient tymes were called barons, and soe divers kinges wrote unto them *Porte-grevio et Baronibus suis London.,* and the auncient seale had this circumscription, *Sigillum Baronum Londonarium.*

FOLIO 78b

December. 1602.

18. I heard that Dr. Smith, M[aste]r of Clare hall, is Vice Chauncellor of Cambridge this yeare.

It was told me by one of St. Johns Colledge that Dr. Playfare hath bin halfe frantike againe, and strangely doted for one Mrs. Hammond, a gent[lewoman] in Kent; is nowe well reclaimed, and hath reade some lectures since.

A mad reader for Divinity! *proh pudor, et dolor!*

Mr. Perkins was buried verry neere with as great sollemnity as Dr. Whitakeres.

The L[ord] Mountjoy in Ireland will never discourse at table; eates in silence. Sir Robert Gardner mislikes him for it, as an unsosiable quality (Hadsor); but great wisdome in soe captious a presence, especially being such a man as desyres to speake wisely.

Mr. Bramstone told howe he sold his bed in Cambridge. Mr. Pym sayd he did wisely, for he knewe those that kept their beds longe seldome prove riche.

21. One Merredeth, a notable coward, when he was in [the] field, and demaunded why he did not fight and strive to kill his enemies, he, good man, told them, he could not finde in his heart to kill them whom he never sawe before, nor had ever any quarrell with them.

FOLIO 79

December. 1602.

19. At Paules, one with a long browne beard, a hanging looke, a gloting eye, and a tossing learing jeasture; his text, "Take heede of false prophets which come to you in sheepes clothinge, but within are ravening wolves; you shall knowe them by theyr fruits."

False prophets, *qui veritatem laudant sed amant mendacia,* preache truely but live wickedly.

He ran over manie heresies, and concluded still "Take heede of them." False prophets which soothe up in synn by pardons for past, and dispensacions for synn to come.

The sheepes clothing: pretended innocency, simplicity, and profitt; they come onely to teache us the auncient, universall, and that relligion which our fathers lived and dyed in; that ours is scarse an hundred yeare old, received but in a corner or twoe, as it were, of the world.

But ours is auncient, theirs newe, all since 600 yeares after Christ, as their universall vicarage. 2. Their singing by note in the Churche. 3. Their lifting up of the breade. 4. Auricular confession and universall pardons, &c.

FOLIO 79b

December. 1602.

19. The multitude noe signe of the churche, for Noah and his family in the old world, Lott in Sodome, &c.

And a true note of the true church, that it hath bin all ways persecuted, and the false the persecutor. Abel slayne, &c.

This cruelty the property of wolves.

His whole sermon was a strong continued invective against the
Papistes and Jesuites. Not a notable villainous practise committed
but a pope, a cardinall, a bishop, or a priest had a hand in it; they
were still at the worst ende.

They come, they are never sent, they come without sending for.

FOLIO 80

December. 1602.

19. In the afternoone, at a church in Fosterlane end, one Clappam,
a black fellowe, with a sower looke, but a good spirit, bold, and
sometymes bluntly witty.

His text Salomon's Song, 4. ca. 3 v.: "Thy lips are like a thred of
skarlett."

For the exposicion of this text he said he would not doe as many
would after the fancy of their owne braine, but according to the
Scripture, expound it by some other place, and that was 2 of Josua,
where he findeth the same wordes, "a skarlet thred," v. 21: "Shee
bound the skarlet threed in the windowe." He told a long story of
Rahab before he came to the threed; and after almost all his sermon was some allusion to that story.

Rabby Shulamo makes this comparison, that the lips are said to be
like a threead of skarlett, to signifie such person in the churche
whose promises are performaunces, whose wordes are workes, as
the red threed was a simbole and a signe unto Rahab.

Rahab was a tavernes, and it signifies alsoe an harlot, because such
kinde of people in that country used to sell their honesty with
their meate.

FOLIO 80b

December. 1602.

19. Like scarlett: the colour sheweth life within, as palenes deathe. Joshua, a type of Jesus, and the wordes the same in severall languages. Moses could not bring the children of Israel into the land of promise, but that was the office of Joshua. The lawe could not be our saviour, but Christ is he that must bring us to heaven. Joshua sent two spies; Christ observed the same number, and always sent two disciples togither.

3. What the spies undertooke and promised according to their commission was firme and ratified by Joshua; whose synnes the disciples, and nowe the ministers, according to their power, remitt or binde on earth shalbe remitted or bound in heaven.

There are enough of Rahabs profession in every place; a man may finde a greate many moe then a good sorte. "I would not give a penny for an 100 of them," said he.

Rahab beleeved and shewed it by hir workes. "Every one will say he beleeves, but except he can showe it to me by his workes, I will not give two strawes for it; lett him carry it to the exchange and see what he can gett for it."

FOLIO 81

December. 1602.

19. An harlot is like a pantofle or slipper at an Inne, which is ready to serve for every foote that comes.

Paule, like the spies, was lett downe out at a windowe, and over a city wall too.

Wee promise in baptisme to fight against Sathan; but, alas, will some say, I finde that I have often strove with him and still I finde I goe away with some wound or other. "Be therefore comforted" (sayd he) "for these woundes are signes of your fighting."

When God delivered his people from the Aegiptians he led them with a pillar of light, but cast a darke cloud betwixt, "and soe the blinde buzardes" (said he) "ran up and downe they knewe not about what."

When he shewed that Salmon was the husband of Rahab, he said "Yf anie nowe, after 44 yeares preaching and the bible being in English, were ignorant of that, it were a horrible shame." And here he sett downe a posicion that none could soundly interpret or understand the Scripture without genealogy, which he commended verry highly.

Of love: they will be at your commaundment, but you may doe it your selfe. You shall commaund and goe without.

FOLIO 81b

December. 1602.

22. When Dr. Colpeper, warden of New Colledge in Oxford, expelled one Payne of that house for some slight offence, this Payne recited that verse alluding to their name.
   Paena potest demi, Culpa perennis erit. (Rous.)

24. I tooke my journey and came to Bradborne.

John Kent told me of a prety cosenning connycatch[ing] trick of late used in London. On[e] that was in execution for debt at the suit of a gent. that dwelt in a far country, procured one of his acquaintaunce to surmise that his creditor was deade, dyed intestate, and he the next of kin, and thereupon to procure letters of administracion, by colour whereof he might have good opportunity to discharge the party, which was effected accordingly.

My Cosen told me that the County of Kent hath compounded by the mediacion of the justices of peace, with the Greene clothe, to be discharged of the purveyors for the Queenes house, for all victualls, &c., except timber and carriage, with the price of wheate raised to 20*d.* the bushell, which before was but 10*d.*, and for this to pay 2100£. per annum, for which the parishes rated, and East Malling at 5£.

27. "Wee have good cardes to shewe for it," said a lawyer to the old recorder Fleetewood: "Well," said he, "I am sure wee have kings and queenes for us, and then you can have but a company of knaves on your syde."

FOLIO 82

December. 1602.

29. I tooke my journey about my Cosens busines, to have a sight of certaine bondes in Mrs. Aldriche handes as executrix to hir husband, wherein my cosen G. Mannyngham, deceased, and his executors, &c., with William Sumner, stoode bound; which bondes by the meanes of my cosen Mr. Wattes I had a sight of and finde that eache of them is in 500£. The condicion of one of them is to pay to Mr. Aldriche during his lyfe 100£. yearely at severall feastes. And yf William Sumner fayle in payment, or not put in nue suertyes upon the death of anie, then to stand in force. Nowe Sumner sayth he did not pay allwayes at the day, and it is apparant that noe suerties are put in since the death of my cosen, nor since the death of one Savil, an other obligor.

The condicion of the other was, whereas Mr. Aldriche had deputed William Sumner to exercise his office, that he should not comitt any thing which might amount to a forfayture of the letters patents whereby Mr. Aldriche held his office; and alsoe that William Sumner should performe all covenantes conteyned in a payre of Indentures bearing the same date with the obligacion, all dated the 20th of June A° *Reginae* 37, A° *Dni.* 1595. These I was to have a sight of, that yf the legataries sue my cosen, as executor in the right of his wife, he might pleade these obligacions in barr.

FOLIO 82b

December. 1602.

29. I lay at my cosen Chapmans at Godmersham.

30. I dined at my cosen Cranmers at Canterbury and by him understoode howe Mr. Sumner had submitted himselfe to the arbitrement of Mr. Ravens and an other, but the arbitrators, not regarding their authority, shuffled it up upon a sudden between Mrs. Aldriche and Sumner, whereas the submission and obligacion was betweene one of Mr. Aldriches sonnes and Sumner; and soe by their negligent mistaking, all was voyd. The cause of controversy was Mr. Aldrich dyed some 2 or 3 dayes before the day of payment, his widdowe executrix desyred the whole, Sumner denied all; yet in regard that Mrs. Aldrich should cancell his bondes and make him a generall acquittaunce, he offred 20 markes and the arbitrators gave but 20£., which Sumner refuseth to pay, and therefore the widdowe threatenes either to sue the bondes or bring an accion of accompt against Sumner for all the monies he received as deputy; but Sumner told me he hath generall acquittances for all accomptes, except the last quarter.

This night I lay at my Cosen Wattes, by Sandwiche, and he rode with me the next morning to Canterbury.

FOLIO 83

December. 1602.

30. Sir Wa. Rawly made this rime upon the name of a gallant, one Mr. Noel:

    (Noe L)

The word of deniall, and the letter of fifty
Makes the gent. name that will never be thrifty.
  And Noels answere (Raw Ly):
The foe to the stommacke, and the word of disgrace
Shewes the gent. name with the bold face.

My cosen Wattes told me more, that the Bishop of Yorke, Dr.
Hutton, was esteemed by Campion the onely man of all our Divines
for the fathers.

That opinion which some hold that Paule did not publishe his
writinges till he and they were confirmed by Peter, as the head of
the Apostles, is plainely everted by the 1[st] and 2[nd] chapters
to the Ga[lla]thians, where it is apparant that Paule withstoode
and contradicted Peter, &c.

31. Dyned with my cosen Wattes, at my cosen Cranmeres in Canterbury. In discourse howe obstinate some are, that they will not confesse a fact, wherefore they were justly condemned, my cosen
Cranmer remembred this story: Not long since one Keyt a
Kentishe man had made [his] will, whereby he bequeathed a great
legacy to one Harris; but after, being displeased, he gave out that
he would revoke his will, and Harris should have nothing, whereupon Harris, thinking to prevent his

FOLIO 83b

December. 1602.

purpose, hired a thrasher to murther him. This poore knave having
effected this villany began to growe resty, could not endure to worke
any more, but would be maynteyned by Harris for this feate, otherwise most desperatly he threatened to reveall the matter. Thus the
fellowe fedd soe long, and spent soe lavishly upon himselfe and his
queanes out of Harris purse, that Harris, growing weary of the
charge, began to thinke howe he might conceale the first by practising a second murther; which he plotted in this manner: he would

invite the knave to dinner at Maidstone, and procure some to murther him as he should come through the woodes. But the fellowe, fearing the worst (because they had bin at some hott words before), imparted his feare to his whore whome he kept, told hir that yf he were murthered shee should accuse the Harrisses, and wisht hir to looke in the bottome of his deske, and there shee should finde that would be sufficent to hang them. As he feared, it happened, for he was murthered; the queane brought all to light, and those papers in his deske shewed the whole manner of the former murther of Keyt, whereupon the Harrises were indited, found gilty, and adjudged to be hanged. The former tooke it upon his death that he was guiltles of the latter murder,

FOLIO 84

December. 1602.

but the other confest it as he was tumbling from the ladder.

When certaine schollers returning from Italy were at the Bishops of Canterbury, amongst other they came about my cosen Cranmer with their newfashioned salutacions belowe the knee. He, like a good plaine honest man, stoode still, and told them he had not learned to dissemble soe deepely.

Hee told mee what dissembling hyppocrites these puritanes be, and howe slighty they regard an oath; Ravens having a booke brought unto him by a puritane to have his opinion of it, the booke being written by B[ishop] Bilson, Ravens as he had reade it would needes be shewing his foolishe witt in the margent, in scoffing at the booke. When the fellowe that had but borrowed it was to carry it home again, he swore it never went out of his hands. After, when it was shewed him what had bin written in it when himselfe could not write, he confessed that Ravens had it; then Ravens forswore his owne hand.

FOLIO 84b

January. 1602.

1. I came from Canterbury to Godmersham.

Cosen Jo. Chapman takes the upper hand and place of his elder brother Drue.

Mr. Jo. Cuttes, Sir Jo. Cuttes sonne and heire, was married some 2 yeares since to Mr. Kemp of Wye his daughter; keepes 4 horse, foure men, his wife a gent[leman] and a mayde, and hath but 200£. per annum in present (mary his meate and drinke and horse-meate) is frank with Mr. Kemps. He shall be heir to Sir H[enry] Cuttes of Kent; is like to be worthe some 1,500£. per annum, after his father and mother and Sir H[enry] Cuttes and his ladyes death.

Stafford, that married Sir Jo[hn] Cuttes daughter, hath brought his yonger brother to this composicion, that there is 300£. per annum for his children, 200£. of it for his wife during hir life, and 100£. for hir husband, shee to keepe hir selfe and children, he to be soe limited because too prodigall.

[fos. 85, 85b, and another leaf (unnumbered) blank in MS]

FOLIO 86

January. 1602.

30. At Paules Crosse one Barlowe, a beardless man of Pembroke hall in Cambridge. After his prayer and before he came to his text, he made a large exordium after this fashion; that yf Paule sayth of himselfe that he was amongst the Corinthians in weaknes, in feare and trembling, much more might he say the like of himselfe: whoe was weake in deliveraunce and methode, &c. Yet he entreated they would not heare, as some say they will heare, the man, but that

they would regard the matter. Of all partes of Scripture the booke of the Preacher may seeme most befitting a preacher, wherein is lively depainted the vanity of the world and all thinges therin; whereof at this time he intended to speake, but not out of the Preacher, but out of the wordes of St. Paule, and those were written in the 8 c. to the Romans, the 19, 20, 21, and 22 verses.

His distribution of this text, or rather context as he called it, because he said it was like Christes garment, soe woven togither that it might not be parted, was into 5 points: 1. That the creature is subject to vanity (v. 20). 2nd. The reason of this subjection, by reason of him which hath subdued it under hope. 3. That the creatures shall be delivered and hope for delivraunce. 4. The effectes of this subjection to vanity: every creature groneth with us (v. 22). 5. The effect of hope, the fervent desyre of the creature wayteth, &c. (v. 19).

He said this place of Scripture is accounted the hardest in all Paules Epistles.

For the first, that the Creature is subject to vanity, he interpreted the words:

FOLIO 86b

January. 1602.

by Creature is ment in this place the heavens, the elementes, all things made of them or conteyned in them except men and Angells.

The vanity of the Creature is in two pointes: 1. In the frustracion of their end, which is twoe fold, the service of God, that made them; 2. and the service of good men, for whom he made them. The 2[n]d vanity, that they are subject to corruption, not of annihilacion, of mater, but decaying in force and virtue.
The creatures, yf they had their owne will, would destroy the

wicked and save the godly alone, as the earth would open hir mouth and swallowe them quicke, as it did Datham and Abiram. The lyons would devoure them, as it did the accusers of Daniel, but shutt their mouths against the innocent. The fier would burne them as it did those which cast the three children into the furnace, &c.

It hath bin observed that as well the influence of the heavens as the futilenes of the earth is decayed and that the whole world is the worse for wearing, the heavens themselves growing old as doth a garment.

2. God hath subdued the creature, for it is he alone that maketh the sunne shine, and powreth downe rayne as well upon the good as the bad, &c. and the reason of this subjection is the synn of man; for all these being created for mans use, when he synned they were punished with him.

3. They shall be delivered from this bondage when there shall be a newe heaven and a newe earth; not that the substance of these shalbe abolished, but a newe forme and perfection added, when they shall enjoy their ends and be ryd [?] of religion.

FOLIO 87

January. 1602.

The elements shall melt with fyre: a comparison from metall, which is melted, not to be consumed, but to be purified and put in a forme.

The morall uses: 1. patiently to endure the afflictions of this life, for as thoughe the Apostle should laye them in a ballance to weighe them, he sayth that the momentary afflictions of this lyfe are not worthy the waight of glory that is layed up for us in the life to come.

We may truely say that the afflictions of these tymes wherein we live are not worthy the glory, for these are non, wee living in abundant prosperity and peace; but tymes of perseqution may come, wherein these may be comfortable argumentes; and he said that for ought he could see the crosse was the proper badge and cognisaunce of a Christian.

There are soe many kindes of takinge: of taking bribes, monie, giftes, &c., that there be fewe will take paynes with the creatures.

The Creatures travayle togither with us: a metaphore taken from travayle with child; which is caused from syn, and is a desyre to be delivered.

When the sonnes of God shall be revealed, i. [e.] when the number of the elect be called, for whose sake the dissolucion of the world is deferred. The Jewes must be converted before the world can be dissolved.

He that before the dissolucion of Abbies had foretold what was to happen unto them for their fault and wickednes which lived in them,

FOLIO 87b

January. 1602.

yf they had thereupon repented and entred into a new course of lyfe, though this could not perhaps have stayed their dissolucion, yet it might have saved themselves in some better state; soe when men are foretold of the dissolucion of the world, which is hastned and caused for our synnes, though our repentaunce and amendment of lyfe cannot hinder the dissolucion, yet may it be good for our selves.

FOLIO 88

January. 1602.

30. In the afternoone, at St. Peters by Paules Wharfe, Mr. Clapham ... Gen. 4: 8, &c.

"Yf a man doth not well, synn lieth at the dore like a dog," sayd he, "that will snap him by the shins."

By primority of birth Kaiñe had the inheritaunce of land, and the rule of his brother Habel. He was Lord over him, and did dominer, a title that was used, and is allowed by all to temporall persons, but by some fantasticall curious heades of late denied to the ecclesiasticall governors. A sort of busie superstitious and factious braines there be, and some in this city, that are afrayed of they know not what, would have something if they could tell what it ment; they are like a goose that stoopes when it comes in at a barne dore, though it knowe not wherefore. These forsoothe crye [?] into the eares of those auditors that like and followe them, that there must be noe such title as Lord given to anie ecclesiastike person, because Christ sayd to his disciples, "Be ye not called Lord," and "The rulers of the gentiles beare dominacion but you not soe." (Math. 20.) Indeede the Scripture talkes after that manner, but not that meaning, and at last they come out with a place, and tell the people they read, (Luk. 22: 25) "The Kings of the gentiles be called gracious lords, but ye shall not be soe:" and this they say cuts home indeede—just as a leaden sawe;

FOLIO 88b

January. 1602.

for they may well say they reade so but I dare say they cannot reade soe in the Scripture. They bely Christ when they say he said soe; he never spake those wordes; it is a punishment for our synnes that wee cannc . .eade right in this age. They are unlearned malitious that read soe. The word in the text originall is εὐεργεται, derived of the particle εὐ, "good," and the other verbe εργαζομαι, "to worke"; in Latin they are called *Benefactores,* we may call them Good Workeres, a title which the kinges of the Southerne nations, those which Daniel describeth to be the kingdome that standes upon black legges, when they had done some litle good to their state they would arrogate. Soe Ptolome Evergetes.

And soe it is forbidden by way of arrogancy for good deedes, because the glory must be ascribed to God.

And by their reason they might as well deny the name of maister, and father, for both are forbidden, as well as the other; and soe they might quickly be amongst the Anabaptistes, and overturne all difference and jurisdicion.

Lord is a name sometyme of place and sometyme of grace; and soe the ecclesiastike may have it as well as the temporall, for to the temporall it is a name of place onely, but the ecclesiasticall by their merit may have it of grace. Neither is it soe strange a title. Jacob useth it to his brother Esau, and the prophet Isay takes it: my Lord, Adoni. Christ acknowledged the name, and some of the apostles did not refuse it.

FOLIO 89

January. 1602.

"Then Kain spake to Habell": it is not sett downe what he said: yet some have adventured to say that he said *Transeamus in campos.* But what soever it was it is not here mentioned, but left to be conceived. As in 3. Gen. v. 22, "Least he put forth his hand [and] take alsoe of the tree of lyfe," it is left what he resolved. Not that yf Adam had tasted of the tree of lyf that he should have lived for ever, noe more then he that receives the Sacrament unworthily shall be a member of Christes body; but that was spoken *ironice.*

It is like he spake fayre wordes, being in the house in presence of his father and mother, and that he used dissembling flattering speeches to draw him to such a place where he might with advantage execute his purpose. A common practise in this world, and an old on[e], you see, a Machivilian tricke; they will match the Divel in this age. To carry fayre countenaunce to him whom they meane to overthrowe; to glose and insinuate, to offer hart roote and all, till he can take him at such a vantage that he may cutt his throate or breake his necke, a familiar fashion amongst the nobility in Court, not altogither unusuall amongst the clergy.

"And when they were in the field Kain rose up against his brother and killed him": a pittifull and a wonderfull matter, will some say, that God will suffer the wicked thus to murther the good. Pittifull indeed, but not wonderfull; for the synnes of the best have deserved greater punishments.

A strang thing, those which were soe great frendes, went arme in arme, are nowe mortall enimies upon the suddeine.

FOLIO 89b

January. 1602.

A marvelous strang thinge that he should knowe he could kill his brother, that he could dy, for he never sawe any man dye before; but many thinges are done, both good and evil, by a secret instinct whereof a man sawe noe reason til after the thing performed, as Moses when he slewe the Agyptian.

Murder an auncient synn, the first open offence after the fall, that was committed in the world. Here a notable pollicy of the divel to have dammed up Godes glory and mans relligion, both at once.

Noe murderer at this day but is guilty of this murder of Kain, and all since, since iniquity is sayd to be a measure which every synner in his kinde by adding his synne strives to make full, and soe assents to all before acted, like a conjuror that subscribes with his bloud.

"Where is Habel they brother?" The Lord careth for the righteous.

Whoe answered, "I cannot tell." He slaps God in the mouth with a ly at the first word; a generall rule that after murder lying followeth, they are links togither, and commonly noe syn committed but a lye runnes after; for none is soe impudent to confesse it, every one would have the face of virtue.

"Am I my brothers keeper?" See a kinges sonne, the heir of the world, what a lob it is! Howe like a clowne, a clunche, an asse, he aunsweres. A synner is the verryest noddy of all. This Kain was the verriest Duns in the world. He thought to have outfact God with [a] ly, and then would excuse it: "Am I my brothers keeper?" I, marry, art thou, as thou wast his brother in love, his elder in government, as the prince is the keeper of his people,

FOLIO 90

January. 1602.

the minister of the congregacion, every one of an other. The greate ones would keepe the minister poore and beggerly, that they might not tell them of their faults, but stopp the preists mouth with a coate or a dynner; "but," said he, "the divel take dynners given to such a purpose."

FOLIO 90b

January. 1602.

30. The papistes make a forril [?] of the Scripture; they sowe up the mouth of it. (Clapham the other Sunday, as Mr. Peter [?] told me.)

SCOTTISH TAUNTS.

Long beardes hartles,
Painted hoodes wittles,
Gay coates graceles,
Makes England thriftles.

FEBRUARY

5. Mr. Asheford told me these verses underwritten are upon a picture of the nowe L[ord] Keeper, Sir Th[omas] Egerton, in the L[ord] Ch[ief] Justice Pophams lodging:
In vita gravitas, vultu constantia, fronte
  Consilium, os purum, mens pia, munda manus.

A gentleman without monie is like a leane pudding without fatt. (J. Bramstone.)

Justice Glandville upon a tyme, when fidlers pressed to play before him, made them sing alsoe, and then askt them yf they could not cry too; they said his wor[ship] was a merry man, but he made them sad fellowes, for he caused them to be used like rogues as they were. (Ch. Davers *na.*)

There is best sport always when you put a woman in the case. (Greene.)

The Attorny Generall [Coke] put a case thus in the Kings benche: "Yf I covenant to stand seised to the use of my Bastard daughter (as I thank God I have none)"—and blusht.

FOLIO 91

February. 1602.

1. There were 11 Sergeantes at Lawe called this day: 2 of the Middle Temple: Mr. Phillips and Mr. Nicholes; 5 of the Inner Temple: Crooke the Recorder of London, Tanfeild, Coventry, Foster, and Barker; 3 of Lyncoln's Inn: Harris, Houghton; 1 of Grayes Inn: Mr. Altam.

When the Queene was moved to have called an other to have made up twelve, she refused, saying she feared yf there were twelve there would be one false brother amongst them.

Sergeant Harris when he heard that Barker was called, "It is well," said he, "there should be one barker amongst soe manie byters."

This day at dynner Mr. Snig tooke Mr. Nicholes by the hand and led him up from the lower end of the table, where his place was, and seated him, on the benche highest at the upper end.

3. I heard by Mr. Hadsore the lawyers Recusantes are admitted to plead at the barr in Irland; that one Everard is preferred of late to be a Justice in the Kinges Bench there, where there are but 2. And yet he a recusant, but an honest man.

4. It is said Mr. Snig offers 800£. to be Sergeant, whereupon Mr. Sergeant Harris said he doubted not but he should shortly salut his Deare brother Mr. Snig.

Argent makes Sargent.

FOLIO 91b

February. 1602.

4. *Out of a poeme intituled The Tragicall History of Mary Queen*
hir ghost   \   *of Scotts & Dowager of Fraunce.*
to Baldwyne \
[4.] In swiftest channell is the shallowest ground,
    In common bruite a truth is seldome found.

[5.] A slight defence repells a weake assault.

[6.] But soe unhappy is a princes state
    That scarce of thousands which on them depend
    One shall be found untill it be too late
    That solid truth shall in their counsell fend [lend],
    But all theyre vainest humours will defend
    Till wee (alas) doe beare the guilt of all,
    And they themselves doe save what ere befall!

[12.] I will not shewe thee howe my body lyes,
    A senceles corps by over hastned death.

[13.] I might bemoane the hap that fell to me
    That yet in grave must still accused bee.

[14.] Lett the faults upon the guilty light.

[19.] But fatall was my Guyssian kin to mee,
    Who built their hopes on hazard of my bloud,
    Like ivy they did clyme up by my tree,
    And skathed my growth in many a likely bud.
    Theyre over kindenes did me little good,
    Whose clyming steps of theyre unbridled mynde
    Makes me (alas) to blame them as unkinde.

[20.] They gave us courage quarrels to pretend
    Gainst neighbours Kings & friends for whom of right
    Our interest and bloud would wish us fight.

FOLIO 92

[21.] Soe did the wise observe my tyme of birth
    To be a day of mourning, not of mirth,

22. For death deprived two brothers that I had,
    Both in a day, not long ere I was borne,
    So that a mourning weede my cradle clad, &c.   ·

24. A greivous chaunce it is to meanest sort
    To leave a widdowe in a forrein land,
    A child whose yeares cannot her selfe support,
    A suckling babe which can ne speak nor stand
    But must depend upon a tutors hand;
    But greatest mischeif is it to a king
    Then which noe hap can greater hazard bring.

25. Ill to the prince, & to the people worse,
    Which giveth meanes to the ambitious mynd

By rapine to enrich their greedy purse
By wreak of commonweale, whilst that they blind
The peoples eyes & shewe themselves unkinde
To pupil princes, whom they doe accuse
As cause of such disorders they doe use.

33. Pride, wealth, and lust, & gredines of mynde
The finest witts wee see doth often blynde.

The choise of the Regent was the beginning of their broyles. Duke
Hamelton a worthie wise prince, chosen regent, purposed a mar-
riag twixt Q. Mary and Ed. 6., interrupted by the Clergy, and
matched with the Dauphine of Fraunce.

41. Thus to and fro, I, silly wretch, was tost,
And made the instrument of either side,
Turmoyled with stormes, with wilfull wynde, & tyde.

FOLIO 92b

47. The Cardinall of Lorraine bare the purse,
The Duke of Guyse the civil wars did nurse.
Our Q[ueene] offered hir 30,000 crownes p[er] annum soe
she would not marry a forreyner.
67. In heaven they say are weddings first decreed,
All though on earth they are solemnized.

70. Soe most unhappy is a princes state
Who must have least respect them selves to ease,
Barr'd of the right men have of meaner state,
Whose choyse is cheife theyr eyes and mynde to please;
Noe outward pompe can inward greif appease;
A sheepherds lyfe with calme content of mynde
Is greater blisse then many princes finde.

78. God graunt in safety long his life may stay
That riper yeares may yeild a plenteous crop
Of virtues which doe kingdomes underprop.

81. Not civil but uncivil wars they were,
     Twixt man & wife, which jealousy did breede.

82. But if my mynde which was not growne soe base,
     Or Davis yeares unfitt for ladyes love,
     As fitt excuses might have taken place.

> Davis hir secretary gave Counsell, that shee should not
> crowne hir husband, L[ord] Darly.

85. Whose rule was like for to eclipse my power.

86. Not any hate unto the prince he had,
     Not unbeseeming love to me he bare.

88. But as they clyme whom princes doe advaunce
     Eache tongue will trip & envyes eye will glaunce.

89. To be advanced from a base estate
     By virtue is indeede a happy thing;

FOLIO 93

> But who by fortune clymes will all men hate,
> Unles his lyfe unlookt for fruit doe bring
> Wherewith to cure the wound of envies sting;
> But seldometymes is found soe wise a man
> That gayneing honour well it governe can.

Of the murther of Davies.

94. I would have wisht some other had him stroke,
     And in a place more farther from my sight,
     Or for his right arraigned he had spoke,
     Or of his death some other sense had light.

95. A Princes presence should a pardon bee,
     A ladyes shout should move a manly mynde,
     A childwifes chamber should from bloud be free,
     A wife by husband should not slaunder finde.

101. To disunite their league I went about,
     For cables crack like threds when they untuist.

> That not the Q[ueen] but others procured Bothwell to
> murther L[ord] Darly.

118. It stoode them well upon to finde a way
     To rid a foe whose power they well might feare;
     The[y] knewe the King did watch revenging day
     And Bothwell did them litle likeing beare,
     They knewe ambition might his malice bleare,
     They knewe the hope of kingdome & of me
     Would win him to the kings decay agree.

119. To fayne my hand to worke soe great effect
     They would not stick to have theyr lives assured.

109. Howe ere it was, by whose soever fact,
     The breache of peace betwixt us growne of late,
     Our parted bed, my love which somewhat slackt,
     Some letters shew'd as myne, importing hate,
     With the slender shewe I make in mourners state,
     Conferred with my match which did ensue,
     Makes most suppose a false report for true.

FOLIO 93b

110. With equall mynde doe but the matter weigh,
     And till thou heare my tale, thy judgment stay.

114. I crave noe priviledge to sheild my cause,
     Lett onely reasons balance triall make,
     A guitles conscience needes not feare the lawes.

> My nay might answere well a bare suspect,
> But likelyhoodes of thinges shall me protect.

That she mourned not.

122. I must accuse the Custome of the place,
Where most our Auncestors themselves doe want
Due monuments theyr memorys to plant.

130. Soe hard it is to Virtue to reclayme
The mynde where pride or malice giveth ayme.

132. Noe cause soe bad, you knowe, but colours may
Be layd to beautifie what princes say.

135. A fetch soe foule as to report I shame,
Even to deprive the life I lately gave,
And shed the bloud I would have dyed to save.

136. A dangerous thing it is once to incur
A common bruit or light suspect of ill;
Fame flyeth fast: the worse she is, more farr
She goeth, and soone a jealous head will fill;
What most men say is held for ghospell still.

Of hir majesties favours.

148. My suit did crave but liberty to live
Exiled from those at home which sought my bloud;
Hir bounty did extend further to give,
With lyfe, eache needefull thing with calling stood
And such repayre of frends as me seemed good;
Which had I used as did a guest beseeme
I had not bin a prisoner, as I deeme.

149. But winged with an overhigh desyre.

FOLIO 94

150. Small provocations serve a willing mynd
Soe prone wee are to clyme against the hill,
If honour or revenge our sayles doe fill.
But woe is me I ever tooke in hand
That to decide I did not understande!

The cause that moved hir to stir sedition.
151. It was the thirst I had both crownes to weare,
    And from a captives state myselfe to reare.

159. Guyse, whoe did lay the egges that I should hatch,
    Sawe subjects hearts in England would not bend
    To treason, nor his force noe hold could catch
    To bring to passe the thing wee did entend,
    He therefore caused the Pope a pardon send
    To such as should by violent stroke procure
    Hir death, whose fall my rising might procure.

Tyborne tippets, i.[e.], halters.
163. At length by full consent of Commonweale
    In Englishe Parliament it was decreed
    By cutting of a withered branche to heale
    Theyre body burdened with a fruitles weede,
    Which was by hir it touched most indeede
    Withstoode by pitty, which could not take place
    Because it did concerne a common case.

165. In body yet wee Adams badge doe wearè,
    And to appeare before Gods throne doe feare.

Appeald to forrein princes.
167. (For of releif I promises had store)
    But when, alas, it stoode my lyfe upon
    I found them fayle; my life and all was gone.

168. Proofes were produced it seemed I should confes
    A murder purposed & some treacherousnes
    Against a queene, my cosen & my frend,
    Whoe from my subjects sword did me defend.

FOLIO 94b

170. And soe the cause did seeme to stand with mee
    That ones decay must others safety bee.

172. Thus I convict must satisfy the lawe,
Not of revenge which hatred did deserve,
But of necessity, by which they say [sawe?]
My onely death would hir in lyfe preserve,
Which I rejoice soe good a turne did serve,
That haples I might make some recompence
By yeilding up the life bred such offence.

173. I did rather others facts allowe
Then sett them on to actions soe unkinde,
Though many tymes my selfe was not behinde
To blowe the fyre which others seemed to make.

174. To doe or to procure, to worke or will,
With God is one, & princes hold the same.

179. What favour should I from my foes expect
If soe unkindely frends did deale with me?
If that my subjects doe my faults detect,
I cannot looke that straungers should me free;
They should have propt or bent my budding tree
In youth, whilst I as yet was pliant wood
And might have proved a plant of tymber good.

180. Howe seldome natures richest soyle doth yeild
A bower where virtue may hir mansion build.

182. Tell them that bloud did always vengeance crave
Since Abels tyme untill this present day;
Tell them they lightly loose that all would have,
That clymers feete are but in ticle stay,
That strength is lost when men doe oversway,
That treason never is soe well contrived
That he that useth it is longest lyved.

FOLIO 95

Some of the Lotteries which were the last Summer
at hir Majesties, being with the L[ord] Keeper.

[1]   FORTUNES WHEELES, TO HIR MAJESTIE.

Fortune must nowe noe more in triumphe ride
The wheeles are Yours that did hir chariot guide.

[3]   A MASKE: LA[DY] SCROOPE.

Want you a maske here fortune give you one
Yet nature gives the rose & lilly none.

[28]   A DIALL: LA[DY] SCUDAMOUR.

The Dial's yours watch tyme least it be lost,
And yet they spend it worst that watch it most.

[6]   A PLAINE RING: LA[DY] FRAUNCIS.

Fortune hath sent to you, hap it well or ill
A playne gold ring to wed you to you will.

[7]   A RING WITH A POSIE AS FAYTHFULL AS I FIND:
       EARLE OF DARBYS COUNTES.

Your hand by fortune on this ring doth light
And yet the word doth fitt your humour right.

[8]   GLOVES: LA[DY] SOUTHWELL.

Fortune these gloves in double challenge sends
For you hate fooles & flatterers hir best frends.

A PURSE: COUNTES OF DARBY DOWAGER.

[2]   You thrive, or would or may, your lottes a purse
       Fill it with gold, & you are ne're the worse.

[12]   A GIRDLE: COUNTES OF KILDARE.

With fortunes girdle happy may you bee
But they that ar lesse happy are more free.

[13]   WRITING TABLES: LA[DY] EFFINGAM

These tables may conteine your thought in part
But write not all that's written in your hart.

FOLIO 95b

[19] A SCISSER CASE: LA[DY] NEWTON

These Scissers doe your huswifry bewray
You love to worke though you be borne to play.

[21] A PRAYER BOOKE (NOT DRAWNE).

Your fortune may be good an other day;
    that day
Till fortune come take you a booke to pray.

[22] A MUFKIN: LA[DY] WARWIKE.

Tis summer, yet a muffkin is your lott
It will be winter one day doubt you not.

[25] A BODKIN: LA[DY] DOROTHY.

Even with this bodkin you may live unharmd
Your beauty is with virtue soe well arm'd.

[33] BLANK: LA[DY] SUSAN VERE.

Nothing's your lott, that's more then can be told
For nothing is more precious then gold.

[32] BLANK: LA[DY] KIDDERMAISTER.

Tis pitty such a hand should drawe in vayne
Though it gaine nothing, yet shall it pity gayne.

BLANK.

You are to daynty to be pleasd God wott
Chance knowes not what to give you for your lott.

Before hir Majesties venturing to the house, a
dialogue betweene the baly and a dary mayd.
Bayly: The mistress of this fayre companie, though shee knowe
the way to all mens heartes, yet shee knowes the way but to fewe
mens houses, except shee love them verry well.

FOLIO 96

February. 1602.

6. At the Temple churche, Dr. Abbottes, Deane of [Winchester.]
His text, 59 of Isay, v. 12: "For our tresspasses are many before
thee, and our synnes testify against us, for our trespasses are with
us, & we knowe our iniquities."

He began with a commendacion of this prophet for the most
eloquent and Evangelique, in soe much that St. Jerome said he
might rather be placed amongst the Evangelistes then the
Prophetes.

All men are synneres. "Our trespasses": When Christ taught his
disciples to pray, it was one peticion, "Forgive us our trespasses;"
to lett them knowe that though they were his chosen disciples, yet
they were not without synn.

Some may say they have lived *sine crimine, sine querela, sed nemo
absque peccato.*

Hence we must learne not to be presumptuous, but to worke out
our salvacion with feare and trembling, since all are synners. 2. Not
to despayre, since the best have synned.

Our synnes are before God, his eyes are 10,000 tymes brighter then
the sunne, nothing hid from his knowledge. Synne is like a smoke,
like fyre, it mounteth upward, and comes even before God to accuse us; it is like a serpent in our bosome, still ready to sting us; it
is the Divels daughter.

A woman hath hir paynes in travaile and delivery, but rejoyceth
when she seeth a child is borne; but the birth of synne is of a
contrary fashion, for all the pleasure is in the bringing forth, but
when it is finished and brought forth, it tormenteth us continually;
they haunt us like the tragicall furies.

FOLIO 96b

February. 1602.

6. In the afternoone, Mr. Clapham; his text, Math. 24: 15: "Lett him that readeth consider it."

He said this chapter is not to be understoode of Doomesday, but of the Destruction of Jerusalem. And that the 28th v., "Wheresoever the dead carcase is, thither doe the Eagles resort," cannot be applied to the resurrection and congregacion of the saintes into state of glory with Christ, as some notes interpret, but of the gathering togither of Christes people in the kingdome of grace; for Christ in his kingdome of glory cannot be sayd a carcase, but nowe he may, because he is crucified.

And the 29th v., "The sunne shall be darkened and the moone shall be darkned, & the moone shall not give hir light, and the stars shall fall from heaven," he expounded thus: that the temporall and ecclesiasticall state of the Jewes in Jerusalem, and the starres, *i.e.* their magistrates, shall loose their authority.

He expounded the opening the 7 seales in the Revelacion to have reference to sundry tymes, and the 6th to the destruction of Jerusalem. 7 tymes 7 makes a weeke of yeares, the Jews true Jubilee wherein 7 trumpets should be blowne.

The best expositor of the Revelacion, a nobleman of Scotland, whoe hath taken Christian and learned paynes therein, yet fayled in the computacion of the beginning of the yeares.

The Revelacion might be better understood if men would better studye it; and that it may be understoode and hath good use, he alledged the word, 1: cap. 3, "Blessed is he that readeth, & they that heare the wordes of this prophesy, & keepe those thinges which are written therein" (which were vayne unles it might be understoode).

FOLIO 97

February. 1602.

6. Towardes the end of his sermon he told his auditory howe it had
bin bruited abroade, as he thought by some Atheistes or papistes,
whose profest enemy he is, that this last weeke he had hanged himselfe, but some of his freindes, he said, would not beleeve it, but
said some other had done it; yet others that like him not for some
opinion said it was noe marvaile yf he hangd himselfe, for he had
bin possest of the Divel a good while. "But I thinke rather," said
he, "they were possessed that said soe; and yet not soe possessed
as some hold possession nowe adayes, that is, essentially." And
here he shewed his opinion that there can be noe essentiall possession: 1. because the divel can effect as much without entering into
the person as yf he were essentially in him, and then it is more then
needes; 2[n]d. because there can not be assigned anie proper token
or signe to knowe that anie is essentially possessed, which signe
must be apparent in all such as are soe possessed, and not in anie
otheres. This opinion of his, he said, he would hold till he sawe
better reason to the contrary. [Next sentence partly cancelled in
MS (see notes).]

In his sermon he told a tale of the Jewes Thalmud, which he said
was as true perhaps as anie in the papists legend of lyes; and it was
howe Rabbi Haley had conference with Elias in a cave, and would
knowe of Elias when Messias should come. Elias told him goe aske
of the Messias himselfe. Rabbi Haly required where the Messias
might be found; Elias told him he should

FOLIO 97b

February. 1602.

6. finde him at Rome gates amongst the poore (a verry scoffe and
a flout, he thought, to the papistes, to shewe that Christ never

came within their City, but they kept him out of dores, and that he was not amongst their Cardinals, but the beggars, &c.)

"I will not believe it, because I will not" is Tom Sculs argument, as they say in Cambridge, and a womans reason, as they say here. (Clapham.)

Mr. Bodley which hath made the famous library at Oxeford was the sonne of a merchant of London; was sometymes a factor for the state; after maried a riche widdowe in Devonshire or Cornewall, whose husband grewe to a greate quantity of wealth in a short space, specially by trading for pilcheres; nowe himselfe having noe children lives a pleasing privat life, somewhile at the City, somewhile at the University; he followed the Earl of Essex till his fall. (Mr. Curle.)

---

7. One came to the fyre and Mr. South gave him place; "You are as kinde," q[uoth] he, "as the South-west winde." (Da.)

---

8. Tom Lancaster met Robbin Snig one day in the Court of Requestes. "Howe nowe, old Robbin," q[uoth] he, "what dost thou here?" "Fayth," said he, "I come to be heard if I can." "I thinke soe," said he; "nowe thou canst be heard in noe other Court thou appealest to Cesar." (Dr. Cesar Master of Requestes.)

---

8. One told Toplife that he would tell him of papist[s] that frequented masse, and would bring him where he should take them At it; but he brought him where he tooke a gent[leman] in bed with his Daughter At it. (Ch. Davers.)

FOLIO 98

February. 1602.

8. Two poore men being at a verry doubtfull demurrer in the Kinges benche, the Justices moved that they would referr the matter to some indifferent men, that might determine soe chargeable and difficult a controversy; and one demaunded of one of them yf

he could be content to have the land parted betweene them; when he shewd himselfe willing, "Doubtles," said Mr. Cooke, the Attorney, "the child is none of his, that would have it divided," alluding to the judgment of Solomon.

9. I offered Mr. Kedgewin as being myne ammiral in the house to cutt before me; he refused with this phrase: "Nay, I regard not men as women doe for their standing."

He sent 3 or 4 dayes after, an hue and cry after him with leaden heeles. (Topham [?]).

7. Turner and Dun, two famous fencers, playd their prizes this day at the banke side, but Turner at last ran Dun soe far in the brayne at the eye, that he fell downe presently stone deade! A goodly sport in a Christian state, to see on[e] man kill an other.

8. One told Sergeant Harrys howe many there were newe prickt sergeantes. "Would I were neweprict to," q[uoth] he; "it would be the better for my wife then." (Hoskins).

11. He that offeres to violate the memory of the deade is like a swyne that rootes up a grave.

The towne of Manitre in Essex holdes by stage playes.

And Rocheford, that they must come at a day unknowne into a field, where the steward keepes court at midnight, and writes with a cole, but the night he goes he must make knowne where he stays; those that are absent, and have none to answer, loose theyr land; grewe upon tenants burn[ing] Lords evidences.

FOLIO 98b

February. 1602.

12. Ben. Johnson the poet nowe lives upon one Townesend and scornes the world. (Tho: Overbury.)

Sir Christopher Hatton and another knight made challenge whoe should present the truest picture of hir Majestie to the Q[ueene]. One caused a flattering picture to be drawne; the other presented a glas, wherein the Q[ueene] sawe hir selfe, the truest picture that might be. (Reeves [?])

13. I heard by Mr. Hull that whereas heretofore the Lord Admirall used to have the tenthe of all reprisall goodes, the state hath nowe thought good, for the encouragement of men to furnishe ships of warr against the enimy, to forgive that imposicion of tenth; but it is thought this indulgence comes too late, the Spaniard having growne soe strong in shipping that fewe dare hazard to venture in small company for incertayne booty.

12. The maysters of the Court of Requestes take their place aboue a knight. (Whitlock.)

Mr. Hadsor, an Irishe gent[leman] of our house, was called to the barre, and tooke his oath to the Supremacy. He is shortly to goe for Irland, there to be Cheife Justice in Ulster, yf the troubles be pacified, as there is great hope they will bee, for the Rebbell Tyrone hath sent an absolute submission.

One Weston, a merchant of Dublin, hath bin a great discoveror.

FOLIO 99

February. 1602.

15. The papistes relligion is like a beggares cloke, where there are soe many patches of pollicy sowed on, that none of the first clothe can be seene. (B. Rudy[erd].)

"I will doe myne endevor," quoth he that thrasht in his cloke. (E. Curle.)

"Non sic fuit ab antiquo," say the Papistes of ours;
"Non sic fuit ab initio," say wee of their religion. (B. Rudyerd.)

14. Impunity is the mother of contempt and impiety, and both those the subverters of all governement. (L[ord] Keeper.)

Qui in os laudatur in corde flagellatur.

I heard that about this last Christmas the Lady Effingham, as shee was playing at shuttlecocke, upon a suddein felt hir selfe somewhatt, and presently retiring hir selfe into a chamber was brought to bed of a child without a midwife, shee never suspecting that shee had bin with child.

The play at shuttlecocke is become soe muche in request at Court, that the making shuttlecockes is almost growne a trade in London.

Praestat otiosum esse quam nihil agere.

FOLIO 99b

February. 1602.

13. At Paules, a yong man, made a finicall boysterous exordium, and rann him selfe out almost dry before he was halfe through. His text:
   "He humbled himselfe to the death, even to the death of the crosse, wherefore God hath glorified him."

He spake much of humility. *Melior est peccator humilis, quam superbus justus. Peccare non potest nisi superbus, nec penitere nisi humilis.*

He first dilated of three meanes to knowe God: by his greatnes, by the prophetes in the old, by his sonne in the newe Testament.

Against pride in beauty: the divel playes the sophister whiles he perswades women to paint that they may seeme fayrer than they are; which painting being discovered, makes them to be thought fouler then they are.

Pride in apparell is pride of our shame, for it was made to cover it, and as yf one should embroyder a sheete wherein he had done pennaunce, and shewe it in bragging manner, &c.

It is said by some that St. Jo[hn] Baptist, for his humility, is rewarded with the place which the divel lost for his pride.

He spake against duellisme, or single combat, and said that yf two goe into the field with purpose to fight, an the one be slayne, he is a murderour of himselfe.

He exhorted the judges to severity, telling them that there is more incouragement taken by one that escapes the punishment due unto him by the lawe, then there is feare wrought by the execution of an hundred.

FOLIO 100

February. 1602.

13. In the afternoone Mr. Clapham at his churche by Paules Wharf. Text, Gen. 4:13: "Then Kain said to the Lord, or Jehovah, My punishment is greater then I can beare, &c." but he reade it "My synne is greater then can be concealed." He noted that translators did very ill to foyst their inventions into the text and sett the originall in the margent, as commonly the common translacions have *synne* in the margent for the word *punishment* in the text, as grosse an absurdity as yf one should shutt the master out of dores and give entertainement to his attendantes.

Nowe Kayne was prest with the horror of his synn; he confesseth, but with a kinde of desperacion and repining, as Judas when he confest and hangd himselfe. If a man will not confesse his faultes, he shall be prest till he confesse, and when his confession comes to late he may confesse and be hangd to, well enough.

For repentant confession must come while grace is offered, while it is called to-day. God deales as the debtor which tenderes his mony till sunne goe downe; when night is come, up goes his money

and a fig for his creditor. Yf men take not tyme while grace is
offered, but delay till the sunne of grace be gonne downe, there
remaines nothing but horrible desperat reprobacion.

A vagabond. An excommunicate person is a vagabond, turned out
of the society of Godes churche both here in earth and in heaven
too, yf it were done by the Spirit of Christ; and therefore lett not
men soe lightly esteeme of this greate censure, nor thinke to
excuse themselves by saying

FOLIO 100b

February. 1602.

it was for trifles; but lett them take heede they deserve it not; and
yf they which gave the sentence abused their authority, lett them
aunswere for it, but always the censure is to [be] reverently regarded.

There be pasport-makers that are as verry rogues as any justice
rogue[s], noble rogues; all that live out of the communion of the
churche are noe better than rogues and vagabonds in the eye[?] of
God.

FOLIO 101

February. 1602.

15.   Paradox. That paynting is lawefull.
Fowlenes is loathesome; can it be soe that helpes it?

What thou lovest most in hir face is colour, and this painting gives
that; but thou hatest it, not because it is, but because thou knowest
it is. Foole, whom ignorance only maketh happie.

Love hir whoe shewes greate love to the[e] by taking this paynes
to seeme lovely to thee.

Hee that weepeth is most wise.

Wee come first unwitting, weeping and crying, into a world of woe,
and shall wee not weepe and cry when wee knowe it? The Reason
of reasons was seene divers tymes to weepe but never to laugh.
Art thou a synner? Wilt thou repent? Weepe. Art thou poore?
Wouldst thou be releeved? Weepe. Hast thou broken the lawes of
thy prince? Hast thou deserved death? Wouldst thou be pittyed?
Wouldst thou live? Weepe. Hast thou injured thy friend? Wilt thou
be reconciled? Weepe.

Laughinge is the greatest signe of wisdome.

Ride si sapis, O puella, Ride. Yf thou be wise, laugh, for sith the
powers of discourse and reason and laughinge be equally proper to
only man, why shall not he be most wise that hath most use of
laughing, as well as he that hath most use of reasoning and discoursing?
I have seene men laugh soe long and soe earnestly that they have
wept at last, because they could weepe [laugh?] noe more.

Laugh at a foolish gallant; soe shall he be knowne a man, because he
laughs; a wiseman, for he knowes what he laughs at; and valiant,
that he dares laugh.

FOLIO 101b

February. 1602.

15.   To keepe sheepe the best lyfe.

The lyfe of man was soe affected to this lyfe that he denyed not to
Crowne his deity with this title: and by this he directed his especiall
charge to his especiall disciple: giving us men this best name of a
beast, of the best nature of beastes. They are innocent, they are

patient, soe would God have man; they love and live togither, soe would man [God?] have man. God made the[e] to behold the heavens and to meditate the wonderes thereof; make thy selfe a shepheard, and thou art still beholding, still meditating. God commaunds the[e] to forsake the world; yf thou art a shepheard thou dost soe, thou withdrawest thyselfe from the world. The private lyfe is the sweetest lyfe; yf thou livest the lyfe of a shepheard, thou liveth the sweetest private. Wilt thou be a king? be a shepeard: thou hast subjectes, thou hast obedient subjectes, thou hast sheepe; thou hast a scepter, thou hast a croke; thy fold is thy counsell chamber, and the greene field thy flourishing pallace. Thy companions are the sunne, the moone, and the stars, of whom thou makest continuall use, and from the viewe of their lightes receyvest thy counsell and advise. Thou art more happie then other kinges, thou art freed from hate and soe from feare, thou reignest quietly and rulest securely; thou hast but one enimie, and thou hast an enimy for that enimy, the dog & wolf. He that was Godes second best beloved was a shepheard and a king; yf thou art a shepeard thou art a king, thou art happie, nay thou art most happie, thou art a happie king, thy subjectes living onely to lengthen thy life, and to shorten their owne, &c.

FOLIO 102

February. 1602.

One fee is too good for a bad lawyer, and two fees too little for a good one.

Hee that will love a man he knowes not why, will hate him though he knowe not wherefore.

When Sir Ed[ward] Hobby heard of Sir H[enry] Nevils disaster with the E[arl] of Essex, he said that his cosen Nevil was ambling towardes his preferment, and would needs gallop in all the hast, and soe stumbled and fell. (Ch. Davers.)

The Bishop of Bathe and Wells, being sent for to the court and there offered the Bishopricke of Ely upon some condicions which he thought inconvenient, he said that Bishopricke was the onely mayden Bishopricke in England, and he would not be the first should deflour it. (Hooper.)

One being entreated to part a man and his wife that were togither by the eares, "Nay," q[uoth] he, "I will never part man and wife while I live."

Dr. Rud made a sermon before the Queene upon the text "I sayd yee are Gods, but you shall all dy like men," wherein he made such a discourse of death that hir Majestie, when his sermon was ended, said unto him, "M[aste]r D[octo]r, you have made me a good funerall sermon; I may dye when I will."

Give the way to any that you meete: yf he have a better horse it is duty; yf a worse, in pity; yf the way be fayre you are in, commonly it is foule hard by, and soe you shall have power to durty him that you give the way, not he you. (Burdett.)

Yf you put a case in the first bookes of the lawe to the auncientes, you may presume they may have forgotten it; yf in the newe bookes, you may doubt whether they have reade it. (Bur[dett].)

FOLIO 102b

Febru. 1602.

Sir Henry Unton was soe cunning a bargayner for landes that they which dealt with him were commonly greate loosers, whereupon Mr. Duns of Barkshire said that he bought landes with witt and sold them with rhetorick. (Chute.)

My taylor Mr. Hill, a little pert fellowe, was upon a tyme brought before the L[ord] Chamberlaine, and accused that he had heard one Harlestone curse the E[arl] of Leister in his house. But Hill denying it, the L[ord] Cha[mberlain] threatning him, called him

rogue and raskall, that would hear noblemen abused and yet justifie to. Hill replyed that he was neither rogue nor raskall, but a
poore artificer, that lived by his labour. The Lord demaund[ed]
what trade. "A taylor," said Hill. "O, then a theife by profession,"
said the L[ord], "and yet yf thou beest a theife thou art but a
prettie little one. But, sirra, you rogue, what say you to the matter
of my L[ord] of Leister?" "O, my L[ord]," said he, "I heard noe
such matter." "I will hang you, you raskall," said the L[ord].
"You shall hang a true man, my L[ord]," sayd Hill. "What, and a
taylor!" said the Lord. Soe leaving Hill when he could not force
him to confesse, he went to the accuser and told him he must not
come and trouble him with such trifles, which were fauls to; and
yf it had bin true, yet yf he should committ every one to prison
that spake evil of Leister or himselfe, he should make as many
prisons in London as there be dwelling houses.

FOLIO 103

Marche. 1602.

20. *Laudo navigantem, cum pervenerit ad portum.* (Ch. Da.)

Si praebendari, si vis alta locari,
  Consilium praesto, de sanguine praesulis esto.
(Burdett.)

Fayth is the evidence of thinges not seene; as wee hold our
temporall inheritaunce by our writinges, which we call our evidence, soe wee clayme our eternall inheritaunce in the heavens by
fayth, which is our evidence. (On[e] King at Paules.)

Risus potest esse causa aliqua, irrisus nulla. Irridere bona nefas,
mala crudelitas, media stultitia, probos impium, improbos saevum,
notos immanitas, ignotos dementia, denique hominem inhumanum.
(Lodov. Vives, *ad. Sap:* intr. 439.)

E bestijs, exiatiatis maxime ferarum est Invidiae mansuetarum
assentatio. (Idem.)

FOLIO 103b

Febr. 28.

One said of Rochester that it had been an Auncient towne, as though it were not more auncient by continuance. (H. Gellibrand *nar.*)

A whore is noe worse then a Catt, for she plays with her tayle, and a whore does noe more. (One in the tillbuow as I came from Lond.)

Dr. Covels booke which he wrote as an appology of Mr. Hooker may be sayd to be all heaven, butt yett Mr. Hookers sentences, and discourses intermixed, are the stars and constellations, the speciall ornaments of it.

One discoursing of a gent[leman], Dr. Cesars wives first husband, that had bin imployed as a Ligier in France, "I well beleeve it," said an other, "that he hath bin a Lecher in Fraunce."

Dr. Caesar's wife was at first but a mayd servant in London; till advanct by hir first marriage. When hir Majesty Dyned at Dr. Caesars, shee gave his wife a checke, because in hir widdowhood she refused to speake with a Courtier whom hir Majesty had commended to hir. (Cose.)

When a minister was reading the wordes in mariage "Wilt thou have this man as thy wedded husband," the Bryde presently cryed, "O God, I, Sir," as though shee had tarried for him.

FOLIO 104

November. 1602.

Upon one Sunday this moneth Dr. Holland, Professor at Oxeford, made a sermon at Paules crosse; his text, Luke 12, v. 13, 14, &c.

"Take heed of covetousnes, for though a man have abundaunce, his life standeth not in riches."

2 partes: a caveat; 2. the reason. The reason: by a negative, 1. Mans lyfe not in abundance; 2. by a similitude.

He noted a difference between the Syriack and the Greeke. The Syriac sayth Christ spake to his disciples; the Greeke, to the brethren that strove for the inheritaunce.

In the caveat considered 1. the giver, Christ; 2. the brevity; 3. the occasion, the falling out of brethren.

All that followe Christ are his disciples.

The giver is Christ, which is Amen, *verax,* omniscient, he that knowes the wave of the serpent upon the stone, of an arrowe in the ayre, and a ship in the sea. *Multa habent auctoritatem propter dicentem.* He can tell us *latet anguis in herba.* The 2 eyes of the Lambe a great watchman to tell us the danger of synn, that it hath the face of a woman, but the sting of a scorpion.

Brevitye: one word of Christ a whole sermon; the ten commaundmentes are called but 10 wordes, Deut. 4:13. The whole lawe but one word, Love, of God and our neighbour, ὁ ὢν, ὁεί, δ ἐρχόμενος, ἀ and ὠ. One word of God overthrewe the whole kingdom of Assiria. Adams synne was the breach but of one commaundement, yet condemned the whole world. Relligion is one,

FOLIO 104b

though questions be infinit, yet all must be determined *per unum verbum domini scriptum. Verbum indicabit,* all must be resolved *per primam veritatem.*

Our soule can never be quiet till it be resolved by the word of God. Neither can wee have any perfection till wee have a seed of Gods.

Some have gone about to shewe the truth of relligion by casting
out divels. David must come out with his two stones, the old and
the newe testament, before Goliah can be slayne.

He would not speake against the good use of riches.

*Divitiae nec putentur mala, quia dantur bonis: neque bona, quia
conferuntur malis.*

Though the soule neede none of these goods of riches, yet the
body doth, *propter victum et vestitum,* and therefore we pray, *Da
nobis hodie panem nostrum quotidianum.*

God is the author of them, and soe being the giftes of God they
cannot be evil in their nature.

Diverse virtues followe and depend upon riches, as magnificence,
munificence, &c; hence have these goodly churches beene builded,
famous colledges found[ed], warrs mainteyned, &c.

The use of riches is to serve our owne necessity, Godes glory, to
doe good to the poore, to lend to the needy, to reward the virtuous,
to make frend of, &c. Yet the gift can not merrit, for yf I give all
that I have, yet yf I want charitie, &c. Yet *facta in fide mediatoris,*
they shall not want a reward: "Come ye blessed of my Father,
when I was naked you clothed me," &c.

The abuse of riches is covetousnes. Covetousnes is an Hydra with
7 heades; i.[e.], the Divel is the author of it; he tempted Christ
with riches, when he shewed him δόεαν, the glory of the world.
The divel could make shewes; he was a cunning Juggler.

FOLIO 105

The 2[n]d heade, the name, which is an ill name, to covet house,
land, &c. allways taken in the ill part; *avaritia,* in Latin, *aviditas
aeris,* φιλαργνρία—not a good name amongst them all. 3rd. The
daughters of Covetousnes: 1. *Rapina,* robbery. 2. Φιλαργνρία.
3. *Oppressio.* 4. *Furtum.* 5. *Homicidium.* 6. *Proditio.* 7. *Fallacia.*

8. *Mendacia.* 9. *Obduratio,* whereof more at this day then the
Bishop of Constance burnt poore people in a barne which came for
a dole. 10. *Usuria:* this rangeth abroad over the whole land. 11.
Bribery. 12. *Symonia,* Lady Symonie, a shameless on[e]. 13. *Sacri-
legium,* the end *Superbia,* which conteines all and holdes all things
to base for himselfe. 4th head, the effects of covetousnes:
1. Hatred. 2. Misery. 3. Contempt. 4. Forgetfulnes of God. 5. *Suffo-
catio,* sorrowe. 6. Danger, death of body and soule; howe many
have bin slayne for riches, or dyed in them. 5th head, it is the
roote of all evill (1 Tim. 6. 10): it is an evill of generality. Some
nations are sicke but of one vice: but he that hath this hath all; it
is hardly cured, it growes by continuance; *peccatum clamans,* it is
maxime inimicum Deo, for hee gave all by creacion to all equally,
but this strives to drawe all to it selfe most unequally. Of such a
man it is sayd *abstulit a pauperibus, congregavit, et manet in
aeternum eius infamia.* 6th head, similitudes, all evill: it is compared to the Dropsy, a disquieting kinde of thirst; to leaches, which
sucke till they burst. 7th, the end: he gathers he knowes not for
whom.

The reason, mans life consistes not in the abundance of riches: 1.
because both when we came into the world, though wee were naked,
yet wee then lived, and before that too;

FOLIO 105b

2. wee shall carry nothing away with us when we dye, yet our soules
shall live; 3. they cannot deliver us from death.

Riches are incertayne, and therefore Eschines compares them to
Euripus, which ebbes and flowes oftentymes in a day. An other
says they are winged, because the[y] passe away soe swiftly; and
fortune hir selfe is allways painted upon a wheeling stone, to note
the inconstancy of riches; and certaine it is that at last yf they part
not from us, wee must part from them.

The parable. A riche man, though he be riche, yet he must dye; for he is but a man. God would have some riche, some poore, for distinction sake, and the mutuall exercise of liberality and patience, whereby the opinion of the Anabaptistes is easily confuted, whoe would have all things alike common. *Admirabilis concatenatio* in the order of thinges and states.

God made noe miraculous provision for his disciples, therefore there ought to be an ordinary provision for the ministery.

As the people love the ministeres for their spirituall blessinges, soe the ministers love the people for their temporall commodities.

The order of professions: 1. relligion; 2. husbandry; 3. merchandise; 4. souldiery.

Abuse in acquirendo, concupiscendo, consumendo.

The covetous man reasons with himselfe in his bed, where wee should *bonum omissum, malum commissum, tempus amissum, deflere.* David sayth, "Lord, I remember the in my bed."

"I will pull downe;" surely he was a man of this age, pul downe colledges, Churches, cyties, kingdomes; every one cryes "Down with Jerusalem!" An easy matter to pull downe that which was in building forty yeares; he will build it agen;

FOLIO 106

soe will not many an other doe.

The foole when his owne belly is full thinkes all the worlde hath enoughe. "Eate, soule! drinke, soule!" a hog may say as much. "I will pull downe, I will build." Here is all "I," nothing but himselfe.

Presumption that he shall enjoy all; whence he noted his infidelity, security, carnality, ευτραπελία

Of the soule. The soule is the image of God, *Christi redempta sanguine, haeres cum Angelis, capax coelestis beatitudinis, simplex, immortalis, incorporea.* It useth *organa*, instuments. God giveth, not man begge[tte]th it. 21 Exod. 22. *Creando infunditur, infundendo creatur.* God is the father of soules, and the soule returneth to God that gave it (Ecclesiastes).

Anima imago Dei, in justitia et dominio.

Relligion of the Turk more towards their Alcoran then our[s] to the Scripture; speake but against that there, it is death.

He that dishonoureth his father, or disobeyeth the magistrat, every where punished, but for Godes dishonour fewe take care or vengeance.

This thought he spake to himselfe, but God puls him by the sleeve, and calls him by his name, "Thou foole!"

The godly give up their soules, but the soules of the wicked are taken from them.

FOLIO 106b

Marche. 1602.

> Femme que dona s'abandona,
> Femme que prende se vende;
> Femme que regarde son honneur
> Non veult prendre, ne donner. (My Cosen.)

1. My cosen told me: That about some 24 yeares since, the Prince of Aurange, being driven to some necessity, sent for reliefe to hir Majesty, with protestation that yf shee fayled to supply their wantes he must turne pirate. And soe receyving but a cold aunswere, all they of Flushing and other partes adjoining instantly of merchantes became good men of warr, and tooke our merchantes fleete & forced them to lend 50,000£., which was never repayd. Yet when they had served their turnes for that extremity, and after divers complaintes made by our merchants to our Q[ueen] against their

piracys, had receyved message from hir Majesty to desist from those courses, they presently retyred themselves on a sudden, every one to his former trade. Of soe apt a nature is that nation for any purpose.

There was a company of yong gallantes sometyme in Amsterdame which called themselves the Damned crue. They would meete togither on nightes, and vowe amongst themselves to kill the next man they mett whosoever; soe Divers murthers committed, but not one punished. Such impunity of murder is frequent in that Country. (My Cosen *narrav.*)

FOLIO 107

Marche. 1602.

1: My cosen repeated *memoriter* almost the first booke of Virg[ils] AEniads.
3. And this day he rehersed without booke verry neere the whole 2[n]d booke of the Aeneads, viz. 630 verses without missing one word. A singular memory in a man of his age: 62.

You shall never see a deares scutt cover his haunche, nor a fooles tongue his frendes secrett.

FOLIO 107b

Notes of a sermon upon the 15th ch. to the Corinth. verse 22: "As in Adam all dye, soe in Christ shall all men be made alive."

The judgement of the first disobedience was Death. And in truth, God could doe noe lesse, unlesse he would be unjust, for as in wisdome he had ordayned that man should dye when he tasted the fruit of the forbidden tree, soe in justice he was to execute what in wisdome he had decreed.

Christ was like Adam in his preheminence, in being the cheife and having government over all creature[s]. But yet unlike in this, that Adam was the cause of death, but Christ is the cause of lyfe unto all that beleeve in him.

There is a tyme for all to dye; and this act of dying is done by us, and upon us. It is a sentence which comprehendeth all though all apprehend not it.

Adam was one before all, one over all, and all in one, by whose synn all taynted; soe Christ, by whom all saved: 1 Tim. 2:4.

Man is the principall cause in the course of generacion, but woman was in the fall of Adam. 1 Tim. 2:14.

Those which are sicke of the wantonnes make many answereles, end-les, needeles questions, about the fall of Adam, &c.

There be synnes p[er]sonall and synnes naturall; these wee derive ofttymes from our parents, as a synne in us and punishment of them. Soe Adultery, and drunkennes of father, is oft tymes punished in an adulterous and cupshott childe.

FOLIO 108

Death 3^x: externall, internall, eternall. 1. Separacion of body and soule. 2. Of sowle from Christ, which is our lyfe; soe was that spatterlashe widdowe, 1 Tim. 5:6, dead while she lived. 3. Of body and soule in hell fyre.

It was an errour of Pelagius that man should have dyed though he had neve[r] synned.

FOLIO 108b

Notes of a sermon upon Matth. 5:17: "Thinke not that I am come to destroy the lawe, or the prophets: I am not come to destroy them, but to fullfill them."

The best could not live free from slaunders, as Nehemias was charged to have rebelled, &c. and Christ him selfe could not escape the malitious censures of the wicked. When he cured the sicke of the palsy saying, "Thy synnes bee forgiven thee," these whispered in their hartes, and called that speach blasphemy. When he disposs[ess]ed the man that was vexed with a Devil, they said he cast out Devils by Beelzebub the prince of the Devils. When he suffered for us they sayd he was plagued for his owne offences.

But Augustine sayth well of these men: *Hoc facilius homo suspicator in altero, quod sentit in seipso.*

The lawe stretcht noe further then the outward action, but Christ layes it to the secret thought.

Synnes in our thoughtes are like a snake in our bosome, which may kill us yf wee nurse it; it is like fyre to gunpowder.

Wee must shake synn from our thoughtes as wee would a spark from our garments, lest yf wee be once sett on fyre with them all our teares shall not quenche them.

The divel puts synn in our thoughtes as a theife thrustes a boy in at a windowe, to open the dore for the great ones.

FOLIO 109

Yf syn enter into the heart it becomes like a denn of theeves, and like a cage of uncleane birdes.

Synn a sly thing; it will enter at the windowe at the casement, at a chinke of our cogitations.

The more free wee are to syn, the more slaves are wee to Sathan.

Will a theife steale in the sight of the Judge? and shall a man presume to synn in the sight of God?

AT A SPITTLE SERMON.

Yf our synnes come out with a newe addicion, Godes punishmentes
will come out with a newe edition.

Ambrose sayd of Theodosius: *Fides Theodosii vestra fuit victoria;*
soe he of Q[ueene] Elizabeth.

FOLIO 109b

March. 1603.

June. 1603

8. My cosen told me the strange manner of the wolves in their generation. The bitche, when shee growes proud, gathers a companie of
the doges togither and runnes before them soe long, that having
tyred them and hir selfe, she lyes downe, and they fall a sleepe about
hir; then she riseth alone and singles out one which shee likes best,
and he does the deede; but instantly after all the rest fall upon him,
and teare him in peeces for it.

   Observe: The wolfe dyes with gettinge his yong, as the Viper doth
by bearing hir yong ones. 2. an old man that kills him selfe to gett a
child.

FOLIO 110

Marche. 1602.

23. I was at the Court at Richemond, to heare Dr. Parry one of hir
Majesties chapleins preache, and to be assured whether the Queene
were living or dead. I heard him, and was assured shee was then

living. His text was out of the Psalme [96:18,19]: "Nowe will I pay my vowes unto the Lord in the middest of the congregacion," &c. It was a verry learned, eloquent, relligious, and moving sermon; his prayer, both in the beginning and conclusion, was soe fervent and effectuall for hir Majestie that he left few eyes drye.

The doctrine was concerning vowes, which were growne in contempt and hatred because the Jews of old and the papistes of later tymes have used them, whereas the thing it selfe, in i[t]s owne nature, is reasonable and commendable. Wee owe all that wee have, that wee are, unto God; and all that we can doe is but our bounden duty, yet those offices may seeme to please him best, and be most gratefull, which even besydes those dutyes which he requires, wee doe enter of our owne will as it were into a newe, a neere[r] bond. And he defined it to be a promise made unto God, to performe some service in such manner as wee are not otherwise bound by duty to p[er]forme. It must be made to God, soe it differs from other promises; it must be voluntary, and soe differs from required dutyes; it must be deliberate, which takes away rashnes; it must be of thinges possible within our power, of things that are good, and tending to Godes glory and our bettering.

And they are generally either *penitentiae,* of a strict course of life, in punishing our synfull bodies

FOLIO 110b

Marche. 1602.

23. by spare dyet, &c.; *gratitudinis,* for benefites received; 3. *amicitiae:* testimonyes of our love, *dona.*

Vowes of p[er]petuall chastity and solitude exculed [exculcated?] because of a generall impossibility. Noe merit to be hoped by them, soe the papisticall abolished.

Certaine impediments which being removed any man may walke the way without stumbling.

1. Wee cannot performe what wee are commaunded; howe can wee then add anie thing of our owne?
2. The danger of breaking them should stay us from making them.
3. They were ceremonious with the Jewes, and supersticious amongst the papistes, therefore not to be reteyned.

These were present at his sermon: the Archbishop of Canterbury [Whitgift]; the L[ord] Keep[er] [Egerton]; the L[ord] Treasuror [Buckhurst]; L[ord] Admiral [Howard]; E[arl] of Shrewsbury; E[arl] of Worster; L[ord] Cobham; L[ord] Gray; Sir William Knollys; Sir Ed[ward] Wotten, &c.

FOLIO 111

Marche.

23. I dyned with Dr. Parry in the Privy chamber, and understood by him, the bishop of Chichester, the deane of Canterbury, the deane of Windsore, &c. that hir Majestie hath bin by fittes troubled with melancholy some 3 or 4 monethes, but for this fourtnight ex-treame oppressed with it, in soe much that shee refused to eate anie thing, to receive any phisike, or admit any rest in bedd, till within these 2 or three dayes. Shee hath bin in a manner speacheles for 2 dayes, verry pensive and silent; since shrovetides sitting some-tymes with hir eye fixed upon one object many howres togither, yet shee alwayes had hir perfect senses, and memory, and yesterday signified by the lifting up of hir hand, and eyes to heaven, a signe which Dr. Parry entreated of hir, that shee beleeved that fayth which shee hath caused to be professed, and looked faythfully to be saved by Christes merits and mercy only, and noe other meanes. She tooke great delight in hearing prayers, would often at the name of Jesus lift up hir handes and eyes to Heaven. Shee would not heare the Arch[bishop] speake of hope of hir longer lyfe, but when he prayed or spake of Heaven and those joyes, shee would hug his hand, &c. It seemes shee might have lived yf she would have used meanes; but shee would not be persuaded, and princes must not be

forced. Hir physicians said shee had a body of a firme and perfect constitucion, likely to have lived many yeares.

A royall majesty is noe priviledge against death.

FOLIO 111b

Marche. 1602.

24. This morning about 3 at clocke hir Majestie departed this lyfe, mildly like a lambe, easily like a ripe apple from the tree, *cum leve quadam febre, absque gemitu*. Dr. Parry told me that he was present and sent his prayers before hir soule; and I doubt not but shee is amongst the royall saintes in heaven in eternall joyes.

About 10 at clocke the Counsell and diverse noblemen, having bin a while in consultacion, proclaymed James the 6, K[ing] of Scots, the King of England, Fraunce, and Irland, beginning at White hall gates, where Sir Robert Cecile reade the proclamacion, which he carried in his hand and after reade againe in Cheapside.

Many noblemen, lords spirituell and temporell, knightes, 5 trumpets, many herauldes.

The gates at Ludgate and portcullis were shutt and downe, by the Lord maiors commaund, who was there present, with the aldermen, &c., and untill he had a token besyde promise, the L[ord] Treasurers George, that they would proclayme the K[ing] of Scots King of England, he would not open.

Upon the death of a king or Q[ueene] in England the L[ord] maior of London is the greatest magistrate in England. All corporacions and their governors continue, most of the other officeres authority is expired with the princes breath.

There was a diligent watch and ward kept at every gate and street, day and night, by housholders, to prevent garboiles: which God be thanked were more feared then perceived.

FOLIO 112

Marche. 1602.

24. The proclamacion was heard with greate expectacion, and silent joye, noe great shouting. I thinke the sorrowe for hir Majesties departure was soe deep in many heartes they could not soe suddenly shewe anie great joy, though it could not be lesse then exceeding greate for the succession of soe worthy a King. And at night they shewed it by bonefires, and ringing.

Noe tumult, noe contradicion, noe disorder in the city; every man went about his busines, as readylie, as peaceably, as securely, as though there had bin noe change, nor any newes ever heard of competitors. God be thanked, our king hath his right: *magna veritas et prevalet.* Doubtles there was a grave, wise counsell and deliberacion in fact; *sed factum est hoc a Domino,* we must needes confesse. And I hope wee may truly say, *Nobis parta quies.* The people is full of expectacion, and great with hope of his worthines, of our nations future greatnes; every one promises himselfe a share in some famous action to be hereafter performed, for his prince and Country. They assure themselves of the continuance of our church government and doctrine.

Their talke is of advauncement of the nobility, of the subsidies and fifteenes taxed in the Q[ueenes] tyme; howe much indebted shee died to the commons, notwithstanding all those charges layed upon them.

FOLIO 112b

Marche. 1602.

They halfe despayre of payment of their privey seales, sent in Sir William Ceciles tyme; they will not assure themselves of the lone.

One wishes the E[arl] of Southampton and others were pardoned,
and at liberty; others could be content some men of great place
might pay the Q[ueenes] debtes, because they beleeve they
gathered enough under hir.

But all long to see our newe king.

This evening prayer at Paules the King was publikely prayed for,
in forme as our Q[ueene] used to be.

The L[ord] Hunsdon was in his coache at paules hill beyond
ludgate, to attend the proclamacion.

It is observed that one Lee was maior of London at hir Majesties
comming to the Crowne, an[d] nowe another Lee at hir decease.

25. This day the proclamacions were published in print, with names
of many noblemen, and late Counsellors.

The feares of wise men are the hopes of the malitious.

26. Mr. Francis Curle told me howe one Dr. Bullein, the Q[ueenes]
kinsman, had a dog which he doted one, soe much that the
Q[ueene], understanding of it, requested he would graunt hir one
desyre, and he should have whatsoever he would aske. Shee demaunded his dogge; he gave it, and "Nowe, Madame," q[uoth] he,
"you promised to give me my desyre." "I will," q[uoth] she.
"Then I pray you give me my dog againe."
    A foole will not loose his bable for a ——— [MS imperfect].

FOLIO 113

Marche. 1603.

26. *Quod taceri vis, prior ipse taceas. Arcanum quid aut celandum
maxime amico quum committis, cave ne jocum admisceas, ne ille
jocum ut referat occultum retegat.* (Ludovic. Vives, *Ad Sapient,*
introd. 487.)
29. *Corrumpitur atque, dissolvitur officium imperantis, si quis ad*

id quod facere jussus est, non obsequio debito, sed consilio non desiderato respondeat. (A gellius.)

He that corrupts a Prince and perverts his government is like one that poisons the head of a conduit; all inquire after him to have him punished.

30. Three thinges which make other[s] poore make Alderman Lee, nowe maior, riche: wine, women, and dice; he was fortunat in marrying riche wives, lucky in great gaming at dice, and prosperous in sale of his wines. (Pemberton.)

FOLIO 113b

Marche. 1603.

27. At White hall, Dr. Thomson, deane of Windsore, whoe at thys tyme attendes still with Dr. Parry as chaplein, was by course to have preached this day, but Dr. King was appointed and performed that duty. His text was the gospell for this day, the 11th. of Luke and the 14th verse, and soe foreward. He prayed for the King, that as God had given him an head of gold, soe hee would give him a golden brest, golden leges, and feet alsoe; that as he had a peace-able and quiet entrance, soe he would graunt him a wise and happie government, and a blessed ending, when soever he should take him from us; that it would please God to laye his roote soe deepe that he may flourishe a long tyme, and his braunches never fayle.

The summe of his text in these partes: 1. a Divel cast out; 2. the Dumb speake; 3. the multitude wonder; 4. the scribes and pharisees slander; 5. Christ confuteth; 6. a woman confesseth.

The ende of Christes comming was to dissolve the workes of the divel, whereof possession was not the meanest. Can there be a greater then to take the temple of the Holy Ghost, and make it the sell and shrine of the divels image?

Non requiritur intelligendi vivacitas, sed credendi simplicitas.

Indocti coelum rapiunt, dum nos cum doctrina nostra trudimur in infernum.

The workes of Christ, his miracles, were manifest, *posuit in sole tabernaculum:* he cast out a divel, they sawe it, they could not deny it; but then, what malice could, they deprave the fact or diminishe and eclipse his glory.

Judei signum quaerunt. Julian cals it the Rusticity of faythe, as though none but the simple rude multitude beleve.

FOLIO 114

Marche. 1603.

27. *Invidia non quaerit, quid dicat, sed tantum ut dicat.* The envious and malitious live onely in contradiction, like the bettle in dung and filthines.

They said not that Christ could not cast out a divel, and soe denyed his power, which is a synn against the Holy Ghost, but they said him selfe was possessed, nay more that he was belzebub.

Belzeebub signifies an Idoll of flyes: because there was soe much bloud spilt in sacrifice before it that many flyes bred and lived upon it.

Christ confuted them by 4 reasons: 1. From autority: a maxime and rule in all policy that a kingdome divided against it selfe cannot stand. 2. From example: by whom doe your children, his apostles and disciples he meanes, cast them out? Yf they doe it by the finger of God, then must I, except the same thing be not the same, yf other persons doe it. Atticus and Ruternus [?] (*idem non idem si non p[er] eundem*) unles they will allowe the thing and condemne the person.

But he said, *Testes mei Judices vestri.* 3. From a similitude: of a stronge and a stronger man, two warlike men, yf one kepe possession, he must be stronger that puts him out; soe he must be greater than the divel that can cast him out. 4. From the contrary: the repugnancy betwixt Christ and the divel.

He insisted most upon his first reason, of intestine discord, which he said is like a consumption; as yf the head should pull out the eye, or the mouth refuse to eate because the belly receives it, &c. This is that plague that Aegypt shall fight against Aegypt, brother against brother, &c.

FOLIO 114b

Marche. 1603.

27. In the 11th of Zacharia there are two staves mentioned, the one of beauty, the other of bondes; it is a grevous plague which is there threatened, *dissolvam germanitatem eorum:* their brother-hood, of Judah and Israel. Ephraim against Manasse and Manasse against Ephraim, two tribes of the same family; the incomparable miseryes of Jerusalem by intestine sedicion.

Auxilia humana firma consensus facit.

Agesilaus shewed his armed men a mind in consent for defense of the city, and said, *Hii sunt Muri Spartae, scutum haerens scuto, galeae galea, atque viro vir.*

Friendes at discord are most deadly enimyes, and those thinges which before were *ligamenta amoris* became then *incitamenta furoris.*

The greatest wronges are most eagerly pursued; such are commonly the causes for which frendes fall out.

Quasi musto inebrientur sanguine.

Even the divel must have his due; it was commendable that a legion of them could dwell togither in one man, without discord amongst themselves.

Scarse a few in one house but some jar betwixt them.

Yet their concord was not *ex amicitia, sed ex communi malitia,* like Herod & Pilat.

Aliquod bonum absque malo, sed nullum malum absque aliquo bono; even in the divels their essence and their order is good.

There is a tyme to gather, said he, and a tyme to scatter, but he had scattered what he had scarce any tyme to gather; his comming up to this place being *tanquam fungus e terra,* an evening and a morning being the whole tyme allotted for meditacion, and disposicion.

FOLIO 115

Marche. 1603.

27. Wee may not be undmindefull of our late soveraigne whom God hath called to his mercy, nor ought wee be unthankefull for our newe suffected joy, by the suddein peaceable succession of our worthy king.

The finger of the Spirit directed the churche, and the order of [the] Church lead me (said he) to the choise of this text, being the gospell for this day.

There are that have slandered, but they are Scribes and Pharisees; and that being the worst part of this text, he would passe over it.

There were feares and foretellinges of miseries like to fall upon us at these times, but blessed be the God of peace, that hath setled peace amongst us. Blessed be the God of truth, that his kingdome came unto us long since, and I hope shall continue even till the comming of Christ; and blessed be the father of lights, that wee see the truth, and be not scattered.

The miracle of dispossession. Wee have seene the exile of the divel out of our Country, his legendes, his false miracles, exorcismes, supersticions, &c., and lett him goe walking through dry places; wee are watered with heavenly deawe, and wee hope he shall never returne againe; but the favour of God towards us shall be like the kindenes of Ruth more at the latter end than it was at the beginning.

Our state hath sustayned some Division of late. "I mean not," sayd he, "of the myndes of great nobles and Counsellors, wherein to our good and comfort wee have found *idem velle et idem nolle;* but such a division as of the body and soule,

FOLIO 115b

Marche. 1603.

27. of the Vine and the branches, of the husband and the wife, of the head and the body: the prince and the land hath bin divided by hir death, a division without violence. This applying the axe to the roote made the tree bleed at the verry heart."

This gospell makes mention of an excellent woman that sang not to hir selfe and hir muses, but went amongst the multitude, and blessed an other woman more excellent then hir selfe; yet soe blessed hir as a mother for hir babe's sake.

Soe there are two excellent women, one that bare Christ and an other that blessed Christ; to these may wee joyne a third, that bare and blessed him both: shee bare him in hir heart as a wombe, shee conceived him in fayth, shee brought him forth in aboundaunce of good workes, and nurst him with favors and protection; shee blessed him in the middest of a froward and wicked generacion, when the bulls of bazan roared, and the unholie league, and bound themselves with oethes and cursings against the Lord and his annoynted.

"And am I entred into hir prayses," said he; "and nowe is the tyme of prayse, for prayse none before their death; and then *gratissima laudis actio cum nullus fingendi aut assentandi locus relinquitur.* Yet such prayses are but like a messe of meate sett upon a dead mans grave which he cannot tast, or like a light behind a mans back which cannot direct him."

He would say little, *non quod ingratus, sed quod oppressus multitudine et magnitudine rerum dicendarum*; onely he would say that

FOLIO 116

Marche. 1602.

27. hir government had bin soe clement, temperat and godly, that he may say *Sic imbuti sumus, non possumus nisi optimum ferre.* Those which in Theodosius the Emperours tyme went to Rome called their travel *felix peregrinatio,* because they had seen Rome, they had seen Theodosius, they had seene Rome and Theodosius togither; soe have and may strangeres that have bin to visit our kingdome thinke them selves happie that they had seene England, and Q[ueene] Elizabeth, and England and Q[ueene] Elizabeth togither. But there are panegyricks provided for hir, faythfully registred, and as she merited. Shee was *preteritis melior,* better then those which went before hir, and may be a precedent to those that shall followe hir; the taking hir from us was a great division, but God hath sowed it up again; it was greivous sore, but God hath healed it; he hath given us a worthy successor, a sonne of the nobles; one that is fleshe of our fleshe. God seemes to say to us, "Open thy mouth wide and I will fill it with aboundant blessinges"; he may say as he did to his vine, "what should I have done that I have not done unto thee, O England?" Noe vacancy, noe interregnum, noe interruption of government, as in Rome an[d] other places, where in such tymes the prisons fly open, &c.; but a quiet, a peace[a]ble, and present succession, of such a king *quem populus et proceres voce petebat,* the best wished and the onely agreed upon. The Lord from his holy sanctuary blesse him in his throne.

FOLIO 116b

Marche. 1603.

27. It was noe shame for Solomon to walke in the wayes of his father David; neither can it be a dishonour for our K[ing] to walke in the steps of his mother and predecessor. Lett the foster-sonne and sonnes sonne continue their glory, grace and dignity, and never lett him want one of his seede to sit upon his seate.

Then to the nobles, for their wise menaging those greate affayres: *"Utinam retribuat Dominus,"* said he, "and, as Nehemias prayed for him selfe, 'Remember them, O God in goodnes.' Your peace" (said he) "continued ours, and long may you continue in firme alledgeance to doe your prince and Country service in wisdome, honour, and piety."

"And this is noe *detractio, sed attractio, impius in tenebris latet,* he holds his peace; but Lord open thou our lips, and our mouth shall shewe forth thy prayse: *Paratum est cor meum,* my heart is ready, my heart is ready," &c.

FOLIO 117

Marche.

27. It was bruited that the L[ord] Beauchamp, the E[arl] of Hart-fordes sonne, is up in armes, and some say 10,000 strong. Mr. Hadsor told me the Lords sate about it upon
28. Satterday night, and have dispatcht a messenger to entreat him to come unto them, or els to be in danger of proclamacion of treason. An other bruit that Portsmouth is holden for him, that the Frenche purpose against us, that the Papistes are like to rise with Beauchamp (they may trouble us, but I hope shall not prevaile).

"He is up," said one. "He is risen," said an other. "True, I thinke," said I, "he rose in the morning and meanes to goe to bed at night."

Ch. Davers said he could tell the K[ing] what he were best to doe (not to change his officers). "Nay then it were best to choose you first for a Counsellor," said I.

I sawe this afternoone a Scottishe Lady at Mr. Fleetes in Loathebury; shee was sister to Earl Gowre, a gallant tale gent[lewoman], somewhat long visage, a lisping fumbling language. Peter Saltingstone came to visit hir.

29. I askt Mr. Leydall whether he argued a case according to his opinion. He said noe, but he sett a good colour upon it. I told him he might well doe soe, for he never wants a good colour; he is Rufus.

Mr. Rudyerd tels that to muster men in these tymes is as good a colour for sedicion, as a maske to robbe a house, which is excellent for that purpose.

FOLIO 117b

Marche. 1603.

29. Mr. Rous said that the Q[ueene] began hir raigne in the fall and ended in the spring of the leafe. "Soe shee did but turne over a leafe," said B. Rudyerd.

30. Was reported that the K[ing] had sent for some 5,000£. to bring him into England. It is said the Q[ueenes] jewe[l]s shee left were worth 4 millions [?], i.e. 400,000£.; in treasury present, 50,000£. (noe soe much this long tyme).

The Kinges booke Basi[li] con Doron came forth with an Epistle to the reader apologeticell.

A man may doe an other a good turne though he cannot performe it for himselfe, as the barber cannot trimme himselfe though he can others. (Pim.)

It was sayd our K[ing] is proclaymed nowe Duke of Gelderlaund.

29. Jo[hn] Grant told me that the K[ing] useth in walking amongst
his nobles often tymes to leane upon their shoulders in a speciall
favour, and in disgrace to neglect some in that kindenes.

30. It is sayd Sir R[o]b[er]t Cary, that went against the Counsells
directions in post toward the K[ing] to bring the first newes of the
Q[ueenes] death, made more hast then speede; he was soe hurt with
a fall from his horse that an other prevented his purpose and was
with the K[ing] before him. This Cary had an office in the Jewell
house.

31. This night there came a messinger from the K[inges] Majestie
with letteres directed to the nobles and Counsellors of his late
sister the deceased Q[ueen]: all to continue their places, and keepe
house, and order matteres according to their discretion till he come.
(Isam.)

A puritane is such a one as loves God with all his soule, but hates
his neighbour with all his heart. (Mr. Wa. Curle.)

FOLIO 118

Marche. 1603.

31.   Of a beggar that lay on the ground (Dun)
He can not goe nor sitt nor stand, the beggar cryes;
Then though he speake the truthe yet still he lyes.

I was in Mr. Nich. Hares companie at the Kinges Head. A gallant
yong gent[leman], like to be heir to much land; he is of a sweet
behaviour, a good spirit, and a pleasing witty discourse.

It was soe darke a storme, that a man could never looke for day,
unles God would have said againe *fiat lux.*

Two were going to washe them selves; one spied the others prepu-
tian discovered: "I pray you be coverd," q[uoth] he.

A wenche complained that she was ravished in a chamber, and being asked howe chaunce shee cryed not, "Why, there were some in the next roome," said shee, "and the[y] would have heard mee!" An other said shee could not cry for laughing. (Mr. Hare).

A gent[lemans] nose fell a bleeding verry late in a night, and soe causing his boy to light him downe to a pumpe to washe the bloud away, he spied written upon the pump that it was built at the proper cost and charges of a physician which lay nere the place, whom he presently sent for to come to a lady that was dangerously sicke; but when he came he shewed that his nose was bloudy, that he went downe to have washt at the pompe, but espying it to be built at his proper costes and charges, he thought good manners to aske leave of him before he would washe at [it]. (Mr. N. Hare.)

FOLIO 118b

Aprill. 1603.

1. Dr. Some, upon a tyme speaking of the popes in a sermon, said that Pius 5th. sent out his bulles against the Queene like a calfe as he was. (Mr. Isam.)

2. I heard that one Griffin, Q[ueene] Marys Attorney, purchased some 24 mannors togither; his sonne hath sold 10 of them and yet is in debt; *male parta male dilabuntur.*

One Mr. Marrow, late Sherife of [Warwickshire], useth his wife verry hardly, would not allowe hir mony nor clothes fit for hir, nor trust hir with any thing, but made hir daughter sole factres. (Mr. Wagstaffe.)

A covetous fellowe had hangd himselfe, and was angry with him that cutt the rope to save his lyfe.

A covetous man rather will loose his lyfe then his goodes.

One when the house was on fyre, and himselfe ready to be burnt, fell a seeking for his girdle, amidst the fyre.

Homo impius quid aliud quam immortale pecus. (Ludovicus Vives.)

Faelices essent artes, si nulli de eis judicarent nisi artifices. (Mr. Maynard.)

He thinkes the statut of wills will be as greate a nurse of controversies as the statut of tayles and uses in common.

The egges are [?] layd, and are nowe in hatching. (*Idem.*)

FOLIO 119

Aprill.

1. Wee are purged from our corruption, *non per gratiam naturae, sed p[er] naturam gratiae.* (Dr. Dod.)

Wee worshipt noe saintes, but wee prayd to ladyes, in the Q[ueenes] tyme. (Mr. Curle.) This superstition shall be abolished, we hope, in our kinges raigne.

One reading Horace happened upon that verse
Virtus est vitium fugere, et sapientia prima stultitia caruisse.
"Here is strange matter," said he. "*Virtus est vitium.*" "Read on," said an other. "Nay first lett us examine this," and would not goe a word further. "Nay," said the other, "yf you gather such notes, I will finde an other as strange as that in the same verse: *Et sapientia prima stultitia.*" (T. Cranmer.)

Natura brevium. (Fitch.) The nature of Pigmies (said B. Rudyerd.)

3. Dr. Spenser upon the 1 Mark, v. 29 etc. to the 36. Christes sabboths dayes work, to cure the diseased; a miracle, a work of his mercy that he would, of his power that he could.

A man must take the tyme that Christ offereth himselfe: yf he was with Simon and Andrew at night, he parted into the wildernes in the morning.

The fever left hir, and shee ministred, v. 31.

Hence he collected the conveniency of Church-going for women to give publique thankes for safe deliverance.

FOLIO 119b

Aprill. 1603.

3. In the afternoone Clapham. He prayed for the King and his sonne Henry Frederick and Frederick Henry; prayed for a further reformacion in our Churche.
Note: the 7th moneth amongst the Jewes, according to their civil computacion, was but the first in their ecclesiasticall.

Close fisted, that will give nothing to the ministers, and musty doctors, that lett learning mould and rust in them for want of use.
4. Gluttony and lechery dwell togither, *Venter et genitalia sunt membra vicina* (Mr. Key.), as they are placed in that prayer, Ecclesiasticus 23. v. 6: "Lett not the gredines of the belly, nor the lust of the flesh, hold me." A great spender in leachery must be a great ravenour in glutony, to repayre what he looseth.

Dr. Parry told me the Countess Kildare assured him that the Queene caused the ring wherewith shee was wedded to the Crowne, to be cutt from hir finger some 6 weekes before hir death, but wore a ring which the Earl of Essex gave hir unto the day of hir death.

This day a letter gratulatory from the King to the Maior and City was read in publique in their Court.

FOLIO 120

Aprill. 1603.

5. I heard that Sir Robert Carewe lay in the Kinges chamber the first night he brought the newes of hir Majesties death, and there related the whole discourse; whereupon he was made one of his chamber. A place of confidence and meanes to preferment.

It is certaine the Queene was not embowelled, but wrapt up in cere cloth, and that verry il to, through the covetousnes of them that defrauded hir of the allowance of clothe was given them for that purpose.

6. There was a proclamacion published in the K[inges] name conteining his thankefullnes to the people for continuance in their duty in acknowledging him and receiving him as their rightfull successour, and a restraint of concurse unto him, especially such as were in office and had great place in their countryes, with a clause for continuing officers of justice in their place.

4. A letter gratulatory to the L[ord] Maior, Alderman, and Citizens was read in their court, which letter came from his Majestie, dated at Halliroode house, 28 Martij, 1603; it conteined a promise of his favour, with an admonission to continue their course of government for matters of justice.

FOLIO 120b

Aprill. 1603.

6. Dr. Overall, deane of Paules, made a sermon at Whitehall this day; his text,

> "Watch and pray that yee enter
> not into temptation."

He discoursed verry scholastically upon the nature of temptations, their division, &c.

fit for those tymes, in this change, least wee be tempted to desyre innovacion, &c.

He held that God permits many things to worke according to their nature, not forcing their actions by his decre; soe wee enter into temptacions unforced, of our owne accord, by his permission.

FOLIO 121

Aprill. 1603.

7. Mr. Timo[thy] Wagstaffe and my self brought in a moote where-at Mr. Stevens, the next reader, and Mr. Curle sate.

I heard there had bin a foule jarr betwixt Sir Robert Cecile and the L[ord] Cobham upon this occasion because the Lords and late Counsell, upon the Q[ueenes] death, had thought good to appoint an other captaine of the gard, because Sir Walter Rhaley was then absent, which the L[ord] Cobham tooke in foule dudgeon, as yf it had bin the devise of Sir Robert, and would have bin him selfe deputy to Sir Walter rather [than] any other.

The L[ord] Cobham likewise at subscribing to the proclamacion tooke exception against the E[arl] of Clanricard. *Inepte, intempestive*, but he is nowe gone to the King, they say.

The occasion of the bruite that was raysed of the L[ord] Beauchamps rising was but this: he had assembled diverse of his followers and other gent[lemen] to goe with him to proclayme the king, which a good lady not understanding, gave intelligence that he assembled his followeres; but upon the effect, hir self contradicted hir owne letter.

FOLIO 121b

Aprill. 1603.
At White Hall

8. Dr. Montague, M[aste]r of Sydney Colledge in Cambridge, made
a sermon; his text Matt. 18, v. 11:
"The Sonne of Man came to save that which was lost."

In his prayer: "Wee give our selves to synn, without restraint in our
conscience before, or remorse after."

He considered 3 pointes; 1. The stile of Christ, the Sonne of Man.
2. To whom he came, to the lost. 3. The end of his comming, to
save.

Where men come of an honorable parentage or beare an office of
dignity, it is their use to stile themselves in the name of their auncestors, as Solomon the sonne of David, &c. But where they have
none, the Jewes call them Ben Adam, the sonne of man.

Howe happens it then that Christ which is *Salvator mundi,* Εωτήρ,
the best word the Greekes have, that he takes upon him this stile
of basenes? For two reasons: 1. Because the nearer he came to our
nature, the neerer he came to our name; first before the lawe he
was called *Semen mulieris,* then *Shilo,* after *Messias,* and nowe himselfe gives himselfe this name, the Sonne of Man; by speciall effectes
changing his name; when he was Silo wee were but servantes, &c.
He layd downe his name to take up ours, that wee might for his
sake lay downe our lives to take up his glory.

He would not have his glory upon earth;

FOLIO 122

Aprill. 1603.

8. he would never suffer himselfe to be called God upon earth, nor
suffer his miracles to be blazoned; he would have his fame spread

by the inward persuasion of the Spirit, not the outward applause
of the mouth. And hence he noted the difference betwixt the fame
of a magistrate and of a minister; for from the outward action of
the magistrat we come to an inward approbacion of his virtue; but
contrary in a minister, from our inward perswasion of his virtue to
the outward approbacion of his actions.

Exinanition of Christs glory on earth typified in the auncient Jewish
manner of coronacion, and enthronizing their kinges, when they
powred a horne of oyle upon his head, to shewe that as the horne
was emptied to annoint him, soe out of his fullnes he should inrich
others. Oyle is taken for grace.

2. point, to those that were lost. The Rabbins devide all the people
into three sorts: *Sapientes,* such were the Scribe[s] and Pharises.
2. *Sapientum filij,* such as held nothing for opinion, nor did any
thing for action, but that which was approved by the Pharisees, etc.
3. *Terrae filij,* the children of the world—publicans, and synners,
reputed as lost sheepe—to these Christ came; and for conversing
with these he was obrayded.

FOLIO 122b

Aprill. 1603.

8. To teache men what a different course there is in the managing
of heavenly and earthly things: the greate affayres of the world
begin at the prince, and soe are derived by a long course to the
people, but the matters of heaven begin in the people, and soe rise
up to the prince. The first newes of Christs birth was brought but
to a company of silly shepheards, from them to a poore city,
Bethleem, from thence to Jerusalem, and soe by calculacion it was
neere 2 yeares before it came to the kings eare.

There are two kingdomes in this world, a temporall and a spirituall
or mysticall, eache needing other; where the rich, feeling their
poverty in spirituall, come to the minister, to be furnished in that

commodity, and the minister, feeling his wants in the riches of this lyfe, followeth great men, to be relieved in that necessity. *Communis indigentia est societatis vinculum*, mutuall necesity is the surcingle of the world.

2nd reason; Christ came to these, as the fittest to receive his doctrine, and yet it is clapt in amongst his miracles that the poore beleeved.

The promises of a kingdome in heaven is a greate matter which greate men according to their course in earth will hardly beleeve can be effected without greate meanes, and therefore a miracle yf princes receive Christ. Our princes did, and our king doth, continue this miracle; for shee did, and he doth hold

FOLIO 123

Aprill. 1603.

8. and maintaine the truth of the gospell, and this hath king'd him (said he).

Two conclusions: better to be a lost sheepe in the wild field then put up safe in the fold of the Pharisies.

There have bin three great monarchies in the world, the first of synn, the 2nd of the lawe, the 3[r]d of grace; and these have severall ends: the first was death, the next Christ, and the last is lyfe; and these were attained by severall meanes, for synn brought us to death by concealment of our faults, the lawe brought us to Christ by knowing our syn, by revealing our syn, and Christ by his grace leads us to everlasting lyfe. In each soule those three kingdomes have their succession, yf it be saved.

Though the lawe was delivered with thunder, yet there insued comfort in the first word, "I am thy God."

The lawe like a bason of water with a glas by it; serves to discover, and scower away the filthines.

2nd conclusion: noe syn soe greate that should discourage us from comminge to Christ. Aesculapius, as the poetes faine, devised more remedys against poison out of a serpent then any other creature, yet the serpent more poisonous in it selfe then anie man. Soe from syn.

Our confidence, *i.e.* from the nature of God, whoe regards not soe muche what a man hath bin, but what he is, and will bee. Whereas the judgment of man, on the contrary,

FOLIO 123b

Aprill. 1603.

is ground[ed] upon *vita anteacta,* and forepassed actions; soe Ananias made conjecture of Paule.

God more delights to pardon the synner then to punishe the synne.

2. From the nature of Christ, more mild and mercyfull than Moses, for Christ never executed any point of judgment. He is an intercessor, and shalbe our judge; but that tyme is not come, soe our creede notes "from thence he shall come to judge"; and this seemes to be the reason that under the lawe, yf anie strang syn had escaped the hand of the magistrat, yet it was usually punished by the hand of God: whereas nowe, yf offences slip the magistrat, they are seldome or never revenged from heaven.

Christ is not soe muche a remedy for easy synns, but even for such synners as even beginn to stink and rott in them as Lazarus did in the grave. Shee that had hir issue 12 yeares was healed with the touch of his garment, &c.

He is more ready to pardon a synner upon repentance then to punishe him upon perseverance.

3. The end: To save. *Christus salvat; solutione debiti, et applicatione remedij.*

Debitum nostrum 2^x; $\begin{cases} Obedientiae, \\ P[o]enae. \end{cases}$

Wee must obey the lawe or indure the punishment.

Christ by his lyfe hath payd the dett of our obedience, and by his death hath cleered the debt of our punishment. Both were necessary to our plenary redemption: his life to ripe age to accomplishe our righteousnes; his passion by death to meritt of [*sic*] our salvacion. Righteousnes of his lyfe—merit of his passion.

FOLIO 124

Aprill. 1603.

The applicacion: by taking upon him our syns, and imputing unto us his righteousnes.

In all synn, three things: $\begin{cases} culpa \\ reatus \\ P[o]ena. \end{cases}$

And the remedy must have something contrary to the malignant quality of the disease; soe Christ cureth the fault by his obedience, the guilt by his innocency, and the punishment by his passion; soe by applicacion all our synns are his, all his righteousnes is become ours. But heere surges a doubt, howe it comes to passe that synce the imputacion of his merits makes us righteous, the imputacion of our synn can not make him synfull.

Ferrum candens absorbet aquam, and the drop of our synn cannot infect the ocean of his innocency; *finiti ad infinitum nulla proportio.*

The applicacion of our syn to him is but a mere imputacion, but his merits, beside an imputacion, worke in us alsoe an inherent righteousnes.

For applicacion: the commaundments are given in the 2d person; and the bible written in fashion of a story, not precepts and rules, because it is more for practise then speculacion, and God would have us rather good christians then good schollers.

Without particular applicacion all is nothinge, but like the rude chaos; for before the incubacion of the Spirit of God, there was noe separation, noe vivificacion, noe animacion. In the sacrifice in the old lawe it was noe idle thing that they were to sprinkle the right eare,

FOLIO 124b

Aprill. 1603.

the right thombe, and the right foote too, to shewe the inward affection must be moved by the eare, and the action by the thomb and the toe.

The Virgin liked the newes well which was brought hir, "but howe shall this come to passe?" q[uoth] shee; soe it is welcome to every one to heere that he shall be the sonne of God, but howe shall he knowe that?

There is but thre wa[y]s of knowing himselfe to be the sonne of God: 1[st]. *Scientia unionis,* and soe Christ onely knowes himselfe to be the Sonne of God. 2[n]d. *Scientia visionis,* and soe the Saints. 3[r]d. *Scientia revelationis,* and soe every Christian. And this last is two fold, either by a descendant course, whereby Gods spirit comes downe to us, and this those knowe which have it. Philosophy sayth, every lambe knowes his owne damme, *non per eundem sonum sed per eundem spiritum,* as the uniting of the father and the sonne in the trinity is *per communionem Spiritus.* "My sheepe heare my voyce," by inward perception. "Did not our harts glowe within us?" The difference is knowne to them that have it. Samuel, before he was acquainted with it, thought it had bin the voyce of a man, but Ely could discerne it.

2. Wee knowe by our Spirit ascending to God: the spirit like fyre, still ascendeth, like a steele toucht with the magnet, turnes northward; soe this heavenward.

FOLIO 125

Aprill. 1603.

wee are placed twixt heaven and earth like an iron betwixt two loadstones.

wee incline still to one of them.

8. I heard the Q[ueene] left behinde hir in mony, plate and jewels, the value of 12,000,000£., whereof in gold is said 400,000£.

It was said for a truth that the Countes of Essex is married to the E[arl] of Clanricard, a goodly personable gent[leman] something resembling the late E[arl] of Essex.

The L[ord] Keeper Sir Th[omas] Egerton hath married his sonne, before the Q[ueene] dyed, to the Countes of Darby's daughter, his Ladys daughter—bloud-royall—*superbe satis.*

This afternoone a servingman, one of the E[arl] of Northumb[er-land], fought with swaggering Eps, and ran him through the eare.

I heard that the K[ing] hath or will restore the L[ord] Latimer to the Earldome of Westmorland; some 3 or 4000£. *p[er] annum.*

FOLIO 125b

Aprill. 1603

9: There came forth a proclamacion for making certaine Scottish coyne currant in England; as a peice of gold for 10s., and the sylver at 12 d. *ob.,* and this for the menaging of commerce betwixt these nations.

Mr. Barrowes called Seminaryes *Semmimaries.*

10. I heard that my cosen Wingat is married to a riche widdowe in Kent.

At the Court at Whitehall, Dr. Thomson, Deane of Windsore, made a sermon; he hath a sounding laboured artificiall pronunciacion; he regards that soe muche that his speache hath no more matter then needes in it. His text 2 Psal. 10, 11: "Be wise nowe, O ye Kings, be learned, O ye Judges; serve the Lord with feare, and rejoyce unto him with reverence."

Be learned: *scientia conscientiae* rather then *scientia experienciae.*

Serve the Lord: a strang doctrine, that those whom al[l] desyre to be servants unto should be taught that themselves must serve an other: yet this the highest point of their honour, to serve God: for the excellency of man is in his soule, the glory of his soule in virtue, the height of virtue in relligion, and the ende of relligion to serve God.

As strang to teach that they whom others feare should feare an other.

FOLIO 126

Aprill. 1603.

10. Mr. Layfeild; his text, "Not preaching our selves." Noe heretike ever preached himselfe directly, for they never can be heretikes except they professt Christ, and such as preach them selves for saviours deny Christ; but preaching themselves undirectly is when by preaching men stake their owne glory or advauncement as the cheifest end of their preaching. "Labour not for meat;" that is, make not meate the chiefest end of labour, but the service of God in that vocation, and the benefit of the State; soe labour in all your trades as yf you laboured for God, making not the hyer the maine end, though it be an end allsoe.

Every man spends more then he can gett; untill thirty yeare commonly men doe nothing but spend, and then when they begynn to gaine, yet expenses runne on with their tyme.

Every manuary trade is called a mystery, because it hath some slight or subtlety of gayning that others cannot looke into.

Every man cannot be a carpentour of his owne fortune.

The faults of preachers in preaching themselves and false doctrine, like a physicion that poisoneth his medicines, or a mintmaister that adulterates the coine; he kils under pretence of safety, and this robbes all under pretext of honest gaine.

Mr. Hill told me that Mr. Layfeild married a rich wife, worth above 1,000£. He speakes against covetousnes, but will exact the most of his dutyes in his parishe.

FOLIO 126b

April. 1603.

10. At Whitehall in the afternoone in the Chappell, Dr. Eaton, Bishop of Ely. His text, "Come unto mee all yee that labour, and are heavy laden, and I will refreshe you," *ego reficiam.*

"Come unto me." God the father hath given all power in heaven and earth unto Christ; therefore in our prayers to obtaine any thing wee must goe unto him, and in him wee may be sure to obteine, for this is hee in whom the father is well pleased.

He consider[ed] the subject, "All yee," &c.; the invitacion, "Come unto me"; and the promise, "I will ease you."

"All yee" is heere speciall, limited, to those that labour, and are laden, which are [have?] greate synnes and feele the waight of them.

Noe synn soe dangerous to men, soe odious in the sight of God, as contempt of synn. (Amongst many synns which he mentioned as greivous and haynous offences not one word of sacriledge.)

Synne makes a man turne from God like a runagate that having committed some offence for which he feares punishment runnes away from his maister; but their [*sic*] is noe place, noe tyme, can hide him from the presence of God, but onely one, [the] wing of Jesus Christ his mercy. Adam was soe foolishe to thinke he might have hidden himselfe, but David sayth "Yf I goe into the wildernes, etc."

Qui recedit a facie irati, for synn, *accedit ad faciem placati,* in the merit of Christ, in whom onely he is well pleased.

"Which labour, and are laden." All labour under synne and all are laden with it, but such as have greivous synns and are greived for them, and almost pressed downe to despayre, lett them come.

FOLIO 127

Aprill. 1603.

10. *Reficiam;* he will ease them; not take away the roote, but *reatum;* for the old man will be in us as long as we live, and as fast as wee rise by grace, the fleshe is ready still to pull us downe againe to synn.

FOLIO 127b

Aprill. 1603.

10. Jo[hn] Davis reportes that he is sworne the Kinges Man, that the K[ing] shewed him great favors. *Inepte.* (He slaunderes while he prayses.)

There is a foolishe rime runnes up and downe in the Court of Sir H[enry] Bromley, L[ord] Tho[mas] Haward, L[ord] Cobham, and the deane of Canterbury Dr. Nevil, that each should goe to move the K[ing] for what they like:

> Nevil for the protestant, L[ord] Thomas for the papist,
>
> Bromley for the puritane, L[ord] Cobham for the Atheist. (Mr. I. Ysam *nar.*)

Jo[hn] Davys goes wadling with his arse out behinde as though he were about to make every one that he meetes a wall to pisse against. (B. Rudyerd, or Th. Overb[ur]y). He never walkes but he carries a clokebag behinde him, his arse stickes out soe farr.

11. I heard that the E[arl] of Southhampton and Sir H[enry] Nevil were sett at large yesterday from the Tower; that Sir H[enry] Cock the cofferer was sent for by the King, and is gone unto him.

Was with the L[ady] Barbara. Shee saith the K[ing] will not sweare, but he will curse and ban, at hunting, and wishe the divel goe with them all.

In the frenche court, the gard is all of Scottishmen, and to distinguishe betwixt a frenche and a scot in admitting anie to a place of present spectacle, the[y] give the word "Bread and chese," which the frenche cannot pronounce ("bret and sheese").

FOLIO 128

Aprill. 1603.

11. Mr. Tho[mas] Overbury spake much against the L[ord] Buckhurst as a verry corrupt and unhonest p[er]son of body.

12. He spake bitterly against the Bish[op] of London, that Darling, whoe was censured for a slaunderous libellor in the starchamber, and had bin convict for a counterfaitour of passes [?], was a better scholler then the bish[op]; that the bish[op] was a verry knave. I contradicted.

11. He would not have the bishops to have anie temporalties, or temporall jurisdicion, but live upon tithes, and nothing but preach, &c.

When I was mentioning howe dangerous and difficult a thing it would be to restore appropriacions, he said, *"Fiat justicia et coelum ruat,"* which applicacion I termed a doctrine of Jesuits.

12. He said Sir Rob[ert] Cecile followed the E[arl] of Ess[exes] death not with a good mynde.

This day the 2 cheife judges Sir Jo[hn] Popham and Sir Ed[mund] Anderson, with the rest of the judges, were sworne.

I sawe divers writs or commissions sealed by the L[ord] Keep[er], with the old seale of Q[ueene] Elizabeth. It is verry like wee shall have a terme.

FOLIO 128b

Some Partes out of
Jo[hn] Hawards answere to
Dolmans booke of Succession

To offer excuse for that which I needed not to have done were secretly to confesse that having the judgment to discerne a fault, I wanted the will not to committ it. (in the epist[le] to the K[ing])
    The title of the 1st Chapter:
That Succession to government by neerenes of bloud is not by Lawe of nature or divine, but onely by humaine & positive lawes of every particular commonwealth, & consequently that upon just causes it may be altered by the same.

The lawe of nature $\begin{cases} \text{primary, principles in grossed[?]} \\ \text{secondary, in } \begin{cases} \text{collection} \\ \text{execution} \end{cases} \end{cases}$ of the first

the 2[n]d is the lawe of nations: *quod naturalis ratio inter omnes homines constituit, id apud omnes peraeque custoditur, vocaturque jus gentium. In re consensio omnium gentium lex naturae putandae est;* (Cic.)

not all in grosse, but which most nations in the world embrace.
Such is the weakenes or wilfulnes of our judgment, that they whoe
are not onely admitted but admired for wise men doe manie tymes
disagree in determining what is most agreable to nature.

Three rules leade us to the knowledge of the Lawe of nature: 1. To
appeale unto sense. *Omne malum aut timore aut pudore natura
perfudit,* quoth Hayward (Tertullian). *Licet possint negare non
possunt tamen, non erubescere* (Ambros.). 2[n]d. To observe what
hath bin allowed by those whoe are of greatest both wisdome and
integritie; that is probable which approved men doe approve: in
the first ranke the writers of holy scripture; next, counsels & fathers
of the Church; then the authors of the civil lawe whose judgment
hath bin these many 100 yeares admired by manie, approved by all,
& at this day accepted for lawe almost in all states of

FOLIO 129

the Christian commonwealth; 3rd place, to philosophers,
hystoriographers, oratours, and the like, whoe have not unprofit-
ably laboured to free nature of twoe Cloudes wherewith shee is
often over cast: grosse ignorance & subtile or curious errour. The
3[r]d rule: To observe the common Use of all nations. I dare not
disallowe that which the world alloweth. (Baldus). In this custome
of the world 3 circumstances: antiquity, continuance, and generality.

Notorious points the more wee proove, the more wee obscure; you
doe but gild gold in labouring to prove it.
After the deluge magistrates not knowne untill kings did arise;
Jewes were without magistrate or government. (Judges 17:6).
Nature is immutable *in abstracto, non in subjecto;* in it selfe, not
in us, by reason of our imperfections, or rather it is not changed,
but transgressed; for in manie nations evil custome hath driven
nature out of place. (All this bundle of wordes is like a blowne
bladder full of winde but of no weight.)

Yf many kingdomes be united into one, yf one be divided into manie, the nature of government is noe more altered then is the tenure of land, either when particion is made or many partes accrue unto one.

The verry sinewes of government consist in commaunding and in obeying, but obedience cannot be performed where the commaundments are either repugnant or incertaine; neither can these inconveniences be any way avoyded but by union of authority which doth commaund; which union is either when one commaundeth or when manie doe knit in one power and will; the first is naturall, the 2[n]d by meane[s] of amity; aequality and amity scarse compatible.

FOLIO 129b

All multitude beginneth from one: from unity all thinges proceede and are resolved againe into.

The world is nothing but a greate state, a state is noe other then a greate familie, and a familie noe other then a great body; as one God ruleth the world, one maister the familie; as all the members receive both sence and motion from the head, which is the seate and tower both of the understanding and will, soe it seemeth noe lesse naturall that one state should be governed by one commaunder.

Inconveniences of Election: 1. outrages during the vacancy; every one that is either greived or in want, assuming free power both for revenge and spoile. 2. the bouldest wins the garland oftener then the best; 3. for that they whoe leave not their state to their posterity will dissipate the domaine and work out of it, either profit or frendes; 4. occasion of warr, upon repulse, etc.

At most tymes in all nations, and at all tymes in most, the royalty hath passed according to the propinquity of bloud.

The autority of the people in state matters may be bound or streightned 3 ways: 1. by cession or graunt, for anie man may relinquishe the authority which he hath to his owne benefit and favour; neither is he againe at pleasure to be admitted to that which he once did think fitt to renounce; and as a privat man may altogither abandon his free estate and subject himselfe to servile condicion, soe may a multitude passe away both their authority and their liberty by publique consent; 2. by pres[crip]tion and custome, least matteres should allwayes floate in uncertainties, and controversies remaine immortall. One reason is, one in the 3[rd] place of arithmeticke may stand for 100. Every thing may be prescribed wherein prescription is not prohibited; therefore in this case.

FOLIO 130

Generally custome doth not onely interpret lawe but correcteth it and supplieth where there is noe lawe. *Quae praeter consuetudinem & morem maiorum fiunt, neque placent, neque recta videntur.* (A. Gellius).
3. by conquest.

2nd CHAPTER.

Of the particular forme of Monarchies & kingdomes & the different lawes whereby they are to be obtayned, holden, and governed in divers countries, according as each common wealth hath chosen & established.
(Plato one of natures choise secretaries.)
Kings in auncient tymes did give judgment in person, not out of any formality in lawe but onely according to naturall equity. *At cum jus aequabile ab uno viro homines non consequerentur, inventae sunt leges* (Cic.)

An other originall of lawes, to keepe the conquered in subjection. In K. Henry the first tyme the 16th yeare of his raigne the first parliament in England.

Utopicall state writers, whoe being mellowed in idlenes, and having neither knowledge nor interest in matteres of government, make

newe models upon disproportioned joints borrowed from nations
most different in rule.

Concerning our conquest and title of fraunce:
Rammes recoile to strike harder: wee are gone rather backe then
away. I will not presage, but anie man may conjecture, that our
mynds & our meanes will not allways want the favour of tyme.
You speake fayre, but the maine drift of your discourse is nothing
but a tempestuous doctrine of rebellion, you being therein like
the boteman, whoe looketh one way and pulleth an other, or like
the image of Janus, which looked twoe contrary wayes at once.

FOLIO 130b

Protestatio actui contraria non relevat.

An infidel moore, when he violated the fayth given to Christians,
said, "Wee have no bone in our tongues, that wee cannot turne
them which way wee please."

Will you make a king of worse condicion then the L[ord] of a
mannour, then a parishe preist, then a poore schoolemaister, whoe
cannot be removed by those that are under their authority and
charge?

Noe offence soe greate as may be punished with paricide. Obedience
in performing lawfull commaundments; subjects in suffring, for ill
actions injoyned.

It concernes princes in pollicy "to breake those proceedings which
may forme precedents against them."

THE 3rd CHAPTER:

That princes may be Chasticed by their subjects (a logger-
headed lye).

They terme the slaughter of Emperours but interludes (a foundred
judgment). Three causes alledged why a king may be deposed:
tyranny, insufficiency, impiety.

Opinion is partiall and report erronius, yet those the guides of the multitude.

The possession of the crowne purgeth all defects and maketh good the acts of him that is in authority although he want both capacity and right.

THE 4th CHAPTER:

Omnia rex imperio possidet, singuli dominio (Seneca).

They whoe have given authority by commission doe all retayne more then they graunt, and are not excluded either from commaunding or judging, by way of prevention, concurrence, or evocation, even in those cases which they have given in charge.

FOLIO 131

In those offices which are mutuall betweene anie persons by the lawe of nature or of God, as betweene the father and the child, the husband and the wife, the maister and the servant, the prince and the subject, although the same be further assured by oath, the breache of duty in the one is noe discharge unto the other.

Three ways a prince may worke violence against his subjects: upon their goods, their persons, their consciences.

Profanely abuse the Scriptures in maintaining rebellion, as conjurours doe in invoking the divel.

CAP. 5:

Magistrates are judges of privat men, the prince of magistrates, and God of princes.

If princes voluntarylie promise to see the lawes of God and nature performed, this is noe condicion to restrayne him selfe, but an honourable promise of endeavour to discharge his duty. *Expressio eius quod tacite inest nihil operatur.*

Scattered a fewe loose speeches, which noe man would stoope to gather togither. Put those speeches in the reckoning of monie accounted not received. Those evils are alwayes just for us to suffer which are manie tymes unjust for them to doe.

CAP. 6:

The Parliament court of Paris doth accompanie the funerall obsequies of those that have bin their kings, not in mourning attyre, but in scarlett, the true ensigne of the never dying majesty of the Crowne.

FOLIO 131b

Soe soone as the kinge departeth this lyfe, the royalty is presently transferred to the next successor.

All states, all persons are bound to beare his alleageance.

Soe the D[uke] of North[umberland] executed before Q[ueene] Mary was crowned, for treason against hir.

CHAPTER 7:

(a long harvest for a small deale not of corne but of cockle.)

CAP. 8:

The miseryes of Fraunce by the Jesuits procurement. The good did feare, the evil expect; noe place was free either from the rage or suspicion of tumult; fewe to be trusted, none assured, al[l] in commixtion; the wisest too weake, the strongest too simple, to avoyd the storme which brake upon them.

The victour may freely dispose of the succession of that state which he hath obteyned by the purchase of his sword.

Where the kingdome was in the father by succession and soe the dignity inherent in the stocke, the eldest sonne shall succeede although he were borne before his father were king.

(Teache men to breake oathes with as great facility as a squirril can crack a nut.)
(I arrest your word; lay hold of it til an other tyme.)

A shameles tongue governed by a deceitfull mynde can easily call faction the commonwealth; rebellion a just and judiciall proceeding; open and often perjury an orderly revoking of a sentence; Gods secret judgment in permitting injustice to prevaile, a plaine defense and allowance thereof.

You doe wisely to give a light touch, it is soe hott it will scald your throate.

FOLIO 132

CHAPTER 9.

Diogenes said of a tumbler, he never sawe man take more paynes to breake his owne necke. It is hard to finde a man that hath more busied his witts to overthrowe the opinion of his wisdome.

The people noe judge in their owne cause; noe inferior hath jurisdicion over the superior; therefore people not to judge of sufficien[c]y, etc., of kings.
Jesuites are a nursery of war in the commonwealth and a seminary of schisme and division in the Church.
They make shew of care to preserve the state but they are like the ivy which seemeth outwardly both to imbrace and adorne the wall whereinto it doth inwardly eate and undermine.

There are two principall parts of the lawe of God: the one morall, or naturall, which conteineth 3 parts: sobriety in our selves, justice towards others, and generally reverence and piety towards God; the other is supernaturall, which conteyneth the true fayth of the mysteries of our salvacion and the speciall kinde of worship that God doth require. Most nations have fayled in this; during the tyme of the lawe the flourishing empires of the world knewe it not, yet the Jewes under their tyranny were by the prophets enjoyned obedience. In the tyme of grace the meanes to propagate the gospell were neither by pollicy nor power; and when princes did persecute, the apostles did encounter and overcome, not by resisting, but by persisting, and enduring. Strange to the discourse of reason to plant relligion under the obedience of kinges, not onely careles thereof, but cruel against it; yet it is observed that the church was more pure, more zealous, more entire when she travayled with the storme in hir face then when the winde was eithe[r] prosperous or calme.

FOLIO 132b

Every man professeth his war to be holy; every man termeth his enimies impious. Sanctity and piety is in every mans mouth, but in advise; and action nothing lesse. (Paulus Emilius.)
Relligion must be perswaded, not inforced. (Tertullian, Bernard.)
You always have bin like a winter sunne, strong enough to rayse up vapours, but unable to dispell them; most cowardly companions may sett up strife, but it is maintained with the hazard, and ended with the ruine, of the worthiest.

Surely wee must be better informed of the soundenes of your judgement before we dare depend upon the authority of your word.
God did create the world not to participate anie thing thereof, but to communicate from himselfe unto it.

(I did not take you for such a widdower of witt.
I allowe that a good action contrary to conscience is unprofitable, but that it is always a damnable synne I dare not affirme.
It were a deflowring of tyme to dive into this question.)
This is the eagles feather which consumeth all your devotion: reason of state. You wrest scriptures, corrupt hystories, counterfait reason.
You acknowledge noe relligion but your will, noe lawe but your

power; all lyes, treacheries & fraudes doe change their nature and become both lawefull and laudable actions when they beare for the advantage of your affayre.

FOLIO 133

Aprill. 1603.

13. Dr. Parry was sollicited by the Archebishop to make a kinde of funerall oracion for the Q[ueene], to be published, not pronounced, and hath given him instruccion. Mr. Savil or he must doe it. Savil fitter, for better acquaintance with the Q[ueenes] private accions and reddier stile in that language; both scarse have leisure. Dr. Parry warned to be provided of a sermon, against the Kinges coming. He told that the Bishop of Durrham hath tendered his duty in all humility, craving pardon for his opposicion heretofore, with promise of faythfull service; hath preacht at Berwike before the K[ing] and said grace at his table twise or thrise.

The Q[ueene] nominated our king for hir successor; for being demaunded whom shee would have succede, hir answere was there should noe rascals sitt in hir seate. "Who then?" "A king," said shee. "What king?" "Of Scotts," said shee, "for he hath best right, and in the name of God lett him have it."

The papists verry lately put up a supplicacion to the king for a tolleracion; his aunswere was, yf there were 40,000 of them in armes should present such a petition, himselfe would rather dye in the field then condiscend to be false to God. Yet seemed he would not use extremity, yf they continued in duty like subjects.

The Q[ueene] would sometymes speake freely of our K[ing] but could not endure to heare anie other use such language.

The L[ord] of Kenlosse, a Scott, told our nobles that they shall receive a verry good, wise, and relligious King, yf wee can keepe him soe; yf wee mar him not.

L[ord] H[enry] Howard would come and continue at prayers when the Q[ueene] came, but otherwise would not endure them, seeming to performe the duty of a subject in attending on his prince at the one tyme, and at the other using his conscience. He would runne out of the Q[ueenes] chamber in hir sicknes when the chaplein went to prayer. Their prayer, for him, like a conjuracion for a spirit.

FOLIO 133b

Aprill. 1603.

13. The E[arl] of Southampton must present him selfe with the nobles, and Sir H[enry] Nevill with the Counsellors; like either shall be one of their rankes.

It is a common bruit, yet false, that Sir W[alter] Rhaly is out of his captainship of guard. *Facile quod velint credunt, quod credunt loquuntur.*

Sir Amias Preston, an auncient knight, sent a challendge a while since to Sir W. Ra. which was not aunswered. Sir Ferd[inand] Gorge is out with him, as some say.

14. "He hath a good witt, but tis carried by a foole," said Cobden of W. Burdet.

Crue invited Cobden to a fyre, and there cald him foole; "It is one comfort," said Co[bden], "that I am in a Crue of fooles."

13. Dr. Parry's note saith the Q[ueene] was soe temperat in hir dyet from hir infancy, that hir brother K[ing] Ed[ward] 6. did usually call hir Dame Temper.

14. Mr. Hemming, sometyme of Trinity colledge in cambridge, in a sermon at Paules crosse: Speakinge of wome[n], said yf a man would marrie, it were 1000 to one but he should light upon a bad one, there were soe many naught; and yf he should chaunce to find a good one, yet he were not suer to hold hir soe: for women are like a coule full of snakes amongst which there is one eele: a

thousand to one yf a man happen upon the eele, and yet if he gett
it in his hand, all that he hath gotten is but a wett eele by the tayle.
(Mr. Osborne.)

Tis certaine that Tyrone hath submitted absolutely but as to the
late Q[ueene], not knowing of hir death; he is nowe at Dublin with
the L[ord] Mountjoy, and Tirrell is come in with him.

THE LIFE OF MANNINGHAM

The Life of John Manningham, Esq.

The scholarly author of the entertaining book known as Manningham's Diary became not only a prominent Middle Temple barrister, acquainted with many of the eminent men of the kingdom during the last years of Queen Elizabeth and the first two decades of James I, but also squire of Bradbourne, at East Malling in Kent, the manor that he often visited during the period covered by the Diary. He lived a short but eventful life of about 48 years. Long after his death a grandson became a notable Restoration churchman, a bishop of Chichester, and a great-grandson earned fame in the eighteenth century as a medical doctor, a pioneer in obstetrics. Because research has turned up a number of biographical facts, we know more about John Manningham than we did a century ago.

He was fortunate in his ancestry and parentage, being born into a family of means and respectability—that is, of the landed gentry—and was thereby fortunate in his education. From his father he inherited, besides property, a family tradition, several centuries old, of political and clerical administration, business acumen, and scholarly learning.

ANCESTRY AND PARENTAGE

John Manningham, named for his grandfather, was born about 1575 to Robert Manningham, gentleman, of Fen Drayton, Cambridgeshire, a rural parish surrounding a charming village between Cambridge and St. Ives, and his wife, Joan, third daughter of John Fisher, gentleman, of Bedlow, in Bedfordshire.[1]

Manninghams had been prominent in medieval Yorkshire, where the family name had been taken from that of a berewick or village attached to the manor of Bradford.[2] In the thirteenth century some members of this family removed to Bedfordshire, where they became prominent.[3] Among the more notable in the fifteenth century were Sir "John Manyngham of Wrastlingworth," whose first wife was related to Edward IV,[4] and Sir Oliver Manningham of Wrestlingworth, London, York, and Stoke Poges.[5] A brother of the latter, John Manyngham, enjoyed eminence as an early humanist at Oxford and served from around 1448 through 1451 as Registrar of the University, the first whose name is known for certain.[6]

In the time of Queen Mary the Diarist's great-grandfather, Thomas Madyngham (*sic*) of Luton, Beds., served as a burgess of St. Albans (1553) and then became Mayor of that city (1555). Here he and his wife, Emma, owned a "Messuage in St. Peters Street."[7] By 1548 he was involved in a legal settlement of tenements in Baldock and Hychyn (Hitchen),[8] some of which property appears to have become part of the Diarist's inheritance.

When Thomas died in 1559—he was buried June 11 in St. Albans Abbey[9]—his property in Baldock, Herts., passed to his son and heir, John Manningham, the grandfather of the Diarist. He and his wife, Elizabeth, daughter of John Boteler, or Butler, of Waresly, Hunts.,[10] owned a messuage called "le Swan" and lands in Baldock and Wyllyen, which were subject of a legal settlement in 1557.[11] Sometime before 1575 John and Elizabeth moved to Swavesey, near Cambridge, so that in the official Visitations the Diarist's grandfather is referred to as "John Manningham of Swasey [Swavesey] in Com. Cambridge." They produced at least four children, Robert (the Diarist's father), Thomas, Allice, and Elizabeth.[12]

During his childhood and adolescence young John, growing up in Fen Drayton, scarcely a stone's throw from Swavesey, must have known his grandmother, as well as his two aunts and uncles. For the grandmother, Elizabeth Manningham, "Late while she lived of Swavesey in the diocs. of Elye widowe," was alive until the year of the Armada, as indicated by her nuncupative will, dated June 15, 1588, now preserved in the University Archives at Cambridge.[13] This will mentions "the Rents at Baldock," which with other money she bequeathed to George Bigges, "thacher," the son of her daughter Elizabeth, who had married John Bigges of Stewkley and "Honygton" in Huntingdonshire.[14]

The older of the Diarist's aunts, Allice (or Alice), was wife to John Gastley,[15] then evidently a widow until 1584, when she remarried. The Fen Drayton parish register has the following entry for 1583/84: "Thomas Roberts and Alice Maningham were married the 4th of Februarye."[16] It is a curious though perhaps natural error that when Robert Manningham, the Diarist's father, made his last will in 1588, he continued to refer to Alice as "my sister Gastley";[17] but John was later to call William Robardes (Roberts) of Enfield, Doctor of Divinity, "my very loving Cosin."[18]

John's uncle, Thomas Manningham, served from 1573 to 1603 as vicar of the church of St. Andrew at Swavesey,[19] the ancient "priory," so-called because in pre-Reformation times a monk had been its rector.[20]

From the 1588 will of Robert Moningham (*sic*) we learn a little about the Diarist's father. He had come into possession of houses and lands in Baldock, Bigrave, Clapthall (Clothall), Weston, and Wyllien in Hertfordshire, as well as property in "Fendrayton." It may be inferred from the items he bequeathed to his wife Joan (née Fysher or Fisher): his silver plate—a "double gilte tankerd, a double gilte salte with a cover, a silver pott, parcell gilte, and a dozen silver spoones"—and the gown that he wore on "holye-dayes," that he and his family lived in an Elizabethan style and comfort befitting their station. That Robert felt a sense of responsibility, not only toward the future maintenance of his property by his son, but also toward the local parish, is suggested by his gift of twenty shillings "toward the mending of the bridge against the Parsonage" and of a like amount to be "equally distributed amongst the poore householders of Fenne Drayton," ten shillings at Christmas and ten at Easter.[21]

After John's father died, in September 1588, and until John attained his majority, his mother was duly entrusted with management of the estate.

Joan Fisher too came of good stock. Her father, John Fysher, a prosperous Bedfordshire gentleman with extensive holdings in Sheforde and Campton, owned the farm of Bedlow with its woods and meadows, near Clophill, and other property. He was well-connected, being related to the Lords of Clifton Manor, Sir John Fysher, a justice of the Common Pleas (d. 1510), and his son Sir Michael Fysher of Clifton (d. 1548 or 49). He was friendly with Oliver St. John, the future first baron of St. John, who married Sir Michael's daughter Alice and whom John Fysher named a supervisor of his will.[22]

The Fyshers of Bedlow were a large family, Joan being apparently the third of five daughters: Alice, Elizabeth, "Jone," Rose, and Anne. She also had four brothers, Henry, George, Richard, and Stephen.[23] Henry the eldest, who seems to have been destined for Cambridge and the Inns of Chancery, entered Trinity Hall as a pensioner in 1553 but took no degree.[24]

When and where Joan married the Diarist's father is uncertain, the marriage settlement not having been discovered. Theirs was to be a small family.

FEN DRAYTON: EARLY LIFE AND SCHOOLING

The young boy grew up without brothers or sisters. In 1580, when he was about five, his brother Thomas Manningham was born at Fen Drayton and baptized in the village church by the curate, William Warde, on May 12, but lived less than two months.[25]

There is no record of where he went to school. Whether he was privately tutored at home in "Fendrayton," where George Nicholson, "Schoolmr." was active around 1582,[26] or whether he was sent to an elementary school at St. Ives[27]—where in 1574 Urian Kirke and John Wood had received licenses from the bishop to perform the office of school master[28]—we can only surmise. Later on, young John was probably sent to one of the free grammar schools, at Huntingdon or Godmanchester.

There the curriculum, if we may judge from the statutes of the similar school at Bury St. Edmunds, which were modeled on the *Tabula Legum Pedagogicarum* of Winchester College,[29] consisted largely of the rules of grammar and the learning of Latin and Greek through the best classical authors. The pupils were to talk Latin continually. Studies began at 6 A.M. and did not end till 5 P.M. (till 3 on Saturdays). On Thursdays only, if the weather were fine and they had been industrious, they could enjoy a little recreation —some gentlemanly (*honesto*) sport such as running, throwing darts, and archery. Under this rigorous system—competitive but effective —many boys throve and went up to Cambridge.[30]

In the year of the Armada, when young John Manninghan was about 13 and probably in the 4th Form, his father died and was buried from the parish church at Fen Drayton by the curate William Ward on the 6th of September.[31] Thereafter interest in the boy was shown by his uncle Thomas Manningham in nearby Swavesey; by Dr. Bartholomew Chamberlaine, the rector of Holywell, Hunts., just east of St. Ives; and especially by a generous relative in Kent, Richard Manningham, a retired member of the Mercers' Company of London who had purchased the manor of Bradbourne at East Malling, near Maidstone.[32] Though married, Richard was childless. Finding in John the heir he lacked, he adopted him, to their mutual advantage and satisfaction. In the Diary, as well as in his will, John refers to his foster-father as "My Cusen" and "my father-in-love."

Born in St. Albans about 1539, Richard was apparently a younger brother of the Diarist's grandfather John. He was well-educated, fluent in Latin, French, and Dutch, and blessed with a keen memory. At 62, we learn from the Diary (fo. 107), he could repeat from memory almost all of the first two books of the *Aeneid*. John also came to have respect for the older man's knowledge of trade and commerce.

When the adoption was arranged can only be conjectured. It may have begun on an informal basis before John went up to Cambridge, in 1592—Richard was then already settled at East Malling[33]—or more likely in 1598, after the death of Richard's first wife, Jane.[34] (She was a native of Holland and a relative of the Lady Palavicino, who later became the wife of Sir Oliver Cromwell, uncle of the future Protector. In 1595 she persuaded her husband to lend £400 to her kinsmen Arnold Verbeck, Abraham Verbeck, and Goris Besselles, "merchant strangers.")[35] Richard was to remarry, in 1601, "Mistris Jane Maningham of Maydstone Widdow,"[36] a woman of spirit whom the Diarist apparently liked and who comes alive in some of the domestic scenes of the Diary (fos. 10b, 38b).

Though John entered the Middle Temple as the son and heir of Robert Manningham of Fen Drayton, deceased, he regarded Richard as his foster-father and frequently visited him at Bradbourne. In 1610 (3 Jan. 1609/10) the old merchant formalized his relationship to John by executing a deed of gift for the mansion house and lands at Bradbourne, confirming it in his will two years later.[37]

Through his "father-in-love" John became acquainted with his numerous Kentish kinsmen: Drewe Kent, a son of Richard's half-brother Robert Kent; the Chapman brothers, John and Drew, at

Godmersham; Cousin Watts at Sandwich; Cousin Cranmer at Canterbury; and others, many of them sons of female descendants of George Manningham, who had settled in Kent. (That George had enjoyed some status has been inferred from the fact—see fo. 82—that he "was bound as surety with William Somner, father of the well-known antiquary of Canterbury," for the father's performance of the duties of registrar of the Ecclesiastical Court.)[38]

MAGDALENE COLLEGE YEARS

In 1592 John entered Cambridge University, matriculating pensioner and becoming a member of Magdalene, the only college north of the Cam.[39] It was a good choice, if Fuller is correct in declaring that because of its "remote situation" its scholars could live "cheaper, privater, and freer from town temptations" than other undergraduates.[40]

There is no mention of Manningham in the few extant Magdalene College records of that period,[41] but he was there during a time of growth and lively change. Sir Christopher Wray, a distinguished alumnus and Lord Chief Justice (mentioned in the Diary on fo. 33b), had enlarged the endowment and built new chambers, and in 1596 his widow, Lady Ann, who had founded two scholarships, gave generously for books for the college library.[42]

The power behind the government of the college, Sir Thomas Howard, nominated the masters who served, in rapid succession, during Manningham's student years.[43] Thomas Nevile, the future Dean of Canterbury (see fo. 127b) had been master since 1582; in 1593 he resigned to become master of Trinity, which he improved and where he is immortalized by Nevile's Court. His successor was the fair-minded, practical, efficient Richard Clayton, who at the end of 1595, after the death of the illustrious William Whitaker, became master of St. John's.[44] The next master of Magdalene was the colorful but "unfortunate" John Palmer, Fellow and senior bursar at St. John's under Whitaker and future Dean of Peterborough: Palmer had acted Richard III in Legge's play, before the Queen in the hall at St. John's, and was often in trouble for debt.[45] Within a year of Palmer's tenure at Magdalene, the college itself was in debt.[46]

Among the Fellows at Magdalene were Barnabe Goche, or Goge (also spelled Gooche, or Googe), son of the aeclogue-writer and kinsman of the Cecils and of Thomas Nevile; and James Wattes, who as praelector, would sign Manningham's *supplicat* for his degree. Manningham was undoubtedly acquainted with his classmates at Magdalene, Clement Lancaster and William Todde,[47] and with students at other colleges, such as Thomas Kedgwin of Emmanuel, who is twice-mentioned in the Diary (fos. 1, 98).

Probably Manningham had to endure the usual matriculation procedures, swearing of customary oaths and paying of fees,[48] and in November 1592, during his first month, the initiation known as "Salting." In this ordeal every Freshman was summoned to the college hall to make the acquaintance of his seniors, the senior and junior sophisters. There he was called on for a statement: if it were witty, he was rewarded with sack and beer; if he failed, he was given salt and water, or a caudle mixed with salt, to drink, and received a "tucking," an incision made in the lip by the fingernail, or an abrasion from chin to lip, causing the blood to flow. Then to each newcomer the senior cook administered an oath, sworn upon an old shoe that each had to kiss reverently.[49]

He may well have visited the Cross Keys Inn in Magdalene Street to relax the tensions created by a system in which Cambridge undergraduates were treated as schoolboys under "a series of minute regulations enforced by a rigorous system of fines and punishments."[50]

The curriculum was diversified—encyclopedic. Chief staples in the academic diet of the 1590's were Rhetoric—in the second and third years Logic—Aristotle, Cicero, and especially the controversial Peter Ramus. In those years students from abroad were resorting to Cambridge as a center of Ramistic logic, and to be well up on Ramus was to be a good logician.[51]

Greek and Hebrew, especially the latter, and also history, though regarded as inferior, received a large share of attention.[52]

Although most of the instruction was given by college appointees rather than by University-appointed Regent masters,[53] the Regius chairs were held by illustrious scholars, such as Edward Lively and Andrew Downes, Regius professors of Hebrew and Greek, respectively, both destined to contribute their learning and taste to the King James Bible translation. Manningham, who later would hear

Downes preach in London (Diary, fos. 7-7b), may have heard him
at Cambridge too; for students were required to attend services not
only at their college chapel but also on Sunday at Great St. Mary's
to hear the University sermon, absence from which incurred a fine
of 6d.[54] If, as the sermon notes in the Diary suggest, Manningham
had a serious layman's interest in theology, he undoubtedly sampled
the pulpit oratory of various divines. Besides William Whitaker, the
Regius professor of Divinity, young John probably heard Whitaker's
most distinguished pupil, William Perkins, then drawing large crowds
of undergraduates to St. Andrew's.[55]

The early 1590's were marked by renewed theological conflict,
particularly over Calvinistic discipline. Following the appearance
of the Martin Marprelate tracts in 1588, the Puritan party had re-
sumed its activity. The voice of Thomas Cartwright, leader of those
advocating a Presbyterian system, was still being heard from Geneva.
Opposing the Puritans, two of the more moderate of whom had become masters of colleges—Whitaker, of St. John's, and Laurence
Chaderton, of Emmanuel—were the Lady Margaret Professor of
Divinity, Peter Baro, and his supporter William Barret of Gonville
and Caius. On the 29th of April in 1595—Manningham's third year
—Barret's sermon *ad Clerum*, for his B.D. degree, before the University at Great St. Mary's, rocked Cambridge with a blast at the
authority of Calvin. Six days later Barret was forced to read a recantation,[56] which was subsequently condemned "as savouring of
Popish doctrine," whereupon he appealed to Archbishop Whitgift,[57] who rebuked those who had forced the recantation; and Dr.
Clayton, the master of Magdalene, was directed to bring Whitgift's
letter from London.[58]

Far from settled, the controversy now waxed hotter, culminating
in the defeat of Barret and the drawing up of the intolerant Lambeth
Articles, which were hailed by the Calvinist party in the University
as a great victory[59]—a hollow triumph, since it resulted in the untimely death in December 1595 of Whitaker, the University's
"greatest living ornament." From a comment in the Diary (fo. 78b)
it seems likely that Manningham witnessed the pageantry marking
the elaborate funeral ceremonies for Whitaker.[60]

Elected to succeed Whitaker in the Regius professorship was one
less sympathetic to Calvinist doctrine and the Puritan party: John
Overall of Trinity,[61] soon to become Dean of St. Paul's. (Eight

years later the Diarist would hear him preach at Whitehall—see fo. 120b.) Shortly afterward Baro incensed the Puritans by criticizing the Lambeth Articles in a sermon at Great St. Mary's[62] but was saved from proceedings by support from Lord Burghley, who himself disapproved of the Articles, and by an influential minority including Overall, Clayton, Harsnet of Pembroke (a future archbishop of York), and Lancelot Andrewes.[63]

Thus it is clear that during Manningham's college years Calvinism was tottering, giving way to the more tolerant, liberal Arminianism championed by Overall, Harsnet, and Andrewes at Cambridge and by Buckeridge and Laud at St. John's, Oxford.[64]

The influence and experience of these years confirmed in the future Diarist-lawyer the rightness, for him, of a central, moderate Anglicanism. It was a stance that would permit him to repeat the conventional jibes at extreme or fanatical Puritans while enabling him to enjoy the preaching of Godly moderate, conforming Puritans such as Stephen Egerton (fo. 76b).

Student life in Tudor Cambridge was of course not limited to serious study and passionate theological disputes, for there was leisure for sports and pastimes—archery with the crossbow, quoits, football, and cock-fighting. Latin plays were performed in the college halls and public shows at such inns as The Black Bear, The Eagle, and The Falcon.[65]

Whether the young man from Fenny Drayton made the Honours List cannot be ascertained, since the lists for 1591/2 to 1596/7 are missing (his friend from Bristol, Thomas Kedgwin of Emmanuel, is on the list for 1597/8);[66] but in the University Archives among the *Supplicats* for 1596 are the formal petitions from Magdalene College to the University for the A.B. degree—those of Clement Lancaster, William Todde, and "Johannes Maningham."[67] On July 12 the following year Manningham's degree was incorporated at Oxford.[68]

Besides exposing him to the New Learning—that great tradition of humanist education sponsored by John Fisher and Lady Margaret Beaufort; nourished by Erasmus, and by Cheke and Ascham at St. John's; and affected by the leaders of reform, Cranmer, fellow of Jesus College, Ridley of Pembroke, and Latimer of Clare—Manningham's experience at Cambridge may well have whetted his interest in the common law, which had gained in favor as the civil law had declined.

TRANSITION (1596-1598)

Where he was or what he did between graduation in the spring of 1596 and his admission to the Middle Temple nearly two years later is not known. Study like John Donne's in one of the Inns of Chancery must be ruled out, since it was not mentioned in his Middle Temple admissions record. Instead of traveling on the Continent as many gentlemen's sons were doing, or sailing on Essex's expeditions against the Spanish, it appears likely that he resided at Fen Drayton taking care of his estate. This supposition is given support by a *finalis concordia*, or concluding agreement in the Feet of Fines for Hertfordshire (Hilary Term, 40 Elizabeth). It records that on Feb. 9, 1597/98 "John Manyngham, gentleman, and Bartholomew Chamberleyne, Doctor of Sacred Theology, and Joan his wife" appeared before Justice Edmund Anderson, Thomas Walmsley, Francis Beaumont, and Thomas Owens at the Queen's court at Westminster and sold to William Pomford, for £200, six messuages, six gardens, seventy acres of land, and six acres of pasture with appurtenances, in Baldock, Weston, Willian, Clothall, and Bygrave.[69]

At least some of this property was undoubtedly part of his patrimony from his great-grandfather, Thomas Manyngham of Luton and St. Albans, property had had passed to his grandfather, John of Baldock and Swavesey, thence to his father, Robert of Fen Drayton, and finally to himself.

This document offers external evidence of Manningham's friendship and association with the Oxford-educated divine, Dr. Chamberlaine, then still rector of Holywell, Hunts., though soon to become vicar of Hemingford Abbots, between Fen Drayton and St. Ives. According to Wood, Chamberlaine had achieved some fame as a preacher.[70] At that time (1598) he was 52, John about 23. A few entries in the Diary (fos. 37, 37b) reflect Manningham's continuing friendship with Chamberlaine.

AT THE MIDDLE TEMPLE, 1598-1605

In late Tudor and early Stuart times the Inns of Court,

261 : Life of Manningham

that third university, termed by Ben Jonson "the noblest nurseries
of humanity and liberty in the kingdom,"[71] constituted a natural pro-
fessional school for young graduates of Oxford and Cambridge. Legal
studies could prove profitable, for in this litigious age "a competent
barrister could net £600 a year," we learn from James Whitelocke,
who became one of Manningham's friends at the Middle Temple.[72]

On March 16, 1597/8, Manningham was admitted to membership in the Ancient and Honourable Society of the Middle Temple,
then perhaps the finest of the Inns of Court.

The Queen herself was fond of it and a frequent visitor. Its great
gate, known as "the Middle Temple Gate," toward "Fleetstreet,"
had been built by Sir Amias Paulet about the seventh year of
Henry VIII. Close to the Thames, almost at water's edge, stood its
magnificent new hall, large and stately, built under the leadership
of the great Plowden, the Promoter of the Hall, and completed in
1572. This commodious building, with its double hammer-beamed
roof, its screen of carved oak, its colorful armoreal displays in the
windows (coats of arms of many of the eminent lawyers and judges
whom Manningham mentions or quotes in the Diary)[73] was the
center of the society's activities.

Here were held the instructional exercises, festivals, with their
banquets, plays, and dancing, and other special events, both pro-
fessional and social. Here many a notable event had taken place—
Drake's dramatic appearance in 1586 and more recently the performance of the clever, witty, Christmas revels of 1597/8, "Le
Prince D'Amour," featuring Donne's friend Richard Martin in the
title role—and Manningham would witness or participate in many
another during the next two decades.

Extending northward from the Hall were the buildings known
as Brick Court, erected by Thomas Daniel, Treasurer, in 1569.[74]
Nearby were several other Elizabethan structures not listed by
Dugdale but referred to in Middle Temple records, such as "the
new buildings erected by Messrs. Edward Stampe and George
Ryvers" in 1581.[75] Near Temple Bar was Garnet's Building, where
Richard Hadsor, the expert on affairs in Ireland, had chambers.[76]

The Middle Temple, a voluntary society governed by the Masters
of the Bench, made every effort to encourage self-discipline. Peri-
odically the Benchers issued regulations to maintain order and to
cultivate unity and amity among the members. In 1584, for instance,

dicing, cardplaying, and making "outcries in the night" had been proclaimed illegal; and the old way of celebrating Candlemas by setting up a Lord of Misrule had been forbidden.[77] In both 1590 and 1591 offenders—including Fleetwood, Martin, John Davies, and others—were punished by fines of 50 shillings each (though later 20 shillings was "redelivered to them").[78]

During Manningham's own residence, night-disturbers and play-boys were expelled or fined. Records of the society also refer to several instances of physical violence. In the Hall on 21 Nov. 1601, for instance, a Saturday night, Mr. Hugh Boscawen of Tregothnan, Cornwall, struck Mr. William Bowghton of Lyttle Lawford, War-wicks., with his dagger, giving him two wounds on the head, for which misdemeanor the assailant was fined £10 and expelled.[79]

On 30 June 1598, only three months after the Diarist's admission, the Benchers passed an ordinance designed to eliminate certain unpleasant habits, as follows:

> Divers grievances are daily committed by reason of water, chamberpots, and other annoyances cast out of gentlemen's chambers to the great offence of gentlemen of good worth passing by, as well as of the House and others; in future the owner of a chamber where such an offense is committed shall be fined 40 s.[80]

Failure to take Communion at least once a year resulted in a forty-shilling fine or loss of one's chamber.[81]

But the Diary itself affords the best indication of what Manningham's life as a student was like. It epitomizes the experience of those seven memorable years, in which he read a variety of legal, historical, political, polemical, and poetical works; attended the official "Readings" in the Hall and there took part in the moots (the arguing of hypothetical cases at law); listened to sermons in numerous churches in and about the City; and rubbed shoulders with the great or near-great.

Upon his admission he was "bound" with his kinsman John Chapman of Godmersham, Kent, and with Ben Jonson's witty poetical friend John Hoskyns,[82] who was then writing or about to write his *Dirreccōns for Speech and Style* and on his way to becoming Serjeant-at-Law. (That is, Chapman and Hoskyns, as Manningham's sureties, entered into bond with him to observe the orders and discharge the duties of the Fellowship.) Thus almost from his first entrance Manningham began to associate with a group of wits enjoying the friendship of John Donne, Ben Jonson, and Henry Goodere. Besides Hoskyns, the group included Richard Martin, Benjamin Rudyerd, and young Thomas Overbury, all quite naturally antipathetic to the recently expelled Middle Temple poet John Davies—now in disgrace for his brutal cudgeling of Martin in the Hall on February 9, just a month or so before the Diarist entered the Society.

Among those who became his closest friends were Charles Danvers of Edington, Wilts., and Edward Curle of Hatfield, as the many references and attributions to them in the Diary bear witness. Danvers was to become father-in-law to the poet George Herbert. To Curle, Manningham would owe his introduction to his future bride, Curle's sister Anne, as well as preferment to a post in the Court of Wards and Liveries.

Students like Manningham who were admitted to commons were required to continue for two years' vacations or to pay a fine of 20 s. for each absence.[83]

Middle Temple records show that Manningham was fined only twice, once in his first year when he was among twenty-six members "fined 20 s. each for absence and being out of commons" at Christmas, and again during the Christmas of 1599.[84] (Presumably he went to Bradbourne then; as he tells us in the Diary that he did at Christmas time in 1602.)

From such external evidence as well as from the Diary itself an impression is given that, at a time when the Inns of Court were enrolling many men bent more on pleasure and prestige than on pursuing legal studies,[85] Manningham was seriously dedicating himself to his calling.

His habit was a student's gown "of sad colour" and in term time a round cap, which he and his fellows wore both in the Hall and in the Temple Church.[86] He was entitled to purchase a share in a chamber—all but Benchers lived two to a chamber—from any other in the Society, or from the House when any fell vacant by death; actually, however, he may have had to wait four years, since the first mention of his assignment to chambers is that of 5 Feb. 1601/2.[87] (Where he lived till then has not been recorded.) A member had an estate in his chamber for life as long as he continued his affiliation and kept commons at least six weeks a year, and the Diarist did so until his death in 1622.

After two to three years he had to perform certain exercises. These consisted of reciting the Pleadings of such barristers as mooted in term time, of mooting also in vacations, and shortly afterward of mooting "abroad" in the Inns of Chancery. For failing to moot, he would incur a fine.[88]

After seven years a successful candidate would be admitted to the Degree of Utter Barrister.

Such a system of training lawyers was chiefly oral, by means of Readings, in the Great Hall, as well as the moots. There were two Grand, Learning, or Reading, Vacations each year: the Lent, which began on the first Monday in Clean Lent, and the Autumn (Summer) Vacation, which began on the first Monday after Lammas Day (August 1). Each lasted three weeks and three days.[89] In these vacations the Readers, normally two elected each year—one for the Autumn and one for the Lent Readings—performed, usually discussing some statute.[90] To assist him each Reader had two Benchers who had already served as Readers, and four Stewards for the special, elaborate feast over which the Reader presided at the close of his Reading. The Cupboard men—so named because they had to stand at a square or oblong table placed near the Bench table called the "cupboard," which became the center of ceremonies in the Hall—had to attend, of course, and debate points of law raised by the Reader.[91]

A Reading took place on alternate days (Monday, Wednesday, Friday)[92] extending over three to four weeks, during which time the Reader was expected to dispense hospitality generously, apart from the lavish and sumptuous final feast; thus besides the help of the four Stewards, he had a retinue of serving men dressed in his livery.[93]

The Reader's principal reward for his pains and expense was his admission to the governing body of the society, the Masters of the Bench. He could also admit a new member to the society free of any admission fine and call students to the bar during his Reading. In addition he was entitled to wear a special gown in the courts and to receive special recognition from the judges.[94]

During his first three years Manningham—since he was not fined for absence as several of his fellows were—was evidently present for the Readings of George Snigge, Francis Morgan, Bartholomew Mann, and Nicholas Overbury (the father of the young wit Thomas).[95]

On the main festival days, All Saints' (November 1) and Candlemas (February 2) the Society extended themselves to entertain with appropriate splendor the Judges and Serjeants who had been members of the Inn. Usually the banquet was graced by a play, such as the performance witnessed by Manningham of *Twelfth Night* on Candlemas Day in 1601/2 by Shakespeare's own company, the Lord Chamberlain's men (fo. 12b).

The year in which the Diary opens, 1601, was a busy and interesting one. The Lent Reading was conducted by John Cavell of Maidstone, assisted by Nicholas Overbury. Some of Manningham's friends, Edward Blunte, Chapman, T. Forde, Hoskyns, and Rudyerd, missing both this reading and the customary Reader's Feast, were fined 20 *s.* each for absence and being out of commons.[96] In August came the reading by James Walrond, with Mr. Cavell assistant.[97] On October 14 the poet John Marston was expelled "for nonpayment of commons and other causes."[98]

On All Saints' Day another expelled poet, John Davies, esq., the cudgeler of Richard Martin, was permitted to apologize to Martin and make his submission "at the Cupboard in the Hall immediately before dinner," in the presence of the assembled Judges and Serjeants. These included Sir John Popham, Chief Justice and Privy Councillor; Sir William Periam, Chief Baron of the Exchequer; Edward Fenner, Justice of the Queen's Bench; John Savile, Baron of the Exchequer; Thomas Harris and David Williams, Serjeants-at-Law; and others.[99]

Two weeks later (November 16) John Ford, the future dramatist, was admitted, even though he was not yet seventeen years of age.[100] On the 27th Marston was restored to fellowship in the Society.[101]

Christmas that year was kept solemnly but not grandly, and Manningham was not fined for absence,[102] though as the Diary indicates (fo. 96), he was at Bradbourne. By 22 Jan. 1601/2 he was back in London (fo. 11), well in advance of the Candlemas Feast with its revels and the performance of *Twelfth Night* (fo. 12b and n.). Three days later, February 5, Richard Martin, the erstwhile Prince of Love, who may have had something to do with arranging the Candlemas entertainment by Shakespeare's company, was called to the bar;[103] and that same day the Diarist was assigned

Thomas Streynsham's place as Edward Curle's chambermate, for a fee of 20 s.[104]

By an odd coincidence theirs was the same chamber that John Davies had occupied before his expulsion.[105] Earlier (1589-91) it had belonged to Robert Cotton, the antiquarian.[106] It may have been located in the buildings of Brick Court,[107] or more likely in "the new buildings" erected in 1581 by Stampe and Ryvers.[108]

On February 18 Manningham returned to Bradbourne (fo. 13b). On the 24th he attended the assizes at Rochester (fo. 16) and visited the cathedral there (fo. 16b); but he was evidently back at the Middle Temple for the Lent Reading by Henry Haule.[109]

In March he was hearing a fiery debate between his friend Charles Danvers and William Watts and jotting down the now-celebrated anecdote about Shakespeare and Burbage as reported by his Inner Temple acquaintance William Towse (fo. 29b).

That he enjoyed visiting friends and relatives is reflected in his travels during the following month. First we glimpse him at Hemmingford, visiting Dr. Chamberlaine (fo. 37). By April 15 he was again in Kent with Richard Manningham, his "father-in-love" (fo. 37b); on April 16 he was with Dr. Henry Parry, the Queen's chaplain, perhaps at Bradbourne (fo. 38), and again on the 20th at Sundridge or Chevening (ibid.), returning to Bradbourne on the 21st (fo. 38b). On the 26th he returned to London (fo. 39).

On May 14 his chambermate, Edward Curle, was called to the degree of the Utter Bar (fo. 35b). The only ceremony involved in this proceeding, according to Dugdale, occurred the day after the announcement of such calls, when just before dinner the successful candidates were summoned to the Cupboard to take the Oath of Supremacy, which was administered by the Treasurer, with some of the Benchers assisting.[110]

In both May and June 1602 Manningham continued his practice of attending service at the Temple Church, at Paul's Cross, at Westminster—where he heard the learned dean, Lancelot Andrewes, preach on May 23 (fo. 21b)—and at St. Paul's. He also heard more anecdotes from Towse (fo. 31b).

In August Manningham heard Augustine Nicolls perform his Reading.[111] In the Autumn he recorded news and gossip, read Samuel Rowlands' popular verses *'Tis Merry When Gossips Meet*, and heard Dr. John King, the future Bishop of London, preach at

St. Andrew, Holborn (fo. 46b), and Dr. John Dove at St. Paul's
(fo. 54b), as well as several preachers at Paul's Cross.

In November the custom of ringing the handbell in each court
of the Middle and Inner Temple was begun by Thomas Middleton,
Clerk of the Temple Church (a service for which he was granted
10 s. a year).[112] That same month, on the 21st, Jervaise Maplesden,
son of the Maidstone lawyer and gentleman Edward Maplesden,
was admitted to the society, for a fee of only 40 s., at the request
of Mr. Cavell, and bound with Manningham and Richard Freston.[113]
Five days later, on the 26th, several of the Diarist's acquaintances
were called to the bar: John Bramston (the future Lord Chief
Justice), Marcellus Ryvers, Richard Bennett, William Brodnax, and
John Gibbes.[114]

Since Christmas that year was not kept grandly, vacationers
were not required to attend. On Christmas Eve John Manningham
traveled to Bradbourne (fo. 81b), afterward going on a business
trip for Richard Manningham, visiting Cousins Chapman at Godmersham, Cranmer at Canterbury, and Watts near Sandwich (fos.
81b-84b).

Back at the Middle Temple, on 11 Feb. 1602/3, his friend
Richard Hadsor, the expert on Ireland, was called to the Bar.[115]
For the Lent Reading of "Mr. Nycolles" and John Doddridge,
Manningham was apparently present.[116]

But now anxiety concerning the succession, mingled with grief
for the Queen's death and subsequent excitement and relief over
the coming of King James, filled every heart during those crucial
spring months of 1603. When it was clear that the Queen was dying, Manningham went with his friend Dr. Parry to the palace at
Richmond and was deeply moved by the momentous events un-
folding (fos. 110-111).

Because of the plague in the summer of 1603 no Reading was
held at the Middle Temple. Commons broke up on Saturday after
Trinity term, and everybody was ordered to depart—all gentlemen,
clerks, and serving men—"until such time that it shall please God to
cease the sickness."[117] The next Middle Temple parliament was
held at Winchester, November 23.

The following year, "by reason of the daunger of the plauge"
there was neither Reading in Lent nor vacation, and members were
not required "to keep commons of the House."[118]

Undoubtedly Manningham spent those long and fearful months at Bradbourne. The next we hear of him he is being called to the Bar, 7 June 1605, with Charles Danvers.[119] (In this new status he could not wear a Bar-gown openly at any Bar in Westminster Hall or engage in practice for two years; rather he would continue the exercises of mooting in the Inns of Chancery,[120] such as Furnival's.)

MARRIAGE AND CHILDREN

One month after becoming an Utter Barrister, Manningham married Anne, the sister of his Middle Temple chambermate, Edward Curle. The wedding took place at Hatfield, in the parish church known as Bishops Hatfield, near the old Tudor palace, 16 July 1605.[121] Anne's father, William Curle, gent., who as Steward of Hatfield had been close to the Queen[122] and had served as "deputy surveyor of the Queen's possessions in Hertfordshire,"[123] was now Auditor of the lucrative Court of Wards and Liveries. With his wife, Frances, he resided in Woodside, beyond the Hatfield parks.[124]

Anne, the second of William Curle's three daughters, had a sister Petronell, or Petronilla, who was married to Robert Carter (mentioned by the Diarist in his will) and a younger sister, Dorothy, who seems to have married first a member of the Wither family and later Richard Keene.[125] Besides Edward, she had two other brothers, Walter Curle, M.A., now fellow of Peterhouse and destined to a distinguished career in the Church, and Francis.[126]

The match proved to be suitable and fortunate for both John and his bride. Besides bearing eight children, of whom five survived (two dying in infancy and one in childhood), Anne became lady of the manor of Bradbourne, with its attendant duties and privileges, domestic and social, for more than two decades.

When their first son, named Richard to honor John's foster father, was born in 1608[127]—probably at Hatfield—William Curle stood godfather at the christening.[128] A daughter, Susan or Susanna, was born sometime in 1609;[129] and since her baptism was not entered in the parish records at East Malling, it seems likely that John Manningham did not take up residence at East Malling until late that same year or early the next.

Certainly they were living at Bradbourne by the Spring of 1610, when the old squire, Richard, feeling the infirmities of his 70 years, was content to have John take over management of the estate, which he had recently deeded to him.[130]

Richard apparently had been living alone, perhaps for some months or years, his second wife, Jane, "my Cosen Shee" of the Diary, by this time having either died or left; for no mention is made of her in the old gentleman's will, nor is her burial recorded in the East Malling registers.[131]

Bradbourne in the time of Queen Elizabeth and King James was a moated house with a great hall and courtyard. Though in the eighteenth century it was rebuilt into the handsome Georgian house that one may see today, graced by the surrounding orchards and fields of the East Malling Research Station, some of its original Tudor lines are visible at the east end of the house and in the cellars on the north side. The remains of the courtyard are to be seen if one goes into the main passage on the first floor of the 1774 drawing-room extension built on the south side.[132]

Besides the main house with its typical Tudor features, Bradbourne had the usual complements of gardens, outbuildings, pastures and woodlands—about 165 acres, forty years later when the Diarist's son and heir, Richard, sold the Manor to the Twisdens.[133] In his will John Manningham mentions "the barnes stables dovehouses, brewhouse and outhouses gardens orchard lande meadowes and pastures" of Bradbourne.[134] In addition there were two messuages or farms in Well Street to be looked after, besides other lands in Cranbrook, Detling, and Thurnham.[135] It was a considerable estate for John to supervise. Fortunately at Bradbourne he had in Thomas Rayner a bailiff both experienced and trustworthy.[136]

Much of the life of the squire and his household, indeed of the whole village of East Malling, centered in the parish church, St. Mary in the East (now St. James), just a mile or so south of the manor house. Here Manningham worshiped, and here their younger children were baptized and some were buried, by Launcelot Sympson, the vicar.[137]

In the spring of 1610 Anne was delivered of twin daughters, only one of whom survived. Jane was buried on April 1, 1610, and her sister—named Anne—was baptized two days later.[138] She was destined to live only nine and a half years. A boy, named for his father,

came next and was baptized May 16, 1611, but by November of
that year he was dead, the burial entry for November 5 reading
"John Maningham a childe."[139]

The next sorrow to befall the manor was the passing on April
25, 1612, after a lingering illness, of the old squire. He was buried
on the 27th.[140] In his will, of which John was executor, Richard's
bequest of £5 to William Short, a former servant of John's, must
have made the Diarist more conscious than ever of the generosity
of his kinsman. On the north side of the chancel in the church John
had a monument—still well-preserved—erected to Richard's memory. There in a niche, beneath the inscription *Redemptor meus
vivit*, is a half-figure effigy of the old gentleman, bearded and ruffed,
with his left hand over the traditional memento mori, a death's
head. Although the engraver of the tablet below the bust erred in
recording the date (1611 instead of 1612), the well-chosen Latin
phrases—beginning *Richardus Mannyngham, Honesta natus familia*
in a manner reminiscent of the inscription on the monument in
Chelsea church to Sir Thomas More, *familia non celebri sed honesta
natus*[141]—eloquently express John's admiration and sense of loss.

The following February (1612/13) another daughter, Elizabeth,
was born—baptized on the 28th.[142] When she was only two and a
half, another boy arrived and was christened John at his baptism,
September 24, 1615.[143] By then Richard was seven, Susan six, and
Anne five.

If life at the manor was quiet and ordered, it could hardly have
been dull. There must have been diversions, such as the Saturday
market at West Malling;[144] the annual East Malling Fair, on July
15;[145] visits—probably not frequent—for Anne and the children
to London and Hatfield; occasional trips to the nearby hamlets of
Larkfield, Ditton (where the rector, William Prew, was known to
the Manninghams),[146] and New Hythe, and to the thriving mercan-
tile and shipping town of Maidstone, which had its market on
Thursday.[147]

In Maidstone the Manninghams had a wide acquaintance. A few
of their friends there, whose names appear in the Diary or in
Middle Temple records in connection with the Diarist, such as the
Gellibrands (see fos. 10, 10b), are not listed in the registers of All
Saints parish, but others are: John Cavell,[148] Edward and Richard
Maplesden, "Thomas Reve, Jurate," James Francklin, Robert and

Paul Cranmer, the Courthops, William Walter and his son Maning-
ham Walter—the latter perhaps a godson of John[149]—and Henry
Haule. Haule, a prominent Middle Temple bencher, and his wife
Jane, the second daughter of Richard Dering, esq., of Pluckley,
Kent, resided at Bigons, otherwise known as Digons, in Maidstone.[150]

There may have been visits to and from other Kentish friends
and relatives mentioned either in the Diary or in the wills of Richard and John Manningham: Richard Lawrence in Maidstone, the
Chapmans and Brodnaxes in Godmersham, the Cranmers at Canterbury, and Cousin Watts in Sandwich.

News of relatives and friends must have touched their lives: the
wedding of Francis Curle, the youngest of Anne's brothers, in the
autumn of 1614 at the church of St. Margaret, Lothbury, to Mary
Bristowe, the daughter of a Hertfordshire gentleman;[151] the appointment in Feb. 1614/15 of Edward Curle to assist in providing the
Reader's Feast for the Lent Reading;[152] the appointment in July
1616 of John's kinsman by marriage William Roberts, S.T.B., of
Trinity College, Cambridge ("my very loving cousin") to be Vicar
of Enfield;[153] and the death of Anne's father, William Curle, at
Hatfield in the spring of 1617. (On April 17 he was interred in
Bishop's Hatfield Church,[154] where his marble monument—a
sculptural pun, its recumbent effigy lying in a curled position—may
still be seen, next to Sir Robert Cecil's monument. By the terms of
his will his grandson (and godson), Richard Manningham, who was
now 11, was to receive the "bay mare's colt" and £ 5; his daughter
Anne would get "a bowl of silver guilt with cover."[155]

In 1619, when Philipot made his Visitation of Kent, John registered his coat of arms: "Sable, a fess ermine, in chief three griffins
heads erased or, langued gules."[156] But the autumn brought new
grief to Bradbourne when young Anne, only 9, died. She was buried
on the 3rd of October 1619.[157]

Sometime afterward a third son was born, and named Walter for
his uncle, Dr. Walter Curle, who became his godfather. By 1620
Dr. Curle was Vicar of Bemerton, Wilts., which a decade later the
poet George Herbert would serve; then in 1621 he continued his
rise to prelacy by becoming one of King James's chaplains and
Dean of Lichfield.[158] (Many years later, as Bishop of Winchester,
he would remember his nephew and godson by bequeating him
£ 50.)[159]

About this time too John was in contact with a kinsman on his father's side, Beckingham Butler, who had married Elizabeth, the daughter of Thomas Pigott and thus had come into possession of the estate of Wymondley Bury, Herts. In 1620 Butler purchased Tewin (Tewing), Herts.—near Welwyn—and became lord of that manor. Two years later, however, he mortgaged its "capital messuage" to John Manningham.[160]

During these years John seems to have divided his time between his family and estate and his legal work in London and Westminster, probably traveling by water, using the town landing at Maidstone, and on the Thames riding in the tiltboat between London and Gravesend, as he had done in 1602 (fo. 103b). Certainly there is evidence that he actually practiced his profession, including the duties required by his position in the Court of Wards and Liveries.

COURT OF WARDS AND OTHER LEGAL WORK

His appointment to this agency—a profitable one because it controlled revenue to the government by selling wardships, including the right of marriage, and by leasing wards' lands[161]—Manningham owed to the Curles, who enjoyed the favor of Cecil.[162] Sir Robert had succeeded his father in the mastership, after Lord Burghley's death in 1598, and William Curle had been one of two auditors, with Walter Tooke, since 1589.[163] In 1603 Edward Curle wrote to Cecil, asking the reversion of his father's place in the Court of Wards;[164] his brother Francis, however, actually succeeded, in 1615.[165]

Since there were only two auditorships and these were held for a quarter of a century by a succession of Tookes and Curles, who were related,[166] and since there were only two clerkships, held by members of the Hare family[167]—it seems likely that Manningham served as one of the common minor attorneys, whom (after 1581) suitors were compelled to employ,[168] rather than as an auditor or clerk.

With its small though growing staff at Westminster Hall—behind the Court of Chancery and connected to it by a passage[169]—and a feodary in every shire, the Court of Wards involved much work. It tracked down wardships and collected smaller sums for licensing widows' marriages, fines on sheriffs who failed to make proper returns, and fees for managing the affairs of idiots and lunatics.

Some of the cases were arduous. As auditor, William Curle had to conduct inquisitions, such as one "at Kings alias Bishops Hatfield" December 16, 5 James I (1607), when he and his son-in-law Robert Carter (husband to Anne Manningham's sister Petronell), acting "as a feodary of the said court," were commissioned to enquire what lands and tenements John Jeninges knight, lunatic, had and held in co. Hertford. (Sir John had beome lunatic "on the 16th day of August now last past," having lucid intervals.) Testimony had to be taken from fifteen witnesses.[170]

One of Manningham's own cases, recorded on vellum and preserved in the Public Record Office in London—the one clear, tangible proof we have of his connection with the Court of Wards, since it bears his signature—involved no less a personage than Richard Earl of Dorset ("then his Ma:ties Warde"). It charged one "Thomas Banes, Citizen and Sadler of London," with "entering and infringing certain Liberties Francheses Priviledge and Immunities within the P[re]cinc[t] of the Mannor of Salisburye Courte al[ia]s Dorset House in the P[ar]ish of Sainct Bridges neare Fleete Streete in the Suburbs of London beinge the inheritance of the saide Earle . . . ."[171]

In work of this sort the Diarist continued to associate with the legal luminaries of the age, for in other documents of the same bundle appear the signatures of Henry Hobarte, F. Bacon, Chr. Brooke, Lau. Hyde, Nich. Pory, G. Tooke, Curll (his capital C curling, whimsically, counterclockwise from the top of the second l completely around the name to the bottom of the same letter), and Sir James Ley.[172]

That kinsmen as well as the great or near-great valued Manningham's legal abilities is reflected in a document preserved in the Library of the Middle Temple, a vellum deed or indenture, dated 21 Nov. 1611,[173] wherein "William Onslowe of London esquire" settled the manor of Norton in Suffolk on his wife, Elizabeth; his eldest son and heir, William; and his grandsons, William and George Onslowe, "sonnes of George Onslowe gent." (George, of the Middle Temple,[174] was apparently the "Cosen Onsloe" mentioned on fo. 39 of the Diary.) Witnesses and signatories to this indenture were Sir William Killegrewe [sic], his son Sir Robert Killegrewe, "John Dixe doctor of divinitie" (rector of Little St. Bartholomew-by-the Exchange, the Onslowes' parish, and of St. Andrew Undershaft, where Stow the Antiquary had been buried,)[175] and "Jo: Mannyngham."

The associations revealed in this document offer another instance of the way the lives of Tudor and Stuart worthies touched at many points. Sir William Killigrew, who maintained a large house in Lothbury despite his debts, had been groom of the privy chambers to Queen Elizabeth and chamberlain of the exchequer. His son Sir Robert, a fiery-tempered courtier and parliamentarian, who would pass on his gusto to his offspring, including the dramatist Thomas Killigrew, Henry Killigrew the divine, and a granddaughter (Elizabeth Boyle), one of King Charles the Second's mistresses,[176] had connections with two Middle Temple friends of Manningham— Sir James Whitelock (mentioned on fos. 57 and 98b) and the ill-fated Sir Thomas Overbury. To the former Sir Robert gave a seat in Parliament for Helston, Cornwall, in 1614.[177] After the murder of the latter, he found himself enmeshed in official investigations into the cruel poisoning, because as a concoctor of drugs and cordials, from the making of which he had gained a reputation for scientific attainments, he had supplied the favorite, Somerset, with three powders—all harmless—for an emetic by Overbury.[178]

Among other notables, Manningham probably came in contact with Sir Roger Wilbraham, another lawyer-diarist, who, after fourteen years as solicitor-general in Ireland, served as Surveyor in the Court of Wards and Liveries from 1607 until his death in 1616. Undoubtedly he continued his association with his poetical Middle Temple friend Benjamin Rudyerd, who during Easter Term in 1618 became Surveyor of the same court.[179]

Probably, too, he knew Sir Walter Cope, the antiquary, who succeeded Sir George Carew as Master of the Court of Wards in 1613, then died within a year.[180] Surely he was acquainted with Walter Pye (to be knighted in 1630), a favorite of Buckingham, who made him Attorney of this court in 1621,[181] for Manningham was one of those chosen to provide the Reader's Feast at the Middle Temple during Pye's Reading in the spring of 1618.[182]

As required, he had for the next few years after his call to the degree of the Utter Bar in 1605 attended nearly all the readings,[183] and with Danvers, Bramston, Hadsor and the rest he had shared in the instructional exercises of mooting, held in the Hall after supper every Tuesday and Thursday night of the term.[184]

Numerous references in the Society's records show that he kept his chambers. Not until May in 1612 did he give up the chambers he had been sharing with Edward Curle, and apparently this step was taken to allow Curle's (and Anne Manningham's) nephew William Carter to move in with his uncle Edward.[185] The following November he received "half a chamber on the third story on the north side of the new brick building by Middle Temple Lane." With his new chambermate, a younger Kentishman, Richard Parker of Northfleet,[186] he formed an association that continued for several years. In May 1617 he and Parker became sureties for a newly admitted Kentishman, Richard Best, eldest son of John Best of Allington Castle. At that time Best went into Manningham's half of the chambers.[187]

Thereafter Manningham shared chambers with John Angell of London;[188] with William Smyth of Binderton, Sussex, who took his own life, under mysterious circumstances, sometime early in 1620;[189] and finally with Benjamin Tichbourne, son and heir of Sir Walter Tichbourne, of Aldershott, Hunts.[190]

When the Benchers honored Manningham by naming him one of the Stewards of the Reader's Feast for Lent, 1618, they appointed three others to share the cost—Sir Richard Lydall, R. Weston, and [Thomas?] Waldram[191]—since traditionally such a dinner, with its attendant drinking, attracted a crowd of high-placed guests as well as members of the Society, entailing enormous expense.[192] Assisting the Reader, Walter Pye, were Nicholas Hyde and Richard Hadsor[193] (often cited in the Diary—e.g., fo. 44); and appointed to stand at the Cupboard during these Lent Readings were the poet and playwright John Ford, Henry Sterrell, William Ryvers, and James Whitelocke.[194] This brilliant event with its music, ceremonial dancing, and lavish cuisine climaxed Manningham's association with his Inn.

He continued to be active in the Society, serving as surety, with Edward Curle, for such newly admitted members as Adrian Scroope of Wormesley, Oxon.[195] Curle, Lent Reader in the spring of 1620, was appointed to be Autumn Reader in 1621, but by August of that year he fell ill and died in his Middle Temple chamber.[196]

The following February Manningham was appointed, with his old friends Danvers and Bramston, and with Aegremont Thynne, "to stand at the Cupboard" during the reading of Thomas Southe, "next Lent."[197] Thus it is apparent that after nearly twenty-four years' association with the Middle Temple, he was about to be chosen Reader and soon thereafter a Master of the Bench.

In July 1622 he was again appointed to stand at the Cupboard, with Bramston, Danvers, and William "Freeston" [Freston], during the Autumn reading by Thynne;[198] but his illness, the nature of which has not been recorded, prevented him from serving. As the records of a "Parliament holden 25 Oct., 20 Jac. I, 1622" tell us,

> Messrs. John Manningham and William Freston are fined 3£ 6s. 8d. each for not being at the Cupboard during Mr. Aegremont Thynne's reading last Autumn, according to the Act of Parliament of 26 May 1620.[199]

John Bramston and Charles Danvers were chosen Readers for the following Lent and Autumn, respectively,[200] but Manningham's turn would never come. He died toward the end of November, 1622, at Bradbourne, the burial record at East Malling reading "25 John Manningham Esqr"[201]. His will, which he had prepared and executed the preceding February, was probated on 4 Dec. 1622, by his brother-in-law, Dr. Walter Curle, then Dean of Lichfield.[202]

The final mention of the Diarist in the Middle Temple records is the following:

> 2 Dec. Mr. James Scudamore to the chamber of Messrs. Benjamin Tichbourne and John Manningham, on the death of the latter; fine 50£.[203]

The next year, 1623, Charles Danvers served as Autumn Reader and was elevated to the Bench.[204] Thus it appears virtually certain that if Manningham had maintained good health, he too would have moved up the ladder to Reader, Bencher, and possibly even Serjeant (a rank which both Hoskyns and Bramston attained in 1623),[205] or beyond.

THREE DESCENDANTS

Several of the Diarist's descendants added luster to

the family name, especially John's grandson Thomas Manningham, who became a famous preacher and bishop after the Restoration, and his great-grandson Richard, who became a notable obstetrician in the eighteenth century. (Articles in the *Dictionary of National Biography* err in failing to connect them with the Middle Temple barrister.)

John Manningham's eldest son and heir, Richard (1608-1682), inherited Bradbourne but later, in the 1650's, sold it to the Twysden family. Had the Diarist lived a decade longer, he would have been proud of his son's academic achievements at Cambridge. Seven months before his admission as pensioner at Peterhouse, which occurred in October 1624, he was awarded a Blithe (or Blythe) scholarship, which he resigned at the end of 1626 to become Perne Scholar. Under the guidance of his tutor, the brilliant Luke Skippon, formerly of Caius,[206] he proceeded B.A. in 1628. In the Honours Lists of 1628/9 his name follows that of "John Milton, of Christ's."[207] In 1632 he received the M.A. and was elected Fellow of Peterhouse.[208]

Sometime between these events and his marriage, in December 1636 (at St. Faith's, London, to Bridget Blackwell of Broxborne, Herts.),[209] he took holy orders.[210] He and his bride were living at Bradbourne when their first child, Anne, was born in December 1637.[211] Beginning in May 1638, he served as rector of Michelmersh, Hampshire, until being sequestered in 1646.[212] In 1649 a son Thomas (the future bishop) was born in the parish of St. George, Southwark.[213]

In that same year Richard's younger brother Walter sold to Thomas Twisden "with his mother's consent, those properties which are called the Well Head House and the Well Head Cottage."[214] Twisden, an Inner Temple barrister, was now Recorder of Maidstone.[215] A few years later, between 1656 and 1659, Richard sold Bradbourne to him.[216]

After the Restoration Richard was restored to his rectory at Michelmersh, holding it until his death in 1682.[217]

His brother Walter, the Diarist's other surviving son, inherited lands in Detling and Thurnham in Kent. He, too, married a girl named Bridget, who bore him at least two children, Henry and Mary. In the spring of 1658 he was at Bourbrough in West Flanders, where, feeling "sick in body," he made his will and named Captain

John Maning (Manning) executor. Sometime after Walter's will was proved at London, 9 Sept. 1658[218] and before 1663, when Captain Manning is mentioned in New England, he married Walter's widow and brought her and her children to New York. His name is commemorated in Manning's Island, for which he held a patent.[219]

When Richard Manningham made his will at Michelmersh, 12 June 1682 (probated the following November), he mentioned three sons, Richard, Nicholas, and Thomas, and a daughter, Bridget.[220] (His first-born, Anne, had predeceased him.) It is Thomas who next warrants attention.

For Thomas Manningham (1649-1722), the Diarist's grandson, like his great-uncle, Walter Curle, the Bishop of Winchester, rose to prominence in the Church. By way of Winchester and New College, Oxford (B.A., 1673) and the rectory of East Tisted, Hampshire, he became "a high flown preacher," in Wood's phrase, earning such admiration from Charles II that in 1684 he was made preacher at the Rolls. After a three-year stint as headmaster of Westerham Grammar School in Kent (1689-1692) he became rector of St. Andrew's, Holborn, where his grandfather had heard many a fine sermon; within three months of his appointment, in September 1691, he was awarded the degree of Doctor of Divinity. Other appointments followed: he became chaplain to William and Mary, and canon, then dean, of Windsor. His consecration as bishop of Chichester took place 13 Nov. 1709. Since at the time of his death in 1722 he had been residing in Greville Street, Holborn, he was buried in St. Andrew's.[221]

A large number of his sermons have been published, including one preached at St. Andrew's 30 Dec. 1694, on the death of Queen Mary, and printed shortly afterward.[222]

Of his ten children, by his wife Elizabeth (1657-1714), two became prominent in the Church: Thomas, D.D., his eldest son, and Simon Manningham.[223]

Another, his second son, Richard, attained medical fame as the chief "man-midwife" of his time. Sir Richard Manningham (1690-1759), was born at Eversley, Hampshire. Although he was intended for the Church and sent to Cambridge, graduating LL.B. in 1717, he later took the degree of M.D. In 1720 he was elected Fellow of the Royal Society and admitted to the College of Physicians. On 18 Feb. 1721 he was knighted by George I.[224]

So much in demand did he become thereafter, that Sterne portrayed him, in Chapter 18 of *Tristram Shandy*, as too busy to take Mrs. Shandy's case.

It was Sir Richard who in 1726 exposed the fraud of Mary Toft, who pretended to have given birth to several rabbits.[225] This affair, the talk of the town and the subject of a Hogarth drawing, enhanced his reputation.

To advance the art of obstetrics he not only wrote on the subject but established, in the parish infirmary of St. James, Westminster, a word for parturient women, the first of its kind in Great Britain. Here he lectured on midwifery until his death in May 1759.

One of his sons, another Thomas Manningham, graduated M.D. from St. Andrews in 1765 and became a physician.[226]

APPENDIXES

Appendix A
Final Agreement on Ownership of Land

This is the final concord made in the Court of Queen Elizabeth at Westminster in the Octave of the Purification of the blessed Mary in the fortieth year from the conquest [i.e. February 9, 1598] of the reign of Elizabeth by the grace of God queen of England France and Ireland defender of the Faith &c before Edmund Anderson Thomas Walmsley Francis Beaumont and Thomas Owen Justices and others of the queen's faithful then present there between William Pomford plaintiff and John Manyngham gentleman and Bartholomew Chamberlayn Doctor of Sacred Theology and Joan his wife deforciants for 6 messuages 6 gardens 70 acres land and 6 acres pasture with appurtenances in Baldock Weston Willian Clothall and Bygrave whereof a plea covenant was summoned between them in that Court Namely that the aforesaid John Bartholomew and Johanna acknowledged the aforesaid tenements with appurtenances to be the right of the same William For this the said William has of the gift of the aforesaid John Bartholomew and Joan And they remitted and quit-claimed for the same John Bartholomew and Joan and the heirs of the aforesaid John to the aforesaid William and his heirs in perpetuity And moreover the said John Bartholomew and Joan undertook for themselves and the heirs of the said John that they would warrant the aforesaid tenements with appurtenances for the aforesaid William and his heirs against the aforesaid John Bartholomew and Joan and the heirs of the same John in perpetuity And for this acknowledgement remission quitclaim warranty fine and agreement the same William gave to the aforesaid John Bartholomew and Joan two hundred pounds sterling.

Hertford.

[Dorse]   According to the form of the Statute.
The first proclamation was made on the 13th February Hilary Term in the fortieth year of the within written Queen, the second proclamation was made on the 12th May Easter Term in the fortieth year of the within written Queen, the third proclamation was made the 23rd June Trinity Term in the fortieth year of the within written Queen, the fourth proclamation was made the 13th October in the Michaelmas Term in the fortieth year of the within written Queen [1598]

Appendix B
Will of Richard Manningham

In the name of the most holy blessed and glorious Trinitie
Father Sonne and holy ghost one eternall and immortall God Amen I Richard
Manyngham of the the p[ar]ishe of Estmallinge in the Countie of Kent gent
beinge in tollerable health of body in regard of myne age and infirmities but of
p[er]fecte mynde and memorie endewed w[i]th all my sences I laude and prayse
God therefore Doe make and declare this my last will and Testament all written
w[i]th myne owne hand the xxith daye of Januarie in the yeare of our lord
God one thousand six hundred and eleven and in the yeares of the raigne of
our soveraigne Lord James by the grace of God kinge of England Scotland
Fraunce and Irelande defendor of the faith &c That is to saye of Englande
Fraunce and Ireland the nynth and of Scotland the five and fortith in manner
and forme followinge And first I commende and comitt my soule into the
handes of almighty God my heavenly Father that gave it my body to the earth
to be buried (if God so please) in this parishe Church of Estmallinge by my
first wyfe, Item I geve unto the poore inhabitantes of this p[ar]ishe of this
saide p[ar]ishe of Estmallinge where I dwell the summe of Tenne poundes,
Item I give unto the poore inhabitantes of the Towne of S[t] Albans in Hartford
there where I was borne the like summe of Tenne poundes, Item I give unto
Edmond Manyngham my kinsman the summe of Twentie poundes and further
I forgive him the Twenty poundes he oweth me, Item I give unto William
Manyngham his sonne the summe of five poundes And to Marion Maningham
the daughter of the said Edmond the summe of five markes, Item I give unto
Will[ia]m Maningham brother to the said Edmond the summe of Fortie poundes,
Item I give unto Charles Manyngham his brother the summe of Thirtie poundes,
Item I give unto the three sisters of the saide Charles Anna Marie and Elizabeth
or whatsoever their names maye be the summe of Tenne poundes a peece And
yf any of the said sisters be dead or shall die before me then I will the sur-
vivors shall enjoye the deades p[ar]te to be equally devided betweene them
Item I give unto Elizabeth Houghton and Mary Cleyton daughters of my late
half brother Robert Kent the summe of Tenn poundes a peece, Item I give to
the widdowe of Drewe Kent one of the sonnes of the said Robert the summe
of five poundes, Item I give unto Gregory Arnolde eldest sonne of my late
half sister Elizabeth Arnold the summe of Tenn poundes, Item I give unto
Marie Lawrence and Sara Peters daughters of my saide halfe sister Elizabeth
Arnold the summe of Tenn poundes a peece, Item I give unto the fower
daughters of the said Marie Lawrence whatsoever their names be the summe
of Tenn poundes a peece Item I give unto Susan Hardy daughter of my other
half sister Marie the summe of Tenn poundes, Item I give unto Janeken Vermeren daughter of my first wyfes sister the summe of Twentie poundes,

Item I give unto the only daughter of one George Herne late paynter of London the summe of Tenn poundes to be paid her at her daye of marriage,
Item I give unto James Ashpoole my tayler the summe of Tenn poundes,
Item I give unto John Demua and Isabell his wife some tymes my servantes
the summe of five poundes a pece, Item I give unto Thomas Whithead my
late servant the summe of five poundes, Item I give unto poore Joane Hawkyns
sometymes my servant the summe of Fortie shillinges, Item I give unto Jane
Owen my mayd servant the summe of Twentie markes to be paid her at her
daye of marriage, Item I give unto Arthur Wyse my husbanman the summe of
Five markes, Item I give unto my man John Haslet and to Edmond Gibson
my boye the summe of Fortie shillinges a peece, Item I give unto my two
mayde servantes Katherin and Annis Wood the summe of Five markes a peece
Item I give unto my other maydservant Ales the summe of Fortie shillinges,
Provided that all these my men and maydeservantes be dwellinge w[i]th me
at the tyme of my death, Item I give unto William Short late servant unto my
Cosen John Mannyngham the summe of Five poundes, Item I give unto the
right worshipfull the Master and wardens and liverye of the Company of the
Mercers of London whereof I am the summe of Five and Twentie poundes to
make them a dynner, Item I give unto my honest waterbearer of London
goodman Pigeon if he be livinge the summe of Twentie shillinges, Item I give
unto my two poore laborers Edmond Gibson and Thomas Rogers the summe
of Fortie shillinges a peece, Item I give unto my kinsman William Cranmer the
merchant the summe of five poundes, Item I remitt and forgive unto these
p[er]sons hereunder named all such summes of money w[hi]ch they or any
of them doe owe me either by booke bill or bond that is to saye unto William
Kent, John Kent, Roger Kent Nicholas Kent Drewe Kent and Stephen Kent
all sonnes of my aforesaid half brother Robert Kent, unto George Arnold unto
Barnabie Lawrence and Jacob Peeters sonnes in law of my late half sister
Elizabeth Arnold, unto William Pawley and Thomas Pawley unto Thomas
Whithead James Ashpoole Alexander Brickenden and [canceled] and Edmond
Pierson, Item I remitt and forgive unto Arnold Verbeck Abraham Verbeeck
and Goris Besselles marchantstrangers kinsmen unto my first wife and to their
heires all those fower hundreth poundes sterlinge w[hi]ch I lent them at my
said wifes request and for her sake in the yeare of our Lord God 1595 uppon
their joynt bill w[i]th all interest due unto me ever since uppon this Condiccon
that they their executors or Administrators shall paye or cause to be contented
or payed unto the two daughters of the said Arnold Verbeeck called Margarita
and Susanna and unto their nicht [niece] Janeken Vermeren afore remembred
if the said Margarita Susanna or Janeken or any of them be livinge at my death
the summe of fortie poundes sterlinge a peece w[i]in one whole yeare next after
my Executor hereunder named shall have given them or sent them intimaccon
and warninge so to doe w[i]th coppie aut[h]enticall of this part of my last
will only, And here I nominate appoynte and declare my kinsman and sonne
in love John Maningham gentleman of the Middle Temple of London to be
sole and onely executor of this my last will and testament and my good friend
Emanuell Drom of London Merchant overseer of the same unto whome for
his paynes therein to be taken I give the summe of Tenn poundes The Rest of

all my goodes Chattles debtes and moveables whatsoever my debtes first paid
funeralles p[er]formed and legacies in this my last will first and last given discharged I wholy give unto my said Executor John Manyngham, And here I
require Charge and adjure him the said John Maningham by all the love and
dutie w[hi]ch he oweth me for all my love and liberalitie w[hi]ch I have allwayes borne him and his heretofore but cheifly in this my last will and Testament that he p[er]forme and paye all and every legacie in this my last will
given w[i]thin six monethes at the farthest after my death those excepted
that are appoynted to be paid at certen dayes lymmited and those also to be
duly paid at their dayes appoynted and limited all accordinge to my my true
intent and meaninge as my trust is in him and as he will answere afore God
and me at the latter daye hetherto concerninge the disposinge of my goodes
and moveables,/ Nowe this is alsoe the last will and Testament of me the said
Richard Manyngham of Estmallinge in the saide Countie of Kent gent concerninge the disposinge of all my landes Tenementes and hereditamentes published the daye and yeare above written in manor and forme followinge And
first I doe by these presentes (if it be needfull) ratifie and confirme unto my
above named Executor and Kinsman John Manyngham and to his heires for
ever all that my graunt gift and feofment formally by me unto him made of
all this my mansion house called Bradborne w[i]th all the landes and tenementes of me the said Richard Manyngham situate lyinge and beinge in
Estmallinge aforesaide in this said Countie of Kent (exceptinge and fore-
prisinge as in the said gifte of feofment is excepted and foreprised) In which
saide deed of feofment amonge other thinges I have reserved unto myself a
power to dispose of the premisses either by my last will or otherwise in my
lyfe time to what p[er]son or p[er]sons I list for the space of five yeares next
after my decease as by the said deede of feofment bearinge date the third
daye of January in the seaventh yeare of the raigne of the Kinges Ma[jes]tie
that nowe is over great Brittayne Fraunce Ireland more at large doth and
maye appeare, Now I doe by these presentes utterly renounce and disclayme
all that saide power of disposinge aforesaid and doe hereby remitt and leave
the premisses to be enjoyed by the said John Manyngham and his heires for
ever ymmediatlye after my death any thinge in the said deed to the contrary
hereof in any wyse not w[i]thstandinge and further I doe nowe give unto the
said John Manyngham all other my landes tenementes and hereditamentes
w[i]th all and singuler their appurtenances whatsoever sett lyinge and being
in Estmallinge aforesaide and to his heires for ever exceptinge that my one
Tenement barne and orchard w[i]th th[e] appertenances w[hi]ch I lately
purchased of one John Goldsmyth now in the occupaccon of one Harry
Metcalfe And also exceptinge that other my smale tenement in Melstreet
garden and barne w[i]th the orchard adjoyninge called Hackstables w[hi]ch
I lately purchased of one John Dowle Both w[hi]ch said Tenementes barnes
and orchardes w[i]th all and singuler their appurtenances whatsoever I nowe
give unto my baylife Thomas Rayner and to his heires for ever And also exceptinge and reservinge unto my poore servant Thomas Whithead his dwellinge use and profitt of that my small cottage nowe called poore Johns and
the orchard thereto appertayninge dureinge his naturall life only, Item I give

unto the said John Manyingham all my landes tenementes and hereditamentes
w[i]th all and singuler their appurtenances whatsoever sett lyinge and beinge
in the Towne and p[ar]ishe of Cranbrooke in this said Countie of Kent To
have and to hold to hym the said John Manyngham and to his heires for ever,
Lastly I give unto my kinsman John Arnold of Saint Albans and to my kinsman Richard Lawrence of Maydstone and to my mayd servant Annis Hull
and to their heires for ever all this my Thirtie acres of land more or lesse
called larkhale [Larkhall] set lyinge and beinge in the p[ar]ishe of Hadlow
or els where w[i]thin this Countie of Kent w[hi]ch I lately purchased of one
Thomas Tutsom now in the occupaccon of one John Bredger or his Assignes
to be equally parted and devided betwene them. And further I give unto each
of them the summe of Twentie nobles a peece in money Haveinge thus I
thanke God finished this my last will and Testament and sett an order in my
wordly affayres I will nowe henceforeward awayte Gods mercifull will and
pleasure to depart hence in peace when his blessed will shall be to call for me
Most humblie beseachinge him of his infinite goodnes and mercy that when
the finall daye of my dissoluccon shalbe come I maye by his grace be armed
w[i]th a true and lively faith firme hope and constant pacience agaynst all
the assaultes and temptaccons of my ghostlye enemye the dyvell and to be
willinge and reddy to forsake all to goe to my blessed Saviour and Redeemer
Jesus Christ Amen good Lord And in witnes that this is my very last will
and Testament all written w[i]th myne owne hand contayned in five whole
pages and eight lynes of the sixt[h] page I have fastened them all together
w[i]th my seale in m[er]chantes waxe and under every pagesubscribed my
name and to the last page sett my seale in the presence of these witnesses
thereunto called and required the daye and yeare above written viz the xxith
day of Januarie 1611,/ [signed] Richard Manyngham, The w[i]thin written
Richard Manyngham Testator hath acknowledged declared and published
before us witnesses here under written that this is his last will and Testament
all written w[i]th his owne hand contayned in five whole pages or leaves and
eight lines of the sixt[h] page And hath in our presence fastned them all
togeather w[i]th his seale in merchantes and hard wax and hath under every
page subscribed his name And under the last page sett his seale the daye and
yeare above written, [signed:] William Prew rector de Ditton, Richard Brewer,
Mathew Prowhurst, William Whiller,/[in Latin:] PROVED was the Testament
above written at London . . . before Dr. Thomas Edwardes . . . in the Prerogative Court of Canterbury . . . the first day of May, A.D. 1612, by John
Maningham, Executor.

Appendix C
Inscription on
Richard Manningham Monument

Richardus Mannyngham, honesta natus familia, mercaturam juvenis exercuit satis copiosam; aetate provectiore ruri vacavit literis et valetudini, in studiis tam divinis quam humanis eruditus; Latine, Gallice, Belgice dixit, scripsit, eleganter et proprie; nec alieni appetens nec profusus sui, amicos habuit fideliter et benigne, pauperes fortunis suis sublevavit, affines et consanguineos auxit; animi candore, vultus suavitate et gravitate conspicuus; sobrie prudens, et sincere pius. Languido tandem confectus morbo, fide Deum amplexus orthodoxa, expiravit 25° die Aprilis, anno salutis 1611 et aetatis suae 72° Desideratus suis, maxime Johanni Mannyngham haeredi, qui monumentum hoc memor moerensque posuit.

*The monument stands on the north side of the chancel, in a niche, over which is inscribed "Redemptor meus vivit."

Appendix D
Will of John Manningham

In the name of God amen the one and Twentieth daye of January in the yeare of our Lorde God one Thousand six hundred twenty and one, and in the nyneteenth yeare of the raigne of our Sov[e]raigne Lord James by the grace of God of England France and Ireland king defendor of the faithe &c and of Scotland the five and fiftieth I John Mannyngham [sig.] of East Malling in the Countie of Kent Esquire, being in reasonable good health of bodie and in p[er]fect and sound memorye God bee thanked doe make and ordaine this my last will and Testament in manner and forme followinge First I give and render up my soule into the handes of the holy blessed and glorious Trinitie God the father, God the sonne and God the holy ghost, assuredly beleeving to be saved body and soule by the infinite meritts and mercies of my Lord and Savyour Jesus Christ Item I give unto the poore inhabitantes of the said p[ar]ish of East Malling the summe of Five poundes to be paid and distributed amongst them upon the daye of my funeralls Item I give unto the poore Inhabitantes of the parish of Fennydrayton in the Countie of Cambridge the summe of Five poundes to be payd and distributed amongst them within three monethes after my decease Item I will that mine executors shall Cause ringes of gould to be made of the valewe of twentie shillinges apeece to be given to every one of my servantes that shall be dwelling w[i]th me at the time of my decease to each of them one as a remembrance of mee Item I give unto my daughter Susan the some of three hundred poundes Item I give unto my daughter Elizabeth two hundred and fiftie poundes Item I give unto my sonne Walter one hundred poundes, and if it shall happen that either of my said daughters Susan and Elizabeth shall dye before shee shall [canceled] accomplishe her age of Eighteene yeares or be maryed, then my will is that her portion and legacie shall be equally devided, amongst my two younger sonnes John and Walter, and my daughter that shall survive and likewise if my sonne Walter happen to dye before he shall accomplish his age of one and twenty yeares then my will is that his said legacie shall be equally devided amongst his sisters and his brother John or such of them as shalbe then living And my Will and meaning and desire is that myne executors hereafternamed will within convenient tyme after my decease rayse and imploy the legacies unto my said Children bequeathed as aforesayd and out of the profittes therof by their care and industry to be raysed to allowe to each of them respectively as they shall thinke fitt for their mayntenance, and the residue to remaine for increase of their portions and legacies Item I give unto mine executors hereafter named the summe of twenty nobles apeece The Residue [?] of my goods and Chattells my debts and legacies being satisfied I give unto my deare and wel-beloved wife Anne Mannyngham, and to my

sonne Richard equally to be devided betweene them And of this my last will
and testament I doe make nominate and appointe my loving brother in lawe
Walter Curle Do[cto]r of Divinitie and Deane of Lichfeild and my very loving
Cosin Will[ia]m Robardes of Enfeild Do[cto]r of Divinitie Executors./-./.-./
This is alsoe the last will and testament of mee the said John Mannyngham,
made the day and yeare abovewritten, of for and Concerning all my messuages
houses landes tenementes and hereditamentes whatsoever in the sayd County
of Kent Firste Whereas there was one fine sur conisans [?] de droyt come
ceo &c had and levied in the terme of St Michaell in the tenth yeare of our
sayd sov[e]raigne Lord King James his reigne of England &c betweene my
late brother in lawe Edward Curll of the Middle Temple London esquire now
deceased, and my Cosin Beckingham Boteler of Tewing in the County of
Hartford esquire Compl[ainan]tes and myselfe the sayd John Mannyngham,
Edmund Mannyngham, Will[ia]m Mannyngham and Charles Mannyngham
Defendantes of all the messuages landes tenementes and hereditamentes of
me the sayd John Mannyngham in the sayd Countie of Kent by such names
and quantities as in the sayd fine are expressed, w[hi]ch fine was had and
levyed, and was and is to the use of me the sayd John Mannyngham and of
mine heires and assignes untill by my last will and testament in writinge or
otherwise by my deed Indented, I should declare nominate limitt or appoynt
other uses and estates therof, and then to such uses intentes and purposes
as by my last will and testament in writinge or by my deed Indented I should
declare nominate limit or appoint as in and by one deede Indented made
betweene me the said John Mannyngham, Edmund Will[ia]m and Charles
Mannyngham of the one p[ar]t and the said Edward Curll and Beckingham
Boteler of the other part bearing date the first daye of October in the sayd
tenth yeare of our said sov[e]raigne Lord King James his Raigne of England
&c whereunto reference be had amongst other thinges doth at large appeare
Nowe therefore for and Concerninge all that my Capitall Messuage and
mansion house called Bradborne in the sayd parish of East Malling and all
the barnes stables dovehouse brewhouse and outhouses gardens orchardes
landes meadowes pastures and hereditam[en]tes whatsoev[e]r with all and
singular their appurtenances in East Malling aforesaid w[hi]ch my late deare
Cosin and father in love Richard Mannyngham esquire deceased purchased
to him and his heires of George Catlin gent of John Pathill gent and Nicholas
Miller gent or any of them joyntly or sev[er]ally or otherwise, and for noe
more my will and meaning is And I doe hereby will declare limit and appoint
that immediately after my decease the said fine shall be, and be construed
and adjudged to be to the use of my said welbeloved wife Ann Mannyngham
for and during her naturall life in lieu [?] recompense and barr of all such
joyneture Dower, fifee estate Clayme and demaund whatsoever w[hi]ch by
any lawe Custome or conveyance or meanes whatsoev[e]r shee may or might
have clayme or demaund, of into or out of all or any of the landes tenementes
& hereditamentes wherof I am or was or shalbe at any time duringe her
Coverture seised of any estate of inheritance alwayes provided that shee my
said wife and her assignes and all & every person and p[er]sons that shall or
may by her meanes have any estate fifee or interest in the said Capitall

Mesuage and premisses to her bequeathed or limited hereby as aforesayd, or
in any p[ar]cell therof shall maintaine and keepe the same in Convenient and
decent reparations, and that by the meanes of her and her assignes or any that
hereafter may have any estate or interest from by or under her, or in her right
of in or to the said Capitall Messuage and pr[e]misses to her bequeathed or
limited as aforesaid or in any p[ar]te or p[ar]cell therof there be noe Waste
or spoile willfully done suffered or Committed either in houses, gardens,.
orchardes meadowes timber, fences, or inclosures therof, or of any part therof.
And my Will and meaninge is, and I doe hereby will declare limitt and appoint,
that for and Concerning my said Capitall Messuage landes, tenementes, hereditamentes and pr[e]misses to my wife hereby before bequeathed limited or
appointed, the sayd fine immediately after the decease of my said wife or
other determinaccon of her estate in the pr[e]misses shall be construed taken
and adjudged to be to the use and behoofe of my sonne Richard Mannyngham
and of the heires males of his body lawfully to be begotten and for want of
such heires of his body then to the use of my sonne John, and of the heires
males of his body lawfully to be begotten and for want of such heires of his
body to the use of my sonne Walter, and of the heires males of his body lawfully to be begotten, and for want of such heires of his bodie then to the use
of my right heires for ever, And for and concerning my two messuages or
farmes, and all my landes tenementes & hereditamentes unto the same belonging or therewith used or occupied lyeing & being at or neare a Certaine place
Called wellstreate in the said parish of East Malling, and now or late in the
sev[er]all tenures or occupations of Thomas Pennyall, Moses Wattes and
Nicholas Beeching my will & meaninge is, and I doe hereby limitt declare and
appoint that imediately after my decease, the said fine shall be, and be construed taken and adjudged to be to the use of my sonne John & of the heires
of his body, and for want of such heires then to the use of my sonne Walter
and of the heires of his body, and for want of such heires then to the use of
my right heires for ever. And for and concerning my messuage landes tenementes farme and hereditamentes, with theppurtenances in the parishes of
Detling and Thurnham in the sayd Countie of Kent, my will and meaninge is
and I doe hereby limitt declare and appoint that the said fine from and immediately after my deceasse, shall be and be construed taken and adjudged,
to be to the use of my sonne Walter, and of the heires of his body lawfully
to be begotten, and for want of such heires, to the use of my sonne John and
of the heires of his body and for want of such heires to the use of my sonne
Richard and of the heires of his body and for want of such heires to the use
of my right heires for ever, / And for and Concerninge all that Capitall
messuage or tenement landes, meadowe pastures woodes and hereditamentes
whatsoever w[hi]ch my said late deare Cosin, and father in love Richard
Mannyngham (whoe for ever is gratefully to be remembred by me and myne)
purchased to him and his heires of Sir Will[ia]m Gratewick knight deceased
and of Edmund Catlin gent. deceased, and all and singuler other my landes
tenementes and hereditamentes whatsoever in the sayd County. of Kent
hereby before by mee not disposed of, my Will and meaning is, & I doe hereby
declare limitt and appointe that the said fine immediately after my decease

shall be and be construed taken and adjudged to be, to the use of my said
sonne Richard Mannyngham, and of the heires males of his body and for
want of such heires of his body then to the use of my sonne John and of the
heires males of his body and for want of such heires of his body then to the
use of my sonne Walter and of the heires males of his body, and for want of
such heires of his body then to the use of my right heires for ever. And my
will is further that my said wife shall be guardian to my sayde sonne Richard
and the rest of my Children soe long as shee shall continue my widdowe and
unmarried. And if shee fortune to marry, then myne executors abovenamed
shall have the Care and government of all my children and their estates untill
they be marryed, or come to their ages of one & twentie yeares. And in witnes that this is the true and last will and testament of me the sayd John
Mannyngham, and that I doe hereby revoke make voyd and annull all former
wills and testaments that I have written all this with myne owne hand in these
three sheetes of paper and fixed the same together w[i]th a labell at the head
of them and sealed the same with my seale and subscribed my name as well
to this third sheete as to both the former Jo: Mannyngham./ Published and
declared by me the said John Mannyngham to be my last will and testament,
the one and twentieth daye of Februarie Anno D[omi]ni 1621./ in the
presence of [signed] Sackville Pope, Richard Butler, John Roberdes, John Gwy/

[in Latin:] PROVED: was the testament above-written at London, . . .
before Sr William Byrde . . . in the Prerogative Court of Canterbury . . . the
4th day of December, 1622, by [Dr.] Walter Curle (*Sacre Theologie pro-
fessoris*), [Dr.] William Robertes having renounced.

NOTES TO THE TEXT
OF THE DIARY AND TO
THE LIFE

Notes to the Diary

Adm.	*Register of Admissions to the Honourable Society of the Middle Temple, I, Fifteenth Century to 1781,* ed. H. A. C. Sturgess, London, 1949.
B	*The Diary of John Manningham,* ed. John Bruce, Camden Society, 1868.
Chamberlain	*The Letters of John Chamberlain,* ed. Norman E. McClure, 2 vols., Philadelphia, 1939.
Chambers	E. K. Chambers, *The Elizabethan Stage,* 4 vols., Oxford, 1923.
CSP	*Calendar of State Papers, Domestic,* Elizabeth and James I.
DNB	*Dictionary of National Biography,* ed. Sidney Lee, 1908-09 reissue, 22 vols. and supplements, including *The Concise Dictionary, 1939.*
Foss	Edward Foss, *Biographia Juridica, Biographical Dictionary of the Judges of England from the Conquest to the Present Time, 1066-1870.* Boston, 1870.
Foster	Joseph Foster, *Alumni Oxonienses: The Members of the University of Oxford, 1500-1714, Early Series,* 4 vols., 1891, 1892.
Fuller	Thomas Fuller, *The Worthies of England,* ed. John Freeman, London, 1952.
Gray's Adm.	*Register of Admissions to Gray's Inn: 1521-1887,* ed. Joseph Foster, London, 1889.
Hardy's Le Neve	John Le Neve and T. Duffus Hardy, *Fasti Ecclesiae Anglicanae, or a Calendar of the Principal Ecclesiastical Dignitaries in England and Wales,* 3 vols., Oxford, 1854.
Harrison	G. B. Harrison, *The Elizabethan Journals, 1591-1603,* New York, 1939.
Hasted	Edward Hasted, *The History and Topographical Survey of the County of Kent,* 2nd ed., 1798.
Inderwick	Frederick A. Inderwick, Q. C., *The Inner Temple: Its Early History as Illustrated by its Records,* London, Vol. I, 1896, Vol. II, 1898.
I. T. Adm.	*Students Admitted to the Inner Temple 1547-1660,* ed. W. H. Cooke, London, 1878.
L. I. Adm.	*Lincoln's Inn Admission Register: 1420-1799,* Records of the Honourable Society of Lincoln's Inn, The Black Books, I, 1896.

Min.*   *Minutes of Parliament of the Middle Temple,* ed. Charles
               T. Martin, in *Middle Temple Records,* ed. Charles H.
               Hopwood, London, 1904.
MS   British Museum *MS. Harley* 5353: The Diary of John
               Manningham.
OED   *Oxford English Dictionary: A New Dictionary on
               Historical Principles,* ed. James A. H. Murray, et al.,
               10 vols., Oxford, 1888-1928, with Supplement, 1956.
STC   A. W. Pollard and G. R. Redgrave, *A Short-Title Catalogue
               of Books Printed in England, Scotland, & Ireland And
               of English Books Printed Abroad 1475-1640,* London,
               1946.
Venn   John and J. A. Venn, *Alumni Cantabrigienses,* Part I,
               From the Earliest Times to 1751, 4 vols., Cambridge,
               1922-27.
Wood   Anthony Wood, *Athenae Oxonienses,* 2 vols., 2nd ed.
               London, 1721.

Fo. 1. "A puritan is . . . indifferent.": Examination of the MS diary con-
firms the following comment by B: "This and the subsequent memoranda up
to fo. 5 have been apparently jotted down at odd times upon the fly-leaves of
the little book in which . . . the Diary was written."

"Rec[?] . . . Windsor": Omitted by B; nearly illegible in MS.

"Song to the Queene . . . Maske": Little is known about this masque except that Elizabeth was at Richmond at the time (Nov. 1602) and that in the
previous spring Sir Robert Cecil and Sir John Popham on behalf of the Middle
Temple had been negotiating for an entertainment to please the Queen, one for
which the Benchers were willing to contribute 200 marks. (Chambers, I, 170
and nn. 2-3). But Middle Temple records make no reference to such a masque,
and it is not listed by Alfred Harbage and S. Schoenbaum in *Annals of English
Drama 975-1700* (Philadelphia, 1964).

The sort of masque presented, however, is suggested by the description
of a masque given at court during the famous Middle Temple Christmas revels
of 1597/98, in which Richard Martin played the Prince of Love and John
Hoskyns and John Davies had leading roles (see notes to fo. 12b). The account,
penned by one of Manningham's fellow Templars, the future Sir Benjamin
Rudyerd, is prefaced with the information that on Wednesday, Jan. 4, Martin
deferred an invitation to the Lord Mayor's in order to rehearse and that he and
the maskers also rehearsed on Thursday the 5th. The masque itself was per-

---

*Adopted for convenience despite its being a modern term, the true title being
Benchers' "Orders Books."

formed on "Twelfth Day at Night," when "there went to the Court 11. Knights and 11. Esquires, 9. Maskers, and 9. Torchbearers. Their setting forth was with a peal of Ordnance, a noise of Trumpets alwayes sounding before them, the Herald next, and after two Esquires and two Knights. The Knight[s] for their upper parts in bright Armor, their hose of cloth of gold and silver; the Esquires in Jerkins laced with gold and silver, and their hose as fair; all upon great horses, all richly furnished. Then came the Maskers by Couples upon Velvet Foot-clothes, their short cloaks, doublets, and hose of cloth of gold and silver of nine several colours, representing nine several passions; to every Masker a Torchbearer upon a Foot-cloth carrying his devise, besides a hundred Torches born by servants. Never any Prince in this Kingdom, or the like made so glorious and so rich a shew. When they came to the Court the Knights broke every man a Lance & two swords; the nine Maskers like Passions issued out of a Heart. All was fortunately performed, and received gracious commendation." (*Le Prince d'Amour, or the Prince of Love, with a Collection of Several Ingenious Poems and Songs By The Wits of the Age* (London, 1660), p. 86, quoted from Huntington Library copy.)

Fo. 2. "*In Motleyum* . . . Holland": Probably the poet Hugh Holland, wit, member of the Mermaid Club, writer of commendatory verses, including a sonnet prefixed to the 1623 first folio of Shakespeare, whom he may have known personally, as well as a poem to Tom Coryate's *The Odcombian Banquet* (1611)—DNB, IX, 1040. Wood, I, 583, records his studies at Westminster School and Trinity College, Cambridge; his travels to Jerusalem and Constantinople; his early fame as a poet; and his burial (1633) in the Abbey, "near to the door entering into the Monuments." Manningham may have met Holland at Cambridge, where the latter received the B.A. in 1593/94 and M.A. in 1597 (Venn, I, 393).

"*In Spenserum*": Edmund Spenser, author of *The Faerie Queene*, had died Jan. 16, 1598/99.

"I sawe Dr. Parryes picture": The Rev. Henry Parry, D.D., one of the Queen's chaplains and prebendary of York, a personal friend of the Diarist and his chief channel of communication with the court. Scholar and later Greek reader at Corpus Christi College, Oxford, Parry translated polemical works and preached eloquently. At this time he held benefices at Sundridge and Chevening in Kent. Subsequently he became Dean of Chester (1605), Bishop of Gloucester (1607), then of Worcester (1610 until his death in Dec. 1616). His sister Pascha was married to the physician Peter Turner (see fo. 34 and note). Wood records Parry's epitaph in Worcester Cathedral: ". . . *trium linguarum cognitione, assidua verbi divini praedicatione, provida Ecclesiae gubernatione, mentis pietate, morumque integritate spectatissimus*," &c. (*Athenae*, I, 416, quoting *Hist. & Antiq. Univer. Oxon*, lib. 2, p. 238.)

In 1606 Dr. Parry was given the honor of preaching before King James and his brother-in-law, Christian IV of Denmark, at Rochester. Of this event the poet Donne's Cambridge friend John Pory, M.A.—an energetic newsletter writer destined to become the first secretary of state in Virginia—wrote as follows to Sir Robert Cotton, Aug. 12: "On Sunday the kings, queen, and prince, lying the night before in the bishop's palace at Rochester, had a Latin sermon in the cathedral church preached by Dr. Parry, who delivered so good matter with so good a grace, as their majesties were very well pleased to hear him. His text was 'Fac judicium, et videtis faciem Domine'." (*Court and Times of James the First*, ed. Birch, 1848, I, 65.)

Other references to Parry appear in the Diary on fos. 13b, 34, 110, 133, and 133b.

"Epigr[am] (Mr. Kedgwyn)": Thomas Kedgwin, son and heir of Christopher Kedgwin of Bristol, gentleman, was a fellow student of the Diarist at the Middle Temple, mentioned in records of the Society in May 1596 when he was surety for William Vawer, son of a Bristol merchant (*Min.*, I, 363), though not formally admitted until 14 October 1598 (*Min.*, I, 388; *Adm.*, I, 74). Meanwhile he had been at Cambridge, where he was admitted pensioner from Emmanuel College, Sept. 24, 1594, and received the B.A., 1597/98 (Emman. Coll. *MS. CHA.* 1.4 and Venn, III, 2). Prof. Philip Finkelpearl of Vassar College has kindly informed me that Kedgwin contributed a dedicatory poem to John Weever's *Epigrammes in the Oldest Cut and Newest Fashion*, 1599; this volume of satire by an Emmanuel man took the side of John Marston of the Middle Temple against Hall, who was then in residence at Emmanuel. Manningham mentions Kedgwin again on fo. 98.

"Tom Hortons nose.": A Londoner of this name was admitted pensioner at Emmanuel College, Cambridge, May 13, 1597; he proceeded B.A., 1600/01: M.A., 1604; and was ordained deacon and priest (London) in 1606, at age 26— Emman. Coll. *MS. CHA.* 1.4, and Venn, II, 411. Kedgwin would certainly have known him.

"Eiusdem in Luce Morgan . . . lyes.": Omitted by B. Lucy Morgan has not been identified, though there were several Morgans at the Middle Temple, including Francis Morgan of Kingesthorpe, Northants., gent., who entered 1 August 1598, and was called to the degree of the utter bar, with Manningham, Charles Danvers, John Bramston, Alban Piggott, Timothy Wagstaffe, and others, 7 June 1605. Francis' father, also Francis Morgan, a member of the society since 1574, had become a Bencher and served as Autumn Reader in 1599 (*Adm.*, I, 74, 38). John Chamberlain mentions "one Morgan a lawiers sonne of good estate" who slew James Egerton, eldest son of Sir John Egerton, in a duel and who, though himself wounded, ended in Newgate (2 May 1610— I, 298).

Fo. 2b. "the Chauncery at Sandey": Chancel or chantry? (B). OED does not list this usage but does list *chauncery* as a worn-down form of *chancelry* and *chancer* as an obsolete Scottish form of *chancel* (II, 266). In 1593 the Diarist's friend Dr. Bartholomew Chamberlaine, mentioned on fos. 36b and 37, was rector of Sandy, about nine miles from Bedford.

Fo. 3. "Certayne Devises . . . Whitehall": The Shield Gallery at Whitehall is twice mentioned in Pepys' Diary (ed. Richard, Lord Braybrooke, 1848-49, I, 89, 113). Hentzner's *Journey into England* (1757), p. 29, describes among other things to be observed there "Variety of emblems on paper, cut into the shape of shields, with mottos, used by the nobility at tilts and tournaments, hung up there for a memorial."—B. Such paper, or pasteboard, shields painted with their devices and emblems were of course not used in actual encounter (Chambers, I, 143, and n. 1). See also Diary, fo. 66b and note.

Fo. 5. "Marche 28: 1602.": Palm Sunday.

"At the Temple:": According to Stow, the Temple Church had a "Maister and foure Stipendiary Priestes with a clarke," for the "ministration of diuine seruice there . . ." (*Survey of London*, ed. Kingsford, II, 1908, p. 51), but it seems clear from Middle and Inner Temple records that the principal personnel of the Temple Church were the Rector, called the Master of the Temple; the Reader, who read prayers in the Temple Church twice daily, at eight and four; and the Afternoon Preacher, either a fixed lecturer or a series of hired preachers, paid 10s for each sermon, the charge being shared by the two societies—*Master Worsley's Book on the History and Constitution of the Honourable Society of the Middle Temple*, ed. Arthur R. Ingpen (London, 1910), p. 197; Inderwick, II, 1898, p. 86. In the 1581-92 period, when Walter Travers was Reader, under the Mastership of Richard Hooker, the Reader preached the Afternoon Sermon; it is said of Travers that, "Though friendly with Hooker, he preached the doctrines of Geneva in the afternoon, while Hooker as Master, stood for Canterbury in the morning"—J. Bruce Williamson, *Middle Temple Bench Book*, 2nd ed. (1937), p. 307.

Who preached this remarkable message on Palm Sunday, 1602, can only be conjectured. The Reader at this time, Richard Baker, had formerly been Clerk of the Church but had sold the office of Clerk to one Thomas Middleton in 1593; he was allowed a life estate in a little house he had built, at his own cost, adjoining the Church, with certain shops—Inderwick, I (1896), pp. lix-lx. I think it unlikely that Baker was the preacher. The Master was Thomas Masters of St. John's and Merton Colleges, Oxford, a fellow of Merton and future canon of Lichfield (Williamson, 301); he was the third son of Dr. Masters, Physician to the Queen. He succeeded Nicholas Balguy, or Balgay, D.D., of Magdalen College, Oxford, after Balgay's death in August 1601, and continued as Master until the end of his life (1628), although in June, 1627, a suitor in the name of both Societies urged the King to "prefer Mr. Masters, the present Master of the Temple, to a Prebend at Windsor, and appoint Mr. [Paul] Micklethwayte their preacher to the Mastership"—J. E. Martin, *Masters of the Bench of the Honourable Society of the Inner Temple*, 1540-1883, privately printed (London, 1883), p. 132. See also Foster, III, 986.

I am grateful to the Rev. Frederick Shriver for helpful discussions concerning the theological stance of this finely tempered sermon, reflecting as it does the non-Calvinist and Erasmian doctrine that just and honest pagans are saved. Although Thomas Masters migrated to Merton after only two years at St. John's, in 1577, the year before Dr. John Buckeridge, Laud's tutor, became a scholar of St. John's, he may have caught some of the atmosphere of that college in advance of Buckeridge and Laud and may well have been the preacher whom Manningham heard.

As Canon T. R. Milford, Master of the Temple, has kindly suggested in a letter to the writer, Jan. 4, 1967, since Manningham does not mention that anyone other than the Master was preaching, we may take it that Thomas Masters was the man.

In Elizabethan times the Temple Church consisted of three parts: (1) *The Round,* built in the form of the Temple near the Holy Sepulchre at Jerusalem, but smaller, had been consecrated in 1185 by Heraclius the Patriarch of Jerusalem, on a mission from Pope Lucius III to Henry II. Its domed roof was supported by six clusters of pillars of polished Purbeck marble. Beneath it were recumbent monumental effigies and a circular sedile. (2) *The Choir or Oblong,* 82 feet long, 53 feet wide, and 37 feet high, had been added later and consecrated on Ascension Day, 1240, in the presence of Henry III and many noblemen. Built in the Lancet or Early English Style, it had middle and side aisles of corresponding height and roofs supported by graceful groined vaulting emanating from clustered columns of Purbeck marble. (3) On the southwest side, near the junction of the Round and Oblong, stood *the Chapel of St. Ann,* later ruined by fire (1678) and razed (1825). It had 13 lancet windows, each of three lights, and an organ, possibly under the center arch between the Round and Choir.

The communion plate had two chalices inscribed with the name of the Middle Temple Treasurer, "Nicholas Overburye." T. H. Baylis, *The Temple Church* (London, 1895), passim.

Fo. 5b. "agent": MS a gent

Fo. 6. "At St. Clementes": The Church was St. Clement Danes, in the Strand, of which Dr. John Layfield, of Trinity College, Cambridge, had recently become rector (1602). Later he would work with the Hebrew group of Bible translators at Westminster, under Lancelot Andrewes.

Layfield had had a harrowing experience sailing to the West Indies, in 1598, as chaplain to George Clifford, the third Earl of Cumberland. Upon his return he had written a colorful, detailed description of the voyage, printed in *Purchas, His Pilgrims.* See Gustavus S. Paine, *The Learned Men* (New York, 1959), pp. 35–39. They sailed from Portsmouth, March 6, 1597/98, bound for Puerto Rico and Dominica, returning October 3. Chamberlain commented rather caustically on the arrival home of the expedition and its dubious success: "they tooke the towne and castell of Porto-ricco where they found no great riches," because the Spanish, forewarned, had carried off their chief wealth; they brought back only 15,000 or 16,000 pounds worth of goods, mostly sugar and ginger—not even half the cost of the expedition—and lost 600 men by sword and sickness—*Letters,* I, 46–47. Manningham also heard Layfield preach twice on a Sunday in December 1602 (see fos. 73–74) and again in April 1603 (fo. 126).

"*Medicina*": MS medicinia; B reads medicine.

Fo. 6b. "the Picture of a Perfect Commonwealth": Not capitalized in MS. The book was entitled *The Picture of a perfit Common wealth, describing aswell the offices of Princes and inferiour Magistrates ouer their subiects, as also the* *duties of subiects towards their Gouernours. Gathered forth of many Authors, aswel humane, as diuine, by Thomas Floyd, master in the Artes.* This tiny (approximately 2 in. by 4 in.) moralistic work was "Printed at London by Simon Stafford, dwelling on Adling hill, 1600" (STC 11119), with a dedicatory epistle to Sir Thomas Egerton, in Latin. The passage comparing a wicked king to a crazed ship is from pp. 48-49 of the section on Tyrants: "Like as a battered or a crazed ship by letting in of water, not only drowneth herselfe, but all that are in her: so a king or a vitious tyrant, by vsing detestable enormities, destroyeth not himselfe alone, but all others beside that are vnder his gouernment . . ." Chapter 36 discusses "Pleasures and delights," but Floyd does not actually use the simile of "sweete singing birds." Rather, on pp. 215-216 of Chapter 31, "Of Friendship," he indirectly compares the third object of Friendship, pleasure, which is the pastime of youths and children and which is ephemeral, to "birds of the same feathers," which "do flocke and resort together."

"Dr. Mounfordes Sermon.": Dr. Thomas Mountford was prebendary of Westminster from 1585 to 1631/32 (Hardy's Le Neve, III, 350). The son of John Mountford of Norwich, "this worthy Doctor," as Wood terms him, received the D.D. 4 July 1588; by then he was also prebendary of Harleston and residentiary of St. Paul's (*Fasti*, I, 135-136).

"(Ch. Davers.)": Charles Danvers, or Davers, of Edington, Wilts., a close friend and fellow student of Manningham at the Middle Temple; admitted 31 October 1597; called to the degree of the Utter Bar at the same time as the diarist, 7 June 1605; became a Bencher and Autumn Reader, 1623 (*Adm.*, I, 72). Later one of his daughters, Jane, married the poet George Herbert (see Introduction). There are many references to him in the Diary. Evidently Manningham copied the notes of Dr. Mountford's sermon from Danvers' notebook.

"broken fishes": In MS "broken" is underlined, perhaps indicating that the diarist meant it to be canceled.

"Matt. 12.": The section headed by this citation may be notes from another sermon, since MS has a separation line across the page above it. On the other hand, B may have been right in regarding it as part of the Mountford sermon, inveighing as it does against envy as well as gluttony.

Fo. 7. "great person": In MS substituted for *Emperour* (which has been crossed out) without change of article.

"Mr. Downes": Andrew Downes, appointed Regius Professor of Greek at Cambridge in 1595 (B, citing Hardy's Le Neve, III, 660). Born about 1549, he attended grammar school at Shrewsbury, then went up to St. John's College, Cambridge, where he distinguished himself in Greek. One who heard his lectures on Demosthenes described him as tall, long-faced, elderly, with ruddy complexion and bright eyes, addicted to sitting with his legs on the table, and talking without stirring his feet or body. (Paine, *The Learned Men*, , p. 64.) An anecdote in Sir Nicholas L'Estrange's "Merry Passages and Jests" (*MS Harl.* 6395) reports an occasion when, preaching at Great St. Mary's, Downes was so "pitifully out" that some of his auditors jeered him: "Well, he rubb'd thorough, and gave them a short benediction; but, as he came downe from the pulpitt, 'By——,' sayes he, 'I'le never come here againe,'" In *Anecdotes and Traditions Illustrative of Early English History and Literature*, ed. William J. Thoms, Camden Society, V (1839), 41. Downes served with the New Testament group of translators at Cambridge, one of his former students, John Bois, or Boyes, who served with him, praising him as "our most subtle thinker in words" (Paine, p. 115).

Fo. 7b. "Mr. Phillips.": Probably Edward Philips, Oxford-educated, at Broadgates Hall, now Pembroke College, where he entered in 1574. He had a large auditory at St. Saviour's in Southwark, mostly of zealous Puritans, according to Wood, for he was "a zealous Calvinist." Henry Yelverton of Gray's Inn (afterwards a judge), son of Justice Christopher Yelverton, took down Philips' sermons and published them in 1605, two years after Philips' death. (*Athenae*, I, 321–322; STC 19853, *Certaine godly and learned sermons.*)

Fo. 8. "(Cha. Davers.)": Charles Danvers of the Middle Temple (see Introduction and note to fo. 6b).

Fo. 8b. "Mr. Munnes of Peterhouse": Edward Munnes, or Muns (1568-1603), M.A., fellow of Peterhouse, 1591-98, vicar of Stepney, Middlesex (appointed Mar. 16, 1597/8), and rector of East Barnet (1601). Second son of John Munns, merchant, of St. Andrew Hubbards, London, he had attended St. Paul's as an exhibitioner and Pembroke College, Cambridge (B.A., 1587/88). He was ordained deacon and priest at Peterborough 15 Aug. 1596, became prebendary of Gloucester the following year, and prebendary of Chichester in 1599. He died in May 1603, leaving his goods to his widow Anne, and was buried, it is supposed, in Gloucester Cathedral. George Hennessy, ed., *Novum Repertorium Ecclesiasticum Parochiale Londinense* (1898), pp. 411, clxi; Venn, III, 227; Hardy's Le Neve, I, 449; T. A. Walker, ed., *Biographical Register of Peterhouse Men*, Part II, Camb. (1930), p. 138. B mistranscribed Munnes as "Munoes."

"*Stultus Populus Quaerit Romam*": MS Stultus populus quaerit Romam.
"as the Divel is": MS as the diuel is.

Fo. 9. "Serchfeild": Dr. Rowland Searchfield of St. John's College, Oxford; admitted Doctor of Divinity, 16 May 1605; Bishop of Bristol 1619-22 (Wood, *Fasti*, I, 169; *Athenae*, I, 726).

"Mr. Scott, Trinit. Cant'br.": Robert Scott of Trinity College, Cambridge. At this time, 1601-02, he was Junior Dean, a position earlier held by such luminaries as John Overall, in 1591–92, and William Redman, 1572-73. Scott matriculated Pensioner, 1584/5; became Scholar, 1588; received the B.A., 1588/9; became Fellow, 1591; and received the M.A., 1592. *Admissions to Trinity College, Cambridge*, II, 1546-1700, ed. W. W. Rouse Ball & J. A. Venn (London, 1913), pp. x, 151. In 1599 he received the B.D. and was ordained deacon and priest at Peterborough. From 1608 till his death early in 1621, he seems to have served as rector of West Grinstead, Sussex. (Venn, *Alumni Cantabrigienses*, IV, 32.)

"Offer noe love rights . . . seldome like them.": Omitted by B.

Fo. 9b. "At Bradborne with my Cosen": The "cousin" or kinsman, frequently mentioned in the Diary, was Richard Manningham, esq., who had acquired the manor of Bradbourne, in East Malling, Kent, approximately 30 miles from London on the Maidstone Road. Childless, he had chosen young John Manningham to be his "son-in-love" and heir. Since the older man had been a successful merchant in London and a member of the Mercers' company, John tended to respect his comments on commercial topics and foreign countries. His first wife, Jane, having died in January, 1597/8, Richard had married in 1600/01 "Mistris Jane Manningham of Maydstone Widdow" (Register I, St. James, East Malling, under date of 26 Jan.). Richard died 25 April 1612, aged 72, and was buried at East Malling Church, where he is commemorated by a wall monument in the sanctuary (see Introduction).

"Mr. Richers": John Richers of Kent, son of a Lincoln's Inn bencher, specially admitted to Lincoln's Inn Jan. 27, 1574/5 (*L. I. Adm.*, 81). The John Rychers mentioned in Sir Roger Twysden's Book of Musters in Kent as one of the justices of the peace in the South Division of the Lathe of Aylesford is probably the same person; he was obliged to impress men for service in France, 1591/2. (*Calendar of Sir Roger Twysden's Collection of Lieutenancy Papers*, 1583-1622, pp. 77 ff.) Mr. Richers, as the Diarist tells us, was a first cousin of Mr. Hugh Cartwright, about whom see below and notes to fos. 13b and 35. The name "John Richeres, esquire" appears in the Court Rolls of Ightham, 1586-1618 (*Archaeologia Cantiana*, XLIX, 1937, p. 60).

"his cosen Cartwright": Hugh Cartwright, esq., of East Malling, Kent, who came into possession of the manor of East Malling and its premises from Pierpoint (buried in Town Malling Church), who had had it from Sir Henry Brooke (seventh son of George Lord Cobham), who had received it on lease from the Queen (12 Eliz.). Cartwright also had a grant of the chapel at New Hythe (see fo. 35). (Ref: Hasted, IV, 509, 511. See also fos. 13b, 14b, and notes.)

"Peter Courthope": Member of a prominent Kentish family and evidently a friend and neighbor of Richard Manningham. His kinsman "George Courthop" is mentioned in the registers of All Saints Church, Maidstone, where he married Ruthe Gooreley 11 Feb. 1578. Two earlier "Courthopps" contributed to a loan to the King in 1542: Richard Courtopp of Cranebrook and "Petir Courtop of Cranebroke yoman." James Greenstreet, "Kent Contributors to a Loan to the King. A.D. 1542," *Arch. Cant.*, XL (1877), p. 402. There were also Courthopes living in East Malling, for Susan "Courtup" was buried there 30 Aug. 1591 (St. James, E. Malling, Reg. I).

Fo. 10. "Sir Moyle Finche . . . Hastinges daughter": Sir Moyle Finch, a Gray's Inn man (admitted, 1568), knighted in 1584, was created 1st Baronet of Eastwell, Kent, in 1611; he died in 1614, aged about 64. Sir Francis Hastings, educated at Cambridge and in Magdalen College, Oxford, under Dr. Lawrence Humphrey, was a politician, champion of the Puritan party, and a pamphleteer against Fr. Robert Parsons, S.J. (DNB, IX, 116-117). Apparently Manningham is recording an earlier marriage of Moyle Finch, one not known to Dugdale (Bar., II, 445) or Collins (III, 382, ed. Brydges) and not mentioned in DNB. On 4 Nov. 1572, at Heneage House in London, Moyle Finch and Elizabeth

Heneage, only daughter and heir of the Queen's Vice-Chamberlain Sir Thomas Heneage, were married by the Dean of St. Paul's, Alexander Nowell. *The Complete Peerage*, ed. G. E. C., Geoffrey White, and R. S. Lea, XII, Part II (1959), 773. They had eleven children, including Ann Finch, who became 1st Lady Twysden; Thomas Finch, who became 1st Earl of Winchelsea; and Sir Heneage Finch (1580-1631), their fourth son, who became Speaker of the House of Commons in 1625 (ibid.). The illustrious mother became Viscountess Maidstone in 1623 and 1st Countess of Winchelsea in 1628. Thomas Philipot, *Villare Cantianum: or Kent Surveyed and Illustrated*, London (1659), p. 228. At Bradbourne House, East Malling, are miniatures of Sir Moyle and his Lady, as well as Sir Heneage. R. G. and C. H. Hatton, "Notes on the Family of Twysden and Twisden," *Archaeologia Cantiana*, LVIII (1946), 59. At the time of Manningham's entry, Heneage was at the Inner Temple (admitted, 1597; called 1606)—DNB, VII, 7. Eastwell was the seat of the Finch family and, according to Izaak Walton, Henry Wotton's mother was the daughter of Sir William Finch of Eastwell—*Life of Sir Henry Wotton* (London, 1685), b 2.

"(Drue Chapman.)": Drew Chapman of Godmersham, Kent, elder brother of John Chapman, one of Manningham's sureties at the Middle Temple, a kinsman of the Diarist. Mistranscribed by B as "Dene Chapman." See fo. 44 and note; also Manningham's comment on the Chapman brothers, fo. 84b.

"at Mr. Gellibrandes": The Gellibrand family appears to have enjoyed preeminence in Kent in the early part of the seventeenth century. Henry Gellibrand, M.A., a Fellow of All Souls College, Oxford, was father of Henry Gellibrand (1597-1636) the mathematician and astronomer (DNB, VII, 996). Among other properties he owned a residence at St. Paul's Cray, Kent. The DNB records his death as of 15 Aug. 1615; more than likely he was the Henry Gellibrand whose inquisition *Post Mortem*, dated 14 Feb. 14 James I—i.e., 1616—is in the Public Record Office (C142/357/36, and Wards 7/55/165). His will names another Henry as his son and heir and mentions Boxley, Chiselherst (sic), and division of the manor of Footescray into two parts (ibid.). Manningham, on fo. 103b of the Diary, mentions an "H. Gellibrand," presumably Henry the elder, but whether this was the Maidstone physician is unclear. The name Gellibrand does not appear in the pertinent parish registers of All Saints, Maidstone. There are, however, gaps in the baptismal records from March 1588 to 1593 and in the burials, Sept. 1596-1611. Dr. Felix Hull, Kent County Archivist, has kindly informed me that Thomas Gellibrand of Sandwich (died 1607) is listed in indexes of wills proved in the Canterbury Diocesan Courts 1602-1670: PRC 17/56, fo. 141. It is quite possible that he was the "Th. Gellib." mentioned as brother to the physician on fo. 10b of the Diary (q.v.).

In other branches of the family, two Edward Gellibrands were prominent: one, of Magdalen College, Oxford, was a strong Puritan, B.D. 1584, and Fellow 1573-88, minister at the English Church of Middelburg, Holland, where he died in 1601 (Venn, II, 206); the other was a Lincoln's Inn lawyer, ordered to be called to the bar 27 June 1596 (actually nominated 5 June 1596) and one of the stewards of the Reader's Dinner, Autumn 1601 (*Black Books*, fo. 23, 33, 88, in *L. I. Adm.*, II, 48, 51, 70). Among others were Thomas and Roger Gelibrande, of Blackborne, co. Lancs., when in August 1567 they were among fifty appointed governors of the Free Grammar School of Queen Elizabeth there—*Calendar of Patent Rolls, Eliz. I, 1566-69* (1964), p. 90. Probably more closely related to Henry was Edmund Gellibrand ("Gillibrande"), whose *Inq. P. M.* dated 7 Nov., 14 James I (1616), mentions the manor of Footescray and "Elizabetha Gillibrand Widwe," but whose sister Elizabeth was his sole heir (Public Record Office, C 142/357/8; Wards 7/51/169).

From Bradbourne to Maidstone was a short ride of 4-5 miles by the old Turnpike.

"Mr. Fr[ancis] Vane": Statesman and parliamentarian, soon (at the coronation of King James) to be made K.B., and later (1642) to be created Baron Burghersh and Earl of Westmoreland (B). His father-in-law, Sir Anthony Mildmay, of the Mildmays of Apethorp, Northants., had become ambassador to France in 1596 (Harrison, II, 135, citing Stow's *Annals*).

"(Mr. Tutsham.)": Probably Thomas Tuttesham of West Peckham, Kent, uncle to Thomas Stanley of Hamptons, near Tunbridge. He is variously reported to have married in 1581 a widowed Cecilia Leiston of Gravesend and Elizabeth Pettey (*Arch. Cant.*, XV, 380; XVII, 357 n). From Thomas "Tutsom" Richard Manningham purchased Larkhall in Hadlow, Kent (according to his will). Or the Diarist may be referring to Anthony Tuttesham, owner of Oxenoth, a fifty-acre estate in West Peckham and Wrotham. As resident of Nordiham in Sussex in 1606, he sold Oxenoth, 11 August, to John Stanley, who married Dorothy Tuttesham (his daughter?), settling half of it upon Dorothy as a dowry, in case of widowhood (ibid., XV, 388). The ancestor of Thomas and Anthony, one John Tuttesham, gent., had acquired lands in West Peckham and Wrotham in 1495/6 (ibid., XV, 387-8). One Richard Tutsam was buried at All Saints Church, Maidstone, 30 March 1631 (Register of Burials, 1576-1670).

"The Duke of Albues [Alva's] negligence . . . Flushinge": Alvarez de Toledo, third Duke of Alva (1507-1582), Spanish general sent by Philip II in 1567 to "pacify" the Netherlands. Flushing (Vlissingen), a fortified port of Zealand province controlling the approach to Antwerp, was the first town to throw off the Spanish yoke, in 1572.

"(Cos [en].)": The Diarist's kinsman and foster-father Richard Manningham, of Bradbourne, East Malling, Kent (see note to fo. 9b).

Fo. 10b. "My Cosen shee": Jane, or Joan, second wife of Richard Manningham of Bradbourne, East Malling, the Diarist's "father-in-love." Parish registers at St. James, East Malling, record their marriage in 1600 (i.e., 1600/01): "Jan: 26 Richard Maningham & Mistris Jane Maningham of Maydstone Widdow." Richard's first wife, also Jane, had died three years earlier (Buried at East Malling Jan. 30, 1597/8—Reg. I). We may infer that the second wife had been married to one whom she called "Marche" (see subsequent entry on fo. 10b) and then to a kinsman of the Diarist's foster father, perhaps to George Manningham, referred to as "deceased" on fo. 9b and note, and fo. 14b.)

"like a payre of turtles": MS liue a payre . . .

"Th. Gellib[rand] said . . . cuckold.": Omitted by B. Concerning the Gellibrands, see note to fo. 10.

"Husband, said a wife . . . what shee gave him).": B omitted this cryptic little indecency, with its suggestion of an almost international gesture. One sense of the phrase *put downe* is outdo or overcome; compare an example of this usage in the second entry of fo. 11. Also compare Kate to Hotspur in Act II, Scene 4, of Shakespeare's *Henry IV, Part I*: "In faith, I'll break thy little finger, Harry, / An if thou wilt not tell me all things true."

"My Cos., . . . straungelly.": Omitted by B. "Haston's house," though not listed in OED and in Partridge and other dictionaries of slang or informal usage, is apparently a colloquial term for privy—a punning euphemism. Compare the similar usage in Dryden's *MacFlecknoe* which has long puzzled editors: "Echoes from *Pissing*-Ally, Sh----call/ And Sh---- they resound from A [ston] Hall." *Seventeenth-Century Verse and Prose*, II, ed. Helen C. White, Ruth C. Wallerstein, and Ricardo Quintana (New York, 1952), p. 280, ll. 47-48.

"Wee were at Mrs. Cavils": From Middle Temple and Kent records it may be inferred that Mrs. Cavill, or Cavell, was Elizabeth, wife of John Cavell, Bencher and Reader who became Treasurer of the Middle Temple (1604, 1605). The Diarist seems to have been present for his reading, Lent, 1600/01 (*Min.*, I, 413). On 21 Nov. 1602 Jervaise Maplisden, or Maplesden, son and heir apparent of the Maidstone lawyer Edward Maplisden, gent., was admitted "at the request of Mr. Cavell, a Master of the Bench" and was "Bound with Messers. Manningham and Richard Freston." (*Min.*, I, 427.) Registers of All Saints parish, Maidstone, record the burial of "Maister John Caveell connesyller" on March 20, 1611 (Reg. Burials, 1576-1670). The following March 12th (1612/13) his property was granted to Elizabeth, his relict (Act Books of P.C.C., fol. 52, in "Kentish Administrations, 1604-1649," ed. Leland L. Duncan, *Arch. Cant.*, XX, 1893, p. 7).

Fo. 11. "one Lovell of Cranebrooke (a good honest poore silly puritane)": Unidentified. Cranbrook Church, about 13 miles south of Maidstone, Kent, had been the scene of a notorious Sessions trial for heresy—of John Bland by Sir John ("Bloody") Baker—during the Marian persecutions. By the end of the seventeenth century the Anabaptists were strong in this parish. (J. Cave-Brown, "Cranbrook Church," *Arch. Cant.*, XXII, 1897, pp. 228, 229.)

"in a booke of newes from Ostend": *News from Ostend of the oppugnation*, etc., (V. Simmes for T. Pavier, 1601), 4to—STC 18893; or *Extremities urging Sir F. Veare to the anti-parle with the Archduke Albertus* (STC 24651). Toward the end of December, 1601, the garrison besieged at Ostend since late June, having endured hot fighting in the intervening months, badly needed reinforcements, for the Archduke, then in person before the city, was preparing another assault. During a truce and parley, the Lord General, Sir Francis Vere, employed a delaying stratagem to gain time for reinforcements to arrive and to improve his defenses. Refusing to admit the Archduke's envoys and their attendance of about 60 horses, Vere sent them back; meanwhile, the tide having arisen, the Spaniards were obliged to travel nearly twelve wearying miles around the drowned lands to return to their headquarters, which they could not reach until noon the following day. On their next try Vere admitted them and put on a fish and egg supper, letting claret make up for the lack of meat; that night, while the Spaniards rested, three warships carrying six companies of Zealand soldiers arrived to strengthen the English Forces. (Harrison, III, 246-8.) Then Sir Francis "sent the Commissioners back disappointed of their hopes," and "flouting them with a nipping Jest, he desired them to pardon him, if in case of urgent necessity he should do the like again." (William Camden, *History of . . . Elizabeth Late Queen of England,* Book IV, 4th ed., 1688, p. 633.)

"Leake": Whether Thomas Lake or Francis Leake is meant is uncertain. The former, one of the clerks of the signet, was knighted in May, 1603, and became secretary of state from Jan., 1615/16, until his ruin in Feb., 1618/19. (DNB, XI, 417-19; Shaw, *Knights of England,* II, 109). In 1588 he had been one of the bailiffs of the Barons of the Cinque Ports to the town of Great Yarmouth and the town and port of Dover, with Henry Lennarde of Dover (see their report, "A True Record . . . at . . . Great Yarmouth," in *Arch. Cant.,* XXIII, 1898, pp. 162-183).

On June 30, 1599, he was granted the office of clerk of York Castle and the county courts of York (CSP, *Dom., Eliz., 1598-1601,* p. 224). His house was near Charing Cross (ibid., 82). He was knighted as Thomas Leake of Co. Derby (Shaw, loc. cit.).

Francis Leek, or Leake, of Sutton in Le Dale, Derbyshire, was knighted in August, 1600 or 1601 (Shaw, II, 98). His son Francis, specially admitted to the Middle Temple 1 Feb. 1599/1600 (*Min.* I, 400), was also knighted, March 14, 1603/04, at the Tower (Shaw, II, 131). See also fo. 35b.

"Theroles[?] *nar.*": Probably Therold or Thorold, hence one of several Thorolds listed in *Gray's Adm.,* pp. 76, 89, 97: Alexander Thorold or his brother Robert from Hough, co. Lincoln; or a cousin, Edmund, of the same place; or William or John, of Morton, co. Lincoln; or John, a younger brother of Alexander and Robert. The last, admitted to Gray's Inn, May 7, 1599, would have been contemporary with the Diarist. Robert and John Thorold were admitted pensioners at Emmanuel College, Cambridge, in 1586 (*Emman. Coll. MS. CHA.* 1.4). John was knighted April 23, 1603 (Shaw, *Knights of England,* II, 103). His wife was a niece of Robert Cranmer of "Cheeveninge," Co. Kent, esq., and was mentioned in his uncle's will, dtd. 17 Dec. 1616 (*Abstracts of Wills in P.C.C. at Somerset House,* ed. J. Henry Lee, Boston, 1904, p. 131).

"The companie of pewterers much greived at a licence . . . to one Atmore to cast tynne,": Atmore's name is not mentioned in Charles Welch's two-volume *History of the Worshipful Company of Pewterers of the City of London* (1902), but it clearly appears from the Company's records that they felt it their exclusive right, granted by committees of the Council, "to nomynat and chuse fower bretheren of the company to be casters of tynne into barres ffor the space of one yere next followyng and that no other pewterer shuld vppon penalty to be farther agreed vppon cast any." (Company court of 14 Jan. 1602/03—Welch, II, 36.) The main question at issue was whether the Crown had the right to pre-empt and export tin. Thomas Brigham and Humphrey Wemes had been granted a patent by the Queen for pre-emption of tin in Cornwall and Devon (CSP

Dom. James I, 1603-1610, pp. 14, 335). The Pewterers, unhappy about the export of raw (unwrought) tin, petitioned Her Majesty that no tin in blocks be transported out of the realm unless first cast into bars and ingots by the Company or made into vessels by pewterers in England (undated, *Hist. MSS. Comm., Salisbury Papers*, XIV, 1923, p. 310). In 1603 by contributing heavily to the City's entertainment of the King and charges for the coronation, the Company succeeded in procuring James' proclamation to suppress the pre-emption of tin (Welch, II, 37-38): "giuen at our Mannour of Greenwich the 16. Day of Iune . . . 1603." (*Book of Proclamations*, 1609, p. 22). But this was not to be the end of the matter, which continued to be controverted for six years by the aggrieved patentees, the Company under Richard Glover, the Privy Council, and the Court of Star Chamber. Eventually the Pewterers who had induced the King to relinquish the pre-emption of tin were prosecuted and fined, and the pre-emption was re-established (CSP, *Dom., James I, 1603-10*, pp. 84, 152, 157, 335, 608).

Fol. 11b. "(Leydall)": One of two brothers Lydall, or Leydall, at the Middle Temple: Edward, "son and heir of Thomas L., of Redinge, Berks., gent."—admitted 21 Jan. 1591/92 (*Adm.*, I, 63); or Richard, the second son, specially admitted 24 Jan. 1597/98 (less than two months before Manningham), and "bound with Messers. Francis Moore and Edward Lydall, his brother." (*Min.* I, 380). One of the Lydalls was called with William Burdett "by Mr. Doddridge during his first reading," confirmed 3 June 1603 (*Min.* II, 440). *Adm.*, ed. Sturgess, 1949, makes this out to be Edward's call (I, 63), but the index of *Records*—i.e., *Min.*, ed. Martin, 1905—implies that it was Richard's. Probably the latter is correct, since there is no specific mention of Edward after Jan. 1597/98, whereas Richard's name appears several times from 10 Feb. 1603/04 until 1637. Sometime between 20 Nov. 1614 (*Min.*, II, 587) and 6 Feb. 1617/18 Richard was knighted, for an entry of the latter date reads: "Sir Richard Lydall, Messers. Manningham, R. Weston, and Waldram are appointed to provide the Reader's feast" (*Min.*, II, 625). The name was mistranscribed "Archdall" by B. See also fos. 58, 59, and 117.

"Rashnes ridiculous: . . . (Mr. Davers).": Omitted by B. The raconteur was Charles Danvers (see note to fo. 6b).

"some reverence": excrement. Neither OED nor Eric Partridge's *Shakespeare's Bawdy* (New York, 1948) records this usage, which is apparently an abbreviation of an abbreviation: i.e., a shortening of *sir-reverence*, which term represented a slurring of *save-your-reverence*, used apologetically before mentioning something unpleasant or when coming across a lump of (human) excrement. Compare Ben Jonson's expression for a commode or privy: "the stoole of worship"—ll. 122-123 of Epigram CXXIII, "On the Famous Voyage," in *Complete Poetry of Ben Jonson*, ed. William B. Hunter (New York, 1963), p. 71.

"Hide to Tanfeild": Probably Nicholas Hyde to Robert Tanfield. All four sons of Lawrence Hyde of West Hatch, Tisbury, Wilts., were affiliated with the Middle Temple: Robert, Lawrence, Henry and Nicholas. The last was admitted 14 July 1590 (three months after Benjamin Rudyerd and in the same month as Richard Hadsor), called to the bar 24 Nov. 1598, served in Parliament, became Bencher and Lent Reader in 1616, and Treasurer in 1625 (*Adm.*, I, 61). Though a leader of the popular party, against the prerogative of impositions in 1610 and one of the speakers in the conference of the houses on impositions in 1614, he rose to eminence in 1626/27, being knighted, called to Serjeant-at-law, and made Chief Justice all within a space of eight days. (DNB, X, 399). B suggests Nicholas' older brother, Lawrence, citing Foss's *Judges*, VI, 335: he was admitted 19 Nov. 1580, called 7 Feb. 1588/89, and made Bencher and Autumn Reader in 1608, Treasurer in 1616. (*Adm.*, I, 48). Both were uncles to Edward Hyde, Lord Chancellor Clarendon of the Restoration.

Robert Tanfield was admitted 6 March 1598/99, "late of New inn, gent., son and heir of Robert T., late of Northampton, esq., dcd. Called 27 Nov., 1607. Bencher 1623. Reader Lent 1623. Treasurer 1631." (*Adm.*, I, 75). B, citing Foss's *Judges*, VI, 365, identifies "Tanfeild" as Lawrence Tanfield, of the Inner Temple, "the future Lord Chief Baron, whose only daughter was mother to Lucius Lord Falkland."

See also fo. 44 and note; fo. 91.

"The L[ord] Paget": William Paget (1505-1563), first Baron Paget of Beaudesert, was the son of William Paget, a serjeant-at-mace of the city of London. His "low birth" was often objected to by the courtiers. He was educated at St. Paul's under William Lyly and at Trinity Hall, Cambridge, and rose to eminence in the reigns of Henry VIII, Edward VI, and Mary. Known as Lord Paget of Drayton, he was buried at West Drayton, Middlesex, but a monument was erected to his memory in Lichfield Cathedral. (DNB, XV, 60-62.) Of his four sons, at least two were members of the Middle Temple: Thomas and Charles "Pagett," second and third sons of "lord P. of Draiton," were admitted Oct. 9, 1560 (*Adm.*, I, 25). Thomas became third Lord Paget; his son William, who became the fourth Lord, was admitted Feb. 20, 1610/11 (*Adm.*, I, 96).

"Sir Tho. White": Sir Thomas White (1492-1576), a founder of St. John's College, Oxford, and—with Richard Hilles—of the Merchant Taylors' School. This benefactor to education, son of a Hertfordshire clothier, prospered in his father's trade and became a resident of Cornhill in the parish of St. Michael. He was elected alderman in 1544 and Lord Mayor in 1553. (DNB, XXI, 76-77.)

Fo. 12. "(Reeves.)": There were two Reeves at the Middle Temple at this time: William Ryves, admitted 4 Feb. 1592/93, and Richard Ryves, admitted 30 July 1597. Both came from Dorset but from different families. (*Min.*, I, 369, 376.) William was called on 2 May 1600 and became a Bencher in 1618 (*Adm.*, I, 64). The "R. R." mentioned on fo. 70 of the Diary may have been Richard Reeves.

"Tarlton": Richard Tarlton, famous Elizabethan stage clown or comic actor, a favorite of the Queen and the populace. The Earl of Leicester had brought him to court, and Sir Philip Sidney had stood god-father to Tarlton's son. Though he had died in 1588, his memory was being kept green by various publications issued under his name, such as *Tarltons newes out of purgatorie*,

1590 (STC 23685), and *Tarltons Jests,* 1638. Stow, in his *Annals,* 1615, said that "for a wondrous plentifull pleasant extemporall wit, hee was the wonder of his time." (DNB, XIX, 369.) Donne listed him in the satirical *Catalogus Librorum Aulicorum (The Courtier's Library)* as the author of a book on 'The Privileges of Parliament,' a jibe at the Parliamentarians (see Nonesuch Press edition, 1930, ed. Evelyn M. Simpson).

"(Ch. Davers.)": Charles Danvers, or Davers, of the Middle Temple (see Introduction and note to fo. 6b).

"Mr. Curle": Edward Curle, or Curll, the Diarist's chambermate and future brother-in-law; admitted to the Middle Temple Nov. 29, 1594, as "son and heir of William C., of Hatfeild, Herts., gent. Called 14 May, 1602. Bencher 1620. Reader Lent, 1620." (*Adm.,* I, 67). Middle Temple records show that Manningham took Thomas Streynsham's place as Curle's "chamberfellow" on 5 Feb. 1601/02 (*Min.,* I, 418). The punning on *bind* and *loose* was evidently commonplace, for Donne so joked in a letter of 1600, probably written to his friend Henry Wotton: ". . . at least I would not haue beene well by so ill a meanes, as taking phisick: for I am bound by making myself loose." (As printed in E. M. Simpson, *A Study of the Prose Works of John Donne,* 2nd ed., Oxford, 1948, p. 315.)

"Overbury *recit.*": Thomas Overbury (1581-1613), the young, brilliant but ill-fated courtier and writer, son of the Middle Temple Bencher Nicholas Overbury, of Aston Sneege (i.e., Aston Sub edge), Glos. Thomas had been admitted to the Middle Temple 30 July 1597 (*Min.,* I, 72) at the age of 16 or 17, perhaps—like James Whitelock at St. John's, Oxford,—shuttling between Queen's College and London, until he received his B.A., at the end of 1598 (*Min.,* I, 376). Handsome, talented, and cultivated, Overbury was much admired by his contemporaries, including Ben Jonson, who praised him and enjoyed his company until they quarreled over the Countess of Rutland (see Jonson, to Drummond of Hawthornden, in *Works,* ed. Herford and Simpson, I, 137-8, 170, 214-218; and DNB, XIV, 1275). Manningham probably knew both father and son. On several occasions he quotes Thomas, who was known for his outspokenness (see the next passage and the entry on fo. 39b). John Chamberlain told Carleton that Overbury "is too plain for the tender ears of the age." (Dec. 23, 1613; *CSP Dom. James I, 1611-1618,* p. 216.) He would meet a gruesome end in the Tower from cruel poisoning by confederates of the vindictive Frances Countess of Essex, the Jacobean Jezebel. (See William McElwee, *The Murder of Thomas Overbury,* New York, 1952, p. 41.)

"They say London stones . . . fall.": Omitted by B.

Fo. 12b. "Mr. Lancastre": Probably Thomas Lancaster of Gray's Inn, admitted 1569 (*Gray's Adm.,* fo. 604, p. 40). See also Manningham, fo. 45b and fo. 97b.

"Margaret Westfalinge": Margaret Westphaling, daughter of Harbert (Herbert) Westphaling, Bishop of Hereford from 1585 until his death in March, 1601/02. She married the illustrious poet-playwright Richard Eedes, or Edes, D.D., (1555-1604), who since 1596 had been Dean of Worcester. According to Wood, Dr. Eedes was "held in great admiration at Court, not only for his preaching, but most excellent and polite discourse." (*Athenae*, I, 314, 326). That she herself was given to word play is shown by her having inscribed on her husband's tomb a punning epitaph in verse, in the form of a dialogue between the monument (Lapis) and a traveller (Viator) meditating among the tombs. (See inscription and plate in Thomas' *Survey of the Cathedral Church of Worcester*, pp. 47, 48, and in Willis, *Survey of Cathedrals*, II, 659—DNB, VI, 364.)

"Streynsham *nar.*": Probably Thomas Streynsham of the Middle Temple, admitted May 18, 1596, "late of New Inn, gent., son and heir of Richard S., late of Feversham, Kent, dcd." He was Edward Curle's chambermate for a time, until Manningham took his place (see note to fo. 12). Streynsham was called to the degree of the Utter Bar on the same day as Charles Danvers, John Bramston, and the Diarist, 7 June 1605 (*Adm.*, I, 70, 72, 73). Another Streynsham from Kent, George, a barrister of Clifford's Inn, was admitted to Lincoln's Inn Dec. 12, 1580 (*L. I. Adm.*, 91).

"Dauis . . . (Martin.)": John Davies, the Middle Temple lawyer and poet, author of *Orchestra, Nosce Teipsum*, epigrams, posies, and "gulling" sonnets; and Richard Martin, friend of Jonson, Donne, Hoskyns, Rudyerd and other poetical wits—he would achieve fame in Parliament and become Recorder of London before his death in 1616.

Davies and Martin had been close friends at the Middle Temple, having participated together in the riot growing out of the prohibited Lord of Misrule festival in 1591. In the autumn of 1592 they had been together in the Netherlands, where they had visited the Dutch scholar Paul Merula (Bodl. *MS. D'Orville* 52, f. 50, cited by Robert Kreuger, "Sir John Davies: *Orchestra* Complete, *Epigrams*, Unpublished Poems," *R.E.S.*, XIII, 1962, p. 25). In a letter the following spring Davies had sent Martin his greetings (ibid.). Then Davies had dedicated his *Orchestra* (publ. 1596) to Martin.

During the Christmas revels of 1597/98, however, "Le Prince d'Amour or the Prince of Love," Martin gained the title role, over Davies, who, in spite of his playing an important part and even writing a portion of the entertainment, was so ridiculed as "Milorsius Stradilax" by the other revellers that he conceived a violent animosity towards "Sir Martino." The revels ended on Candlemas Day, 2 Feb. One week later, 9 Feb., Davies marched into the Great Hall, armed with a bastinado, and brutally cudgelled his erstwhile friend sitting at supper. (See P. J. Finkelpearl's "Sir John Davies and the 'Prince D'Amour'," *Notes and Queries*, Aug., 1963, pp. 301-2; also *Min.*, especially I, 379, 381, 416; and the detailed account by Benjamin Rudyerd in *Le Prince d'Amour, Or the Prince of Love*, London, 1660—Wing STC 2189).

For his offense Davies was expelled. Then after a long "vacation" and through the mediation of Lord Chief Justice (Sir John) Popham and Master Secretary (Sir Robert) Cecil—see Chamberlain, I, 126—he made an official submission, on All Saints Day, 1601, receiving Martin's pardon and being reinstated.

Although Manningham was not admitted to the Society until five weeks

after the infamous cudgelling, others whom he came to know well, such as
John Hoskyns, Edward Curle and Charles Danvers, had probably been eye-
witnesses. Thus in this anagram and in other passages the diary reflects the
approbrium heaped upon Davies by his Middle Temple associates. (See fo. 127b,
for instance.) Henceforth too, Davies-baiting became a popular sport, indulged
in by Jonson, Donne, and other friends of Martin, as well as by Middle Templar
John Marston. Jonson's scorn of Davies' verses is expressed in his *Conversations
with Drummond*, sect. 15, ll. 387–91. Donne ridiculed Davies' posies and
anagrams in his mock-library, *Catalogus Librorum Aulicorum*, in which No. 16
slyly adverts to Davies' absence from the Middle Temple: "English Law-
vacations. Holiday exercises of John Davies on the Art of forming Anagrams
approximately true, and posies to engrave on Rings." (in Simpson, *Study of
the Prose Works of Donne*, 1948, p. 155). Marston satirized both *Orchestra*
and its author in Satire I appended to *Pygmalion* (1598) and in Satire X (see
Waldo F. McNeir, "Marston versus Davies and Terpsichore," *Philological
Quarterly*, XXIX, IV, October 1950, pp. 430-4).

  According to Rudyerd, who described him in his stellar role as the
Prince of Love, Martin was "of Face thin and lean, but of a cheerful and
gracious countenance; black haired, tall bodied, and well proportioned; of a
sweet and fair conversation to every man that kept his distance. Fortune never
taught him to temper his own Wit or Manhood." (*Le Prince d'Amour*, 1660,
pp. 89-90, from Huntington Library copy).

  Martin is commemorated by a fine Jacobean alabaster effigy in the
restored Temple Church, on the south side between the Round and the Nave,
its inscription reading as follows:

> "Salve Lector
> MARTINUS Jacet Hic si nescis caetera quaere
>   Interea Tumuli sis Memor ipse tui

> "Vale Ivrisconsvlte
> Accedat totum precibus quod cunq recedit
> Litibus, aeternum sic tibi tempus erit."

  "At our feast . . . a play called 'Twelve night . . .'": In MS Manningham
wrote "Mid" then crossed it out before writing "Twelve," undoubtedly at first
thinking of *A Midsummer Night's Dream*. And he makes rather little of this
notable event, a performance in the Great Hall of the Middle Temple of what
Leslie Hotson has rightly called Shakespeare's "most musical and festive" high
comedy (*The First Night of 'Twelfth Night*,' 1954, p. 16); but he was there,
on Candlemas Night (one of the two major festivals at the Inns of Court, the
other being All Saints, Nov. 1); he saw it and enjoyed it.

  On this Grand Day of the Feast of the Purification the judges and serjeants belonging to the society assembled for the entertainment provided, which
included dinner, an interval of retirement to the garden while the Hall was
cleansed and prepared for the festivities to follow, a play performance, then
the ceremony of dancing and singing known as the "solemn revels." The
illustrious and handsomely dressed audience included divers Noblemen, some

of them Knights of the Garter, "invited as Guests to the Dinner in regard they were formerly of the Society" (William Dugdale, *Origines Juridiciales*, 1666, p. 205. See also Alfred Ainger, "Shakespeare in the Middle Temple," *The English Illustrated Magazine*, March 1884, pp. 366-76; J. Bruce Williamson, *The Temple Hall*, 2nd ed., 1934, pp. 37, 40-45, 59; James P. Cunningham, *Dancing in the Inns of Court*, London: Jordan & Sons Ltd., 1965, 44 pp.)

The play was presented by the Lord Chamberlain's company of the Globe Theatre. Whether the author was among the actors can only be conjectured, as Ainger has done, suggesting that Shakespeare played Malvolio if Burbage declined it, or perhaps Orsino (p. 374). Was it a new play—especially written for performance at the Middle Temple? J. D. Wilson, pointing out that the prose scenes are full of legal jests, has declared them "penned expressly for performance at the Inns of Court" (Sir Arthur Quiller-Couch and John Dover Wilson, eds., *Twelfth Night or What You Will*, 2nd ed., Camb. 1949, p. 95); but Prof. Hotson has argued that the play had had its first performance at the palace of Whitehall Jan. 6, 1600/01, as part of the Queen's entertainment of Virginio Orsino, Duke of Bracciano, ambassador to the English court (*First Night of 'Twelfth Night'*, esp. pp. 12 ff.). An opposing view, that the comedy was written for the general audience of the public theatre, is offered by Martin Homes, *Shakespeare's Public*, London, 1960, p. 135.

The method of staging is also something of an enigma. Where and how in the Hall was it done? At the upper west end, on the dais supporting the bench table, where dramatic entertainments are now performed? Or at the screen end, using the portals in the screen for entrances and exits? Or in the center, on the floor, arena-fashion, using free-standing, painted units of scenery ("scenic houses" or "mansions"), the audience seated on every side? Having inspected the Hall several times in 1966 and again in 1967, I am disinclined toward the first location, the upper or bench end, on the likelihood that proud noblemen, judges, serjeants, officers (Treasurers and Readers) and ancients, would have preferred to view the show from their honoured and favored (raised) position. The location of the fire, midway laterally and two-thirds of the way up the hall toward the bench table, seems to have precluded a circus-type or theatre-in-the-round performance. The practicability of acting at the screen end of the Hall weighs heavily in its favor, though the minstrel's gallery is probably too high (about 15 feet) to have been used as a balcony or upper stage. Wherever the play was enacted, the smoke and flame of the fire is liable to have interfered with audience vision. It is to be hoped that old accounts in the archives of the Middle Temple Library will shed some light on these problems

That Dick Martin, principal entertainer in the society and a member of the Jonson-Donne circle, may have had something to do with the arrangements is suggested by the fact that he was called to the bar just three days later, some dozen years after his admission (*Min.*, I, 419).

"Inganni": There were *Gl'Inganni* plays by Nicole Secchi, first acted in 1547 and printed at Florence in 1562, and by Curzio Gonzaga, printed in Venice in 1592. Both contain a brother and sister who are much alike, the

sister clothed in man's attire. Since the Lady in Gonzaga's play is called
Cesare, we may infer that Shakespeare probably knew both plays and certainly the latter. More like his *Twelfth Night* in plot, however, is the comedy
Gl'Ingannati (The Deceived Ones), introduced by a poetical induction entitled *Il Sacrificio de gli Intronati,* performed at Siena, 1531, pr. Venice, 1537.
A Latin version of this, called *Laelia,* was acted at Queens' College, Cambridge,
in 1595, when Manningham was an undergraduate, though he may not have
seen it. (See Joseph Hunter, *New Illustrations of the Life, Studies, and Writings of Shakespeare,* I, London, 1845, pp. 390-399, and C. J. Sisson, ed., *The
Complete Works [of William Shakespeare],* 1954, p. 356.) Hunter declares:
"The notice of this play by Manningham not only opens to view a particular
play in the dramatic literature of Italy to which Shakespeare was indebted,
but . . . it opened to view also a new field in which to hunt for other sources
of the plots of Shakespeare. None of his plays had, I believe, before been
traced to the Italian theatre . . ." (pp. 398-399).

"his Lady widdowe": Manningham's reference to Olivia as a widow
suggests that in the original version of the play she was a widow mourning
the loss of her lord and that sometime after the Middle Temple performance
the play was altered to have her appear sorrowing for the loss of a brother
(Hunter, p. 399).

"Cosen Norton": William or Robert Norton, second or third son,
respectively, of the lawyer and poet Thomas Norton (1532-1584) of Sharpenoe, Beds., co-author with Thomas Sackville of the tragedy *Gorboduc*
(publ. 1565), first play in English to employ blank verse. The Nortons and
Cranmers were closely connected with the Grocers' Company, to which
Thomas belonged. (DNB, XVI, 664, 666, 668.) The cause of Cousin Norton's
arrest may have been connected with the situation described on fo. 13, concerning Coppin and the support of Norton's insane mother. (See fo. 13 and
notes below.)

"which remembring, with out being remembred, what . . .": MS punct.
"which remembring with out being remembred, what . . ." I take the chron-
ology and sense of this and the foregoing entry to be that on the eleventh of
February Norton drew up a petition, which he asked his wife to present to
Cecil, who received her on the twelfth and who recalled the circumstances
at issue without having to be reminded; but that Cecil had already decided
for Coppin and against Norton so that on that very day Norton was arrested.
(See fo. 13 and note below.)

Fo. 13. "Copping . . . Mr. Cranmers hand . . . the Lunaticke their mother,":
Thomas Norton, the lawyer and poet, was related to the Cranmers through
two marriages: his first wife was Margery, or Margaret, third daughter of
Archbishop Cranmer; after her death, he married, before 1568, her cousin
Alice, daughter of Edmund Cranmer, Archdeacon of Canterbury. The second
wife, described as a bigoted protestant who fell victim to religious mania, became hopelessly insane by 1582; from at least 1584 until at least 1602 she
lived at Cheshunt under the care of her eldest daughter, Ann, who had married
George Coppin, or Coppen, of Norfolk (DNB, XIV, 668.) Coppin, an informant

of Cecil in Lord Burghley's household in 1598 and 1599 (*Hist. MSS. Comm. Salisbury*, VIII, 259, 276, 280, 286; IX, 282-3), became clerk of the Crown and was later knighted July 23, 1603 (Shaw, II, 114).

"Mr. Cranmer" was probably Thomas Cranmer, brother of Thomas Norton's second wife, Alice, and the poet's executor; he was registrar of the archdeaconry of Canterbury and the father of George Cranmer of Corpus Christi College, Oxford, and of a younger son, Thomas, with whom Manningham was well acquainted (see fo. 66 and notes). The younger Thomas became lunatic in 1607 (Foster, I, 346).

The situation referred to in the Diary may be summarized as follows: Coppin and his wife Ann had agreed to care for Alice Cranmer Norton, the mad mother of Ann and "Cosen" Norton and the sister of Thomas Cranmer, for £20 a year; Norton and Cranmer had supplied Coppin with goods (unspecified) from which he should have deducted the £20; he was now refusing to repay the balance or give an accounting and was deducting £50 instead of £20.

"account": MS accountes

"H. Norton": Henry, eldest son of Thomas Norton the lawyer and poet, and brother of William, Robert, Ann and Elizabeth (DNB, XIV, 668.) In July, 1599, he had a license to transport corn and was in Bayonne with it, when his patron Sir William Bevyll wrote to Robert Cecil (*Hist. MSS. Comm., Salisbury*, IX, 247).

"My Cosen Garnons": Middle Temple and Lincoln's Inn records list several men of this name, spelled Garnauns, Garnaunce, Garnans, Garnons. Which, if any, was Manningham's kinsmen is not yet known. James Garnauns, third son of Nicholas Garnauns of Garnauns, Herefordshire, was specially admitted to the Middle Temple 26 Nov. 1560 and was still there in Nov., 1595 (*Min.*, I, 130, 162, 357). Robert Garnaunce, late of New Inn, from Barrs Court, Herefords., was admitted 13 May 1572 (*Min.*, I, 187, 198, 214, 252). Anthony Garnons "of co. Glouc., barr., Thavies Inn" was admitted to Lincoln's Inn May 9, 1580 (*L. I. Adm., Records*, I, 90).

"Henricus Garnons" was one of the signatories on the October, 1604, petition of 32 Christ Church students to King James, asking that "Johannem Kinge Theologiae Doctorem" be made their new Dean (Bodleian Library MS). See note to fo. 46b.

One "Dr. Garnons," evidently a churchman, is quoted several times in *MS Harl.* 6395, Sir Nicholas L'Estrange's "Merry Passages and Jests," excerpts from which were published in *Anecdotes and Traditions Illustrative of Early English History and Literature*, ed. William J. Thoms, Camden Society, V, 1839, pp. 40, 41, 44-45, 46, 59, 61. Most of the anecdotes attributed to "Dr. Garnons" concern clergy—e.g., Andrew Downes (see fo. 7 and note); Dr. Usher; a Rurall Deane, defined as "an Ecclesiastical High Constable"—though one is about "A New-Made Knight" and another about Edmund Waller in the 1642 Parliament.

"the olde E [arle] of Sussex": Thomas Ratcliffe, third Earl of Sussex, 1556-1583 (B).

Fo. 13b. "at malling with Mr. Richeres": John Richers (see fo. 9b and note).

"The Bishop of London": Richard Bancroft, D.D. (1544-1610), elected Bp. of London in 1597; became Archbishop of Canterbury in 1604. He was noted for his severity and arbitrariness, vigilance in detecting sedition, intolerant sermons, and attacks on puritans (DNB, III, 108-111). Fuller remarked that as a champion of church discipline he "hardened the hands of his soul" (*Worthies*, 301). Hence Mr. Richer's pun on "crosse" in this entry.

"Dr. Parry": The Rev. Henry Parry, D.D., one of the Queen's chaplains and a personal friend of the diarist. See fo. 2 and note.

"Mr. Sedley": Probably William Sedley of the Friars (formerly called the Priory) on the northeast side of the Medway, near Aylesford, about 2 miles from Bradbourne. In 33 Henry VIII the priory and its lands had been granted to Sir Thomas Wyatt the elder. Then Queen Elizabeth had granted it to John Sedley, son of John Sedley, esq., of Southfleet. It passed from John, who died without issue, to his brother William, afterwards knighted and, in 9 James I, created baronet. He was grandfather to Sir Charles Sedley, the Restoration wit. (Hasted, IV, 427-428). His lady was Elizabeth, daughter and heir of Stephen Darell of Spelmonden, and widow of Henry Lord Abergavenny (B, citing Hasted, II, 170, ed. 1782).

"Rotham": Wrotham, not far from Malling in Kent.

"Mr. Cartwright": Hugh Cartwright, esq., of East Malling. (See fos. 9b, 14b, 35, and notes.)

Fo. 14. "Mr. Catlin": George Catlyn, once owner of Bradbourne, was related to the Twysden family through his Royden wife and mother; he sold the manor of Bradbourne to Richard Manningham and died without heir. (Ronald G. and Christopher H. Hatton, "Notes on the Family of Twysden and Twisden," *Arch. Cant.*, LVIII, 1946, p. 44.) He was probably the son and heir of Hew (Hugh) Catlin, Esq., one of the executors of Thomas Royden of East Peckham, in whose will of 10 Aug., 1557, he is mentioned: "to George Cattelenn my gown of taffeta." In the will of Thomas' wife Margaret Royden, 19 Jan., 1575/76, "My daughter's son George Catlyn" is mentioned as owing her £40. (A. R. Cook, *A Manor Through Four Centuries*, 1938, pp. 46-47). What his relationship was to Richard Catlyn, gent., of Malling, whose widow Joyce married John Skott (Scott) of West Malling, is not clear. Scott's will was filed, dated, and proved in 1554; Joyce's, in 1557 (*Kent Records: Wills Proved in the Rochester Consistory Court*, ed. Leland L. Duncan and F. W. Cock, 1924, p. 172).

"Sir Robert Sydney": Younger brother of Sir Philip Sidney, knighted 7 Oct. 1586, created Viscount Lisle in 1605 and Earl of Leicester, 1618. He served as Governor of Flushing, 1588, and aided Sir Frances Vere in the Low Countries 1596, 97. (DNB, XVIII, 236-239). Jonson paid tribute to him and his family in "To Penshurst."

"Otford house": The manor and park of Otford, near Sevenoaks, co. Kent, had once been exchanged by John Duke of Northumberland (letters patent, dtd. March 2, 1553/4) for Knole and other lands in Sundridge, Shoreham, and Sevenoaks (*Pat. Roll, 7 Ed. VI*, p. 8, m 14—cited by A. P. Newton, ed. *Cal. of MSS. of Major General Lord Sackville Preserved at Knole, Sevenoaks, Kent*, I, 1940, p. 316).

"Mr. Jo[hn] Sedley": John Sedley, or Sidley, son of William Sedley of Southfleet, Kent, and Elizabeth, widow of Henry Neville, 6th Lord Avergavenny. In 1613 he married Elizabeth, the only daughter of Sir Henry Savile, to the keen disappointment of Sir Robert Sidney, who "had destinated that young gentleman"—i.e., John Sedley—"for his daughter Phillip[a]." (Chamberlain, I, 415 and n. 3; I, 436).

"The L[ord] Buckhurst": Sir Thomas Sackville, (1536-1608), poet and politician; Baron of Buckhurst (1567), first Earl of Dorset (March, 1603/04), Lord High Treasurer (1599-1608)—DNB, XVII, 585-589. About 1596 he had been eager to obtain a country residence within easy journey to London. Though he had obtained a grant of Knole, it was leased to the Lennards. He was inclined to Otford Park but was opposed by Lord Cobham and Sir Robert Sidney, then Governor of Flushing. In 1603 he obtained possession of Knole, rebuilding and redecorating it at great expense. (Charles J. Phillips, *History of the Sackville Family*, London, n. d.—1932?, I, 209, 216.) See also fos. 53b, 128, and notes.

"a book entitled Quodlibets": William Watson's "A Decacordon of Ten Quodlibeticall Questions concerning Religion and State; wherein the author, framing himself a Quilibet to every Quodlibet, decides an hundred crosse Interrogatorie doubts, about the generall contentions betwixt the Seminarie priests and Jesuites at this present," 1602 (STC 25123).

Fo. 14b. Manningham's notes on 'Quodlibets' do not mention arguments numbered 4 and 5 in Watson's book, suggesting that the Diarist did not regard them important. "Watson's remarks are not so much arguments in favour of toleration abstractly considered, as reasons why it should not answer the purpose of Father [Robert] Parsons and the Jesuits to support its introduction into England."—B

"One Kent, my cosen's brother by his mothers side": Robert Kent. See Appendix, Richard Manningham's will: "my late half-brother Robert Kent."

"the Earle of Lyncolne": Henry Clinton, who succeeded his father, the Lord High Admiral, to the earldom in 1585 and held it until his death in 1616.

"Mr. Cartwright": Hugh Cartwright, esq., of East Malling (see note to fo. 9b). After the death of this acquisitive gentleman, his property passed to his widow Jane, one of 17 daughters of Sir John Newton, to her second husband, Sir James Fitzjames (Hasted, IV, 511).

"My Cosen shee": Richard Manningham's second wife, Jane. See notes to fos. 9b and 10b.

Fo. 15. "A gent. of Nottinghamshire . . . by a whore as thou art.' (My Cosen *narr.*)": Omitted by B.

"S[i]r Jarvis Clifton": Sir Gervais, first Lord Clifton, a wealthy and powerful Nottinghamshire knight, was made a peer in 1608. Chamberlain's comments to Carleton in April, 1612, suggest that he pursued trouble. He quarreled with his daughter Katherine and her husband Esmé Stuart, eighth Seigneur of Aubigny (who became third Duke of Lennox in 1624), speaking of her with unbridled bitterness. In 1617 he was fined 1000£ by the Star Chamber "for some fowle misdemeanure," and was confined in the Fleet, where he violently inveighed against the justice of the land and threatened to kill Lord Keeper Francis Bacon, so that he was sent to the Tower (*Letters*, II, 126). In 1618 this unhappy man took his own life with a penknife (ibid., II, 170). See also the reference to his father, Sir John Clifton, fo. 30b and note.

"in the passage of the yard neere the fundament,": Omitted by B. Stow describes how the catheter was used in this period, to relieve the suffering of Ferdinando, Earl of Derby, who died at Latham, 16 April 1594: "The 14. and 15, was used an instrument called a Catheter, which being conveyed into his bladder, was strongly sucked by the Chirurgion but no water followed." (*Annales*, ed. Howes, 1631, p. 767).

Fo. 15 b (mislabeled fo. 16 in B). "Sir Rich[ard] Martin": Warden of the Mint—not to be confused with the Middle Temple lawyer and wit Dick Martin, who later became Recorder of London.

"Mr. Thomas Scott of Scottes Hall in Kent": A direct descendant of Sir John Scott of Scotts Hall, in the parish of Smeeth. Sir John, one of Edward IV's Privy Council, also acquired Brabourne in the Hundred of Birchott Franchises (Thomas Philipot, *Villare Cantianum*, 1659, pp. 116, 69). Philipot's *Visitation of Kent, 1619-21*, mentions Thomas Scott as *Miles*, married to Elizabeth, daughter of John Baker of Sinsinghurst.

"Tristram Lyde a surgeon": Not mentioned in Sidney Young, *Annals of the Barber-Surgeons of London* (1890).

"admitted to practise by the Archbishops letteres": Such ways of persuading the College of Surgeons to approve medical practitioners were evidently common, in this period, as witness the case of the notorious astrologer and quack Dr. Simon Forman, who, having been sent to prison and fined by the College of Physicians, was released by order of Lord Keeper Egerton, who demanded an explanation of their conduct (DNB, VII, 438-9).

Fo. 16. "Sergeant Daniel": William Daniel from Cheshire, a Gray's Inn man (entered in 1556, reader in 1579, treasurer in 1580 and 1587). He served as deputy recorder of London under Fleetwood and afterward as Judge in the Court of Common Pleas, from 1604 until his death in 1610. (Foss, 213.)

Fo. 16b. "In the Cathedrall Churche at Rochester. Monuments. Of Jo. Somer . . .": The other daughter, the eldest, of John Somer, was Mary, first married to Thomas Peniston, one of the Clerks of the Council to Queen Elizabeth, then to Sir Alexander Temple. According to Thorpe's *Antiquities of Rochester* appended to *Customale Roffense*, p. 244, the monument was a stately table tomb (perhaps not unlike Sir Robert Cecil's in Bishop's Hatfield church); it was battered to pieces in the Civil War. See Edward Hawkins, "Notes on Some Monuments in Rochester Cathedral," *Arch. Cant.*, XI, 1877, pp. 5-6. The tombs of Thomas Willowbee and Walter Phillips, the inscriptions on which Manningham set down in his book, have disappeared from Rochester Cathedral (ibid., p. 9).

Fo. 17 b. "Mr. Towse": William Towes, or Towse, of Hingham, Norfolk, member of the Inner Temple since 1572 and Bencher of that society since 1594, (*I. T. Adm.*, 72) was one of Manningham's chief informants. He had served as M. P. for Bramber in 1586. He knew the leading lawyers and judges of the time, especially those associated with the Inner Temple, such as Edmund Anderson, Chief Justice of the Common Pleas, Edward Coke, George Croke, Francis Gawdy, Dr. Julius Caesar, John Heale, Sir Roger Manwood, and Lawrence Tanfield. To the Diarist, or within his hearing, he told anecdotes about contemporary personages, including men of letters and of the theater. It was Towse—or possibly his son William, admitted to the Inner Temple in 1596, called to the bar in 1603 (ibid., 146)—who gave Manningham the lines Spenser was said to have written for the Queen when he could not get payment for his verses (see fo. 31b), as well as the comical story of Shakespeare's triumph over Burbage with a citizen's wife (see fo. 29b).

Active in his Inn, Towse served on numerous Inner Temple committees, including one in June, 1602, appointed to confer with the Treasurer and Bench of the Middle Temple "touching a convenient pension or yearly contribution" for a preacher and for his reading of two lectures every week in term and vacation, on Sunday and Thursday at Evening Prayer (Inderwick, I, 449). A similar committee on which Towse served in 1605 brought about the appointment of William Crashaw, father of the future Metaphysical poet Richard Crashaw, as preacher at the Temple Church (ibid., II, 9). In 1608 Towse became Treasurer of the Inner Temple (*I. T. Adm.*, 72); in 1614 he was made Serjeant at Law (Foss, *Judges of England*, VI, 29).

According to John Peile, Towse matriculated pensioner from Christ's College, Cambridge, in Oct., 1567. He married Joan French, who bore him the son, whom he outlived, the younger William dying in May, 1632, and the elder on 22 Oct. 1634, aged 83 (*Biographical Register of Christ's College, 1505-1905*, I, Cambridge, 1910, p. 100).

"the olde Earle of Hartford": Edward Seymour, son of the Protector Somerset, was Earl of Hertford from 1559 to 1619. The widow whom he married was Frances, daughter of Thomas, third Viscount Howard of Bindon; eventually she became the celebrated Duchess of Richmond and Lennox of Jacobean and Caroline times. The Earl's first wife was Lady Catherine Grey, sister of Lady Jane Grey. See also fo. 117 and note.

Fo. 18. "Dr. Montague": James Montague, first master of Sidney Sussex College, Cambridge; he became editor of King James's Works, then Bishop of Bath and Wells, and later of Winchester. "Bishop Mountague" and Dr. John Buckridge, president of St. John's College, Oxford, were so warmly regarded as friends of the Middle Temple that they were specially admitted to membership in the society, All Saints Day, 1608 (*Min.*, II, 497). See also fo. 121b.

"the serpent": MS shows that originally for "serpent" the Diarist wrote "wilderness," then crossed it out.

"none other Gods": MS none others god.

Fo. 19b. "one moore of Baliol colledge": Probably Eustace Moore of Warwickshire, pleb. Balliol, matriculated 28 Feb. 1588/89, aged 16. He received his B.A. in 1592 and M.A. in 1595; was licensed to preach 21 Nov. 1601; and received his B.D. in Feb., 1604/05. Eventually he became a canon of Worcester (1617). (Foster, III, 1022.)

Fo. 20b. "At Paules crosse": Traditional outdoor preaching place since the middle ages. According to Stow, it was "a Pulpit Crosse of timber, mounted vpon steppes of stone, and couered with leade," and it stood in the "middest" of St. Paul's churchyard. Here large crowds gathered to hear eloquent and learned Anglican divines preach "euery Sundaye in the forenoone"—and, we may infer, on other, special occasions. (See Stow's *Survey,* I, 331.)

"one Sanders": Identified by Millar Maclure as "perhaps Matthew Sanders, after Rector of Barnston, Essex" (*The Paul's Cross Sermons, 1534-1642,* Univ. of Toronto Press, C 1958, p. 222). A Samuel Sanders, M.A., was a prebendary of Lichfield, collated 9 Aug. 1601 (Hardy's Le Neve, I, 605), and vicar of Gt. Hale, Lincs., 1599-c. 1617 (Venn, IV, 15). Both were Cambridge men. Matthew, of Ely, Cambs., matriculated sizar from Trinity, Easter, 1581, and migrated to Queens' in 1584; he proceeded B.A., 1584/85, M.A. in 1588, and B.D. from Pembroke in 1595. He was buried at St. Michael's, Cornhill, London, Aug. 24, 1629. Samuel, born at South Kirby, Yorks., c. 1563, studied three years at St. John's, was ordained priest at York, and preached in Norwich and Northbrook, Norfolk. (Ibid.)

Fo. 21. "merchant adventu[rer]": MS illegible. B reads "merchant adventures."

Fo. 21b. "At Westminster Dr. Androes": The learned theologian Lancelot Andrewes (1555-1626), whose sermons T. S. Eliot has helped us to admire (see *For Lancelot Andrewes,* 1928). Educated under Richard Mulcaster at the Merchant Tailors' Free School in London and at Cambridge, he is said to have known fifteen languages. Scholar and Fellow of Pembroke Hall, Cambridge, he served as master of his college from 1589 to 1605. From 1601 to 1605 he served as Dean of Westminster, before being appointed Bishop of Chichester and undertaking to help with the Authorized Version of the Bible. Later he was translated to Ely (1609) and then to Winchester (1618). (DNB, I, 401-5.) For a biographical sketch of Andrewes based on the account by his secretary, Henry Isaacson, *An Exact Narration . . .* (1650), see Maurice J. Reidy, S.J., *Bishop Lancelot Andrewes, Jacobean Court Preacher,* (Chicago: Loyola University Press, 1955). The sermon Manningham here records was preached on Whitsunday.

Fo. 24. "inlightens": MS inlightnes.

"rectifies the will": Thus in MS. B's "certifies the will" is clearly in error.

"[Elijah]": Supplied by B (MS blank).

Fo. 24b. "(Ch. Da.)": Charles Danvers of Edington, Wilts., and the Middle Temple. See Introd. and fo. 12.

"Mr. Stevens of our house": Probably Thomas Stevens of Horsley, Glos.: entered the Middle Temple from New Inn, August 2, 1578; called, Oct. 29, 1585; Bencher, 1604; Reader, Autumn 1604; Treasurer, 1612 (*Adm.*, I, 43). Manningham also refers to him on fo. 121. The entire entry concerning Mrs. Fowler was omitted by B.

"Mrs. Fouler": Wife of Richard Fowler, who in 1599 was committed to the Tower on suspicion of plotting against her Majesty's person (Chamberlain, 23 August, 1599, I, 85). She figured in a notorious case of bawdry the next year. As described by Chamberlain to Carleton, June 13, 1600, "Fayre Mistris Fowlers cause held us on, the same day [yesterday, in the Star Chamber, where Lord Keeper Egerton had spoken concerning Essex] till amost five a clocke, the conclusion wherof was that she is to be carted to Bridewell and there whipt, her mignon captaine Heines to stand on the pillorie and imprisoned: her brother Harry Boughton to pay 100^{li} and be imprisoned till he find sureties for the goode behaviour: and Gascoin a souldier to ride with his face to the horse tayle, to stand on the pillorie at Westminster and in Cheapside, and to be marked in the face with a hot yron, and imprisonment during life: the greatest burthen lighted on him, because he was the principall actor, and best proofe came against him: whereas for the rest though every man that heard yt might justly condemne them *in foro conscientiae,* yet the case was not altogether so cleere *in foro judicii,* but there is hope she may finde favor and be dispensed withall, though (as my Lord Keper saide) she is *haec Helena,* the cause of all the evill, carrieng the right picture of a courtesan in her countenaunce, and having rather *frontem meretriciam* (as he called yt) then any such delicate feature as I looked for." (I, 98).

In April, 1602, just two months before Manningham made his entry, "Mistris Fowlers mignon," Capt. Heine, was "hang'd . . . in Smithfield for killing his fellow prisoner in the Fleet, and they say blasoned her armes at the gallowes very brodely, . . ." (Chamberlain, I, 139); and her brother Boughton was reported "stabd and kild in a brabble at bowles" by a page of the Archbishop of Canterbury (ibid.).

"(Th.)": Thomas [Stevens]—see above.

"Were is your husband? . . . a male with one stone. (Ch. Da.)": Omitted by B.

"Mr. Reeves": Perhaps William or Richard Reeves of the Middle Temple (see fo. 12 and note).

Fo. 25. "Junii 6th, 1602.": B, mistaking a slash mark separating *Junii* and 6 in the MS, interpreted the date as the 16th, an error perpetuated by Maclure in *The Paul's Cross Sermons, 1534-1642,* p. 222. Fo. 25 b, is headed "6 Junii, 1602." in both MS and B.

"Mr. Barker": Probably Lawrence Barker, Vicar of St. Botolph's without Aldersgate (see Maclure, p. 222). Wood mentions a Will Barker, D.D., 1602, who became chancellor of Wells (*Athenae,* I, 717).

Fo. 25b. After this page in MS there is a blank leaf—*i.e.*, what would be fo. 26 and 26b—however, the present edition follows the MS and B pagination in numbering the next page of the text fo. 26.

"1. in *ferendo*": MS has "2ᵈ in ferendo," which B also followed, preferring to ignore Manningham's second "2.," which B omitted altogether.

"the old Deane of Paules": Dr. Alexander Nowell, (1507?-1602), had died just four months earlier (Feb. 13). His successor, Dr. John Overall, had been elected May 29, 1602 (Hardy's Le Neve, II, 315). For a fuller account of Nowell see fo. 66 and note.

Fo. 26. "Marti Lib. 10, Epig. 47 . . . Th. Sm.": Several translations of this epigram of Martial have come down to us from the 16th Century. One of the best-known translations of this epigram, *Vitam quae faciunt beatiorem*, is the Earl of Surrey's: "Martiall, the things that do attayn/ The happy life." Jonson, who admired Martial highly (Drummond, *Conversations*, II), also translated this one (T. K. Whipple, *Martial and the English Epigram from Sir Thomas Wyatt to Ben Jonson*, U. of Cal. Publ. in Modern Philology, Vol. 10., No. 4, Mar. 7, 1925, pp. 317, 386). The author of this plain, blunt version, Thomas Smith(?), has not been identified. Franklin B. Williams, Jr., in *Index of Dedications and Commendatory Verses in English Books Before 1641* (London, 1962), lists twelve Thomas Smiths, including several who are known to have written verse (p. 173).

One likely possibility is the great classical scholar, author, and statesman Sir Thomas Smith (1513-1577), of Queens' College, Cambridge (DNB, XVIII, 532-5).

Another is Thomas Smith of Christ Church, Oxford, (B.A., 1574; M.A., 1578; public orator, 1582); he became secretary to the Earl of Essex, later one of the clerks of the Lords' council, secretary of the Latin tongue, and one of the masters of the Requests (Birch, *Court and Times of James the First*, 1848 ed., I, 52 n.2). He was knighted in 1603. Although he never published anything, he was reported to have left behind him "several matters" fit for the press, as well as money to Oxford for books (Wood, I, 352). See also DNB, XVIII, 535-6.

"Georgius Savile": This anagram was omitted by B.

Fo. 26 b. "Vrsula . . . won all.": Omitted by B. Ursula was Lady Walsingham's name (see fo. 37 and note).

"Arbella Stuarta": Arbella Stuart (1575-1615), great-granddaughter of Henry VIII's sister Margaret, (Arbella's father having been Charles Stuart, Earl of Lennox, younger brother of Lord Darnley) and thus a leading claimant to the throne, with her cousin James. Since she had been born in England whereas James had not, her supporters felt hers to be the better claim. Some of the more moderate Catholics would have welcomed her accession as offering more tolerance to them (S. R. Gardiner, *History of England*, I, 1883, p. 79). In the 1590's her name and claim had been continually discussed both in England and on the Continent, particularly after "R. Doleman's" *A Conference About the Next Succession to the Crown of England*, appearing in England in 1594 (see note to fol. 128b, ff.), had kindled new interest in the problem of the succession. "Doleman"—actually Richard Verstegan, though thought to be the Jesuit Father Parsons—had stated that Burghley favored Arbella (P. M. Handover, *Arbella Stuart: Royal Lady of Hardwick*, 1957, pp. 147, 107). In June 1601 a list drawn up by one of Cecil's men, Thomas Wilson, recognized Arbella as second choice, next to James, whom Cecil favored; Lord Beauchamp (Edward Seymour, eldest son of the Earl of Hertford) as third; and Lord Henry Seymour, the old earl's brother, as fourth (ibid., 128). In July 1602 court rumours had it that some persons wanted to marry her with the Earl of Hertford's younger son—i.e., Thomas Seymour, Beauchamp's brother, an error for Edward, Beauchamp's eldest son, since Thomas had died in 1600—and thus "to carry it that way." (Harrison, III 290). Naturally such rumours afflicted the Queen, who ordered the Lady Arbella closely guarded at Hardwick Castle by her grandmother the Countess of Shrewsbury ("Bess of Hardwick").

By Christmas 1602 Arbella herself, realizing or hoping that a combination of her claim with that of the Seymours would be nearly irresistible, may have decided to play for the highest stakes (Handover, 167-8). Emboldened by reports of the Queen's declining health, and perhaps made desperate by her own virtual imprisonment at Hardwick, she boldly made overtures to the Earl of Hertford regarding a marriage with his grandson Edward Seymour, whom she had never seen and who was twelve years younger than herself, only to be coldly rebuffed (ibid., 137, 140). But the rumours persisted: Sir John Carey wrote to Cecil from Berwick, 21 March 1602/03, "The Scots are very discontent and murmur desperately at a rumour of the Lady Arbella's marriage." (*Hist. MSS. Comm., Salisbury*, XII, 1910, p. 699.) They need not have worried, for her frustration and behavior had been naturally feminine enough for supporters of King James' claim to circulate reports that she was mad, thereby destroying public sympathy for her and enabling the succession to be proclaimed without disturbance. (Handover, 163, 165).

After the Queen's death Arbella was appointed to be chief mourner at the funeral, which took place at Westminister, 28 April 1603 (Chamberlain, I, 193). An abortive plot, however, in which Ralegh, opposing Cecil and scheming closely with Lord Cobham and his brother George Brooke, sought "to dispossess James in favor of the Lady Arbella" (James Spedding, *Letters of Francis Bacon*, III, 1868, p. 134)—in order, they supposed, to secure peace with Spain and toleration for Catholics (Philip Magnus, *Sir Walter Raleigh*, New York, 1956, p. 112)—intensified the new King's long-standing antipathy toward her. Thereafter he made her relationship to Queen Elizabeth a source of misery to her. Eventually she did marry a Seymour—William, second son of Lord Beauchamp—but not until 1610; then she was sent to the Tower, where in 1615 she died. (Chamberlain, I, 476, n 25; II, 31, n 6, 174, n 6.)

In 1602, when she was 28, the Venetians, comparing her claim with that of James, reported "her great beauty, and remarkable qualities," which included knowledge of five languages (as quoted, Handover, 147). Like the Queen of Scots an indefatigable letter-writer, she had the scholarly temperament, religious interests, solitary disposition, and love of music of Lady Jane Grey (ibid., 151, 166, 10).

"Henricus Burbonius": See fo. 70, where this anagram is repeated, with an addition.

"(Curle.)": Edward Curle, or Curll, the diarist's chambermate and future brother-in-law; Manningham mentions him frequently (see fos. 12 and 30b, for example).

"(Bradnux.)": William Brodnax of Godmersham, Kent, mentioned in *Min.*, I, 396, 420; II, 450. He was admitted 10 Oct. 1594 (*Adm.*, I, 67). On fo. 70b Manningham lists him among those called to the bar 27 Nov. 1602. By 26 Jan. 1609/10 he was dead, and Giles Overbury (brother of Sir Thomas and son of the Middle Temple bencher and treasurer Nicholas Overbury) was assigned to his chamber (*Min.*, II, 515). William Brodnax was one of ten children (five of each sex) born to "Tho. Brodnex de Godmersham in co' Cantij" and his wife Elizabeth, daughter of John Tayler of Wilsborough; "obijt in juventute." (John Philipot, *Visitation of Kent* . . . 1619-21, ed. Robert Hoveden, London, 1898, p. 73.) Middle Temple records list him as the fourth son, his brother Thomas, "third son of Thomas B . . . gent.," having been a member of the society since 12 Dec., 1583 (*Adm.*, I, 52). Godmersham is about 15 miles east of Maidstone, just north of Wye and west of Waltham.

The "Bradman" of B is clearly a mistranscription of Bradnux.

"Laetus . . . noe more (G. M.)": Omitted by B. Thomas Bastard in *Chrestoleros*, 1598, has the following line: "Laetus did in his mistress' quarrel die." (*Poetry of the English Renaissance, 1509-1660*, ed. J. William Hebel and Hoyt H. Hudson, New York, C 1957, p. 525.) And in the Middle Temple Christmas revels of 1597/98, the famous *Prince d'Amour* (see notes to fo. 12b), one of the performers appeared as "*Amantius Letus* Esquire, Sheriff of Hartfordshire." (1660 ed., p. 50.) For possible identity of "G. M." see note below.

"G. M.": These initials, which in MS seem to have been written with a finer pen and in darker ink than the entry itself, may stand for Gervase, or Jervis, Markham (1568?-1637), soldier, scholar, horse-breeder, and prolific author on multifarious subjects (Franklin B. Williams, Jr., *Index of Dedications*, etc., 1962, p. 125, and DNB, XII, 1051 ff). He edited *The gentleman's academie, or the booke of S. Albans, reduced into a better method by G. M.*, 1595 (STC 3314). According to Sir Clement Markham, in DNB, he shamelessly repeated his books, reissuing them under new titles, etc., and was scorned by Ben Jonson as "But a base fellow." (XII, 1051.) Tobie Matthew used the same initials—G. M.—as a pseudonym in his 1621 translation of Francisco Aria's *The Judge* (STC 741)—*Dictionary of Anon. and Pseudonymous English Literature*, ed. Halkett and Laing, VI (1923), 376.

"(Franklin.)": James Franklin, or Francklyn, of Wye, Kent; admitted to the Middle Temple from Clifford's Inn Feb. 20, 1601/02 (*Adm.*, I, 79). He seems to have enjoyed the favor of Sir Edward Fenner, Justice of the King's Bench, who exerted pressure to have Franklin called to the degree of the Utter Bar in the spring of 1609; the call was held up until the autumn of that year, when it was confirmed Nov. 3 (*Min.*, II, 507). He later became a Bencher, 1626, and Treasurer, 1634 (*Adm.*, I, 79).

Fo. 27. "Kentish tayles . . . all the land he can see.": Both the origin of

Kentish long-tails and the meaning of the punning reference to them here are somewhat obscure. According to Moryson's 1617 *Itin.*, "The Kentish men of old were said to have tails, because trafficing in the Low Countries, they never paid full payments of what they did owe, but still left some part unpaid." (III, i, 53—in 1907-8 ed. III, 463.) But Deloney's *Works* (c. 1600) speaks of "The valiant courage and policie of the Kentish-men with long tayles." (Mann, 383, A)—*Oxford Dictionary of English Proverbs*, 2nd ed. (Oxford, 1960), p. 333.

Fuller offers several explanations of the origin of the term, rejecting a legend connecting Kentish long-tails with the fish-tails of Saint Austin and favoring these interpretations: (1) The English were so-called from their wearing a pouch or poke (a bag to carry their baggage in) behind their backs, "whilst probably the proud Monsieurs had their lackeys for that purpose." (2) "If any demand how this nickname (cut off from the rest of England) still entailed on Kent, the best conjecture is, because that county lieth nearest France," the French being held "the first founders of this aspersion." (3) "But if any will have the Kentish so called from dragging boughs of trees behind them, which afterward they advanced above their heads, and so partly cozened, partly threatened King William the Conqueror to continue their ancient customs: I say, if any will impute it to this original, I will not oppose." (*Worthies*, pp. 258-259.)

That the term enjoyed colloquial usage is suggested by its employment in a 1602 letter from Edward Reynolds to John Rawlins of Wakering, Essex, both followers of the Earl of Essex: "Remember me to your Kentish Tails, where I think you would rather be than in Ireland or any other part of the world." (CSP *Dom., Eliz., 1601-03*, p. 213.)

"Anagr[am] Martyne: myne art. (W[?])": Unaccountably omitted by B, this anagram unquestionably refers to the fun-loving and popular Dick Martin of the Middle Temple—Prince d'Amour of the Middle Temple Christmas revels in 1597/98. See fo. 12b and note.

"Sergeant Heale, . . . the Queens Sergeant,": John Hele, or Heale, a famous Inner Templar, one of the legal butts of the time, noted for his drinking. Since his call to the bar in 1574 he had risen to the status of Bencher (1589) and Reader (Lent, 1591; Lent, 1594) and had been elected Sergeant in 1594. (Inderwick, I, pp. 276, 356, 371, 392, and 393-4.) By October 21, 1600, said Chamberlain, Hele was being cried up for "master of the Rolles" (I, 111), though on the following Feb. 3, he added, "Heale may misse yt." (I, 117.) On Oct. 2, 1602, he wrote that "Sergeant Heale was made the Quenes sergeant this sommer, and rode circuit with Judge [Francis] Gawdie [Justice of the Queen's Bench], in Sussex, Surrey, Kent, Essex, and Hartfordshire, wherin he plaide such pranckes, and so demeaned himself that he is become both odious and ridiculous." (I, 161-2.) Other references to him in the diary are on fo. 29b and 43b. In May, 1601, riding too fast, he nearly ran down three gentlemen near Temple Bar: William Dethick, Garter Principal King of Arms to the Council, Mr. Robert Cotton of Connington, and Mr. Morgan of the Middle Temple (CSP *Dom. Eliz., 1601-1603*, p. 49).

"The L[ord] Keeper": Sir Thomas Egerton, Donne's employer, was Lord Keeper from 1594 to 1603.

"doubt it not": Thus in MS. Though emended by B to "doubted not," Manningham's use suggests a survival of old past tense and past participle forms: *dutte, dute, doute* (see OED, III, 616).

"(Mr. Bennet *nar.*)": Probably Richard Bennet of the Middle Temple, admitted May 31, 1594, "son and heir to Robert B., of Law Whitton, Cornwall, gent. Called 26 Nov., 1602." (*Adm.*, I, 66.) See also fo. 38 and fo. 64b.

Fo. 27b. "At Paules": The old cathedral church of St. Paul, in the city, destroyed in the Great Fire of 1666.

Fo. 28b. "June, 1601": Thus in MS, although the Diarist may have intended to write 1602. If he did so intend, he heard two sermons that day, June 20th, one at St. Paul's in the morning, summarized in fo. 27b and 28, then the one preached by Dr. John Buckridge at the Temple Church in the afternoon. Dr. Buckridge subsequently became President of St. John's, Oxford (1605), and Bishop of Rochester (1611) and Ely (1628). (Hardy's Le Neve, I, 343; III, 573.) He and the Bishop of Bath and Wells, James Mountague, were so cordially regarded as friends of the Middle Temple, that on All Saints Day, 1608, they were specially admitted, *gratis* (*Min.*, II, 497). An illustrious St. John's alumnus and Middle Templar, James Whitelock, friend of Dick Martin, John Hoskyns, and others, tells us in his *Liber Famelicus* that Dr. Buckridge became god-father to his daughter Mary on 16 Oct., 1606 (p. 16).

Fo. 29. "Mr. Foster of Lyncolnes Inn": Probably Thomas Foster, or Forster, though which of the two men of that name is difficult to determine. One was son to William Foster, a prominent officer of Lincoln's Inn mentioned 33 times in the records of that society. William was admitted in 1526, became a Bencher in 1541, and was so listed as late as 1573/74 (*Records of the Honourable Society of Lincoln's Inn, The Black Books*, I, 1897, p. 456.) He may have been the conveyor if not the originator of the anecdotes about More told to the Diarist. The son Thomas was called to the bar in 1560; in a list of 1573/74 he is mentioned as an "Utter Barester." (Ibid., I, 329, 457.)

The other Thomas Foster was admitted to Lincoln's Inn March 11, 1573/74, "of London, late of the barr. of Thavies Inn." (*L.I. Adm.*, I, 81.) He was called to the bar Feb. 7, 1582/83. (*Black Books*, I, 1897, p. 427.) Very likely he was the "Mr Forster" fined, in Nov., 1590, along with six others, £7 each "in respecte they have not performed the charge of the Reader's Dinner" (*Black Books*, II, 1898, p. 18). Several other Fosters were students at Lincoln's Inn: John Forster, of Salop, admitted from Furnival's Inn, May 3, 1582 (*L.I. Adm.*, I, 96); Edward Forster, of Berks., arm., admitted from New Inn, Feb. 25, 1582/83 (ibid., I, 97)—he had been at Trinity College, Oxford (Foster, II, 517); and "Francis Forster of Salop, gent." and University College, Oxford, admitted Oct. 29, 1590 (*L.I. Adm.*, I, 111).

"jeastes of Sir Th. Moore": At the request of Abbé Germain Marc'hadour, editor of *Moreana*, Michael A. Anderegg of Yale University has kindly supplied the following about these anecdotes: Manningham's version of the *Memento morieris* story antedates that of Cresacre More, the first of Sir Thomas's biographers to tell it (*Life of Thomas More*, 1st ed., composed c. 1615-20, published c. 1626, pp. 232-233)—in a briefer, less circumstantial form than Manningham's. Although it does not seem likely that the young lawyer could have been Cresacre's source, the usual sixteenth-century printed works that allude to More and retell his many jests do not mention this one, and its appearance in Manningham's diary indicates that the story was circulating more than a decade before Cresacre wrote his biography.

The second anecdote was well-known by the turn of the sixteenth century. To quote Mr. Anderegg: "The earliest version, which is quite similar to Manningham's, appears in Roper's *Life* (composed in the 1550's and first printed in 1626), p. 55 in the *EETS* edition. Harpsfield incorporates Roper's story verbatim into his own *Life* (*EETS*, p. 66) which was not printed until the present century. The anecdote, in a somewhat expanded version, also appears in Thomas Stapleton's *Tres Thomae* (1588). Ro. Ba., whose biography of More is indebted to both Roper and Stapleton, again tells the story, adding a few more details of his own (*EETS*, p. 84). His *Life of More*, first published in the nineteenth century, was composed c. 1599. Sometime after 1567, Gabriel Harvey wrote a very brief version of the anecdote in the margin of his copy of *The Rules of Reason* (1567); see Samuel A. Tannenbaum, "Some Unpublished Harvey Marginalia," *MLR*, 25 (1930), 327-331, p. 331. And William Camden includes a reference to the story among the handful of More anecdotes in his *Remains Concerning Britain* (1605). Finally, the story appears (with further embellishments) in Cresacre More's *Life of Thomas More*, composed c. 1615-20 and published on the continent around 1626." (Ltr. to the present editor, April 15, 1972.)

See also my article "Thomas More Anecdotes in an Elizabethan Diary," *Moreana*, No. 34, May, 1972, pp. 81f and 115f; and Anderegg, "The Anecdotal Tradition of Thomas More: A Note," *Moreana*, No. 35, Sept., 1972, pp. 55 f.

Fo. 29 b. "Sergeant Yelverton . . . (Mr. Ed. Curle, *n.*)": Omitted by B. The Sergeant was probably Christopher Yelverton (1535?-1612), a Gray's Inn man (entered 1552) who rose to become Justice of the Queen's Bench (2 Feb. 1601/02)—*Gray's Adm.*, I, 23; x. Active in the theatricals of Gray's, he supplied the epilogue to *Jocasta*, translated by Gascoigne and Kynwelmersh (Chambers, III, 518). In 1597 he was elected Speaker of the House (Foss, 778). His anecdotes enliven more than one Elizabethan diary; see, for example, Roger Wilbraham's *Journal*, ed. Harold Scott, Camden Miscel., X (London, 1902), p. 18. Sergeant-at-law in 1589, he was promoted to Queen's Sergeant in 1598 (DNB, XXI, 1230). See also fo. 31 and note. The raconteur was Edward Curle, or Curll, the Diarist's chambermate and brother-in-law-to-be (see notes to fo. 12).

"Sergeant Heale": John Hele, or Heale (see note to fo. 27).

"Mr. Watts": Two of Manningham's fellow students bore this name: William Wattes, second son of John Watts, a citizen and alderman of London, entered Oct. 8, 1594; Edward Watts, son and heir of William Watts, Esq., of Blakesley, Northants, entered Feb., 1, 1594/95. Both were called to the degree of the Utter Bar on 14 May 1602. (*Adm.*, I, 67.) The Diarist had probably known William Wattes at Cambridge, when the latter was a student at Emmanuel, having matriculated fellow commoner Oct. 31, 1593 (*Emman. Coll. MS., CHA.* 1.4). His father, John Watts, Esq., the alderman, was specially admitted to the Middle Temple, Mar. 9, 1595/96 (*Adm.*, I, 70, and *Min.*, I, 362). On fo. 35b William is clearly meant.

"Mr. Danvers": Charles Danvers of Edington, Wilts., and the Middle Temple (see Introduction and note to fo. 6b).

"Upon a tyme when Burbidge played Rich[ard] 3." etc.: This celebrated anecdote, perhaps the best-known passage in Manningham, has oft been cited as evidence not only of Shakespeare's flesh-and-blood existence as a playwright but of his gay temperament and amorous propensities. John Davies of Hereford, in "To our English Terence, Mr. Will. Shakespeare," (from *The Scourge of Folly*, c. 1611) alludes either to the anecdote or to the events it purports to narrate, in the following lines:

"Some say, good Will, (which I in sport do sing)
Hadst thou not played some kingly parts in sport,
Thou hadst been a companion for a king
And been a king among the meaner sort."

(*Poetry of the English Renaissance, 1509-1660*, ed. J. William Hebel and Hoyt H. Hudson, New York, C 1957, p. 536. Emphasis added.)

Professor Allan H. MacLaine has kindly called my attention to James Joyce's use of the anecdote in Chapter II of *Ulysses* (New Random House Edition, 1961, p. 201), q.v.

"grewe": B reads *grone* but MS apparently has "grewe."

"(Mr. Touse.)": William Towse of the Inner Temple (see note to fo. 17b). A word about the ascriptions on fo. 29b of MS is appropriate here. At the end of the first entry "Curle" has had the *C* gone over twice. The *T* of "Touse" may originally have been a *C*, and the *ou* could have been *ur*, but the fourth letter is unmistakably an *s* (whereas on fo. 30b the Diarist had trouble writing the *s* of "Touse"). If anyone has altered the name at the end of this Burbage-Shakespeare anecdote, surely it was the Diarist himself.

"Mr. Fleetewood the Recorder": William Fleetwood (1535?-1594), Recorder of London, a Middle Templar ("double reader in Lent," 1568), noted for his wit and eloquence (DNB, VII, 268). Wood says he was "a learned Man and a good Antiquary; but of a marvellous, merry, and pleasant conceit." (*Athenae*, I, 262.)

"Mr. Bramstone": John Bramston (1577-1654), the future Sir John, Lord Chief Justice. He was one of Manningham's most illustrious associates at the Middle Temple. Admitted Oct. 26, 1597, he was called on the same day as the Diarist: 7 June 1605. In 1622 he became a Bencher and Lent Reader (*Adm.*, I, 72; *Min.*, I, 377), then Serjeant-at-law. He was knighted in 1634. When Dr. John Buckridge became Bishop of Ely, he appointed Bramston Chief Justice of his diocese (1630) (DNB, II, 1116). It is possible that Manningham had known him at Cambridge in undergraduate days, Bramston having been at Jesus College (see his son's *Autobiography*, ed. P. Braybrooke, London, Camden Society, 1845, p. 5, and Venn, I, 204). Other references to Bramston are on fos. 70b and 78.

Fo. 30. "Mr. Hull *narr.*": Henry Hall (Haule), a prominent Middle Templar, admitted Dec. 2, 1571, "late of Staple Inne, gent., son and heir of George H., of Wyè, Kent, gent. Called 9 Feb., 1578. Bencher 1595. Reader Autumn 1595 and Lent 1601. Treasurer 1606." (*Adm.*, I, 35.) He purchased Bigons, alias Digons, in Maidstone and resided there. His wife Jane was the second daughter of Richard Dering, esq., of Pluckley, Kent (Hasted, IV, 297).

Fo. 30b. "Mr. Touse": William Towse of the Inner Temple (see fo. 17b and note; also fo. 29b).

"the Vice President of Yorke": Ralph Eure, Third Lord Eure (1558–1617); Lord Warden of the Middle Marches, 1586; Sheriff of the County of York, 1593-4; Lord President of the Council of Wales, 1607-17 (Gibbs and Doubleday, *The Complete Peerage*, V, 1926, pp. 181-2). The incident here referred to occurred during the summer assizes of 1600. It had been the custom for the Lord President of the North, or in his absence the Vice-President, to go to the castle at York and sit in the chief place between the judges; accordingly Lord Eure, then Vice-President, seated himself next to Baron of the Exchequer Sir John Savile, at the end of the Hall where the gaol delivery was read. Serjeant Christopher Yelverton, appointed with Baron Savile as Justice of the Assize, coming from the other end of the Hall where the commission of *Nisi Prius* was read, thrust past Eure and sat next to Savile, as he had done two days earlier at the Minster sermon.

During the next summer assizes (of 1601), when the President of the North, Thomas Cecil, 2nd Lord Burghley, was present, Yelverton omitted the names of the Lord President and the Council from the gaol delivery; then when Lord Burghley came to sit by him on the Bench for the reading of *Nisi Prius*, Yelverton called for the Abridgement of the Statutes and ordered publicly read the statute of 20 Richard II c. 3 forbidding barons and others to sit by the Justice of *Nisi Prius* when he is on the bench hearing cases. The Lord President, taking umbrage, left the hall. Thereafter the Council of the North complained to the Privy Council, the Queen ordered a search of the Assize Rolls for 25 to 30 years back to determine the precedents, and Sir Robert Cecil, taking up his brother's cause, had Yelverton summoned before the Council sitting in the Star Chamber.

On June 9, 1602, (about a month after Manningham's entry), the Council ordered "That the Vice-President of the Council of York shall take place before the Justice of Assize . . ." (*Acts of the Privy Council, 1542-1603*, ed. J. R. Dasent, XXXII, 488), and on June 11th Secretary Cecil reprehended Judge Yelverton for his conduct toward Lord Burghley. The full story of this controversy is told in the State Papers (see CSP *Dom. Eliz., 1601-3*, pp. 155-6, 178, 195) and in Rachel R. Reid, *The King's Council in the North* (1921), Part III, Chap. 6, especially pp. 346 ff.

"Justice Yelverton": Christopher Yelverton (see note above and fo. 29b and note).

"Justice Manwood": Sir Roger Manwood (1525-1593) of Sandwich in Kent, Justice of the Common Pleas, 1572-78, and Lord Chief Baron of the Exchequer, 1578-93; a member of the Inner Temple (Foss, 429-431), admitted 1548; M. P. for Hastings, 1554-7, and for Sandwich 1557-78; called Serjeant-at-Law, 1567; called to the Bench, 1561; Reader, Lent, 1565 (*I.T. Adm.*, p. 5). He was one of the commissioners sitting at the trial of the Queen of Scots. His birthplace, Sandwich, benefited from his building and endowing a free school there (Fuller, 272), and the parish of St. Dunstan's, Canterbury, from his erecting, in 1592, a house of correction adjacent to the felons' gaol (Hull, *Guide to Kent County Archives*, p. 15); but his public-spirited generosity was outweighed by other qualities less admirable: Manwood was acquisitive, grasping, avaricious, rigorous against the Puritans (A. L. Rouse, *The England of Elizabeth*, 1951, p. 374). Foss says he was much complained of in Kent for oppression, bribery, pardoning a murder, and the like (p. 430). In May, 1591, he was under the Queen's displeasure for accepting money for a place he had the power to give (ibid.); then Burlegh and the Council had him restricted to his house in Great St. Bartholomew's (ibid., 431). Because of his "cheek" and facetiousness, many quips were attributed to him (Rouse, 375), and Donne ridiculed both Manwood and Serjeant Hele in his mock *Courtier's Library, Catalogus Librorum Aulicorum*:

> 21. *A Manual for Justices of the Peace*, comprising many confessions of poisoners tendered to Justice Manwood, and employed by him in his privy; these have now been purchased from his inferior servants and collected for his own use by John Hele.

(Ed. and tr. Evelyn Mary Simpson, London: The Nonesuch Press, 1930). See also Manningham, fo. 70.

"L[ord]e Anderson": Sir Edmund Anderson, of the Inner Temple, became Justice of the Common Pleas in 1578, serving more than 23 years as Lord Chief Justice (Foss, 13-15). He was knighted in 1591. His portrait in the Inner Temple presents him as tough, stern, even cruel-looking, with long hooked nose and pointed chin (reproduced in Inderwick, I, facing p. 290).

"the Lord Sturton": Probably John, 9th Baron Stourton (1553-1588), eldest son and heir of Charles Stourton, the 8th Baron, who was convicted of murder and hanged at Salisbury, 6 March 1556/7. John was restored in blood in Parliament in 1575, the year he matriculated at Oxford (Exeter College), aged 20, and served as commissioner for the trial of Mary Queen of Scots. He married Frances, daughter of William Brooke, 10th Lord Cobham. (*The Complete Peerage*, XII, Part I, 1953, pp. 308-9; Collins' *Peerage*, London, 1779, III, 63; VI, 394.)

"Sir Jo. Clifton": Sir John Clifton of Barrington, Somersetshire, knighted Aug. 23, 1574 (William A. Shaw, ed., *The Knights of England*, London, 1905, II, 76). Manningham also refers, on fo. 15, to his son Sir Gervase Clifton, who was summoned to Parliament as a baron by writ of 9 July 1608, but who later killed himself in the Tower—14 Oct. 1618 (Burke's *Peerage*, 49th ed., 1949, pp. 544-5). See also note to fo. 15.

"My Chamberfellowe": Edward Curle, or Curll, of the Middle Temple, the Diarist's future brother-in-law. (See Introduction and fo. 12 and note.)

"Mr. Longs opposicion": Possibly Edmund Long, "late of Lyons Inne, gent." when admitted to the Middle Temple, 3 Feb. 1576/77 (*Adm.*, I, 41). See also fo. 43b.

"preferment . . . by the Lord Ch[ief] Baron Periams": Curle's account
is corroborated by an entry in the Orders Books of the Middle Temple
parliament concerning his admission: "Mr. Edward, son and heir-apparent of
William Curll of Hatfield, Herts., gent. specially; fine, only 3 *l.*, at the request
of William Periam, knt., Chief Baron of the Exchequer." (29 Nov. 1594—*Min.*,
I, 348.) He was also called to the degree of the Utter Bar at Periam's request,
14 May 1602 (*Min.*, I, 422).

"his father": William Curle, or Curll, of Hatfield, an Auditor of the
Court of Wards and Liveries.

"Auditour Tucke": Probably William Tooke, Auditor-General of the
Court of Wards and Liveries; he had the manor of Popes, co. Herts., near Hatfield (DNB, XIX, 966; *Victoria History of Herts.*, III, 1912, p. 104); or his
eldest son Walter Tooke, who died seised of that manor in 1609 (see *Visitations of Herts. made by Robert Cooke, Esq. in 1572; and Sir Richard St.
George, Kt., in 1634*, ed. Walter C. Metcalfe, London, 1886, p. 99, and *Vict.
Hist. of Herts.*, loc. cit.)

"by . . . Lord Ch[ief] Justice Pophams meanes": John Popham, Lord
Chief Justice of the Queen's Bench since 1592, had been at Balliol, engaging
in manly sports and encounters, then at the Middle Temple, where he is said
to have led a "loose life for a time" before "his juvenile humour was reduced
to gravity." (Wood, I, 342.) As barrister, he became Reader (1568, 1572),
Serjeant-at-Law, Solicitor General (1579), Attorney General (1581), and
Treasurer of the Middle Temple (1580-87). He was a severe judge, according
to Wood's account of the "Martin Marprelate" execution of 1593 (I, 258-261).

"Serjeant Harris": Thomas Harris, Serjeant-at-Law, a member of the
Middle Temple since Plowden's time, having been admitted 16 Feb. 1565/66,
"son and heir of Edward Harrys of Corneworth, Devon., gent." (*Min.*, I, 152.)
He became a Bencher in 1588 and served as Autumn Reader in 1588 and
1589 (*Adm.*, I, 30). He was one of those present on All Saints Day, 1601,
when the expelled poet John Davies made his submission (*Min.*, I, 416). (See
Introduction and fo. 12b.) This "negligent pleader" (Harrison, III, 273) is
also mentioned on fos. 70b and 98. His son and heir-apparent, Edward Harris,
was a student at the Middle Temple in 1594 (*Min.*, I, 347).

"*Quare impedit*": "Wherefore he hinders," a writ or action by the patron
of an advowson against one who has hindered him in his right of patronage,
asking the disturber why he hinders the plaintiff. (*Black's Law Dictionary*,
ed. Henry Campbell Black, 4th ed., St. Paul, Minn., 1957, p. 1409.)

"the Common Place": The Court of Common Pleas.

Fo. 31. "One that would needes be married . . .": This anecdote must have
been circulating freely and widely, for Sir Roger Wilbraham entered a version
of it in his journal, between Whitsunday and September, 1598, as follows:

> Seriant Yelverton said a pore bachelor to be maried had no money
> to pay the prist, only 8^d: the prist in congregation refused to marry him
> without full pay: he desired he might be maried as farr as his money
> wold go & promised to pay the rest: & so was: the prist after asking
> the dett: nay said he, I will geve 10 tymes as much to unmarie us:

(ed. Harold Scott, Camden Miscellany, X, London, 1902, pp. 18-19).

"One when he was in marrying . . . (Mr. Douglas *n.*)": Omitted by B. Mr. Douglas has not been positively identified. The only one of this name connected with the Inns of Court in this period was Sir George Douglas, of Redhouse, knight, admitted to the Inner Temple, Nov., 1604, together with a large number of others of the nobility and Scots knights (*I.T. Adm.*, 167). But several prominent Douglases were in London in 1602, including Archibald Douglas, former parson of Glasgow and Scottish ambassador to England (see DNB, V, 1185-6)—in March he was "at Maister Harvass in Lym streitt" (*Hist. MSS. Comm., Salisbury*, XIV, 212-213, 295-6); and Archibald Douglas of Whittinghame, who had accompanied King James to Norway on his marriage in 1589, and who would be knighted and admitted privy councillor 29 May 1603 ("Members of Parliament—Scotland," in *Collectanea Genealogica,* ed. Joseph Foster, I, 1892, pp. 99, 102). Other possibilities include Sir Robert Douglas, who became treasurer of the Prince's house in 1616 and Master of the Horse to Prince Charles (Chamberlain, II, 58, 402), knighted at Whitehall or Royston in Feb. 1608/09 (Shaw, II, 147), later created Lord Belhaven; George Douglas a Scot knighted at Hatfield Woodhall or Theobalds July 10, 1607 (Shaw, II, 143)—he was "of St. Martin-in-the-Fields" when in 1611 as a "widower, 45" he married the widow of Sir Robert Kennington at St. Andrew Holborn (Foster, *London Marriage Licences*, 1521-1869, Lond., 1887, p. 414); George Douglas, D.D., rector of Stepney, London—he married Cecily, fourth daughter and co-heiress of Sir Robert Drury (William Fraser, *The Douglas Book*, II, Edinburgh, 1885, p. 546). In the Diarist's home village of Fen Drayton there was also a William Dowglasse whom Manningham probably knew (*Feet of Fines for Cambridgeshire*, ed. W. M. Palmer, Norwich, [1908?], p. 103; see under 32 and 33 Eliz., Michaelmas.)

"(Ch. Da[nvers].)": Charles Danvers of the Middle Temple (See Introduction and note to fo. 6b).

Fo. 31b. "Mr. Fleetwood": Probably Thomas Fleetwood, son of Recorder William Fleetwood mentioned on fo. 29b; admitted to the Middle Temple March 10, 1592/93; called 22 May 1601; Associate Bencher 1603 (*Adm.,* I, 64). Later knighted, he became attorney to Henry, Prince of Wales (DNB, VII, 268).

"Mr. Bramston": John Bramston of the Middle Temple, future Lord Chief Justice (see fo. 29b and note).

"It pleased your Grace . . . reason": These verses of Edmund Spenser to the Queen, here quoted to Manningham by William Towse of the Inner Temple (see fos. 17b, 29b, and 30b), are given by Fuller in a slightly different version:

> I was promis'd on a time,
> To have reason for my rhyme;
> From that time unto this season,
> I receiv'd nor rhyme nor reason.

According to Fuller's account, Lord Treasurer Cecil, given discretionary powers to reward Spenser with "what is reason" (after he had demurred at £ 100), neglected to pay; thereupon the poet complained and the Queen ordered Cecil to pay him £ 100. (*Worthies*, 366.)

Fo. 32. "L[ord] H. Howard": Henry Howard (1540-1614), second son of the poet Henry Howard, Earl of Surrey, and thus younger brother of Thomas Howard, fourth Duke of Norfolk. A personal enemy of Lord Cobham and Sir Walter Ralegh, he was created Earl of Northampton, 13 March 1604/05. Lord Howard's translation of Charles V's last advice to Philip II (*Harl. MSS.* 836, 1056; *Cotton MS. Titus* C. xviii; Bodl. Libr. *Rawl. MS.* B 7, f. 32) and his dedication of it to the Queen were evidently part of his effort to ingratiate himself with her, as he did "with suppleness and flattery." (DNB, X, 30.)

As Lord Warden of the Cinque Ports and Privy Councillor he was specially admitted to the Middle Temple 2 Feb. 1603/04 (*Min.*, II, 442).

After his name in MS "E. of Arundell" has been crossed out.

Fo. 33b. "One Mr. Palmes": Probably Guy Palmes of the Inner Temple, a resident of Lanceleby, Hants., and Ashwell, Rutland, admitted in Nov., 1597. He was knighted in 1603, and served as M.P. for Rutland, 1614-49. His father was Francis Palmes, admitted to the Inner Temple in 1573, M.P. for Knaresborough, 1586. (*I. T. Adm.*, 74, 148).

"every one must have": MS every one much have

"Justice Wray": Sir Christopher Wray, Lord Chief Justice of the Queen's Bench, 1574-92, and a generous benefactor to Manningham's college, Magdalene, as indicated by the early account book in the care of Mr. Derek Pepys-Whitely at the Pepys Library at Magdalene. A temperate man and "as exemplary in his private as in his judicial life," he seems to have been fond of "putting his rules of conduct into pithy forms," says Foss (p. 763). David Lloyd, in the next century, wrote that Wray was "choice in five particulars": his friend, his wife, his book, his secrets, and his expression and garb (Foss, 763, quoting *State Worthies*, 580).

Fo. 34. "Dr. Parryes Ale": Henry Parry, D.D. (see fo. 2 and note).

"at Dr. Turners, appothecary, in Bishopgate Streate": Peter Turner, D. Med., Heidelberg (incorp. at Cambridge, 1575, and Oxford, 1599); Licenciat, College of Physicians, 1582; physician to St. Bartholomew's Hospital. He was the son of an earlier physician, writer, and divine, William Turner, D. Med., Dean of Wells (d. 1586). Dr. Peter Turner married Dr. Henry Parry's sister, Pascha, who bore him two sons, Samuel and Peter. (Foster, IV, 1521; Wood, *Fasti*, I, 157, 167.) His prominence in Elizabethan and Jacobean London is suggested not only by the present entry but by other records of his activity. In 1606 (March?), for instance, he certified the ill health of Sir Walter Ralegh, advising his removal to a room near the still-house, which he had built in the Tower garden (CSP, *Dom., James I, 1603-1610*, p. 307). Among the Cecil papers at Hatfield House are a diagnosis and three prescriptions for illness during supposed pregnancy, signed by Peter Turner and five colleagues (*Hist. MSS., Comm., Salisbury*, XIV, 1923, p. 270).

"the olde Earle of Pembroke": Henry Herbert, second Earl of Pembroke, died 19 Jan. 1600/01. He was succeeded in the Presidency of Wales by Edward the last Lord Zouche of Haryngworth (B), concerning whom, see fo. 43b and note.

Fo. 34b. "it came to passe": for *to* MS has *it.*
"Epitaphes in the Temple churche": For information about the Temple Church, see note to fo. 5.
"*H. Bellingham Westmerlandiensis*": Henry Bellingham, second son of Alan B., of Hellsingtone, Westmoreland, esq. admitted to the Middle Temple, 30 Jan. 1582/83 (*Adm.*, I, 50).

Fo. 35. "D: O: M: on the South Syde . . . *Rogerio Bisshopio*": Dugdale, *Origines Juridiciales* (1666), p. 175, printed the epitaph on Roger Bishop as he found it "upon another Tablet fixt to the same South Wall" of the Temple Church, meaning near the round walk, where a large tablet of marble had been placed to commemorate "Johannes Seldenus, 1654." Stow and Strype also mention it in their *Survey of London and Westminster* (1720), Bk. 3, p. 274.
". . . in the church at Hythe in Kent": Presumably New Hythe, on the Medway in the parish of East Malling (not far from Bradbourne). Close to the river, it was called New Hythe (new harbor or haven) because of shipping and reloading of goods here. "A chapel once existed here, called New Hythe chapel", where daily masses were said; it was suppressed in the reign of Edward VI (W. H. Ireland, *History of County of Kent,* London, 1829, III, 602-3). Richard Manningham's neighbor, Hugh Cartwright, esq., acquired it (see note to fo. 14b).

Fo. 35b. "*W. Wats, antagonista.*": William Watts of London. He was called to the Utter Bar with Edward Watts (his Cousin?) by Mr. Haule (Henry Hall) during his reading, Lent, 1602 (14 May)—*Adm.* I, 67. See note to fo. 29b.
"9. [name heavily cancelled] showed me certaine love letteres . . . word him.": Omitted by B.
"29. There have bin 5 Bishops of London . . . nowe.": Omitted by B.
"B. Rud[yerd]": Thus in *MS*; mistranscribed by B, in both instances on this page, as "B. Reid." Benjamin Rudyerd (1572-1658), poet, wit, the future Sir Benjamin, statesman, mediator between Charles I and Parliament, was educated at Winchester and St. John's College, Oxford; he entered the Middle Temple 18 April 1590, "third son of James R., of Winchfield, Hants., and late of New Inn, gent." (*Adm.*, I, 60). He was called to the bar with James Whitelock, 24 Oct. 1600, by Nicholas Overbury in his reading (*Adm.*, I, 60, 64).
Rudyerd numbered among his intimate friends John Donne, John Hoskyns, Henry Wotton, and William Herbert, Earl of Pembroke. With Wotton he enjoyed a lasting friendship, being his traveling companion, says his biographer, James A. Manning (*Memoirs of Sir Benjamin Rudyerd, Knt.,* London, 1841, p. 8). With Pembroke, who patronized the greatest literary men of the time, he wrote some sprightly and satirical verse "by way of

repartee," printed with *Poems written by the Rt. Hon. William Earl of Pembroke* . . . (London, 1660). One of his poems, "Why slights thou her whom I approve?" refers to his future wife, Elizabeth, daughter of Sir Henry Harrington. Among Rudyerd's admirers was Ben Jonson, who in epigrams (cxxi, cxxii, and cxxiii) hailed in him and in Egerton, men who renewed "the aged SATVRNE's age"—"the world's pure gold, and wise simplicitie." (Herford and Simpson ed., II, 364; VIII, 78.)

In 1614, with Wotton and Donne, Rudyerd contributed to the second edition of Thomas Overbury's *Wife* and characters (Simpson, *A Study of the Prose Works of Donne,* 135). In the same year Sir Robert Killigrew gave him a seat in Parliament, for Helston, Cornwall (Whitelocke, *Liber Famelicus,* 41).

In Easter Term, 1618, he became surveyor of the Court of Wards and was immediately afterward knighted (ibid., 61-61). Whitelocke, himself in a gown of wrought velvet, pictures Rudyerd at a memorable dinner in Middle Temple Hall on "all hallowd day" [Nov. 1] in 1620, the Serjeants present "in skarlet": Sir John Davies, the king's serjeant; Sir Frauncis More, Frauncis Hartye, Sir Frauncis Ashlye, and "sir Benjamin Rudyerd knighte. . . ." (*Liber Famelicus,* p. 85).

At some time, unspecified, he and Hoskyns quarrelled, fought a duel in which Rudyerd was wounded in the knee, but "were afterwards friends again." (Aubrey, *Brief Lives,* ed. Dick, 1950, pp. 169-170).

In 1641 and 42 he strove for peace, giving "learned" and "worthy" speeches in the House of Commons, such as the one spoken July 9, 1642, "for accommodation, betwixt His Majesty and His Parliament" and printed soon after for both R. Thrale and R. Lowndes (Wing, *S.T.C.* 2206-2208). He was also interested in colonization and was one of the incorporators of the Providence Company.

In the Diary, Manningham shows that he enjoyed Rudyerd's wit; see, for example, fos. 99, 117 and 119b.

"yong Mr. Leake": Perhaps Francis Leeke, or Leake, son and heir of Francis Leeke, esq., of Sutton in le Dale, Derbyshire, when he was specially admitted to the Middle Temple, 1 Feb., 1599/1600 (*Min.,* I, 400); on 6 June 1600, he was one of those appointed to provide the Reader's Feast for the ensuing Autumn (*Min.,* I, 406). He was knighted at the Tower March 14, 1603/04 (Shaw, *Knights of England,* II, 131). See also fo. 11 and note. Or possibly Thomas Lake, son and heir of Stephen Lake, esq., Master of Chancery; he was admitted to the Middle Temple 13 April 1602, and called 26 May 1609 (*Adm.,* I, 79). One Thomas Leake was also admitted 14 May 1602, son and heir of Thomas L. of Hasland, Derbs., esq., dcd. (ibid.)

Fo. 36.: Blank in MS.

Fo. 36b. "*Dr. Chamberlayne*": Bartholomew Chamberlaine, D.D. (Oxon., 1578/79). Born at Shipton-under-Wychwood, Oxon., about 1546, died 1621. A scholar of Trinity College, Oxford, he received his B.A. in 1566, M.A. in 1570, and B.D. in 1576. He served as vicar of Burford, Oxon., in 1578, then as rector of Holywell, Hunts., from 1579 to 1600, and of Hemingford Abbots, Hunts. (both near St. Ives and Fen Drayton), 1601?-1621 (Foster, I, 257, cited by Venn, I, 316). In 1593 he was also rector of Sandy, Beds., (see fo. 2b and fo. 37). He and the Diarist seem to have enjoyed a close friendship; undoubtedly Chamberlaine was acquainted with John's uncle Thomas Manningham, the vicar of Swavesey. In Hilary Term, 40 Eliz., 1597/98 the Diarist was associated with Dr. Chamberlaine and his wife Joan in a legal settlement (*finalis concordia*) with one William Pomford of six messuages and lands in Baldock, Weston, Willian, Clothall, and Bigrave, Herts.—property formerly in the possession of Manningham's grandfather. (Public Record Office, C.P. 25 (2), 2232. See also *Herts. Genealogist and Antiquary*, ed. William Brigg, III, Harpenden, 1899, p. 233).

"Sapley": The forest of Sapley in Hunts., formerly a royal forest about seven miles in circuit, had been conveyed by Roger, 2nd Baron North, in 1565 to Henry Williams alias Cromwell, son of Sir Richard Williams alias Cromwell, to whom it had been leased in 1542. Thus Henry had become seised in fee of both the forest and the office of keeper. (*Vict. Hist. of Hunts.*, II, 1932, p. 173.) The village of Hartford cum Sapley is on the north bank of the Ouse, along the road from Huntingdon to Ramsey and St. Ives (ibid., II, 171).

"Mr. Oliver Cromwell": Sir Oliver Cromwell of Hinchinbrook, uncle to the future Protector. He was knighted by the Queen in 1598 and created K.B. at the coronation of James I (B).

"Mr. Hynd came behinde": Probably William or Edward Hynde, sons of the eminent and wealthy Sir Francis Hynde, owner of Maddingley Hall near Cambridge, the manor of Anglesey, and other manors, and of his wife Jane, daughter of Sir Edmond Verney (Edward Harlstone, Jr., *History and Antiquities of the Parish of Bottisham and the Priory of Anglesey in Cambridgeshire*, Camb., 1873, Publ. of Camb. Antiq. Soc., XIV, pp. 327-9). William was knighted in 1603 and Edward in 1615 (Shaw, *Knights of England*, II, 105, 157). Ironically, the son and heir of the latter, also Edward Hynde, was killed by a fall from his horse.

Fo. 37. "at Hemmingford Dr. Chamberlayne told me": Bartholomew Chamberlaine, D.D. (see note to fo. 36b) was at this time rector of Hemingford Abbots, on the lovely, winding River Ouse near St. Ives, Hunts. According to wills dated 1537 and 1541, the church there, with its 13th century nave and 14th century tower, was known as All Hallowes, with its "High Altar of St. Margaret"; later it was called the Church of St. Margaret the Virgin. Patrons of this living were Sir Thomas Gorges and his wife Dame Helen, Marchioness of Northampton. Dr. Chamberlaine was also vicar of St. James, Hemingford Grey, 1602-1606. ("Incumbents of County of Huntingdon," *Transactions of Cambridgeshire and Huntingdonshire Archaeological Society*, ed. W. M. Noble, III, Ely, 1914, pp. 119-121.)

"Dr. Bilson": Thomas Bilson (1547-1616), bishop of Winchester; elected and consecrated bishop of Worcester in 1596 but translated to Winchester in 1597 (Hardy's Le Neve, III, 18). In the next reign he, with Miles Smith, his Puritan successor, and others, reviewed the Bible translators' work and made final revisions. (Paine, *The Learned Men,* p. 72.). This "dullish, dogged church-man," says Paine, helped keep the 1611 Bible "within the fixed framework of the Church" (ibid., 127, 140). It also fell to him to pronounce the divorce in the Countess of Essex's infamous nullity suit (Welsby, *George Abbott,* p. 70). See also fo. 84 and note.

"Lady Walsingham": Ursula St. Barbe, widow successively of Sir Richard Worseley and of Sir Francis Walsingham, secretary of state form 1573 until his death in 1590. She was "a woman of means" and "of well-poised practical temper," one who held her husband's confidence throughout their marriage (Conyers Read, *Mr Secretary Walsingham,* Cambridge, Mass., 1925, III, 422). Frances, her daughter by Walsingham, became successively wife to Sir Philip Sidney, Robert Devereux, second Earl of Essex, and Richard de Burgh, Earl of Clanricarde (DNB, XX, 693, 696).

"Dr. Yeilderes decease": Arthur Yeldard, or Yildard, M.A., president of Trinity College, Oxford, died 1 Feb. 1598. Bishop Bilson nominated Ralph Kettell, S.T.P., ("him, that nowe is, President") to succeed him, 12 Feb. 1598 (Hardy's Le Neve, III, 572).

"the Lady Polivizena": Anne, daughter of Egidius Hoostman, or Hoof-man, of Antwerp ("a notable rich man," says the Diarist on fo. 37b), and widow of Sir Horatio Palavicino, a prominent Genoese who had settled at Babraham, Cambridgeshire. Sir Horatio, a financier, speculator, secret agent, and international intriguer, advanced large sums to Queen Elizabeth. (For an account of his career, see Lawrence Stone, *An Elizabethan: Sir Horatio Palavicino,* Oxford, 1956.) Sometime after his death on 6 July 1600, his widow received letters of proposal from both Sir Robert Cecil and the Earl of Shrewsbury supporting the suit of Mr. Oliver Cromwell, son and heir to Sir Henry Cromwell (*Hist. MSS. Comm., Salisbury,* XI, 1906, pp. 260-1); she married him a year and a day after first husband's demise.

It is ironical that Manningham should have mentioned Sir John Cutts and Sir Horatio Palavicino on the same page, for these knights were at odds with each other. Sir John's unfriendliness toward Sir Horatio is revealed in a letter sent by the latter to Sir Robert Cecil, from "Baburham," 30 July 1597 (*Hist. MSS. Comm., Salisbury,* VII, 1899, p. 326); in Cecil's letter to Cutts of Aug. 6, 1597 (ibid., 337); and in Sir John's reply of Aug. 10, (ibid., 343). Palavicino was unappeased on 15 August (ibid., 353).

"Mr. Mayne of Grayes In": Perhaps James Mayne, of Bovingdon, Herts., admitted to Grays Inn 28 Jan., 1599/1600 (*Gray's Adm.,* fo. 478, p. 98), or James Mayne, of Hemel Hempstead, Herts., adm. 5 Nov. 1585 (ibid., fo. 82, p. 68).

Fo. 37b. "The yong Lord North": Dudley, third Baron North (1581-1666), then only 23, succeeded to that title on the death of his grandfather, the second Baron, 3 Dec. 1600. The bride, "Mrs. Brocket," was Frances, daughter of Sir John Brockett of Brockett Hall, Herts. Barely 16, she was not altogether Lord North's choice, but their marriage produced four sons and two daughters. Lord North lived to be 85, and his wife survived him by eleven years. (DNB, XIV, 594-6.) On Sir John Cutts, see notes to fo. 84b and to fo. 37.

"Dr. Chamberlaine": Bartholomew Chamberlaine, D.D. (see fo. 36b and note).

"at Sir Henry Cromwells": Sir Henry Cromwell, "the Golden Knight," was the father of Sir Oliver and grandfather of the Protector. In April, 1603, his son Sir Oliver, in possession of his lands under the arrangement mentioned in fo. 37, entertained James I at Hinchinbrooke as the King made his progress from Scotland to take possession of the throne (B). Sir Henry died the following January.

'his Uncle Warrein": Richard Warren of Claybury, Essex, son of Sir Ralph Warren, Lord Mayor of London in 1536 and 1544. Sir Ralph's daughter Jane was Sir Henry Cromwell's first wife; she inherited her brother's lands, which upon her death then passed to Sir Oliver (B).

Fo. 38. "Ditton": In Kent, on the main road from Maidstone to London, just east of the manor and park of Bradbourne.

"Dr. Parry": Henry Parry, D.D. (see note to fo. 13b).

"Dr. Barlowe": William Barlow, D.D., fellow of Trinity Hall, Cambridge; prebendary of London (1597) and canon of Westminster (1601), dean of Chester (1603), bishop of Rochester (1605), translated to Lincoln (1608)— Hardy's Le Neve, II, 24, 378. Wood speaks of him as "a considerable Benefactor to St. Joh[ns] Coll. in Cambridge," being the founder of the London Fellows and Scholars of that college (*Fasti*, I, 162). He should be distinguished from two other William Barlowes, one of whom was bishop of Chichester and father to William Barlowe (1560?-1625) of Balliol College, Oxford, an expert in navigation and magnetism, as well as prebendary of Winchester, chaplain to Prince Henry, and Archdeacon of Salisbury (*Athenae*, I, 494-495).

"Duke de Neveurs": Charles de Gonzaga, Duke of Nevers (1580-1637), son of Louis de Gonzaga (1539-1595), French military leader, and Henrietta of Cleves, sister and heiress of Francis II of Cleves (*Larousse du XXe Siècle*, Paris, 1930, III, 824). This French visitor made a good impression on the English, except that he was thought "very drie-handed" by the Queen's musicians and other "inferior officers." (Chamberlain, I, 139). His arrival was anticipated 17 March 1602: "The coming of the Duke of Nevers is daily expected, and the Earl of Northumberland is appointed to meet, receive, and conduct him. Many of the most rich hangings are fetched out of the Tower to adorn the Court and great preparations made for his honourable entertainment. The general opinion is that he cometh of curiosity to see the Court and country but some say that he desireth secretly a sight of the Lady Arabella. A house is being prepared here privately in London where the lady, with those with whom she liveth, are expected soon after Easter." (Harrison, 269, citing *Records of the English Province of the Society of Jesus*, ed. Henry Foley, S.J., 1877, etc., I, 23, 24.)

"Vicares": Thomas Vicares, or Vicary, (1495?-1562?), a Maidstone surgeon, author of *The Anatomie of the Bodie of Man*, 1548, reputed to be the first book on anatomy to be published in English. Vicary's curing of Henry VIII's sore leg took place about 1525, when the King was passing through Maidstone. The success of the treatment so pleased Henry that he made Vicary Junior Warden of the Barbers' Company. The next year (1526) Vicary was receiving £ 20 a year as the King's Surgeon. The King also granted him tithes of grain, glebelands, the chief house of the Rectory of Boxley, and ten pieces of land—i.e., of the dissolved abbey of Boxley. (John W. Bridge, "A Famous Maidstone Surgeon," *Arch. Cant.*, LXI, 1949, p. 185; LXII, 1950, pp. 91-93.) He held the office of sergeant-surgeon from 1536 until his death (DNB, XX, 300). In 1540, with other surgeons, he was doing research on blood circulation, by dissecting bodies of those hanged at Tyburn (Bridge, LXII, 92-3). From 1548 on, he was resident governor of St. Bartholomew's Hospital (DNB, XX, 300). The 1548 edition of Vicary's *Anatomie* published by F.J. and Percy Furnivall contains a life of the author.

"rode to Dr. Parryes": From Bradbourne, at East Malling, to Sundridge or Chevening, about 13 miles as the crow flies. Parry was rector of both parishes at this time but probably resided at Sundridge (rectors of Sundridge also held Lambeth appointments and are said always to have resided at Sundridge). Manningham had a choice of two routes: by the Maidstone-West Malling-Sevenoaks-Westerham Road, or by the longer Pilgrim's Way, north of East Malling. At Chevening the rectory is near the church on the Pilgrim's Way. (For this information I am indebted to the Rev. M. G. Hewett, Rector of Chevening, Kent, ltr. of Nov. 31, 1966.)

"He said . . .": MS Shee said . . . But Dr. Parry was unmarried. It is possible, of course, that Manningham meant Parry's sister Pascha, wife of Dr. Peter Turner (fo. 34 and note), or a housekeeper.

Fo. 38b. "deane of Salisbury": Henry Parry the elder was actually Chancellor, rather than Dean. He was collated 24 Sept. 1547, deprived during the reign of Queen Mary, but restored in 1559, shortly after Elizabeth's accession. He died in 1571. (Hardy's Le Neve, II, 651, 652.)

"Cos. shee": Richard Manningham's second wife, Jane (See Introduction and note to fo. 10b.)

Fo. 39. "by fines . . .": Thus in MS. B reads *for* but emends to *from*.

"One Parkins of the Inner house": Probably George Parkins, or Parkyns, of the Inner Temple, mentioned 23 May 1596 (38 Eliz.) as one of those ordered to be "remitted into commons" and to "attend the bench table's end. . . ." (Inderwick, I, 413.) He was ordered called to the bar 3 Nov. 1598 (ibid., I, 425).

"29. 'It is a great thing must stopp a feme covert,' . . . Fennar.": Omitted by B. A *feme covert* (woman covered) meant one under the protection of her husband, hence used for a married woman or, humorously, for a wife (OED, IV, 151). Justice Fenner's word-play here is obvious. Edward Fenner (d. 1612) was a Middle Templar, admitted 16 Oct. 1577, Bencher 1576, Autumn Reader 1576, Serjeant-at-law 1577, Justice of the Queen's Bench, 1590. In Huntingdonshire in 1593 he presided at the trial of "three wytches." (*Adm.*, I, 23; Foss, 248; DNB, XVIII, 319.) His eldest son was also at the Middle Temple, admitted July 3, 1593 (*Adm.*, I, 65).

"Cosen Onsloe": Probably George Onslowe, son and heir of the William Onslowe for whom Manningham prepared and executed an indenture settling the manor of Norton in Suffolk in 1611 (MS. in Middle Temple Library— see Introduction and Appendix). He matriculated pensioner at Trinity College, Cambridge, Easter, 1585, but did not graduate (Venn, III, 281; Ball and Venn, *Trinity College Admissions*, II, 152). He entered the Middle Temple 10 Oct. 1587, as "son and heir apparent of William Onslowe of Littell Saint Bartholamew, London, gent., generally; fine, 53 s. 4d." (*Min.*, I, 292; *Adm.*, I, 58.) Though fined three times for absence in the ensuing year and a half, (*Min.*, I, 297, 298, 304), he was appointed to provide the Reader's feast, 13 June, 1589 (31 Eliz.)—*Min.*, I, 306. I take him to have been the same "George Onslowe of London Haberdasher" whose daughter Hester married Thomas Clerke of London, gent., whose eldest son was living in 1634 (*Visitation of London, A.D. 1633, 1634, and 1635. Made by Sir H. St. George, Kt.*, ed. J. J. Howard and J. L. Chester, I, 1880, p. 171.) He was evidently not elected Sheriff, for John Pemberton and John Swynerton were, Michs., 1602 (*List of Sheriffs for England and Wales*, P.R.O. *Lists and Indexes*, IX, 1898, p. 205).

Fo. 39b. "Mr. Ousley of the Middle Temple": Probably Richard Oseley, "late of New Inn, gent., second son of Richard O., of Curtenhall [Courtenhill], Northants., esq."—admitted Nov. 14, 1591 (*Adm.*, I, 63); his older brother John Oseley, had been admitted 29 October 1585 (*Adm.*, I, 55).

"Mr. Buttler . . . (Overbury.)": Omitted by B. The informant was Thomas Overbury (1581-1613), son of the Middle Temple bencher Nicholas Overbury. (See fo. 12 and note.) The Biblical origin of the pun in this entry is Matthew 9:12.

"Sniges nose": George Snygge, or Snigge, esq., one of the Masters of the Bench of the Middle Temple, and Treasurer (1602). He had been a member since 1567 and had been called to the bar in 1575 (*Adm.*, I, 31). He would serve as Baron of the Exchequer from 1604 to 1617 (Richard C. Mitchell and Lewis W. Morse, *Chronicle of English Judges*, Oswego, N.Y., 1937, p. 60). Or: his son John Snygge, admitted October 24, 1600 (*Adm.*, I, 77).

"Mr. Blundell of the Middle Temple": No one of this name is mentioned in *Adm.* except two Blundells admitted after the Restoration. The Diarist is probably referring to Andrew Blunden, or Blundon, of Bishopcastle, Salop., "a wise and learned lawyer" (Thomas Windebanck and Thos. Lake to Sec'y Cecil—*CSP Dom. Eliz., 1601-1603*, p. 198; see also p. 276). He was admitted to the Middle Temple 19 Oct. 1566 and called 10 Feb. 1584/85 (*Adm.*, I, 31).

'**Fo. 40.** "Dr. Spenser": John Spenser, D.D., (1559-1614) rector of the church of the Holy Sepulchre, London, 1599-1614, and future president of Corpus Christi College, Oxford, 1607-1614. To him, on the death of Richard Hooker, who had been his fellow-student at Corpus, were given Hooker's MSS. for completion of the *Ecclesiastical Polity* (DNB, XVIII, 806-7). The sermon on which Manningham took these extensive notes at Paul's Cross was printed in 1615 under the supervision of Spenser's curate, Hamlett Marshall, by George Purslowe for Samuel Rande, "to be sold at his shoppe

near Holborne Bridge." It occupies 49 quarto pages (Bodleian Library copies).
In a dedicatory epistle to John King, the Bishop of London, Marshall praised
Dr. Spenser as *Lux illuminata* in order that he might be *lux illuminans.*
Spenser had entitled his message "Gods Love to His Vineyard." Comparison
of the Diarist's notes with the printed version shows that the young lawyer
had a keen grasp of Spenser's fundamental points as well as an ear for the
preacher's imagery. It is a remarkably accurate paraphrase and précis, occasion-
ally using the same words as those later printed but more often summarizing
and varying the language. Thus Manningham is clearer, simpler, and less wordy
than the published text; in the passage concerning grafts (section 6), for
example, the Diarist used only 62 words to say what Spenser had developed
in 328. Although terse, plain, and blunt, and lacking the rhetorical flourish
of Spenser's pulpit oratory, Manningham's version is sometimes as poetical.
The final portion in the diary (fo. 43, corresponding to p. 39 of the published
sermon) is a free paraphrase and condensation. That Manningham concluded
at this point suggests both common sense and fatigue, for the sermon goes on
for another ten pages of reiteration, peroration, and final prayer. (For notes
on another sermon by Spenser, see fo. 119.)

Fo. 40b. "Bare naked": *naked* is interlined in MS, after *bare.* In the 1615
published version: "but when winter cometh . . . no plant standeth so poore,
so deformed, so contemptible to the outward eye;"

Fo. 41b. "our countriman Stapleton": Thomas Stapleton, the controversialist, from one of whose works Manningham copied seven pages of extracts (see fo. 60b to fo. 63b and note.)

Fo. 42. "He that receiveth a benefit . . . saith Seneca . . . (not our owne).":
Preached but apparently not included in the 1615 printed version.

Fo. 43b. "the L[ord] Zouche": Edward la Zouche (1556-1625), eleventh
Baron Zouche of Harringworth, became President of Wales—i.e., Lieutenant
of North and South Wales—in June, 1602 (Chamberlain, I, 150). "The Lord
Zouch playes *rex* in Wales," wrote Chamberlain on 15 Oct. 1602, "and takes
upon him *comme un Millord d'Angleterre,* both with the counsaile and
justices, as also with the poor Welchmen, whom they say he punishes extreemly
for pewtry." (I, 166.)
"the Chief Justice of that bench": Sir Edmund Anderson (see fo. 30b
and note).
"Chief Justice Leukenour": Sir Richard Lewkenor, or Lewknor, (1540?-
1616) of the Middle Temple, chief judge at Chester from 1600 until his death
in 1616 at age 76. As second son of Edmund Leucknour of Tangmer, Sussex,
he was admitted to the Middle Temple 9 Oct. 1560; Bencher, 1581; Reader,
Autumn, 1581—also Lent, 1592, but did not read because of the plague. He
served as M.P. for Chichester, 1572-98, and Recorder of Chichester, 1588-
1600. In 1593 he was made Serjeant-at-Law and in 1600 was knighted. (*Adm.,*
I, 25; J. Bruce Williamson, *The Middle Temple Bench Book,* 2nd ed., 1937,
p. 82.) In January, 1602/03, Lewkenor was complained of to Cecil by Lord

Zouche, the Lord President of Wales (see above), for his pride and sensitivity to personal pique (a "jealousy grown between us")—Ludlow, 28 Jan., 1602 (*Hist. MSS. Comm., Salisbury*, XII, 1910, pp. 619-620). Two months later Sir Richard wrote to Cecil from Ludlow regarding the death of his only son and requesting a one-month leave to travel to London and Sussex to settle his affairs there. (ibid., XII, p. 86). See also Foster, III, 911, and Foss, *Judges of England*, V, 1857, p. 414.

"(Th. Overbury)": Thomas Overbury of the Middle Temple (see note to fo. 12).

"Sir Walter Rhaleighs sollicitor on Sheborough": Thus in MS. B has interpreted *on* as *one*, *Sheborough* as the name of Ralegh's solicitor, adding commas (". . . sollicitor, on[e] Sheborough, was . . ."). But Manningham may have been referring to Sherborne Castle in Dorset, the favorite home of Sir Walter and his Lady, and to one of the suits with which his former bailiff, John Meers, was plaguing him. (A. L. Rouse, *Ralegh*, 1962, p. 223.) In the summer of 1601 Meers had refused to give place to a new bailiff, Dolberry; the result was petty violence and public squabbling. Ralegh is said personally to have put Meers in the stocks in Sherborne market place and to have walked off with the keys. Meers, a lawyer, as well as a coin-clipper and forger, had powerful backing and appealed to the Star Chamber; but Ralegh had applied to Cecil for help and Meers was finally jailed. Serjeant John Hele had been Ralegh's attorney in that case. (See Norman Lloyd Williams, *Sir Walter Raleigh*, London, 1962, pp. 157, 173, and *Gentlemen's Magazine*, 1853, II, 435-444; 1854, I, 17-23.)

"Justice Walmesley": Thomas Walmesley (c. 1537-1612), a Lincoln's Inn man from Lancashire (called to the bar June 15, 1567; Reader, 1578, 1580); Judge of the Common Pleas from 1589 until his death; knighted by King James. With Justice Edward Fenner he seems to have traveled the Western Circuit for five consecutive years, from Autumn, 1596, to Spring, 1601 (Foss, 698-9).

"At Guildhall, Mr. Long . . . my lordship.": Omitted by B. Regarding Edmund Long and Serjeant John Hele, see fo. 30b and 27, and notes, respectively.

Fo. 44. "The Irish Earle of Clanrichard": Richard of Kinsale, the fourth Earl, 1601-1635 (B).

"Mr. Hadsor": Richard Hadsor, or Hudsor, of the Middle Temple, admitted July 9, 1590, "son and heir of Nicholas H., of the county of Louide, Ireland, esq., and late of New Inn, gent. Called 11 Feb., 1602-03. Bencher 1617. Reader Autumn 1617. Treasurer 1624." (*Adm.*, I, 61). Hadsor advised Cecil on Irish affairs, endorsing his letters of March 1601/02 "From my chamber in Garnet's Buildings, near Temple Bar." (*Hist. MSS. Comm., Salisbury*, XII, 1910, p. 74). His charitableness or breadth of view enabled him to recommend to Cecil that Tyrrelagh O'Neile be supported even though his grandfather Tyrrelagh Lenaugh had "burned and spoiled my father's living in the country of Louth, within 28 miles of Dublin, at the time of Shane O'Neile's rebellion." (4 March, 1602/03, ibid., XII, 661.)

Manningham quotes Hadsor frequently, particularly on Irish matters; see folios 44b, 57b, 78b, 90, 98b, and 117.

"The E[arl] of Ormond": Thomas Butler, the tenth Earl of Ormond and Ossory, Viscount Thurles (1531-1614). As Chief Butler of Ireland, he was called "Tom Duffe" ("Black Tom"). His daughter and only surviving child, Elizabeth, was married, through the influence of King James, to Sir Richard Preston, subsequently created Earl of Desmond. When he died at Carrick, 22 Nov. 1614, he was 83. (B; DNB, III, 531-3; *The Complete Peerage*, ed. G.E.C., H. A. Doubleday, *et al.*, X, 1945, pp. 144, 147.) A sonnet praising Ormond was prefixed by Edmund Spenser to *The Faerie Queene*, 1590.

"Mr. Tanfeild, . . . to inward with hir.": Omitted by B. Whether Robert Tanfield of the Middle Temple or Lawrence Tanfield of the Inner Temple is meant is unclear. See fo. 11b and fo. 91; in the latter the "Tanfeild" mentioned is of the Inner Temple, indicating Lawrence, the future Lord Chief Baron of the Exchequer and grandfather of Lord Faulkland. His popularity is suggested by the renaming of Bradshaws Rents, his residence at the Temple, "Tanfield Court." He purchased the priory and manor of Great Tew. Upon his death in 1625, one month after the King's, he was buried in Burford Church, Oxfordshire. (Foss, p. 649.)

"one Nic. Hill": Nicholas Hill, astrologer and alchemist patronized by Edward, the "prodigal Earl of Oxford" (Wood's phrase), and by Henry the Earl of Northumberland during his long sojourn in the Tower. Donne satirized Hill in the first item of his mock *Catalogus: the Courtier's Library*; and Jonson made sport of

> *Those atomi ridiculous,*
> *Whereof old* Democrite *and* Hill Nicholas
> *One said, the other swore, the world consists.*

Wood reports that Hill "fell into conspiracy with one Basset," described as "of Umberly in Devonshire, descended from Arthur Plantagonet Viscount Lisle a natural Son of Edward IV," so that he "pretended some right to the Crown." Forced to flee to Holland, Hill practised physic in Rotterdam; when his son Laurence died of the plague, the grieving father swallowed poison and died, about 1610. (*Athenae*, I, 366.)

"Jo. Chap[man]": John Chapman of Godmersham, Kent, whom the Diarist mentions as a cousin (fo. 82b and fo. 84b). Second son of Henry Chapman of Godmersham, he entered the Middle Temple from New Inn, 14 Feb. 1591; his and John Hoskyns' calls to the bar were confirmed 2 May 1600. Hoskyns and he were Manningham's sureties when the Diarist was admitted. (*Adm.*, I, 63; *Min.*, I, 327, *et passim*.) His close relationship with Hoskyns, Martin, and others makes it very likely that he was the John Chapman who contributed one of the 60-odd mock-serious panegyrical poems to Thomas Coryate's *Crudities* (1611) and that he was therefore a member of the Mermaid wits. (See Michael Strachan, *the Life and Adventures of Thomas Coryate*, London, 1962.)

Fo. 44b. "The E[arl] of Sussex": Robert Radcliffe (1569?-1629), the fifth

Earl of Sussex, known as Viscount Fitzwalter from 1583 until 1593; courtier; patron of writers such as Greene and George Chapman; prominent in the capture of Cadiz; one of the peers commissioned to try his former commander Essex in 1601. Bridget, his first wife, praised here by Manningham, was daughter of Sir Charles Morison; Greene had complimented her by subtitling his *Philomela* (1592) "the Lady Fitzwa[l]ter's Nightingale." Before 1602 she had separated from the husband whose cruel taunts are described here. (DNB, XVI, 587-8.)

"Capt[ain] Whitlocke . . . pander,": Edmund Whitelock (1565-1608), older brother of James, the future judge, whom Manningham knew at the Middle Temple, was a learned (five modern languages, besides the classics and Hebrew) adventurer—a soldier, traveler, and boon companion. His friends included Dick Martin, Inigo Jones, and Donne's friend Sir Henry Goodyere; Dudley Carleton lamented his death in 1608. His brother described him as "verye valiant" but "extreme prodigall and wastefull in his expense" (*Liber Famelicus of Sir James Whitelock*, ed. J. Bruce, Camden Society, 1858, p. 10). Because of his connections with men in high place, like the Earls of Rutland and Northumberland, the playboy "Captain" was suspected of participating in both the Essex rising and the Gunpowder Plot, and was in and out of Newgate, the Tower, and the Fleet. (Ibid., Introduction, p. iv.) See also fo. 64.

"whoe is of a verry . . .": MS reads "whoe is a of a verry"

"of preferring strang fleshe before his owne,": Omitted by B.

"J. Bramstone *nar.*": John Bramston of the Middle Temple. See note to fo. 29b.

"(I would be loath . . . Su[ssex].)": Omitted by B.

"(Mr. Hadsor *narr.*)": Richard Hadsor of the Middle Temple (see note to fo. 44).

Fo. 45. "'It is merry when Gossips meete.' S. R.": Samuel Rowlands' popular verses *Tis Merrie when Gossips meete* (STC 21409) had evidently just been printed in 4to, by W. W.[hite] "to be sold by George Loftus at the Golden Ball in Popes-head Alley," for it had been entered in the Stationers' Register on 15 Sept. 1602. It enjoyed several editions and sequels during the next 25 years. Rowlands (1570?-1630?) was a prolific writer of prose and verse tracts, some pious, some bitingly satirical. *Tis Merrie* is a delightful naturalistic sketch in six-line stanzas (rime royal with the fifth line omitted), involving a widow, a wife, and a maiden at a tavern, discussing marriage and men.

The complete poem, which Edmund Gosse termed "one of the best studies of *genre* we possess in all Elizabethan literature," was published in *Complete Works of Samuel Rowlands*, printed for the Hunterian Club of Glasgow, 1880: Gosse's "Memoir" on Rowlands appears in Vol. 1 and has been reprinted in his *Seventeenth Century Studies*, 1883.

Additional interest in this work derives from John Davies' having composed a "device" entitled "A Contention betwixt a Wife, a Widdowe and a Maide" for Sir Robert Cecil's entertainment of the Queen, at his new house in the Strand, near Ivy Bridge. (See fo. 75b.) Since that celebration occurred December 6, 1602, and since Davies' device was admired by John Chamberlain as "a pretty dialogue" that would probably soon be printed (I, 178), Rowlands' poem clearly has the priority, as having furnished the inspiration to Davies, rather than—as the DNB article on Rowlands puts it (XVII, 354)— the other way around. "Rowlands indeed had anticipated Davies with the publication of *Tis Merrie....*" (Hyder Rollins, ed., *A Poetical Rhapsody*, II, Cambridge, Mass., 1932, p. 215.) Davies' skit was published in the second edition (1608) of Francis Davison's *Poetical Rhapsody*, not the first (1602).

"There's many deale... Vintners Syne": Closing couplet of stanza 8 of a twelve-stanza introduction addressed "To the Gentle-women Readers."

"She ply'd him ... bottom up.": Closing couplet of Stanza 9.

"I pray goe ... standing here.": "Widdow: Where shall we bee? Vintner: I pray go vp the staires. / Wife: Good Cousen no, let's take it standinge heere."

"A drapers man ... (lovers)": Speaking about Jane, one of their friends in Soper-lane, the Widow says, "A Drapers man and she were mighty in. / Wife: I pra'y, what she with him, or he with her? / Wid: Fayth both in loue: ..."

"Maydes take ... nay": Spoken by the Widow, "... Lord! Maydes be strange, / They looke for thousand words of sweet and pray / And take few things to which they say not nay."

"Tis maydens modesty ... thrice.": Spoken by the Mayde.

"Wine and Virginity ... drink flatt.": Part of the Widow's reply to the preceding speech, "Put here's a cup of Wine doth stand for tryall, / Your Mayden-ship takes liquor in too nice: / Pray mend your fault, kinde Besse, wee'le none of that, / Wine and Virginitie kept stale, drinke flat."

"Taurus soe rules ... hornework cap.": Spoken by the Mayde. / In this section of the poem she and the Wife dispute as follows:

> Wife: There's an old graue Prouerbe tell's vs that / Such as die Maydes, doe all lead Apes in hell.
> Mayde: That Prouerbs proofe can do you little stead: / But married *Wiues* oft giue and take such claps, / Taurus so rules and guides their husbands head, / That euery night they sleepe in Hornework caps. / I pra'y what Proverbe is it that allowes / The Diuels picture on your husbands browes.

"I knowe tis better ... leades us to it.": The Widow is complaining about her red-haired deceased husband, his infidelities, and her revenge: "I know t'is better to take wrong then do it, / But yet in such a case flesh leades vs to it."

"A man whose beard ... jack an Apes behind.": The Widow is discussing men's hair, approving of any color except red and scorning a ragged chin, as follows:

> A man whose beard seemes scar'd with sprites t'haue bin, / That wants the bountious grace, length, bredth, & thicknes / And hath no differ-ence twixt his nose and chin, / But all his haires haue got the falling sickness, / Whose fore-front lookes like Iack-an-Apes behinde, / She that can loue him beares a scuruey minde.

"A Gossips round . . . a cup.": Spoken by the Wife to Besse, the Mayde: "I pledge thee my Girle: nay sweet now drink it vp, / A *Gossips* round, that's euery one a Cup." "To draw a Gossips cuppe" was a proverbial expression. (Sir Nicholas L'Estrange, 1603-1655, records its use in his *Mery Passages & Jeasts*, # 249, in *MS. Harl.* 6395.) Compare "Gossips are frogs—they drink and talk" (1640)—G. L. Apperson, *English Proverbs and Proverbial Phrases*, 1929, p. 267.

Fo. 45b. *posset*: MS *posse*

"Mr. Prideaux, a great practiser in the Eschequer,": Probably Edmund Prideaux, an eminent lawyer, bencher, and reader of the Inner Temple (ordered "called to the bench" of that society 2 May 1596—Inderwick, I, 447). According to Foss, (p. 539), his practice at the bar netted him about £ 5,000 a year; in addition he received about £ 15,000 a year as inland postmaster. (A competent barrister could earn £ 600 a year—James Whitelock, *Liber Famelicus*, ed. Bruce, 1858, xvi.)

"Lancaster of Grayes In": Thomas Lancaster—see fo. 12b and note, also fo. 97b. Both William Hackwell and Dr. Caesar, Master of Requests, tell anecdotes exemplifying Lancaster's cleverness at repartee.

"Mr. Hackwell *nar.*": William Hakewell (Hackwell), 1574-1655, of Lincoln's Inn, admitted August 3, 1598, from Devon and Staple Inn (*L.I. Adm.*, 127); reader at Lincoln's Inn, Lent, 1624/25 (ibid., 197). He was one of its chief benchers for thirty years. Nephew of Sir John Peryam and a kinsman of Thomas Bodley, he was one of the chief mourners at Bodley's funeral in Oxford and his executor afterward. This able lawyer served in Parliament for Cornwall and on legal commissions, became solicitor-general to the Queen (May, 1617). A friend of Donne, Christopher Brooke, Sir Robert Phelips, and other wits, he became interested in the repair of St. Paul's and served on the commissions (1631, 1634) appointed to effect the work. (DNB, VIII, 894.) See also Wood, II, 112.

Fo. 46. "Mr. Dodridge": John Dodridge, or Doddridge (1560–1628), bencher and reader at the Middle Temple, from Barnstable, Devon, by way of Exeter College, Oxford, and the New Inn. A learned legal antiquary and writer, highly esteemed by King James, he was destined to become serjeant-at-law (20 Jan. 1603), to be knighted (5 July 1607), and to be appointed justice of the King's Bench (26 Nov. 1612). (*Adm.*, I, 42; *Min.*, I, 217; Wood, I, 519-521; Chamberlain, I, 395; II, 387, 399.) Edward Darcy was patentee for playing cards.

"An epitaphe upon a bellowe maker. . . . (*B.J.*)": The initials attributing this epigram to Ben Jonson have apparently been added by a later hand. It has never been included in the published editions of Jonson's poems, but it closely resembles verses in *Chetham MS.* 8012 attributed to "Mr. Hoskines"—i.e., Jonson's witty friend and "father," the Middle Temple lawyer John Hoskyns:

An epitaph on a bellows-maker

Here lies John Goddard, maker of bellows,
His craft's master, and king of good fellows;

But for all that, he came to his death,
For he that made bellows could not make breath.

(in *Poetry of the English Renaissance,* ed. Hebel and Hudson, New York, C 1957, p. 527). Osborne attributes another version to Hoskyns, from the anonymous *MS. Add.* 30,982, f. 36b:

Song vppon a bellowes mender

Here lyes Tom short ye king of good fellowes
Who in his time was a mender of bellowes
But when he came to ye howre of his death
He that made bellowes could not make breath.

(in Louise Brown Osborne, *Life, Letters, and Writings of J. Hoskyns, 1566-1638,* Yale Studies in English, 87, New Haven, 1937, p. 170.) Although many manuscripts of the poem are anonymous, in Camden's *Remaines,* 1605, as well as in MS. *Rawlinson* D. 1377. f.9.a, it is ascribed to Hoskyns (ibid., 281). I suggest that the Manningham version (Ben Jonson's?) is superior to both.

"Mr. Bodly . . . wan a riche widdowe by this meanes: . . .": Thomas Bodley, founder of the Bodleian Library (knighted 1604), married Anne Carew, daughter of a merchant of Bristol and widow of Nicholas Ball of Totnes, from whom she had a considerable fortune. Chamberlain mentions her loss of a son at Ostend and then the death of her eldest son, Captain Ball, in the Low Countries, by sickness. (I, 131, 169). Writing to Alice Carleton, in Feb., 1613, after Bodley's death, Chamberlain was scornful of Sir Thomas' motives in willing "about seven thousand pound to his librarie at Oxford, and two hundred pound to Merton Colledge" instead of taking care of "his wifes children by whom he had all his wealth." (I, 417.) One of these children, Elizabeth, married Ralph Winwood, the future Sir Ralph, on a Tuesday in July, 1603—amid "much thunder, lightning, and raine" (I, 195). Mr. Bodley's "goodly library" was formally opened by the Vice-Chancellor of the University of Oxford on Nov. 8, 1602, just two weeks after Manningham made this entry in his diary (see W. D. Macray's *Annals of the Bodleian Library,* 2nd ed., 1890).

Fo. 46b. "Mr. Dr. King . . . at Paules Crosse": John King, S.T.D., D.D. (1559?-1621), one of the Queen's chaplains and rector of St. Andrew, Holborn, since 1597; he would subsequently become Dean of Christ Church, Oxford (1605), Vice-Chancellor of the University (1607-10), and Bishop of London (1611). Noted for his solid learning, piety, and eloquence, he won King James's praise as "the King of Preachers." Sir Edward Coke declared him "the best speaker in the Star-Chamber in his time." (Wood, I, 458.) King, whose uncle Robert had been the first bishop of Oxford, was educated at Westminster and Christ Church. At the latter, Dudley Carleton had King "for his tutor." (Birch, *Court and Times of James the First,* 1848, p. 5.) In 1602 when he returned to Oxford to proceed D.D., he was welcomed by a delegation of students who had ridden out to meet him (see Manningham's comments on this event, fo. 58 and notes to same). In October, 1604, after the promotion of Thomas Ravis from the Deanery of Christ Church to the see of Gloucester, thirty-two Christ Church students petitioned King James to make Dr. King their new dean, terming him *"nunc clarissimum lumen Anglicanae Ecclesiae"* (Bodl. Library MS.). As Bishop of London it was he who ordained the poet Donne to the ministry; and his poetical son Henry King, who afterward (1642) became Bishop of Chichester, was Donne's executor. This worthy prelate, "full fraught with all Episcopal qualities," says Fuller (*Worthies*, 41), was a severe disciplinarian; but he preached sermons rich in illustrations—drawn from divinity, the classics, and both ancient and modern history—and colorful in imagery.

Concerning the outdoor pulpit at St. Paul's, see note to fo. 20b.

Fo. 48b. "and were [to] be purged with that floud.": MS and were be purged; B and were [to] be purged.

Fo. 49b. "He preserved him safe . . .": In MS just before this clause the following words have been cancelled: "Soe as it may be truly said it was noe meane [?]."

Fo. 50. "as aunciently discended": In MS before "aunciently" the words "greatly d" have been crossed out.

Fo. 51. At the bottom of this page in MS and running into the bottom of fo. 50b is the word "Memorandum," upside down, written in large cursive letters—apparently penned before the notes of Dr. King's sermon were taken.

Fo. 52. "and yet noe partakers of . . .": MS partakers with; B partakers of.

"Their conscience is sett in binde,": Thus in MS. B reads "bonde."

"like Thamar . . . harlott;": The rape of Absolam's sister Tamar is told in 2 Sam. 13: 1–32.

Fo. 53. "In the Chequer, Mr. Crooke, the Recorder . . . betweene the twoe maiors,": John Croke of the Inner Temple (1553-1620), knighted in 1603 (DNB, V, 118), was Recorder of London from 1595 to 1603, Speaker of the House of Commons when Parliament sat, Oct. 27, 1601, and later a Judge of the King's Bench (Foss's *Judges*, VI, 130; Chamberlain, I, 132, 185). The "resigning" mayor was Sir John Garrett, or Garrard; his successor, Robert Lee. Upon the Queen's death in March of 1603, Chamberlain commented to Carleton: "and as one Lee [Thomas Lee or Leigh] was maior . . . when she came to her crowne, so is there one Lee maior now that she left yt." (I, 189.) See also fo. 34 of the Diary, where Manningham mentions Croke's dark or swarthy complexion.

"The L[ord] Chief Baron Periam": Sir William Periam, or Peryam (1534-1604), of the Middle Temple (admitted 28 April 1553; associate bencher 21 June 1577—*Adm.*, I, 20); serjeant-at-law, 1579; judge of the Common Pleas, 1581; promoted to chief baron of the exchequer and knighted in 1593. He was a cousin of Thomas Bodley. His father, John Periam, a merchant, was twice mayor of Exeter. (DNB, XV, 930.)

Fo. 53b. "The L[ord] Treasuror, L[ord] Buckhurst": Sir Thomas Sackville, poet and statesman, Lord Buckhurst, 1567-1604, and Earl of Dorset 1604-8. He became Lord Treasurer in 1599. See fo. 14 and note; also fo. 111b and 28.

"hir Majesties Clemency.": In MS. the word *Clemency*, in large letters and book hand, stands out on the page.

Fo. 54. "Wee call an hippocrite a puritan . . . (*Albions Engl[and]*.): *Albions England, or historicall map of the same island. In verse and prose.* by William Warner (1558?-1609) came out in 1586 (STC 25079); it contained Books I-IV. An enlarged version containing Books I-XIII, was published in 1602 (STC 25083). Manningham's entry seems to be an adaptation or loose paraphrase of a passage in a Chaucerian kind of tale told in Book 12, Chap. LXXV (p. 311 in the 1602 edition), wherein a would-be lover, thinking to kiss the object of his wooing, kisses a yeoman's beard instead, and is caught:

". . . As though he were a Man right good, he stood amaz'd and quaking." When the Host and ostlers,

"with a Light and Tooles
Came in, where he, almost unstript, but wholly skar'de did stande.
They wonder (for they knew him well) that he should be a Theife.
Good Sirs, quoth he, be still, we all deceived are, in briefe."

For other excerpts from *Albions England* see entries on fo. 60.

"(Mr. Gorson).": Not yet identified. His name does not appear in records of the Middle or Inner Temple or of Gray's Inn.

"the Recorder": John Croke (see note to fo. 53).

"Harwell": Not yet identified. A William Harwell of Fetcham, Surrey, was admitted to the Inner Temple in November, 1567 (*I.T. Adm.*, 62). One Henry Harwell, esq., of Coventry, had a son who was specially admitted to the Middle Temple 16 October 1633 (*Min.*, II, 811).

Fo. 54b. "At Paules Dr. Dove": John Dove, D.D. (1562-1618), rector of St. Mary Aldermary, London. A Surrey man, says Wood, he was elected from Westminster School to Christ Church in 1580, aged 18, and afterward became a preacher of note at Oxford. In 1596 he proceeded in Divinity. He wrote and published on various subjects: against atheism, for the Church-Government in England, for the sign of the cross in baptism (under attack from the Puritans), and on *Canticles* (Wood, I, 432-3). Dove's wife was Dudley Carleton's sister Anne (d. 1606), who bore him a daughter (Chamberlain, II, 158). On May 10, 1601, he preached at Paul's Cross on Matthew XIX:9, concerning adultery, declaring that marriage is indissoluble and that not even after divorce may either partner, regardless of the circumstances, marry again. (See Harrison, III, 180.) This sermon was published in the same year as *Of diuorcement, a sermon Preached at Pauls Cross* . . . (STC 7083).

B mistranscribed Dove as *Dene*, an error perpetuated by Maclure in *Paul's Cross Sermons*, wherein, p. 223, Maclure identifies the preacher as "[Nicholas?] Dene."

"Mr. Egerton": Stephen Egerton, M.A., of Cambridge, a popular Puritan divine, learned member of Peterhouse, and minister of St. Anne's, Blackfriars, from 1598 until his death about 1621. As one who wished to abolish the sign of the cross in baptism and the ring from the marriage service, he was one of those chosen to present the Millenary petition for the further reform of the Church, in 1603. One of his books, *A Brief Method of Catechizing*, went through 44 editions between 1594 and 1644. (DNB, XVII, 160.) Egerton is satirized by Donne in number 25 of his mock *Catalogus Librorum* (*The Courtier's Library*): "Egerton's Spiritual Art of Enticing Women; or Petticoat Preachings." (Ed. and transl. E. M. Simpson, Nonesuch Press, 1930.) Two months after hearing Dr. Dove reprehend Egerton, Manningham went to hear the latter preach in his little second-story church in Blackfriars (see fo. 76b and note).

"Mr. Irland": Thomas Ireland, third son of John Ireland, citizen and salter of London, admitted to the Middle Temple, 20 Feb. 1597/98 (one month before Manningham). (*Adm.*, I, 73, and *Min.*, I, 382.) By 25 Oct. 1602, his chamber was declared "void by his discontinuance" (*Min.*, I, 426).

"Mr. Marbury": This inaudible preacher (whom Manningham could not hear well enough to take notes) was Francis Marbury, who—ironically—while preaching at Paul's Cross earlier that year (June 13) had complained about those who walked about and talked during the sermon. (Maclure, *Paul's Cross Sermons*, p. 8). Afterward he became rector of St. Martin-in-the-Vintry, at the south corner of "Royall streete" next to a stone and timber building called the Vintrie, which contained "vaults for the stowage of wines." (Ibid., 222, and Stow, *Survey of London*, ed. Kingsford, I, 239, 248.)

"at the Temple": Thus in MS. B reads "of the Temple."

Fo. 55b. "Cosen Willis *narrav.*": Unidentified.

"One Clapham, a preacher in London": Probably Henoch Clapham, an erudite theological writer and preacher, who worked in Amsterdam as pastor of an English-speaking congregation but who engaged in ministerial work in London both in 1602 and in 1603, during the plague (see DNB, IV, 371). Venn lists an "H. Clapham" who matriculated sizar from Trinity College, Michaelmas, 1560 (III, 339). Hasted's *Kent* has one Henry Clapham appointed Vicar of Northbourne by the Archbishop of Canterbury in 1607, but the DNB writer, the Rev. Ronald Bayne, declares this a mistake for Henoch (IV, 372); and a 1608 preface to one of Clapham's books, *Errour on the Left Hand*, is dated "from my house at Norburne, East Kent, 8 of June." (Ibid.)

STC lists 17 religious, theological, and scriptural works by Clapham, including his best-known, *A Briefe of the Bible drawne into English poesy*, first printed in Edinburgh in 1596 and reprinted in England in three subsequent editions in 1603, 1608, and 1639 (STC 5332-5335). The dedication of the first part of the first edition to "the Right Worshipful Master Thomas Mylot, Esquier," is signed "your poore unworthy kinsman." In 1603 his *An Epistle . . . upon the present Pestilence*, in which he argued that a Christian who died of the plague thereby showed a lack of faith, but not so much as to imperil his soul, was misunderstood and its author clapped into prison (in Nov., 1603) for several years, on a charge of increasing the panic caused by the epidemic. (DNB, IV, 372.)

It may be inferred that Clapham was one of Manningham's favorite preachers since there are eight references to him in the Diary. See fos. 80 and 88 and notes; also 90b, 96b, 97b, 100, and 119b.

"Dr. Witheres, a black man, preached in Paules . . .": Probably George Withers, Archdeacon of Colchester, 1570-1605, and Rector of Danbury, Essex, 1572-1605. A Londoner born, son of an alderman and baptized in All Hallows, Bread Street, 1540, he studied at Cambridge, St. John's and Queens'. A fellow of Queens', 1559-1562, he received his M.A., in 1562, D.D., Heidelberg, 1572. In 1563 he was University Preacher. (Venn, II, 444.) Another possible identification is Henry Withers, fellow of Trinity and D.D., Wittenberg, 1592. Vicar of Kensington, Middlesex, 1572-1608. From 1574 to 1591 he had been Rector of St. Martin, Outwich, London, and then of Theydon Garnon, Essex, 1591-1609. George died in 1605, Henry in 1609. (Ibid.)

"in regard of the heavenly glory . . .": MS has the word *maiesty* cancelled between *heauenly* and *glory*.

Fo. 56. "*ad oras:* . . .": Thus in MS B reads "*ad auras.*"

Fo. 56b. "is like a banquet . . .": MS is a like a banquet.

Fo. 57. "Barker": Francis Barker, chief butler at the Middle Temple. (See *Min.*, I, 357, for example.) In 1623 (Nov. 28) he was honored "for his good and faithful service" by being specially admitted to the society, *gratis* (*Min.*, II, 688). Evidently his position was not an easy one: "Francis Barker, the Master Butler, was amerced in 40 *s* last Christmas by the Utter Barristers and gentlemen in commons because the strong beer proved new. It is agreed that 20 *s.* of this shall be paid out of the Treasury; and if the Butler was in fault, he shall pay the other 20 *s.*, otherwise it is to be cast into commons." (Entry of 10 June, 6 Jac. I, 1608—*Min.*, II, 495.)

"Whitlocke": James Whitelock or Whitlocke (1570-1632), the future Sir James, lawyer, parliamentarian, Steward of St. John's College, Oxford, and of Eton, and judge; author of the family biography *Liber Famelicus*. Admitted to New Inn, Michaelmas Term, 1590, and to the Middle Temple, 2 March 1592/93, while still at St. John's, where his tutor in classics and logic was Rowland Searchfield, afterward Bishop of Bristol (see Manningham's notes to his sermon, fo. 9). Whitelock had numerous friends among the eminent: Humphrey May (at St. John's, and his chambermate at the Middle Temple); William Laud; Ralph Winwood; Benjamin Rudyerd; Richard Martin; Sir Edward Phillips, Master of the Rolls; Sir Henry Savile, provost of Eton and warden of Merton; the Haringtons; and John Hoskyns. With Hoskyns he served in the "Addled Parliament" of 1614, representing Woodstock. Dr. John Buckridge, president of St. John's and future Bishop of Rochester, then of Ely, became godfather to Whitelock's daughter Mary, 16 Oct. 1606. Then in September, 1610, when his fifteen-day-old daughter Dorothy required emergency christening at 7 a.m. (she died six hours later) Dick Martin stood in for Sir Humphrey May.

Whitelock was called to the bar by Nicholas Overbury, father of young Thomas, 24 Oct. 1600; became steward of St. John's College lands in 1601;

married Elizabeth Bulstrode, 1602. In 1619 he became bencher and served as Autumn Reader. (Ref: *Liber Famelicus*, ed. Bruce, 1-77, *passim*; DNB, XXI, 117-119; *Adm.*, I, 64; *Min.*, I, 345.) Concerning his older brother "Captain" Edmund, the playboy-courtier, see fo. 44b.

"(Mr. Gibbes.)": Probably William Gibbes (Gibbs), mentioned many times in Middle Temple records as late as 1615. He was admitted 4 July 1567, "son and heir of Antony Gibbes, of Neitherbury, Dorset, gentleman," one month ahead of George Snygge and Roger Bramstone (*Min.*, I, 160); called 9 Feb. 1574/75 (ibid., I, 204), he became a prominent bencher. Gibbes was Lent Reader in 1589 and 1597 (*Adm.*, I, 31). In April, 1602, John Pym, the future parliamentary leader, was admitted at his request, for a fee of 20 *s*. (ibid., I, 421). Gibbes' son John was also a Middle Templar, admitted 9 May 1595, and called 26 Nov. 1602 (*Adm.*, I, 68; see also fo. 70b); he may, of course, have been Manningham's informant here rather than the father.

"One said Nel Frengtham[?] kisseth . . . inside out. (Fraklin.)": Omitted by B. MS presents difficulties here, for a small *d* appears to have been inserted above the *g*, and the *t* of "tham" could be read as *c* ("cham"). If Manningham intended "Frendcham," the remarkable kisser may have been a member of the family of Henry Frencham, rector of Walpole St. Peter, Norfolk (Venn, II, 179). If "Frengtham," which may be a shortened form of Frothingham, she may have been the sister of two Middle Temple students, Christopher Frothingham, first son and heir-apparent of Edward F., of Frothingham, Yorks., esq. (admitted 10 Nov. 1591) and Francis, his brother (admitted 22 July 1595)—*Min.*, I, 324, 355; *Adm.*, I, 63, 68.

"like a neates foote": The feet of a bullock or heifer could be used as food and were fat and tender if boiled; or the phrase could indicate the oil obtained from the feet. (OED, VI, 58.)

"(Fraklin)": James Franklin (Francklin), Middle Templar from Wye, Kent. See note to fo. 26b.

"Ch[arles] Davers told me . . . to your selfe.": Omitted by B. On Charles Danvers, see note to fo. 24b and Introduction.

"Mr. Curle told me . . .": Edward Curle, or Curll, the Diarist's chambermate and future brother-in-law. See Introduction and note to fo. 12.

"Mr. Cartwright": Probably the Rev. Thomas Cartwright, M.A. (1535-1603), the Puritan leader, who is reported to have lived out his last years in wealth and honor, enjoying the mastership of Leicester's Hospital in Warwick. He was noted for his impulsive temperament and impetuosity in argument. (DNB, III, 1138-9.)

Fo. 57b. "Mr. Hadsor told Mr. Curle and me . . .": Richard Hadsor, Middle Templar from County Louide, Ireland. See note to fo. 44.

"Mr. Plowden": Edmund Plowden (1518-85), jurist, admired by Camden, Coke, and others as the greatest and most honest lawyer of his time. Admitted to the Middle Temple in 1538, he later became its Treasurer (20 June 1561). Under his leadership the Great Hall was built. When he died (6 Feb. 1584/85) he was buried in the Temple Church, his tomb marked by a monument (still preserved) depicting him in his lawyer's robe, with a Latin inscription. (DNB, XV, 1314.) A range of buildings also commemorates his name (B). But his fame chiefly lives in his legal writings, *The Reports (Les comentaries, ou les reportes de Edmunde Plowden, . . .)* London, 1571.

Fo. 58. "Mr. Gardner of Furnivals Inne": Perhaps some member of the "Company of Furnival's Inn" or "the Auncientes" whose name has not come down to us. There were a number of Gardiners at the various inns of court; because of the close connection between Furnival's and Lincoln's Inn, however, he may have been a Lincoln's Inn barrister. See D. S. Bland's Introduction to *Early Records of Furnival's Inn* (King's College, Newcastle upon Tyne, 1957), pp. 10, 11, 14. Furnival's was one of several inns of Chancery that developed in the 14th and 15th centuries into preparatory schools subordinate in an academic sense to the Inns of Court. It was probably at first occupied by clerks of the Exchequer, under Sir William de Furnival, Baron of the Exchequer, who in May, 1376, acquired its property, fronting on the north side of Holborn, about equidistant from Lincoln's Inn and St. Andrew's Church (i.e., between Brooke Street and Leather Lane); Lincoln's Inn purchased it in 1547. By 1587 it was rich enough to build a new hall and about 1600 to build several blocks of new houses. (Ibid., 7, 13, 14.)

It had a handsome building with a large court before it and a fine garden behind it when Strype wrote his appendix to *Stow's Survey of London* (1720 ed., p. 252). It was demolished in 1897 when Furnival's was sold to the Prudential Assurance Co., which built on the site. Unfortunately the records of this Inn of Chancery were not acquired by Lincoln's Inn when the property was sold and their whereabouts is a mystery, neither the Prudential Assurance Society nor the Public Record Office having information about them. (C. W. Ringrose, Librarian of Lincoln's Inn, letter to the present editor, 4 Nov. 1966.)

"Mr. Dr. King, preacher at St. Androes in Holborne,": Dr. John King, afterward Dean of Christ Church and Bishop of London (see note to fo. 46b).

"the E[arl] of Northumberland": Henry Percy, 9th Earl (1564-1632), known as "the Wizard Earl" for his indulgence in astrology and alchemy. Eighth on the list of presumptive heirs to the crown, he had been urged by the Catholics to marry Lady Arbella Stuart (see fo. 26b and note) to strengthen his claim, but he had married instead Dorothy, sister of Robert Devereux, the second Earl of Essex, and widow of Thomas Perrott. They were not compatible and frequently lived apart. The child to whom Manningham alluded was probably Algernon, the tenth earl, baptized 13 Oct. 1602. Henry, the 9th Earl, was an avid smoker, a harsh landlord, and always quarreling with his mother; like Shakespeare's Hotspur, he was volatile, highly sensitive to slights, real or imagined, against his honor, challenging Sir Francis Vere (commander-in-chief in the Low Countries) and quarreling with Lord Southampton, (DNB, XV, 856-8; Collins' *Peerage*, ed. Brydges, II, 346, cited by B).

He did have some redeeming features, however; he befriended John Davies after Davies' expulsion from the Middle Temple (DNB, V, 591), and, during his nearly 16 years in prison after the Gunpowder Plot, he encouraged men of learning like Thomas Harriot and the mathematicians Walter Warner and Thomas Hughes (DNB, XV, 857).

"(W. Scott na[r].)": Probably William Scott of the Inner Temple, admitted 1 June 1595, "at Mr. Tanfield's request, paying only 40 s." (Inderwick, I, 405). There were no Scotts at the Middle Temple during this period.

"Mr. Martin": Richard Martin of the Middle Temple, the wit, and the future Recorder of London (see note to fo. 12b).

"(Of Mr. L.)": Perhaps Edmund Long (see fo. 30b and note, also fo. 43b), or Richard or Edward Lydall, of the Middle Temple. One of the Lydall brothers is quoted on fo. 11b of the diary. There was also a Francis Lyll, from Herefordshire and the New Inn, at the Middle Temple, officially admitted 8 March 1598/99 but actually "Venit in com. 15 die Junii, anno predicto and non antea, 1599."—Min., I, 393. See also the ascription to "L." on fo. 59.

Fo. 58b. "Mr. Overbury": Either Thomas Overbury or his father Nicholas, of the Middle Temple, the latter being a Master of the Bench. See note to fo. 39b.

"Dr. Redman": Dr. William Redman, S.T.P., "accounted one of the wisest of his coate" (Chamberlain, I, 166), was Bishop of Norwich from 1595 until his death on 25 Sept. 1602. (Hardy's Le Neve, II, 470). He was buried in Norwich Cathedral.

"Dr. Juel": Perhaps George Jewyll, or Jewell, of Scoulton, Norfolk, and Gonville and Caius College. The son of John Jewell, *mediocris fortunae*, he studied at Wymondham School, Norfolk, and then was admitted pensioner at Caius May 19, 1565, at age 18, and assigned a cubicle with his tutor and surety, Mr. Warner. He was almost exactly contemporary with the eminent founder of the Perse School in Cambridge, Stephen Pearse (Perse) of Great Massingham, Norfolk, who was admitted to the same college Oct. 29, 1565, and later elected Fellow. (J. Venn and S. C. Venn, *Admissions to Gonville and Caius College in the University of Cambridge*, London, 1887, pp. 10f; also *Biographical History of Gonville and Caius College*, I, 1897, p. 57.) No record of his later career has yet been discovered. The illustrious bishop of Salisbury, John Jewell, who had five sisters, mentioned in his will one whom he called "my loving brother, John Jewel, of Northcote in Devon, gent." (*Works*, ed. John Ayre, IV, 1850, p. xxv); but I have not been able to connect the Diarist's "Dr. Juel" with this gentleman.

"Mr. Perkins of Cambridge": William Perkins, Fellow of Christ's College until his marriage in 1595, and rector of St. Andrew's in Cambridge. The great name in his college for eleven years, he was a well-known Calvinist writer and theologian in the finest Puritan tradition of practical divinity and plain preaching. (Harry H. Porter, *Reformation and Reaction in Tudor Cambridge*, Camb., 1958, pp. 225, 228, 238.) Perkins was much admired for his doctrine and the example of his life, and his painful death 'by reason of the stone,' in October, 1602, was much lamented. He was only 43. Sam Ward of Christ's, now Fellow of Emmanuel, who had earlier confided to his Diary his pride in his former tutor, thought the world almost at an end. (*Two Puritan Diaries*, ed. M. M. Knappen, 104, 130, cited by Porter, 238, 268.) See also fo. 78b.

"(Mr. Curle *nar.*)": Edward Curle, or Curll, Manningham's chamber-mate and future brother-in-law (see note to fo. 12).

Fo. 59. "Wake": Abraham Wake of the Middle Temple, admitted 16 Feb. 1597/98 (*Min.*, I, 382), just one month before the Diarist; son and heir of Arthur Wake, late of Oxford, esq., deceased, and elder brother to Isaac Wake, also a Middle Templar, who became secretary to Sir Dudley Carleton when the latter was ambassador to Venice. (Chamberlain mentions Isaac often and wrote to him in 1614—Letter #212, Oct. 12, 1614, in *Letters*, I, 555-8.) Confirmation of Abraham Wake's call to the degree of the Utter Bar was referred to a future Middle Temple Parliament at least three times in 1603 and 1604 (*Min.*, II, 440-442). From 1610 to 1624 we hear no more of him, apparently. Then on May 7, 1624, he was fined £ 10 for not reading, along with Richard Lydall, knt., Messers. John Freman, William Freston, Jasper Baker, and three others (*Min.*, II, 690).

"he lived upon exhibicion": Upon a scholarship or financial assistance (OED, III, 408-9).

"s[ai]d L.": Edmund Long? or Edward or Richard Lydall? or Lyll? See notes to fo. 30b and fo. 58.

"Mr. Blunt": Edward Blunte, or Blount, of the Middle Temple, "third son of Thomas B. of St. Lawrence, in London," admitted 25 Oct. 1590 and called 26 May 1598 (*Adm.*, I, 61). By the beginning of 1618 he was dead and his chamber reassigned (*Min.*, II, 625); thus he should not be confused with Edward (Ned) Blunte, or Blount, the stationer, who had a shop in "Pouleschurchyard" (Chamberlain, I, 484, 489, 544) and who joined with Isaac Jaggard to publish the 1623 First Folio edition of Shakespeare.

"Mrs. T . . . *quam indigne.*)": Omitted by B.

"Mr. Bacon": Francis Bacon, of Trinity College, Cambridge, the essayist and lawyer. At this time he was a bencher of Gray's Inn. In a document dated 16 Feb. 1602/03, listing nominees from the Inns of Court "touching a solicitor for Ireland" and sent by Lord Buckhurst to Sir Robert Cecil, Bacon is so listed (*Hist. MSS. Comm., Salisbury*, XII, 1910, pp. 646-7).

"the Lord Morley": Edward Parker, 12th baron Morley and *de jure* Lord Marshall (c. 1551-1618). He and his successors called themselves Barons of Rye—i.e., the marshall barony derived from Hubert de Rye. He had been admitted fellow-commoner of Gonville and Caius College in 1562 at age 11. He was subsequently a member of Parliament and served on several commissions, including those for the trials of Mary Queen of Scots (1586) and the Earl of Arundel (1589). He was one of the twenty-five peers that passed upon the trial of the Earls of Essex (in whose rebellion Morley's son had taken part) and Southampton (1601). (*The Complete Peerage*, ed. H. A. Doubleday and Lord Howard de Walden, IX, 1936, pp. 226-7.)

The Parkers appear to have been a quarrelsome family. In 1598 Lord Morley's brother was killed in a quarrel by a man of Sir Thomas Gerard,

Knight Marshal and Lieutenant of the Tower (CSP *Dom. Eliz., 1598-1601,* p. 130); and Lord Morley held messuages and lands in Hertfordshire over which he was frequently involved in litigation (see "Feet of Fines for Herts. from 1583 to 1601," in *Herts. Genealogist and Antiquarian,* II; III, 323).

"the forrest of Hatfeild": The Great Park or Hatfield Wood, a large area of forest, containing, in 1538, about 10,000 oaks and beeches and extending over the southeast projection of the parish of Hatfield, between Essendon and Northaw; it probably stretched from Woodside, the home of the Curles, eastward to the hamlet of Newgate Street—a circuit of about seven miles. It held a fine breed of deer. After Sir Robert Cecil became first Earl of Salisbury and took Hatfield in exchange for Theobalds, he improved it, forming Hatfield Park from part of the Great Wood. (*Victoria History of Herts.,* III, 1912, pp. 99-100.)

"The first Lord Riche": Robert, Lord Rich, Lord Chancellor from 1547 to 1551.

"To stinge a wench. Brod[na]x?)": Omitted by B. The ascription is probably to William Brodnax, of the Middle Temple and Godmersham, Kent. See fo. 26b and note.

"They have lockt . . . (Darston.)": Omitted by B. The ascription is probably to Richard Daston, a Bencher (and later Treasurer, 1608, 1609) of the Middle Temple. He was admitted Nov. 16, 1572, from New Inn and Wormyngton, Glos., "Commended for Call 2 July, 1582," and Autumn Reader in 1598, the year of his elevation to Master of the Bench (*Adm.,* I, 38). As M.T. Treasurer he was associated with William Towse (see fo. 17b and note), his counterpart at the Inner Temple; both are named in a royal patent of 6 James I (6 Aug. 1608)—Inderwick, Introd., II, xv.

"In the Starr chamber, . . . Mr. Moore . . .": Probably Francis Moore, or More, of the Middle Temple, admitted 6 Aug. 1580, "late of New Inn, gent." (*Min.,* I, 235) and called 30 June 1587. He became an Associate Bencher 23 Nov. 1603 (*Adm.,* I, 47) and Autumn Reader in 1607 (*Min.,* II, 480). Later he was knighted and made a Serjeant-at-Law (see *Min.,* I, 625, under date of 20 Feb. 1617/18).

"the B[ishop] of L.": Richard Bancroft, D.D. (1544-1610), Bishop of London from 1597 to 1604; afterward Archbishop of Canterbury.

"(Mr. Cu.)": Edward Curle, or Curll, of the Middle Temple. See notes to fo. 12 and 58b.

Fo. 59b. "Blackborne": Perhaps Henry Blackbourne of the Inner Temple, admitted Nov. 1598, from Wymondham, Norfolk (*I.T. Adm.,* 151).

"The old L[ord] Treasurors witt . . . Sir R[o]b[er]t": The reference is to William Cecil, Lord Bughley (1520-1598) and his son Sir Robert Cecil. The attributions at the end of this and the next entry have been cancelled in MS.

"A drunken Cunt . . . noe porter.": Omitted by B. This proverb is listed by Morris P. Tilley, *A Dictionary of the Proverbs in England in the Sixteenth and Seventeenth Centuries* (Ann Arbor, 1950), p. 134: "C901 A drunken Cunt has no porter." Among his sources Tilley cites David Fergusson's "Ane druken cunt had neuer ane good dore bar," of around 1598 (in

Fergusson's Scottish Proverbs from the Original Print of 1641 . . . ed. E.
Beveridge, S.T.S., 1924, No. 144).

"The Dutch . . . (Sir Robert Mansell.)": Chamberlain said of this
episode, writing to Carleton Nov. 4, 1602, "The Dutch men had set out a
relation of the fight with the gallies which we allow not, neither do theyre
owne tales agree: whereupon I thought goode to send you this report [*A*
true report of the service done upon certain galleys—STC 17259] of Sir Rob:
Mansell in aunswer of those druncken companions." (I, 170.) Mansell was
a colorful Elizabethan sea-dog from Norfolk; in October, 1602, he was
engaging and defeating enemy ships off the Low Countries (ibid., I, 161).

"Mr. Attorny [Coke]": Edward Coke, or Cooke, of Norfolk (1552–
1634), Attorney General under Queen Elizabeth—appointed, 1593—and
Chief Justice under King James. Educated at Norwich Grammar School,
Cambridge (Trinity College), and the Inner Temple, of which he became
Treasurer in 1596, Coke rose to prominence as Queen's prosecutor in such
trials as those of Dr. Roderigo Lopez, the Queen's physician, who was
accused of conspiring to murder the Queen, tried at the Guildhall, found
guilty, and in June, 1594, executed at Tyburn; and of the Earl of Essex
(Feb., 1600/01). By 1601 Coke had become so wealthy (by marriages to
Bridget Paston in 1582 and Lady Elizabeth Hatton, Lord Burghley's granddaughter, in Nov., 1598) and powerful that he could entertain the Queen
lavishly at his house in Stoke Poges. Knighted in May, 1603, he was later
created Serjeant and Chief Justice of the Common Pleas at once, in the
summer of 1606. In 1613 Sir Edward was unwillingly translated to Lord Chief
Justice of the King's Bench, to make room for Sir Henry Hobart in Common
Pleas and Sir Francis Bacon as Attorney General.

The long, bitter rivalry between Coke and Bacon, partly reflected in
the Manningham entry here, began in 1598 when Coke won the lucrative
post of Solicitor General sought by both. It seemed to reach a climax in
1616 with Coke's dismissal but actually culminated in Bacon's impeach-
ment five years later. (Catherine Drinker Bowen, *The Lion and the Throne:*
The Life and Times of Edward Coke, Boston, C 1957, *passim.*)

What is perhaps most remarkable about Coke, as Miss Bowen declares,
is his "transmutation" from harsh and ruthless state prosecutor—his vitupera-
tion in the trial of Ralegh, Nov., 1603, is infamous (ibid., Chaps. 15, 16)—
to "wholehearted Commons man, defender of free speech and parliamentary
privilege." (ibid., p. x). In 1628, at age 76, Coke championed the Petition
of Right, helping thereby to father one of the three great documents of
English—and American—liberty (ibid.). Although narrow in his churchman-
ship, he is known for his veneration of the law. He also lives in his written
Reports and *Institutes* (see DNB).

On fo. 90b the Diarist recorded an embarrassing moment in Coke's
career (q.v.).

"Vennar, a gent. of Lincolnes": Richard Vennar, or Venarde, of Lincoln's Inn, admitted 25 July, 29 Elizabeth, from Wiltshire and Barnard's Inn,
but listed under date of June 10, 1581—*L.I. Adm.:* 1420-1892, *Records,*

I, 93. He is described by Manningham in a later entry (fo. 70) as "the graund connicatcher" with the "golden spurres" and "brasen face." He was a rascally practical joker, a forerunner of Mark Twain's Duke and King in *Huckleberry Finn*. Chamberlain (ltr. to Dudley Carleton, Nov. 1602) describes Vennar's hoax show and its circumstances as follows:

> ... I must not forget to tell you of a cousening prancke of one Venner of Lincolns Ynne that gave out bills of a famous play on Satterday was sevenight on the Banckeside [at the Swan], to be acted only by certain gentlemen and gentlewomen of account. The price at comming in was two shillings or eighteen pence at least and when he had gotten most part of the mony into his hands, he would have shewed them a fayre payre of heeles, but he was not so nimble to get up on horseback, but that he was faine to foresake that course, and betake himselfe to the water, where he was pursued and taken and brought before the Lord Cheife Justice [Sir John Popham], who wold make nothing of yt but a jest and a merriment, and bounde him over in five pound to appeare at the sessions: in the meane time the common people when they saw themselves deluded, revenged themselves upon the hangings, curtaines, chaires, stooles, walles and whatsoever came in theyre way very outragiously and made great spoyle: there was great store of goode companie and many noble men. (I, 172.)

Chambers, III, 500–503, gives a full account of this incident. One of Vennar's original playbills has survived and is reproduced in facsimile in W. W. Greg's *Dramatic Documents from the Elizabethan Playhouses*, 1931. The play was originally called *England's Joy* (Harrison, III, 361–2). The broadsheet advertised "The Plot of the Play called England's Joy. To be Played at the Swan this 6 of Nouember, 1602."

Venner, a Balliol man, "lived a shifty life" and ended about 1615 in debtor's prison (Chambers, III, 500).

Fo. 60. "L[ord] Keeper": Sir Thomas Egerton.

"The callender of women saynts . . . yf they be importuned.": From William Warner's *Albions England*, Bk. 12, Chap. LXXIV (in 1602 ed., p. 306):

> "For long agoe the Calendar of Women-Saints was filde,
> Fewe not to opportunitie, importunated, yeild."

The passage occurs in a gay tale about a fair young wife of Lincolnshire who is 'picked up' by a Yorkshire gentleman while on her way to London but who is enjoyed at an inn in Huntingdon by a Southern gentleman, B printed only the first nine words of Manningham's entry. See also fo. 54 and note.

"A Womans love is river-like . . . it often runnes too lowe.": From *Albions England*, Bk. 11, Chap. LXI (in 1602 ed., pp. 269–270):

> "A Womans Loue is Riuer-like, which, stopt, will ouer-flow,
> But when the Currant finds no let it often fals too lowe."

This passage is from a section concerning Sir John Mandeville and "King Edwards Cozen Elenor," who "wisht nothing more than that she might him know."

"shipcoates": sheepcotes, large sheephouses or barns (OED, VIII, 664).

"(Mr. Pigott na.)": Probably Alban Pigott of the Middle Temple, admitted 20 August 1597, from Colewick, Bucks., and called with Manningham and others on 7 June 1605 (Min., I, 354; Adm., I, 72).

"Posies for a jet ring lined with sylver.": The custom of inscribing "posies" on rings is an ancient one, thought to be of Roman origin. In the 14th and 15th centuries the motto was inscribed on the outside but in the 16th and 17th on the inside. H. B. Wheatley, in his edition of Pepys' Diary (I, C 1892, p. 40), calls attention to a small volume published in 1674 entitled Love's Garland: or Posies for Rings, Handkerchers and Gloves, and such pretty tokens that Lovers send their Loves. John Davies composed "posies" for Lord Keeper Egerton's entertainment of the Queen at Harefield, in the summer of 1602 (see fo. 95 and note). Donne must have had such "posies" in mind when he ridiculed Davies in his mock Courtier's Library —Catalogus Librorum Aulicorum incomparabilium et non vendibilium—wherein item 16 reads:

"The Justice of England. Vacation exercises of John Davies on the Art of forming Anagrams approximately true, and Posies to engrave on rings."

(Ed. and transl. E. M. Simpson, London: The Nonesuch Press, 1930.) See also Donne's poem "A Ieat [Jet] Ring sent." (in Poems of John Donne, ed. Herbert J. C. Grierson, I, Oxford, 1912, pp. 65-66.)

Fo. 60b.: Blank in MS.

Fo. 61-Fo. 63b.: Omitted by B.

"Ex oratione Academica Stapletonii.": From an Academic Oration by Thomas Stapleton, D.D. (1535-98), author of books on Thomas More (e.g., Tres Thomae, Douay, 1588), translator of Bede, and professor of theology at Louvain. He was famed throughout Europe for his learning and his skill as a Catholic controversialist. His Orationes Academicae, Miscellaneae was published in Antwerp "Apud Ioannem Keerbergium," in 1600, in two books, twenty orations comprising the first book and fourteen the second. An politici horum temporum in numero Christianorum sint habendi is the third oration of the first book, occupying pp. 49-105. In Stapleton's Opera, II (Paris, 1620), it occupies pp. 514-527. In both these editions it has following its title the notation "Oratio quodlibetica Duaci habita, Anno, 1589." Some of Stapleton's "Miscellaneous Academic Orations" were published in 1602, but whether Manningham read a 1602 edition of the An Politici is not known. That contemporary interest in this work continued unabated is suggested by its publication in Munich in 1608. The version as printed in the 1600 Antwerp edition is hereafter referred to as 1600.

One of those who took up the cudgels against Stapleton was the much-admired Cambridge divine William Whitaker, in *Disputatio de sacra scriptura, contra huius temporis Papistas, inprimis R. Bellarminum . . . & T. Stapletonum* (Cantabrigiae, 1588) and in other works of 1594 and 1600. For a recent study of the Catholic controversialist see Marvin Richard O'Connell, *Thomas Stapleton and the Counter Reformation.* Yale Publications in Religion, 9, New Haven, 1964.

Fo. 61. "Isti politici contendunt, Multa esse . . .": In *1600 contendunt* is the final word of the preceding sentence: it begins "Contra enim Politici isti, multa esse . . . etc.

Fo. 61b. "Nec Christianus . . . deserit.": This is Manningham's shortening of Stapleton's "nec Christianus existimandus, qui periclitantem aliquando religionem penirus deserit" (*1600*, p. 65).

Fo. 62. "(Matt. 22).": Manningham sometimes encloses Biblical sources in parentheses, whereas *1600* has these sources in the margin.

"At tu dictis Albane maneres.": In *1600* this is a section heading, centered, with question mark, on p. 83.

Fo. 63. "Controuersiae modernae . . . grauissimae.": In *1600* this is the marginal heading on p. 94.

"An Romana Ecclesia sit vera.": In MS following this line the words *et Catholica* have been canceled.

"Iudaeorum vox Christo": This is Manningham's version of "Iudaeorum haec vox fuit Christo Redemptori nostro in Cruce pendenti." (*1600*, p. 96.)

Fo. 63b. "ad Herodem extremum . . .": *1600, extrenum*

Fo. 64.: Blank in MS.

Fo. 64b. "(Benet[?].)": Perhaps Richard Bennet of the Middle Temple, adm. 31 May 1594, "son and heir of Robert B., of Law Whitton, Cornwall, gent. Called 26 Nov., 1602." (*Adm.*, I, 66.) See fo. 70b. He died before 16 April 1619 (*Min.*, II, 635). B reads "Benn," which, if correct, probably refers to Anthony Benn, or Benne, admitted 26 Oct. 1583—"eldest son of Robert B., of St. Nycholas Colde Abbay, London. Called 8 Feb., 1593-4. Bencher 1611. Reader Lent 1611." (*Adm.*, I, 52.) He was knighted 15 Sept. 1617, and became Recorder of London (Chamberlain, II, 62, n6; II, 134).

"Captaine Whitlocke, a shuttlecock:": Edmund Whitelocke (see fo. 44b and note).

Fo. 65. Dr. Dawson of Trinity in Cambridge, at Paules Crosse": Not positively identified. Admitted to Trinity College were William Dawson, B.A., 1565-6; M.A. 1569, who was Chaplain of the college 1566-74 and Curate of St. Michael's Church, Cambridge (W. W. Rouse Ball and J. A. Venn, *Admissions to Trinity College, Cambridge*, 1913, I, 48; II, xvi, 75); and Alexander Dawson, who matriculated pensioner 1588-9; Scholar, 1590; B.A. 1593-4; M.A., 1597 (ibid., II, 168). One Philip Dawton matriculated pensioner in 1581 and did not graduate (ibid., II, 135) yet was ordained deacon and priest at Peterborough 13 Nov. 1590 as Philip Dawson, M.A., of Trinity (Venn, II,

22). Maclure (*Paul's Cross Sermons*, 223) queries Ralph Dawson, but Ralph, D.D., 1601, was at Clare, Peterhouse, and Corpus Christi—a Fellow of Corpus, 1586-97 (Venn, II, 22); he was rector of St. Mary Abchurch, 1597-1611 (George Hennessey, *Novum Repertorium Ecclesiasticum Parochiale Londinense,* 1898, p. 297).

Fo. 65b. "Christ cals . . .": MS Christes cals.
"Bishop Bonner made bonefires . . . Maries days.": Edmund Bonner, alias Savage (1500?-1569), Bishop of London. Wood says he "shew'd himself the most severe of all Bishops against Heretics, as they were then called," in Queen Mary's time (*Athenae*, I, 191), and Fuller declares contemptuously that "he caused the death of twice as many martyrs as all the bishops in England." (*Worthies*, 627.) Holinshed records that Queen Elizabeth, at Highgate on her accession in Nov., 1558, when huge crowds were watching the procession of bishops kneel by the wayside to offer their allegiance, refused her hand to him. (*Chron.*, III, p. 1748, cited in *Victoria History of Middlesex*, II, 1911, p. 34).

Fo. 66. "(of Dr. Reynold;": Dr. John Reynolds (Rainolds), President of Corpus Christi College, Oxford, famed for his prodigious learning and memory. Wood says he had an astonishing memory of St. Augustine's works and all classic authors; "he was a living library and a third University." (*Athenae*, I, 340). Fuller says, "His memory was little less than miraculous . . ." (*Church-History of Britaine* (1655), Bk. X, p. 48. His proposal at the 1604 Hampton Court Conference led to the translation of the Authorized Version of the Bible (1611), he himself working on Isaiah through Malachi, in the Oxford Old Testament group.
"Th. Cranmer.": Thomas Cranmer (1571-1641), son of the Thomas Cranmer who was registrar of the archdeaconry of Canterbury (see fo. 13 and notes). Thus he was the grandson of Edmund Cranmer, Archdeacon of Canterbury, and grand-nephew of Archbishop Thomas Cranmer. He studied at Oxford, matriculating pleb. from Magdalen, 1581, but subscribed as of Corpus Christi College, 2 July 1585, and was granted the exhibition vacated by his brother George; he graduated B.A., 1589, and received the M.A. in 1593 and B.C.L. in 1599. (Foster, I, 346.) He is said to have become lunatic before 1607, (ibid.)—pathetic, if true, in view of the reference to his father's "lunaticke" sister on fo. 13.
His brother George (1563-1600) studied under Hooker at Corpus Christi College, Oxford, received his M.A., 1589 (Wood, *Fasti*, I, 138) and helped compile the *Ecclesiastical Polity* (*Athenae*, I, 305); he served as secretary to a succession of eminent men: William Davison, Secretary of State; Sir Henry Killigrew, Ambassador to France; Sir Edwin Sandys; and Charles Blount, Lord Mountjoy (DNB, V, 18). Middle Temple minutes for 11 Feb. 1589/90 mention a Mr. Cranmer with whom Edwin Sandys, second son of the Archbishop of York, was bound; then immediately afterward they record the admission of George Cranmer, "son and heir-apparent of Thomas Cranmer, gent., specially; fine 3 *l.* Bound with Mr. Edwin Sandis."

(*Min.*, I, 312; *Adm.*, I, 60). Both Thomas and George were first cousins of Izaak Walton (DNB, V, 18).

See also mention of "T. Cranmer" on fo. 119.

How the Diarist was related to the Cranmers does not appear, except that Richard Manningham in his will speaks of "my kinsman William Cranmer, the merchant." Undoubtedly he was the same William Cranmer who in 1619, with Richard Bull, received "the some of forty-five poundes too pence" from John Ferrar, Sir Edwin Sandys' Deputy Treasurer in the Virginia Company, for gartering, leather points, and stockings that Bull and Cranmer had paid for (Miscel. Account dtd. 16 July 1619, in Magdalene College *MS. Ferrar Papers*, Box XIII, Peckard # 1286).

"cockcrowen pottage": "cock-crown. Poor pottage. *North.*" (B., citing Halliwell, *Arch. Dict.* I, 260.)—"that [which] the cock has crowed on, . . . no longer fresh; stale" (OED, II, 570).

"The olde Deane of Paules, Nowell, told Dr. Holland . . .": MS reads "Dr. Holland did [cancelled] the old Deane . . ." Alexander Nowell (1507?-Feb. 13, 1602) was Queen Elizabeth's confessor and annual Lenten preacher. He was educated at Brasenose, Oxon., and taught at Westminster. An avid fisherman (praised by Walton in *The Complete Angler*), he is supposed to have left a bottle of ale in the grass, then to have found it several days later; whereupon the explosion of its being opened started the bottled ale industry in England (Fuller, 295). During the reign of Queen Mary, says Fuller, "whilst Nowell was catching of fishes, [Bishop] Bonner was catching of Nowell" and designing him to the shambles, but the merchant Francis Bowyer, afterwards sheriff of London, helped Nowell escape "beyond the seas." Returning in 1558, he was made dean of St. Paul's and chosen by parliament and convocation to make a catechism for public use. (Ibid.) This learned and pious angler once riled the Queen, when in his Lenten sermon at Paul's, Elizabeth and the Spanish ambassador being present, he spoke slightingly of the crucifix: "To your text, Mr. Dean," the Queen called aloud; "leave that, we have heard enough of that." The abashed preacher was unable to continue and Elizabeth left in a rage. (Ibid., Freeman's note 1.)

Thomas Holland was Fellow of Balliol, Regius Professor of Divinity in Oxford 1589-1611, and rector of Exeter College. (Maclure, *P.C. Sermons*, 68; Hardy's Le Neve, III, 509.) He was *"mersus in libris* (drowned in his books)" (Fuller, 483) and so "mighty in the scriptures" that he served with Dr. John Harding, the president of Magdalen College, and Dr. John Reynolds, president of Corpus Christi, in the Oxford group of King James translators who worked on the Prophets and Lamentations (Fuller, *Church History of Britain*, X, 45).

See fos. 104-106 for notes of a sermon Manningham heard Holland preach at Paul's Cross this same month, Nov. 7, 1602.

Fo. 66b. "Jo[hn] Marstone": John Marston (1576-1634), the "sharp-fanged satirist," playwright, and future clergyman (see Anthony Caputi, *John Marston, Satirist,* 1961), enjoyed a desultory and intermittent association with the Middle Temple. He was officially admitted 2 August 1592 (only six months after his matriculation at Brasenose), as "son and heir-apparent of John Marston of Coventry, esq., specially, by Mr. Marston, his father, Reader." —*Min.*, I, 330. Taking up residence at the Middle Temple in 1595 (Caputi, p. 7), he was there in 1596—June 24, when Richard Kelley was bound with "John Marston, jun" and John Armitage (*Min.*, I, 367)—and in June, 1597, when he went into the chamber of his father with Isaac Johnson (*Min.*, I, 376). In Feb., 1599/1600 he "was readmitted to the chamber to which his father was lately admitted with Mr. Haule." (*Min.*, I, 400). On 14 October 1602, he was "expelled . . . for non-payment of commons and other causes," but a parliament of 27 Nov. 1602, restored him "to the Fellowship and his antiquity, but restoration to his chamber will be further considered." (*Min.*, I, 418). On 24 Nov. 1606 he was declared to have "forfeited" his chamber with Henry Haule, esq., Treasurer, "for discontinuance," Robert Weevill being given his place (*Min.*, II, 471). So there is strong probability that Manningham was acquainted with Marston.

"Alderman Mores wives daughter, a Spaniard borne": John More was alderman of Queenhithe Ward, 1597-1603, having been sheriff 1597-8 and Master of the Skinners' Company 1597 and 1601; he died April 20, 1603, his will being adm. (P.C.C., 26 Bolein) April 21. (A. B. Beaven, *The Aldermen of the City of London*, II, 1913, p. 46, and P. E. Jones, NQ, April, 1957, p. 180.) As a factor in Spain he had met and married about 1590 the widow of Alonso Perez de Recalde, son of a former viceroy to the West Indies (Brit. Mus. *Add. MSS.* 39829, f. 129). Her daughter had come with her to England known as Mary Perry or Mary Recalde. In the Christmas season of 1601/02 she was 22. Despite her lack of appeal to Marston, she married in March, 1603, Lewis Tresham of the Inner Temple, second son of Sir Thomas Tresham of Rushton, Northants., with the consent of both fathers (Harl. Soc. Publ., *London Marriage Licenses*, 1520-1610, 1887, p. 276)—Gladys Jenkins, "Manningham, Marston and Alderman More's Wife's Daughter," NQ, CCII, June, 1957, p. 243.

"Mr. Tho. Egerton, the L[ord] Keepers sonne": Manningham probably meant grandson, Sir John Egerton's son James, later slain in a duel, in 1610. Sir Thomas Egerton, the Lord Keeper's eldest son, died in Ireland in 1599 and was buried in Chester Cathedral. (See Chamberlain, II, 65, and notes there.)

"this tilting": The tilting on the Queen's Day, 1602—Wednesday, Nov. 17, the anniversary of Her Majesty's accession. As Chamberlain described it on Friday, Nov. 19, "the ordinarie solemnitie of preaching, singing, shooting, ringing and running: the bishop of Limmericke Dr. [John] Thornborough made a dull sermon at Paules Crosse [unlisted by Maclure, *P.C. Sermons*, 1958]. At the tilt were many younge runners . . . : your foole Garret made as fayre a show as the prowdest of them, and was as well disguised, mary not altogether so well mounted. for his horse was no bigger than a goode bandogge [bloodhound or mastiff], but he delivered his scutchion with his *impresa* himself and had goode audience of her Majestie and made her very merry." (I, 172.) The elaborate ceremonies usually accompanying the sports took place 'at the foot of the staires vnder the gallery window in the Tilt-yard at Westminster' [i.e.,

Whitehall], says W. Segar, *Honor, Military and Ciuill,* (1602) Bk. III, Ch. 54, quoted by Chambers, III, 403. See also Chambers, III, 269; I, 18ff.; and see also Manningham, fo. 3 and note.

Fo. 67. "At Paules Crosse: Mr. Fenton, Reader of Grays Inn": Roger Fenton, D.D. (1565–1616), from Lancashire, became fellow of Pembroke Hall, Cambridge, and minister of St. Stephen's, Walbrook, London (Fuller, 304). As preacher at Gray's Inn, to which post he was elected about July, 1599 (*Pension Book of Gray's Inn,* p. 141, where "Richard" Fenton is un-doubtedly an error for "Roger"), he won the admiration of Francis Bacon, who in August, 1610, requested Fenton to preach "at my mother's funeral." To a friend Bacon wrote, "I dare promise you a good sermon to be made by Mr. Fenton; for he never maketh other." (As quoted, Benjamin Farrington, *Francis Bacon, Philosopher of Industrial Science,* N.Y., 1949, pp. 22-23.) In 1604 Fenton became chaplain to Sir Thomas Egerton, the Lord Chancellor. It is hardly surprising, then, to learn that this bright young man, favored by the elite of the state, should have been chosen to serve in the New Testament group at Westminster, translating the Epistles, with William Barlow, Dean of Chester, and Dr. John Spenser (Paine, *The Learned Men,* 43-44). Fuller speaks of him as a "painful, pious, learned and beloved minister" (304). After Fenton's death Donne wrote an "Elegy on the worthy and learned Dr. Roger Fenton, lecturer of Gray's Inn" (fol. 136 of *C.C.C. MS. cccxvii, Codex chartaceus,* in 4to minori, ff. 38, sec. xvii, A Collection of elegies, sonnets, and other verses by Dr. John Donne, dean of St. Paul's, and others).

Fo. 67b. "hee aunswered his disciples wonder,": Thus in MS. For "wonder" B has "words."

"Hardly can he runne after Christ": Thus in MS. B prints "runne after God."

Fo. 68b. "(Jame)": Omitted by B. The reference is to James 5.4.

Fo. 69. "noe sufficient repentaunce;": Thus in MS. B has "nor."

Fo. 70. "one Daniel, an Italian . . . one Mowbray, a Scott . . .": Daniel Archideaquila, or Archdeacon, described by Chamberlain as "a little pigmee Italian fencer" (Oct. 15, 1602, I, 166), who accused Mowbray of suborning him "to have slaine the king of Scotts: the other denies yt constantly, whereupon he was demaunded by the Lord Hume [Sir George Hume, Lord High Treasurer of Scotland] to be sent and tried there." On 19 Nov. 1602 Chamberlain wrote of their "combat in Scotland, or on the borders, wherin they are both slaine, . . ." (I, 173); but on Dec. 4 he corrected this report and declared that both men were still alive and in Edinburgh Castle (I, 174). Then on Feb. 11 he wrote that Mowbray, trying to escape with sheets and ropes too short, had fallen and died within two hours. (I, 184).

"–foughten verry lately, wherein they were slayne.": Omitted by B.

"L[ord] Cheife Baron Manwood,": Sir Roger Manwood, chief baron of the Exchequer from Hilary Term, 21 Elizabeth (1578) until his death in 1593. See fo. 30b and note.

"Mr. Nichols, of Eastwell in Kent, . . . a booke . . . called the Plea of Innocents;": Josias Nichols, rector of Eastwell from 1580 until deprived in 1603 (B, citing Hasted's *Kent*, fol. edition, III, 203). His book was entitled *The Plea of the Innocent: wherein is averred That the Ministers and People falslie termed Puritanes are iniuriouslie slaundered for enemies and troublers of the state.* 12 mo. 1602 (STC 18541).

"(J. Coupers motto)": John Cowper, admitted to the Middle Temple from Dunston, Staffs., 2 Nov. 1599 (*Adm.*, I, 75). See also fo. 77b.

"*Anagrammata* . . . Bright Lady Bes.": Entire passage omitted by B.

"John Sweete:": Middle Templar, admitted 26 Jan. 1593/94, from Modburye, Devon (*Adm.*, I, 65).

Fo. 70b. "There were called to the bar . . . Shurland . . . Crue.": Except for orthographical differences Manningham's list of new utter barristers tallies exactly with that given in Middle Temple records, as follows: [Thomas] Shurland, Brandeston [i.e., John Bramston—see fo. 29b], W. Brodnax, Bennett, Jo. Gybbes, A. Jenour, M. Ryvers, Ja. Pagytt, R. Horton, Crewe. (*Min.*, I, 428.) James Paget (Pagytt, or Pagitt) was the son of Thomas Pagytt, Middle Temple Reader and master of the Bench. (*Adm.*, I, 68; *Min.*, II, 579, 586.)

"Bradnux": Thus in MS. B reads *Bradnum*. William Brodnax of Godmersham, Kent, is mentioned on fo. 58 and described in a note, q.v.

"A wenching gent[leman] . . . his festcue (i.[e.] his p').": Omitted by B.

"Serjeant Harris,": Thomas Harris, Serjeant-at-Law, the "negligent pleader" (see fo. 30b and note).

"Vennar the graund connicatcher": Richard Vennar of Lincoln's Inn (see fo. 59b and note).

"R.R.": Possibly Richard Reeves (Ryves) of the Middle Temple (see notes to fo. 12), admitted 30 July 1597, from Randleston, Dorset (*Adm.*, I, 72); or Robert Rouse of Halton, Cornwall—the older brother of Francis Rouse—admitted 12 Nov. 1597 (ibid.); or Robert Reade, "third son of Andrew R. of Faccombe, Hants., esq. and late of Clementes Inn, gent.," admitted 10 May 1590. (*Adm.*, I, 61.) R. Rouse and Manningham were fined 20 *s.* for absence and being out of commons at Christmas, 1598 (*Min.*, I, 391).

Fo. 71. "At Paules Mr. Tolson of Queenes Colledge in Cambridge;": Robert Townson or Tolson (Toulson), D.D. (1575-1621), a fellow of Queens', having been admitted at the age of 12. He became one of King James' chaplains, then in 1617 Dean of Westminster (succeeding George Montaigne), and in 1620 Bishop of Salisbury (Fuller, 57, and Chamberlain, II, 105, 122, 240, 296, 312). When he died of the smallpox in May, 1621, he left his widow with 13 children (Chamberlain, II, 375, 379). Fuller (p. 57) tells us that this learned preacher could recite the second book of the *Aeneid* "without missing a verse." As Dean of Westminster he was not always in the King's graces, for in the winter of 1619/20, misinterpreting the King's commands as passed along by the Bishop of London (John King) "against the insolence of our women" in wearing men's attire and other unseemly apparel, Townson strictly prohibited yellow ruffs, both ladies' and gentlemen's, and thereby offended the King (Chamberlain, 25 January and 11 March, II, 286, 294).

Fo. 72b. "the sword of persecution be . . .": Thus in MS. B reads "the sword, persecution, be . . ."

Fo. 73. "Mr. Layfeild at St. Clementes": Dr. John Layfield of Trinity College, Cambridge, rector of St. Clement Danes, and future translator of the Authorized Version. See fo. 6 and note.

Fo. 74b. "In Justice Catlines tyme": There were two judges named Catlin, Richard Catlin of Lincoln's Inn, serjeant in 1551 and Queen's serjeant in 1556, and Robert Catlin, of the Middle Temple, reader in 1547, judge of the Common Pleas in 1558, and after Elizabeth's accession, head of the Court of Queen's Bench. As Sir Robert he presided as chief justice for 16 years, dying in 1574. (Foss, pp. 158-159.)

"a Replegiar": A *replegiare* (Medieval Latin, from O.F., *repleger*, to give or become surety for a person) was a *replevin*, meaning restoration to, or recovery by, a person of property taken from him, upon his giving security to have the matter tried in a court of justice and to return the goods if the case is decided against him (or a writ impowering a person to recover his goods by replevin)—OED, VII, 469, 471.

"(Colebrand.)": Probably George Colberne, a Middle Templar from Hadley, Middlesex. Neither *Adm.* nor *Min.* gives his admission date, but on 30 Dec. 1589/90, he purchased Francis Tusser's father's buildings in the Middle Temple, for 72 *l.* (*Min.*, I, 313) and on 9 May 1605 his son and heir-apparent, James Colberne, was specially admitted and bound with his father (*Min.*, I, 454). The "Colberne" mentioned 10 Feb. 1582/83 as one fined for absence and being out of Commons "last Christmas," was probably the same person. (*Min.*, I, 266.) A Henry Calborne, or Colborne, of Suffolk, entered Lincoln's Inn, from Furnival's Inn, May 29, 1592, just 23 days after "John Donne, of London, gen., of Thavies Inn" (*L.I. Adm.*, I, 114).

"Mr. Deering held . . . (Mr. Colebrand.)": Entire passage omitted by B. Edward Deering or Dering (1540?-1576) was a celebrated Puritan divine from an ancient Kentish family and a Fellow of Christ's College, Cambridge. Fuller speaks of him as a pious and "painfull *Preacher*," but "disaffected to *Bishops* and *Ceremonies*" (*Church Hist. of Britain*, 1655, Bk. IX, p. 109). Of a definite and reforming spirit, says Rouse, he anticipated lines in Milton's *Lycidas* in calling for a "preaching ministry of active pastors who directed their sheep." (*The England of Elizabeth*, 467-8.) When he preached before Elizabeth, he told her "That when in persecution under her sister *Queen Mary*, her *Motto* was *Tanquam ovis* as a sheep, but now it might be, *Tanquam indomita juvenca* as an untamed heifer." The Queen is reported to have endured this public reproof patiently, not punishing Dering except to forbid his preaching at Court again. (Fuller, *Church Hist.*, Bk. IX, p. 109.) In 1569 he was chosen Margaret Professor of Divinity, obtained the living of

Pluckley in Kent, and became chaplain to the Duke of Norfolk (Hutchinson, *Men of Kent and Kentishmen*, p. 38).

Fo. 75. "a little booke . . . *Buccina Capelli in Laudem juris*": Probably the work of Jacques Cappel (1525-1586) a French jurisconsult and sieur du Tilloy, whose *De etymologiis juris civilis* is dated 1576, from Sedan. For five years Cappel served as counsel to the parliament of Rennes until, embracing Protestantism, he retired to his estate of Tilloy (Brie). The St. Bartholomew Massacre forced him to seek asylum at Sedan. (*Nouveau Larousse Illustré*, 1898-1904, II, 479.) It may be inferred from a digest of *De etymologiis* printed at the end of Carolus Dukerus' *Opuscula Varia de Latinitate Jurisconsultorum Veterum* (1711), pp. 462 ff., that Manningham is quoting from Book I, Section 1, "princ. de Justit. et Jure."

Fo. 75b. "Dunne is Undonne; . . . against his Lordes pleasure.": John Donne liked to pun on his name; this one, widely circulated at the time, he himself seems to have originated. His "lord" was Sir Thomas Egerton, the Lord Keeper, whom he served as secretary. Donne's courtship of and secret marriage with Anne More, daughter of the irascible Sir George More and niece to Lady Egerton, put Donne in prison and cost him his position. His friend—and best-man—Christopher Brooke and the latter's brother, the Rev. Samuel Brooke, who performed the ceremony, were also incarcerated. "On this occasion," says Walton, ". . . Donne subscribed a letter with his wife, 'John Donne, Anne Donne, *undone*.'" (A. J. Kemp, *The Loseley Manuscripts*, 1836, p. 322.) In a letter to Sir George dated 2 Feb. 1601/02 ("From my lodginge by the Savoy") Donne said, ". . . about three weeks before Christmas we married. . . . it is irremediably donne." (Ibid., 328, 329.)

"the Queene . . . at Sir Robert Secils . . . Sundry devises;": This party on Dec. 6, 1602, a warming of Cecil's new house in the Strand near Ivy Bridge, had been delayed a few days because of cold and foul weather (see Chamberlain, I, 175, and n). The skit of the three women ("a maid, a widdowe, and a wife, eache commending their owne states") was the work of John Davies. See note to fo. 45. Afterward Chamberlain wrote to Carleton: "You like the Lord Kepers devises so yll, that I cared not to get Master Secretaries that were not much better, saving a pretty dialogue of John Davies twixt a maide, a widow, and a wife. . . ." (I, 177-8.) It was registered 2 Apr. 1604 as *A Contention Betwixt a Wife, a Widdow, and a Maide* (Arber, III, 258) and it appeared in Davison's *Poetical Rhapsody*, 2nd ed., 1608, with initials "I.D." (See Chambers, III, 248-9; also *Annals of English Drama 975-1700*, ed. Alfred Harbage and S. Schoenbaum, 2nd ed., Philadelphia, 1964, pp. 82-83+.) Minor differences between Manningham's description and the version in Brit. Mus. *Tanner MS.* 79 of Davies' "Dialogue between a Gentleman Usher and a Post" (published by A. B. Grosart in *Memorial-Introduction to Sir John Davies's Works*, p. 15) are pointed out by Br. Nicholson, *Notes and Queries*, 7th Ser., IV, Oct. 15, 1887, pp. 305-6: The Dialogue makes no mention of presents, and Post describes himself as the bearer of letters from China.

Fo. 76b. "At the Black Friars, Mr. Egerton": Stephen Egerton (c. 1555-c.

1621), of Peterhouse, Cambridge, M.A. 1579 (incorporated at Oxford, July 9, 1583), described by Wood as "a zealous Puritan in his time, and Preacher at the *Black Fryers* in *London*" (*Fasti*, I, 125). St. Anne's, Blackfriars, was William Gouge's church for half a century. Here that devout Puritan lectured every Wednesday morning, men coming from the City and the Inns of Court to hear him. (Harry Porter, *Reformation and Reaction in Tudor Cambridge*, 1958, p. 223). The "little church or chappell up stayres," according to Stow, was "a lodging chamber aboue a staire," which had been rebuilt and enlarged in 1597, after having collapsed. Sir Thomas Carden had pulled down the parish church of St. Anne, in the precinct of the Black Friars, with the Friars' Church; then in Queen Mary's reign, when forced to find a place of worship for the congregation, he had allowed them this second-story chamber. (*Survey of London*, I, 341). Egerton became minister of St. Anne's in 1598 (DNB, VI, 578) and kept this cure till his death. See also fo. 54b and note.

Fo. 76b–77. "glad like one that": MS. glad like a glad as one that

Fo. 77. "for hir husband": Thus in MS. B has "for a husband."
"his answere": Thus in MS. B has "he answered."
"—intimating shee was a whore, as well as he a theife.": Omitted by B.
"with a white . . .": Thus in MS. B has "and a white."

Fo. 77b. "Sterrill": Probably Henry Sterrel, or Stirrel, admitted to the Middle Temple 24 Jan. 1592/93, "late of New Inn, gent., second son of Henry S., of Gaynsbrowghe, Lincs., esq." and called to the bar 24 Oct. 1600 (*Adm.*, I, 64).

"J. Cooper": John Cowper, Middle Templar from Dunston, Staffordshire. See note to fo. 70.

"Nic. Girlington": Nicholas Girlington of Lincoln's Inn, admitted Nov. 11, 1599, "of co. Linc., gen., at request of Anthony Irby, a Master of the Bench." (*L.I. Adm.*, folio 103; *Records*, I, 129.) He was a nephew of Sir Christopher Wray, the benefactor of Magdalene College, Cambridge, who had married Anne, daughter of Nicholas Girlington of Normanby (E. K. Purnell, *Magdalene College*, 1904, pp. 82, 85).

"on[e] Blackewell": George Blackwell, (1545?-1613) of Trinity College, Oxford, appointed by Pope Clement VIII arch-priest over the secular clergy, March, 1598. On Jan. 17, 1599, Chamberlain wrote to Carleton, "The Quene is very angry with Sir Thomas Gerrard for the escape of one Blackwell an arch-priest out of the Marshallsee." (I, 63 and n.) Evidently Manningham's reference is to his recapture. (See also DNB, II, 606-8.)

Fo. 78. "a moote with Jo. Bramstone.": John Bramston, the future Sir John, and Lord Chief Justice (see fo. 29b and note). A moot was an exercise in arguing a point of law before one or more benchers. "The point for argument, termed the case, was started by an inner barrister, who acted as counsel for an imaginary plaintiff to whom another inner barrister answered. The case was argued by two utter barristers, and the decision given by the benchers." (Inderwick, I, 515.)

"Stowe the Antiquary.": John Stow, or Stowe (1525-1605), author of

A Survey of London, 1598, (enlarged 1603). His modern editor, Charles Kingsford, terms him "the first painful searcher into the reverend antiquities of London."—Introd., *A Survey of London*, I, (Oxford, 1908), vii. Stow was about 78 when Manningham talked with him. According to Howes in his edition of Stow's *Annales* (1631), he was tall, lean, his "eyes small and crystaline," pleasant and cheerful, keen of sight and memory, "sober, mild, and courteous." In Manningham's report, however, Stow sounds a bit crotchety. The brass engraving referred to was copied by John Swain and republished in the *Gentleman's Magazine* for Jan., 1837; the latter version forms the frontispiece of Kingsford's edition. Ironically, after Stow had complained to the Diarist about "the defacers of the monuments of others," his own grave suffered a similar desecration, when in 1732 his corpse was removed 'to make way for another.' (Ibid., I, xxvii.)

How did Manningham meet Stow? Probably through Stow's friend Francis Tate, Utter Barrister (and later Bencher and Treasurer) of the Middle Temple; or through one of the Cottons—Sir Robert, or one of his brothers, Thomas or Henry, admitted to the Middle Temple in 1588, and 1601, respectively (*Min.*, I, 295, 389, 411). Or if he did not know Tate or the Cottons personally, he was certainly acquainted with Robert Tanfield, the younger, who was admitted 8 March 1598/99, and became Tate's chambermate in place of his own deceased father. (*Min.*, I, 392-3, 401. See also Kingsford, I, xxiii, xxxii, and note, and fo. 44 of the present edition.)

Possibly Manningham visited Stow at his house in Leadenhall Street, Cornhill (Kingsford, I, lxviii n.).

Fo. 78b. "Dr. Smith, M[aste]r of Clare Hall": Dr. William Smith, S.T.P., was master of Clare from 1598 to 1612, when he became provost of King's College (Hardy's Le Neve, III, 671, 683).

"Dr. Playfare": Dr. Thomas Playfere (1561?-1609), fellow of St. John's College, Cambridge, and Lady Margaret Professor of Divinity from 1596 until his death (Hardy's Le Neve, III, 654). On Nov. 4, 1602, Chamberlain wrote to Carleton that "another eclipse is befaln that universitie, for Dr. Plaifer the divinitie reader is lately crackt in the headpeece, for the love of a wench as some say." (I, 169). A note in the College Register of Admission to Fellowships implies that Playfere in later years was not altogether of sound mind, "a statement of which I have found no corroboration," wrote J. B. Mullinger (*The University of Cambridge*, II, 1884, p. 347, n. 2), evidently unaware of the Manningham and Chamberlain comments. That this distinguished preacher and Latinist regained his balance is suggested by the fact that Bacon requested him to translate *The Advancement of Learning* into Latin; Bacon's letter is undated but probably was written after Nov., 1605, when the book was published (*Add.MSS.* 5503, f. 29, b, in James Spedding, *Letters and Life of Francis Bacon*, III, 1868, p. 300). Among those who admired Playfere as a 'witty' preacher was Nashe, who praised him as "Mellifluous Playfere" (*Strange News*, 1592, quoted by George Williamson, *The Senecan Amble*, 1951, p. 95 n). A Jacobean monument in the chapel of St. Botolph's, Cambridge, commemorates "Thomam Plaiferum . . . Theologiae Doctorem."

"Mr. Perkins": William Perkins, the esteemed Puritan writer and theologian, Fellow of Christ's College (see fo. 58b and note). Fuller described the funeral as solemn and sumptuous, all charges being borne by the college and "the Vniversity and Town lovingly contending which should express more sorrow thereat." Fittingly a Christ's alumnus, Dr. James Montague, later Bishop of Winchester, preached the sermon on the text "Moses, my servant is dead." (*Holy State*, 1840 ed., p. 71).

"as Dr. Whitakeres": William Whitaker (1548-1595) studied at St. Paul's School and Trinity College, Cambridge, being chosen "emperor of the schools" over two older competitors. He served as Regius Professor of Divinity at Cambridge, 1580-95. Master of St. John's College when he died, at age 47, he was solemnly interred therein. He was nephew to Alexander Nowell, the dean of St. Paul's. In his time he was an important exponent of Calvinism. (Fuller, *Holy State*, quoted in *Worthies*, ed. Freeman, 1952, p. 302.)

"Hadsor": Richard Hadsor, Manningham's informant on Irish affairs (see fo. 44 and note).

"Mr. Bramstone": John Bramston (see fo. 29b, fo. 78, and notes to same).

"Mr. Pym": John Pym, the future Parliamentary leader, admitted to the Middle Temple, 23 April, 1602, "son and heir of Alexander Pym, late of Brymour, Somerset, esq., decd." (*Adm.*, I, 79) and bound with his kinsman Francis Rowse and William Whitaker, of Westbury, Wilts., Whitaker being in turn bound with Pym and Rowse (*Min.*, I, 421). Pym maintained a family tradition, for his father had been at the Middle Temple from 1565 until his death in 1584 (*Min.*, I, 149, 273), and in 1629 his son Alexander entered and was bound with him and John Bayliffe, esq. (*Min.*, II, 757).

"One Merredeth, a notable coward,": Possibly Sir William Meredith, paymaster of English garrisons in the Low Countries. His death was noted by Chamberlain to Ralph Winwood, Feb. 16, 1605 (I, 204).

Fo. 80. "at a church in Fosterlane end, one Clappam,": Exactly which church is meant is difficult to determine. Stow describes S. Fosters as "a fayre church lately new builded," in Foster Lane, in Faringdon ward (*Survey*, I, 314, 306) but he also mentions "the smal parrish Church of S. Leonardes, "on the west side of Fauster lane," in Aldersgate ward. (I, 306). The preacher was probably Henoch Clapham (see fo. 55b and note).

Fo. 81b. "When Dr. Colpeper . . . expelled . . .": Dr. Martin Culpeper, warden of New College, Oxford, 1573-1599 (Hardy's Le Neve, III, 555). Wood mentions a "scandalous" work by John Penry, or ap Henry—i.e., "Martin Marprelate"—containing "several reflecting Stories on Dr. Martin Culpeper Warden of New-College, and on Dr. Nich. Bond of *Magd.* College, and on his excellent dancing." This work, printed in 1589 in quarto, was entitled *Dialogue, wherein is plainly laid open the tyrannical dealings of the Lord Bishops against God's Children.* (*Athenae*, I, 259.)

"(Rous)": Which of the Rouse brothers is meant here is unclear. Robert, second son of Antony Rowse of Halton, Cornwall, esq., was admitted to the Middle Temple 12 Nov. 1597 (just two weeks after Charles Danvers), but is not mentioned in *Min.* after 26 Oct. 1599, until his son Antony entered in 1621 (*Min.*, I, 378, 397; II, 666). Francis, the fourth son of Antony Rowse was admitted 5 May 1601 (*Min.*, I, 412.) See other references on fos. 17b, 29b, possibly 30b, 31b, and 71 ("R.R."), and 117b. See also note to fo. 79b on John Pym.

"John Kent told me . . .": One of several sons of Richard Manningham's half-brother Robert Kent. (See Richard Manningham's will, Appendix, and note to fo. 14b.)

"the Greene clothe": A board or court of justice held in the counting house of the queen's household and composed of the lord steward and inferior officers. It received its name from the green cloth spread over the board at which it was held. (*Black's Law Dictionary*, 4th ed., 1957, p. 831.)

"the old recorder Fleetewood": William Fleetwood (see note to fo. 29b).

Fo. 82. "I tooke my journey about my Cosens busines . . .": Folios 82 through 84b tell the story of this trip. On 29 Dec. Manningham seems to have gone from Bradbourne, East Malling, to Godmersham, some 18 miles, staying with "my cosen Chapmans"—i.e., John Chapman of the Middle Temple (see Introd., and his older brother Drew Chapman (see fo. 84b). On 30 Dec. he went to Canterbury, dining at his cousin Cranmer's—perhaps William Cranmer, the merchant, mentioned in the will of Richard Manningham as a kinsman; or Thomas (see fo. 66 and note). Then he rode to his Cousin Watts' place near Sandwich, spending the night there. On 31 Dec. he and Cousin Watts rode into Canterbury together, where both dined at Cousin Cranmer's. On Jan. 1 he returned to Godmersham.

"G. Mannyngham": George Manningham, a Kentish kinsman of the Diarist. B infers that his female descendants' marriages produced the numerous "cousins" in Kent that the Diarist refers to (Preface, v).

"William Sumner": Father of a well-known antiquary of Canterbury (B, Preface, iv-v). He was registrar of the Ecclesiastical Court, preceding his son in that office (ibid., v).

Fo. 83. "Sir Wa. Rawly made this rime upon . . . Mr. Noel:" : The gallant was probably Henry Noel, esquire, a gentleman to the Queen. He was the younger son of Sir Andrew Noel of Dalby in Leicestershire. Fuller describes him as "of the first rank in the court" for his "person, parentage, grace, gesture, valour, and many excellent parts," including skill in music; despite his modest means, "in state, pomp, magnificence, and expenses" he equalled the great barons. His end was sad and sudden: "Being challenged by an Italian gentleman to play balloon [in this game a large leather ball was struck to and fro by the arm, which was protected by a guard], he so heated his blood, that falling into a fever, he died thereof, and, by her majesty's appointment, was buried in the abbey of Westminster, and the chapel of St. Andrew, anno 1597." (*Worthies*, 318-319.)

Though Agnes Latham declares the identity of Noel uncertain, she lists other MSS. in which the verses appeared, including *MS. Rosenbach* 187, p. 195, where Ralegh's opponent is termed "H. Noell, Courtier." (*Poems of Sir Walter*

Ralegh, London, 1951, pp. 131, 132, 138.) The attribution to Dr. Alexander Nowell, the Dean of St. Paul's, in *MS. Douce*, F.5, fo. 31, and *MS. Folger*, 128, fo. 135, makes little sense, for though the worthy churchman and fisherman had a sense of humor, he was hardly "a gallant" in the usual sense.

The pun on Ralegh's name is one of many contemporary answers provoked by Ralegh's poem "The Lie," written probably in 1593-96, says Miss Latham, p. 133. One in *Chetham MS.* 8012, quoted by Latham, reads:

> Go Eccho of the Minde,
> A careless troth protest;
> Make answere that rude Rawly
> No stomack can digest.

Of which verse l. 3 of *MS. Rawl. Poet.* 212 reads:

> "Make answere that so raw a lye."

For all his brilliance and power, Ralegh had a reputation for arrogance. As S. R. Gardiner says, "To the greater number of the men amongst whom he moved, he was simply the most unpopular man in England," and except by a few men like Sir John Harrington who knew his loyal heart, he "was regarded as an insolent and unprincipled wretch." (*History of England*, I, London, 1883, pp. 88-89.)

"The Bishop of Yorke, Dr. Hutton . . . esteemed by Campion . . .": Dr. Matthew Hutton (1529-1606), Archbishop of York, 1595-1606 (Hardy's Le Neve, III, 115). At Cambridge he had been Margaret Professor of Divinity, Master of Pembroke Hall, and Regius Professor, before being made Dean of York in 1567 and Bishop of Durham in 1589. (Fuller, 298-299). Campion was probably the Jesuit martyr Edmund Campion (1540-1581), a scholar of St. John's College, Oxford, noted for his eloquence. After his conversion to Roman Catholicism, he became a Jesuit in 1573 and was sent by Pope Gregory XIII to England in 1580, with Fr. Robert Parsons. Wood describes his writings, his arrest, his disputations, and his execution at Tyburn, 1 Dec. 1581 (I, 206-208).

Fo. 84. "My cosen Cranmer": See folios 66, 82b, 83, and notes.

"slighty": Thus in MS. B has "lightly."

"Ravens": Not positively identified. A learned clergyman Dr. Ralph Ravens, dean of Wells, served in the Greek group of Bible translators at Oxford (Paine, *The Learned Men*, pp. 50, 156). Wood lists a John Ravens of Queen's College, Oxford, (M.A., July 7, 1595); in 1607 he became "sub-dean of *Wells* and Prebendary of *Bishop's Compton* in that church." (*Fasti*, I, 149-150.)

"the booke . . . by B[ishop] Bilson": Thomas Bilson (1547-1616). Bishop of Winchester and a Privy Counsellor. His "Sermons . . . preached at *Paul's* Cross made great alarms against the Puritan Brethren," says Wood. In 1599 they were published as "The effect of certain Sermons touching the full redemption of Mankind by the death and Blood of Christ Jesus; . . . The clearing of certain Objections made against the aforesaid Doctrine." Then the

Puritans put Henry Jacob, of Kent, "an old Dissenter," to work, to refute Bilson. (I, 404.) See also fo. 37 and note.

Fo. 84b. "1" [in margin]: Thus in MS. Mistaken by B for 7.

"Mr. Jo. Cuttes, Sir John Cuttes sonne and heire, . . . married . . . to Mr. Kemp of Wye his daughter": John Cutts, son of Sir John Cutts of Childerley, Cambs., and his second wife, Margaret, eldest daughter and co-heir of Sir John Brockett of Brockett Hall in Hertfordshire, married Anne Kempe, the eldest daughter and co-heir of Sir Thomas Kempe of Olantigh in Kent, by the daughter of Sir Thomas Moyle. She lived 48 years, dying 13 March 1631. In the church at Swavesey, Cambs., is an unusual monument to her memory, in the form of a cabinet with two folding doors of black marble, each having five pieces of white marble that answer one another. (*Monumental Inscriptions and Coats of Arms from Cambridgeshire*, ed. W. M. Palmer, Camb., 1932, pp. 110, 164-5.) From his mother, Lady Margaret, John Cutts inherited the manour of Boxworth in Cambridgeshire (ibid., 110). According to Philipot, Sir Thomas Kempe (whose father had acquired the manor and castle of Chilham, 10 Eliz.) had four daughters and co-heirs, whose marriages Philipot partly confused by linking Dorothy to John Cutts, Ann to Sir Thomas Chichley, Amy to Sir Henry Skipworth, and Mary to Sir Dudley Digges (*Villare Cantianum*, 1659, p. 116).

Fo. 85-fo. 85b. Blank in MS. Also blank is another leaf, unnumbered.

Fo. 86. "At Paules Crosse one Barlowe, a beardless man of Pembroke hall in Cambridge": Ranulph, or Randolph, Barlow, M.A. of Pembroke Hall, afterwards D.D. He became Archdeacon of Winchester, 1609, and Archbishop of Tuam in Ireland, 1629. Incorporated, Oxford, July 16, 1600, as "Randolph Barlow M.A. of Cambridge"—Wood, *Fasti*, I, 160. Maclure identifies the preacher heard by Manningham as "Ralph Barlow, after[ward] Dean of Christ Church in Dublin" (*P.C. Sermons*, p. 223).

Fo. 88. "at St. Peters by Paules Wharfe, Mr. Clapham": St. Peter the Little, by Paul's Wharf, a small parish church, hence called *parva*, or little, in Queene Hithe Ward. Paul's Wharf was "a large landing place with a common stayre vpon the Riuer of Thames, at the end of a streete called powles wharfe hill. which runneth downe from Powles chaine"—i.e., from "the South chaine of Powles churchyarde." (Stow, *Survey of London*, II, 6, 12, 13.) Evidently Henoch Clapham was rector of this parish, for on fo. 100 Manningham wrote: "Mr. Clapham at his Churche by Paules Wharf." See fo. 55b and note.

Fo. 89b. "like a conjuror that subscribes with his bloud.": An allusion to Doctor Faustus in Marlowe's tragedy?

"slaps": Thus in MS. B reads "flaps."

"lob": a clown, clumsy fellow

"clunche": a clod-hopper

Fo. 90b. "a forril[?]": Somewhat blotted in the MS. and thus doubtful. A "forel" was a cloth or canvas covering used to wrap up a book (B) or manuscript, "or into which it is sewn" (OED, IV, 436).

"Clapham": Probably Henoch Clapham, the divine (see fo. 88 and note).

"Mr. Peter[?]": MS. illegible; thus in B. One John Peter of Bowhay, Devon, was admitted to the Middle Temple 1 Dec. 1598 (*Adm.*, I, 74).

"Scottish taunts.": Printed by Camden in *Remaines* (ed. 1637, p. 194) and assigned to the reign of Ed. III, though not to the Scots.—B.

"Mr. Asheford": There were two men of this name at the Middle Temple: Henry Ashforde, son and heir of Roger A., of Ashforde, Devon, esq., admitted 26 April 1594 (*Adm.*, I, 66) and his younger brother Thomas, admitted 17 May 1599, called 4 July 1606 (*Adm.*, I, 75).

"(J. Bramstone.)": John Bramston (see fo. 29b and note).

"Justice Glandville": John Glanville of Tavistock and Lincoln's Inn, Justice of the Common Pleas, 30 June 1598 until his death 27 July 1600. He was called to Serjeant at the same time as Thomas Harris. His monument in Tavistock Church represents him as corpulent. (Foss, p. 303.)

"(Ch. Davers *na.*)": Charles Danvers (see note to fo. 12).

"(Greene.)": Thomas Greene, or Grene, of the Middle Temple, admitted 20 Nov. 1595, "late of Staple Inne, gent., son and heir of Thomas G. of Warwick, gent. dcd. Called 20 Oct. 1602. Bencher 1621. Reader Autumn 1621. Treasurer 1629." (*Adm.*, I, 69). At the time of his admission his sureties were "Messrs. John Marston of the Bench and John, his son." (*Min.*, I, 357.) Afterwards Greene, practising law in Stratford, lived at New Place, where he and his wife Letitia shared the household with Shakespeare's wife Anne. (See Marchette Chute, *Shakespeare of London*, 1949, pp. 296–8.)

Fo. 91. ". . . 11 Sergeantes at Lawe called this day:": Manningham names only ten, omitting Henry Hobart, or Hubert, of Lincoln's Inn. Chamberlain lists them all, as follows: [James] Altham of Gray's; [Henry] Hubert [i.e., Hobart]. [Robert] Hawton [Houghton], and [Arthur] Harris of Lincoln's; [Edward] Phillips [Phelips] and [Augustine] Nicols [Nicolls] of the Middle Temple; [John] Crooke the recorder, [Thomas] Coventrie, [Lawrence] Tanfield, [Thomas] Foster, and [Robert] Barker of the Inner Temple. (Feb. 11, 1602/03: I, 185.)

The Thomas Foster mentioned here is clearly not the "Mr. Foster of Lyncolnes Inn" who told "jeastes" about Sir Thomas More on the way to Westminster, fo. 29 and note. (The index of B confuses the two Fosters.) Serjeant Foster, from Hunsdon, Herts., entered the Inner Temple in 1571, became Reader in Autumn, 1596. He was later knighted, served as counsel to Queen Anne and Prince Henry, and in Nov., 1607, was named Judge of the Common Pleas. Thomas Sutton nominated him to be one of the first judges of his hospital—the Charterhouse. He died in May, 1612, and is buried at Hunsdon, under an arched marble monument with effigy in his judge's robes. (Foss, 279; Chamberlain, I, 349).

"Sergeant Harris": Thomas Harris of the Middle Temple (see note to fo. 30b).

"Mr. Snig": George Snygge, or Snigge, Bencher and Treasurer of the Middle Temple. (See fo. 39b and note.)

"Mr. Nicholes": Augustine (Austin) Nicolls of the Middle Temple, son

of a Bencher, Thomas Nicolls of Hardwicke, Northants; admitted 5 Nov.
1575; called 10 Feb. 1583; Reader Autumn 1602 and Lent 1602/03; Serjeant,
1603, and knighted in that year; Recorder of Leicester, 1603; Justice of the
Common Pleas, 1612, and Chancellor to Charles, Prince of Wales. He died
at Kendal while on summer circuit in 1616 and was buried there. He is said
to have been "renowned for his judicial endowments and integrity." (J. Bruce
Williamson, citing Foss, in *Middle Temple Bench Book,* 2nd ed., 1937, p. 90.)

"Mr. Hadsore": Richard Hadsor of the Middle Temple (see fo. 44 and note).

"one Everard": Sir John Everard, a noted lawyer and a recusant, described
by Chamberlain as "a very sufficient and grave man" (June 10, 1613—I, 456.)

Fo. 91b. "*a poeme intituled The Tragicall History of Mary Queen of Scotts*":
Manningham's "disjointed extracts" (B) are from a poem attributed to Thomas
Wenman, M.A. (1590), afterwards Fellow of Balliol, and Public Orator of the
University of Oxford, 1594—though John Fry, of Bristol (d. 1822), who found
a manuscript version dated 1601 and published it in 1810, admits its authorship is "a knotty point, impracticable of resolve, except by conjecture." (*The
Legend of Mary, Queen of Scots, and other Ancient Poems now first Published
from MS.S. of the Sixteenth Century. with an Introduction, Notes and an
Appendix.* London: Printed for Longman, Hurst, Rees, and Orme, 1810,
p. xi.) Fry described the manuscript as a small quarto of 52 leaves, though
originally containing 55, written in three hands; the Queen of Scots poem
takes up 32 leaves. The poem is in 186 stanzas of rime royal. According to
Fry, everything to p. 75 is by Wenman, whose name appears on the last page:

"Thomas Wenman, Bonus—
Homo Timens Deum
J.H.S. Maria.
1601,
Londoni datum
die 10 Jully."

(Ibid., Appendix 3, p. xvi.) (See also Wood, I, 493, and *Fasti,* I, 139; Hardy's
Le Neve, III, 534.)

Except for bracketed numbers added by B and here retained, the marginal numbers are printed as in MS (Manningham's).

Fo. 92. "The choise of the Regent . . . with the Dauphine of Fraunce.":
Manningham's abstract of stanzas 34-40.

Fo. 92b. "Our Q[ueene] offered . . . not marry a forreyner.": Manningham's abstract of stanzas 48-66.

"Davis her secretary . . . hir husband, Lord Darly.": Abstract of stanzas
83-84.

Fo. 93. "That not the Q[ueen] . . . murther L[ord] Darly.": Abstract of
Stanzas 102-117.

"might his malice bleare,": Thus in MS. B: teare.

"With the slender shewe I make in mourners state,": This line does not
occur in Fry's publication—B.

Fo. 94. "Tyborne tippets, i, [e.], halters.": Manningham's note on a phrase in stanza 160–B.

Fo. 95-Fo. 95b. "Some of the Lotteries . . . last Summer at hir Majesties, being with the L[ord] Keeper.": Omitted by B on the grounds that these mottoes had already been printed by the Percy and Shakespeare Societies and in Nichol's *Progresses*. Composed by the Middle Temple poet John Davies, the 34 lots were part of the "devices" sponsored by the Lord Keeper, Sir Thomas Egerton, to entertain the Queen at his house at Harefield, Middlesex, (near Uxbridge) July 31–Aug. 3, 1602 (Chambers, IV, 67–68).

The second edition (1608) of Francis Davison's *Poetical Rhapsody* prints a version, misdated 1601, containing this account: "A Marriner with a Box vnder his arme, containing all the severall things following, supposed to have come from the Carrick, came into the presence singing this Song.

"Cynthia Queene of seas and lands . . ."

The song is in three 6-line stanzas, each with a refrain ending

"There is no fishing to the sea, nor seruice to the King."

Then the Marriner makes a short speech of greeting and compliment to "a company of the fairest Ladies that euer I saw. Come Ladies," he says, "try your fortunes, and if any light vpon an vnfortunate blank, let her thinke that fortune doth but mock her in these trifles, and meanes to pleasure her in greater matters." (See *Poetical Rhapsody*, ed. Hyder Rollins, Harvard University Press, 1932, II, 202-210—hereafter referred to as *P.R.*)

Manningham's version has been checked against that of *P.R.* and also that of the MS. in the Conway Collection, ed. Peter Cunningham and printed in *Shakespeare Society Papers*, II, (1845), 65-75, headed "The devise to entertayne hir Ma^{ty} at Harfielde, the house of Sr Thomas Egerton Lo. Keeper and His Wife the Countess of Darbye."

In the present text bracketed numbers in the margin indicate the position in the *P.R.* text.

In most instances Manningham's identifications and wording agree with the Conway MS., rather than with *P.R.*

Fo. 95. "La[dy] Scudamour.": Wife to Sir James Scudamore, a gallant soldier, with Essex at Cadiz, noted for his tilting prowess and held up as the very pattern of chivalry as Sir Scudamour in Spenser's *Faerie Queene*, Bk. IV, and mother of Sir John Scudamore, first Viscount Scudamore, 1601-1671, Charles I's scholarly ambassador in Paris (DNB, XVII, 1092 ff.).

[28] "And yet they spend it worst that watch it most." Thus in MS. and Conway. *P.R.* reads "Yet they most loose it that do watch it most."

[6] "Fortune hath sent to you,...": Thus in MS and Conway. *P.R.* "Fortune doth send you,..."

[7] "A ring with a posie As faythfull as I find.": *P.R.* "*this* posie."

"Earle of Darbys countes.": Conway "Lo. Derbyes Wife."

"And yet the word doth fitt ...": *P.R.*: "And yet the words doth hit ..." Conway: "And yet the words do fitt."

[8] "Fortune ... hir best frends.": Thus in MS and Conway. *P.R.* reads: "Fortune these gloues to you in challenge sends / For that you loue not fooles that are her frends."

[12] "With fortunes girdle": Thus in Conway MS. *P.R.* "By fortunes girdle"

[13] "Writing tables.": *P.R.* "A Paire of writing-tables."

"your thought": *P.R.* "your thoughts"

Fo. 95b. [19] "A scisser case.": *P.R.* "A paire of Sizzers."

"though you be borne": *P.R.* "though you were borne"

[21] "A prayer booke (not drawne).": Conway MS. "This onely lefte undrawne." Percy copy, however, gives it to Lady Digby.

"may be good": *P.R.* "may proue good"

      that day

"Till fortune come": *P.R.* "Till fortune come,"

[22] "A Mufkin:" *P.R.* "A Snuftkin"

"'Tis summer, yet a muffkin is your lott / It will ...": *P.R.* "'Tis Summer yet a Snuftkin is your lot, / But 'twill ..."

[32] "Though it gaine nothing,": *P.R.* "Though it gaine nought,"

Fo. 96. "At the Temple churche, Dr. Abbottes, ... : Dr. George Abbot (1562-1623), dean of Winchester, 1599/1600 to 1609, when he was appointed Bishop of Coventry and Lichfield; in 1611 he was made Archbishop of Canterbury, owing to the posthumous influence of his patron, the Earl of Dunbar, on King James. (Paul Welsby, *George Abbot, The Unwanted Archbishop*, London: S.P.C.K., 1962, pp. 35-37.) Welsby, his latest biographer, says of him, "Of the eight Archbishops between the Reformation and the Revolution, one (Reginald Pole) was an anachronism and two (Edmund Grindal and George Abbot) were a mistake." (Ibid., p. 1.) But he could preach. He had "the gift of composing a vivid phrase" and, to drive home his point, could make "telling use of illustrations." (Ibid., p. 10.)

Fo. 96b. "In the afternoone, Mr. Clapham;": Henoch Clapham, one of the Diarist's favorite preachers (see fo. 55b, 80, 88, and notes to same).

"... a nobleman of Scotland, ... fayled in the computacion of the beginning of the years.": John Napier of Merchiston, inventor of logarithms. His work *A plaine discouery of the Whole Reuelation of Saint John*, printed at Edinburgh in 1593 by Waldgrave (STC 18354), went through several editions and was translated into the major European languages.

Fo. 97. "In his sermon he told a tale of the Jewes Thalmud,": MS, partially cancelled, reads thus: "... he told another report of himselfe that he was sent for by some mini ..."

Fo. 97b. "(Clapham.)": Henoch Clapham, (see fo. 96b, 55b, 80, 88 and notes)

"Mr. Bodley": Thomas Bodley (see fo. 46 and note).

"trading for pilcheres;": The pilchard is "allied to the herring but smoother and rounder . . . taken in large numbers on the coasts of Cornwall and Devon," and therefore "a considerable article of trade." (OED, VII, 854). "Pilcher" was also used as term of abuse at the beginning of the 17th century; e.g., "To take sturgeons with pilchards" meant "to get large returns from small outlays." (Ibid.)

"(Mr. Curle.)": Edward Curle (see note to fo. *12*).

"Mr. South": Probably Thomas South of the Middle Temple, admitted 27 Feb. 1595/96, "late of New Inn, gent., son and heir of Thomas S., of Northley, Hants., gent. Called 12 Oct., 1604. Bencher 1621. Reader Lent 1621. Treasurer 1630." (*Adm.*, I, 69.) Edward South, "son and heir Thomas S., of Swallowcliff, Wilts., esq." was admitted 12 Oct. 1601 (*Adm.*, I, 78) but is not mentioned in *Minutes* beyond that date (*Min.*, I, 415). Another Edward South, from Kerrington, Lincs., and Clementes Inne, entered 16 May 1595 (*Adm.*, I, 68).

"(Da.)": Charles Danvers, usually spelled Dauers (Davers) by the Diarist.

"Tom Lancaster met Robbin Snig . . .": Thomas Lancaster of Gray's Inn (see fo. 12, fo. 45, and notes to same). Robbin Snig is probably Robert Snegge or Snagg of the Middle Temple, mentioned in records of the society as far back as 28 Feb. 1566/67, in Plowden's time, and until 1585, when he is described as "of the Bench" and involved in a dispute with Mr. Ferrers (*Min.*, I, 158, 279). He became a Bencher in 1580 and served as Lent Reader in that year (*Adm.*, I, 25).

"(Dr. Cesar Master of Requestes.)": Julius Caesar, LL.D. (1558-1636), Master of Requests in Ordinary since 1591, and a Bencher of the Inner Temple (admitted, 1580; called to the Bench 24 Jan. 1590/91). (Inderwick, I, 372, 488.) He became Treasurer of the Inner Temple at a parliament held at St. Albans, 11 Nov. 1593 (ibid., I, 391-392), and was reelected the following year. In 1595 or 6 he contributed 300 *l.* towards the erection of chambers between the Inner Temple Hall and the Temple Church, long known as Caesar's buildings (DNB, III, 657). In 1603 he was knighted and went on to higher posts as Chancellor of the Exchequer, 1606, and Master of the Rolls, 1614 (ibid., 488). He and the poet Donne enjoyed a cordial relationship. See also fo. 103b and note.

"One told Toplife . . . (Ch. Davers)": Omitted by B. "Toplife" was Richard Topcliffe (1532-1604), a Magdalene College alumnus (matriculated 1565) who became an Admiralty Judge and then a cruel and detested informer against Catholics. (Edward K. Purnell, *Magdalene College*, London, 1904, p. 59.) He was one of a special commission appointed 8 Jan. 1591/92 to deal with imprisoned recusants, particularly prisoners suspected of being Jesuits or Seminaries from overseas (Harrison, I, 100). In 1581 Parliament had made it high treason to withdraw from the Church of England to that of Rome, and anyone saying or hearing Mass was liable to a large fine or a year's imprisonment. (Rouse, *The England of Elizabeth*, p. 444). The execution of the Jesuit Edmund Jennings and six other Catholics in Dec., 1591, has been cited as evidence of Topcliffe's participation in vile butchery (Harrison, I, 83–84). He also took a prominent role in the arrest, torture, and trial of Fr. Robert Southwell, who was arraigned before Lord Chief Justice Popham 20 Feb. 1595 (ibid., II, 13–15; I, 140, 150). The verbs *topcliffizare* and *topclifferize* became synonymous with *to hunt a recusant* or *to inform*. To persuade his victims, he is said to have invented an instrument of torture much worse than the rack (Purnell, p. 59).

Topcliffe, together with Roger Wilbraham and Dr. Giles Fletcher, uncle of dramatist John Fletcher and father of poets Giles and Phineas Fletcher, was one of the commission appointed by the Privy Council to apprehend and interrogate the players of the "lewd . . . seditious & sclandrous" play *The Isle of Dogs*, (August, 1597)—for which Ben Jonson was imprisoned. (See letter quoted by Hereford and Simpson in Appendix III of *Ben Jonson*, I, Oxford, 1925, 217.)

Fo. 98. "Mr. Cooke, the Attorney,": Edward Coke (knighted 1603). See fo. 59b and note.

"I offered Mr. Kedgewin . . . for their standing.": Omitted by B. The wit here referred to and quoted was Manningham's fellow student at the Middle Temple, Thomas Kedgwin from Bristol and Emmanuel College, Cambridge (see fo. 2 and note).

"being myne ammiral in the house": My superior, outranking me in seniority. *Ammiral* is a form of *admirall* or *admiral*, from Arabic *amir*, commander (OED, I, 118). Kedgwin's connection with the Middle Temple seems to have commenced in May, 1596, while he was still an undergraduate at Cambridge (*Min.*, I, 363)—some two years before the Diarist joined the Society. (See above and fo. 2n.)

"He sent . . . leaden heeles. (Topham[?]).": Omitted by B. Topham has not been identified. There were two young men at Cambridge about this time: John Topham of Peterhouse, son of Thomas T. of Cracoe near Skipton, Yorks., yeoman; matriculated Lent, 1597/98; Scholar, 1600-2; B.A., 1601/02; and Robert Topham, of Derbyshire admitted to Queens', 1597; matriculated pensioner, St. John's, Easter, 1598; B.A., 1600/01, M.A., 1604 (Venn, IV, 253). But could the Diarist have meant Topcliffe? (See fo. 97b and note.)

"Turner and Dun": John Turner and John Dun, famous master fencers. Their ill-fated challenge match took place at the Swan Theatre, on the Bankside in Southwark, on Monday, 7 Feb. 1602/03. As reported by Chamberlain, "Dun had so yll lucke . . . that he fell downe starke dead, and never spake word nor once moved: the case is, and wilbe much argued by Lawiers whether yt will prove chaunce medley, manslaughter or murder, by reason of malice and many challenges past betweene them before." (I, 184.) Doubt on the accidental nature of this violence is cast by a statement of Joseph Swetnam, a Master of Defence, in a booke called *The Schole of the Noble and Worthy Science of Defence* (1617): "Turner did speedily kill John Dun with a Thrust in the Eie. He by his unluckie Hand did thrust out two or three

Eies, and was praised by the Publick for his Skill."—quoted by J. D. Aylward, "The Creighton Case," *Notes and Queries,* CCII, June, 1957, pp. 249-250. Aylward's article recounts another mishap, in August, 1604, at a house party given by Turner's patron, Francis, Second Baron Norreys, at Rycote, near Thame, Oxfordshire. Among the guests, most of whom thought it a privilege to "play at foils" with the celebrity, was one who regarded himself a skilled fencer and who had resolved to discredit the Master. This was Robert Crichton, or Creighton, sixth baron Sanquhar, who pretended to be a novice and claimed the scholar's privilege of sparing the face but whose deception was detected by Turner as soon as they crossed swords. Turner, provoked, then pressed his opponent and put out one of his eyes. Though contemporaries regarded it as an accident, Crichton brooded, meditated revenge for seven years and, after several abortive attempts, finally succeeded in having Turner assassinated (ibid., 245-250)—on May 11, 1612. On May 20, 1612, Chamberlain reported that Turner, while "drincking with certain Scottes belonging to the Lord Sanquir," was "sodainly slaine with a pistoll." (I, 348.) After a trial in the King's Bench, Crichton was hanged, 29 June 1612, in the Great Palace yard of Westminster (Gibbs & Doubleday, *Complete Peerage,* III, 541).

"One told Sergeant Harrys . . . (Hoskins).": Omitted by B. The punster was Thomas Harris, Sergeant-at-Law, the "negligent pleader" (see fos. 30b, 70b, and notes to same). Hoskins was John Hoskyns, Middle Templar, wit, author of *Directions for Speech and Style,* future M.P. and Serjeant-at-Law. He had recently married, at Bath, 1 Aug. 1601, Benedicta ("Bennet") Bourne, daughter of Robert Moyle of Buckwell, Kent, widow of a fellow Middle Templar, Francis Bourne of Witlington, Somersetshire, and mother of three young children. With his beloved "Ben," a woman of charm and wisdom as well as of considerable fortune, the volatile Hoskyns was, as his warm, intimate letters reveal, passionately in love. (*Life, Letters and Writings of John Hoskyns,* ed. Louise B. Osborne, New Haven, 1937, pp. 22, 62, 229; C. S. Lewis, *English Literature in the Sixteenth Century,* Oxford, 1954, p. 546.) (See Introd.)

"The towne of Manitre in Essex . . . stage playes.": Thomas Heywood's *An Apology for Actors,* 1608(?), states that "to this day in divers places of England there be townes that held the privilege of their faires and other charters by yearely stage-plays, as at Manningtree in Suffolke, Kendall in the North, and others . . ." (Shakespeare Society Edition, p. 61, as quoted in Chambers, IV, 253).

"And Rocheford . . . keepes court at midnight . . .": At the "Lawless Court" of Rochford, near Southend in Essex, the parties assembled at a post in a close called the King's Hill; whatever was spoken during the proceedings was whispered to the post (Morant's *Essex,* I, 272: W. H. Black, F.S.A., *Notes and Queries,* IX, 11). This curious rite was celebrated about midnight of the first Tuesday after Michaelmas (Karl Baedeker, *Great Britain,* 7th ed., 1910, p. 508).

Fo. 98b. "Ben Johnson . . . lives upon one Townesend . . .": Jonson's host at this time was Sir Robert Townshend, an accomplished patron of writers, including John Fletcher, whose sprightly verses prefixed to *The Faith-*

ful Shepherdess address him as "the perfect Gentleman, Sir. R. T." (*Ben Jonson*, ed. Herford and Simpson, I, 30n, 31, 31n.) At Townshend's home the poet "found the leisure at last to write his Roman tragedy *Sejanus*." (Marchette Chute, *Ben Jonson of Westminster*, 1960, p. 112.) In 1602/03 he exchanged this hospitable haven for that of Esmé Stuart, Lord of Aubigny. (Herford & Simpson, I, 31.) B's identification of Townshend as Aurelian, Jonson's later rival in masque-making, is incorrect.

"(Reeves[?])": Perhaps William or Richard Reeves, or Ryves, of the Middle Temple (see fo. 12 and note). Or possibly John Reves, jun., admitted 23 Nov. 1574, and called 10 Feb. 1583/84 (*Adm.*, I, 39). B queries "(Free- wer?)"; if B is substantially correct, the informant may have been Edward Frere of Oxford, admitted to the Inner Temple Nov., 1584. He became a Baronet in 1620 and died in 1630. His seat was at Water Eaton. (*I.T. Adm.*, 109.) Or possibly John Freeman at the Middle Temple, called to the degree of the Utter Bar 3 June 1603, with Blounte, A. Wake, T. Palmer, *et al*; these were referred to the next parliament for confirmation and again referred 8 July 1603 (*Min.*, I, 440, 441).

"Mr. Hull": Henry Hall, or Haule, of the Middle Temple. (see fo. 30 and note).

"(Whitlock.)": James Whitelock of the Middle Temple (see fo. 57 and note).

"Mr. Hadsor": Richard Hadsor of the Middle Temple, from County Louide in Ireland. He had been called to the degree of the Utter Bar the day before Manningham made this entry. (See fo. 44 and note.)

"One Weston, a merchant of Dublin, . . . a great discoveror.": Nicholas Weston, "agent of the city of Dublin," victualer to the Queen's Army, and Alderman. In 1596 he supplied fish to the English army in Ireland and was named in a warrant to be paid for so doing (Jan. 9, 1596/97, CSP *Dom. Eliz.*, *1595-97*, p. 345). In 1601 he said he had been a suitor for ten months for £ 1,700 due the citizens of Dublin for dieting the army quartered there, in time of scarcity of victuals, at the rate of 5d per diem, which they could not afford at less than 8d per meal. (*Hist. MSS. Comm., Salisbury*, XIV, 1923, p. 196.) After July 1, 1606, he lent money (£ 150) to the army. (CSP *Ireland, James I, 1603-1606*, p. 534). According to the context of Manningham's entry, Weston was "discovering" information about the Irish rebels, though B queries: "of concealed lands."

Fo. 99. "The papistes relligion . . . (B. Rudy[erd].)": Benjamin Rudyerd. It is interesting to find the future Sir Benjamin (see fo. 35b and note) antici- pating Swift's *Tale of a Tub* by 100 years.

"(E. Curle.)": Edward Curle, or Curll, of the Middle Temple (see Introd. and note to fo. 12).

"(L[ord] Keeper.)": Sir Thomas Egerton.

"the Lady Effingham . . . at shuttlecocke,": Anne, wife of William, Lord Howard of Effingham, daughter and heir of Oliver, Lord St. John of Bletsoe. The Effinghams had married 7 Feb. 1597/98. (Faulkner's *Chelsea*, II, 124, cited by B.)

Fo. 100. "Mr. Clapham at his churche by Paules Wharf.": See note to fo. 88.

"*Synne* in the margent . . . *punishment* in the text": Emphasis (italics) added by present editor.

"out of dores": MS out of out dores.

"Nowe Kayne . . . horror of his synn; he confesseth, but . . .": No punctuation after *synn* in MS.

Fo. 101-101b. On these leaves Manningham copied versions of several paradoxes by John Donne, including "That Women Ought to Paint" (MS title: "That paynting is lawefull") and "That a Wise Man is Known By Much Laughing" (MS title: "Laughinge is the greatest signe of wisdome."). In the first edition of Donne's *Juvenilia: or certaine paradoxes and problemes,* 1633 (STC 7043), these are Paradoxes II and X, respectively. Another, entitled in MS "Hee that weepeth is most wise," corresponds to no known paradox by Donne, but R. E. Bennett ("John Manningham and Donne's Paradoxes," *Modern Lang. Notes,* May, 1931, XLVI, pp. 309-313) has proved beyond reasonable doubt that Donne composed it. The most serious and poetical of the four, "To keepe sheepe the best lyfe," on fo. 101b, may be Donne's also. These are the earliest dated references to Donne's Paradoxes.

This genre, though within the broad tradition of Martial and Erasmus' *The Praise of Folly,* was, in a sense a new literary form derived from Italy, particularly from the *Paradossi* of Ortensio Lando, first published in 1543. Twelve of these were translated by Anthony Munday and published by him in 1593 as *The Defence of Contraries.* Drawing heavily from Lando, Sir William Cornwallis the younger, in 1600, wrote such paradoxes as "That it is happiness to be in debt" and "That Inconstancy is more commendable than Constancie." (Simpson, *A Study of the Prose Works of John Donne,* p. 143.)

Such ironic reversals or defense of outrageous propositions appealed to the legal mind. Because of their interest in disputation, Inns of Court students like Manningham, who probably had manuscript copies from Martin, or Hoskyns, or John Chapman or Rudyerd, would naturally have enjoyed the paradoxes of Donne and of other wits.

Fo. 102. "Sir Ed[ward] Hobby": Sir Edward Hoby (1560-1617) of Bisham, Berkshire, eldest son of Sir Thomas Hoby and Elizabeth, daughter of Sir Anthony Coke. On Jan. 24, 1583/84, "Edward Hobbey, knight" was admitted to the fellowship of the Middle Temple (*Adm.,* I, 52). He was active in the lower house of Parliament (1597, 1601, 1614); translator of Don Bernardino de Mendoza's *Theorique and practise of War* (1597); author of *A curry-combe for a cox-combe* (1615), STC 13540, one of several polemical exchanges between Hoby and the Jesuit John Floyd, 1613-15. (Harrison, II, 231, 233, 236; III, 210; II, 179. Chamberlain, I, 568 and Maclure's n. 10.) He was noted for proficiency in logic, wide reading, and love of the arts. (Wood, *Athenae,* I, 417.) To his house in the "Blacke Friers," Sir Henry Savile, his lady, and his whole household went to keep Christmas in 1612 and to spend most of the winter (Chamberlain, I, 397, 398).

"Sir H[enry] Nevils disaster with the E[arl] of Essex,": Sir Henry Neville was Ambassador to France in 1599 and 1600. For his part in the Essex rebellion of Feb. 8, 1600/01, he was confined in the Tower for two years. See fo. 127b for news of his release.

"The Bishop of Bathe and Wells,": Dr. John Still, Master of Trinity College, Cambridge; Bishop of Bath and Wells, 1592-1607/8 (B).

"(Hooper.)": George Hooper of the Middle Temple, admitted 11 Feb. 1591/92: "late of New Inn, son and heir of Thomas Hooper of Carhampton, Somerset, gent." (*Min.*, I, 326.) He is mentioned in Middle Temple records until 1629 (ibid., II, 753). When Henry and John Ford, sons of "Thomas Forde of Islington, Devon, esq." were admitted, 18 Oct. 1600 and 16 Nov. 1602, respectively, they were bound with George Hooper and Thomas Ford (ibid., I, 407, 427).

"Dr. Rud . . . before the Queene": Probably Anthony Rudd, D.D., of Trinity College, Cambridge; Dean of Gloucester, 1584-94; consecrated Bishop of St. David's, June 9, 1594, "being then accounted a most admirable Preacher." (Wood, *Fasti*, I, 110, 116; *Athenae*, I, 710). He published four or more sermons, including one preached before King James, 13 May 1604 (W. Fraser Mitchell, *English Pulpit Oratory from Andrews to Tillotson*, p. 441.) He died 7 March 1614 (*Fasti*, I, 116).

"(Burdett.)": William Burdett of the Middle Temple, "second son of Humfrey Burdett, late of Sunninge, Berks., esq.," admitted 12 Feb. 1594/95, and bound with Messrs. Francis Moore and Edward Lydall. (*Min.*, I, 351.) See also Cobden's disparagement of him, fo. 133b.

Fo. 102b. "Sir Henry Unton": Sir Henry Umpton, or Unton, (1557-1596) diplomat and soldier, Ambassador to France. He entered the Middle Temple 11 Feb. 1574/75, just two weeks before Walter Ralegh. (*Min.*, I, 204.) He served in the Low Countries, 1585-86, and was knighted in the latter year (DNB, xx, 32).

"Mr. Duns of Barkshire": Perhaps William Dunch, son and heir of Edmund Dunch of Witnam, Berks., Esq.; he entered Gray's Inn, June 21, 1596 (*Gray's Adm.*, p. 90).

"(Chute.)": Perhaps Charles Chute, who entered the Middle Temple specially, 20 Feb. 1586/87, and was bound with Mr. Edward Comes (*Min.*, I, 290). In 1599 (May 17), he was assigned "to the chamber of Messrs. Henry Savile and Thomas Lewes in place of the latter." (*Min.*, I, 398.) In 1606 (7 Feb. 1606/07) he was one of those appointed to provide the Reader's Feast (*Min.*, II, 462). We also hear of him in 1621 (*Min.*, II, 663). On 23 May 1623, called to the bar were Simondes Dewes, Benjamin Tichbourne, and others including "Ch. Chute," who may have been Charles or his son Chaloner. (*Min.*, II, 682.) After Chaloner's admission, 11 Nov. 1621, father and son were assigned to the new buildings and chambers built by Sir Walter Cope and Sir Arthur Gorges, "adjoining the east side of Middle Temple Gate." (*Min.*, II, 572, 689.)

Or possibly Manningham's informant was George Chute, second son of George Chute, of Bread, Sussex, esq., specially admitted 19 April 1594,

(*Min.*, I, 366). Whether or not this is the same man mentioned in 1642 as Sir George Chute, of Stockwell, Surrey, is not evident. Sir George's son George entered 24 June 1642, and was bound with his father and Chaloner Chute, esq., mentioned above. (*Min.*, II, 926.)

"the L[ord] Chamberlaine": George Carey, second Lord Hunsdon (1547-1603), was appointed Lord Chamberlain in March 1596/97 (DNB, III, 975), but his predecessor, his own father, may have been meant. Sir Henry Carey, the first Lord Hunsdon (1524?-1596), was a first cousin to Queen Elizabeth, his mother being Ann Boleyn's sister Mary. (Fuller, *Worthies*, p. 236 and ed. note 2). He was described by Fuller as a hard-swearing man, "very choleric, but not malicious." (Ibid.) He was raised to the peerage in 1559 and admitted with Robert Lord Dudley and Charles Lord Nevile, to the Inner Temple in 1561 (*I.T. Adm.*, 42-43).

"one Harlestone": Perhaps Henry Harleston, described as of "poore estate," "sometyme one of the men at armes," 2 April 1584, when he was granted an annuity or pension of twenty marks, in a warrant signed by Sir Walter Mildmay to "Mr. Tho. Egerton, esquire, hir Mat[ies] Soliciter Generall." (*The Egerton Papers*, ed. J. Payne Collier, London: For the Camden Society, 1840, p. 99.) What claim he had on the Queen's bounty is not clear.

Fo. 103. "(Ch. Da.)": Charles Danvers of the Middle Temple.

"(Burdett.)": William Burdett of the Middle Temple (see fo. 102 and note).

"(On[e] King at Paules.)": Undoubtedly not the famous Dr. John King, of Christ Church, Oxford, rector of St. Andrew, Holborn, and future bishop of London, whom Manningham had heard the previous October (fo. 46b, ff.), had mentioned again in November (fo. 58), and would soon hear preach at Whitehall, three days after the Queen's death. Rather this must have been Jeffrey King, a fellow of King's College, who became Regius Professor of Hebrew at Cambridge; he also became a Bible-translator, one of Lancelot Andrewes' Westminster Hebrew group, with the Dean of Paul's, Dr. Overall, and the rector of St. Clement Danes, Dr. Layfield. He died in 1630. (Fuller, *Church History of Britain*, X, 45; *History of University of Cambridge*, 1655, p. 125; Paine, *The Learned Men*, pp. 98, 164.)

"*Risus potest* . . . (Lodov. Vives, *ad Sap*: intr. 439.)": Joannes Ludovicus Vives, in *Ad sapientiam introductio*, in *Works*, 8-vol. 4to ed., Valencia, 1782-90, I, 35. The treatise quoted was a popular favorite, several editions of Richard Moryson's translations being published 1540-1564 by T. Berthelet, John Daye and H. Wykes (STC 24847-24851) (B). Vives (1492-1540) was a Spanish scholar and teacher (at Louvain, Corpus Christi College, Oxford, etc.) to whose writings Thomas More directed Erasmus' attention and whose aid Erasmus subsequently sought in preparing a new edition of St. Augustine. Vives published his *Introduction to Wisdom* on the occasion of his marriage in 1524. (See DNB, XX, 377-9.) Other passages from or references to Vives are on fos. 113 and 118b.

"*E bestijs* . . . *assentatio.* (Idem.)": B suggests that Manningham, "probably copying from a manuscript," had difficulty with this passage, which reads in the Spanish edition of Vives mentioned above: *"Ex bestiis, exitiabiles maxime, inter feras invidia, inter mansuetas adulatio."* (I, 42.)

Fo. 103b. "(H. Gellibrand *nar.*)": [Henry?] Gellibrand, see fo. 10 and note. "A whore . . . from Lond.)": Omitted by B.

"in the tillbuow": The tilt-boat was a large passenger boat with an awning, rowed from London to Gravesend. ". . . I was resolved to go in a tilt-boat," says the narrator of *The Tinker of Turvey* (London, 1630); but while waiting at Billingsgate to go to Gravesend, he chose the barge over the tilt-boat, which was covered. (*Anchor Anthology of Short Fiction of the Seventeenth Century*, ed. Charles C. Mish, 1963, p. 120.)

"Dr. Covel's booke . . . an appology of Mr. Hooker . . .": William Covell, D.D., *A just and temperate defence of the five books of Ecclesiastical policie by R[ichard] Hooker*, against an uncharitable Letter of certain English Protestants . . . (London, 4to, 1603). STC 5881.

"a Ligier in France,": A ligier, or ledger (lieger), was an ordinary or resident ambassador (OED, VI, 172).

"When hir Majesty Dyned at Dr. Caesars,": Queen Elizabeth, on her way to Nonsuch, visited Dr. Julius Caesar at his house at Mitcham, Surrey, on 12 Sept. 1598, spending the night there and dining with him the next day (DNB, III, 657). He entertained her lavishly, with costly presents (ibid.). According to Chamberlain, he "had provided for her eight severall times." (*Letters*, I, 45.) See also fo. 97b and note.

"(Cose)": Richard Manningham of Bradbourne, East Malling, the Diarist's guardian or foster-father.

Fo. 104. "Dr. Holland, Professor at Oxeford,": Dr. Thomas Holland, Fellow of Balliol and Regius Professor of Divinity (see fo. 66 and note).

"by a negative,": MS negatives.

Fo. 104b. *"putentur"*: MS *putenta;* B *putentur.*

Fo. 106. "begge [tte]th": MS beggeth; B begge[tte]th.

Fo. 106b. ". . . in Amsterdame . . . the Damned crue.": These roisterers were not confined to Amsterdam, for a group with the same name under the leadership of Sir Edmund Baynham (Bainham) disturbed London. On the death of Queen Elizabeth, Sir Edmund was briefly committed to prison (the Marshalsea) by the Council for declaring that the King of Scotland was a schismatic "and that he would not acknowledge him as King." In 1605 the Gunpowder Conspirators sent him to Rome as their agent," "to communicate with the Pope after the plot should have taken effect." Henry Garnet, Supervisor of the Jesuits in England, helped him on his way to Rome by a letter to the Pope's Nuncio in Flanders. (B, citing Jardine's *Gunpowder Treason*, 58, 318. See also Chamberlain, I, 190.)

Fo. 107b. "cupshott": drunken, overcome with liquor, from an older form, *cuppe-shotten* (OED, II, 1258).

Fo. 109. "At a Spittle Sermon.": A sermon preached at the pulpit cross in the churchyard of St. Mary Spittal. The church took its name from a dissolved priory and hospital in Bishopsgate ward, dating from 1197. (The hospital contained, says Stow, "180 beds well furnished, for receipt of the poore. For it was a Hospitall of great reliefe.") On Good Friday afternoon "some especiall learned man" was appointed by the bishops to preach at Paul's Cross on Christ's passion; then on the three holy days following Easter, to preach at the "Spittle" on Christ's resurrection. On Low Sunday another learned preacher at Paul's Cross would "make rehearsall of those former sermons," commending or reproving them, and would offer a sermon of his own. The Mayor and Aldermen attended "in Violets" at Paul's Cross on Good Friday, "in Scarlets" at the Spittal on the holy days (except Wednesday, when they wore violet), and again in scarlet on Low Sunday at Paul's Cross. (Stow, *A Survey of London,* I, 166-168.)

> "On Easter Tuesday in the morn
> He rides unto the Spittle,
> And there he sits three hours long,
> And brings away but little."

—so jibed one of the wits in an anonymous poem called "London," printed in Benjamin Rudyerd's *Le Prince d'Amour, or the Prince of Love, with a Collection of Severall Ingenious Poems and Songs by the Wits of the Age.* (London . . . for William Leake . . . 1660), p. 160.

Fo. 109b. "March. 1603 . . . to gett a child.": Entire page omitted by B. In MS two blank leaves (4 pp.) separate fo. 109b and fo. 110.

Fo. 110. "Dr. Parry": Manningham's friend Henry Parry, D.D., of Corpus Christi College, Oxford, rector of Sundridge and Chevening, and future Dean of Chester, and Bishop of Worcester. (See fos. 2, 13b, 34 and notes.)

Fo. 110b. "exculed [exculcated?]": MS exculed; B queries "exculcated": OED defines *exculcate* as to tread or trample out, does not list *excule,* but does define *excude* as to beat or strike out (as well as to find out with study) (III, 389). The word *reculed,* forced back or delayed, was used in late Elizabethan times (see Chamberlain, 30 March 1603, I, 191).

"L[ord] Cobham;": Omitted by B from the list of those who attended Dr. Parry's sermon at Richmond.

Fo. 111. "the Privy chamber": In the palace at Richmond, whither the Queen had removed from Westminster on the last day of January, a windy and rainy day (William Camden, *The History of . . . Elizabeth, Late Queen of England,* 4th ed., 1688, Bk. IV, 659).

"the bishop of Chichester": Anthony Watson, Lord Almoner and Bishop of Chichester.

"the deane of Canterbury": Thomas Nevile, S.T.P., dean from 1597 until his death in 1615 (Hardy's Le Neve, I, 33).

"the deane of Windsore": Dr. Giles Thompson, or Tomson, a Londoner educated at University College, Oxford; Fellow of All Souls (elected, 1580);

Proctor of the University and Divinity Reader at Magdalen; one of the Queen's chaplains. He had only recently been appointed Dean of Windsor (25 Feb. 1602/03) and installed (2 March), "being then Doctor of Divinity, Scribe or Registry of the Most Noble Order of the Garter, and a most eminent Preacher" (Wood, I, 721). Thompson was noted for his natural *ex tempore* wit. He served as translator in the Oxford New Testament group, with Abbot, Thomas Ravis, and Henry Savile (ibid.) and became Bishop of Gloucester in 1611 (Hardy's Le Neve, III, 374). After his death, 14 June 1612, he was buried in Bray's Chapel at Windsor (Wood, I, 721). For notes of sermons Manningham heard him preach, see fos. 113b and 125b.

"hir Majestie . . . by fittes troubled with melancholy some 3 or 4 monethes": Camden tells us that after her removal to Richmond, "the Almonds in her Throat swelled, and soon abated again; then her appetite fell by degrees; and withall she gave herself over wholly to Melancholy." Her grief, he adds, was aggravated by overtures being made by courtiers to her successor: "They have yoaked my Neck; I have none whom I can trust; my condition is strangely turned upside down." (*History of Elizabeth*, 4th ed., 1688, Bk. IV, 659.)

Fo. 111b. "at White hall gates . . . Cecile reade the proclamacion,": The solemn and awesome document of March 24, 1602, as it appears in *A Booke of Proclamations*, 1609, pp. 1-3 (STC 7759, Emmanuel College copy) is entitled "A Proclamation, declaring the vndoubted Right of our Soueraigne Lord King James, to the Crovvne of the Realme of England, France, and Ireland." Cecil had earlier composed it; in fact it had been sent to Scotland in anticipation of the Queen's death and had received James' approval (S. R. Gardiner, *History of England*, 1883, I, 84). Stow tells us that about 11 o'clock it was "distinctly and audibly" read by Cecil "at the West side of the high Crosse in Cheape-side, where were assembled the most part of the En. Princes, Paers, diuers principall Prelates, and extraordinary and vnexpected number of gallant Knights, and braue Gentlemen of note well mounted, besides the huge number of common persons." They all listened reverently, then afterward cried aloud, "God saue King Iames." (*Annales*, ed. Howes, 1631, p. 817.)

"a token . . . the L[ord] Treasurers George": The George is the jewel forming part of the insignia of the Order of the Garter. The Great George is thus described by Ashmole: "At the middle of the Collar before, is to be fastned the Image of St. George armed, sitting on Horseback, who having thrown the Dragon upon his back, encounters him with a tilting Spear. This Jewel is not surrounded with a garter, or row of Diamonds, as is the lesser George . . ." (*Order of the Garter*, 1672, p. 221, quoted in OED, IV, 128.) The Lord Treasurer at this time was Thomas Sackville, Lord Buckhurst, soon to become first Earl of Dorset (see fos. 14, 128, and notes).

Fo. 112b. "The E[arl] of Southampton and others . . .": Henry Wriothesley, third Earl of Southampton, and Sir Henry Neville, ambassador to France in 1599 and 1600, had been in the Tower for two years, for their part in the

Essex rebellion. King James had them released on April 10, 1603. (See Chamberlain, I, 192, and Stow, *Annales*, ed. Howes, 1631, p. 819; also fo. 102, above, and fo. 127b.)

"The L[ord] Hunsdon": George Carey, second Lord Hunsdon, the Lord Chamberlain (see fo. 102b and note).

"one Lee was maior . . . at hir Majesties comming . . . another Lee at hir decease.": Thomas Lee, or Leigh, and Robert Lee, respectively. (See also Pemberton's jibe at the latter, on fo. 113.)

"the proclamacions . . . with names": Thirty-seven notables signed the Proclamation of March 24 "Anno. 1602."—i.e., 1603—declaring James King of England, beginning, according to custom, with the Lord Mayor (Robert Lee) and including the Archbishop of Canterbury (Whitgift), Lord Keeper Egerton, Lord Treasurer Buckhurst, the Earl of Oxford and the principal nobility, bishops, officers of state and of the household then in town, and ending with John Popham, Lord Chief Justice of the Common Pleas (*(Booke of Proclamations, published since the beginning of his Maiesties most happy Reigne ouer England, &c Vntill this present Moneth of Febr. 3 Anno Dom. 1609.* [STC 7759, Emmanuel College copy], p. 3). It was immediately printed (24 March 1602/03) for Robert Barker, who became "Printer to the Kings most Excellent Maiestie." [STC 8301.]

"Mr. Francis Curle": Son, probably the third, of William Curle, or Curll, of Woodside, near Hatfield, Herts., and brother to Edward, Walter, Richard, Petronilla (m. Robert Carter), and Anne (see Introduction). In 1607 he was listed as one of those "gentlemen in particular counties" fit to hold the office of escheater (*Cranfield Papers*, Doc. 1463, in *Cal. of MSS. of Major-General Lord Sackville Preserved at Knole, Sevenoaks, Kent*, ed. A. P. Newton, I, 1940, p. 320).

In 1615 he succeeded in getting the reversion of his father's place as second auditor in the Court of Wards and Liveries, a post his brother Edward had sought in 1603 (H. E. Bell, *Introduction to the History and Records of the Court of Wards and Liveries*, Cambridge, 1953, p. 25; see also CSP, *Dom., James I, 1611-1618*, p. 269, under date of Jan. 16th). Then on June 5, 1616, he was admitted to Gray's Inn, the date subsequently being corrected to "before June 12, 1614" (*Gray's Adm.*, 144, 152). A marriage license allegation dated Oct. 26, 1614, shows that "Francis Curll, Gent., of S^t. Botolph, Aldersgate, Bach^r, 37," intended to marry "Mary Bristowe, Maiden, 22, dau. of Nicholas Bristowe, of Lawrence Ayott, Co. Herts., Gent., who consents; at S^t. Margaret's, Lothbury." (*Allegations for Marriage Licenses Issued by the Bishop of London, 1611 to 1828*, ed. J. L. Chester & George J. Armytage, Publ. of Harl. Society, XXVI, 1887, p. 29; *A Calendar of the Marriage Licenses in the Registry of the Bishop of London*, I, 1597-1648, ed. Reginald Glencross, 1937, p. 30.)

"Dr. Bullein, the Q[ueenes] kinsman": Probably George Bulleyn (Boleyn) the Divine, (d. 1603), or William Bulleyne (Boleyn) the Physician (d. 1576). Both were descended from Thomas Bullen of Blyckling, Norfolk, the great-great-grandfather of Queen Anne Boleyn; but George was more

closely related to Queen Elizabeth, being the son of George Boleyn, Viscount
Rochford, (d. 1536), who was the son of Sir Thomas Bullen, Earl of Wiltshire,
the father of Anne Boleyn. (DNB, II, 781-2.) George Bulleyn, D.D., became
Dean of Lichfield in 1576, succeeding Lawrence Nowell, brother of Alexander
Nowell, Dean of Paul's; he died in January, 1602/03 (Wood, I, 186).

For an account of William the physician, author of *Bulleins Bulwarke of
Defence against all Sicknes, Sornes, and Woundes* (1562), dedicated to Lord
Henry Carey, Baron of Hunsdon, and of other works, see DNB, III, 244-246.
Wood claimed him for Oxford (I, 186), and Stow noted his monument in the
parish church of St. Giles, Cripplegate, along with monuments to his brother
Richard, also a physician, who died in 1563, and to "W. Bolene Phisition,
1587." All three of these shared a grave in the choir with Robert Crowley,
the vicar there, and with "the learned *Iohn Foxe* writer of the Actes and
Monumentes of the English church 1587." (*Survey of London*, ed. Kingsford, I, 1908, p. 300).

The parallel between this anecdote, told by Francis Curle, about Dr.
Bulleyn and his dog, and an episode in Shakespeare's *Twelfth Night*, V, i,
was pointed out by G. Crosse, *Notes and Queries*, 9th ser., VII, March 16,
1901, p. 205:

> "*Fabian.*   Now, as thou lovest me, let me see his letter.
> *Clown.*   Good Master Fabian, grant me another request.
> *Fab.*   Anything.
> *Clo.*   Do not desire to see this letter.
> *Fab.*   This is, to give a dog, and in recompense desire my dog
>   again."

If the anecdote were a new or current one, referring to Dr. George Boleyn,
the Dean of Lichfield, Crosse may have been right in concluding that *Twelfth
Night* had not long been written, though his further inference that the performance of the play at the Middle Temple was the *first* performance is
scarcely warranted. (See W. H. Welpy, "An Unanswered Question, Bullein
and Hilton," *NQ*, CCII, Jan., 1957, p. 4.)

Fo. 113. "(Ludovic. Vives, *Ad Sapient*, intro. 487.)": *Ad sapientiam
introductio* by Joannes Ludovicus Vives. See also quotations from Vives on
fos. 103 and 188b.

"(A gellius.)": Aulus Gellius (117-180 A.D.), Roman author of the
twenty books of *Noctes Atticae*, containing extracts from many lost authors
on literature, history, philosophy, philology, and natural science. Manningham
quotes from I, xiv.

"(Pemberton.)": William Pemberton of the Middle Temple, admitted
26 May 1598 (two months after the Diarist): "late of New Inn, gent., second
son of Robert P., of Rusden, Northants., esq." (*Adm.*, I, 73.)

Fo. 113b. "At White hall, Dr. Thomson, deane of Windsore,": Dr. Giles
Thompson or Tomson (see note to fo. 111). After his election as Bishop of
Gloucester in 1611 he held the Deanery of Windsor *in commendum* until
his death, 14 June 1612. (Hardy's Le Neve, III, 374.)

"Dr. King": Dr. John King, rector of St. Andrew, Holborn, and one of the Queen's chaplains. (See note to fo. 46b.)

Fo. 114. ". . . that many flyes . . .": MS that that many flyes

Fo. 115b. ". . . of the husband . . .": MS of the hubsband
". . . for hir babe's sake.": MS for hir bab'es sake.

Fo. 117. "L[ord] Beauchamp, the E[arl] of Hartfordes sonne, is up in armes . . .": Edward, son of Edward Seymour, Earl of Hertford, and Catherine Grey (sister of Lady Jane Grey) was a claimant to the throne through his mother, of the Suffolk line, although his legitimacy was questioned because of doubts about the validity of his parents' marriage. The Suffolk family had title by an Act of Parliament that gave Henry VIII power to dispose of the succession by will; Henry had directed that after his own children, the Lady Frances, eldest daughter of his sister Mary, Duchess of Suffolk, should succeed. The rumour of Lord Beauchamp's "rising" soon proved false (see fo. 121 and note); see also note on Arbella Stuart, fo. 26b).
    "the Lords sate about it": In MS the word *Council* has been canceled.
    "Portsmouth is holden for him.": In MS *taken by* has been canceled.
    "Ch. Davers": Charles Danvers of the Middle Temple (see fo. 66 and note).
    "a Scottishe Lady at Mr. Fleetes in Loathebury; . . . sister to Earle Gowre,": Barbara Ruthven, sister of the scholarly John Ruthven, third Earl of Gowry (Gowrie), and his brother Alexander Ruthven, both of whom had been killed in the Gowry Conspiracy of 16 August 1600, which had nearly cost King James his life (Harrison, III, 104-9). One of James' first official acts as King of England was to issue "A Proclamation for the discouery and apprehension of William Ruthen [*sic*] and Patricke Ruthen, brethren to the late Earle of Gowrie."— the Earl being described therein as "a dangerous traitour" and the brothers as "malicious persons" who were uttering "cankered speeches" and "practicing and contriuing dangerous plots" against the King's person. ("Giuen at Burghley the 27. day of Aprill, 1603. In the first yeere of our Reigne. Anno Dom. 1603" —in *A Booke of Proclamations*, 1609, STC 7759, Emman. Coll. copy, pp. 9-10.)
    The host on this occasion was probably William Fleete of the Middle Temple (admitted 15 Oct. 1589), son and heir of William Fleete of Godmersham, Kent, esq., deceased (*Min.*, I, 308). Lothbury, a street in Coleman Street ward, was occupied mainly by founders of candlesticks, chafing dishes, spice mortars, and similar copper and laton works, the workmen turning them with the foot, and not with the wheel, to smoothe and brighten them, causing a loathsome scrating noise; but the south side of the street had "some faire houses and large for marchantes." (Stow, *Survey*, I, 277.)
    "Peter Saltingstone": Peter Saltanstall, fourth son of Richard Saltanstall, citizen (goldsmith) and alderman of London; specially admitted to the Middle Temple, 26 Jan. 1596/97 (*Min.*, I, 371; *Adm.*, I, 71.) By an odd coincidence he had come into possession of property in Hertfordshire, Moor Hall in Ardeley, just south of Clothall, where Manningham had inherited "messuages and lands." (See Introd. and notes on Bartholomew Chamberlayne, fo. 36b.) Richard

Saltanstall purchased it in 1598 from George Shurley; then two years later, when Peter married Anne Waller, the daughter of Edmund Waller, he settled it on his son. (*Vict. Hist. of Herts.*, III, 1912, p. 197, citing Chauncy, *Hist. Antiq. of Herts.*)

"Mr. Leydall": Edward or Richard Leydall, or Lydall, of the Middle Temple (see note to fo. 11b).

"Mr. Rudyerd": Benjamin Rudyerd of the Middle Temple, poet, future statesman (see note to fo. 35b).

Fo. 117b. "Mr. Rous": Francis Rowse, or his brother Robert, of the Middle Temple (see notes to fo. 81b; also to fo. 79b on Pym).

"Basi[li]con Doron": *Basilicon Doron. Or His Maiesties instructions to his dearest sonne Henry, the prince.*, written by King James "in nature of his last will or remembrance to his sonne, when himself was sicke" (Chamberlain, I, 167) and first published in Edinburgh in 1599 (STC 14348). It was now given official publication by being reprinted in Edinburgh in 1603 (STC 14349) and in England (entered 28 March) (STC 14350). Five more editions appeared in 1603.

"(Pim.)": John Pym of the Middle Temple, the future Parliamentary leader (see fo. 79b and note).

"Gelderlaund": Gelderland, or Guelderland, province in the Netherlands. Lower Gelderland had joined the revolt of the Protestant Netherlands in 1579; Upper Gelderland had been kept by Spain.

"Jo[hn] Grant": Perhaps John Grant, M.A. (1601), Fellow of Trinity College, Cambridge (1599). He matriculated sizar from Manningham's college, Magdalene, c. 1596, but migrated to Trinity; Scholar, 1596, B.A., 1597/98. His father, Edward Grant, was Head Master of Westminister. Later John took orders—B.D., 1608; D.D., 1614—and held rectories at Benefield, Northants., 1616-23 and St. Bartholomew-by-the-Exchange, London, 1623. He was Vicar of South Benfleet, Essex, till 1641, and died in 1653. His brother Gabriel was admitted to Lincoln's Inn June 15, 1598, but became a clergyman, in charge of St. Leonard's, Foster Lane, 1604-22. (Venn, II, 248.) A John Grent of Detford [*sic*], Kent, had a son and heir William Grent who was admitted to the Middle Temple 3 July 1617 (*Min.*, I, 619). According to Wood, Sir Benjamin Rudyerd had a "faithful and loving Servant" named John Graunt, who, after Rudyerd's death in May, 1658, had a monument set up to his master's memory in the Church of West Woodhey, Berks., where Rudyerd was buried (II, 226).

"Sir R[o]b[er]t Cary": Robert Cary or Carey (1560?-1639), a kinsman and favorite of Queen Elizabeth; knighted by Essex in 1591; created first Earl of Monmouth by Charles I in 1626. In 1601 he was admitted to fellowship in the Inner Temple (*I.T. Adm.*, 159). His own account of his stupendous and controversial ride to Scotland is given in his *Memoirs*, published in 1759 and 1808. As Warden of the Marches he had pacified the border, then gone to London and the Court. On March 19, a Saturday night, the Queen summoned him. "Robin," said she with heavy heart, "I am not well." (*Memoirs*, 1759 ed., p. 136; Harrison, III, 324). Thereafter, worried about the loss of his livelihood and eager to win favor by being the first to carry the news of the Queen's death, Carey wrote to James in Edinburgh, telling him "not to stirr." Then, having stationed post horses along the road, and becoming impatient with efforts of the Council to delay him, he slipped away, six or seven hours after the Queen's demise was certain. (*Memoirs*, 1759, pp. 144-148.) On March 30, 1603, Chamberlain wrote that there was "much posting" toward Scotland, "as yf yt were nothing els but first come first served." Among those who hoped "to be with the formost" were Henry Brooke, Lord Cobham, and John Davies the poet; and Francis Bacon sent Tobie Matthew with a letter to the King. But Carey was acknowledged to be "the first that of his owne motion" carried the news (I, 189, 192). Stow said, ". . . at the first sir Rob. Cary unknowne to the Lords ryd post unto his Maiestie with wondrous expedition, and by the way sent certaine knowledge of all thinges to Berwicke unto his brother sir John Cary, who presently proclaimed the Kings right." (*Annales*, ed. Howes, 1631, p. 817.) Although one George Marshall is said by other authorities to have beaten Sir Robert, he was taken into favor by James, who made him gentleman of his bed chamber and "groom of the stoole." (Gardiner, *History of England*, I, 86-87; Chamberlain, I, 192.) See also fo. 120.

"(Isam.)": John Isham of the Middle Temple, admitted 6 March 1601/02 (about six weeks before John Pym), "son and heir of Thomas I., of Lamport, Northants." (*Adm.*, I, 79); or Zacheus Isham, "late of New Inn, gent., third son of Henry I., Citizen Mercer of London," admitted 8 March 1594/95 (*Adm.*, I, 68).

"(Mr. Wa. Curle.)": Walter Curle, or Curll (1575-1647), of Peterhouse, second son of William Curll of Hatfield and thus brother to the Diarist's chambermate Edward and to his future bride Anne. He was destined to become Dean of Lichfield and Bishop of Winchester. Born at Strafford, near Hatfield, Herts., he matriculated pensioner from Christ's College, Cambridge, c. 1592, but migrated to Peterhouse, receiving the B.A. around 1594-5 and the M.A. in 1598. In August, 1598, he was admitted Fellow of Peterhouse. In 1602 he took holy orders. He served as Vicar of Little St. Mary's, Cambridge, in 1605-6, and received the B.D. in 1606, before going on to other cures in Kent and Wiltshire, including Bemerton. He was made D.D. in 1612, chaplain to the King in 1615, and Dean of Lichfield in 1621. He attained the see of Winchester by way of Rochester (1628) and Bath and Wells (1629). (Venn, I, 433; Foster, I, 363.) His suffering in 1645 when he was besieged in Winchester and deprived is described by Wood (*Fasti*, I, 162). (See also Introduction.)

Fo. 118. "Of a beggar . . . (Dun) . . . still he lyes.": A version of John Donne's epigram "A lame begger":

> "I am unable, yonder begger cries,
> To stand, or move; if he say true,
> hee *lies*."

(*The Poems of John Donne*, ed. Grierson, I, 1912, p. 76.) Grierson notes a similar couplet in a 1607 work by Thomas Deloney, *Strange Histories of Songes & Sonets of Kings, Princes, Dukes, Lords, Ladyes, Knights and Gentlemen. Very pleasant either to be read or songe, &c:*

> "Dull says he is so weake, he cannot rise,
> Nor stand, nor goe; if that be true, he lyes."

(Ibid., II, 59.) B misreads ("Dun") as "D[r]unk."

"in Mr. Nich. Hares companie": Nicholas Hare was the son of the Inner Temple bencher, John Hare (1546-1613), chief clerk in the Court of Wards and Liveries (Inderwick, I, 336, 369, 379), a post that he held jointly with his brother Hugh (P.R.O. Ind. 16776, 32 Eliz. f. 4—cited, H. E. Bell, *Introduction to the History of the Court of Wards and Liveries*, Cambridge, 1953, p. 26). In 1604 John obtained a new patent, a grant of the clerkship naming his son Nicholas in survivorship (CSP, *Dom., James I, 1603-1610*, p. 152). Then in 1613, on the death of John Hare, Nicholas succeeded as sole clerk, till 1618—though he did not actually serve, his fee being paid to his deputy, Richard Chamberlain (Bell, p. 58). John Chamberlain, writing to Carleton, then in Venice, 10 June 1613, implies that Nicholas is "there with you." (I, 457.) Nicholas Hare was of course friendly with the new Master of the Court of Wards, Sir Walter Cope, to whom he was writing in October of that year (Chamberlain, I, 478). Whether Nicholas benefited from his uncle Hugh's fortune is doubtful, for as reported by Chamberlain March 11, 1619/ 20, "The last weeke died Hugh Hare an old rich man of the [Inner] Temple, who left behind him 80000^li whereof 60000^li he devided equally twixt two of his nephewes Sir Rafe Hare of Norfolke, and a younger brother [Hugh Hare, created Lord Hare of Coleraine, 1625] of him that was at Venice." (II, 293.) Nevertheless Nicholas seems to have fulfilled Manningham's expectations to some degree, for Chamberlain wrote on Jan. 19, 1621: "Master Nicholas Hare that was at Padoua died here the last weeke and made Captain John Harvie his executor, which is saide to be three or fowre thousand pound in his way." (II, 422.)

"at the Kinges Head.": Probably the King's Head in Fish Street, an ancient tavern having an unrivalled position near the northern end of old London Bridge and the Stairs at Billingsgate and Old Swan. It was doubtless visited by Shakespeare, Jonson, Beaumont, Fletcher, and other famous writers, since every passenger across the old bridge could see its sign displaying the well-known features of Henry VIII. The vintner there from around 1594 to 1610 was Bryan Kynaston, who had succeeded John Edwards. Samuel Pepys visited this King's Head on October 29, 1664. (*Diary*, ed. Henry B. Wheatley, C 1894, IV, 260.) Even after the Great Fire had ravaged it, the reconstructed tavern had a magnificent staircase and twenty rooms. (Kenneth Rogers, *Signs and Taverns About Old London Bridge*, 1937, pp. 72, 76-77.) It was one of three favorite resorts of Inns of Court men at the end of the Elizabethan age, for to patronize it, or the Mermaid, or the Mitre, was a matter of prestige, if we may judge from a passage in the Middle Temple Christmas revels of 1597/

98 (in which Dick Martin was the Prince of Love—see note to fo. 12b); one of the mock Articles of the "Order of the Honourable Knights of the Quiver," read by the Herald purportedly out of Ovid's *de arte amandi*, goes as follows: "15. That riding in the street after the new French fashion, he salute all his Friends with an affected Cringe; and being asked where he dined, he must not say at the Tavern or the Ordinary, but at the Miter, the Mearmaid, or the Kings-head in old Fish-street." (Sir Benjamin Rudyerd, *Le Prince d'Amour, or the Prince of Love*, 1660, p. 44.) The Mermaid was the actor's tavern in Cheapside (M. Bateson, *Social England*, ed. H. D. Traill & J. S. Mann, III, p. 782). There were several Mitre taverns, including one in Chancery Lane and one built at Ely Place for servants of the bishop of Ely's London Palace, still standing, a popular public house today. The King's Head was demolished about 1898, King's Head Court, No. 34, marking the site today. Another King's Head Tavern "by Chancery Lane" is mentioned by Pepys, April 2, 1668 (*Diary*, ed. Wheatley, VII, p. 362), and it is of course possible that Manningham is referring to it.

"It was soe darke a storme . . . *fiat lux.*": A rather garbled version of lines 71-2 of Donne's *The Storm*: ". . . so that we, except God say / Another *Fiat*, shall have no more day." F. P. Wilson, who first noted this paraphrase, says he does not know of an earlier reference to Donne's verse. The same lines are quoted in Dekker's *A Knight's Conjuring*, 1607 (*Elizabethan and Jacobean*, Oxford, 1945, p. 55). This entry and Manningham's version of the Lame Beggar epigram on the same page show how MS. versions of Donne were "corrupted . . . by memories of conversation and garbled quotation in societies of wit," says W. Millgate, "The Early References to John Donne," NQ, cxciv, (27 May 1950), 229.

"Two were going to washe . . . q[uoth] he.": Omitted by B. The informant's name has been heavily canceled in MS.

"A wenche complained . . . laughing. (Mr. Hare).": Omitted by B.

"(Mr. N. Hare.)": Nicholas Hare (see note above).

Fo. 118b. "Dr. Some,": Dr. Robert Some, or Soame, of Queens' College, Cambridge, Master of Peterhouse, 1589-1609, and three times Vice-Chancellor of the University, 1591-92, 1600 (Grace Book ϵ and Venn, IV, 119). J. B. Mullinger terms him "an intolerant and narrow-minded Calvinist," although indebted to Whitgift for his preferment to the mastership of Peterhouse (*The University of Cambridge*, II, 1884, 335-6).

"(Mr. Isam.)": Either John or Zacheus Isham of the Middle Temple (see note to fo. 117b). On fo. 127b Manningham specifies "Mr. J. Ysam *nar.*"

"one Griffin, Q[ueene] Marys Attorney,": Edward Griffith, or Griffin, Esq., Queen Mary's Attorney General, appointed during the last years of Edward VI's reign, and removed Nov. 17, 1558, when changes were made in the chiefs of all the courts (Edward Foss, *Judges of England*, London, 1857, V, 346, 412). He was a prominent member of Lincoln's Inn, mentioned 61 times in the *Black Books*, the records of that society, from 1523 until his death in 1570. He was appointed Attorney General May 21, 1552, and is referred to as such in *Black Books*, fo. 253, under date of October 12, 1552, rendering Foss's date inaccurate. (*Records*, I, 1897, p. 301 and note.) In the first year of Edward VI, on 16 Dec., he with William Roper and Richard Heydon, Esq., purchased Furnivall's Inne from Francis the Earl of Shrewsbury (who had inherited it) for the use of Lincoln's Inn, who supplied them with £ 100 to pay for it (Dugdale, *Origines Juridiciales*, 1661, p. 270). Later (April 30, 1551) with Roper and Heydon, Griffith, in his capacity as Solicitor General, was ordered to arrest the Principal of Furnival's for non-payment of rent by that Inn (*Black Books*, fo. 239; *Records*, I, 297).

"One Mr. Marrow, late Sherife of [Warwickshire]": Samuel Marrowe, Esq., of Berkswell, Sheriff of Warwickshire from 28 Nov. 1598 until Dec., 1599 (*List of Sheriffs for England and Wales, from the Earliest Times to A.D. 1831*, P.R.O. Lists and Indexes No. IX, 1898, p. 146). He was the son of a prominent landholder in mid-sixteenth century Warwickshire, Thomas Marrow, Esq., of Rudsyn and Barkswell, to whom in the third and fourth year of her reign Queen Mary granted the inheritance of Bermingham, together with the Burgh of Bermingham and patronage of the rectory (Dugdale, *Antiquities of Warwickshire Illustrated*, 1745 ed., p. 633a). Samuel's wife was Margaret, daughter of Sir John Littleton, of Frankley, Worcestershire (*Visitation of County of Warwick* Taken by William Camden in 1619, ed. John Fetherston, 1877, p. 69); of their nine children, Margaret, who married Thomas Compton of Stowe in Staffords., seems to have been the oldest (ibid.).

"(Mr. Wagstaffe.)": Timothy Wagstaff of the Middle Temple, admitted 12 May 1597, "late of Furnifalles Inne, gent., son and heir of Thomas W., of Harbury, Warwicks., gent." (*Adm.*, I, 71.) He and Manningham were called to the bar the same day, 7 June 1605 (ibid.). See also fo. 121. In 1624 he was holding the manor of Metley (*Victoria History of County of Warwick*, IV, 1947, p. 72).

"(Mr. Maynard.)": Probably Alexander Maynard, or Maynarde, admitted to the Middle Temple 7 May 1587, "fourth son of John M., of Sherforde, Devon, gent., and late of New Inn, gent." (*Adm.*, I, 57.)

Fo. 119. "(Dr. Dod.)": John Dod (1549-1645), Puritan divine, scholar and fellow of Jesus College, Cambridge; soon to be known as "Decalogue Dod" from his *Plain and familiar Edition of the Ten Commandments*, published in 1604, in which year he was suspended for nonconformity (DNB, V, 1050). Fuller, who praised him as a godly divine, said that Dod "made to himself a cabin in his own contented conscience" (*Worthies*, I, 279, quoted by Porter, *Reformation and Reaction in Tudor Cambridge*, p. 221). Like Perkins he had a gift for similitudes, preaching plainly but with homely imagery—e.g., he called the Sabbath "the Market Day of the Soul." (Porter, pp. 224, 225.) He preached at the funeral of Cartwright, who died 27 Dec. 1603 (Fuller, *Church History of Britain*, 1655, Bk. IX, p. 6).

"(Mr. Curle.)": Presumably Edward Curle of the Middle Temple, though possibly his brother Walter, the future bishop (see fos. 12, 117b, and notes).

"*Virtus est vitium fugere . . . caruisse.*": Horace, *Epistles*, Bk. I, 1., 11. 41-42.

"(T. Cranmer.)": Thomas Cranmer, perhaps a kinsman of the Diarist (see fo. 66 and note).

"(Fitch.)": William Fitch, or Fitche, of the Middle Temple, admitted specially, 30 Nov. 1602, and bound with Andrew Jenour (see fo. 70b) and Richard Weston. He was "son and heir of Thomas Fitche of High Easter, Essex, esq., deceased." (*Min.*, I, 418.)

"(said B. Rudyerd.)": Benjamin Rudyerd (see note to fo. 35b).

"Dr. Spenser": Dr. John Spenser of Corpus Christi College, Oxford (see fo. 40 and note).

Fo. 119b. "In the afternoone Clapham.": Henoch Clapham (see fos. 55b, 80, 88, and notes).

"(Mr. Key.)": Possibly John Kaye, from Woodsom, Yorks., admitted to the Middle Temple 17 March 1596/97 (*Adm.*, I, 71); or Edward Kye, from Aston, York, admitted to the Inner Temple in Nov. 1594 (*I.T. Adm.*, 140); or Abraham Kaye, of Yorks., admitted to Lincoln's Inn 8 Feb. 1598/99 (*L.I. Adm.*, I, 127).

"Dr. Parry": Henry Parry, D.D. (see fo. 13b and note).

"the Countess Kildare": Frances, daughter of Charles Howard, first Earl of Nottingham; widow of Henry Fitzgerald, twelfth Earl of Kildare Her marriage to Lord Cobham (Henry Brooke), which had been rumored for years, had taken place by May, 1601. In 1598 she began receiving 700 £. a year by order of the Queen. (Chamberlain, *Letters*, I, 52, 64, 86, 123.)

"This day a letter gratulatory . . . in their Court.": Omitted by B, probably because in MS the last two lines are partly canceled.

Fo. 120. "I heard that Sir Robert Carewe laye . . .": Sir Robert Cary, or Carey, future Earl of Monmouth (see Manningham's report of Carey's ride to Scotland, fo. 117b, and note.) For Carey's pains in bearing the tidings of Queen Elizabeth's death to Edinburgh, King James rewarded him by making him Gentleman of his bed-chamber, thereby irritating the envious Lord Mayor and lords of the Privy Council in England so much that he was obliged to withdraw the appointment (Carey's *Memoirs*, ed. 1759, pp. 152-7), though later he made him chamberlain to Prince Charles. Manningham's report of Carey's lying in the King's chamber the night of his arrival in Edinburgh is contradicted by Carey's own account (ibid., 152).

"a proclamacion . . . in the K[inges] name . . . and a restraint of concurse unto him,": This proclamation, given at Whitehall, April 5, is entitled in the *Booke of Proclamations* (1609), pp. 3-5, "A Proclamation, signifying his Maiesties pleasure. That all men being in office of Gouernment at the death of the late Queene Elizabeth, should so continue till his Maiesties further direction." It commended the "earnest and longing desire in all his Maiesties Subjects, to enjoy the sight of his Royall person and presence" which had "mooved very many of good degree and quality . . . to hasten and take their iourneys at this time unto his highnesse"; but it alleged that because of "overmuch, and too frequent resort and concourse" the country was in such danger of being "overcharged with multitude," that "scarcity &

dearth" were "like ynough to proceed." (Ibid., STC 7759, Emmanuel College Library copy.) James left Edinburgh that same day and entered Berwick on the 6th. Among the many state officers who ignored the ban and rushed to see their new monarch was Sir Walter Ralegh (Willard M. Wallace, *Sir Walter Raleigh*, Princeton, 1959, p. 190).

"A letter gratulatory . . .": Printed in Stow's *Annales*, ed. Edmund Howes, London, 1631, p. 818.

Fo. 120b. "Dr. Overall, dean of Paules,": Dr. John Overall (see fo. 25b and note).

Fo. 121. "Mr. Timo[thy] Wagstaffe": Timothy Wagstaff, Middle Templar from Warwickshire (see note to fo. 118b).

"a moote . . . Mr. Stevens, the next reader, and Mr. Curle sate.": Thomas Stephens, chosen for the following Autumn (*Min.*, II, 440). See also fo. 24b and note. "Mr. Curle" is probably Edward Curle (Curll), the Diarist's chamber-mate and future brother-in-law. (See fo. 12 and note.)

"the L[ord] Cobham": Sir Henry Brooke, eighth Lord Cobham (d. 1619), warden of the Cinque Ports (1597)—DNB, VI, 423. This "poor mean-spirited" man was one of the few who attached themselves to the unpopular Ralegh, says Gardiner (*History of England*, I, London, 1883, p. 90). Soon after King James' accession he and his brother George Brooke were arrested on a charge of high treason; they implicated Ralegh, leading to a trial in November, 1603, a mockery of justice in which Ralegh was charged with conspiring with the Spaniards to bring England under a Roman Catholic monarchy—and condemned. (Agnes Latham, *Poems of Sir Walter Ralegh*, London, 1951, Introd., xix.) "Cobham, fighting wildly for his life, said one thing to one person and another to the next, affirmed one day what he denied the day after." (Ibid.) See also Manningham's reference to him on fo. 127b.

"the bruite . . . of the L[ord] Beauchamps rising": Edward Seymour, son of the Earl of Hertford, a possible successor to the throne (see fo. 117 and note.) Chamberlain wrote to Carleton 30 March 1603: "Here was a rumor two dayes since that the Lord Beauchamp stoode out and gathered forces, but yt was a false alarm for word is come since that his father was one of the for-most in his countrie to proclaime the Kinge." (I, 190.)

Fo. 121b. "Dr. Montague, M[aste]r of Sydney Colledge in Cambridge,": James Montague, first master of Sidney Sussex College and future bishop of Bath and Wells (see fo. 18 and note).

Fo. 122. "Exinanition": Emptying or pouring out. OED, III, (1897), 413, cites an example of this word used in the sense of ridding oneself of pride, self-will, etc., in a 1627 sermon (V, 45) of Donne: "This exinanition of our-selves is acceptable in the sight of God."

Fo. 124. "culpa": Thus in MS; *culpas*, B.

Fo. 124b. "his own damme": Thus in MS. B's reading, *dame*, is awkward and misleading.

Fo. 125. "Countes of Essex . . . married to the E[arl] of Clanricard": Frances, daughter of Sir Francis Walsingham, wife (and widow) successively to Sir Philip Sidney and Robert Devereux, second Earl of Essex, married Richard Burke, fourth Earl of Clanrickard. Chamberlain's report of 12 April 1603 reflects a public reaction somewhat at variance with Manningham's: "Here is a common bruit that the earle of Clanrikard hath maried the Lady of Essex wherewith many that wisht her well are nothing pleased, . . ." (I, 194.)

"The L[ord] Keeper . . . Egerton hath married his sonne . . . to the Countes of Darby's daughter, his Ladys daughter": Sir Thomas Egerton's Lady was Alice Spencer, daughter of Sir John Spencer of Althorpe and widow of the fifth Earl of Darby (Ferdinando Stanley). His son John Egerton (knighted, 1603; created Earl of Bridgewater, 1617) married Frances Stanley, his step-sister; the match was rumored in October, 1600, and again in June, 1602, but confirmation of the nuptials did not come until the end of March, 1603. (See Chamberlain, I, pp. 111, 153, 190.)

"a servingman, one of the E[arl] of Northumb[erland's] men, fought with swaggering Eps,": MS has *E. of Northub.* written above the phrase *Lieutenant of the toweres men*, which has been underscored or partly canceled. Northumberland was Henry Percy, the 9th earl; the lieutenant of the Tower was Sir John Peyton. "Swaggering Eps" has not been positively identified. He may have been William Eppes, who (with Roger Marshall) reported "a great victory obtained over the rebels by the Lord Deputy," using only 1500 foot and 800 horse against Tyrone and O'Neil and their force of 6000 Irish and Spanish. According to Eppes' and Marshall's "Advertisements" from "Haverfordwest, 27th Dec. 1601," the English "made execution of 1,000" of the enemy "and took seven colours" (CSP, *Dom., Eliz., 1601-1603*, pp. 132-3). If this was the same William Eppes admitted pensioner from Emmanuel College, Cambridge, 20 May 1594 (Venn, II, 105), and listed in the *Ordo Senioritatis*, B.A., 1597, along with Hollande, Reive, and thirteen others, he must have been known at Cambridge to Manningham and Tom Kedgwin.

Professor Grierson has printed a poem attributed to Donne but probably by Sir John Roe, mentioning an Epps in l. 26; entitled "To Sr Nicholas Smyth," it describes "Natta, the new Knight," an arrogant fool who seized on the poet and offered him the benefit of his experience:

> "I found him throughly taught
> In curing Burnes. His thing hath had more scars
> Then Thinges himselfe; like Epps it often wars,
> And still is hurt."

(*Poems of John Donne*, ed. Herbert J. C. Grierson, I, 1912, p. 402). Grosart declares Epps to be the soldier described in Dekker's *Knights Conjuring* as behaving with great courage at the siege of Ostend, (1601-4), where he was killed (ibid., II, 264 and 264n).

"the L[ord] Latimer": Edward Neville, "that pretends to be Lord Latimer and earle of Westmorland," (Chamberlain, 30 March 1603, *Letters,*

I, 189). He, like Sir Robert Carey (fo. 117b) and Middle Templar poet John Davies (fo. 127b), was among those who posted to Scotland shortly after the Queen's death, to gain preferment (ibid.). Neville also claimed the title of Lord Abergavenny and was so summoned to Parliament 25 May 1604 (ibid., I, 56 and 56n.).

"some 3 or 4000 *l. p*[*er*]*annum*.": Thus in MS and B, although in MS a small zero in darker ink appears to have been inserted after *3* and another after *4000*.

Fo. 125b. ". . . a proclamacion for making certaine Scottish coyne currant in England;": Given at Whitehall 8 April 1603, it is headed in *A Booke of Proclamations* (1609), p. 6, "A Proclamation declaring at what values certaine Moneys of Scotland shall be currant within England." It declared the Scottish "five-pound piece, of golde . . . of twentie and two Carrects" to be worth ten shillings sterling and "The Marke-piece of silver . . . currant . . . at the value of thirteene pence halfe-peny."

"Mr. Barrowes": Probably Isaac Barrow, second son of Philip Barrowe of Moulton, Suffolk, admitted to the Middle Temple, 13 August 1591 (*Min.*, I, 323). Apparently his older brother Samuel, "late of Thavies Inn, son and heir-app. of Philip Barrowe of Issilham, Cambridgeshire, esq.," preceded him (admitted 27 Jan. 1581/82), but is not mentioned in the records after 28 October 1588 (*Min.*, I, 246, 301).

"my cosen Wingat": Unidentified; evidently one of the Diarist's numerous kinsmen in Kent or elsewhere.

"Dr. Thomson, Deane of Windsore,": Giles Thompson, or Tomson, Fellow of All Souls College, Oxford, and future Bishop of Gloucester, 1611-1612 (see fos. 111, 113 and notes to same).

Fo. 126. "Mr. Layfeild.": Dr. John Layfield of Trinity College, Cambridge, rector of St. Clement Danes, and future Bible translator (see fo. 6 and note). MS has a blank space between "his text," and "not preaching. . . ."

"Mr. Hill": Probably Manningham's tailor, mentioned in fo. 102b as "a little pert fellowe," or perhaps Edward Hill of Devon and the Middle Temple, admitted 2 Aug. 1600 (*Adm.*, I, 76).

Fo. 126b. "Dr. Eaton, Bishop of Ely.": Dr. Martin Heton, (1552-1609), Bishop of Ely 1598-1609 (Hardy's Le Neve, I, 343). Born in Lancashire, he studied at Westminster School, then at Christ Church, Oxford, (B.A., 1578), later (1582) becoming a Canon there. In 1589 he became Dean of Winchester, at age 36. (Wood, *Athenae*, p. 719.) Queen Elizabeth gave him the bishopric of Ely after twenty years' vacancy, and according to Fuller, he became a good "housekeeper in that see," (*Worthies*, ed. Freeman, 304), though this favorable judgement is qualified by Wood, who mentions that Cambridge men reported that Heton impoverished "the said See, *by sealing many good deeds of it, and till they were cancelled, it would never be so good as it should be.*" (*Athenae*, I, 719.)

". . . speciall, limited, to those that labour,": Thus in MS. Compare B: "specially limited to"

Fo. 127. In MS after "10. Reficiam; . . . pull us downe againe to synn."
appears a fragment of disconnected Latin verses from Ovid and Virgil, in a
cursive Italian hand apparently not that of the Diarist, as follows:

"O mihi post nullos Juli memorande sodales
O fortunatos nimium bona si sua norint

"Foelix ille animi quem non de transiterceto
Impia sacrilegae flexit contagio turbae

"Si mihi centum"

The second line, beginning "O fortunatos," is a variant of *Georgicon*, Lib.
II, 11. 458-9: "O fortunatos nimium, sua si bona norint, Agricolas!" (P.
Virgili Maronis, *Opera*, ed. A. Sedgwick, Cambridge, 1907, p. 126).

Fo. 127b. "Jo[hn] Davis reportes . . . greate favors.": John Davies, the
poet and reinstated Middle Templar (see notes to fo. 12b, 119, 125, and
the description of his appearance and gait on this same page). Davies was
one of several, including Ralegh, who rushed to Scotland to curry favor with
the new King (fo. 117b, 120, 125, and notes to same). "John Davies is sworne
his [i.e., the King's] man." (Chamberlain, I, 192.)
    "a foolishe rime . . . of Sir H[enry] Bromley, L[ord] Tho[mas] Haward,
L[ord] Cobham, and . . . Dr. Nevil": Among others posting to Scotland, besides Sir Robert Carey, Edward Neville, John Davies, and Tobie Matthew (see
notes to fo. 117b and 125), were Sir Henry Bromly, Sir Thomas Challoner,
John Peyton, son of the Lieutenant of the Tower, and Henry Brooke, Lord
Cobham, Warden of the Cinque Ports. "The Lord Henry Howard [second
son of Henry Howard, Earl of Surrey; created Earl of Northampton in 1604]
was sent thither to possesse the Kinges eare and countermine the Lord Cobham." (Chamberlain, I, 192).
    "(Mr. J. Ysam *nar.*)": John Isham of the Middle Temple (see fo. 117b,
118b, and notes).
    "Jo[hn] Davys goes wadling . . . his arse stickes out so farr.": Omitted
by B.
    ". . . the E[arl] of Southampton and Sir H[enry] Nevil were sett at large
. . . from the Tower;": Henry Wriothesley, third Earl of Southampton (Shakespeare's patron) and Sir Henry Neville, ambassador to France in 1599 and 1600,
had been confined to the Tower for two years, for their part in the Essex
rebellion, Feb. 8, 1600/01. King James had them released as part of his
amnesty toward political prisoners. Stow also dates the discharge the 10th
of April. (*Annales*, ed. Howes, 1631, p. 819.)
    "Sir H[enry] Cock the cofferer": Sir Henry Cocke, appointed Cofferer
of the Royal Household in 1597 (Chamberlain, *Letters*, I, 31).
    "Was with the Lady Barbara.": Lady Barbara Ruthven, the Earl of
Gowrie's sister, whom he had met at Mr. Fleete's in Lothbury a fortnight before (see fo. 117).

Fo. 128. "Mr. Tho[mas] Overbury spake . . . against the L[ord] Buckhurst . . .":
Overbury, brilliant young Middle Temple wit, was noted for his outspokenness.

Here his first target is Sir Thomas Sackville, the Lord Treasurer who in 1604 would become first Earl of Dorset. (See fo. 14.)

"the Bish[op] of London": George Bancroft, Bishop of London from 1597 to 1604, when he became Archbishop of Canterbury (Hardy's Le Neve, II, 302). See fo. 13b and note.

"Darling": Thomas Darling, of Burton-on-Tweed. In 1596, at age 14, he was exorcised by John Darrel, who two years later was prohibited from preaching and then in 1599 was imprisoned by an ecclesiastical commission. Alice Goodrich, who was supposed to have bewitched Darling, was tried and convicted at Derby. (Samuel Harsnet, *A Discovery of the fraudulent practises of J. Darrel*, 1599, STC 12883). On 28 Feb. 1602/03 Chamberlain wrote that "The last starchamber day one Darling a youth of Merton Colledge, (that pretended heretofore to be dispossessed of a devill by Darrell) was censured to be whipt and loose his eares, for libelling against the vice-chauncellor of Oxford and divers of the counsaile." (I, 186 and n 4.)

"passes [?],": In MS this word may be "posts."

"Sir Ed[mund] Anderson": See fos. 30b, 43b, and notes.

Fo. 128b-Fo. 132b. "Some Partes out of Jo[hn] Hawards answere to Dolmans booke of Succession": This work of John Hayward (1564?-1627) (knighted, 1619) was *An Answere to the First Part of a Certaine Conference concerning Succession, published not long since under the name of R. Dolman,* (London, for Simon Waterson and Cuthbert Burbie, 1603), 4to. STC 12988. Entered in the Stationer's Register 7 April 1603. The work resulted from Hayward's effort to seek favor by publicly justifying James' succession and the divine right of kings. R. Dolman, or Doleman, was the pen name of an English-born Catholic writer, Richard Verstegan, who had fled abroad when, in 1582, his secret printing press was discovered (P. M. Handover, *Arbella Stuart*, London, 1957, pp. 101-2). But Dolman was generally regarded as a pseudonym for Father Robert Parsons, S.J., formerly fellow of Balliol College, Oxford, and in 1587 rector of the English College in Rome. Actually Parsons had only aided in revising and rewriting Verstegan's work (ibid., 101). He was (erroneously) thought by Protestants to have urged the Catholics to depose Queen Elizabeth and had published books in Latin and English. *A conference about the next succession to the crowne of Ingland* (STC 19398) circulated on the Continent late in the Autumn of 1593; a large edition was then printed in Antwerp in 1594, with a dedication to the Earl of Essex, for the English market (ibid.). The first part discussed what constituted a claim to the throne and minimized primogeniture and nearness of blood; the second tried in a concealed way to prove that the Infanta of Spain was legal heir to the Crown of England. (Wood, I, 358; Handover, p. 102.)

Publication of this work had profound repercussions, "startling" contemporary interest in the problem of succession to the throne of Elizabeth "into vigorous life." (Ibid., 107.) Hayward's dedication to King James characterizes his work as a "Defence, both of the present Authority of Princes, and of Succession according to Proximity of Bloud; wherein is maintained, that the People have no lawful Power to remove the one, or repel the other."

Interest in the work did not end in the 1600's, for it was reprinted in 1683 with a dedication to Charles II, "for the Satisfaction of the Zealous Promoters of the Bill of Exclusion." (The Yale University Library copy of this edition has been consulted.)

Since Manningham quotes the titles of only the first two chapters of Hayward's *Answer* to Dolman, the other chapter titles are here given:

Chap. 3: An Answer to the third Chapter, which is entitled, 'Of the great Reverence and respect due to Kings, and yet how divers of them have been lawfully chastised by their Commonwealths for their mis-government; and of the good and prosperous success that God commonly hath given to the same, and much more to the putting back of an unworthy Pretender.'

Chap. 4: An Answer to the fourth Chapter, which beareth title, 'Wherein consisteth principally the lawfulness of proceeding against Princes, which in the former Chapter is mentioned. What interest Princes have in their Subjects goods or lives. How Oaths do bind or may be broken, of Subjects towards their Princes; and finally, the difference between a good King and a Tyrant.'

Chap. 5: An Answer to the fifth Chapter, which is intituled, 'Of the Coronation of Princes, and manner of admitting to their Authority; and the Oaths which they do make in the same unto the Commonwealth for their good Government.'

Chap. 6: An Answer to the sixth Chapter, whereof the title is, 'What is due to onely Succession by Birth; and what interest or right an Heir apparent hath to the Crown, before he is crowned or admitted by the Commonwealth; and how justly he may be put back, if he hath not the parts requisite.'

Chap. 7: An Answer to the Seventh Chapter, which beareth title, 'How the next in Succession by propinquity of Blood, have oftentimes been put back by the Commonwealth, and others further off admitted in their places, even in those Kingdoms where Succession prevaileth; with many examples of the Kingdom of Israel and Spain.'

Chap. 8: An Answer to the eighth Chapter, which is entituled, 'Of divers other examples out of the States of France and England, for proof, that the next in Blood are sometimes put back from Succession, and how God hath approved the same with good Success.'

Chap. 9: An Answer to the Ninth Chapter, which beareth this Title: 'What are the Principal Points which a Commonwealth ought to respect, in Admitting or Excluding any Prince; wherein is handled largely also, of the Diversity of Religions, and other such Causes.'

Fo. 128b. "*quod naturalis . . . jus gentium.*": The 1683 ed. identifies the source as Gaius.

"In re concensio . . . putandae est": Cicero (1683 ed.)

"Omne malum . . . perfudit,": This appears in the margin of the 1683 ed.; in the text itself is the following English version: *"And Likewise Tertullian: 'Nature hath tainted* all Evil either with fear or shame.'" (1683, p. 10).

"Licet possint . . . non erubescere (Ambros.)"*: "Whereto agreeth that which S. Ambrose saith: *although they deny it, they cannot but show some tokens of shame."* (Ibid.)

"that is probable . . . doe approve.": "For as Aristotle saith; that is probable which proved men do approve." (Ibid.)

Fo. 129. "(Baldus)": Perhaps Bernardino Baldi (1553–1617), abbot of Guastalla, a learned Italian mathematician and miscellaneous writer of a hundred different works, including *La nautica,* a didactic poem on seafaring; eclogues; prose dialogues; historical works. A linguist who knew 16 languages, he produced Arabic, Persian, and Hungarian grammars. (Chambers' *Biographical Dictionary,* ed. J. O. Thorpe, 1962, p. 81; *Encyclopedia Britannica,* III, 11th ed., p. 243.) Another Baldus was Hucbald, a monk of St. Amand, born about 840; he wrote a short Latin poem *Eclogue de calvis,* known to Donne, for at the end of his mock *Catalogus Librorum,* in the Trinity College Library version (in a manuscript commonplace book, *MS.* B.14.22), Donne appended "Baldus in laudem Calvitiej." (VII, fo. 3. See also R. E. Bennett, "The Additions to Donne's *Catalogus Librorum,*" MLN, March, 1933, pp. 167 ff.)

"aequality and amity scarse compatible.": "For as *Tacitus* saith: *equality* and amity are scarse compatible." (1683 ed., p. 16).

Fo. 129b. "from unity all thinges proceede and are resolved againe into.": 1683 has ". . . resolved againe into the same."

Fo. 130. "*Quae praeter . . . videntur* (A. Gellius).": In the margin of Hayward's work; the text itself reads (in 1683) "and *Aul. Gellius:* 'Those things which are beside the custom and fashion of the Elders, are neither pleasing, nor to be adjudged right.'" (p. 34).

Fo. 130b. "*Protestatio actui contraria non relevat.*": Printed in margin of 1683 ed., p. 46, where the text reads: "It is a Rule in Law; that a Protestation contrary to a mans Act, will not serve to relieve him."

". . . with paricide.": "by parricide." in 1683.

"Obedience in performing lawfull commaundments; subjects in suffering, for ill actions injoyned.": Hayward's text reads, "If he commandeth those things that are lawful, we must manifest our obedience by ready performing. If he enjoyn us those actions that are evil, we must shew our subjection by patient enduring." (1683, p. 52).

"They terme the slaughter of Emperours but interludes . . .": "You terme . . ." in 1683.

"*Omnia rex . . . dominio* (Seneca).": Seneca, *De Beneficiis,* Lib. VII, cap. 5, cited in Hayward: "The King hath Empire, every man his particular propriety in all things." (1683, p. 80).

Fo. 131. "Profanely abuse . . . divel.": Hayward's text makes clear that he is continuing to inveigh against Dolman (*i.e.*, Verstegan-Parsons): "Surely, if you had been advised, . . . you would not thus profanely have abused the Scriptures in maintaining Rebellion, as Conjurers do in invocating the Devil." (1683, pp. 90-91).

"Magistrates . . . princes.": "even as *Marcus Aurelius* said, That Magistrates were Judges of private men, and the Prince of Magistrates, and God of the Prince." (1683, p. 92).

Fo. 132. ". . . which conteineth 3 parts:": For *parts*, 1683 has Points (p. 162).

Fo. 132b. "Sanctity and piety . . . but in advise; and action nothing lesse.": So punctuated in Hayward, 1683 ed. This makes better sense than the MS reading, "Sanctity and piety is in every mans mouth, but in advise and action nothing lesse."

"(Paulus Emilius.)": Paulus Lucius Aemilius, surnamed Macedonius (c. 229-160 B.C.), an aristocratic Roman general and Consul. He finished the Macedonian war and organized Macedonia as a Roman province. Although he brought in vast sums to the Roman treasury from Spain and Macedonia, he is said to have kept nothing for himself. (*Encyclopedia Britannica*, XVIII, 1964, p. 401.)

"a deflowring of tyme": "wasting time" in 1683 ed., p. 170.

"reason of state": "reasons of state," 1683, p. 173.

Fo. 133. "Dr. Parry": Dr. Henry Parry (see fo. 110 and note).

"the Archebishop": Dr. John Whitgift.

"Mr. Savil": Henry Saville (1549-1622), the future Sir Henry; warden of Merton College, editor of the works of St. Chrysostom, and provost of Eton. As a Bible translator he would serve in the Oxford group of eight scholars working on the Gospels, the Acts, and the Apocalypse (Fuller, *Worthies*, p. 659, and *Church History of Britain*, 1655 ed., Bk. X, p. 46).

"the Bishop of Durrham": Dr. Tobie (Tobias) Matthew (1546-1628), of Bristol, future archbishop of York. Educated at Wells and Oxford (University College and Christ Church), B.A. 1564/65, M.A. 1566, he had become fifth President of St. John's College in 1572; Dean of Christ Church in 1576; vice-chancellor of Oxford in 1579 (nominated by Robert Dudley, Earl of Warwick); and Dean of Durham in 1583. His previous "opposicion" to the succession of James goes back to his early years, for when the Queen visited Oxford in 1566, he took part in a disputation before her at St. Mary's Church, September 3, arguing in favor of an elective as opposed to an hereditary monarchy. Then, while Dean of Durham, he had acted as government political agent in the north, giving information to the Queen's advisors about Scotland—"a court and kingdom as full of welters and uncertainties as the moon is of changes," he wrote to Walsingham, 15 Jan. 1593. (DNB, XIII, 61-62.)

On his way to London the King heard the Bishop preach at Newcastle, Sunday, April 10. Three days later the Bishop, "with 100. Gentlemen in Tawnee liuery coates," "royally received" the King at Durham. On the 14th "his Maiestie tooke leave of the Bishoppe of Durham, whom he greatly graced, and commended for his learning, humanitie, and grauitie, promising to restore diuers things taken from the Bishoprike." (Stow, *Annales,* ed. Howes, 1631, p. 819.)

B's identification "Dr. Matthew Hutton" is clearly in error. Bishop Matthew took a prominent part in the Hampton Court Conference, preaching at the close before the King, who admired his sermons, and was appointed Archbishop of York, 18 April 1606, on the death of Matthew Hutton, whom he had succeeded at Durham (ibid.).

"The L[ord] of Kenlosse, a Scott,": Sir Edward Bruce, Lord Bruce of Kinloss, who had come to England in 1601 to pave the way for James' succession by effecting an understanding with Sir Robert Cecil. He was appointed Master of the Rolls in 1604. (B).

"L[ord] H[enry] Howard": Second son of Henry Howard, Earl of Surrey; created Earl of Northampton in 1604. See note to fo. 127b.

Fo. 133b. "The E[arl] of Southampton . . . and Sir H[enry] Nevill": See fo. 127b and note.

"Sir Amias Preston . . . sent a challendge to Sir W. Ra.": Sir Amyas de Preston was known for his valor as a soldier and active seaman against the Spanish in 1588 and in the West Indies in 1595. He quarreled with Ralegh and challenged him, but Sir Walter, who was opposed to dueling, declined to accept; later the two knights were reconciled. (Fuller, *Worthies,* 501).

"Sir Ferd[inand] Gorge": Sir Ferdinand Gorge, or Gorges, of Ashton, Somerset, and M.A., Cambridge, 1594/95, was a naval and military commander and a father of English colonization in America. He served under Essex in Normandy, 1591, was wounded at the siege of Rouen, and knighted. In 1597 he joined Essex on the Islands Voyage. During the Essex "rising" he tried to persuade Essex to let him go to the Earl's house to release the Lord Keeper and the rest of the Council whom Essex was holding there, then to accompany them to the Queen to intercede for a pardon, but Essex would allow only the Lord Chief Justice Popham to be released. (Harrison, 1939 ed., III, 146-147.) Arrested with the Earl, during the trial, on 19 Feb. 1601, he declared that he had been "a great dissuader of the Earl from his attempts." (Ibid., III, 157). Later he formed the settlement of New Plymouth (1628) and became lord proprietary of the Province of Maine (1639). He died in May, 1647. (Venn, II, 16.)

"Crue invited Cobden to a fyre,": Probably Thomas Crewe of the Middle Temple, admitted 25 January 1594/95, "fourth son of James Crewe, late of London, gent., specially; fine 5 *l.* Bound with Messers Simon Wismann and Benjamin Rudyerd." (*Min.,* I, 348). He was called to the bar with Shurland, "Branstone," Brodnax, Horton, *et al.,* 26 Nov. 1602. (*Min.,* I, 428). Cobden may have been John Cobden, admitted to the Middle Temple 15 Feb. 1579/80, "of Wesdon, Sussex, and late of New Inn, gent." (*Min.,* I, 231.) The following entry, dated 24 Nov. 1615, may refer to him: "If Mr. Cobden, who has practised as a Counsellor and worn the habit of an Utter Barrister, to which degree he has never been called, practises henceforth as an Utter Barrister, he shall be *ipso facto* expelled." (*Min.,* II, 600)

"Dr. Parry's note": See fo. 133.

"Dame Temper.": Thus in MS. B adds *ance* in brackets: "Dame Temper[ance]."

"Mr. Hemming, sometyme of Trinity colledge in cambridge . . . at Paules crosse:": Robert Hemming, matriculated pensioner from Trinity College in 1579; Scholar, 1582; B.A., 1582-3; Fellow, 1585; M.A., 1586; B.D., 1593 (Ball and Venn, *Trinity College Admissions,* II, 126). Wood mentions his incorporation at Oxford, Feb. 23, 1590/91: "Robertus Hemmingius, M.A." (*Fasti,* I, 142.) He was vicar of Brabourne and Meopham, Kent, 1593; vicar of Alkam and Chislet, 1594; rector of Harbledown, 1597-1601; and supposedly died in 1601 (Venn, II, 353, citing Foster, *Al. Oxon.*).

"(Mr. Osborne.)": John Osborne of the Middle Temple, admitted 12 Jan., 1593/94, "son and heir apparent of Edward Osborne of Stockbery, Kent, gent." (*Min.,* I, 335). His call to the bar by Mr. [Henry] Haule (see fo. 30 and note) during Haule's reading was confirmed on 14 May 1602, along with the call of Edward Curll, W. Wattes, Ed. Wattes, and [George] Bonner (*Min.,* I, 422). Osborne is mentioned as of the Utter Bar as late as 21 Jan. 1644 (*Min.,* II, 993).

"Tyrone": Hugh O'Neill, third Baron of Dungannon and second Earl of Tyrone (see reference to him on fo. 98b and in note on Eps, p. 398). Called "The Great Earl," he was famed for his leadership and skill in the Irish cause. In 1603 he was pardoned and had his titles and estates confirmed by James I—P.S. McGarry, *New Catholic Encyclopedia,* X (1967), p. 697.

"the L[ord] Mountjoy": Charles Blount, eighth Lord Mountjoy, lord deputy of Ireland; created first Earl of Devonshire in 1603.

"Tirrell": Richard Tyrrel, senior officer under Tyrone. Having served with the English, he used his experience to improve the training of the Irish forces. At the decisive battle of Kinsale on Christmas Eve, 1601, he led the vanguard of the Irish army, together with 200 Spanish mercenaries. When Mountjoy launched his attack, "the Irish melted away," but the Spaniards fought on until three-fourths of them had been killed.—Cyril B. Falls, *Elizabeth's Irish Wars* (London, 1950; New York, 1970), pp. 72, 307.

Notes to the Life

1. *The Visitation of Cambridge Made in A°1575. Continued and Enlarged with the Vissitation [sic] of the Same County made by Henry St George in A° 1619,* ed. John W. Clay, F.S.A. (London, 1897), p. 97 (hereafter referred to as St. George). I am inferring that Manningham was born and baptized in Fen Drayton, where the earliest extant parish registers begin with baptisms of 1576. John is not mentioned among them, though the christening—and burial—of his brother Thomas in 1580 are recorded in the Fen Drayton registers. It is possible, of course, that John was born at his mother's home, at Bedlow, though extant registers of Clophill and neighboring parishes do not record his baptism there.

2. William Cudworth, *Manningham, Heaton, and Allerton (Townships of Bradford) Treated Historically and Topographically* (Bradford, 1896), p. 10. See also *Yorkshire Pedigrees,* ed. J. W. Walker, Harl. Society, *XCVI* (1944), 479.

3. John Ross Delafield, *Delafield the Family History,* II (privately pr., 1945), 516.

4. A. V. Richards, *Victoria History of County of Beford,* II (London, 1908), 219, 257. Delafield, II, 517-518. His father, Thomas Maningham, is mentioned in Fuller's *Worthies* (1662) as one of the gentry of Bedfordshire in 12 Henry VI; see *Bedfordshire Notes and Queries,* ed. F. A. Blaydes, II (Bedford, 1886), 169, 171.

5. Delafield, II, 514.

6. An example of one of the books he compiled is in the Library of Trinity College, Dublin, MS. D.4.24, ca. 1451. See William O'Sullivan, "John Manyngham: An Early Oxford Humanist," *Bodleian Library Record,* VII (June 1962), 28-39, from which I have drawn biographical facts. For calling my attention to this Oxford Manyngham and to the Trinity College MS, I am indebted to Drs. Robert Kreuger and Clare Murphy.

7. "Some Bedfordshire Wills," *Bedfordshire N.Q.,* ed. Blaydes, III (Bedford, 1893), pp. 24-25. Delafield, II, 520, citing Clutterbuck's *History of Herts. Feet of Fines for Herts., The Herts. Genealogist and Antiquary,* ed. William Brigg, I (Harpenden, 1895), 108, 245.

8. *Feet of Fines for Herts.,* I, 201.

9. According to the St. Albans register (Delafield, II, 520).

10. *Visitation of the County of Kent Taken in the Year 1619* by John Philipott, Rouge Dragon, printed from a copy in handwriting of Sir Edward Dering, with additions, in *Archaeologia Cantiana,* IV (1861), 255. This source lists John Butler as of Waisley [Wavesley?] "in co. p'dict"; but the "Waresley, Hunts." given by Delafield, II, 520, is, I think, correct. Butler is mentioned

in the will of his brother-in-law, Edward Butler, 1 Dec. 1561 (ibid.).

11. *Feet of Fines for Herts.*, Trinity Term, 3 and 4 Philip and Mary (1557), *Herts. Geneal. & Antiquary*, ed. Brigg, I, 251.

12. St. George, p. 97.

13. *Archdeaconry Court of Ely, Wills*, 1582-1591, No. 4, pp. 175-176. I am indebted to Miss H. E. Peek, Cambridge University Archivist, for assistance in finding this will.

14. Ibid. See also St. George, p. 97.

15. St. George, p. 97.

16. For permission to examine the Fen Drayton registers, I am indebted to the Cambs. County Archivist, Mr. J. Michael Ferrar, and the incumbent vicar, the Rev. Raymond Pearson.

17. Will of Robert Mannyngham, 1 Leicester, 2 Aug. 1588.

18. Will of John Manningham, 112 Savile, 21 Jan. 1621/22.

19. Through the kindness of the Rev. Harold J. Scott, Vicar of Swavesey, I have been privileged to examine the original MS. Parish Register, Bk. I, which has the name "Manningham" neatly inscribed in bold letters at the top of the first page, followed by the words (barely legible) *Vicarius p[ar]ochialis.* It is followed by the baptismal entries for Nov.-March 1576. In the church building itself Thomas is listed as Vicar there 1573-1603.

20. W. W. Palmer and Catherine Parsons, "Swavesey Priory," *Trans. of Cambs. & Hunts. Arch. Soc.*, I (Ely, 1904), 29 ff. The patronage of this church had been given to Jesus College in 1554, but no evidence has been found to connect the Rev. Thomas Manningham with that college. In fact, as a helpful note from Dr. F. Brittain of Jesus College, dtd. 3 July 1968, has reminded me, the Vicar of Swavesey is not listed in the Venns's *Alumni Cantabrigienses.* An interesting document in the Cambridge University Library (MS Add. 6605, 246), headed, "Parte of Penance Inioyned vnto Richard [Bridgewater] Squire of Swavesye" and dtd. 27 Jan. 1586—when the Diarist was about eleven—bears the signature of Thomas Maningham as Vicar. He died in June 1603 and was buried on the 15th (A. Gibbons, *Ely, Episcopal Records*, Lincoln, 1891, p. 364).

21. 1 Leicester, 2 Aug. 1588.

22. *Visitations of Bedfordshire, Annis Domini 1566, 1583, 1634*, ed. Blaydes (London, 1884), p. 54. See also *DNB*, XVII, 639.

23. Probate of Will of John Fysher, 31 Oct. 1552 (proved at London 14 Nov. 1553), Bedford County Record Office, provided through the courtesy of Miss Patricia Bell, Assistant Archivist.

24. John & J. A. Venn, *Book of Matriculations and Degrees*, 1544-1609, p. 251; *Alumni Cantabrigienses*, II, 142.

25. See n. 16, above.

26. *Ely Episcopal Records*, ed. Gibbons, G 2, p. 183.

27. For this suggestion I am indebted to Mr. Donald Missen, librarian, antiquarian, and collector—himself a resident of Fen Drayton.

28. *Lincoln Episcopal Records*, Bp. Cooper, cited by C. Guy Parsloe, "Schools," *Victoria History of Hunts.*, II (1932), 115n.

29. Brit. Mus. Lansd. MSS 119, printed by Lord Francis Hervey, 1888;

cited by A. F. Leach, *Victoria History of Suffolk*, II (1907), 40-42.

30. Ibid.

31. Fen Drayton parish registers. Robert's will, 1 Leicester, is dated 2 Aug. 1588.

32. The house was purchased from George Catlyn (referred to in the Diarist's will), who died in 1590 without an heir. Catlyn was connected, through his Royden wife and mother, with the Twisdens, who later acquired the property from the son of the Diarist. Ronald G. and Christopher Hatton, "Notes on the Family of Twysden and Twisden," *Archaeologia Cantiana*, LVIII (1946), 44.

33. "Richard Manningham of East Malling, gentleman" is mentioned in Sir Roger Twysden's Book of Musters in Kent, fo. 63, under date of 20 Oct. 1591, when Sir John Levenson sent Twysden the names of nine men who were "either departed out of the Lymitt, decayed or dead." *Kent Records: The Twysden Lieutenancy Papers, 1583-1668*, X, (Ashford, 1926), 78.

34. Died in January, 1597/8, and buried Jan. 30: "Jane the Wyfe of Richard Maningham Esqr"—Register I of St. James, East Malling. I am indebted to the Vicar, the Rev. Derek Chapman, for his kindness in allowing me to inspect his copies of the registers.

35. John Bruce, Preface, *The Diary of John Manningham* (Camden Society, 1868), pp. v-vi. See also Will of Richard Manningham, 30 Fenner, 21 Jan. 1611/12.

36. At East Malling, 26 Jan. 1600/1, Register I of St. James, East Malling. The widow of a blood relative, perhaps of a brother of Richard Manningham, perhaps of George Manningham, referred to as "deceased" in the Diary (fo. 82), she was almost certainly not the Diarist's mother, as Gen. Delafield infers she was (*Delafield: the Family History*, II, 520).

37. Bruce, Preface, vii, and Will of Richard Manningham, 30 Fenner, 21 Jan. 1611/12.

38. Bruce, Preface, v.

39. *Alumni Cantabrigienses*, ed. Venn, Part I, Vol. III (1924), 136.

40. Thomas Fuller, *History of the University of Cambridge*, ed. James Nichols (London, 1840), p. 171.

41. Through the courtesy of the Magdalene librarians Mr. Alan Maycock and Mr. Derek Pepys-Whitely, I have been privileged to examine the MS college records.

42. Magdalene College Register 1, fo. 27b; fo. 4, Oct. 4, 1590; fo. 30a, under "Receiptes of Magdalen Colledge from December 12, 1595, to December. 11. 1596." Also "The Master's Private Book," Magd. Coll. MS, quoted by Robert Willis and John Willis Clark, *The Architectural History of the University of Cambridge*, II (Cambridge, 1886), 364-5.

43. Except where otherwise noted, information in this paragraph and the next is summarized from Edward K. Purnell, *Magdalene College* (London, 1904), pp. 85ff.

44. The Fellows would have preferred the eloquent Latinist Dr. Playfere, one of their own, but the choice narrowed to Clayton and Lawrence Stanton, the Queen favoring Stanton until she learned he was married! Clayton was

elected on 22 Dec. 1595: J. B. Mullinger, *University of Cambridge*, II (1873), 346; Harry H. Porter, *Reformation and Reaction in Tudor Cambridge* (Cambridge, 1958), pp. 204-205.

45. Porter, *Reformation and Reaction in Tudor Cambridge*, p. 195.

46. Magd. Coll. Register 1, fo. 31a. According to a statement signed with the mark of one Thomas Lake, "The 14 of May [1597] ther was remayning of the tymber wch was given to the colledge by o^{ur} founder the Lord Thomas Howard ten stone": ibid., fo. 31b.

47. *Supplicats* for 1596, in Cambridge University Archives, examined with the kind assistance of the Archivist, Miss H. E. Peek.

48. Venn, *Oxford and Cambridge Matriculations* 1544-1906, p. 5. The Magdalene oath reads as follows: "Jurabis quod et singula statuta huius Collegeij inuiolabiliter obseruabis, commoditatem huius Collegij quantum in te est procurabis et obedientiam debitam ergo superioris p^r stabis, sicut te deus aduivet": Coll. Reg. 1, fo. 164b. If the pensioner's admissions fee at Magdalene was the same as at Emmanuel in this period, Manningham had to pay five shillings (Emman. Coll. MS CHA.1.4).

49. Mullinger, II, 401.

50. Ibid., p. 391.

51. Ibid., pp. 401-412 passim.

52. Sir John Hayward, whose treatise on the Succession Manningham would read (see Diary, folios 128b to 132b), had contributed to the luster of Pembroke College by his research into the reigns of Edward and Elizabeth; and the Latin version of Bodin's *de Republica*, 1586, was a textbook in the University (ibid., II, 422).

53. Michael Grant, *Cambridge* (London, 1966), p. 86.

54. Mullinger, II, 428.

55. V. H. H. Green, *Religion at Oxford and Cambridge* (London, 1964), p. 118.

56. On 10 May 1595. In his recantation, as printed in Fuller's *History of Cambridge* (1840 ed., pp. 209-211), Barret acknowledged that he had called Peter Martyr, Theodore Beza, Jerome Zanchius, and Francis Junius, these "lights and ornaments of our church . . . by the odious name of 'Calvinists'" (p. 24).

57. Mullinger, II, 322-329.

58. Strype, *Life of Whitgift*, IV, C.14, cited by Mullinger, II, 334.

59. Mullinger, II, 339.

60. For a detailed account of these obsequies, see Fuller, *Hist. of Cambridge*, 1840 ed., p. 212; Mullinger, II, 340; and Porter, 202-203.

61. Mullinger, II, 345.

62. 12 Jan. 1595/6. Ibid., II, 347.

63. In effect Baro was forced out, but he escaped the fate of Barret by resigning and moving to London. "*Fugio, ne fugarer.* I fly, for fear to be driven away," quoted by Fuller, p. 213. Dr. Thomas Playfere, Fellow of St. John's, mentioned by Manningham, fo. 78b, was elected to succeed him as Lady Margaret Professor (Mullinger, II, 348-350).

64. Green, 125-128.

65. Mullinger, II, 430-431. Grant, 97-98.

66. C. M. Neale, *Early Honours Lists of the University of Cambridge* (1909), p. 64.

67. "Magd: Coll: Supplicat reverentiis vestris Johannes Maningham, vt duodecim terminis completis, in quibus ordinarias lectiones audiverit (licet non omnino secundum formam statuti) vnà cū [cum] oppositionibus, responsionibus, reliquisque exercitijs, per ̧regia statuta requisitis, sufficiant ei ad respondendum quaestioni. Jacobus Wattes p^r lector."

68. Joseph Foster, ed. *Alumni Oxonienses*, III, 966.

69. P.R.O., CP 25 (2), Bundle 160, File 2232. See also *Herts. Genealogist and Antiquary*, ed. William Brigg, III (Harpenden, 1899), 233. The places mentioned are contiguous. Bygrave and Clothall are in the western side of Odsey Hundred, which is bordered by Bedfordshire on the northwest and by Cambridgeshire on the north; to the west are Baldock, Weston, and Willian, in the northern end of Broadwater Hundred, which includes Bishop's Hatfield at its southern end. Between Baldock and Clothall Church lies Clothall Field, about 600 acres of open, arable land noted for barley. *Victoria History of Herts.*, III (1912), 220. For assistance in obtaining a transcription and translation of this document I am indebted to the Keeper and Head of the Search Department of the Public Record Office and to Miss Mildred Wretts-Smith of London. An excellent account of the nature of a "Fine" is given by Frank W. Jessup in his introduction to *Kent Records: Calendar of Kent Feet of Fines to the End of Henry III's Reign* (1955), pp. xiii-xvii and passim.

70. 7 June 1563: Wood, *Athenae Oxon.*, 2nd ed., I (1721), 254.

71. *Dedication to Every Man Out of His Humour* (1600).

72. *Liber Famelicus*, ed. John Bruce (1858), p. xiv, cited by E. W. Ives, "The Law and the Lawyers," *Shakespeare in His Own Age*, Shakespeare Survey, 17 (Cambridge, 1964), p. 80.

73. Six under the Queen's Arms at the east end, above the carved oak screen added in 1575; eight in each of five windows on the south side, but none in the bay window there; ten on the north side in the bay window there, and eight in each of the other five windows on the north side; and, according to Master Ingpen in the *Middle Temple Bench Book*, twenty-one at the west end. Ingpen's count has been questioned by the late Master of the Middle Temple, J. Bruce Williamson, in a signed typescript prefacing an illustrated folio MS volume entitled "Record of the Arms in the Windows of the Hall of the Middle Temple in the year 1602, preserved at the College of Arms." For information about this work, which is in the Middle Temple Library, and for other facts about the Coats of Arms in the windows of the Great Hall of the Middle Temple, I am indebted to the former Librarian and Keeper of Records of the Society. Mr. D. V. A. Sankey (letter of January 22, 1968). Since each of the five side windows is divided by four mullions and a transom into eight parts, each of these eight divisions probably contained one coat of arms, so that in 1602 the armorial display on both sides and at both ends had the appearance of being complete. (Master Ingpen, Introduction to Appendix VII of *Middle Temple Bench Book*, 1912.)

74. Dugdale, *Origines Juridiciales* (1666), p. 188.

75. *Minutes of Parliament of the Middle Temple,* ed. Charles T. Martin, in *Middle Temple Records,* ed. Charles H. Hopwood (London, 1904), I, 246. (This work is, as before, referred to as *Min.*)

76. At least in August, 1602: *Historical Manuscripts Commission Reports,* Salisbury, XIII (1910), 281.

77. 25 Nov. 1584 (*Min.,* I, 272).

78. *Min.,* I, 311, 318, 320.

79. *Min.,* I, 409.

80. *Min.,* I, 386.

81. Order of 18 June 1602 (*Min.,* I, 424).

82. Ibid., I, 382; *Register of Admissions to the Honourable Society of the Middle Temple,* ed. H. A. C. Sturgess, I (London, 1949), 73 (this work, as before, cited as *Adm.*).

83. Dugdale, 201-202.

84. *Min.,* I, 391-392, 401.

85. Ives, p. 79.

86. Boots, spurs, cloaks, and excessively long hair had been banned since 1584 (Dugdale, 202, 191). Earlier, by order of 25 June 1557 sent by the Judges to all four Inns of Court, gay apparel had also been banned, along with the wearing of gowns into the city; no Spanish cloak, sword or buckler, or rapier could be worn in commons; no one under the degree of knight could wear a beard. And moots were not to contain more than "two points argumentable." Charles Worsley, *Observations Historical and Chronological on the Constitution Customs & Usage of the Middle Temple,* 1733, ed. Charles Hopwood (1896), pp. 32-33.

87. *Min.,* I, 418.

88. On 27 Nov. 1602 "Mr. Flettwood Dormer and Mr. Sefton Jones, Utter Barristers, were fined 40 *s.* and then 4 £ each for failing of moots" (*Min.,* I, 418.)

89. F. A. Inderwick, *The Inner Temple* (London, 1896), p. 502.

90. J. Bruce Williamson, *The Middle Temple Bench Book,* 2nd ed. (1937), p. xviii.

91. Ibid., xix.

92. Ibid., xxi.

93. Ibid., xix.

94. Ibid., xx.

95. *Min.,* I, 392, 395, 397, 404, 408. Both of the Diarist's sureties, Chapman and Hoskyns, were fined for absence during Nicholas Overbury's reading, Autumn, 1600 (ibid., I, 408).

96. *Min.,* I, 413.

97. Ibid., p. 416.

98. Ibid., p. 418.

99. Ibid., p. 416.

100. *Adm.,* I, 80.

101. *Min.,* I, 418.

102. Ibid.

103. Ibid., p. 419. Martin and Benjamin Rudyerd seem to have been the leading thespians at the Middle Temple in this period.

104. *Min.*, I, 418.

105. Ibid., pp. 322, 381, 395.

106. Ibid., p. 306.

107. See n. 74, above.

108. *Min.*, I, 246. At a Middle Temple parliament of 28 Nov. 1581 Edward Amerydeth (Amerideth), Treasurer 1574–79, complained of being annoyed by these buildings (ibid.).

109. *Min.*, I, 418. Chapman, Hoskyns, Rudyerd, and thirty-one others were fined 20 *s.* each for absence (ibid.).

110. *Origines Juridiciales*, 202.

111. *Min.*, I, 426.

112. F. A. Inderwick, *Calendar of Inner Temple Records*, I (1896), Introduction, p. lxii.

113. *Min.*, I, 427.

114. Ibid., p. 428. *Adm.*, I, 66, 68.

115. *Adm.*, I, 61.

116. *Min.*, II, 440.

117. Ibid., p. 441.

118. Ibid., p. 442.

119. *Adm.*, I, 73.

120. Dugdale, p. 203.

121. Recorded in Bishops Transcripts, in Herts. County Record Office, and communicated to the present editor by Mr. Peter Walne, County Archivist, letter of 4 Jan. 1967. The sixteenth and early seventeenth century parish registers of Hatfield have not survived.

122. Thomas A. Walker, ed., *A Biographical Register of Peterhouse Men*, Part II, 1574–1616 (Cambridge, 1930), p. 114. William Curle is said to have "earned promotion" in the Queen's service by assisting "in the detection of conspirators" (ibid.).

123. He was thus referred to on 4 Jan. 1594/5: *Cal. of MSS. Hatfield*, Part XIII (1915), p. 524.

124. *Victoria History of Herts.*, III (1912), 91.

125. Will of William Curle, P.C.C. 44 Meade, cited by Delafield, II, 523.

126. Edward is mentioned on fo. 30b and in several other passages in the Diary; Walter, the future bishop of Winchester, on fo. 117b; and Francis, on fo. 112b. The oldest of the Curle sons, William Curle the Younger, had died while in residence at Peterhouse in 1586 and had been buried in Little St. Mary's (Walker, 114).

127. Listed in 1619 as "Richardus, fil. et haer., aet. 11 annor' et amplius": *Visitation of Kent Taken in . . . 1619* by John Philipot, as printed from a copy in handwriting of Sir Edward Dering, with additions, in *Arch. Cant.*, IV (1861), 255.

128. Will of William Curle, P.C.C. 44 Meade, proved 2 May 1618 (Delafield, II, 523).

129. Philipot, *Visitation of Kent.*

130. 3 Jan. 1609/10 (Bruce, Preface., p. vii). Mentioned in will of Richard Manyngham, 38 Fenner, 21 Jan. 1611/12.

131. Bruce (p. vi) concluded that she died between 1602-11, though the span can perhaps be narrowed to 1603-09.

132. For these observations I am indebted to Dr. S. C. Pearce of the East Malling Research Station; to an article by the late Sir Martin Conway, "Bradbourne, Kent, the Seat of Sir John R. Twisden, Bt.," in *Country Life,* Aug. 1918, and reprinted by the Committee of the East Malling Research Station; and to the Vicar of East Malling, the Rev. Derek Chapman, who personally guided me through both the manor house and the nearby parish church. Dr. Pearce declares: "More clearly visible is the floor of the so-called marble hall, which is usually taken to be the paving of the Elizabethan court yard." (Letter to me, 5 Dec. 1966.)

133. S. C. Pearce & D. W. P. Greenham. *A Short History of Research Land in the Parish of East Malling* (1955), p. 56.

134. Will of John Manyngham, 112 Savile, 21 Jan. 1621/2.

135. According to wills of both Richard Manningham and the Diarist.

136. Will of Richard Manyngham, 38 Fenner, 21 Jan. 1611/2.

137. Sympson (1576-1627) was vicar of East Malling during much of the Manninghams' residence at Bradbourne (Grindal, 563).

138. East Malling Register I.

139. Ibid.

140. Not in the transcripts at East Malling but verified by Dr. Felix Hull from the original parish registers at the Kent County Archives Office in Maidstone.

141. Bruce, Preface, iv, citing Faulkner's *Chelsea,* I, 207.

142. East Malling Register I.

143. Ibid.

144. Thomas Philipot, *Villare Cantianum: or Kent Surveyed and Illustrated* (London, 1659), p. 232.

145. Trans. C. H. Fielding, *Memories of East Malling And Its Valley* (West Malling: Henry C. H. Oliver, 1893), p. 71.

146. Prew witnessed the will of Richard Manningham.

147. Philipot, *Villare Cantianum,* 228.

148. Buried 20 March 1611/2 was "maister John Caveel connesyller" (All Saints' Parish, Maidstone, Reg. Burials, 1576-1670). I am indebted to the Rev. Canon N. K. Nye, Rural Dean, to his secretary, Mrs. K. L. Kidman, and to the Verger of All Saints', Maidstone, for their courtesy in allowing me to peruse transcripts of these and other registers in the sacristy of the church.

149. Maningham Walter was buried from All Saints' on 28 May 1619, according to the Register of Burials, 1576-1670.

150. Hasted, *Kent,* IV, 297. Bigons was "a seat of some note," formerly in the possession of the Maplesden family, until forfeited to the crown in the first year of Queen Mary (ibid.).

151. The marriage license allegation is 26 Oct. 1614. Francis Curle was

37, his bride 22. Her father was Nicholas Bristowe, of Lawrence Ayott, gent. See Joseph Foster, ed., *London Marriage Licenses, 1521-1869* (London, 1887), p. 367.

152. *Min.*, II, 592.

153. *Novum Repertorium Ecclesiasticum Parochiale Londinense*, ed. George Hennessy (London, 1898), p. 149.

154. Information from Bishops Transcripts, courtesy of Mr. Peter Walne, County Archivist, Hertfordshire, letter of 4 Jan. 1967.

155. The Will of William Curle, P.C.C. 44 Meade, was proved at London, 2 May 1618, with Edward Curle executor (Delafield, II, 523). By its terms Edward received "my mannor of Buttermer in co. Wilts." and other property in Wiltshire, Southampton, and Hertford (ibid.).

156. Hasted, *Kent*, IV, 512. Compare "argent a chevron sable between three birds gules" in *T. C. D. MS* D.4.24, fol. 4, perhaps the arms of the fifteenth-century Oxford humanist and registrar John Manyngham (see above); also "Maningham; argent a chevron between three crows sable," in *T. C. D. MS* E.1.32, fol. 60, cited by O'Sullivan, *Bodleian Library Record*, VII, 31 and n. 2.

157. East Malling Reg. I.

158. Venn, *Alumni Cantab.*, I, 433.

159. Will dated 15 March 1646/7 (*Lansdowne MS* 985, cited by Bruce, x).

160. *Victoria Hist. of Herts.*, III (1912), 191, 481. Will of John Manningham, 112 Savile, 21 Jan. 1621/2. Chancery Inquests, *post mortem*, Series II, Vol. 399, no. 137.

161. See H. E. Bell, *Introduction to the History and Records of the Court of Wards and Liveries* (Cambridge, 1953), p. 30; J. Hurstfield, "Lord Burghley as Master of the Court of Wards, 1561-98," in *Transactions of the Royal Historical Society*, 4th Series, XXI (1949), pp. 95-114; and A. L. Rowse, *The England of Elizabeth* (1951), pp. 288 n. 3, 319 n. 2, 322.

162. See fo. 30b of Diary text.

163. Bell, p. 25.

164. *Cal. of MSS. Hatfield* (1930), p. 371.

165. *CSP Dom., James I, 1611-1618*, p. 269, Bell, 25.

166. In his will William Curle bequeathed to "My cousin Nicholas Tooke" £ 5 and a cloak (Delafield, II, 523).

167. Bell, pp. 26-28.

168. Bell, pp. 30-31.

169. Prof. Ward of Gresham College, *Vetusta Monumenta*, I, as quoted by James A. Manning, *Memoirs of Sir Benjamin Rudyerd, Knt.* (London, 1841), p. 39.

170. Chancery Inquests, *post mortem*, Series II, Vol. 298, No. 63, cited in *Herts. Genealogist and Antiquary*, ed. Brigg, III, 60.

171. P.R.O., Wards 13/88, Pleadings. This vellum document of 1610 (9 Fev^r.) bears the signature of "Jo: Mannyngham" together with that of [Sir] James Ley and, just above the Diarist's, that of Amherst, perhaps John

Amherst, great-grandfather of Geoffrey, of Jeffrey, the first Lord Amherst
(Venn, *Alumni Cantab.* I, 28, mentions a John Amherst who was a bencher
of Gray's); or, more likely, Richard Amherst of Kent, also of Gray's:
barrister-at-law, 1592; bencher, 1612; reader, serjeant-at-law; died about
1632 (Foster, *Alumni Oxon.*, Early Ser., I, 22).

172. Wards 13/88, Pleadings. "Curll": probably Manningham's father-
in-law, William Curle.

173. For calling this document to my attention, I am indebted to the
Librarian and Keeper of the Records of the Middle Temple, Mr. D. V. A.
Sankey, and for permission to have it photographed I am indebted to the
Master Treasurer of the Society, William Latey, Esq., C.B.E., Q.C.

174. Admitted 10 Oct. 1587 (*Min.*, I, 292; *Adm.*, I, 58). See note to
fo. 39 of the Diary.

175. Hennessy, *Novum Repertorium*, p. 56. See also Venn, *Matriculations
and Degrees*, I (1913), 212.

176. Thomas Seccombe, *DNB*, XI, 111.

177. *Liber Famelicus*, p. 41.

178. *DNB*, XI, 110-111.

179. According to Wood, when Sir Humphrey May was appointed Chancellor of the Duchy of Lancaster, 9 March 1617, he made Rudyerd his
successor and on the 30th of the same month honored him with knighthood—
as cited by Manning, *Memoirs of Rudyerd*, p. 32.

180. *CSP Dom., James I, 1611-1618*, p. 246, cited by Bell, 246. *DNB*,
IV, 1093.

181. *Min.*, II, 711-712. *DNB*, XVI, 514.

182. Ibid., p. 625 (M.T. Parl. of 6 Feb. 1617/8).

183. He seems to have missed only the readings of Autumn 1606 and of
the following Lent (*Min.*, II, 470, 476).

184. Dugdale, pp. 203, 206.

185. "20 May [1612] Mr. William Carter to the chamber of Edward Curll
and John Mannyngham, esqs., on surrender by the latter; fine of 50 s." (*Min.*,
II, 549). Young William, son and heir-apparent of Robert Carter of Hatfield,
Herts., gent., was specially admitted 10 Dec. 1611 (*Min.*, II, 544) and called
7 May 1619 (*Adm.*, I, 97).

186. Richard, son and heir of Henry Parker, of Northfleet, Kent, gent.,
deceased, was specially admitted 23 Oct. 1605 (*Min.*, II, 457), and his call
to the bar of 14 May 1613 was confirmed 4 June 1614. He would go on to
become a Bencher and Autumn Reader, 1632, and Treasurer, 1641-46 (*Adm.*,
I, 84). Manningham received his new chambers by the last assignment of
George Hodder, gent., of Lytton, Dorset; no fee had to be paid, in accordance
with Middle Temple regulations, which required none for a late assignment
(*Min.*, II, 556). The new range, put up in the kitchen garden by "Francis
Warnett and John Puleston, fellows of this society," had been authorized
in 1609. It extended "from the corner of the chamber of Mr. [Nicholas]
Overbury northwards towards the brick wall dividing the kitchen garden
from the Town Buildings, the outsides and the ends to be made of good and

well burned bricks from the foundation to the top": M.T. Parliament of 24 Nov. 1609 (ibid., II, 514). It was ready for occupancy at least by May 1610 (ibid., II, 522).

187. On 21 May 1617 (*Min.*, II, 575).

188. From July 1617 to November 1618; a second-story chamber on the same (north)side of the same building, Manningham having received this assignment from Angell's former chambermate (Sir) Thomas Norcliffe of Nonnington, Yorks (*Min.*, II, 452, 536, 546). By this time Angell, a high-spirited man who had escaped expulsion for illegal reveling during the Christmas season of 1613/14 (*Min.*, II, 624-625), may have settled down, there being no other unfavorable notices of him in the records.

189. Admitted 30 June 1609 and bound with Edward Powell and Talbot Pepys (*Min.*, II, 510); called to the bar February 1616/7 with R. Hyde, R. Pepys, Giles Overbury, and eleven others (*Min.*, II, 614); moved into chambers with Manningham, in Angell's place, November 1618 (*Min.*, II, 633). In 1620—sometimes before 26 May—he "wounded himself" mortally (*Min.*, II, 649, 650).

190. Admitted 13 May 1616; called 23 May 1623 (*Adm.*, I, 105; *Min.*, II, 606, 682).

191. On 6 Feb. 1617/8 (*Min.*, II, 624-625), Waldram, son of Sir Richard Waldram of Charley, Essex, had only recently been admitted, specially, 10 Feb. 1616/7 (*Min.*, II, 614).

192. See *Calendar of Inner Temple Records*, ed. Inderwick, I, 228, relating to a comparable occasion in Queen Elizabeth's time.

193. Hadsor, an expert on Irish affairs, had been Reader the previous autumn, and the Diarist's friends Charles Danvers and John Bramston had been among those providing the feast (*Min.*, II, 620).

194. *Min.*, II, 624-625.

195. Ibid., p. 645.

196. Despite this loss, the Society performed its customary ceremonies, "in amplitude of feasting, and only his personal presence wanted, which would have lent life to learning and moved more mirth to the multitude, all which ceased by God disposing the whole to the contrary." *Brerewood MS*, as quoted by J. Bruce Williamson, *The Middle Temple Bench Book*, 2nd ed. (1937), p. 103.

197. *Min.*, II, 670.

198. Ibid., p. 673.

199. Ibid., p. 676.

200. Ibid.

201. Register II.

202. Will of John Mannyngham, 112 Savile.

203. *Min.*, II, 679. Scudamore, second son of Sir James Scudamore of Homelacye, Herefords., decd. was admitted 9 Nov. 1622 (*Adm.*, I, 113). His elder brother, John, who was destined to become 1st Viscount Scudamore of Sligo in 1628 and Ambassador to Paris in 1634, preceded him, having been admitted in December 1617, at age 16 (*Adm.*, I, 107). Their father, a soldier

under Essex at Cadiz, is portrayed as a pattern of chivalry in Book IV of Spenser's *Faerie Queene* (*DNB*, XVII, 1092).

204. *Min.,* II, 683, 686.

205. Ibid., p. 684.

206. T. A. Walker, *Admissions to Peterhouse or St. Peter's College* (Cambridge, 1912), p. 29.

207. Neale, *Early Honours Lists of the University of Cambridge,* p. 71.

208. Walker, p. 29.

209. Joseph Foster, ed. *London Marriage Licenses, 1521-1869* (London, 1887), p. 882.

210. The marriage license allegation in the Bishop of London's office, dated 21 Dec. 1636, identifies him as "clerk, of East Malling, Kent, bachelor" (ibid.).

211. East Malling Parish Reg. II.

212. A. G. Matthews, *Walker Revised* (Oxford, 1948), p. 187. *Calamy Revised* (Oxford, 1934), p. 480.

213. *DNB*, XII, 960, gives the date as "1651?" Foster, *Alumni Oxon.,* III, 966, gives Thomas' matriculation date at New College as 12 Aug. 1669, aged 18; but on his death, 25 Aug. 1722, he was aged 73 (*Ath.*, IV, 555; Rawl., I, 30; Herne, II, 61—as cited, ibid.).

214. Sir John Ramskill Twisden, *The Family of Twysden and Twisden* (1929), p. 350. Dr. Felix Hull, Kent County Archivist, has kindly supplied me with this information, letter of 23 Dec. 1966. I have been unable to ascertain when Anne Manningham, widow of the Diarist and mother of young Richard and Walter, died. By his will, of 15 March 1646/7, Bishop Curll left legacies to her and to his godson, Walter. She may have lived out her remaining years at Bradbourne. Sidney Lee, taking Hasted's approximate date for the sale of Bradbourne to Thomas Twisden, infers that she died before 1656 (*DNB*, XII, 959).

215. According to Dr. Pearce (see n. 132, above), Twisden "appears to have lived in a number of houses in East and West Malling before finally purchasing Bradbourne House" (letter of 5 Dec. 1966). On 3 Sept. 1653 his daughter Isabella Twisden was baptized in the parish church at East Malling (Reg. III). Dr. Pearce has suggested, plausibly I think, that he may have been living at that time in a large cottage at Springhead—i.e., Well Head—East Malling.

216. Hasted, the great Kent county historian, gives the date as "about 1656" (*History of Kent*, II, 1782, p. 213), though Sir John Ramskill Twisden has declared the date "not certainly known," adding, however, that Thomas Twisden was living at Bradbourne by 1659 (*The Family of Twysden and Twisden,* p. 350). According to Dr. Hull, there is nothing among the deeds relating to Bradbourne, on which Sir John Ramskill Twisden based his work, to narrow the purchase date. These facts and views must be compared with those of the Rev. W. E. Buckland, who said that Richard Manningham sold the manor to Justice Twisden about 1646 (*Notes on East Malling Church,* 1907).

The new owner of Bradbourne, brother of the scholar and antiquary
Sir Roger Twysden, was a shrewd and politic man who enjoyed the favor of both
Cromwell and Charles II. It was he who emparked the lands around Bradbourne.
See Sir Martin Conway, "Bradbourne, Kent, the Seat of Sir John R. Twisden,
Bt.," *Country Life,* August 1918 (reprint, p. 3).

217. Matthews, *Walker Revised,* 187.

218. P.C.C., 466 Wotten.

219. Delafield, II, 522.

220. Ibid.

221. Gordon Goodwin, *DNB,* XII, 960-1.

222. Wing *STC* 504-506 (three editions in 1695).

223. *DNB,* XII, 961.

224. Norman Moore, *DNB,* XII, 959-960.

225. Sir Richard Manningham, *An exact diary of what was observed during
a close attendance upon Mary Toft, the pretended rabbet-breeder, of Godalming
in Surry; from Monday, Nov. 28, to Wednesday Dec. 7 following. Together with
an account of her confession of the fraud.* (London, 1726). I have been privileged
to study a copy of this odd work in the Medical Library of Dartmouth College,
Hanover, New Hampshire.

226. *DNB,* XII, 960.

Index

(Abbreviations: G.I.—Gray's Inn, I.T.—Inner Temple, L.I.—Lincoln's Inn, M.T.—Middle Temple)

Abbot, George, archbishop of Canterbury, 13, 183, 350, 377, 387
Abergavenny (title). *See* Neville
Academic Oration. *See Oratio Academica*
Actes and Monuments of these latter and perillous dayes, touching matters of the Church, 24, 389
"Addled" Parliament, 351
Adling Hill, London, 301
Admiralty, court of, 378
Ad sapientiam introductio, 195, 210, 384, 389
Aeneas, 98
Aeneid, 202, 255, 365
Aesculapius, 228
Alane, Mr., preacher, 20, 44
Albert (Albertus), Archduke, co-ruler of Spanish Netherlands, 45, 121, 306
Albions England, or historicall map of the same island. In verse and prose, 22, 114, 124, 349, 358
Alcoran (Koran), the, 201
Aldersgate, London, 388; ward of, 370
Aldershott, Hunts., 275
Aldrich, Mr. and Mrs., of Kent, 160, 161
Ale, recipe for, 82
Alice, maidservant of Richard Manningham, squire of Bradbourne, 285
Alkam (Alkham), Kent, 406
All Hallows, church of, Bread Street, London, 351

All Hallows, church of, Hemingford Abbots, Hunts., 336
All Saints' Day, Festival at M.T., 265, 311, 312, 319, 326, 331
All Saints, parish church of, Maidstone, Kent, 270, 303, 304, 305, 306, 414
All Souls College, Oxford, 304, 386, 399
Allington Castle, Kent, 275
Altham, James, G.I., 172, 374
Althorp, Northants., 398
Alva, Duke of. *See* Alvarez de Toledo
Alvarez, de Toledo, third Duke of Alva, Spanish general, 43, 305
"Amantius Letus, Esq., Sheriff of Hertfordshire," 324
America, American, 12, 357, 405
Amerideth (Amerydeth), Edward, M.T., 413
Amherst, Geoffrey (Jeffrey), first Lord Amherst, 416
Amherst, John, 415–6
Amherst, Richard, G.I., 416
Amsterdam, the Netherlands, 202, 350, 385
Anabaptists, 60, 169, 200, 306
Anatomie of the Bodie of Man, 338, 339
Anaxagoras, Greek philosopher, 149
Anderson, Sir Edmund, I.T., 3, 10, 76, 95, 236, 260, 283, 319, 330, 341, 401
Andrewes, Lancelot, 11, 13, 14, 61, 259, 266, 300, 320, 384
Androes, Mr., of Sandy, Beds., 86
Anecdotes and Traditions Illustrative

of Early English History, 2n, 302, 315

Angell, John, M.T., 275, 417

Anglesey, manor of, Cambs., 336

Anglicanism, 259, 299, 340, 378

Annales of England from the first inhabitation, 305, 310, 318, 369, 387, 388, 392, 397, 400, 405

Annals of the Stage, 2, 11

Anne of Denmark, Consort of James I, 297, 374

Answere to the First Part of a Certain Conference concerning Succession, published not long since under the name of R. Dolman, 3, 22, 23, 236, 401–4, 410

Antiquities of Rochester, 318

Antiquities of Warwickshire Illustrated, 395

Antwerp, Belgium, 305, 337, 359, 401

Apethorp (Apethorpe), Northants., 305

Apollo, the, room in Old Devil Tavern at Temple-Bar, 4

Apology for Actors, 380

Apology: written by R. Venner abusively called Englands Joy, 11

Arbella, or Arabella, Lady. *See* Stuart

Archduke. *See* Albert

Archideaquila (Archdeacon), Daniel, fencer, 140, 364

Archives, University of Cambridge, xi, 252, 259, 408, 409

Ardeley, Herts., 390

Aria, Francisco, 324

Arianism, 111

Aristotle, 257, 403

Armada, Spanish, 252, 254

Arminianism, 259

Armitage, John, M.T., 363

Army, royal, in Ireland, 381

Arnold, Elizabeth, 284, 285

Arnold, George, 285

Arnold, Gregory, 284

Arnold, John, of St. Albans, 287

Artois, in Flanders, 88

Arundel (title). *See* Howard

Ascham, Roger, 259

Ashforde, Devon, 374

Ashforde, Henry, M.T., 172, 374

Ashforde, Roger, 374

Ashforde, Thomas, M.T., 172, 374

Ashley, Sir Francis, 335

Ashmole, Elias, antiquary, 387

Ashpoole, James, tailor, 285

Ashton, Somerset, 405

Ashwell, Rutland, 333

Assyria, 197

Aston Hall, 306

Aston Sub edge, Glos., 310

Aston, Yorks., 396

Atmore, licensed to cast tin, 45, 307

Atticus, Titus Pomponius, Roman literary patron, 212

Aubigny (title). *See* Stuart, Esmé

Aubrey, John, 10, 335

Augustine. *See* St. Augustine

Aurelius, Marcus, 404

Authorized Version of the Bible, 12, 13, 14, 257, 300, 302, 320, 361, 362, 364, 366–7, 372, 384, 387, 399, 404

Autobiography of Sir John Bramston K.B., of Skreens, 328

Aylesford, Kent, 50, 316; Lathe of, 303

Aylmer, John, bishop of London, 84

Babraham, Cambs., 337

Bachellor, Joane, 19, 52

Bacon, Sir Francis, Viscount St. Albans, 3, 8, 12, 100, 122, 273, 318, 323, 355, 357, 364, 369, 392

Baker, Jasper, M.T., 355

Baker, John, of Sinsinghurst, Kent, 318

Baker, Sir John, 306

Baker, Richard, 299

Baldi, Bernardino, abbot of Guastalla, 403

Baldock, Herts., 252, 253, 260, 283, 336, 411
Baldus, 237, 403. *See also* Hucbald
Baldwyne [William Baldwyn, printer?], 173
Balguy (Balgay), Nicholas, 299
Ball, Captain, 347
Ball, Nicholas, 347
Balliol College, Oxford, 58, 71, 320, 331, 338, 358, 362, 375, 385, 401
Balloon, game of, 371
Bancroft, George, bishop of London, afterward archbishop of Canterbury, 16, 49, 84, 122, 235, 316, 356, 401
Banes, Thomas, citizen and sadler of London, 273
Bankside, Southwark, 10, 187, 358, 379
Barbers' Company, 339
Barker, Francis, M.T., master butler, 89, 118, 340, 351
Barker, Lawrence, preacher, 67, 321
Barker, Robert, I.T., 172, 173, 374
Barker, Robert, King's printer, 388
Barker, Will, 321
Barlow, Randolph, preacher, 164, 373
Barlowe, William, bishop of Chichester, 338
Barlowe, William, bishop of Rochester, 14, 18, 87, 338, 364
Barlowe, William, chaplain to Prince Henry, archdeacon of Salisbury, 338
Barnard's Inn, 357
Barnstable, Devon, 346
Barnston, Essex, 320
Baro, Peter, Lady Margaret Professor of Divinity, 258-9, 410
Barret, William, master of Gonville and Caius College, 258, 410
Barrington, Somerset, 330
Barrow (Barrowe), Isaac, M.T., 231, 399
Barrowe, Philip, 399

Barrowe, Samuel, M.T., 399
Barrs Court, Herefords., 315
Basilicon Doron, Or His Maiesties instructions to his dearest sonne Henry, the prince, 218, 391
Basset, Sir Richard, 97, 343
Bastard, Thomas, 324
Bath, Somerset, 380; bishop or diocese of Bath and Wells, 5, 194, 319, 326, 383, 392, 397
Bayliffe, John, M.T., 370
Baynham (Bainham), Sir Edmund, 385
Bayonne, France, 315
Bear-baiting, 52
Beauchamp (title). *See* Seymour
Beaufort, Margaret Lady, 259
Beaumont, Francis, judge of Common Pleas, 260, 283
Beaumont, Francis, poet, 393
Beckingham (b. Pigott), Elizabeth, 272
Beckingham, Steven, 7, 99
Bede (Baeda) (Beda), the Venerable, 40, 59, 359
Bedford, Beds., 298, 408
Bedfordshire, 253, 407, 408, 411
Bedlow, Beds., 251, 253, 254, 407
Bedlow Farm, near Clophill, Beds., 253, 407
Beeching, Nicholas, 291
Belhaven (title). *See* Douglas
Bellarmine, Robert, cardinal, 360
Bellingham, Alan, 334
Bellingham, Henry, M.T., epitaph of, 83, 334
Bemerton, Wilts., 271, 392
Benedict, Saint, of Nursia, pope, 60
Benefield, Northants., 391
Benn (Benne), Anthony, M.T., 360
Benn (Benne), Robert, 360
Bennet, Richard, M.T., 71, 130, 141, 267, 326, 360, 365
Bennett, Mr., surgeon, 87
Bennett, Robert, 326, 360

Berkshire, 124, 194, 326; nude dancers in, 124
Berkswell, Warwicks., 395
Bermingham (Birmingham), Warwicks., 395
Bernard. *See* St. Bernard
Berthelet, Thomas, royal printer, bookseller, bookbinder, 384
Berwick, Northumberland, 245, 323, 392, 397
Besselles, Goris, merchant, 255, 285
Best, John, 275
Best, Richard, M.T., 275
Bevyll, Sir William, 315
Beza, Theodore, 410
Bible, King James Version. *See* Authorized Version
Bible, translations, 12, 13, 14, 159, 190, 257, 300, 302, 320, 336-7, 361, 362, 364, 366, 372, 384, 387, 399, 404
Bigges, George, thatcher, 252
Bigges (b. Manningham), Elizabeth, Diarist's aunt, 252
Bigges, John, 252
Bigons (Digons), Maidstone, Kent, 271, 329, 414
Bigrave (Bygrave), Herts., 253, 260, 283, 336, 411
Billingsgate, London, 385, 393
Bilson, Thomas, bishop, 85, 163, 336, 337, 372-3
Binderton, Sussex, 275
Bindon (title). *See* Howard
Birchott Franchises, Hundred of, Kent, 318
Bisham, Berks., 382
Bishop, Roger, I.T., epitaph of, 83, 334
Bishopcastle, Salop, 340
Bishop's Compton, prebendary of Wells Cathedral, 372
Bishopsgate, London, 15; street, 15, 82, 333; ward, 386
Bishop's Hatfield, Herts., 268, 271, 273, 318, 411, 413

Black Bear, Cambridge inn, 259
"Black Tom." *See* Butler, Thomas, tenth Earl of Ormonde
Blackbourne, Henry, I.T., 123, 356
Blackburn (Blackborne), Lancs., grammar school, 305
Blackfriars, London, 151, 350, 367, 368, 382
Blackwell, **Bridget**. *See* Manningham
Blackwell, George, arch-priest, 154, 368
Blakesley, Northants., 327
Bland, John, 306
Bletsoe, Beds., 381
Blithe (Blythe) scholarship, at Peterhouse, 277
Blount, Charles, eighth Lord Mountjoy, first Earl of Devonshire, lord deputy of Ireland, 96, 119, 155, 247, 361, 398, 406
Blundell. *See* Blunden
Blunden, Andrew, M.T., 89, 340
Blunte (Blount), Edward, M.T., 122, 265, 355, 381
Blunte (Blount), Edward, bookseller, 355
Blunte (Blount), Thomas, 355
Blyckling, Norfolk, 388
Bodin, Jean, 127, 410
Bodleian Library, Oxford, 186, 347
Bodley (b. Carew) (Ball), Anne Lady, 100, 186, 347
Bodley, Elizabeth. *See* Winwood
Bodley, Sir Thomas, 5, 9, 100, 186, 346, 347, 348, 378
Bois (Boyes), John, 302
Boleyn, Anne, Queen of England, 384, 388, 389
Boleyn (Bulleyn), George, D.D., 210, 388-9
Boleyn, George, Viscount Rochford, 389
Boleyn, Mary, 384
Boleyn (Bolene), Richard, physician, 389

Boleyn (Bullen), Sir Thomas, Earl of Wilts., 389
Boleyn (Bullen), Thomas, 388
Boleyn (Bulleyn), William, physician, 210, 388-9
Bond, Nicholas, 370
Bonner, Edmund, bishop of London, 132, 361
Bonner, George, M.T., 406
Booke of Proclamations, 308, 387, 388, 390, 396, 399
Booth, indicted for forgery, 97
Boscawen, Hugh, M.T., 262
Bothwell (title). *See* Hepburn
Boughton, Harry, 321
Bouillon, Duc de. *See* D'Auvergne
Bourbrough, West Flanders, 277
Bourne, Benedicta ("Bennet"), 5, 380. *See also* Hoskyns
Bourne, Francis, M.T., 380
Bovingdon, Herts., 337
Bowghton, William, M.T., 262
Bowhay, Devon, 374
Bowyer, Francis, 362
Boxley Abbey, Kent, 339
Boxley, Kent, 304, 339
Boxworth, manor of, Cambs., 373
Boyle, Elizabeth, 274
Brabourne, Kent, 318, 406
Bradbourne, manor of, East Malling, Kent, 1, 19, 41, 50, 51, 88, 159, 251, 255, 263, 265, 266, 267, 268, 269, 270, 271, 276, 277, 286, 290, 291, 303, 305, 316, 334, 338, 339, 371, 385, 414, 418-9
Bradford, manor of, Yorks., 251, 407
Bradnux. *See* Brodnax
Bradshaws Rents. *See* Tanfield Court
Bramber, Sussex, 319
Bramston, John, M.T., future Lord Chief Justice, 3, 18, 75, 78, 97, 141, 154, 155, 172, 267, 274, 275, 276, 298, 311, 328, 332, 344, 365, 368, 370, 374, 405, 417
Bramston, Sir John, the Younger, 328

Bramston (Bramstone), Roger, M.T., 352
Brasenose College, Oxford, 362, 363
Bray's Chapel, Windsor, 387
Bread Street, London, 351
Bread, Sussex, 383
Bredger, John, 287
Brerewood MS, 417
Brewer, Richard, 287
Brick Court, M.T., 261, 266
Brickenden, Alexander, 285
Bridewell, London, 321
Bridget, Elizabeth Lady, 141, 365
Bridgewater, Richard, 408
Bridgman, John, mayor of New Hythe, Kent, epitaph of, 83
Brie, France, 367
Brief Lives, by Aubrey, 10, 335
Briefe of the Bible drawne first into English Poësy, and then illustrated by apte Annotations, 350
Brief Method of Catechizing, 350
Brigham, Thomas, 307
Bristol, Glos., 259, 298, 347, 375, 379, 404; bishop of, 302, 351
Bristowe, Mary, 271, 388, 415
Bristowe, Nicholas, 388, 415
Broadgates Hall, Oxford. *See* Pembroke College
Broadwater Hundred, Herts., 411
Brockett Hall, Herts., 337, 373
Brockett, Sir John, 337, 373
Brockett, Mrs. *See* North
Brodnax family, of Godmersham, Kent, 271
Brodnax (b. Taylor), Elizabeth, 324
Brodnax, Thomas, 324
Brodnax, Thomas, M.T., 324
Brodnax, William, M.T., 70, 122, 141, 267, 324, 356, 365, 405
Brome, Alexander, 4n
Bromley (Bromly), Sir Henry, 23, 235, 400
Brooke, Christopher, 273, 346, 367

Brooke, George, 323, 397

Brooke, Henry, eighth Lord Cobham, 17, 23, 41, 207, 224, 235, 317, 323, 333, 386, 392, 397, 400

Brooke (b. Howard) (Fitzgerald), Frances, Lady Cobham, formerly Countess of Kildare, 17, 181, 222, 396

Brooke, Samuel, preacher, 367

Brooke Street, London, 353

Brooke, William, tenth Lord Cobham, 330

Broxborne, Herts., 277

Bruce, Edward, Lord Bruce of Kinloss, 245, 405

Bruce, John, editor, 1 and passim; omissions by, 21–22

Brymour (Brymore House), Somerset, 370

Buccina Capelli in Laudem juris, 149, 367

Buckeridge (Buckridge), John, bishop of Rochester, 73, 259, 299, 319, 326, 328, 351

Buckhurst (title). *See* Sackville

Buckingham, Earl of, Duke of. *See* Villiers

Buckwell, Kent, 380

Bull, Richard, 362

Bulleins Bulwarke of Defence against all Sicknes, Sornes, and Woundes, 389

Bulleyn, Bullen. *See* Boleyn

Burbage, Richard, actor, 3, 10, 75, 266, 313, 319, 328

Burby (Burbie), Cuthbert, bookseller, 401

Burbonius, Henricus. *See* Henri IV

Burchely, Mr., lawyer, 148

Burdett, Humfrey, 383

Burdett, William, M.T., 194, 195, 246, 308, 383, 384

Burford, Oxon, 335, 343

Burghersh. *See* Vane, Francis

Burghley House, gate of, 46

Burghley House, Northants., 390

Burghley, Lord. *See* Cecil, William

Burke (or de Burgh), Richard, of Kinsale, fourth Earl of Clanrickard, first Earl of St. Albans, 96, 224, 231, 337, 342, 398

Burke (b. Walsingham) (Sidney) (Devereux), Frances, Countess of St. Albans, 231, 337, 398

Burkes, adherents to the Lord Deputy in Ireland, 119

Burnham, watergate officer at Flushing, 52

Burton, Robert, x

Burton-on-Tweed, 401

Bury St. Edmunds, Suffolk, 254

Butler (Boteler), Beckingham, 272, 290

Butler (Boteler), John, 252, 407–8

Butler, Edward, 408

Butler (b. Pigott), Elizabeth, 272

Butler, Richard, 292

Butler, Thomas, tenth Earl of Ormonde and Ossory, Viscount Thurles, 96, 154, 343

Buttermere, manor of, Wilts., 415

Buttler, Mr. *See* Barker, Francis

Byrd, Sir William, 292

Cadiz, Spain, 344, 376, 418

Caesar (b. Greene) (Dent), Alice Lady, 196

Caesar, Gaius Julius, 128

Caesar, Dr. Julius, 3, 9, 186, 196, 319, 346, 378, 385

Caesar's buildings, 378

Calborne (Colberne), Henry, L.I., 366

Calendar of Sir Roger Twysden's Collections of Lieutenancy Papers, 303

Calendar, Jewish, 222

Calling, doctrine of the, 151, 232

Calvin, John, 258

Calvinism, Calvinists, 258, 259, 299, 302, 354, 370, 394, 410

Cam, river, in Cambs., 256

Cambridge, Cambs., city of, 251, 336, 354; university of, 5, 39, 86, 116, 121, 131, 142, 151, 155, 164, 186, 225, 246, 252, 254, 255, 256, 258, 261, 277, 278, 297, 298, 301, 302, 303, 320, 328, 333, 369, 370, 372, 373, 379, 384, 392, 394, 395, 397, 398, 399, 408, 410, 411, 413
Cambridgeshire, 289, 411
Camden, William, 307, 327, 347, 352, 374, 386, 387, 395
Campion, Edmund, 162, 372
Campton, Beds., 253
Candlemas Day, celebration of, 11, 262, 265, 312
Canterbury, archbishop of, 13, 15, 16, 53, 68, 163, 207, 245, 258, 259, 314, 316, 318, 321, 350, 356, 361, 377, 388, 401; archdeacon of, 314, 361; city in Kent, 161, 162, 164, 256, 267, 271, 371; dean of (Thomas Nevile), 16, 207, 235, 256, 257, 386, 400; doctrines of, 299; Prerogative Court, 287, 292, 304; registrar of Ecclesiastical Court, 256, 315, 371
Canticles (Song of Songs), 349
Cappel, Jacques, 149, 367
Carden, Sir Thomas, 368
Carew, Sir George, 274
Carey, George, second Lord Hunsdon, 210, 384, 388
Carey, Henry, first Lord Hunsdon, 194, 384, 389
Carey, Sir John, 323, 392
Carey, Robert, first Earl of Monmouth, 23, 219, 223, 391-2, 396, 399, 400
Carhampton, Somerset, 383
Carleton, Sir Dudley, afterward first Viscount Dorchester, 25, 310, 318, 321, 344, 347, 348, 349, 355, 357, 358, 367, 368, 369, 393, 397
Caroline period, 3
Carpe diem, theme of, 190-1, 222

Carr (b. Howard) (Devereux), Frances, Countess of Somerset, 6, 310, 337
Carr, Sir Robert, Viscount Rochester, Earl of Somerset, 6, 274
Carrick, Ireland, 343
Carter (b. Curle), Petronell or Petronilla, 268, 273, 388
Carter, Robert, 268, 273, 388, 416
Carter, William, M.T., 275, 416
Cartwright, Hugh, 41, 50, 51, 303, 316, 317, 334
Cartwright (b. Newton), Jane. See Fitzjames
Cartwright, Thomas, puritan divine, 118, 258, 352, 395
Cary, Lucius, second Viscount Falkland, 309, 343
Cassandra, 123
Catalogus Librorum Aulicorum (The Courtier's Library), satire by Donne, 8, 310, 312, 330, 343, 350, 359, 403
Catheter, use of, 52, 318
Catholics, 353, 359-60, 372, 375, 401; persecution of, 51, 378-9; moderate English, 322; toleration for, 323. See also Papists
Catlin, Richard, L.I., 366
Catlin, Sir Robert, 148, 366
Catlyn (Catlin), Edmund, 291
Catlyn (Catlin), George, 50, 290, 316, 409
Catlyn (Catlin), Hugh, 316
Catlyn, Richard, 316
Cato, Marcus Porcius, 129
Cavell (Cavill), Elizabeth, 44, 306
Cavell, John, M.T., 265, 267, 270, 306, 414
Cecil, Robert, Viscount Cranborne, first Earl of Salisbury, 3, 16, 23, 48, 76, 96, 119, 123, 150, 208, 224, 236, 257, 271, 272, 296, 311, 314, 315, 318, 323, 329, 337, 340, 341, 342, 344, 355, 356, 367, 387, 405
Cecil, Thomas, second Lord

Burghley, first Earl of Exeter, 329

Cecil, William, first Lord Burghley, 46, 70, 98, 123, 209, 257, 259, 272, 315, 323, 330, 332-3, 356, 357, 415

Certaine godly and learned sermons, 302

Cesare (*Gl'Inganni*), 314

Chaderton, Laurence, 13, 258

Chaloner (Challoner), Sir Thomas, 400

Chamberlain, John, letter-writer, 11, 25, 298, 300, 310, 317-8, 321, 323, 325, 341, 344-5, 347, 348, 355, 357, 358, 360, 363, 364, 365, 366, 367, 368, 369, 370, 374, 375, 379, 380, 382, 385, 386, 388, 390, 391, 392, 393, 396, 397, 398, 400, 401

Chamberlain, Richard, 393

Chamberlaine (Chamberlayne) (Chamberleyne), Bartholomew, 85, 86, 255, 260, 266, 283, 298, 335-6, 338, 390

Chamberlaine (Chamberlayne) (Chamberleyne), Joan, 260, 283, 336

Chancery, court of, Westminster, 272

Chancery, Inns of. *See* Inns

Chancery Lane, London, 394

Chapman, Drew, 1, 43, 164, 255, 267, 304, 371

Chapman family, of Godmersham, Kent, 267, 271

Chapman, George, poet, 344

Chapman, Henry, 343

Chapman, John, M.T., 1, 4, 7, 9, 97, 161, 164, 255, 262, 265, 267, 304, 343, 371, 382, 412, 413

Charing Cross, London, 307

Charles I, King of England, 332, 334, 335, 375, 376, 391, 396

Charles II, King of England, 274, 278, 402, 419

Charles V, Holy Roman Emperor, 78, 333

Charles de Lorraine, archbishop of Rheims and cardinal of Lorraine, 175

Charles Emmanuel, Duke of Savoy, 154

Charles, Prince. *See* Charles I

Charley, Essex, 417

Charterhouse, the, London, 374

Chaucer, Geoffrey, 41; Chaucerian tale, 349

Cheapside, London, 16, 53, 208, 321, 387, 394

Cheke, John, 259

Chelsea, church at, Middlesex, 270

Cheshire, 318

Cheshunt, Herts., 314

Chester, Cheshire, cathedral, 363; chief judge at, 344; dean of, 15, 297, 338, 364, 386

Chevening, Kent, 266, 297, 307, 339, 386

Chichester, West Sussex, bishop of, 16, 207, 251, 278, 320, 338, 348, 386; M.P. for, 341; recorder of, 341; prebendary of, 302

Chichley, Sir Thomas, 373

Child, Mr., epitaph of, 47

Childerley, Cambs., 373

Chilham, manor and castle of, Kent, 373

China, country of, 367

Chislehurst, Kent, 304

Chislet, Kent, 406

Chrestoleros, by Bastard, 324

Christ Church, Dublin, 373

Christ Church, Oxford, 29, 315, 322, 347-8, 349, 353, 384, 399, 404

Christian IV, King of Denmark, 15, 297

Christmas revels 1597/8, at Middle Temple. *See* Prince d'Amour

Christ's College, Camb., 277, 319, 354, 366, 370, 392

Chronicles of England, 361
Church-History of Britaine, 361, 362, 366, 384, 395, 404
Church of England, 94, 111, 222, 299, 349, 378. *See also* Foxe, Hooker, et al.
Chute, Chaloner, M.T., 383, 384
Chute, Charles, M.T., 194, 383
Chute, George, of Bread, Sussex, 383
Chute, George, M.T., son of George C. of Bread, 383
Chute, George, M.T., son of Sir George C. of Stockwell, Surrey, 384
Chute, Sir George, of Stockwell, 384
Cicero, Marcus Tullius, 40, 74, 236, 239, 257, 403
Cinque Ports, the, 307, 333, 397, 400
Civil War, 318
Clanrickard (title). *See* Burke
Clapham, Henoch, preacher, 12, 13, 116, 157, 167, 171, 184, 186, 190, 222, 350-1, 370, 373, 374, 377, 382, 396
Clapthall. *See* Clothall, Herts.
Clare Hall (College), Camb., 155, 259, 361, 369
Clarke, Mr., of Ford, Kent, 52
Claybury, Essex, 338
Clayton, Richard, 256, 258, 259, 409
Clement VIII, pope, 368
Clement's Inn, 365, 378
Clerke (b. Onslowe), Hester, 340
Clerke, Thomas, 340
Clerum, ad, sermon at Great St. Mary's, Camb., 258, 410
Cleyton (b. Kent), Mary, 284
Clifford, Anne Lady. *See* Sackville
Clifford, George, third Earl of Cumberland, 75, 300
Clifford's Inn, 311, 324
Clifton, Sir Gervais, first Lord, 52, 317, 330
Clifton, Sir John, 76, 318, 330
Clifton Manor, 253

Clinton, Edward Fiennes de, ninth Lord Clinton and Saye, Earl of Lincoln, 317
Clinton, Henry, second Earl of Lincoln, 51, 317
Clophill, Beds., 253, 407
Clothall, Herts., 253, 260, 283, 336, 390, 411
Cobden, John, M.T., 246, 383, 405
Cobham, George Lord, 303
Cobham, Sir Henry, otherwise Brooke, 303
Cobham, Lord. *See* Brooke, Henry
Cocke, Sir Henry, 235, 400
Cofferer, of royal household, 400
Cokayne (Cockayne), Mr., of Herts., 49
Coke, Sir Anthony, 382
Coke (Cooke), Edward, 123, 172, 187, 319, 347, 352, 357, 379
Coke (b. Hatton), Elizabeth Lady, 357
Coke (b. Paston), Bridget, 357
Colberne, George, M.T., 148, 149, 366
Colberne, James, M.T., 366
Colchester, Essex, archdeacon of, 351
Colebrand. *See* Colberne
Coleman Street, London ward, 390
Colepepper, Thomas, 54
Colpeper. *See* Culpeper
Coleraine. *See* Hare
Colewick, Bucks., 359
Collier, John Payne, 2, 11, 384
Comes, Edward, M.T., 383
Common Pleas, court of, 149; justice of, 70, 76, 96, 253, 318, 319, 329, 330, 331, 342, 348, 357, 366, 374, 375, 388
Commons, House of, 304, 335, 357, 382; speaker of, 327, 348
Complete Angler, The, 362
Compton (b. Marrowe), Margaret, 395
Compton, Thomas, 395

Conference about the next succession to the crowne of Ingland, 23, 236, 322-3, 401-2

Connington, Hunts., 325

Constance, Germany, 199. *See also* Otto, bishop of

Constantinople, Turkey, 92, 297

Constantius, Roman emperor, 127

Contention betwixt a Wife, a Widdow, and a Maide, 150, 367

Conversations with Drummond, 312

Conway MS, 21, 22, 376, 377

Cony-catchers, 47, 159

Cooke, Robert, 331

Cooper, bishop of Lincoln, 254, 408

Cooper. *See* Cowper, John

Cope, Sir Walter, 274, 383, 393

Coppin (Coppen), George, 48-9, 314, 315

Coppin (b. Norton), Ann, 314, 315

Cordell, Mrs., medicinal remedy of, 84

Corneworth (Cornworthy), Devon, 331

Cornhill, London, 309, 320, 369

Cornwall, county, 186, 307, 346, 378

Cornwallis, Sir William, the younger, 382

Corpus Christi College, Camb., 361

Corpus Christi College, Oxford, 11, 297, 315, 340, 361, 384, 386, 396

Coryate, Thomas, 297, 343

Coryats crudities; hastily gobled up in five moneths travels, 343

Cotton, Henry, M.T., 369

Cotton, Sir Robert, antiquarian, 15n, 266, 297, 325, 369

Cotton, Thomas, M.T., 369

Courtenhill, Northants., 340

Courthope family, in Kent, 271, 303

Courthope, George, 303

Courthope (b. Gooreley), Ruth, 303

Courthope, Peter, 42, 303

Courthope, Peter, yeoman of Cranbrook, 303

Courthope, Richard, 303

Courthope, Susan, 303

Courtier's Library. See Catalogus Librorum Aulicorum

Covell, William, 196, 385

Coventry, Thomas, I.T., 172, 374

Coventry, Warwicks., 349, 363; bishop of, 377

Coverdale, Miles, 14

Cowper (Cooper), John, M.T., 140, 153, 365, 368

"Cozen Elenor," King Edward's, 359

Cracoe, near Skipton, Yorks., 379

Cranbrook, Kent, 44; 269, 287; church at, 306; sessions trials for heresy, 306

Cranmer, Edmund, archdeacon of Canterbury, 314, 361

Cranmer, family, at Canterbury, Kent, 271, 314

Cranmer, George, 315, 361-2

Cranmer, Paul, M.T., 271

Cranmer, Robert, M.T., 270, 307

Cranmer, Thomas, archbishop, 259, 314, 361

Cranmer, Thomas ("Cosen"), 1, 20, 132, 133, 161, 162, 163, 221, 256, 267, 315, 361-2, 372, 396

Cranmer, Thomas, registrar of archdeaconry of Canterbury, 48, 315, 361

Cranmer, William, merchant, 285, 362, 371, 372

Crashaw, Richard, poet, 25, 319

Crashaw, William, preacher, 319

Cresilaus of Athens, 144

Crewe, James, 405

Crewe, Thomas, M.T., 141, 246, 365, 405

Crichton (Creighton), Robert, sixth baron Sanquhar, 380

Croke (Crooke), John, I.T., 112, 114, 319, 348, 349

Cromer, Frances, 55
Cromer, James, 54
Cromer (b. Somer), Frances, 54
Cromwell, Sir Henry, 85, 86, 337, 338
Cromwell, Oliver, the Protector, 255, 336, 337, 338, 419
Cromwell, Sir Oliver, 85, 86, 255, 336, 338
Cromwell (b. Warren), Jane Lady, 338
Crooke (Croke), John, I.T., 112, 172, 348, 374
Cross Keys Inn, Camb., 257
Crowley, Robert, vicar, 389
Culpeper, Dr. Martin, 159, 370
Cumberland (title). See Clifford
Cupboard, in Middle Temple Hall, 70, 264, 265, 266, 275, 276
Cupboard men, 264
Curle, Dorothy. See Keene
Curle (Curll), Edward, M.T., 5, 7, 47, 70, 74, 76, 81, 84, 90, 98, 101, 118, 119, 121, 122, 124, 140, 186, 188, 221, 224, 263, 266, 268, 271, 272, 275, 290, 310, 311, 312, 324, 327, 328, 330, 331, 352, 355, 356, 378, 381, 388, 392, 395, 397, 406, 413, 415, 416, 417
Curle, family of, 272, 356, 388, 392
Curle, Frances, 268
Curle, Francis, 210, 268, 271, 272, 388, 389, 413, 414
Curle, Petronell (Petronilla). See Carter
Curle, Walter, afterward bishop of Winchester, 219, 268, 271, 276, 278, 290, 292, 388, 392, 395, 413, 415, 418
Curle (Curll), William, 268, 271, 272, 273, 310, 331, 388, 392, 413, 415, 416
Curle, William, the younger, 413
Curry-combe for a cox-combe, 382
Customale Roffense, 318
Cutts (b. Brockett), Margaret Lady, 164, 373

Cutts, Sir Henry, 164
Cutts, Sir John, 86, 164, 337, 373
Cutts, John (son of Sir John C.), 164, 373
Cutts (b. Kempe), Anne, 164, 373

Dalby, Leicestershire, 371
Daly (Daylie), Dr., 97
Damned crew, the, 202, 385
Danbury, Essex, 351
Daniel, Italian fencer. See Archideaquila
Daniel, Thomas, M.T., 261
Daniel, William, sergeant at law, 18, 54, 318
Danvers (Davers), Charles, 5, 18, 36, 39, 46, 47, 67, 74, 77, 81, 89, 96, 97, 118, 172, 186, 193, 195, 218, 263, 266, 268, 274, 275, 276, 298, 301, 302, 308, 310, 311, 312, 321, 328, 332, 352, 370, 374, 378, 384, 390, 417
Darcy (Darsie), Edward, groom of Privy Chamber, patentee for playing cards, 100, 346
Darrell, Stephen, 316
Darius, the Great, fourth King of Persia, 81
Darling, Thomas, 235, 401
Darnley (title). See Stuart
Darrel, John, 401
Daston, Richard, M.T., 122, 356
Dauphin. See Francis II
D'Auvergne, Charles de Valois, Duc, 121
Davers. See Danvers
Davies, John, M.T., poet, 3, 7, 8, 23, 48, 234, 235, 262, 263, 265, 266, 296, 311-2, 331, 344-5, 353, 359, 367, 392, 399, 400; his Orchestra, 7; his devices for entertainment of the Queen, 344-5, 376
Davies, John, of Hereford, 328
Davis (Davies) (Davie), secretary to Mary, Queen of Scots. See Rizzio, David

Davison, Francis, 21–22, 345, 367, 376
Davison, William, 361
Dawson, Alexander, 360
Dawson, Dr., 131, 360-1
Dawson (Dawton), Philip, preacher, 360
Dawson, Ralph, preacher, 361
Dawson, William, preacher, 360
Day (Daye), John, printer, 384
De arte amandi (Ovid), 394
De Civitate Dei. See St. Augustine
De etymologiis juris civilis, 367
de Republica (by Bodin), 410
Decacordon of Ten Quodlibeticall Questions concerning Religion and State, 51, 317
Defense of Contraries, The, 382
Dekker, Thomas, playwright, 394, 398
Delafield, John Ross, 407, 409, 413, 415, 419
Deloney, Thomas, 325, 393
Democritus, 343
Demosthenes, 149, 301
Demua, Isabel, 285
Demua, John, servant of Richard Manningham, squire of Bradbourne, 285
Dent, John, 196
Deptford, Kent, 391
Derby (title). *See* Stanley and Egerton
Derby, Countess of. *See* Egerton
Derby, Derbyshire, 401
Derbyshire, 379
Dering, Sir Edward, 407, 413
Dering (Deering), Edward, 149, 366
Dering, Richard, 271, 329
Dethick, William, 325
Detling, Kent, 269, 277, 291
Devereux (b. Howard), Frances, Countess of Essex. *See* Carr
Devereux, Robert, second Earl of Essex, 15, 17, 18, 85, 87, 89, 186, 193, 222, 231, 236, 260, 321, 322, 325, 337, 344, 353, 355, 357, 376, 383, 387, 391, 398, 400, 401, 405, 418
Devereux (b. Walsingham) (Sidney), Frances, Countess of Essex. *See* Burke
Devonshire, 186, 307, 346, 378, 395, 399
D'Ewes (Dewes), Simonds, 25, 383
"Dialogue between a Gentleman Usher and a Post," 367
Dialogue, wherein is plainly laid open the tyrannical dealings of the Lord Bishops against God's Children, 370
Dido, Queen of Carthage, 98
Digby (b. Walcot) (Dyve), Beatrix, Countess of Bristol, 377
Digges, Sir Dudley, 373
Digons. *See* Bigons
Diodorus Siculus, 149
Dirreccōns for Speech and Style, 4, 262, 380
Discovery of the fraudulent practices of J. Darrel, 401
Disputio de sacra scriptura, contra huius temporis Papistas, 360
Ditton, Kent, 87, 270, 287, 338
Dix (Dixe), Dr. John, 273
Dod, Dr. John ("Decalogue"), 221, 395
Dodridge (Doddridge), John, M.T., 100, 267, 308, 346
Dolberry, bailiff, 342
Dolman, R. (pseudonym). *See* Verstegan
Dominica, West Indies, 300
Donne (b. More), Anne, 8, 150, 367
Donne, John, L.I., poet, 3, 4, 8, 9, 12, 14, 24, 150, 260, 261, 263, 297, 310, 311, 312, 313, 325, 330, 334, 335, 343, 344, 346, 348, 349, 359, 364, 366, 367, 378, 382, 397, 398, 403; paradoxes by, 191–3, 382; epigrams by, 219, 392–3, 394; "The Storm," 219, 394; *Courtier's*

Library, 8, 310, 312, 330, 343, 350, 359, 403; elegy on Dr. Fenton, 364
Dormer, Fleetwood (Flettwood), M.T., 412
Dorothy, Lady. *See* Hastings
Dorset, county, 309, 342
Dorset, Earl of. *See* Sackville, Richard
Dorset House (Salisbury Court), 273
Douglas, Archibald, of Whittingham, 332
Douglas, Archibald, parson, 332
Douglas (b. Drury), Cecily, 332
Douglas, George, 332
Douglas, George, D.D., preacher, 332
Douglas, Sir George, of Redhouse, I.T., 332
Douglas, Mr., 77, 332
Douglas, Sir Robert, Lord Belhaven, 332
Douglas (Dowglasse), William, 332
Dove (b. Carleton), Anne, 349
Dove, John, preacher, 114, 267, 349, 350
Dover, Kent, 307
Dowle, John, 286
Downes, Andrew, Regius Professor of Greek, Cambridge University, 11, 13, 37, 257-8, 301, 302, 315
Drake, Sir Francis, 261
Drom, Emanuel, merchant, 285
Drummond, William, 22, 310, 322
Drury, Sir Robert, 332
Dryden, John, poet, 306
Dublin, Ireland, 188, 247, 342, 373, 381, 407
Dudley (b. Russell), Anne, Countess of Warwick, 182
Dudley, John, first Duke of Northumberland, Viscount Lisle, Earl of Warwick, 242, 316
Dudley, Robert, Earl of Leicester, 49, 194-5, 309, 384
Dudley, Robert, Earl of Warwick, 404

Duels, duelling, 190, 298, 363
Duffe, Tom. *See* Butler, Thomas, tenth Earl of Ormonde
Dugdale, Sir William, 24, 261, 266, 303, 313, 334, 395, 412, 413, 416
Dukerus, Carolus, 367
Dun, John, fencer, 10, 20, 187, 379
Dunbar (title). *See* Home
Dunch, Edmund, G.I., 383
Dunch (Duns), William, 194, 383
Dunstable, Beds., 24, 70
Dunston, Staffordshire, 365, 368
Durham, diocese of, 404; dean of, 404; bishop of, 245, 372, 404, 405
Dutch fleet, 123, 357
Dyer, Sir James, M.T., 70

Eagle, the, Cambridge inn, 259
East Barnet, Herts., 302
East Malling, Kent, 19, 49, 160, 251, 255, 268, 269, 276, 277, 284, 286, 289, 290, 291, 303, 305, 316, 317, 339, 371, 385, 414, 418; fair at, 270; parish church of St. Mary in the East (St. James), 269, 409; research station, 269, 414
East Peckham, Kent, 316
East Tisted, Hants., 278
Eastwell, Kent, 140, 303, 304, 365
Eaton, Dr. *See* Heton
Ecclesiastical Court. *See* Canterbury
Eclogue de calvis, 403
Edes (Eedes), Richard, D.D., poet, dean of Worcester, 310-11
Edes (Eedes) (b. Westphaling), Margaret, 48, 310-11
Edinburgh, Scotland, 350, 377, 391, 392, 396, 397; castle, 364
Edington, Wilts., 5, 263, 301, 321, 328
Edward II, King of England, 359
Edward III, King of England, 374
Edward IV, King of England, 252, 318, 343

Edward VI, King of England, 175,
246, 309, 334, 394, 395, 410
Edwards, John, vintner, 393
Edwards (Edwardes), Dr. Thomas,
287
*Effect of certain Sermons touching
the full redemption of Mankind,
The,* 372
Effingham (title). *See* Howard
Egerton, James, 298, 363
Egerton, John, Earl of Bridgewater,
231, 298, 363, 398
Egerton (b. More) (Polstead) (Wolley),
Elizabeth Lady (second wife of
Sir Thomas Egerton), 367
Egerton Papers, 384
Egerton (b. Spencer) (Stanley),
Alice, Viscountess Brackley,
formerly Countess Dowager of
Derby, 21, 181, 231, 376, 377,
398
Egerton (b. Stanley), Frances,
Countess of Bridgewater, 181,
231, 398
Egerton, Stephen, preacher, 12,
259, 350, 367-8; criticized by
Dr. Dove, 115; sermon by, 151
Egerton, Sir Thomas, Lord Elles-
mere, Viscount Brackley, 16, 21,
39, 70-1, 122, 124, 133, 150, 172,
180, 189, 207, 231, 236, 300, 318,
321, 325, 335, 358, 359, 363, 364,
367, 376, 381, 384, 388, 398, 405
Egerton, Sir Thomas, eldest son of
Sir Thomas E., 133, 363
Eleanor of Clare, granddaughter of
Edward I, 359
"Elegy on the worthy and learned Dr.
Roger Fenton, lecturer of Gray's
Inn" (by Donne), 364
Eliot, T. S., 320
Elizabeth I, Queen of England, 2, 3,
10, 14, 15, 16, 17, 18, 21, 23, 29,
32, 45, 51, 53, 75, 78, 79-81, 84,
87, 88, 89, 90, 96, 112, 113, 121,
130, 131, 150, 154, 160, 172, 175,

179, 180, 181, 188, 194, 196, 201,
205, 207, 208, 209, 210, 215, 216,
218, 219, 220, 221, 222, 223, 224,
227, 231, 236, 245, 246, 247, 251,
256, 261, 266, 267, 268, 274, 283,
296, 297, 299, 303, 304, 307, 308,
309, 313, 316, 318, 319, 321, 323,
329, 330, 332-3, 336, 337, 338,
339, 344, 346, 347, 348, 357, 359,
361, 362, 363, 366, 367, 368, 371,
375, 376, 383, 384, 385, 386, 387,
390, 391-2, 396, 399, 401, 404,
405, 409, 410, 413, 417
Ely, Cambs., 320; archdeaconry court
(wills), 408; bishop of, 233, 320,
326, 328, 351, 394, 399; diocese of,
5, 194, 252; episcopal records, 408
Ely Place, London, 394
Emilius (Aemilius). *See* Macedonius
Emmanuel College, Camb., 257, 258,
259, 298, 307, 328, 354, 379, 387,
388, 390, 397, 398, 410
Empresas. *See* Whitehall, Shield
Gallery
Enfield, Middlesex, 253, 271, 290
England's Joy, 11, 358
Englefield, Sir Francis, 89
English Church. *See* Middelburg
English College, at Rome, 401
*Epigrammes in the Oldest Cut and the
Newest Fashion,* 298
*Epistle . . . upon the present Pesti-
lence,* 350
Eppes, "Swaggering," 231, 398
Eppes, William, 398
Erasmian doctrine, 299
Erasmus, Desiderius, of Rotterdam,
259, 382, 384
Errour on the Left Hand, 350
Eschine, Athenian orator, 199
Essendon, Herts., 356
Essex, Countess of. *See* Devereux or
Carr, and Burke
Essex, county, 148, 325, 380
Essex "rebellion," 344, 383, 387, 400,
405. *See also* Devereux, Robert

Eton College, 351, 404
Eure, Ralph, third Lord Eure, 76, 329
Euripus (strait), 199
Everard, Sir John, 173, 375
Eversley, Hants., 278
Every Man Out of His Humour, Dedication to, 411
Exact diary of what was observed during a close attendance upon Mary Toft, the pretended rabbet-breeder, 279, 419
Exact Narration of the Life and Death of Lancelot Andrewes, late Bishop of Winchester, 320
Exchange, the, London, 158
Exclusion Bill, 402
Exeter College, Oxford, 330, 346, 362
Exeter, Devon, 348
Extremities urging Sir F. Veare to the anti-parle with the Archduke Albertus, 306

Fabian (*Twelfth Night*), 389
Faccombe, Hants., 365
Faerie Queene, The, 297, 343, 376, 418
Faithful Shepherdess, The, 380-1
Falcon, the, Cambridge inn, 259
Falkland (title). *See* Cary
Faringdon Ward, London, 370
Faustus, Doctor, in Marlowe's play, 373
Feet of Fines, for Hertfordshire, 260, 407, 411
Fen Drayton, Cambs., 251, 252, 253, 254, 255, 259, 260, 289, 332, 336, 407, 408, 409
Fenner, Edward, M.T., 3, 89, 265, 324, 339, 342
Fenner, Edward, the younger, M.T., 339
Fenton, Roger, preacher, 12, 13, 14n, 134, 364
Fergusson, David, 356
Ferrar, John, 362

Ferrar Papers, 362
Ferrers, Mr. (Henry or Richard), M.T., 378
Fetcham, Surrey, 349
Feversham, Kent, 311
Finch (b. Heneage), Elizabeth, Viscountess Maidstone, first Countess of Winchelsea, 303-4
Finch, Sir Heneage, 304
Finch, Sir Moyle, first baronet of Eastwell, 42, 303
Finch, Thomas, first Earl of Winchelsea, 304
Finch, Sir William, 304
Fish Street, London, 219, 393, 394
Fisher, Saint John, cardinal, 251, 253, 259
Fitch, Thomas, 396
Fitch, William, M.T., 221, 396
Fitzgerald, Henry, twelfth Earl of Kildare, 396
Fitzgerald (b. Howard), Frances, Countess of Kildare, 17, 181, 222, 396
Fitzjames (b. Newton) (Cartwright), Jane Lady, 317
Fitzjames, Sir James, 317
Fitzwalter, Viscount. *See* Radcliffe, Robert
Flanders, papal nuncio in, 385; river Lis in, 88
Fleet Street, London, 261, 273
Fleet, the, prison in London, 318, 321, 344
Fleete, William, M.T., 218, 390, 400
Fleete, William, the elder, 390
Fleetwood, Thomas, M.T., 18, 77, 332
Fleetwood, William, M.T., 18, 75, 154, 160, 262, 318, 328, 332, 371
Fletcher, Dr. Giles, 379
Fletcher, Giles, poet, 379
Fletcher, John, poet, 380-1, 393
Fletcher, Phineas, poet, 379
Fletcher, Richard, bishop of London, 84

Florence, Italy, 313
Floyd, John, S.J., 382
Floyd, Thomas, 301
Flushing, Zeeland (the Netherlands), 43, 52, 201, 305, 316, 317
Flushingers, 42
Foote, John, minister, epitaph of, 47
Foots Cray, Kent, manor of, 304, 305
Ford, Henry, M.T., 383
Ford, John, M.T., 265, 275, 383
Ford, Kent, 52
Ford, Thomas, 383
Forde (Ford), Thomas, M.T., 265, 383
Forman, Dr. Simon, 318
Forster, Edward, L.I., 326
Forster, Francis, L.I., 326
Forster, John, L.I., 326
Fossar, a joiner, 99
Foster Lane, London, 13, 157, 370, 391
Foster, Thomas, I.T., 172, 374
Foster, Thomas, L.I., 3, 9, 73, 326, 374
Foster, William, L.I., 326
Fowler, Mrs., wife of Richard Fowler, 67, 321
Fowler, Richard, suspected plotter, 321
Foxe, John, 24, 389
France, 87, 121, 153, 173, 217, 242, 325, 402; English ambassador to, 154, 305, 361, 376, 383, 387, 400; ligier in, 196, 385; royal court of, 235
Francis II of Cleves, 338
Francis II, King of France, 175, 375
Francis of Lorraine, second Duke of Guise, 175, 179
Frankley, Worcestershire, 395
Franklin (Francklin), James, M.T., 70, 118, 270, 324, 352
Freeman (Freman), John, M.T., 355, 381
Frencham, Henry, preacher, 352
Frengtham (Frencham) (Frothing-

ham), Nell, 118, 352
Frere, Edward, I.T., 381
Freston, Richard, M.T., 267, 306
Freston, William, M.T., 276, 355
Friars' Church, Blackfriars, London, 368
Friars, or Priory, the, near Aylesford, Kent, 316
Frothingham, Christopher, M.T., 352
Frothingham, Edward, 352
Frothingham, Francis, M.T., 352
Frothingham, Yorks., 352
Fry, John, 375
Fuller, Thomas, 2, 2n, 256, 316, 325, 326, 332, 348, 361, 362, 365, 366, 370, 371, 372, 384, 399, 404, 405, 407, 409, 410
Furnival, Sir William de, 353
Furnival's Inn, 120, 268, 326, 353, 366, 395
Fysher, Anne, 254
Fysher, Alice, 254
Fysher, Alice, daughter of Sir Michael F. See St. John
Fysher, Elizabeth, 254
Fysher, George, 254
Fysher, Henry, 254
Fysher, Joan. See Manningham
Fysher (Fisher), John (father of Joan F. and grandfather of Diarist), 251, 253, 408
Fysher, Sir John, 253
Fysher, Sir Michael, 253
Fysher, Richard, 254
Fysher, Rose, 254
Fysher, Stephen, 254

Gainsborough, Lincs., 368
Gaius (Caius), Roman jurist, 402
Gardner (Gardiner), Mr., of Furnival's Inn, 120, 353
Gardiner, Sir Robert, lord chief justice of Ireland, 119, 155
Gardiner, Stephen, bishop of Winchester, 12

Garnauns, Herefords., 315
Garnauns, James, M.T., 315
Garnauns, Nicholas, M.T., 315
Garnauns (Garnaunce), Robert, M.T., 315
Garnet, Henry, S.J., 385
Garnet's Building, near Temple Bar, London, 261, 342
Garnons, Anthony, L.I., 315
Garnons, "Cosen," 49, 315
Garnons, Dr., cleric, 315
Garnons, Henry, 315
Garret, court fool or page, 363
Garrett (Garrard), Sir John, 113, 348
Garter, Order of, knights of, 313, 387
Gascoigne, a soldier, 321
Gascoigne, George, poet, 327
Gastley, John, 252
Gawdy, Francis, I.T., 319, 325
Gelderland (Guelderland), the Netherlands, 219, 391
Gellibrand, Edmund, 305
Gellibrand, Edward, Puritan minister, 304
Gellibrand, Edward, lawyer, 304
Gellibrand, Elizabeth, sister of Edmund G., 305
Gellibrand, Elizabeth, widow, 305
Gellibrand, family of, 43, 270, 304, 305
Gellibrand, Henry, the elder, 196, 304, 385
Gellibrand, Henry, the younger, 304
Gellibrand, physician at Maidstone, 20, 43, 44, 304
Gellibrand, Roger, 304-5
Gellibrand, Thomas, 20, 43, 304, 305
Gellibrand, Thomas, of Blackburn, 304-5
Gellius, Aulus, 211, 239, 389, 403
Geneva Bible, the, 14
Geneva, Switzerland, 154, 258
Gentleman's academie, or the booke of S. Albans, reduced into a better method by G. M., The, 324
Gentleman's Magazine, 342, 369

George I, King of England, 278
George, the, Garter insignia, 208, 387
Georgicon, by Virgil, 400
Gerard, Sir Thomas, 355, 368
Gibbes, Antony, 352
Gibbes, John, M.T., 141, 267, 352, 365
Gibbes (Gibbs), Mrs., 118
Gibbes (Gibbs), William, M.T., 118, 352
Gibson, Edmond, laborer, 285
Girlington, Nicholas, L.I., 153-4, 368
Glanville, John, 172, 374
Glasgow, Scotland, 332
Glastonbury, Somerset, 55
Gl'Inganni, plays by Secchi and Gonzaga, 48, 313-4
Gl'Ingannati, 314
Globe, the, playhouse, 313
Gloucester, bishop of, 15, 297, 348, 387, 389, 399; cathedral, 302; dean of, 383; prebendary of, 302
Gloucestershire, 95, 315
Glover, Richard, 308
"G.M." See Markham and Matthew
Goa, burning women with husbands in, 19, 82
Goche (Googe), Barnabe, fellow of Magdalene College, 257
Godalming, Surrey, 419
Goddard, John, bellows-maker, 346
Godmanchester, Hunts., 254
Godmersham, Kent, 1, 4, 161, 164, 256, 262, 267, 271, 304, 324, 343, 356, 365, 371, 390
Golden Ball, bookseller's shop, 344
Goldsmyth, John, 286
Gonville and Caius College, Camb., 258, 277, 354, 355
Gonzaga, Charles de, Duke of Nevers, 87, 338
Gonzaga, Curzio, 313
Gonzaga, Louis de, 338
Goodere (Goodyere), Henry, 263, 344

Goodrich, Alice, 401
Googe, Barnabe, aeclogue writer, 257
Gorboduc, tragedy of, 314
Gorges, Sir Arthur, 383
Gorges (Gorge), Sir Ferdinando, 246, 405
Gorges, Sir Thomas, 336
Gorges (b. von Suavenberg), Eleanor Lady, formerly Marchioness of Northampton, 336
Gorson, Mr., 114, 349
Gouge, William, 368
Gowry Conspiracy, 18, 390
Gowry (Gowrie) (title). *See* Ruthven
Grant, Edward, 391
Grant, Gabriel, L.I., 391
Grant, John, 219, 391
Gratewick, Sir William, 291
Graunt, John, 391
Gravesend, Kent, 22, 272, 305, 385
Gray's Inn, London, 86, 100, 134, 172, 302, 303, 307, 310, 318, 327, 337, 346, 349, 355, 364, 374, 378, 383, 388, 416
Great Fire of 1666, London, 326, 393
Great Hale, Lincs., 320
Great Massingham, Norfolk, 354
Great St. Bartholomew's, London, 330
Great St. Mary's, church of, Camb., 258, 259, 301
Great Tew, priory and manor, Oxon, 343
Great Yarmouth, Norfolk, 307
Green cloth, the, 160, 371
Greene, Robert, poet, 344
Greene, Thomas, M.T., 172, 374
Greenwich, royal manor of, 308
Gregory XIII, pope, 372
Grent, John, 391
Grent, William, M.T., 391
Greville Street, Holborn, 278
Grey (b. Brandon), Frances Lady, 390

Grey, Catherine Lady, 319, 390
Grey, Jane Lady, 319, 323, 390
Grey, Thomas, fifteenth Lord Grey of Wilton, 207
Griffith (Griffin), Edward, 220, 394, 395
Grindal, Edmund, bishop of London, 84, 377
Grocer's Company, 314
Guildhall, the, London, 96, 342, 357
Guise, Duke of. *See* Francis of Lorraine
Guise, Mary of, consort of James V of Scotland (mother of Mary, Queen of Scots), 351
Guisian (Guyssian), kin of Mary Queen of Scots, 174
Gunpowder Plot, 344, 354; conspirators in, 385
Gwy, John, 292
Gylburne, Mr., at the Assizes in Rochester, 54

Hackstables, tenement in Melstreet, East Malling, Kent, 286
Hadley, Middlesex, 366
Hadsor, Nicholas, 342-3
Hadlow, Kent, 287, 305
Hadsor, Richard, M.T., 96, 98, 119, 154, 155, 173, 188, 217, 261, 267, 274, 275, 309, 342, 344, 352, 370, 375, 381, 417
Hakewell (Hackwell), William, L.I., 9, 100, 346
Hall, Joseph, 298
Halton, Cornwall, 365, 370
Haly (Haley), Rabbi, 185
Hamilton, James, second Earl of Arran, 175, 375
Hamlet, Shakespeare protagonist, 1
Hammond, Mrs., 155
Hampton Court Conference, 361, 405
Hamptons, near Tunbridge, Kent, 305
Harbledown, Kent, 406

Harbury, Warwicks., 395
Harding, Dr. John, 13, 362
Hardwick Castle, 323
Hardwicke, Northants., 374
Hardy, Marie (Mary), half-sister of
  Richard Manningham, squire of
  Bradbourne, 284
Hardy, Susan, daughter of Mary H.,
  284
Hare, family of, 272
Hare, Hugh, I.T., 393
Hare, Hugh, first Lord Hare of
  Coleraine, 393
Hare, John, I.T., 393
Hare, Nicholas, 219, 220, 393, 394
Hare, Sir Rafe (Ralph), 393
Harefield, Middlesex, entertainment
  of Queen at, 21, 180-182, 359,
  376-7
Harleian manuscripts, British Museum,
  1
Harleston, Henry, 194, 384
Harleston, prebendary of, 301
Harpsfield, Nicholas, 327
Harriot, Thomas, 354
Harrington, Sir Henry, 335, 351
Harrington, Sir John, 14, 15n, 351,
  372
Harris, Arthur, L.I., 172, 374
Harris, Edward, M.T., 331
Harris (Harrys), Edward, 331
Harris, Mr., murderer, 162-3
Harris, Thomas, M.T., 4, 76, 141,
  173, 187, 265, 331, 365, 374,
  380
Harsnet, Samuel, archbishop of York,
  259, 401
Hartford cum Sapley, Hunts., 336
Harty, Francis, 335
Harvass, Master, 332
Harvey, Gabriel, 327
Harvey (Harvie), Captain John, 393
Harwell, Henry, 349
Harwell, William, 114, 349
Hasland, Derbyshire, 335
Haslet, John, valet of Richard

Manningham, squire of Brad-
  bourne, 285
Hastings, Dorothy Lady, 182
Hastings, Sir Francis, 42-3, 303
Hastings, Sussex, 330
Haston's house, 44, 306
Hatfield, Herts., 5, 263, 268, 270,
  271, 310, 331, 388, 392, 413, 416;
  forest of, 122, 356; manor of, 356.
  See also Bishop's Hatfield and
  Woodside
Hatfield House, Herts., 333
Hatfield palace, 268
Hatfield Woodhall, 332
Hatton, Sir Christopher, 188
Haule (Hall), George, 329
Haule (Hall), Henry, M.T., 3, 75, 188,
  266, 271, 329, 334, 363, 381, 406
Haule (b. Dering), Jane, 271, 329
Haverfordwest, Pembrokeshire, 398
Hawkyns (Hawkins), Joan, servant
  of Richard Manningham, squire of
  Bradbourne, 285
Hawthorden, Midlothian, 22, 310
Hayward, Sir John, 3, 22, 23, 236,
  237, 401-4, 410
Heidelberg, Germany, 333, 351
Heines (Heine), Captain, 321
Hele (Heale), John, I.T., 3, 9, 70, 74,
  96, 319, 325, 327, 330, 342
Hellsingtone (Helsington), Westmore-
  land, 334
Helston, Cornwall, 274, 335
Hemel Hempstead, Herts., 337
Hemingford Abbots, Hunts., 85, 260,
  266, 336
Hemingford Grey, Hunts., 336
Hemming, Robert, preacher, 246,
  406
Heneage House, London, 303
Heneage, Sir Thomas, 304
Henri IV, Henry of Navarre, king of
  France, 70, 121, 140, 324
Henrietta of Cleves, 338
Henry Frederick, Prince of Wales, 222,
  298, 332, 338, 374, 375

Henry I, King of England, 239
Henry II, King of England, 300
Henry III, King of England, 300
Henry the Fourth, Part One, by
  Shakespeare, 306
Henry VI, King of England, 407
Henry VIII, King of England, 87, 261,
  309, 316, 322, 338-9, 390, 393
Hentzner, Paul, 298
Hepburn, James, fourth Earl of
  Bothwell, 177
Heraclius, Patriarch of Jerusalem, 300
Herbert, George, poet, 5, 25, 263, 271,
  301
Herbert, Henry, second Earl of Pem-
  broke, 82, 334
Herbert (b. Danvers), Jane, 5, 301
Herbert, William, third Earl of
  Pembroke, 6, 334
Herefordshire, 95, 310, 354
Heretics, 361
Herne, George, painter, 285
Hertford (title). *See* Seymour
Hertford, Herts., 415
Hertfordshire, 7, 49, 97, 99, 260,
  268, 271, 273, 283, 290, 309, 325,
  356, 373, 390, 407, 408, 413, 415
Hertfordshire, Feet of Fines for, 407,
  408
Heton, Dr. Martin, bishop of Ely,
  233, 399
Heydon, Richard, 395
Heywood, Thomas, playwright, 380
High Easter, Essex, 396
Highgate, London, 361
Hill, Edward, M.T., 233, 399
Hill, Nicholas, astrologer and
  alchemist, 97, 343
Hill, Mr., tailor, 12, 194-5, 233, 399
Hilles, Richard, 309
Hinchinbrook (Hinchingbrooke),
  Hunts., 86, 336, 338
Hingham, Norfolk, 319
*Historie of the most renowned and
  victorious princesse Elizabeth, late
  Queene of England . . . composed*

by way of Annals, 307, 386, 387
*History of the University of Cam-
  bridge,* 256, 384, 409, 410
Hitchen (Hychyn), Herts., 252
Hobart, Sir Henry, 172, 273, 357,
  374
Hobart (b. Sidney), Philippa, 317
Hoby, Sir Edward, 193, 382
Hoby (b. Coke), Elizabeth, 282
Hoby, Sir Thomas, 382
Hodder, George, M.T., 416
Hogarth, William, artist, 279
Holborn, London, 101, 120, 267,
  278, 353, 384
Holborn Bridge, 341
Holinshed, Raphael, 361
Holland. *See* Low Countries
Holland, Hugh, poet, 30, 297
Holland, Dr. Thomas, 12, 13, 133,
  196, 362, 385
Holy Sepulchre, church of the, Lon-
  don, 340
Holy State, The, 2, 2n, 370
Holywell, Hunts., 255, 260, 336
Holyrood Palace, 223
Home (Hume), George, first Earl of
  Dunbar, 377
Homelacy, Herefordshire, 417
*Honor, Military and Ciuill, contained
  in foure bookes,* 363-4
Honours List, University of Cam-
  bridge, 259
Hoofman, Egidius, 86, 337
Hooker, Richard, 196, 299, 340,
  361, 385
Hooper, George, M.T., 194, 383
Hooper, Thomas, 383
Horace (Quintus Horatius Flaccus),
  Roman poet, 221, 395, 396
Horsley, Gloucestershire, 321
Horton, Roger, M.T., 141, 365, 405
Horton, Thomas, 30, 298
Hoskyns (Hoskins), John, M.T., poet,
  4, 5, 7, 9, 187, 262, 263, 265, 276,
  296, 311, 312, 326, 334, 335, 343,
  346-7, 351, 380, 382, 412, 413

Hoskyns, Mary, 326
Hoskyns (b. Moyle) (Bourne),
    Benedicta, 5, 380
Hotspur (in Shakespeare's *1 Hen. IV*),
    306, 353
Hough, Lincs., 307
Houghton (b. Kent), Elizabeth, 284
Houghton (Hawton), Robert, L.I.,
    172, 374
Howard, Charles, second Lord
    Howard of Effingham, first Earl
    of Nottingham, 17, 39, 98, 207,
    396
Howard, Lord Henry, Earl of North-
    ampton, 23, 78, 235, 246, 333,
    400, 405
Howard, Henry, first Earl of Surrey,
    poet, 23, 322, 333
Howard (b. St. John), Anne, Lady
    Howard of Effingham, 181, 189,
    381
Howard, Philip, first Earl of Arundel
    and Surrey, 355
Howard, Thomas, Earl of Surrey,
    third Duke of Norfolk, 367
Howard, Thomas, fourth Duke of
    Norfolk, 333
Howard, Thomas Lord, first Earl of
    Suffolk, 256, 410
Howard, Thomas, third Viscount
    Bindon, 55, 319
Howard, William, Lord Howard of
    Effingham, 381
Howes, Edmund, chronicler, 318,
    369, 387, 388, 392, 397, 400,
    405, 410, 418
Hucbald, monk of St. Amand, 403
Huckleberry Finn, 358
Hughes, Thomas, mathematician, 354
Huguenots, 154
Hull, Annis, maidservant of Richard
    Manningham, squire of Bradbourne,
    287
Hull, Mr. *See* Haule (Hall)
Humanism, humanist education
    at Cambridge, 259; early Oxford

humanist John Manyngham, 407
Hume, Sir George, Lord High Trea-
    surer of Scotland, 364
Humphrey, Dr. Lawrence, 303
Hunsdon, Herts., 374
Hundson (title). *See* Carey
Hunter, Joseph, 1, 23, 314
Huntingdon, Hunts., 85, 252, 254,
    336, 358
Huntingdonshire, 260, 339
Hutton, Dr. Matthew, archbishop of
    York, 162, 372, 405
Hyde, Edward, first Earl of Clarendon,
    309
Hyde, Henry, M.T., 308
Hyde, Lawrence, the elder, 273, 308
Hyde, Lawrence, the younger, M.T.,
    308, 309
Hyde, Nicholas, M.T., 46, 275, 308,
    309
Hyde, Robert, M.T., 308, 417
Hynde, Edward, 336
Hynde, Edward (son of Edward H.),
    336
Hynde, Sir Francis, 336
Hynde (b. Verney), Jane, 336
Hynde, William, 85, 336
Hythe. *See* New Hythe

Ightham, Kent, court rolls of, 303
Il Sacrificio de gli Intronati, induc-
    tion to *Gl'Ingannati*, 314
India, 72
Infanta, the, of Spain, 401
Ingpen, Arthur R., Master, M.T.,
    298, 411
Inner Temple, 3, 9, 20, 88, 172, 266,
    267, 277, 299, 304, 309, 319, 325,
    328, 329, 330, 332, 333, 339, 343,
    346, 348, 349, 354, 356, 357, 363,
    374, 378, 381, 384, 391, 393, 396,
    413, 417
Inns of Chancery, 120, 254, 260, 264,
    268, 353
Inns of Court, 3, 4, 8, 9, 13, 21, 22,
    25, 260–1, 263, 312, 313, 332,

353, 355, 368, 382, 393, 412
Institutes of the Lawes of England, 357
Irby, Anthony, 368
Ireland, 119, 121, 155, 173, 188, 247, 261, 267, 274, 343, 355, 363, 370, 381, 398, 406, 417
Ireland, John, salter, 350
Ireland, Thomas, preacher, 115, 350
Isaacson, Henry, 320
Isham, Henry, 392
Isham, John, M.T., 219, 220, 235, 392, 394, 400
Isham, Thomas, 392
Isham, Zacheus, M.T., 392, 394
Islam, religion of, 201
Islands Voyage (Azores, 1597), 405
Islington, Devon, 383
Isle of Dogs, The (play), 379
Isocrates, Athenian orator, 149
Issilham, Cambs., 399
Italy, 50, 153, 163, 382; theatre in, 314
Itinerary written by Fynes Moryson, Gent. First in the Latine Tongue, and then translated by him into English, 325
Ivy Bridge, London, 344, 367

Jacob, Henry, 373
Jacobean period, 2, 333
Jaggard, Isaac, printer, 355
James I, King of England, 3, 6, 15, 16, 17, 18, 23, 208, 209, 210, 211, 217, 218, 219, 222, 223, 227, 231, 234, 235, 236, 245, 251, 267, 269, 271, 284, 286, 289, 290, 297, 299, 308, 315, 319, 322, 323, 332, 335, 336, 338, 342, 343, 346, 347, 348, 356, 357, 362, 364, 365, 366, 377, 383, 385, 387, 388, 390, 391, 392, 396-7, 400, 401, 406, 415, 416
Jardine, David, 385
Jarrett. *See* Garrett
Jeninges, Sir John, 273
Jennings, Edmund, S.J., 379

Jenour, Andrew, M.T., 141, 365, 396
Jerusalem, 92, 184, 200, 297, 300
Jesuits, 372; polemics against, 51, 95, 114, 157, 236, 242, 243, 317, 323, 372, 378-9, 382, 385
Jesus College, Camb., 259, 328, 395, 408
Jewell (Jewyll), Dr. George, 121, 354
Jewell, John, bishop, 354
Jewell, John, of Northcote, Devon, 354
Jewell, John, of Scoulton, Norfolk, 354
Jocasta, tragedy by Euripides, 327
Johnson, Isaac, M.T., 363
Jones, Inigo, 344
Jones, Sefton, M.T., 412
Jonson, Ben, poet, playwright, 3, 4, 22, 24, 100, 187, 261, 262, 263, 308, 310, 311, 312, 313, 316, 322, 324, 335, 343, 346, 347, 379, 380-1, 393
Journal of Sir Roger Wilbraham. Solicitor-General in Ireland and Master of Requests, for the Years 1593–1616, 327
Journey into England, in the year MDXCVIII, 298
Joyce, James, 10, 328
Judge, The, by Aria, 324
Julian "the Apostate," Roman emperor, 127, 212
Junius, Francis, 410
Just and temperate defence of the five books of Ecclesiasticall policie by R Hooker, A, 196, 385
Juvenilia: or certaine paradoxes and problems, 382

Kaye, Abraham, L.I., 396
Kaye, John, M.T., 396
Kedgwin, Christopher, 298
Kedgwin, Thomas, M.T., 30, 187, 257, 259, 298, 379, 398
Keene (b. Curle) (Wither), Dorothy, 268

Keene, Richard, 268
Keerbergius, Joannes, printer and bookseller, 359
Kelley, Richard, M.T., 363
Kempe, Amy, 373
Kempe, Anne, 373
Kempe, Dorothy, 373
Kempe, Mary, 373
Kempe, Mr., King's Bench, 81
Kempe, Sir Thomas, 164, 373
Kendal, Westmorland, 375, 380
Kennington, Sir Robert, 332
Kensington, Middlesex, 351
Kent, county of, 1, 42, 43, 53, 86, 155, 160, 162-3, 231, 255, 256, 266, 271, 275, 284, 286, 287, 289, 291, 303, 304, 316, 325, 330, 366, 371, 373, 392, 407
Kent, Drewe, 255, 284, 285
Kent, John, 159, 285, 371
Kent, Nicholas, 285
Kent, Robert, half-brother of Richard Manningham, squire of Bradbourne, 51, 255, 284, 285, 317, 371
Kent, Roger, 285
Kent, Stephen, 285
Kent, William, 285
Kentish tails, 70, 324-5
Kerrington, Lincs., 378
Kettell, Ralph, S.T.P., 85, 337
Key (Kaye) (Kye), Mr., 222, 396
Keyt, thresher, of Kent, 162-3
Kiddermaister (Kiddermister) (Kitterminster), Lady, 182
Kildare (title). See Fitzgerald
Killigrew, Sir Henry, 274, 361
Killigrew (Killegrewe), Sir Robert, 273, 274, 335
Killigrew, Thomas, playwright, 274
Killigrew (Killegrewe), Sir William, 273, 274
King, Henry, poet and bishop, 348
King, Jeffrey, Regius Professor of Hebrew, 14, 195, 384
King, John, bishop of London, 11, 13, 211, 266, 315, 341, 348, 353, 365, 390; sermon at Paul's Cross, 101-112, 347, 384; refuses to preach at funerals of Furnival's Inn members, 120; reception at Oxford, 120
King, Robert, first bishop of Oxford, 347
Kingesthorpe, Northants., 298
King's College, Camb., 14, 369, 384
King's College, Newcastle upon Tyne, 353
King's Head Court, London, 394
King's Head Tavern, by Chancery Lane, 394
King's Head, tavern in Fish Street, London, 219, 393-4
King's Hill, close at Rochford, Essex, 380
Kinloss (title). See Bruce
Kinsale, Ireland, 247, 406. See also Burke
Kirke, Urian, schoolmaster, 254
Knaresborough, Yorks., 333
Knight's Conjuring, A, 394, 398
Knole, Kent, 317
Knollys, William, first Lord Knollys, Viscount Wallingford, Earl of Banbury, 207
Kye, Edward, I.T., 396
Kynaston, Bryan, vintner, 393
Kynwelmersh (Kinwelmersh) (Kindlemarsh), Francis, G.I., poet, 327

La nautica, poem by Baldi, 403
Lady Margaret Professor of Divinity, 258, 366, 369, 372, 410
Laelia, Latin play, 314
Laetus, 324
Lake, Stephen, 335
Lake, Thomas, M.T., 45, 84, 307, 335, 340. See also Leek
Lake, Thomas, 410
Lambeth, 339; Articles, 258, 259; Commissioners at, 140

Lamport, Northants., 392
Lancashire, county, 342, 364, 399
Lancaster, Clement, 257, 259
Lancaster, Duchy of, 416
Lancaster, Thomas, G.I., 47, 100,
    186, 310, 346, 378
Lanceleby, Hants., 333
Lancet style of architecture, 300
Lando, Ortensio, 382
Larkfield, Kent, 270
Larkhall, Hadfield parish, Kent, 287,
    305
Latham, Lancs., 318
Latimer, Hugh, bishop, 24, 259
Latimer (title). *See* Neville
Laud, William, future Archbishop of
    Canterbury, 259, 299, 351
Laudanum, use and effects of, 82
Law Whitton, Cornwall, 326, 360
Lawrence (b. Arnold), Marie (Mary),
    284
Lawrence Ayott, Herts., 388, 415
Lawrence, Barnaby (Barnabie), 285
Lawrence, Richard, kinsman of
    Richard Manningham, squire of
    Bradbourne, 271, 287
Layfield, Dr. John, preacher, 12, 13,
    145, 232, 300, 366, 384, 399
Leadenhall Street, Cornhill, London,
    369
Leake, William, bookseller, 386
Leather Lane, London, 353
Lee (Leigh), Thomas, 210, 211, 348,
    388
Lee, Robert, 113, 210, 222, 223,
    348, 388
Leek (Leake), Francis, M.T., 84, 307,
    335. *See also* Lake
Leek (Leake), Sir Francis, 45, 307,
    335. *See also* Lake
Leek (Leake), Thomas, 335
Leek (Leake), Thomas, M.T., 335
*Legend of Mary, Queen of Scots, and
    other Ancient Poems,* 375
Legge, Thomas, 256
Leicester, recorder of, 375

Leicester (title). *See* Dudley
Leicester's Hospital, Warwick, 352
Leiston, Cecilia, 305
Lenaugh (Luineach). *See* O'Neill
Lennard, family of, 317
Lennarde, Henry, 307
"le Swan," Baldock, Herts., 252
*Les comentaries ou les reportes de
    Edmunde Plowden,* 353
L'Estrange, Nicholas, 2, 301, 315, 346
Levenson, Sir John, 409
Lewes (Lewis), Thomas, M.T., 383
Lewknor (Lewkenor), Edmund, 341
Lewknor (Lewkenor), Sir Richard,
    M.T., 95, 341–2
Ley, Sir James, 273, 415
Leydall. *See* Lydall, Sir Richard
Liber Famelicus, 326, 335, 344, 346,
    351, 352, 411, 416
Lichfield, Staffords., bishop of, 377;
    canon of, 299; cathedral, 309;
    dean of, 271, 276, 290, 389, 392;
    prebendary of, 320
"Lie, The," poem by Ralegh, 18,
    162, 372
Life of Sir Henry Wotton, 304
Life of Thomas More, by Cresacre
    More, 326; by Roper, 327; by Ro.
    Ba., 327; by Harpsfield, 327
Lime Street, London, 332
Limmerick, Ireland, bishop of, 363
Lincoln (title). *See* Clinton
Lincoln, diocese of, 338; bishop of,
    254, 408; episcopal records, 408
Lincolnshire, 43, 51, 307, 358
Lincoln's Inn, 3, 8, 9, 11, 73, 123,
    172, 303, 304, 311, 315, 326, 342,
    346, 353, 357, 358, 365, 366, 368,
    374, 391, 394, 395, 396
Lis, river in Flanders, 88
Little Lawford, Warwickshire, 262
Little St. Bartholomew-by-the-
    Exchange, 274, 340
Little St. Mary's, Camb., 392, 413
Littleton, Sir John, 395
Lively, Edward, Regius Professor

of Hebrew, 13, 257
Lloyd, David, 333
Loftus (Loftis), George, bookseller, 344
London, 22, 42, 45, 47, 48, 86, 88, 89, 113, 159, 186, 189, 195, 196, 252, 258, 262, 265, 266, 270, 272, 273, 275, 278, 285, 292, 298, 303, 310, 316, 317, 332, 333, 338, 342, 350, 351, 358, 366, 368, 369, 375, 385, 386, 391, 392, 393, 410; alderman of, 46, 133, 327, 363; bishop of, 49, 84, 122, 235, 266, 334, 347, 348, 353, 356, 361, 365, 384, 401, 418; Bridge, 393; chief citizens of, in ancient times, 155; compared to Ephesus, 60; entertainment for King James, 308; Fellows and Scholars of St. John's College, Cambridge, 338; legal fraud in, 159; lord mayor(s), 46, 112, 113, 208, 210, 222, 223, 296, 309, 338, 348, 388, 396; making shuttlecocks in, 189; preacher in, 116; recorder of, 18, 75, 112, 114, 172, 311, 318, 328, 348, 349, 354, 360; sheriffs of, 89. For *streets, wards, churches, etc., see individual listings.*
"London," anonymous poem, 386
Long, Edmund, M.T., 76, 96, 120, 122, 330, 342, 354, 355
Long Parliament, 5, 335
Lopez, Dr. Roderigo, Queen's physician, 357
Lord Admiral. *See* Howard, Charles
Lord Chamberlain's company, players, 265, 313
Lord Keeper of the Great Seal. *See* Egerton, Sir Thomas
Lord Mayor. *See* London
Lord Treasurer. *See* Sackville, Thomas
Lords' Council, 322
Lorraine, Cardinal of. *See* Charles de Lorraine

Lothbury, London, 218, 274, 390, 400; church of St. Margaret, 271, 388
Lotteries. *See* Harefield, Middlesex
Louth (Louide), county, Ireland, 342, 352, 381
Louvain, Belgium, 359, 384
Lovell, Mr., puritan, 44, 306
Love's Garland: or Posies for Rings, Handkerchers and Gloves, and such pretty tokens that Lovers send their Loves, 359
Low Countries, the, 19, 43, 50, 75, 121, 123, 255, 305, 311, 316, 325, 343, 347, 353, 357, 370, 383, 391
Lower Gelderland, the Netherlands, 391
Lowndes, Richard, bookseller, 335
Lucian, Greek author of Dialogues, 133
Lucius III, pope, 300
Ludgate, gates at, London, 208
Ludlow, Salop, 95, 342
Luther, Martin, 92
Luton, Beds., 252, 260
Lycidas, poem by Milton, 366
Lydall (Leydall), Edward, M.T., 45, 218, 308, 354, 355, 383, 391
Lydall (Leydall), Sir Richard, M.T., 45, 218, 275, 308, 354, 355, 391
Lydall (Leydall), Thomas, 308
Lyde, Tristram, surgeon, 53, 318
Lyll, Francis, M.T., 354, 355
Lyly, William, 309
Lyons Inn, 330
Lytton, Dorset, 416

Macedonius, Paulus Lucius Aemilius, Roman general, consul, 404
Mac Flecknoe, satiric poem by Dryden, 306
Machiavelli, Niccolo, 169
Machyn, Henry, 25
Maddingly Hall, Cambs., 336
Magdalene College, Oxford, 299, 303, 304, 361, 362, 370, 387

Magdalene College, Camb., 256-9, 333, 362, 368, 378, 391, 409, 410, 411

Magdalene Street, Camb., 257

Magnalia Christi Americana, 24

Maidstone, Kent, 20, 43, 87, 163, 255, 265, 267, 270, 271, 272, 277, 303, 304, 305, 306, 323, 324, 329, 338-9, 414

Maidstone Road, 303

Maine, Province of, 405

Maitland, Frederic W., 4

Malling, Kent, 49, 316. *See also* East Malling and Town Malling

Malvolio, in *Twelfth Night*, 11, 313

Mandeville, Sir John, 359

Manitre. *See* Manningtree

Mann, Bartholomew, M.T., 265

Manners, Roger, fifth Earl of Rutland, 97, 344

Manners (b. Sidney), Elizabeth, Countess of Rutland, 310

Manning (Maning), Captain John, 278, 419

Manningham, Alice, Diarist's aunt, m. John Gastley, 252, 253

Manningham, Anna (Anne), sister of Edmund, William, and Charles M., 284

Manningham, Anne, daughter of Richard M. rector of Michelmersh, 277, 278, 418

Manningham, Anne, infant daughter of Diarist, 269, 270, 271

Manningham (b. Blackwell), Bridget, wife of Richard M. rector of Michelmersh, Hants., 277, 418

Manningham (b. Boteler or Butler), Elizabeth, grandmother of Diarist, 252

Manningham, Bridget, daughter of Richard M. rector of Michelmersh, 278

Manningham, Bridget, wife of Walter M., 277, 278, 419

Manningham, Charles, brother of Edmund and William M., 284, 290

Manningham (b. Curle), Anne, wife of Diarist, 5, 263, 268, 269, 270, 271, 273, 275, 277, 289, 290, 291, 292, 392, 418

Manningham, Edmund, kinsman of Richard M. squire of Bradbourne, 284, 290

Manningham, Elizabeth, aunt of Diarist, 252

Manningham, Elizabeth, daughter of Diarist, 270, 289

Manningham, Elizabeth, sister of Edmund, William, and Charles M., 284

Manningham, Elizabeth, wife of Thomas M. bishop of Chichester, 278

Manningham (b. Fysher), Joan, mother of Diarist, 251, 253

Manningham, George, 160, 256, 305, 371, 409

Manningham, Henry, son of Walter M., 277

Manningham, Jane, infant daughter of Diarist, died in infancy, 269

Manningham, Jane, first wife of Richard M. squire of Bradbourne, 161, 255, 284, 285, 303, 305, 409

Manningham, John, grandfather of Diarist, 251, 252, 255, 260, 336

Manningham, John, of the Middle Temple, the Diarist: ancestry and parentage, 251-4, 407; early life at Fen Drayton, 252, 253, 408; schooling, 254; adoption by Richard Manningham, 255, 303; at Magdalene College, 256-9, 297, 298, 379, 409, 410; A.B. degree, 259, 410; incorporation of, at Oxford, 259; religious stance, 259; friendship with Dr. Chamberlaine, 260; sells property in Herts., 260, 283; admission to Middle Temple, 261, 311-12; "bound" with Chapman and Hoskyns, 262, 304, 343;

association with Donne-Jonson circle of wits, 263; friendship with Danvers and Curle, 263, 301; garb at Middle Temple, 263; assignment to chambers, 263; legal exercises, 264-5, 412; attends *Twelfth Night* performance, 48, 265, 312; activities in 1601-02, 265-7, 299, 300; brings in moot with Bramston, 154, 368; with Wagstaffe, 224, 397; business trip in Kent, for Richard Manningham, 160-4, 371; at Richmond, records death of Queen, 16-17, 207-8, 267; called to Utter Bar, 268, 311, 359, 395; marriage with Anne Curle, 268, 413; children, 268-71, 413, 414; named executor by foster-father, 270, 285; becomes squire of Bradbourne manor, 269, 414; erects memorial to Richard, 270, 288; life at Bradbourne, 269, 270; friends in Maidstone, 270; registers coat of arms, 271, 415; grants mortgage to Beckingham Butler on Tewing manor, 272; legal work of Court of Wards, 272-4, 415; continued association with Middle Temple, 274-5, 416-7; named Steward of Reader's Feast, 275, 308, 417; appointed to stand at Cupboard, 276, 417; makes will, 289-92, 408, 414, 415, 417; illness and death, 276, 417; descendants, 276-9; Diary, 1 *sqq.*, 18-25, 262, *et passim.*

Manningham, John, son of Diarist, 270, 289, 291, 292

Manningham (Madyngham), Emma, 252

Manningham (Madyngham) (Manyngham), Thomas, of Luton, Beds., mayor of St. Albans, great-grandfather of Diarist, 252, 260

Manningham (Maningham), Jane, second wife of Richard M. squire of Bradbourne, 20, 42, 44, 52,
88, 255, 269, 303, 305, 317, 339, 414

Manningham (Maningham), John, infant son of Diarist, died in infancy, 270

Manningham (Maningham), Thomas, father of Sir John M. of Wrestlingworth, 407

Manningham (Manyngham), Sir John, of Wrestlingworth, 252, 407

Manningham (Manyngham), John, Oxford humanist, 252, 407, 415

Manningham, Marian (Marion), daughter of Edmund M., 284

Manningham, Marie (Mary), sister of Edmund, Charles, and William M., 284

Manningham, Mary, daughter of Walter M., 277

Manningham, Nicholas, son of Richard M. rector of Michelmersh, 278

Manningham, Sir Oliver, of Wrestlingworth, 252

Manningham, Richard, squire of Bradbourne ("father in love"), 1, 19, 41, 42, 44, 49, 50, 51, 52, 53, 85, 86, 87, 89, 160, 161, 196, 201, 202, 205, 255, 266, 267, 268, 269, 270, 271, 290, 303, 305, 316, 317, 334, 339, 361, 371, 385, 409, 414; will of, 284-7, 409, 414; memorial, 288

Manningham, Richard, son of Diarist, rector of Michelmersh, Hants., 268, 270, 271, 277, 278, 290, 291, 292, 413, 418, 419

Manningham, Richard, son of Richard M. rector of Michelmersh, 278

Manningham, Sir Richard, M.D., obstetrician, son of Thomas M. bishop of Chichester, 251, 277, 278-9, 419

Manningham, Robert, father of Diarist, 251, 252, 253, 254, 255, 260, 408, 409

Manningham, Simon, son of Thomas

M. bishop of Chichester, 278

Manningham, Susan (Susanna), daughter of Diarist, 268, 270, 289

Manningham, Thomas, brother of Diarist, 254, 307

Manningham, Thomas, D.D., son of Richard M. rector of Michelmersh, bishop of Chichester, 251, 277, 278, 418, 419

Manningham, Thomas, M.D., son of Sir Richard M., 279

Manningham, Thomas, D.D., son of Thomas M. bishop of Chichester, 278

Manningham, Thomas, uncle of Diarist, vicar of Swavesey, 252, 253, 255, 336, 408

Manningham, Walter, son of Diarist, 271, 277, 278, 289, 291, 292, 418, 419

Manningham, William, brother of Edmund M., 284, 290

Manningham, William, son of Edmund M., 284

Manning's Island, New York, 278

Manningtree, Essex, 187, 380

Mansell, Sir Robert, 123, 357

Manwood, Sir Roger, I.T., 10, 76, 140, 319, 329-30, 364

Maplesden, Edward, M.T., 267, 270, 306

Maplesden, family of, 414

Maplesden, Jervaise, M.T., 267, 306

Maplesden, Richard, M.T., 270

Marbury, Francis, preacher, 11n, 115, 350

Marche, first(?) husband of Jane Manningham, 20, 44, 305

Marcus Aurelius, 241, 404

Margaret Tudor, Princess, 322

Marian persecutions, 306

Markham, Gervase (Jervis), 70, 324

Marlowe, Christopher, 373

Marrow (b. Littleton), Margaret, 395

Marrow, Samuel, 220, 395

Marrow, Thomas, 395

Marshall, George, 392

Marshall, Hamlett, curate, 340, 341

Marshall, Roger, 398

Marshalsea, prison, London, 368, 385

Marston, John, M.T., 363, 374

Marston, John, M.T., poet, satirist, playwright, 3, 10, 133, 265, 298, 312, 362-3, 374

Martial (Martialis), Marcus Valerius, Roman poet, 69, 111, 322, 382

"Martin Marprelate," 370; tracts, 258; execution, 331

Martin, Richard, M.T., 4, 6, 7, 8, 9, 48, 70, 120, 261, 262, 263, 265, 296, 311-2, 313, 318, 325, 326, 343, 344, 351, 354, 382, 394, 413

Martin, Sir Richard, 53, 318

Martyr, Peter, 410

Mary, Duchess of Suffolk, 390

Mary Stuart, Queen of Scots, 23, 173-80, 323, 330, 355, 375

Mary Tudor, Queen of England, 132, 220, 242, 252, 309, 339, 361, 362, 366, 368, 394, 414

Mary, Queen of England. *See* William and Mary

Massachusetts, 18

Master of the Horse, 332

Master Worsley's Book on the History and Constitution of the Honourable Society of the Middle Temple, 299

Masters, Dr., physician to the Queen, 299

Masters, Thomas, master of the Temple, 299, 300

"Master's Private Book, The," Magdalene College MS, 409

Mather, Cotton, 24

Matthew, Dr. Tobie (Tobias), bishop of Durham, 70, 245, 324, 392, 400, 404, 405

Maurice, Count of Nassau, Prince of Orange, 201

May, Sir Humphrey, 351, 416

Maynard, Alexander, M.T., 221, 395
Maynard, John, 395
Mayne (b. Androes), Mary, 86
Mayne, James, G.I., 86, 337
Mayne, James, 337
Mead, Joseph, of Christ's College, 25
Meade, Mr., lawyer, 148
Medicinal remedies, 84, 85
Medway, the, river, 316, 334
Meers, John, bailiff, 342
Melstreet, East Malling, Kent, 286
Memoirs of the Life of Robert Cary,
    Baron of Leppington and Earl of
    Monmouth. Written by himself,
    391-2, 396
Menaechmi, comedy by Plautus, 48
Mendoza, Don Bernardino de, 382
Meopham, Kent, 406
Mercers Company of London, 42,
    255, 285, 303
Merchant Adventurers, company of,
    75; their court, 75-6
Merchant Taylors' School, 309, 320
Merchiston, Scotland, 377
Meredith, Sir William, 155, 370
Mermaid Tavern, Cheapside, 393,
    394; wits, 5, 297, 343
Merton College, Oxford, 299, 347,
    351, 401, 404
Merula, Paul, Dutch scholar, 311
Mery Passages & Jeasts, 2, 301, 315,
    346
Metcalfe, Harry, 286
Metley, Warwickshire, 395
Michelmersh, Hants., 277, 278
Micklethwayte, Paul, preacher, 299
Middelburg, Zeeland, the Nether-
    lands, 304
Middle Temple, Ancient and Honour-
    able Society of, 1, 3, 4, 5, 6, 7, 8,
    10, 11, 18, 21, 24, 25, 83, 89, 115,
    172, 251, 260-8, 274, 275, 285,
    296, 298, 299, 301, 304, 306,
    307, 309, 310, 311, 313, 319, 321,
    326, 327, 328, 330, 331, 332, 333,
    334, 335, 339, 340, 341, 342, 343,
    344, 346, 348, 349, 350, 351, 352,
    353, 354, 355, 356, 359, 360, 361,
    362, 363, 364, 365, 366, 368, 369,
    370-1, 374, 375, 378, 379, 380,
    381, 382, 383, 384, 385, 386, 389,
    390, 391, 392-3, 394, 395, 396,
    397, 399, 400, 411, 412, 413, 416,
    417; Bench Book, 299, 411, 412,
    417; Candlemas celebrations, 262,
    265, 311; Christmas revels, 6, 261,
    296-7, 311, 324, 325, 393-4; gate,
    261, 383; Hall, 4, 7, 11, 24, 70, 261,
    262, 263, 264, 265, 275, 311, 313,
    324, 335, 352, 411; lane, 275;
    library, x, 273, 411, 416; masque
    at court, 296; parliament, 84, 267,
    276, 331, 355, 363, 381, 412, 413,
    416, 417
Middleton, Thomas, clerk of Temple
    Church, 267, 299
Midsummer Night's Dream, play by
    Shakespeare, 312
Mildmay, Sir Anthony, 43, 305
Mildmay, Sir Walter, 384
Millenary petition, 12, 350
Miller, Nicholas, 290
Miller, yeoman, 50
Milton, John, poet, 277, 366
Misrule, Lord of, in Middle Temple
    Candlemas celebrations, 262, 311
Mitcham, Surrey, 385
Mitre, the, London tavern, 393, 394
Modbury, Devon, 365
Montague (Montagu), Dr. James, 55,
    225, 319, 326, 370, 397
Montaigne (Mountain), Dr. George,
    365
Montaigne, Michel Eyquem, Seigneur
    de, 153
Moore, Eustace, preacher, 58, 320
Moore (More), Francis, M.T., 122,
    308, 335, 356, 383
Moor Hall, Ardeley, Herts., 390
Mooting, at Inns of Court, 154, 224,
    262, 264, 274, 368, 412
More, Cresacre, 9, 326-7

More, Sir George, 367
More, John, alderman, 133, 363
More, Sir Thomas, L.I., 3, 9, 73–4,
    270, 326–7, 359, 374, 384
Morgan, Francis, M.T., 265, 298, 325
Morgan, Francis, son of Francis M.
    of the M.T., 298, 325
Morgan, Lucy (Luce), 30, 298
Morgan, Mrs. Sylvester, 97
Morison, Sir Charles, 344
Morison (Moryson), Lady, 97
Morley (title). See Parker
Morton, Lincs., 307
Moryson, Fynes, 325
Moryson, Richard, translator, 384
Moulton, Suffolk, 399
Mountford, John, 301
Mountford, Thomas, D.D., prebendary
    of Westminster, 36, 301
Mountjoy (title). See Blount
Mowbray, a Scot, 140, 364
Moyle, Robert, 380
Moyle, Sir Thomas, 373
Mulcaster, Richard, 320
Munday, Anthony, 382
Munich, Germany, 359
Munnes (Muns), Anne, 302
Munnes (Muns), Edward, preacher,
    39, 302
Munnes (Munns), John, 302
Musters, in Kent, Twysden's book of,
    303
Mylot, Thomas, 350

Napier, John, 184, 377
Narrative of the Gunpowder Plot,
    385
Nashe, Thomas, 369
Navy, the, 154
Nazianzen, Saint Gregory of, 111
Neitherbury (Netherbury), Dorset,
    352
Netherlands, the. See Low Countries
Neveurs (Nevers) (title). See
    Gonzaga
Nevile, Charles, Lord, 384

Nevile, Thomas, S.T.P., 16, 207, 235,
    256, 257, 386, 400
Nevile's Court, Trinity College, Camb.,
    256
Neville, Edward, Lord Latimer, eighth
    Lord Abergavenny, 23, 231, 398–9,
    400
Neville (Nevil) (Nevill), Sir Henry,
    23, 43, 193, 235, 246, 383, 387–8,
    400, 405
Neville, Henry, sixth Lord Abergavenny,
    316, 317
Newcastle-on-Tyne, 404
New College, Oxford, 159, 278, 370
New England, 278, 405
Newgate Street, London, 356
Newhide. See New Hythe
New Hythe, Kent, 52, 83, 270, 334;
    chapel at, 303
*New Illustrations of the Life, Studies,
    and Writings of Shakespeare,* 1, 23,
    314
New Inn, 309, 311, 315, 321, 326,
    334, 340, 342, 343, 346, 351, 354,
    356, 368, 378, 383, 389, 392, 395,
    405
Newland, Kent, 54
New Learning, the, 259
New Plymouth, in New England, 405
News from Ostend of the oppugnation,
    45, 306. See also *Extremities
    urging Sir F. Veare to the anti-
    parle*
Newton, Sir John, 317
Newton, Katherine Lady, 182
Nichols, Josias, rector of Eastwell,
    Kent, 140, 365
Nicholson, George, schoolmaster, 254
Nicolls (Nicholes), Augustine, M.T.,
    24, 172, 173, 266, 267, 374–5
Nicolls, Thomas, 374
Niepson, Mr., grandfather of Lady
    Palavicino, 86
Nisi Prius, commission of, 329
Noctes Atticae, 389
Noctes Templariae. See *Prince d'Amour*

Noel, Sir Andrew, 371
Noel, Henry, 161-2, 371
Nonnington, Yorks., 417
Nonsuch, Surrey, 385
Norcliffe, Sir Thomas, 417
Nordiham, Sussex, 305
Norfolk, county, 357, 393
Norfolk (title). *See* Howard
Norman Conquest, 151
Normanby, Lincs., 368
Normandy, 405
Norris (Norreys), Francis, second
   Lord, first Earl of Berkshire,
   380
North (b. Brockett), Frances Lady,
   86, 337
North, Dudley, third Baron North,
   86, 337
North, the, Lord President of, 329;
   council of, 329. *See also* York
North, Roger, second Baron North,
   336, 337
Northampton, Northants., 309
Northampton (title). *See* Howard
Northamptonshire, 81
Northaw, Herts., 356
Northbourne, Kent, 350
Northbrook, Norfolk, 320
Northcote, Devon, 354
Northfleet, Kent, 275, 416
Northley, Hants., 378
Northumberland (title). *See* Dudley;
   Percy
Norton (b. Cranmer), Alice, 48, 314,
   315
Norton (b. Cranmer), Margery, or
   Margaret, 314
Norton, Elizabeth, 315
Norton, Henry, 49, 315
Norton, "Cosen," William or Robert,
   48, 49, 314, 315
Norton, manor of, Suffolk, 273, 340
Norton, Thomas, 314, 315
Norway, 332
Norwich, Norfolk, 301, 320; bishop
   of, 121, 354; cathedral, 354;

grammar school, 357
Nosce Teipsum, poem by Davies,
   311
Nottingham (title). *See* Howard,
   Charles
Nottinghamshire, 52, 317
Nowell, Dr. Alexander, "old" dean
   of St. Paul's, 68, 133, 304, 322,
   362, 370, 372, 389
Nowell, Lawrence, dean of Lichfield,
   389
Nugae Antiquae, 14, 15n

*Observations Historical and Chrono-
   logical on the Constitution Customs
   & Usage of the Middle Temple*, 412
Odcombian Banquet, The, 297
Odsey Hundred, Herts., 411
*Of divorcement, a sermon Preached
   at Pauls Cross*, 349
Of the Lawes of Ecclesiasticall Politie,
   340, 361
*Of the proficience and advancement
   of Learning, divine and humane*,
   369
Olantigh, Kent, 373
Old Swan, London, 393
Olivia, *Twelfth Night*, 314
O'Neill, Hugh, second Earl of Tyrone,
   188, 247, 398, 406
O'Neill, Shane, or John, 342
O'Neill, Sir Turlough (Tyrrelagh),
   Luineach, Earl of Clanconnell,
   342
O'Neill, Turlough (Tyrrelagh), 342,
   398
Onslowe, Elizabeth, 273
Onslowe family, 274
Onslowe, George, son of William O.
   the elder, 89, 273, 340
Onslowe, George, the younger, 273
Onslowe, William, son of George O.,
   273
Onslowe, William, 273, 340
Onslowe, William, the younger, 273
Opera quae extant omnia . . .

quaedam jam antea Anglice scripta, nunc primum studio doctorum virorum Anglicorum Latine reddita, T. Stapletoni, 359
Opuscula Varia de Latinitate Jurisconsultorum Veterum, 367
Orange, Prince of. *See* Maurice
Oratio Academica; an politici horum temporum in numero christianorum sint habendi, 22, 125–30, 359–60
Orationes Academicae, Miscellaneae, 359
Orchestra, or a poem of dancing, by Davies, 7, 8, 311, 312
Order of the Garter, 387
Ordo Senioritatis, University of Cambridge, 398
Origen of Alexandria, 104
Origines Juridiciales, 24, 313, 334, 395, 412, 413
Ormonde (title). *See* Butler
Orsino, *Twelfth Night,* 313
Orsino, Virginio, Duke of Bracciano, 313
Osborne, Edward, 406
Osborne, John, M.T., 247, 406
Oseley, John, M.T., 340
Oseley (Ousley), Richard, 340
Oseley (Ousley), Richard, M.T., 18, 89, 340
Ostend, Belgium, 45, 306, 347, 398
Otford, manor of, Kent, 50, 316
Otford Park, Kent, 316, 317
Otto, bishop of Constance, 199
Ouse, river, 336
Overall, John, dean of St. Paul's, London, 13, 68, 223, 258, 259, 302, 322, 384, 397
Overbury, Giles, M.T., 324, 417
Overbury, Nicholas, M.T., 6, 121, 265, 300, 310, 324, 334, 340, 351, 354, 412, 416
Overbury, Thomas, M.T., 3, 6, 7, 47, 89, 95, 187, 235, 263, 265, 274, 310, 324, 335, 340, 342,

351, 354, 380, 400–1
Ovid: Lucius Publius Ovidius Naso, 394, 400
Owen, Jane, maidservant of Richard Manningham squire of Bradbourne, 285
Owens (Owen), Thomas, 260, 283
Oxenoth, estate of, Kent, 305
Oxford, Diocese of, 347
Oxfordshire, 85, 343, 362, 381
Oxford (title). *See* Vere
Oxford, University of, 5, 7, 11, 12, 58, 71, 85, 90, 100, 159, 196, 252, 259, 260, 261, 278, 315, 322, 333, 335, 346, 347, 349, 361, 362, 368, 372, 373, 375, 381, 385, 387, 389, 396, 399, 401, 404, 406, 415; Bodley's library, 100, 186, 347; reception of John King, 120, 347

Padua, Italy, 49, 393
Paget, Charles, M.T., 309
Paget, James, M.T., 141, 365
Paget (Pagytt), Thomas, M.T., third Lord Paget, 309, 365
Paget, William, first Baron Paget of Beaudesert, Lord Paget of Drayton, ·46, 309
Paget, William, fourth Lord, M.T., 309
Paget, William, sergeant-at-mace, 46, 309
Palavicino (b. Hoostman) (Hoofman), Anne Lady, 85, 255, 337
Palavicino, Sir Horatio, 86, 337
Palmer, John, 256
Palmer, Thomas, M.T., 381
Palmes, Francis, I.T., 333
Palmes, Guy, I.T., 333
Papists, Papism, 34, 92, 100, 111, 143, 144, 145, 146, 154, 157, 171, 185–6, 188, 206, 207, 217, 245, 360, 381, 401; supplication to King James for toleration, 245
Paradossi, by Lando, 382
Paris, France, 242, 376, 417

Parker, Edward, twelfth Baron Morley, 122, 355-6
Parker, Henry, 416
Parker, Richard, M.T., 275, 416
Parkins, George, I.T., 20, 88, 339
Parliament, 5, 179, 239, 274, 309, 310, 311, 315, 330, 334, 335, 346, 348, 351, 355, 362, 370, 378, 382, 390, 391, 399
Parry, Henry, the elder, 87, 339
Parry, Henry, D.D., chaplain to Queen Elizabeth, 14, 15, 16, 30, 49, 82, 87, 88, 205, 207, 208, 211, 222, 245, 246, 266, 267, 297, 298, 316, 333, 338, 339, 386, 396, 404, 406
Parry, Sir Thomas, 154
Parsons, Robert, S.J., 303, 317, 323, 372, 401, 404
Patents, for playing cards, 100, 346; for tin, 45, 307
Pathill, John, 290
Paul V, pope, 385
Paulet, Sir Amias, 261
Paul's Cross, 13, 59, 67, 90, 101, 266, 267, 348, 360; sermons at, 131, 134, 164, 196, 246, 320, 340, 347, 349, 350, 362, 363, 364, 372, 373, 384, 386, 406
Paul's Hill, London, 210
Paul's Wharf. See St. Peter the Little
Paulus Lucius Aemilius, 244, 404
Pawley, Thomas, 285
Pawley, William, 285
Payne, Mr., of New College, 159
Peeters (Peters), Jacob, 285
Pelagius, theologian, 203
Pemberton, John, sheriff, 340
Pemberton, Robert, 389
Pemberton, William, M.T., 211, 388, 389
Pembroke College, Oxford, 302
Pembroke College (Hall), Camb., 164, 259, 302, 320, 364, 372, 373, 410
Pembroke (title). See Herbert

Peniston, Thomas, 318
Pennyall, Thomas, 291
Penry (ap Henry), John, 370
Pentecost, 62
Pepys, Sir Richard, M.T., 417
Pepys, Samuel, diarist, 19, 298, 359, 393, 394
Pepys, Talbot, M.T., 417
Percy, Algernon, tenth Earl of Northumberland, 353
Percy (b. Devereux), (Perrot), Dorothy, Countess of Northumberland, 120, 353
Percy, Henry, ninth Earl of Northumberland, 120, 231, 338, 343, 344, 353, 398
Percy, Lady, "Kate," in Shakespeare's 1 Hen. IV, 306
Perkins, William, Puritan theologian, 121, 155, 258, 354-5, 370, 395
Perne scholarship, at Peterhouse, 277
Perrott (Perrot), Thomas, 353
Perry (Recalde), Mary. See Tresham
Perse (Pearse), Stephen, 354
Perse School, Cambridge, 354
Persian law regarding offending noblemen, 115
Peryam (Periam), John, 348
Peryam (Periam), Sir John, 9, 346
Peryam (Periam), Sir William, 76, 113, 265, 331, 348
Peter, John, M.T., 171, 374
Peterborough Cathedral, 302, 360; dean of, 256
Peterhouse, St. Peter's College, Camb., 39, 268, 277, 302, 350, 361, 368, 379, 392, 394, 413, 418
Peters (b. Arnold), Sara, 284
Petition of Right, 357
Pettey, Elizabeth, 305
Pewterers, Company of, 45, 307-8
Peyton, Sir John, 398, 400
Philip II, King of Spain, 78, 305, 333
Philipot (Philipott), John, Rouge Dragon, 271, 324, 407, 413, 414

Philipot, Thomas, 304, 318, 373, 414

Philips (Phillips), Edward, preacher, 12, 38

Phillips (Phelips), Sir Edward, M.T., 172, 302, 351, 374

Phillips (Phelips), Sir Robert, 346

Phillips, Walter, first dean of Rochester, 55, 319

Philomela, The Lady Fitzwalters Nightingale, 344

Physicians, College of, 278, 318, 333

Piccard, a, 153

Picture of a perfect Common wealth, by Floyd, 36, 300-1

Pierpoint, lord of manor of East Malling, 303

Pierson, Edmond, 285

Pigeon, waterbearer of London, 285

Pigott, Alban, M.T., 124, 298, 359

Pigott, Thomas, 272

Pilgrim's Way, north of East Malling, 339

Piracy, 201-2

Pissing-Alley, London, 306

Pius V, pope, 220

Plain and familiar Edition of the Ten Commandments, 395

Plaine discovery of the Whole Revelation of Saint John, 377

Plantagenet, Arthur, Viscount Lisle, 343

Plato, 239

Plautus, Roman dramatist, 48

Playfere, Dr. Thomas, 155, 369, 409, 410

Pleas of the Innocent: wherein is averred that the Ministers and People falslie termed Puritans are iniuriouslie slaundered for enemies and troublers of the state, The, 140, 365

"Plot of the Play called England's Joy," 358

Plowden, Edmund, M.T., 4, 119, 261, 331, 352-3, 378

Pluckley, Kent, 271, 329, 367

Poems written by the Rt. Hon. William Earl of Pembroke, 335

Poetical Rhapsody, A, 21-22, 345, 367, 376

Pole, Reginald, cardinal, 377

Polivizena. *See* Palavicino

Pomford, William, 260, 283, 336

Pompey (Cneius Pompeius) the Great, 128

Poor John's, cottage in East Malling, Kent, 286

Pope, Sackville, 292

Popes-head Alley, 344

Popes, manor of, Herts., 331

Popham, Sir John, M.T., 76, 172, 236, 265, 296, 311, 331, 358, 379, 388, 405

Popish doctrine, 94, 258

Portsmouth, Hants., 217, 300, 390

Pory, John, newsletter writer, 15, 25, 297

Pory, Nicholas, 273

Posies on rings, 124

Potterell, John, bellows-maker, 100

Poverty, of clergy, 227

Powell, Edward, M.T., 417

Praise of Folly, The, 382

Pranell, Henry, 55

Pranell (b. Howard), Frances. *See* Stuart

Prerogative Court of Canterbury, 287, 292, 304

Prerogative, royal, 100

Presbyterian, 258

Preston, Sir Amyas de, 246, 405

Preston (b. Butler), Elizabeth Lady, 154, 343

Preston, Sir Richard, first Lord Dingwall, first Earl of Desmond, 343

Prew, William, cleric, 270, 287, 414

Prideaux, Edmund, I.T., 100, 346

Prince Charles. *See* Charles I

Prince d'Amour, or the Prince of Love, with a Collection of Several Ingenious Poems and Songs By

the Wits of the Age, 6, 8n, 261, 265, 297, 311, 312, 324, 325, 386, 394
Prince of Love. *See* Martin, Richard; *Prince d'Amour*
Privy Chamber, in palace at Richmond, 16, 207, 386
Privy Council, 45, 96, 98, 101, 119, 208, 210, 215, 219, 224, 246, 265, 307, 308, 318, 329, 332, 333, 372, 379, 385, 392, 396
Proclamations, royal, 208, 209, 210, 223, 224, 388, 390, 396, 399; for value of Scottish coinage, 231, 399; regarding tin, 308
Protestants, 143, 385, 401
Providence Company, 335
Prowhurst, Matthew, 287
Ptolemy III, surnamed Evergetes, 168
Public Record Office, London, x, 273, 304, 353
Puerto Rico, 300
Puleston, John, M.T., 416
Purchas, His Pilgrims, 300
Puritans, Puritan party, 12-13, 25, 29, 44, 77, 114, 124, 140, 163, 219, 258, 259, 296, 299, 302, 303, 304, 306, 316, 330, 336, 349, 350, 352, 354, 366, 367, 368, 370, 372-3, 395
Purslowe, George, printer, 340
Pye, Walter, 274, 275
Pygmalion, 312
Pym, Alexander, M.T., father of John Pym, 370
Pym, Alexander, M.T., son of John Pym, 370
Pym, John, M.T., 3, 155, 218, 352, 370, 371, 391, 392

Quare impedit, 76, 331
Quarles, Francis, L.I., emblem poet, 25
Queenhithe Ward, 363, 373
Queens' College, Camb., 142, 151, 310, 314, 320, 322, 351, 365, 379, 394
Queen's College, Oxford, 372
Quodlibets. See *Decacordon*

Rabelais, François, 4, 8, 22
Radcliffe (b. Morison), Bridget, Countess of Sussex, 97, 344
Radcliffe, Robert, fifth Earl of Sussex, 97, 98, 343-4
Radcliffe (Ratcliffe), Thomas, third Earl of Sussex, 49, 315
Ralegh (b. Throckmorton), Elizabeth Lady, 18, 342
Ralegh, Sir Walter, 3, 18, 23, 66, 96, 161-2, 224, 246, 323, 333, 342, 357, 371-2, 383, 397, 400, 405
Ramsey, Hunts., 336
Ramus, Peter, 257
Rande, Samuel, bookseller, 340
Randleston, Dorset, 365
Ravens, Mr., arbitrator, 161, 163
Ravens, John, 372
Ravens, Dr. Ralph, 372
Ravis, Thomas, 13, 347, 387
Rawlins, John, 325
Rayner, Thomas, bailiff, 269, 286
Reade, Andrew, Clement's Inn, 365
Reade, Robert, M.T., 365
Reading, Berks., 308
Reading, legal exercises of, 262, 264, 265, 266, 267, 271, 274, 275, 276, 306, 308, 334, 355, 412, 416, 417
Recalde, Alonzo Perez de, 363
Recalde, Mary. See Tresham
Recusancy, recusants, 98, 173; lawyers in Ireland, 173
Redhouse, Perthshire, 332
Redman, William, bishop of Norwich, 121, 302, 354
Reeves (Reves), John, M.T., 381
Reeves (Ryves), Richard, M.T., 46, 67, 141, 188, 309, 321, 365, 381
Reeves (Ryves), William, M.T., 46, 67, 188, 309, 321, 381

Regent masters, 257
Regent of Scotland. *See* Hamilton
Regius professorships, 11, 12, 14, 257, 258, 301, 362, 370, 372, 384, 385
Remaines of a Greater Work Concerning Britain, 327, 347, 374
Rennes, France, 367
Reports de Edward Coke, les, 357
Requests, Court of, 186, 188, 322, 346
Reve, Thomas, M.T., 270
Reynolds, Edward, 325
Reynolds, Dr. John, 13, 20, 132, 361, 362
Rich, Robert, first Lord, 122, 356
Richard III, King of England, protagonist of play, by Legge, 256; by Shakespeare, 10, 75, 266, 328
Richers, Frances, Mrs. 50
Richers, John, 41, 49, 50, 303, 316
Richmond, Palace at, 16, 205, 267, 296, 386, 387
Ridley, Nicholas, bishop of London, 259
Rivers (Ryvers), George, M.T., 261, 266
Rivers (Ryvers), Marcellus, M.T., 141, 267, 365
Rivers (Ryvers), William, M.T., 275
Rizzio (Riccio), David, 176, 375
Ro. Ba. *See Life of Thomas More*
Roberts (Roberdes), John, 292
Roberts, Thomas, 252
Roberts (Robardes), William, 253, 271, 290, 292
Rochester, Kent, 196; cathedral, 24, 54, 55, 266, 297-8, 318, 319; dean of, 15, 52, 55, 266; custom searcher, 52; assizes at, 18, 53, 54, 266; bishop's palace, 298; bishop of, 326, 338, 351, 392
Rochford, Essex, "Lawless Court," 187, 380
Roe, Sir John, 398

Rogers, Thomas, 285
Rolls, the, preacher at, 278
Roman Catholic Church, 128, 148, 221, 231, 270, 372, 378, 397; magnificence of Mass, 154. *See also* Papists
Roman occupation (of Britain), 151
Rome, Italy, 216, 385; English College at, 401
Rooke, an infant, 100
Roper, William, 327, 395
Rotham. *See* Wrotham
Rotterdam, Holland, 343
Rouen, France, 405
Rous or Rouse. *See* Rowse
Rowlands, Samuel, verse-writer, 11, 22, 98, 266, 344-5
Rowse, Anthony, of Halton, Cornwall, 370-1
Rowse, Anthony, M.T., 371
Rowse, Francis, M.T., 159, 218, 365, 370, 371, 391
Rowse, Robert, M.T., 141, 159, 218, 365, 370, 391
R.R. *See* Reeves, Richard, and Rowse, Robert
Royal Society, 278
Royall Street, London, 350
Royden, Margaret, 316
Royden, Thomas, 316
Royston, Herts., 332
Rudd, Anthony, D.D., bishop of St. David's, 194, 383
Rudsyn, Warwicks., 395
Rudyerd (Ruddier), Benjamin, M.T., 4, 5, 7, 8, 9, 84, 188, 218, 221, 235, 263, 265, 274, 296, 309, 311, 312, 334-5, 351, 381, 382, 386, 391, 396, 405, 413, 416; his *Noctes Templariae*, 6; *Memoirs of*, by Manning, 6n, 415, 416
Rudyerd (b. Harrington), Elizabeth Lady, 335
Rudyerd, James 334
Rules of Reason, The, 327
Rusden, Northants., 389

Rushton, Northants., 363
Rutland, county, 333
Rutland (title). *See* Manners
Ruthven, Alexander, 390
Ruthven, Barbara Lady, 18, 218, 235, 390, 400
Ruthven, John, third Earl of Gowrie (Gowry), 218, 390, 400
Ruthven (Ruthen), Patrick, 390
Ruthven, William, 390
Rye, Hubert de, 355
Rycote, near Thame, Oxon, 380

Sackville (b. Clifford), Anne, Countess of Dorset, afterwards of Pembroke and Montgomery, 25
Sackville, Richard, third Earl of Dorset, 273
Sackville, Thomas, Baron Buckhurst, first Earl of Dorset, 48, 50, 113, 207, 208, 235, 314, 317, 349, 355, 387, 388, 400–1
St. Albans, Herts., 24, 70, 122, 252, 255, 260, 284, 287, 378, 407
St. Albans Abbey, 252
St. Amand, France, 403
St. Ambrose, bishop of Milan, 205, 237, 403
St. Andrew, church of, Camb., 258, 354
St. Andrew, church of, Holborn, London, 11, 101, 120, 267, 278, 332, 347, 353, 384, 390
St. Andrew Hubbard, London, 302
St. Andrew, Priory Church of, Swavesey, Cambs., 253
St. Andrew Undershaft, London, 274
St. Andrews, University of, 279
St. Ann, chapel of. *See* Temple Church
St. Anne's, Blackfriars, 12, 350, 367–8
St. Augustine, bishop of Hippo, 36, 39, 62, 72, 204, 325, 361, 384; *De Civitate Dei*, 72
St. Austin. *See* St. Augustine

St. Bartholomew by the Exchange, London, 391
St. Bartholomew Massacre, 367
St. Bartholomew's Hospital, London, 333, 339
St. Bernard, 72, 94, 244
St. Botolph's, Camb., 369
St. Botolph's without Aldersgate, London, 321, 388
St. Bride's (Bridget's), Fleet Street, London, 273
St. Chrysostom, 404
St. Clement Danes, church of, London, 12, 35, 300, 366, 384, 399; sermon at, 145, 151
St. David's, bishop of, 383
St. Dunstan's, parish of, Canterbury, 330
St. Dunstan's, 29
St. Faith's, church in London, 277
St. George, 387
St. George, Henry, 340, 407, 408
St. George, parish in Southwark, 277
St. George, Sir Richard, 331
St. Giles, Cripplegate, London, 389
St. Ives, Hunts., 251, 254, 255, 260, 336
St. James, church of, East Malling, Kent (formerly St. Mary in the East), 269, 276, 284, 288, 289, 303, 305, 409, 414, 418
St. James, Hemingford Grey, Hunts., 336
St. James, Westminster, parish infirmary, 279
St. Jerome, 183
St. John (b. Fysher), Alice Lady, 253, 254
St. John, Oliver, first Lord St. John of Bletsoe, 253, 381
St. John's College, Camb., 155, 256, 258, 259, 301, 320, 338, 351, 369, 370, 379, 410
St. John's College, Oxford, 6, 21, 40, 259, 299, 302, 309, 310,

319, 326, 334, 351, 372, 404
St. Lawrence, London, 355
St. Leonard, church of, Foster Lane, London, 370, 391
St. Margaret the Virgin, church of, Hemingford Abbots, Hunts., 336
St. Margaret, church of, Lothbury, London, 271, 388
St. Martin-in-the-Vintry, London, 350
St. Martin Outwich, London, 351
St. Martin-in-the-Fields, Westminster, 332
St. Mary Abchurch, London, 361
St. Mary Aldermary, London, 349
St. Mary in the East, church of, East Malling, Kent. See St. James
St. Mary Spittal, church of, London, 205, 385-6
St. Mary the Virgin, university church, Oxford, 404
St. Michael's Church, Camb., 360
St. Michael, parish of, Cornhill, London, 309, 320
St. Nicholas Cole Abbey, London, 360
St. Paul's Cathedral, 12, 14, 18, 29, 71, 114, 210, 266, 267, 301, 326, 346, 348, 349, 365; churchyard, 99, 320, 355, 373; dean of, 12, 68, 87, 133, 223, 304, 322, 362, 364, 370, 372, 384, 389, 397; sermons preached at, 71, 114, 116, 142, 156, 189, 195; reader at, 149; repair of, 346
St. Paul's Cray, Kent, 304
St. Paul's School, 302, 309, 370
St. Peter the Little, Paul's Wharf, London, 13, 167, 190, 373, 382
St. Peter's Street, St. Albans, Herts., 252
St. Saviour's, church in Southwark, 302
St. Stephen's, Walbrook, London, 364
Salisbury Court, Dorset House, 273

Salisbury, Wilts., 330; archdeacon of, 338; bishop of, 354, 365; cathedral or see, 29, 87; chancellor of, 14, 339
Salomo Ben Melech, Rabbi, 157
Saltingstone. See Saltonstall
Saltonstall (Saltanstall), Peter, M.T., 18, 218, 390-1
Saltonstall (Saltanstall), Richard, 390-1
Saltonstall (b. Waller), Anne, 391
Salting, initiation of, 257
Sanders, Matthew, preacher, 59, 320
Sanders, Samuel, preacher, 320
Sandwich, Kent, 1, 161, 256, 267, 271, 304, 329, 330, 371
Sandy (Sandey), Beds., 30, 86, 298, 336
Sandys, Edwin, bishop of London, archbishop of York, 84, 361
Sandys, Sir Edwin, 361, 362
Sanquhar (title). See Crichton
Sapley, Hunts., forest of, 85, 336
Sappcottes, Mr., 81
Saturday market, West Malling, Kent, 270
Savil, Mr., deceased, 160
Savile (b. Dacres) (Garrard), Margaret Lady, 382
Savile, George, 69, 322
Savile, Sir John, baron of the Exchequer, 265, 329
Savile (Saville), Sir Henry, 13, 245, 351, 382, 383, 387, 404
Savoy, Duke of. See Charles Emmanuel
Savoy, the, London, 46, 367
Schole of the Noble and Worthy Science of Defence, The, 379
Scotland, 16, 184, 338, 364, 377, 387, 391-2, 396, 399, 400, 404
Scots, Scottish, 323, 374; court, 23; guards at French court, 235; knights, 332; lady (Barbara Ruthven), 218, 390; Lord Sanquhar's men, 380; Scottish coin, 399

Scott (b. Baker), Elizabeth, 318
Scott, John, 316
Scott, Sir John, 318
Scott (Catlyn), Joyce, 316
Scott, Robert, preacher, 41, 302
Scott, Thomas, sheriff of Kent, 53,
    318
Scott, William, I.T., 120, 354
Scottish taunts, 171, 374
Scotts Hall, Smeeth, Kent, 53, 318
Scoulton, Norfolk, 354
Scourge of Folly, The, 328
Scroope, Adrian, M.T., 275
Scrope (Scroope) (b. Carey),
    Philadelphia Lady, 181
Scudamore, James, M.T., 276, 417
Scudamore, Sir James, 376, 417
Scudamore, Sir John, first Viscount
    Scudamore of Sligo, M.T., 376,
    417
Scudamore (b. Throckmorton)
    (Baskerville), Mary Lady, 181,
    376
Searchfield, Dr. Rowland, 21, 40,
    302, 351
Secchi, Nicole, 313
Sedan, France, 367
Sedley, Sir Charles, 316
Sedley (b. Darrell) (Neville), Eliza-
    beth Lady, 49, 316, 317
Sedley, John, 316, 317
Sedley, John, son of John S., 50,
    316
Sedley (b. Savile), Elizabeth, 317
Sedley, Sir William, 49, 50, 316,
    317
Segar, Sir William, 364
Sejanus, 381
Selden, John, 334
Selwyn College, Camb., 299
Seminary priests, 231, 378
Seneca, Roman philosopher, 93,
    126, 241, 341, 403
Sermons, at Great St. Mary's, Camb.,
    University, 258; Barret's *ad
    Clerum,* 258

Sevenoaks, Kent, 316, 317, 339
Seymour, Edward, Earl of Hertford,
    55, 217, 319, 323, 390, 397
Seymour, Edward, Lord Beauchamp,
    23, 217, 224, 323, 390, 397
Seymour (b. Grey), Catherine Lady,
    319, 390
Seymour, Henry Lord, 323
Seymour (b. Howard), Frances,
    Countess of Hertford, 55, 319
Seymour, Thomas, 323
Seymour, William, second Earl of
    Hertford, second Duke of Somer-
    set, 323
Seymours, the, 3
Shakespeare (b. Hathaway), Anne,
    374
Shakespeare, William, 3, 5, 10, 11,
    23, 75, 265, 266, 297, 306, 312,
    313, 314, 319, 328, 353, 355,
    389, 393, 400
Shakespearean, 1
Shandy, Mrs., in Sterne's *Tristram
    Shandy,* 279
Sharpenoe (Sharpenhoe), Beds., 314
Sheborough. *See* Sherborne
Sheforde, Beds., 253
Sherborne, Dorset, 342; castle, 96,
    342
Sherforde, Devon, 395
Shield Gallery, Whitehall, 25, 31,
    298
Shipton-under-Wychwood, Oxon, 335
Shoreham, Kent, 317
Short, Tom, bellows-mender, 347
Short, William, servant of Diarist,
    270, 285
Shrewsbury grammar school, 301
Shrewsbury (title). *See* Talbot
Shropshire, 326
Shulamo. *See* Salomo
Shurland, Thomas, M.T., 141, 365,
    405
Shurley, George, 391
Shuttlecock, game of, 11, 189,
    381; comparison of Capt. White-

lock to a shuttlecock, 130, 360
Sidney, Sir Philip, 309, 316, 337, 398
Sidney (Sydney), Sir Robert, 50, 316, 317
Sidney Sussex College, Camb., 225, 319, 397
Siena, Italy, 314
Sion, Middlesex, 120
Sinsinghurst, Kent, 318
Skinners' Company, master of, 363
Skippon, Luke, 277, 418
Skipton, Yorks., 379
Skipworth, Sir Henry, 373
Smeeth, parish of, Kent, 318
Smith, Miles, bishop, 336
Smith, Sir Thomas, 69, 322
Smith, Thomas, 44
Smith, Thomas, translator, 69, 322
Smith, Dr. William, 155, 369
Smithfield, London, 321
Smyth, Sir Nicholas, 398
Smyth, William, M.T., 275
Snegge (Snagg), Robert, M.T., 186, 378
Snig, Robbin. See Snegge
Snigge (Snygge), George, M.T., 6, 20, 24, 89, 173, 265, 340, 352, 374
Snigge (Snygge), John, M.T., 340
"Sociable Rules for the Apollo," Jonson's Leges Convivales, 4
Solon, Athenian statesman, 149
Some (Soame), Dr. Robert, 220, 394
Somer, John, 54, 318
Somer (b. Ridge) (Colepepper), Martin, 54
Somerset, Earl of. See Carr
Somerset, Edward, Lord Herbert of Chepstow, fourth Earl of Worcester, 207
Somersetshire, 76
Somner (Sumner), William, 160, 161, 256, 371
Songs and Other Poems, 4n
South Benfleet, Essex, 391

South, Edward, M.T., of Lincs., 378
South, Edward, M.T., of Wilts., 378
South, Thomas, of Wilts., 378
South, Thomas, the elder, 378
South, Thomas, the younger, M.T., 186, 276, 378
Southampton, Hants., 415
Southampton (title). See Wriothesley
Southe, Thomas, M.T., 276
Southend, Essex, 380
Southfleet, Kent, 316
South Kirby, Yorks., 320
Southwark, 10, 187, 358, 379
Southwell (b. Howard), Elizabeth Lady, 181
Southwell, Robert, S.J., poet, 379
Spain, 114, 154, 323, 363, 391, 401, 402, 404
Spaniards, Spanish, 51, 133, 154, 397, 398; ambassador, 362; at Ostend, 306–7; cloak, 412; expeditions against, 260, 300, 405; hold on Low Countries, 305; language 78; scholar and teacher (Vives), 384; soldiers at Flushing, 43; in Ireland, 406; naval strength, 188
Spelmonden, Kent, 316
Spenser, Edmund, poet, 3, 10, 30, 78, 297, 319, 332–3, 343, 376, 418
Spenser, John, D.D., 11, 13, 14n, 90, 221, 340–1, 364, 396, 398
Spittal Sermon. See St. Mary Spittal
Springhead. See Well Head
S.P.Q.R., Bede's interpretation, 40
Stafford, Simon, 301
Stafford, Mr., son-in-law of Sir John Cutts, 164
Stampe, Edward, M.T., 261, 266
Stanley, Ferdinando, fifth Earl of Derby, 318, 377, 398
Stanley, Frances Lady. See Egerton
Stanley, John, 305
Stanley, Thomas, 305
Stanley (b. Vere), Elizabeth, Countess of Derby, 181

Stanton, Lawrence, 409

Staple Inn, 329, 346, 374

Stapleton, Thomas, D.D., 11, 22, 93, 125, 341, 359-60; *Academic Oration*, 125-30, 359; *Tres Thomae*, 327, 359

Star Chamber, court of, 89, 122, 235, 308, 318, 321, 329, 342, 347, 356

State Worthies, 333

Stationers' Register, London, 344, 401

Stephens (Stevens), Thomas, M.T., 67, 224, 321, 397

Stepney, Middlesex, 302, 332

Sterne, Lawrence, novelist, 279

Sterrel (Stirrel), Henry, M.T., 153, 275, 368

Sterrel, Henry, the elder, 368

Still, John, bishop of Bath and Wells, 5, 194, 383

Stockbury, Kent, 406

Stockwell, Surrey, 384

Stoke Poges, Bucks., 252, 357

Storm, The, verse letter by Donne, 394

Stourton (b. Brooke), Frances Lady, 330

Stourton, Charles, eighth Baron Stourton, 330

Stourton, John, ninth Baron Stourton, 76, 330

Stow, John, antiquary, 18, 154, 274, 299, 305, 310, 318, 320, 334, 350, 353, 368-9, 370, 373, 386, 387, 388, 389, 390, 392, 397, 400, 405

Stowe, Staffords., 395

Stradilax. *See* Davies, John, M.T.

Strafford, Herts., 392

Strand, the, London, 46, 150, 300, 344, 367

Strange Histories of Songes & Sonets of Kings, Princes, Dukes, Lords, Ladyes, Knights, and Gentlemen, 393

Streynsham, George, 311

Streynsham, Richard, 311

Streynsham, Thomas, M.T., 48, 266, 310, 311

Strype, John, 334, 353

Stuart, Arabella (Arbella), 3, 23, 69, 322-3, 338, 353, 390, 400

Stuart, Charles, Earl of Lennox, 322

Stuart (b. Clifton), Katherine, Duchess of Lennox, 318

Stuart, Esmé, Lord Aubigny, Earl of March, third Duke of Lennox, 318, 381

Stuart (b. Howard) (Pranell) (Seymour), Frances, Duchess of Lennox and Richmond, 55, 319

Stukeley, Hunts., 252

Stuart (Stewart), Henry, Lord Darnley, 176, 177, 322, 375

Subsidies, 123

Suffolk, county, 366, 390, 409

Suffolk family or line, 390

Sundridge, Kent, 14, 266, 297, 317, 339, 386

Sunning, Berks., 383

Supplicats, University of Cambridge, 259, 410

Supremacy, Oath of, 188, 266

Surgeons, College of, 318

Surrey, county, 325, 349

Survey of London and Westminster, 154, 299, 320, 334, 350, 353, 368, 370, 373, 386, 389, 390

Sussex, county, 275, 325, 342

Sussex (title). *See* Radcliffe

Sutor, John, 51

Sutors Croft, Kent, 51

Sutton in Le Dale, Derbyshire, 307, 335

Sutton, Thomas, 374

Swain, John, 369

Swallowcliff, Wilts., 378

Swan, the, playhouse, 11, 358, 379

Swavesey, Cambs., 252, 255, 260, 336, 373, 408

Sweete, John, M.T., 141, 365

Swetnam, Joseph, 379
Swift, Jonathan, 381
Switzers, 121
Swynerton, John, sheriff, 340
Sympson, Launcelot, vicar, 269, 414
Syria, 57

Tabula Legum Pedagogicarum, 254
Tacitus, Roman historian, 403
Talbot, Francis, fifth Earl of Shrews-
  bury, Lord President of the North,
  395
Talbot, Gilbert, seventh Earl of
  Shrewsbury, 207, 337
Talbot (b. Hardwick) (Cavendish),
  Elizabeth, Countess of Shrews-
  bury, "Bess of Hardwick," 323
Tale of a Tub, A, 381
Talmud, the, 185, 377
Tanfield Court, 343
Tanfield, Lawrence, I.T., 97, 172,
  309, 319, 343, 354, 374
Tanfield, Robert, 309
Tanfield, Robert, the younger, M.T.,
  46, 97, 308, 309, 343, 369
Tangmer, Sussex, 341
Tarlton, Richard, actor, 46, 309
Tarltons Jests, 310
Tarltons newes out of purgatorie,
  309
Tate, Francis, M.T., 369
Tavistock Church, Devon, 374
Tavistock Inn, 374
Taylor, John, 324
Temple Bar, London, 261, 342
Temple Church, 11n, 13, 34, 55, 58,
  73, 83, 115, 263, 266, 267, 299,
  300, 312, 319, 326, 334, 350, 352,
  377, 378; Chapel of St. Ann, 300;
  preachers at, 115, 121, 134, 183
Temple, Sir Alexander, 318
Temple (b. Somer) (Peniston), Mary,
  318
Terence, Roman playwright, 328
Tertullian, Carthaginian theologian,
  237, 244, 403

Tewin (Tewing), manor of, 272, 290
Thame, Oxon, 380
Thames, the river, 261, 272, 373
Thavies Inn, 315, 326, 366, 399
Themistocles, Athenian statesman,
  61
Theobalds, Herts., 332, 356
Theodosius, "the Great," Roman
  Emperor of Eastern Roman
  Empire, 205, 216
Theophrastan characters, 6
Theorique and practice of War, 382
Theroles. *See* Thorold
Theydon Garnon, Essex, 351
Thompson, Dr. Giles, 12, 13, 207,
  211, 232, 386-7, 389, 399
Thoms, William J., 2n, 302, 315
Thornborough, Dr. John, 363
Thorold, Alexander, G.I., 307
Thorold, Edmund, G.I., 307
Thorold, John, G.I., 307
Thorold, John, G.I., brother of
  Alexander and Robert T., 307
Thorold (Therold), Robert, G.I.,
  45, 307
Thorold, William, G.I., 307
Thorpe, John, the elder, M.D., 318
Thrale, Richard, bookseller, 335
Thurnham, Kent, 269, 277, 291
Thynne, Aegremont, M.T., 275, 276
Tichbourne, Benjamin, M.T., 275,
  276, 383, 417
Tichbourne, Sir Walter, 275
Tilloy, estate of, Brie, France, 367
Tilt-boat (tillbuow), 22, 196, 272,
  385
Tilting, 133, 363; Scudamore's skill
  at, 376
Tin, pre-emption of, 307-8
Tinker of Turvey, The, 385
Tisbury, Wilts., 308
'Tis Merry When Gossips Meet, by
  Rowlands, 22, 98-9, 266, 344-5
Todde, William, 257, 259
Toft, Mary, 279, 419
Tolson. *See* Townson

Tom Sculs argument, 186
Tooke, G., 273
Tooke, Nicholas, 415
Tooke (Tucke), Walter, 76, 272, 331
Tooke (Tucke), William, 331
Topcliffe, Richard, informer, 186, 378-9
"To our English Terence, Mr. Will. Shakespeare," 328
"To Penshurst," poem by Jonson, 316
"To Sʳ Nicholas Smyth," poem by Roe, 398
Topham, John, 379
Topham, Mr., 187, 379
Topham, Robert, 379
Topham, Thomas, 379
Totnes, Devon, 347
Tower, the, of London, 6, 23, 235, 307, 310, 318, 321, 323, 330, 333, 335, 338, 343, 344, 383, 387, 398; lieutenant of, 356, 400
Town (West) Malling, Kent, 270, 316, 339; Abbey church, 41, 51, 303
Townshend, Sir Robert, 187, 380-1
Townson (Tolson), Robert, D.D., 142, 365-6
Towse (b. French), Joan, 319
Towse, William, I.T., 3, 9-10, 55, 75, 76, 78, 114, 266, 319, 329, 332, 356
Towse, William, the younger, I.T., 319
Tragicall History of Mary Queen of Scotts (poem), 173, 375
Travel, foreign, 151, 153-4, 163
Travers, Walter, 299
Tregothnan, Cornwall, 262
Tresham (b. de Recalde), Mary, 133, 363
Tresham, Lewis, I.T., 363
Tresham, Sir Thomas, 363
Tres Thomae, 327, 359
Trinity College, Camb., 41, 131, 246, 256, 258, 271, 297, 300, 302, 320, 340, 350, 351, 355, 357,
360, 366, 370, 383, 391, 399, 403, 406
Trinity College, Dublin, 407
Trinity College, Oxford, 85, 326, 335, 337, 368
Trinity Hall, Camb., 254, 309, 338
Tristram Shandy, 279
True report of the service done upon certain galleys, A, 357
Tuam, Ireland, archbishop of, 373
Tucke, Auditor. See Tooke
Tunbridge, Kent, 305
Tunbridge, William, 87
Turkey, 54; costume of a Turk, 150; religion of, 201
Turner, John, fencer, 10, 20, 187, 379-80
Turner (b. Parry), Pascha, 82, 297, 333, 339
Turner, Peter, physician and apothecary, 15, 82, 297, 333, 339
Turner, Peter, son of Peter T., 333
Turner, Samuel, 333
Turner, William, 333
Tusser, Francis, M.T., 366
Tuttesham, Anthony, 305
Tuttesham, Dorothy, 305
Tuttesham, John, 305
Tuttesham, Richard, 305
Tuttesham (Tutsham) (Tutsam), Thomas, 43, 287, 305
Twain, Mark, 358
Twelfth Night, performance at Middle Temple, 11, 48, 265, 312-3, 314, 389
Twisden, Isabella, 418
Twisden, Thomas, I.T., 277, 418-9
Twysden (b. Finch), Ann Lady, 304
Twysden, Sir Roger, 303, 409, 419
Twysden (Twisden), family of, 269, 277, 304, 316, 409, 418
Tyburn, London, execution place, 179, 339, 357, 372, 376
Tyndale, William, 14
Tyrone (title). See O'Neill
Tyrrel, Richard, 247, 406

Ulpian: Domitius Ulpianus, Roman
   jurist, 149
Ulster, Ireland, 188
Ulysses, 10, 328
Umberly, Devonshire, 343
University College, Oxford, 326,
   386, 404
University sermon, Camb., 258
Unton (Umpton), Sir Henry, M.T.,
   194, 383
Upper Gelderland, the Netherlands,
   391
Ursula. *See* Walsingham, Ursula Lady
Usher, Dr., cleric, 315
Uxbridge, Middlesex, 21, 376

Vacations, Grand, Learning, Reading,
   at Middle Temple, 264
Vane, Francis, 43, 305
Vawer, William, M.T., 298
Venetians, the, 323
Venice, Italy, 313, 314, 355, 393
Vennar (Venarde), Richard, L.I.,
   11, 123, 141, 357-8, 365
Verbeck (Verbeeck), Abraham, 255,
   285
Verbeck (Verbeeck), Arnold, 255,
   285
Verbeck (Verbeeck), Margarita, 285
Verbeck (Verbeeck), Susanna, 285
Vere, Edward, seventeenth Earl of
   Oxford, 343, 388
Vere, Sir Francis, lord general, 45,
   306-7, 316, 353
Vere, Susan Lady, 182
Vermeren, Janeken, niece of Jane
   Manningham first wife of Richard
   M. squire of Bradbourne, 284, 285
Vermeren, John, 86
Verney, Sir Edmond, 336
Verstegan, Richard (alias R. Dolman),
   3, 22, 23, 236, 322-3, 401-2,
   404
*Vetusta Monumenta, quae, ad
   rerum Britannicarum memoriam
   conservandam, Societas Anti-*
*quariorum Londini sumptu suo
   edenda curavit,* 415
Vicares (Vicary), Thomas, sergeant-
   surgeon, 87, 338-9
*Villare Cantianum: or Kent Surveyed
   and Illustrated,* 304, 318, 373, 414
Villiers, George, Duke of Bucking-
   ham, 274
Vintrie, the, stowage place for wines,
   350
Virgil: Publius Virgilius Maro, Roman
   poet, 202, 400
Virginia, colony of, 15, 297; London
   company, 362
*Visitation of Cambridge Made in A°
   1575. continued and Enlarged...
   by Henry St George in A° 1619,* 407
*Visitations of Bedfordshire, Annis
   Domini 1566, 1583, 1634,* 408
Visitation of County of Warwick,
   taken by William Camden in 1619,
   395
*Visitation of Herts. made by Robert
   Cooke, Esq. in 1572; and Sir
   Richard St. George, Kt., in 1634,*
   331
*Visitation of Kent Taken in the Year
   1619,* 318, 324, 407, 413, 414
*Visitation of London, A.D. 1633,
   1634, and 1635. Made by Sir H.
   St. George Kt.,* 340
Vitam quae faciunt beatiorem, 322
Vives, Joannes Ludovicus, 195, 210,
   221, 384-5, 389
Vlissingen. *See* Flushing
Vulgate, 14

Wagstaffe, Thomas, 395
Wagstaffe, Timothy, M.T., 220, 224,
   298, 395, 397
Wake, Abraham, M.T., 122, 355,
   381
Wake, Arthur, 355
Wake, Isaac, M.T., 355
Wakering, Essex, 325
Waldgrave, Robert, printer, 377

Waldram, Sir Richard, 417
Waldram, Thomas, M.T., 275, 308, 417
Wales, Lord President of Marches of, 82, 95, 329, 334, 341; Prince of, *see* Henry Frederick
Waller, Edmund, poet, 315, 391
Walmsley, Thomas, L.I., 96, 260, 283, 342
Walpole St. Peter, Norfolk, 352
Walrond, James, M.T., 265
Walsingham (b. St. Barbe) (Worseley), Ursula Lady, 69, 85, 322, 337
Walsingham, Sir Francis, 337, 398, 404
Walter, Maningham, of Maidstone, Kent, 271, 414
Walter, William, M.T., Maidstone, Kent, 271
Waltham, Kent, 324
Walton, Izaak, 304, 362, 367
Ward, John, 415
Ward, Samuel, Puritan divine, 25, 354-5
Warde, William, curate, 254, 255
Wards and Liveries, Court of, 49, 263, 268, 272, 273, 274, 331, 335, 388, 393, 415
Waresly (Waresley), Hunts., 252, 407
Warner, Mr., tutor at Caius College, 354
Warner, Walter, mathematician, 354
Warner, William, poet, 22, 114, 124, 349, 358
Warnett, Francis, M.T., 416
Warren, Sir Ralph, 338
Warren, Richard, 86, 338
Warwick (title). *See* Dudley
Warwick, Warwicks., 374
Warwickshire, 119, 220, 320, 352, 395, 397
Water Eaton, Oxon, 381
Waterson, Simon, bookseller, 401
Watson, Anthony, bishop of Chichester, 207, 386
Watson, William, secular priest, 51, 317

Wattes, James, fellow of Magdalene College, 257, 411
Wattes (Watts), Moses, 291
Watts, Cousin, of Sandwich, Kent, 1, 160, 161, 162, 256, 267, 271, 371
Watts, Edward, M.T., 327, 334, 406
Watts, John, M.T., 327, 328
Watts, William, M.T., 74, 84, 266, 327, 328, 334, 406
Watts, William, 327
Weevill, Robert, M.T., 363
Weever, John, 298
Well Head Cottage, East Malling, Kent, 277, 418
Well Head House, East Malling, Kent, 277, 418
Well Street, East Malling, Kent, 269, 291
Wells, Somerset, 319, 321, 326, 404; bishop of Bath and, 5, 194, 383, 392, 397; dean of, 333, 372; subdean of, 372
Welwyn, Herts., 272
Wemes, Humphrey, 307
Wenman, Thomas, 375
Wesdon, Sussex, 405
Westbury, Wilts., 370
West Drayton, Middlesex, 309
Westerham Grammar School, Kent, 278
Westerham Road, Kent, 339
West Flanders, 277
West Grinstead, Sussex, 302
West Hatch, Tisbury, Wilts., 308
West Indies, 300, 363, 405
West, or Town, Malling, Kent. *See* Town
West Woodhey, Berks., 391
Westminster, abbey church, 266, 297, 323, 371; St. Andrew chapel, 371; Bible translators, 300, 364, 384; birthplace of John Foote, 47; canon of, 338; dean of, 14, 61, 300, 320, 365; Great Palace yard or Tiltyard (Whitehall), 133,

363, 380; Hall, 4, 268, 272, 374, 386; law courts, 9, 73, 260, 272, 283; pillory at, 321; prebendary of, 301; sermon at, 320; School, 297, 347, 349, 362, 391, 399

Westmoreland, 83; earldom of, 231, 305, 398

Weston, Herts., 253, 260, 283, 336, 411

Weston, Nicholas, merchant, 188, 381

Weston, Richard, M.T., 275, 308, 396

West Peckham, Kent, 305

Westphaling, Herbert, bishop of Hereford, 310

Westphaling (Westfaling), Margaret. *See* Edes (Eedes)

Whiller, William, 287

Whitaker, Dr. William, 155, 256, 258, 360, 370

White, Sir Thomas, 46, 309

Whitehall, Palace of, 332; chapel, 12, 223, 233, 259, 313; deanery, 389; gates, 16, 208, 387; gallery (Shield), 25, 31, 298; preacher at, 211, 225, 232, 384; proclamation at, 396, 399

Whitelock (b. Bulstrode), Elizabeth, 352

Whitelock, Dorothy, 351

Whitelock, Edmund, Captain, 97, 130, 344, 352, 360

Whitelock, Sir James, M.T., 3, 25, 118, 188, 261, 274, 275, 310, 326, 334, 335, 344, 346, 351-2, 381

Whitelock, Mary, 351

Whitgift, John, archbishop of Canterbury, 15, 68, 207, 245, 258, 318, 321, 388, 394, 404, 410

Whithead, Thomas, servant of Richard Manningham squire of Bradbourne, 285, 286

A wife now the widdow of Sir T. Overbury, 335

Wilbraham, Roger, 25, 274, 327, 331, 379

William I, King of England, the Conqueror, 10, 75, 325

William III, King of England, and Mary, 278

Williams, David, sergeant-at-law, 265

Williams, Henry, alias Cromwell, 336

Williams, Sir Richard, alias Cromwell, 336

Willian (Wyllien), Herts., 252, 253, 260, 283, 336, 411

Willis, "Cousin," 116, 350

Willowbee, Thomas, dean of Rochester, 55, 319

Wilsborough, Kent, 324

Wilson, Thomas, 323

Wiltshire, 67, 357, 392, 415

Winchester, Hants., 267; archdeacon of, 373; bishop of, 85, 271, 278, 319, 320, 336, 370, 372, 392, 413; dean of, 183, 377, 399; prebendary of, 338

Winchester College, 6, 254, 278, 334

Winchfield, Hants., 334

Windebank, Thomas, 340

Windsor, 296; chapel at, 29, 299, 387; dean of, 12, 16, 207, 211, 232, 278, 386, 387, 389

Wingate, Cousin, 231, 399

Winwood (b. Bodley), Elizabeth, 347

Winwood, Sir Ralph, 347, 351, 370

Wisbishe (Wisbech), Castle, Isle of Ely, Cambs., 98

Wiseman (Wissman), Simon, M.T., 405

Witchcraft, trials for, 339

Witnam, Berks., 383

Wither family, 268

Withers, George, preacher, 116, 351

Withers, Henry, 351

Witlington, Somerset, 380

Wittenberg, Germany, 351

Wood, Annis, maidservant of

Richard Manningham squire of
Bradbourne, 285
Wood, Anthony, 260, 278, 296, 297,
301, 302, 311, 321, 322, 328, 331,
333, 338, 343, 346, 347, 349, 361,
368, 370, 372, 373, 375, 382, 383,
387, 389, 391, 392, 399, 401, 406,
411, 416
Wood, John, schoolmaster, 254
Wood, Katherin, maidservant of
Richard Manningham squire of
Bradbourne, 285
Woodside, near Hatfield, Herts., 268,
356, 388
Woodsom, Yorks., 396
Woodstock, Oxon, 351
Worcester (title). *See* Somerset
Worcester, cathedral, 297; canon of,
320; dean of, 310; bishop of, 15,
297, 336, 386
Wormesley, Oxon, 275
Wormington, Glos., 356
Worseley, Sir Richard, 337
Worsley, Charles, 412
Worthies of England, 316, 325, 332–
3, 348, 361, 362, 365, 370, 371,
372, 384, 395, 399, 404, 405, 407
Wotton, Edward, first Lord, 207
Wotton (b. Finch) (Morton), Eleanor,
304
Wotton, Sir Henry, 22, 304, 310,
334, 335
Wray, Sir Christopher, 81, 256, 333,
368

Wray (b. Girlington), Anne Lady,
256, 368
Wrestlingworth, Beds., 252
Wriothesley, Henry, third Earl of
Southampton, 23, 210, 235, 246,
353, 355, 387, 400, 405
Wrotham, Kent, 50, 305, 316
Wyatt, Sir Thomas, the elder, 316
Wye, Kent, 164, 324, 329, 352, 373
Wykes (Wekes), Henry, printer, 384
Wymondham, Norfolk, 356; school,
354
Wymondley Bury, Herts., 272
Wyse (Wise), John, husbandman, 285

Yeldard (Yilderd), Dr. Arthur, 85, 337
Yelverton, Christopher, 74, 76, 302,
327, 329, 331
Yelverton, Sir Henry, 3, 9, 302
York, 252, 320; archbishop of, 162,
259, 361, 372, 404, 405; assizes,
24; assize justice, 329; county
courts, 307; dean of, 372; prebendary of, 297; sheriff of, 329;
vice-president of, 76, 329. *See
also* North, The
York Castle, 307
Yorkshire, 76, 251, 358, 396, 407

Zanchius, Jerome, 410
Zeeland, province of, 305, 307
Zouche, Edward la, eleventh Baron
of Harringworth, 82, 95, 334,
341-2

This book was designed by Richard Hendel, composed in IBM Selectric Baskerville, and printed by Halliday Lithograph Corporation, West Hanover, Massachusetts.